CYBER SECURITY PRACTITIONER'S GUIDE

CYBER SECURITY PRACTITIONER'S GUIDE

Editor

Hamid Jahankhani

Northumbria University London, UK & QAHE, UK

World Scientific

NEW JERSEY • LONDON • SINGAPORE • BEIJING • SHANGHAI • HONG KONG • TAIPEI • CHENNAI • TOKYO

Published by

World Scientific Publishing Co. Pte. Ltd.
5 Toh Tuck Link, Singapore 596224
USA office: 27 Warren Street, Suite 401-402, Hackensack, NJ 07601
UK office: 57 Shelton Street, Covent Garden, London WC2H 9HE

Library of Congress Control Number: 2019945885

British Library Cataloguing-in-Publication Data
A catalogue record for this book is available from the British Library.

CYBER SECURITY PRACTITIONER'S GUIDE

ISBN 978-981-120-445-6

For any available supplementary material, please visit
https://www.worldscientific.com/worldscibooks/10.1142/11390#t=suppl

Desk Editor: Nur Izdihar Binte Ismail

Typeset by Stallion Press
Email: enquiries@stallionpress.com

Printed in Singapore

About the Editor

Hamid Jahankhani

(Hamid.jahankhani@northumbria.ac.uk)

Professor Hamid Jahankhani gained his PhD from the Queen Mary College, University of London. In 1999 he moved to the University of East London (UEL) to become the first Professor of Information Security and Cyber Criminology at the university in 2010. Over the last 15 years Hamid has also been involved in developing new and innovative programmes and introducing the "block mode" delivery approach at UEL. The programmes he has developed include an MSc in Information Security and Computer Forensics, and a Professional Doctorate in Information Security.

Hamid's principal research areas for a number of years have been the fields of cyber security, information security and digital forensics. In partnership with the key industrial sectors, he has examined and established several innovative research projects that are of direct relevance to the needs of UK and European information security professionals, digital forensics industries, Critical National Infrastructure and law enforcement agencies. Hamid has planned, proposed and managed several collaborative projects, and secured a substantial research income of several million Euros.

Under Hamid's supervision, 13 PhD and Professional Doctorate students in information security have completed their theses. Hamid has also been leading international and national research projects in a number of areas.

Professor Jahankhani is the Editor-in-Chief of the *International Journal of Electronic Security and Digital Forensics* (www.inderscience.com/ijesdf), published by Inderscience, and general chair of the annual International Conference on Global Security, Safety and Sustainability (ICGS3). Hamid has edited and contributed to over 15 books and has over 150 conference and journal publications. In the summer of 2017, Hamid was trained as a GCHQ "cyberist" to train the next generation of cyber security experts through the GCHQ CyberFirst initiative. Professor Jahankhani has a number of books forthcoming, namely, Cyber Criminology, Blockchain and Clinical Trials — Securing Patient's Data, Cyber Security Practitioner's Guide, Digital Twins Technologies and Smart Cities.

Contributors' Biographies

Ali G. Hessami (hessami@vegaglobalsystems.com) — **Introduction**
A trusting and persuasive leader with a talent for big picture strategic and creative thinking and experience/leadership in large scale national and international projects with high level interfacing and accountabilities. A team player taking pride in the group accomplishment whilst striving for continual betterment and excellence in himself, the team and the task. An innovator in business strategy, resilience/continuity, advanced risk assessment & management in financial/safety/environmental aspects, systems safety, security, sustainability and operational decision support. A track record in technology R&D, international business development, design and implementation of advanced processes, methodologies and frameworks for safety and security risk management, knowledge management, competence/talent management, legal compliance, and European/International standards.

David A.E. Haddon (david.haddon@northumbria.ac.uk) — **Chapter 1**
David graduated with an honours degree in electronics from Imperial College in 1980. He worked in defence and broadcasting before joining The Processor Centre in 1983, a computer services company operating in the Channel Islands that he has owned since 1990. The business provides managed IT services to clients in the hospitality and financial services sectors with several clients dating back to the 1980s. David's passion as an engineer extends to his hobby of maintaining and touring with his old cars. He bought an

Atlas lathe from his grandfather in 1985. He has a vintage Lagonda and spare engines and gearboxes that he has personally rebuilt. Married since 1986, David is a proud father and grandfather. He is a regional secretary of the BCS. Whilst studying for a Master's degree and running a business David organised the Jersey Old Motor Club's tour to France for the 2018 Le Mans Classic!

Thomas Welsh (twelsh37@gmail.com) — **Chapter 2**
Tom Welsh is Cyber Security Analyst at a London FinTech company, where Tom not only focusses on policy, procedures and providing guidance to other teams but is also heavily involved in the day-to-day defence and response to cyber security incidents. The company, which has over 19 offices spread across three continents, keeps Tom's life interesting.

Tom has worked in Infrastructure and Operational roles for more than 30 years and in that time has amassed a wealth of knowledge from a large range of companies from multi-national telcos like BT and Nokia to dot com startups. Throughout this time Tom has contributed back to the community in which he works by testing, beta testing, coding and adding features to open source software. You will find his name mentioned in much open source software but majorly in Nagios Monitoring software as well as Op5 Software such as Merlin.

This diverse knowledge base and Tom's drive to learn more made him take up an MSc in Cyber Security during 2017-2018 in which he earned a distinction. His dissertation on "A cyber security threat model for the detection of a ransomware cyberweapon in a networked computing environment" built on a subject close to his heart: threat detection and response.

Tom is currently researching "detection and remediation of a security breach" and will focus on how an incident responder should act on detection of a security breach.

When Tom is not working on his computer he can be found pottering about with his 1998 Land Rover Defender or down by the river fishing.

George Copeland (george.copeland@outlook.com) — **Chapter 3**
George is a freelance senior manager with a strong technical background and proven track record in programme, project and service management. His significant experience and expertise was gained in both development and support environments ranging from mainframe to global networks. He has enjoyed a wide variety of roles and has been successful in the management of change and introduction of best practices in the most challenging environments. This has included projects in various countries as well as at home in the UK. Most recently, he has focused on cyber-physical system implementations and associated cyber security, and has driven the introduction of cyber security controls and supporting management capabilities for Industry 4.0 on behalf of his clients in the railway industry. He has recently completed an MSc Degree in Cybersecurity.

Jon Cosson (jon.cosson@jmfinn.com) — **Chapter 4**
As JM Finn Head of Information Technology (IT) and Chief Information Security Officer (CISO), Jon Cosson has had more than 32 years' experience in the IT Industry. He has held numerous IT positions since he started his career programming Mainframe computer systems at Jones Lang Lasselle in the mid-1980s. Jon has directed the IT department for JM Finn, an established wealth management organisation, for more than 20 years. Jon is a technical leader and security specialist with extensive experience delivering transformative security solutions. He has a passion for IT security and is risk-focussed, understanding the bigger picture and delivering secure business objectives through a grasp of broad industry trends and new technologies. Jon holds numerous industry-recognised cyber security certifications including CISSP, CISM, CCISO, CEH, CHFI and MBCI. Jon has also just completed a Master's degree (with Distinction) in Cyber Security and plans to start a PhD in a related field later this year. Jon is a regular speaker at cyber security events and through his extensive knowledge and passion, is able to address common cyber security concerns.

Stephen Sampana (steve.sampana@refinitiv.com) — **Chapter 4**
An experienced cyber security professional with a demonstrated history of working in the information technology industry. Skilled in Security Operations, IT operations, Incident Response and Forensics, Vulnerability Assessment, and Information Governance and Assurance. Strong technologist and researcher with a Master of Science (MSc) focused in Cybersecurity from Northumbria University.

Haider M. al-Khateeb (H.Al-Khateeb@wlv.ac.uk) — **Chapter 4**
Dr. al-Khateeb specialises in Cybersecurity, Digital Forensics and Incident Response (DFIR). He is a Fellow of the Higher Education Academy (FHEA) and holds a first-class BSc (Hons) in Computer Science, and a PhD in Cybersecurity. Haider is a Senior Lecturer and conducts his research at the Wolverhampton Cyber Research Institute (WCRI), on the University of Wolverhampton city campus.

Haider has delivered a range of hands-on technical training on topics such as Ethical Hacking as part of a proactive approach to protect computer systems. He has many years of experience with Transnational Education (TNE) as a Link-coordinator of franchised courses and a flying faculty team, supports MSc programmes at Northumbria University, and delivers Executive Master's degrees in Cybersecurity through leading IT training providers in the UK such as QA Ltd.

He has published numerous professional and peer-reviewed articles. His research interests include User Authentication Methods, Distributed Digital Forensics and Remote Incident Response and Security for Cyber-Physical Systems (CPS). Additionally, Haider is interested in multiciliary projects to mitigate cyber-related challenges such as online anti-social behaviour.

Usman Javed Butt (usman.butt@brunel.ac.uk) — **Chapter 5**
Usman Butt has extensive industry and academic experience. He worked in the industry as a Network Engineer and Systems Administrator and has had the hands-on experience of managing and configuring Windows/Unix servers and Cisco devices. He is a Certified Ethical Hacker (CEH), holds a Certificate in Information

Security Management Principles (CISMP) awarded by the British Computer Society (BCS), and trained as a Certified Information Systems Security Professional (CISSP). The latter two courses are both Government Communications Headquarters (GCHQ) certified courses. He also trained in CompTIA Security+.

Usman is currently managing a portfolio of MSc Cyber Security technologies and Web and Mobile programmes and is involved in delivering Network Security, Ethical Hacking and Web Application Security modules. He also holds a Fellowship of the Higher Education Academy (FHEA) and is currently doing his PhD in Cyber Security. He is also an active researcher and has interests in penetration testing, ransomware and blockchain technologies.

Arvind Kumar (arvind.kumar@northumbria.ac.uk) — **Chapter 5**
Arvind has a Master's degree in Information and Computing Technology from Northumbria University with a background in Network Engineering. Arvind graduated with his Bachelor's degree in Science majoring in Electronics and Communication from the Far Eastern University Institute of Technology in the Philippines. He has done several pioneering research studies for his Bachelor's degree and his current research focusses on the technical issues of cyber security. Arvind has authored papers in IEEE journals and conference proceedings due to his involvement in research on the ransomware cyber security threat and its impact on Supervisory Control and Data Acquisition (SCADA).

Stefan Kendzierskyj (stefan.kendzierskyj@northumbria.ac.uk) — **Chapter 6**
Stefan Kendzierskyj is a commercial director with over 25 years' experience gained in a number of technology companies covering industries such as telecommunications, software development, outsourcing, publishing, eLearning and content transformation. Stefan has a strategic approach when presenting solutions at board level and finding innovative ways for businesses to transform their models and reach new markets. This has been in the form of collaborating with some high-profile publishers and large associations that need

to reach a global audience with their vision and messaging, particularly in the healthcare and commercial sector.

Stefan also provides publisher services for the United Kingdom Disaster Victim Identification team and Interpol in the form of process tools to aid in investigation work for mass fatalities in which it may not be possible to identify the victims by visual recognition. This consultative approach has, over the years, led to improvements to the methodology and constant attention is applied to ensure those in the field apply an agile and adaptive approach that increases efficiency.

Stefan holds an MSc in Cyber Security and has attained a level of distinction. He has also published a number of articles and books with large publishers concerning blockchain, security/privacy of data (particularly in the healthcare sector) and securing critical national infrastructure, and is in the process of publishing other works. Stefan is also a speaker at conferences and other thought leadership events.

Jaime Ibarra Jimenez (jaime.jimenez@northumbria.ac.uk) — **Chapter 7**
Jaime Ibarra is a Cyber Security Analyst and researcher currently finishing his Master's programme in London. His curiosity and passion to learn have allowed him to write academic papers and chapter contributions for scientific books edited by Springer, providing him with skills and expertise in multiple topics within the field.

Orret R. Grey (orret.grey@northumbria.ac.uk) — **Chapter 8**
Orret Grey is currently an MSc student at Northumbria University where he is pursuing post graduate studies in Cyber Security and specialising in information security and data privacy. Orret has been working as an information security analyst in both the public and private sectors for more than 10 years and demonstrates keen interest in and passion for formulating security policies and innovative solutions for protecting personal and sensitive data. This involves creating new ways of countering complex and emerging threats that pose serious risks to valuable data. He has worked extensively in the financial industry, with governments and in the health sector in various parts of the UK. In addition to conducting academic research into GDPR compliance, another professional undertaking of his

involves developing security strategies for protecting personal data with Blockchain technology or other encryption techniques.

Raymond Brown (ray.brown@northumbria.ac.uk) — **Chapter 8**
Raymond Brown is a Visiting Lecturer and Cyber Security Consultant with over 33 years' experience working in the IT sector, the last 10 of which were spent in academia. He teaches students at both undergraduate and post-graduate levels and for a number of UK universities, both in the UK and also in the Middle East. He holds an MSc in Computer Security and Forensics and also commercial certifications in security and forensics. Ray's teaching and research interests include Biometrics, Cyber Security, Digital Forensics, Data Governance, IoT, Networking, Project Management and other areas. He actively researches with the National Centre for Cyber-stalking Research (NCCR) at the University of Bedfordshire and consults collaboratively with academic organisations to provide support and resources to increase teaching and employment opportunities in the field of Cyber Security.

Reza Montasari (R. Montasari@hud.ac.uk) — **Chapter 9**
Dr. Reza Montasari is a Senior Lecturer in Cyber Security and the Course Leader for the BSc/MEng in Software Engineering in the School of Computing and Engineering at the University of Huddersfield. Reza received a BSc (Hons) in Multimedia Computing (with a second upper classification) and an MSc. in Computer Forensics (with distinction) both from the University of South Wales. Following this, he gained his PhD from the University of Derby. His thesis was titled "The Comprehensive Digital Forensic Investigation Process Model (the CDFIPM) for Digital Forensic Practice".

Richard Hill (R.Hill@hud.ac.uk) — **Chapter 9**
After qualifying as a Chartered Production Engineer and working in the manufacturing industry, Richard's career in higher education commenced in 2000 at Sheffield Hallam University. He has held a number of academic teaching, research and academic management posts over the last 17 years.

In 2010 he joined the University of Derby as Head of Subject, Computing, with a remit to renew the existing academic portfolio and develop the School's first submission to an external research assessment exercise (REF2014). During 2011, the Mathematics scheme was added to the School. In 2014 the School became a Department within the new College of Engineering and Technology.

In 2017 he joined the University of Huddersfield as Head of the Department of Informatics.

Victoria Carpenter (Victoria.Carpenter@beds.ac.uk) — **Chapter 9**
An experienced research leader, excellent at building professional relationships, influencing and driving change agendas. Victoria has extensive experience in developing and managing research strategies to align with the national regulatory policies; preparing REF submissions, negotiating and managing funding for research projects; excellent leadership and project management skills, and a strong ability to translate research outcomes into applications within academia, including policy and strategy.

Although her PhD is in a Humanities subject area, she has expanded her area of expertise; this includes application of the theoretical frameworks she has created for her research to other disciplines (e.g. international marketing, service marketing, leadership studies, and digital security). She works well across disciplines, using her analytical skills to discern patterns and thematic clusters, interpret datasets, and prepare reports and business cases for research development based on these findings. She is fully versed in the use of analytical software (NVivo, Leximancer, SPSS, Excel), as well as quantitative and qualitative research methods.

Amin Hosseinian-Far (Amin.Hosseinian-Far@northampton.ac.uk) — **Chapter 9**
Dr. Amin Hosseinian-Far holds the position of Senior Lecturer in Business Systems and Operations at the University of Northampton. Previously, Amin was a Staff Tutor at the Open University, and prior to that a Senior Lecturer and Course Leader at Leeds Beckett University. He has held lecturing and research positions at the

University of East London, and at a number of private HE institutions and strategy research firms.

Dr Hosseinian-Far received his BSc (Hons) in Business Information Systems from the University of East London, an MSc degree in Satellite Communications and Space Systems from the University of Sussex, a Postgraduate Certificate in Research and a PhD which he acquired from the University of East London. His PhD thesis is titled 'A Systemic Approach to an Enhanced Model for Sustainability'. He has more than 50 peer-reviewed publications that are disseminated in the form of journal articles, conference papers and book chapters. Moreover, he has been an editor of two books and two conference proceedings.

Amin holds Membership of the Institution of Engineering and Technology (IET), Senior Fellowship of the Higher Education Academy (HEA), and Fellowship of the Royal Society of Arts (RSA). He is also an associate editor for the International Journal of Systems and Society, and the founding editor and the Editor-in-Chief of the International Journal of Strategic Engineering (IJoSE).

Ian Mitchell (i.mitchell@mdx.ac.uk) — **Chapter 10**

Ian Mitchell is currently an Associate Professor in the Department of Computer Science at Middlesex University. Ian has more than 30 peer-reviewed publications relating to subjects on a range of issues across computer science. Ian completed his PhD in Artificial Neural Networks and continues research in Spiking Neural Networks, Digital Forensics and Blockchain-related technologies. Ian is programme leader for a BSc in Cyber Security and Digital Forensics at Middlesex University and teaches on a range of subjects including Blockchain Engineering.

Sukhvinder Hara (s.hara@mdx.ac.uk) — **Chapter 10**

Sukhvinder Hara is currently a Senior Lecturer in the Department of Computer Science at Middlesex University. Sukhvinder completed seven years' service as a Digital Forensics Analyst at the Serious Fraud Office and completed many cases. Sukhy teaches on Blockchain Analytics and cryptocurrencies to postgraduate students of MA

Criminology. Sukhy is currently completing her PhD, researching cryptocurrencies and related technologies.

David Neilson (d.neilson@mdx.ac.uk) — **Chapter 10**
David Neilson is currently an Associate Lecturer in the Department of Computer Science at Middlesex University. David teaches on a range of topics to undergraduate students of Digital Forensics. David designed and developed an undergraduate curriculum for Bitcoin Forensics and is currently completing his MRes researching digital forensics and cryptocurrencies.

Firas Hazzaa (firas.hazzaa@pgr.anglia.ac.uk) — **Chapter 11**
Firas Hazzaa is currently a Researcher in Cybersecurity and a PhD Candidate at Anglia Ruskin University, School of Engineering and Built Environment, in the UK. He received his MSc in Computer Science and Communications from the Art, Science and Technology University in Lebanon (AUL) in 2010, and his BSc in Computer Engineering from the University of Technology in Baghdad in 2001. He has many publications in computer and network security, in addition to a published book on e-voting security. Since 2003, he has been involved in many projects with the Ministry of Science and Technology and the institutions of higher education in Iraq. He also has many certificates from training courses in Italy, Iraq and the UK. Firas is a member of IEEE, IET and ChPP.

Sufian Yousef (Sufian.Yousef@anglia.ac.uk) — **Chapter 11**
Sufian Yousef is a Director of the Telecommunication Engineering Research Group in the School of Engineering and the Built Environment at Anglia Ruskin University, Chelmsford, UK. His PhD was in Telecommunications Engineering at Anglia Ruskin University; his MSc in Telecommunications Systems Management from the same university; and his BSc in Electrical and Electronic Engineering from Baghdad University. He won the Royal Academy of Engineering award, which resulted in his being seconded to GEC Marconi for one year in 1999. His main area of expertise is Telecommunications Modelling, Security and Analysis. Sufian was involved in a number

of KTP, KEEP and consultancy projects and carried out supervision in the UK and India. Sufian has seen 21 PhD students complete their degree and was keynote speaker at many conferences as well as external examiner for many national and international universities.

John Goldie — Chapter 12

John Goldie provides business specific information and cyber security services to clients and researches machine learning/artificial intelligence for practical applications in cyber security. He is currently having fun on his Honda NC750X and planning a tour in the Picos Mountains region.

John has been involved as a Head of Operational Security at Fujitsu and ING, a GDPR SME at Merlin Entertainments, a Cyber Security Specialist at Monarch Group, an IT Security, Risk and Compliance Manager at CalMac Ferries, and an Interim Head of Information Security for a company that provides financial services.

Ojo Emmanuel Ademola (emmanuel.ademola@northumbria.ac.uk) — **Chapter 13**

Emmanuel is a Professor of Information Technology Management and the current chairperson of three major institutions: the Institute for Enterprise Management and Analytics, the Centre for Citizenship and Leadership, and Power-Age Consulting. He serves in the UK as an Executive Committee Member of BCS ELITE — The Computing Leadership Forum and BCS ISSG — The Information Security Specialist Group. He is also a BCS and CMI Subject Matter Expert. As the trademark owner of Power-Age Consulting and an academic, his research interests include Human-Computer Interactions, Big Data Analytics, IoT, System Thinking and Cyber Security. He regularly publishes in reputable journals, authors books and hundreds of checklists and reviews books for major international publishers.

Nishan Chelvachandran — Chapter 14

Nishan Chelvachandran is a cybersecurity researcher with years of law enforcement and strategic public sector experience, specialising in operational fields such as Digital Forensics, High-Tech Crime and

Intelligence. He has worked at grassroots, tactical, strategic and organisational levels, developing solutions for managing change, training, recruitment and retention, and the standardisation of best practice.

Nishan has also championed equality and diversity through his elected chair-role in the Hertfordshire Black and Asian Police Association, representing otherwise underrepresented officers and staff, and working with the Constabulary to facilitate and shape best working practices, policies and procedures.

Nishan's professional interests lie in organisational consultancy and oversight. He works in C-Suite level leadership roles to instil and steer overarching organisational and cultural change to accommodate the future challenges that will face both industry and society.

Nishan's research interests include keyword and behavioural analytics, cyber legislation and jurisdiction, ethical frameworks for mass data collection and surveillance and privacy.

Nishan holds an MSc in Cyber Security, for which he was awarded a distinction. He also holds a certification in Cyberwarfare, Surveillance and Security. He has published several research papers and contributed book chapters relating to the data analytics of open source big data to identify exploitation and radicalisation. He has presented his work at the International Conference for Governance, Security and Sustainability, and is publishing further work. He is developing streams for doctoral research and furthering the collective knowledge of wider Cyber Security disciplines and industry.

Nishan is a speaker at conferences and thought exploration events, has been invited to guest lecture at UK universities and helps develop core modules of both undergraduate and postgraduate degree programs.

Sérgio Tenreiro de Magalhães (smagalhaes@champlain.edu) — **Chapter 15**

Sérgio Tenreiro de Magalhães has a PhD in Information Systems and Technologies from the University of Minho (Portugal). Currently he is Associate Professor and Chair of Cyber Security at Champlain College (Burlington, VT, USA). He is also a researcher of the Software

Engineering and Management Group (SEMAG) of the Algoritmi Research Centre (University of Minho, Portugal) and was a former Assistant Professor of the Catholic University of Portugal, Braga, where he coordinated the undergraduate degree in Information and Communications Technologies and graduate studies in Information Security. He was also a member of the Board of Directors of the School of Philosophy and Social Sciences of that university. Prior to assuming a position as a researcher/lecturer, he had managing responsibilities in several corporations and also assumed consulting positions. His research interests are in information security, intelligence and performance monitoring. He was a researcher in several projects, including the "Security in the Armed Forces Data Distribution Network", promoted by the Ministry of Defense of Portugal, and he is an academic member of the NATO Multinational Cyber Defence Education and Training project. He is a reviewer of the *IEEE Transactions on Systems, Man and Cybernetics — Part C: Applications and Reviews* and of the *International Journal of Electronic Governance.* He is also a member of the Editorial Committee of the *International Journal of Electronic Security and Digital Forensics* and served on the Editorial Committee of the *International Journal of Cognitive Biometrics.* He serves as a member of the Scientific Committee of many international conferences and was the President of the Scientific Committee of the 8th European Conference on Information Warfare and Security and of the 6th International Conference on Global Security, Safety and Sustainability. He has published a book on the viability, requirements and implementations of behavioral biometric technologies, edited several other books, authored several chapters on biometric authentication related issues, been included in international peer reviewed books, and published more than 60 papers in security related topics, both in international journals and in peer reviewed conference proceedings.

Introduction

It's Time to Make the Case for Ethics

Ali G. Hessami

Vega Systems, London, United Kingdom
Hessami@vegaglobalsystems.com

Since the days of man as hunter gatherers, the success and prosperity of humanity has been associated with one key differentiator against other species, i.e. the invention of tools and artefacts. This inventiveness was inevitably driven by the need to generate a differential advantage against adversity in order to survive. The advent of agriculture brought the use of manmade tools to a higher level. Such tools gave mankind the ability to cultivate land, produce surplus food and transcend beyond the daily challenges of subsistence and survival. Whilst the invention of tools and artefacts bore testament to man's superior cognitive powers, these arose in response to man's needs to complement his feeble physique and powers in a harsh eco-system, and played a largely functional role in the advancement of the species. In this spirit, the quality, efficacy and diversity of tools and artefacts increased to enhance performance. However, the performance of tools, products and services has often been viewed narrowly through a utilitarian perspective often focused on the market mechanisms of price, functionality and desirability/quality. This has held true largely due to the limited impact of products and services on the society at large. This is a condition that is no longer tenable given our overt dependence on technological tools, products, services and artefacts that are transforming our lives and making us dependent on them without giving us the ability to influence their design, production, or functionality or to hold the supply chain accountable. In this setting, a new paradigm is called for that goes beyond concerns over commercial and functional performance and encourages the providers of products, services and systems towards transparency, accountability, explainability and the observance of higher ethical values in their increasingly global roles. This is the era of ethics and moral considerations for all enterprises, public or private, for or not-for-profit. Strangely but not unexpectedly, this also applies to the safety as well as the security of products, services and systems. We will explore the rationale, necessity and the attainment of this laudable emergent property in this introduction.

Facets of Performance

A purposeful aggregate of interconnected parts performing one or a suite of functions is regarded as a system. A system generally resides in an environment (larger eco-system) or as part of a larger system (system of systems) and manifests properties and behaviours that are not attributable to its individual constituents but to their inter-working. This is referred to as emergence or the emergent property of a system. Apart from emergence, a system can also be viewed from specific stakeholder perspectives that constitute nine inter-related facets of performance, comprising the following:

- Technical and functional.
- Commercial, cost and profitability.
- Environmental.
- Integrity (reliability, availability and maintainability).
- Resilience.
- Safety and security.
- Sustainability.
- Quality.
- Social and individual perceived value and preference.

These facets of system performance are inter-related and their individual desired level of attainment often involves a degree of trade-off and the discretion of the stakeholders regarding an acceptable level for each attribute. A desirable product, service or system delivers an optimal blend of these in a given context and at a cross-section in time.

One particular aspect of performance or behaviour that is traditionally not analysed or treated systematically and comprehensively is the value aspect. By default, it is regarded as the forte of the marketing department to cater for consumer preferences and choices to maximise sales opportunities. One key aspect of value is the social/ethical value that is concerned with the cultural, social moral norms of good/decent behaviour and the impact of products, services or systems on the ethical values held in the stakeholders' community or the whole society. This implies that design decisions and structural and behavioural aspects require stakeholder consultation and that the identification of ethical values that may be affected by the system of interest's concept of operation is crucial, in addition to all the other requirements relating to other facets of performance cited earlier.

The Need for a New Dimension

We have finally moved beyond focussing on safety after two millennia, and new concerns over the protection of life and property have emerged in the physical and cyber security contexts. Whilst safety is regarded as freedom from unacceptable levels of human harm that arise from unintended random or systematic errors and failures, security can be broadly defined as freedom from the unacceptable risks of human harm or loss of property arising from intentional acts and causes. The assurance of safety and security is broadly approached from the perspective of the risk of human harm and property loss to the direct users and stakeholders of a product, service or system. The well-being, happiness and overall quality of life in the social context is the next dimension of interest, largely driven by the emergence and advancement of digital technologies that pervade our lives and that may progress further to have an impact on many aspects of our lives normally considered private and personal. This is rather unprecedented in human history and requires urgent review, an evaluation of the existing and emerging social hazards, and the formulation of proactive strategies to preserve and protect moral and ethical values that have evolved over millennia for the advancement and prosperity of human societies.

Ethics and morals

Ethics is the branch of knowledge that deals with moral principles that govern human behaviour. Morals are the measures of right and wrong in the judgements and decisions that we face in life.

The principal ethical philosophies

There are a number of predominant ethical canons and philosophies that offer competing views of human behaviour. The choices a person makes in all walks of human endeavour depend very much on the philosophies he follows. The oldest school is attributed to Aristotle, and it is known as Virtue Ethics. This is largely concerned with individual qualities (virtues) that underpin our behaviours and promote well-being. The focus is largely on virtues rather than the negative individual traits that are referred to as vices. In this individual and bottom-up perspective, the promotion and upholding of individual virtues are considered instrumental to the collective societal well-being and the quality of interactions and relationships. This is analogous to quality ingredients being essential to integrative virtue from the total system/societal perspective. Whilst this approach has its virtues, it evidently lacks the systems perspective in that the emergence of a virtuous society at peace and happy with itself is not necessarily and entirely conditioned on moral choices made by the individual members.

The second school of philosophy regarding ethics is the Consequentialist school, which is more concerned with the system-level emergence of happiness and well-being from the integral of actions, choices and decisions made by the human agents, sub-systems and components of a system of interest. This regards any choice or decision ethical/moral so long as it contributes or is perceived to contribute to maximising the satisfaction, fulfilment and happiness for the largest number of beneficiaries. This is analogous to an economic utility function and the desire for maximisation of return on an investment as a rational course of action. There are many challenges in utilitarianism, least of all estimating, anticipating or rationalising a system-level effect from a component level course of action. This is as much an issue with human affairs as it is with complex technological systems. The nearest analogy with technological systems is a systems analysis technique known as Failure Mode, Effects and Criticality Analysis (FMECA) that strives to identify critical component level failures that have a major impact on system-level reliability, safety and availability.

The third established perspective on ethics emphasises the importance of leadership and stewardship. The Deontological or Duty Ethics proposed by Immanuel Kant explores the ramifications of choices, options and decisions by those who occupy the positions of responsibility, authority and leadership. This is driven by the realisation that senior decision makers' choices and decisions are more influential/impactful and more significant in terms of their effects on the stakeholders, hence the necessity for moral considerations. One key criteria for the morality of a duty holder's decisions and choices is to ensure that all the others impacted by the decisions made are treated fairly and with dignity, and not used as means to the decision makers' ends and objectives. The influential decision makers are also encouraged to consider circumstances in which their decisions could become universal laws and whether they would be willing to endure life influenced and shaped by those laws. Duty ethics demands moral scrutiny, considerations and judgements by those in a position of authority that would impose limits on their choices. In this way, those in a position of authority strive to ensure that every critical decision is made empathetically in an informed moral context.

The three schools of ethical philosophy endeavour to scrutinise the morality of human choices and decisions from the perspectives of individual virtue (component), consequence/utility (system-level) and duty holders (governance). From a holistic systems analytical viewpoint, the three canons of ethical philosophy provide an encompassing framework for understanding, analysing and proactively addressing ethical concerns arising from our choices, decisions and actions from a personal, corporate and collective perspective. However, this ethical framework is drawn from the Western world's philosophical paradigm. The ethical values that underpin our cultural, historical and social morals may also originate from a multitude of other rich and equally pertinent ecosystems that have their origins in ethnic beliefs, behavioural codes, creed and culture. A universal ethical framework should additionally factor in values that are not necessarily traceable to personal virtues, duty holders' maxims or pure utilitarianism. Ancient human societies and associated cultures have largely evolved in relative isolation, each developing their own ethical values and moral codes. These will additionally provide a potent landscape for the exploration of ethical values and moral implications in the design of products, services and systems alongside the three philosophies cited earlier.

The Emerging Reality

The widescale emerging pattern of cyber attacks globally poses an unprecedented threat to governance, economic activities, and the peace and stability of the largely digitally-transformed lifestyle. The recent cyber attacks on the USA power grid and power companies, also known as the so-called grid hacking — a spree of attacks on over 300 universities and some private companies in the USA and beyond resulting in the loss of 31 terabytes of private data estimated to amount to an equivalent of $3 billion worth of intellectual property and a whole host of data breaches including one which yielded 2 terabytes of private information on hundreds of millions of American adults — are illustrative of the unabating current trends. Apart from the colossal economic, strategic and geopolitical impact such breaches have, many of the security breaches of state and private sector enterprises have major ethical dimensions relating to privacy, trust, duty of care/protection and accountability.

Alongside the current concerns over security, there are other technological developments that bring great promise and at the same time pose major risks to mankind if not understood, analysed and mitigated proactively. The emergence of autonomous and smart products, systems and services, and the vast potential of Artificial Intelligence (AI) comprise the most notable and impactful innovations over the horizon — although they already pervade our lives to some degree.

In this dynamic, exciting, promising as well as potentially disruptive setting, the need to focus on the societal macro perspective is more urgent than it has ever been.

Ethics now

On 1 November 2018, thousands of Google employees staged a mass protest against the corporate's sexual misconduct allegations. This protest took the form of a walkout, which was held across Google offices from Tokyo to California to demonstrate against workplace culture. This Walkout for Real Change followed an earlier employee reaction to a large military contract in 2018 in which employees objected to the company's involvement in non-civilian and militaristic projects. The campaigners in the walkout put forward a five point list of demands that comprised issues from i) putting an end to forced arbitration in harassment and discrimination cases, ii) commitment to equal pay and opportunity, iii) transparency over disclosure of sexual harassment, iv) a globally inclusive process for reporting sexual misconduct and v) the appointment of an employee representative on the Board.

These anecdotal cases paint a newly emerging picture in the hierarchical corporate world even for colossal multinational enterprises that dominate many aspects of global transactions with online services. In this newly emerging paradigm, the passive employees of a large enterprise attempted to awaken a sense of social responsibility and to promote ethical and moral behaviour in an otherwise commercial corporation with impact and partial success. This hopefully heralds the emergence of a socially responsive perspective on all business activities, invariably supported by the power of social media and the instant communication of ideals, including cases of abuse and soft power by the technocrats and scientists who do not sit at the pinnacle of power in large corporations and multi-national enterprises.

The need for pragmatism

The legal framework in most developed countries places a duty of care on people and all public and private enterprises regarding the health, safety and welfare of employees, customers, stakeholders and the general public. Physical and cyber security are increasingly regarded as an extension of the duty of care towards the general public but the general public are not yet subject to the same level of protection by laws and regulations in these areas. Interestingly, safety and security are both facets of the ethical values pertaining to a product, service or system. The importance of safety and security necessitates a new pragmatism towards social/public good that transcends mere compliance with legal duty of care imperatives. This demands a new codified ethical framework to enable public and private enterprises to factor in social sensitivities and ethical values in the design and deployment of their products and services. In this new paradigm, the power of the employees and the consumers are brought to bear as a form of highly responsive and effective market regulation, especially in the absence of adequate legal instruments. The development of legal instruments seems to trail behind the fast-paced technological innovations, but the reality is that many immoral and unethical activities are not necessarily illegal. This new form of social soft power is the antidote to the pure private motive and accountability towards shareholders that dominate the current corporate and legal landscape.

What Next?

There are a number of developments that herald a ray of hope in this dynamic, fast paced and often confusing scene. They are largely driven by current necessities and the initiatives of a number of international standardisation and professional institutions.

Within the context of cyber security, a large-scale effort has been under way to develop a global standard for the cyber protection of Industrial Automation and Control Systems (IACS). The ISA-64223 suite, comprising a 14-part series of standards and technical reports that covers models, concepts and processes for the security of industrial automation and control systems, has been developed by the International Society of Automation (ISA) with the goal of uniformity of approach in the field of instrumentation. Each part of the ISA-62443 suite covers a specific aspect of IACS Cyber Security and is aimed at a particular audience — from the designers and developers of complete systems to the suppliers of components and system integrators, operators and maintainers. The 14 parts are grouped in four key categories addressing general principles, policies and procedures and system and component level processes as illustrated in the overview diagram (Fig. 1).

It is worth noting that due to its extensive scale and scope, the ISA-62443 suite is still undergoing further updates and enhancements.

In the larger context of social good and societal impact, the International Institution of Electrical and Electronic Engineers

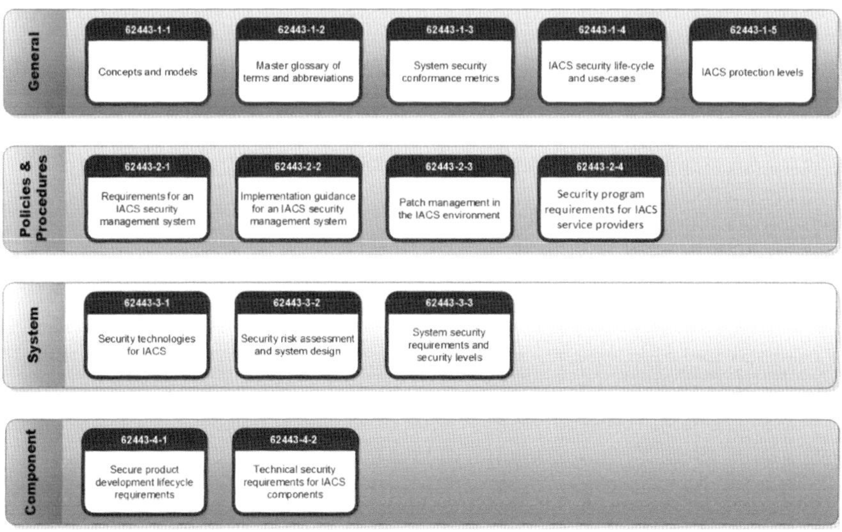

Fig. 1. Overview of the ISA-62443 suite of IACS cyber security standards.

(IEEE) has recently embarked on an ambitious programme of developing standards for Ethically Aligned Design. Apart from giving generic guidance on the Ethically Aligned Design standards, now in second revision, the IEEE Standards Association currently hosts 14 working groups focussed on various aspects of the design and behavioural features of smart, autonomous and AI technologies, products, services and systems. The whole initiative is under the IEEE P7000™ series of standards projects, which was under development at the time this book was written, and which represents a departure from the 1300 IEEE global standards on technology, interoperability and safety. It currently comprises the following:

1. **IEEE P7000™** — Model Process for Addressing Ethical Concerns During System Design
2. **IEEE P7001™** — Transparency of Autonomous Systems
3. **IEEE P7002™** — Data Privacy Process
4. **IEEE P7003™** — Algorithmic Bias Considerations
5. **IEEE P7004™** — Standard on Child and Student Data Governance
6. **IEEE P7005™** — Standard on Employer Data Governance
7. **IEEE P7006™** — Standard on Personal Data AI Agent Working Group
8. **IEEE P7007™** — Ontological Standard for Ethically-Driven Robotics and Automation Systems
9. **IEEE P7008™** — Standard for Ethically-Driven Nudging for Robotic, Intelligent and Autonomous Systems.
10. **IEEE P7009™** — Standard for Fail-Safe Design of Autonomous and Semi-Autonomous Systems
11. **IEEE P7010™** — Wellbeing Metrics Standard for Ethical Artificial Intelligence and Autonomous Systems
12. **IEEE P7011™** — Standard for the Process of Identifying and Rating the Trustworthiness of News Sources
13. **IEEE P7012™** — Standard for Machine Readable Personal Privacy Terms
14. **IEEE P7013™** — Inclusion and Application Standards for Automated Facial Analysis Technology

The current concerns over safety, reliability, security and even ethics require an integrated framework that guides, empowers and supports an inclusive approach to the development of products, services and systems and does not treat each dimension of performance as an independent facet of self-serving significance. This holistic framework is likely to be sustainable in the sense that a product, service or system that does not embody a judicious blend of all the performance requirements cited would fail to be sustainable technically, commercially, environmentally or from a societal point of view. This will pose a challenge but offer the promise of going beyond individual concerns, ethics, safety, security and localism whilst taking a macro perspective. In this new paradigm, the laws and regulations will be supplemented by an agile, responsive and informed global community.

Contents

Chapter 1

Attack Vectors and the Challenge of Preventing Data Theft

David A.E. Haddon

The Processor Centre
david.haddon@ieee.org

ABSTRACT

As a matter of normal business operations, confidential documents, payment instructions and credit card data need to be exchanged between systems easily and securely. To improve efficiency and reduce costs, governments and local authorities provide portals through which data is regularly transmitted in the form of tax returns, social security returns, company registration returns and so on. Email has become the main form of communication in business and as such is the life blood of many organisations. At the same time, it is important that emails are not accidentally or otherwise sent to the wrong recipient, as the content of a misaddressed email could compromise an individual and even expose a company to claims against it. Making sure that data is easily communicated to the correct parties and minimising the likelihood of data being exfiltrated or sent to the wrong location is a challenge every business faces. The challenges of maintaining the availability, confidentiality and integrity of both data and services has never been greater. The evolution of State Sponsored Cyber Attack Units and Cyber Mercenaries (Maurer, 2018) have increased the sophistication of attacks way beyond what some lonely teenager hacking systems from a bedroom could have accomplished. Locking down access rights, patching systems, restricting the ports that are enabled on firewalls and keeping antivirus systems up to date are normal practices on corporate networks. This is a study of the attack vectors and the methods used to mitigate attacks. It is unusual in that it assumes reasonable security precautions have been adopted and its scope is limited to such systems.

Keywords: Next-generation firewall, state-sponsored, data exfiltration, cross-site scripting, emerging threats, threat landscape, advanced persistent threat, tunnelling, covert channel

1.1. Cyber Attack Vectors

Cyber attacks are various. Some are targeted against servers and others are targeted at users and workstations.

According to the Symantec 2018 annual security review the main cyber attack vectors are the following:

- SQL Injection (against web servers).
- Cross Site Scripting (links with hooks to other websites).
- Spear Phishing Emails (links to phony websites made to look like other legitimate sites).
- Business Email Compromise (predominately hacked webmail services).
- Email attachments with embedded code.

Other growing and emerging threats are:

- PowerShell exploits (scripts that exploit PowerShell's vast command library).
- Command and Control exploits (these enable remote shell access to a victim's system).

However, before examining the various methods of performing cyber attacks, we first look at some of the largest leaks to get an insight into the attack vectors used in these attacks. From there an examination will be made of other emerging attack methods, and the way an attacker could subsequently exfiltrate data. Only the methods that could be used on a secure system will be discussed as it is assumed other methods would not be possible on systems where users are logged in with restricted access rights. Then, from a review of exfiltration methods, an analysis is made of the methods and products that can be used to protect a system. Further ideas to prevent data exfiltration are also proposed.

Due to the threats to corporate networks, the potentially large fines resulting from breaches under the 2018 General Data Protection Regulation (GDPR) law and the reputational damage associated with personal data theft, a company director's worst nightmare is to learn that their company's computer systems have been hacked and that client information might have been stolen. By studying this chapter, a company executive will understand some of the issues in protecting data, the vulnerabilities in the systems in which the data is held, and some of the emerging technologies, methods and products for preventing data theft.

Several firewall manufacturers now offer intrusion protection add-ons that use Deep Packet Inspection for detecting and preventing data exfiltration from on-premises networks. Yet, how effective they are at preventing data theft will depend on how well their detection methods are aligned with the exfiltration methods that an attacker or rogue user might use.

If an attack is targeted then an attacker will generally know what they are looking for, otherwise the most likely focus of an attack will be to search for files with credit card details, usernames, passwords, product keys, cryptocurrency wallets (aka crypto-jacking) and other confidential information. The number of files that an attacker would find of interest will generally be small as an attacker would generally have no reason to download all of a company's data unless it is all of interest. An attacker could examine emails for signs of a future large transaction that could be intercepted with a notification telling the company to transfer the money to the attacker's bank account, or he could use stolen user credentials to access other websites and obtain further confidential information. If the amount of data stolen is small, then it will be more difficult to detect the attack.

If a rogue user sends out emails to a personal email account with the company's data attached, how can this be detected when emailing out attachments is an everyday occurrence? Could a rogue user exfiltrate data to a web storage system such as Dropbox, or could a user accidentally launch a "command and control" data exfiltration attack by simply visiting a rogue website through opening an email attachment? These are real concerns not only for company directors but also security professionals.

1.1.1. *A brief look at the attack vectors in high profile leaks*

When leaks are reported, the method by which data is stolen is often glossed over. As far as the news reporter is concerned, the headline generally focusses on how many thousands or millions of personal records or user credentials have been stolen, how many credit card numbers have been taken, the subsequent risks to individuals and the damage to the company. Once confidential data is in the public domain, how it happened is often a secondary issue.

The following is a list of methods used to leak data from historical records accessed on or before March 7, 2019.

1. **Adultfriendfinder** — 412 million accounts were hacked in 2016 due to a Structured Query Language (SQL) injection vulnerability. Of the accounts hacked 103 million were apparently stored in a database in plaintext (Storm, 2016).
2. **Anthem** — The USA's largest healthcare insurers were hacked in 2015. 80 million records were accessed using malware that gave the attackers access to a user's workstation (Abelson and Goldstein, 2015).
3. **Appleby** (Paradise Papers) — 13.4 million documents were leaked. Appleby claimed that the German newspaper *Süddeutsche Zeitung* had obtained these because of a data theft. Appleby are a law firm, and sued newspapers such as the *BBC News* and the *Guardian* — which reported the story — for inaccuracies,

arguing that the data was stolen, not hacked. Though they won this action and managed to prevent further publication, it was a hollow victory, as Appleby are still losing clients (Appleby, 2018).

4. **British Airways** (BA) — 380,000 credit card records were stolen for bookings made between 22 August and 5 September 2018 (FT, 2018). This was the first large theft of personal data in the UK national news since GDPR came into force. The transactions were believed to have been intercepted whilst being processed using an external partner's scripts. As the data controller, British Airways were responsible for reporting the breach even though they do not hold the CCV data. It is interesting to note that Air Canada's data breach over the same period attracted far less publicity (Whittaker, 2018).
5. **Bupa** — 108,000 records were stolen in 2017 by a rogue employee who copied data and tried to sell it (Bupa, 2017). From the Bupa jobs advertised in 2015 we see that Bupa recognised the importance of compliance with security standards ISO27001:2013 and PCI DSS (Bupa, 2015).
6. **Citibank** — A hacker stole 200,000 customer details in 2011 (Packard, 2013). This was the second breach after the bank's internet platform had been hacked (Kitten, 2011). The data was stolen after the hacker realized that once logged in a user could just alter the URL to access another person's bank account, and automated the process (Wilson, 2011).
7. **Deloitte** was hacked through an account that did not have two-factor authentication (Daileda, 2017). This is despite Deloitte implementing ISO27001:2013 and being a company that promotes and assists companies with implementing the ISO27001 standard.
8. **Dixons Carphone** — 5.9 million payment cards and 1.2 million personal data records were stolen in 2017. The cards apparently have not been used maliciously as most of them were protected by their chips and PINs. The names, addresses and email addresses of more than one million people were also taken in the breach (Cellan-Jones, 2018).

9. **eBay** was hacked in 2014 due to the hacker obtaining access credentials from some eBay staff (Finkle, 2014). eBay itself does not process credit card transactions as these are done through a payment gateway provided by PayPal; however, eBay and Paypal would have been audited to the highest Payment Card Industry Data Security Standard (PCI DSS) standards due to the volume of transactions processed. The standard PCI DSS questionnaire D (PCI DSS, 2018) is very stringent and can be very challenging to deploy.
10. **Equifax** had their website hacked due to a security flaw in Apache Struts, an open source Apache Java add-on (Sweet and Liedtke, 2017). The vulnerability is explained by Sophos on the Naked Security website (https://nakedsecurity.sophos.com/) (Ducklin, 2017).
11. **Facebook** — At least 87 million records were breached. An app was developed that scraped details about people's personalities, social networks and engagement on the platform. The breach was disclosed on 17 March 2018 and Facebook were fined £500,000 (Hern and Pegg, 2018). Facebook lost over one million users as a result and its share price fell 20% over two weeks during the Cambridge Analytica scandal before recovering six weeks later, based on strong financial results.
12. **Facebook 2** — A further leak in September 2018 was due to problems with Facebook's code. A quiz app apparently allowed attackers to take control of accounts. Astonishingly, about 50 million accounts were affected (Matsacis and Lapowsky, 2018).
13. **Google** was hacked from China in 2009 and 2011 (Packard, 2013). This was due to a spear phishing attack that gave the attackers access to a Google employee's system. The attack lasted for about one year (Nakashima, 2013).
14. **Heartland Payment Systems** — 134 million accounts of the 6th largest payment provider in the USA were hacked in 2008 using SQL injection (McGlasson, 2009; Vaas, 2018).
15. **JPMorgan Chase** was hacked by criminals who were not expert hackers. The attackers bought the tools to hack JPMorgan Chase (Economist, 2015). Personal data from 83 million accounts were accessed.

16. **Mossack Fonseca** (Panama Papers) — This leak was the result of the Outlook Web Access component of Exchange 2010 not being patched for three years (Wired, 2016).
17. **MyHeritage** — The hack was disclosed on 4 June 2018. A security researcher reached out to the Chief Information Security Officer of online genealogy platform MyHeritage and revealed they had found a file labeled "myheritage" on a private server outside the company. Upon inspection of the file, officials at MyHeritage determined that the asset contained the email addresses of all users who had signed up with MyHeritage prior to 26 October 2017.
18. **RSA** — 44 million account credentials were leaked in 2011. Two separate hacking groups launched a phishing attack against RSA employees. The leak cost the company $66 million (Armerding, 2018).
19. **Sony** warned that users of its PlayStation network might have had their personal information, including credit card details, stolen (Cellan-Jones, 2011). Sony was hacked due to weak passwords. The 2015 hack was extremely sophisticated and used Zero-day malware and sophisticated exfiltration methods. 77 million accounts were compromised and Sony paid $8 m to the affected employees (BBC, 2015).
20. **TalkTalk** was hacked by a teenager on 21 October 2015 (TalkTalk, 2016). 156,959 account details were taken including 21,000 bank details and email addresses. The leak cost TalkTalk £42 m and they were fined £400,000. The cause was SQL injection (ICO, 2016).
21. **Target Stores** — 110 million accounts were hacked in 2013 including 40 million credit card details. Federal law enforcement later discovered 11 GB of data from Target that the hackers had transferred to a temporary server (Smith, 2014).
22. **Tesco** — Cyber attackers exploited deficiencies in Tesco Bank's design of its debit card, its financial crime controls and its Financial Crime Operations Team to carry out the attack. Those deficiencies left Tesco Bank's personal current account holders vulnerable to the cyber attackers for over 48 hours and netted

the cyber attackers £2.26 m. Tesco was fined £16.4 m on 1 October 2018 (FCA, 2018).

23. **Ticketmaster** — 40,000 people were affected over a period from February to June 2018. Ticketmaster revealed that the login information, payment data, addresses, names and telephone numbers of users were at risk. It would turn out that Ibenta Technologies, who operate a chatbot on Ticketmaster's site, had modified a line of JavaScript code to customise its basic product to its client's needs. Ticketmaster then used this code (without Ibenta's knowledge) on its payments page. Hackers discovered this script, and then modified it to extract payment information, harvesting user information from February 2018 onwards (Wired, 2018).
24. **Uber** was hacked in 2016. Uber's chief security officer Joe Sullivan was fired for concealing the October 2016 breach. Uber paid hackers $100,000 to delete data and keep the breach quiet (Wong, 2017). Personal information from 56 million accounts was accessed. Hackers managed to access Uber's accounts on Amazon Web Services by hacking access credentials. The data was unencrypted.
25. **US Office of Personnel Management** — 22 million records were stolen in 2012. The hack was due to a compromised third party (OPM, undated).
26. **Yahoo** — 1 billion account details were stolen (Williams 2017). Yahoo notified users in December 2016 of the breach that occurred in 2014. Farivar (2018) highlights the seriousness of hacking for hire, and how an administrative tool was used to reset passwords for targeted accounts.

The accounts affected by the large data leaks have been collated into a database where one can check using an email address what leaks the email address may have been involved in. The site is run by Troy Hunt and is found at https://haveibeenpwned.com/.

1.1.2. *Overview of the high-profile leaks*

Looking at the high-profile attacks earlier, it is evident that only a few involved a sophisticated attack method (CitiBank, eBay and

Sony). The majority of the attacks were due to SQL injection, deception and carelessness from employees and vulnerabilities due to unpatched systems. Deloitte, eBay and TalkTalk were all supposedly audited to ISO27001:2013; eBay and TalkTalk would have been PCI DSS compliant too. With so many of the systems examined not being patched correctly, the companies were not complying with the standards in practice despite having been audited.

Many of the attacks listed involved insiders. Of those that were outright hacks, the main method of attack was SQL injection. Organisations that have public web servers that interact with SQL servers are therefore particularly vulnerable.

Not all the exfiltration methods used in the listed attacks have been determined. Had there been a secured and properly patched system, only a few would have been successful.

1.1.3. *High profile leaks and insider threat*

The Verizon Data Breach Investigations Report shows that 75% of data exfiltration attacks were from external hackers and 25% from internal actors (Verizon, 2017), which is slightly at odds with the attacks listed, in which internal involvement is seen to have been more prevalent. The Anthem, Appleby, Bupa, eBay, Google, MyHeritage, RSA and Uber attacks all appear to involve insiders, either due to lack of diligence or dishonesty. Techniques that reduce the threat from insiders are therefore important to discuss. Insiders have access to systems and a user with a moderate level of technical expertise will have knowledge of internal systems and their architecture. There are a lot of psychological reasons why an employee may steal data and much has been written on this subject, notably "The CERT Guide to Insider Threats" (Cappelli and Moore, 2012).

> *"Insider IT Sabotage is typically committed by technical users with privileged access, such as system administrators, database administrators, and programmers. The motivation in those crimes is usually revenge for a negative workplace event, and the crimes are often set up while still employed but executed following termination.*

> *Insider theft of intellectual property (IP) is usually committed by scientists, engineers, programmers, and salespeople. The insiders usually steal the information they worked on and take it with them as they leave the organization to start their own business, take with them to a new job, or give foreign government or organization.*
>
> *Insider fraud is usually committed by lower-level employees such as help desk, customer service, and data entry clerks. The crimes are motivated by financial need or greed, and they typically continue for a long time. Many of these insiders are recruited by outsiders to steal information. Collusion with other insiders is very common in crimes involving modification of information for payment from the outside."*

It is clear from this quote from Cappelli and Moore (2012) that Risk Managers and HR departments need to work closely with IT departments to ensure an effective Information Governance security framework. Staff are moved from department to department gaining an ever-increasing knowledge of a company's systems. Rotation of job duties and responsibilities is seen as a form of security control in many large organisations in that it exposes bad practices, but also familiarises the rogue employee with greater knowledge of a company's systems and its vulnerabilities. Although job rotation and compulsory two-week holidays are standard methods that organisations use to expose fraud, build skills and provide variety, it is questionable whether these practices improve security. Office practices are clearly very different to military security practices. In the military, information is conveyed on a need-to-know basis.

1.1.4. *What exfiltration methods are possible on a corporate network?*

Although in practice malware and botnets might be used to exfiltrate data, one would expect these to be picked up by an antivirus scanner. Unwanted applications that come with new machines are removed as a matter of course and Potentially Unwanted Applications (PUAs) and the payloads that are downloaded due to Zero-day exploits are prevented from being installed by restricted access rights. Even so it must be assumed that there is still the possibility that some malware might get installed and not detected. Once installed, malware could provide the means to enable a command and control exploit like the Kali BEEF exploit and subsequently exfiltrate data.

Word macros that can launch fileless malware are a more sophisticated threat as an exploit is run in memory without the need to save a payload. Payloads may also be delivered using steganography to hide code in images which are generally ignored by Antivirus programs. Visiting a website's images causes images with steganographic content to be automatically downloaded into a user's internet cache, providing another means from which code could be extracted. This will be discussed later.

If a firewall is configured correctly, there are no inbound rules generally required other than for incoming email to an email gateway server configured for that purpose, and the only outbound rules allowed should be:

- DNS outbound using UDP DNS port 53 only. (Generally, from a DNS Caching server only).
- HTTPS outbound through a proxy server.
- Email outbound from a Microsoft Exchange Server, or an email gateway.
- NTP outbound for time synchronisation.
- ICMP outbound for diagnosing connectivity issues.

This chapter is therefore limited to these protocols and their related TCP/UDP ports.

1.2. Scope of Discussion on Data Exfiltration Methods

According to Rashid *et al.* (2017) an advanced persistent threat (APT) attack follows three distinct phases.

Stage 1: Reconnaissance, attack staging and initial host infection.
Stage 2: Network intrusion, remote control, data discovery, persistence.
Stage 3: Staging server selection, data preparation and data exfiltration.

This chapter focuses on the last stage where access is obtained to a user's workstation or a server. Therefore,

- Data exfiltration by air-gapped methods is excluded from this discussion.
- Data exfiltration via USB devices is also excluded. Obviously stealing data using USB devices, either as backup media or otherwise is perhaps the easiest way to get substantial amounts of data from an organisation but this involves deception and unauthorised physical access which are outside the scope of this chapter. Also, it is assumed that the use of USB storage devices has been restricted either by a system Group Policy (GPO) or centrally managed antivirus endpoint management system like Sophos EMS. Where USB devices need to be used it would be assumed that they are encrypted and that their loss would not pose a threat.
- It is assumed that user access rights are set correctly, and that users do not have local administrative rights. The focus will be on methods that are theoretically possible using tools which are native to the operating system or that could be possible without installing programs — effectively living off the land (Symantec, 2017).
- Stolen Laptop. This is outside the scope of this discussion, though the following quote must not be forgotten: "The data leaks posed by accidents exceed the risks posed by vulnerable software" (Kaspersky, 2014).
- Wireless vulnerabilities like man-in-the-middle attacks are excluded as wireless connections to a corporate network are assumed to be unacceptable.

1.2.1. *Web server attack — SQL injection*

Structured Query Language injection occurs when code is input in forms. If the data entered is not validated, then any code placed in a search box is sent to the SQL engine with two possible undesirable outcomes. The first is that a buffer overflow is caused resulting in shell access using the SQL connect permissions and the second is that answers to unintended queries can be retrieved. To extract data, many queries might be required to establish a database's structure. This sounds complex but has happened on many occasions, as is clear from the reported hacks.

The reality is and has always been that anything internet facing with an external IP address will be under attack, so web server operating systems need to be hardened and web interfaces need to be robust. Forensic investigations of web attacks on web servers such as Apache can be difficult because even if full forensic logging is turned on, if the attacker is using the TOR browser, then it will be the TOR endpoint IP address that is logged, not the attacker's IP address.

Web servers must therefore be patched and scanned for vulnerabilities regularly, and when accessing confidential information, two-factor authentication should be used where possible.

1.2.2. *Cross Site Scripting*

Cross Site Scripting (XSS) involves appending a JavaScript string to the end of a URL. This is then sent in an email to a user who is meant to think that clicking on that URL will only lead him to a familiar site. This perception is reinforced by the fact that the displayed URL does not show the appended string. When a user clicks on the link they are taken to the site as expected but a JavaScript script also runs. This can be set to pop-up a window asking for credentials, a hook that launches a command and control attack.

According to the European Union Agency for Network and Information Security (ENISA), XSS attacks grew 39% in Q1 of 2017, and XSS vulnerabilities are thought to have grown by 166% in 2017 (ENISA, 2017, p. 36). There are various types of XSS attacks, the most common being a reflected attack whereby no change is made to the web server. Cross Site Scripting attacks are also a common way of stealing cookies for session hijacking and getting user credentials.

Preventing web attacks requires a combination of technology and awareness. XSS attacks commonly happen when users follow links in emails and on the internet to familiar websites. One effective way to prevent XSS attacks is to examine links before clicking on them. Many Antivirus solutions examine weblinks for suspicious content at the end of a web address, as do all the main browsers now, including Internet Explorer 11, Microsoft Edge, Google Chrome and Mozilla Firefox. Trustwave's Blended Threats is an example of an option deployed on the Trustwave Secure Email Gateway that rewrites links in emails so that they can be verified by Trustwave. The primary precaution to avoid the consequences of rogue content is not to have systems that are vulnerable, which is largely achieved by keeping systems patched with the latest security updates.

Cutting edge firewalls that have XSS detection built into IDS/IPS features should be deployed as these can prevent XSS attacks and filter out Denial-of-Service (DoS) attacks. GeoIP filters, which can be used to block traffic from specific geographic locations, are now also a common feature of firewalls. They are seldom used, and their use should be considered.

1.2.3. *PowerShell exploits*

PowerShell exploits are fileless malware using PowerShell, PSExec or WMI that run simple scripts and shellcode directly in memory. They are increasingly being used in attacks by both targeted threat actors and cyber criminals as they avoid detection and make forensic investigations harder (Symantec, 2017). Symantec refer to these attacks as "living off the land" and "fileless attack methods".

1.2.4. *Command and Control*

In a Command and Control attack, a staging server under the control of the attacker is used to mount the attack. This means that any tracing done on the target network will lead to the compromised system that is the staging server. The staging server might be controlled over the TOR network, thus protecting the anonymity of the attacker. An alternative approach that allows an attacker to protect their identity is ngrok (ngrok, 2018), a free utility available from GitHub which allows the attack to be proxied via ngrok's server using a temporary URL (Hackersgrid, 2018). ngrok was developed as an educational tool to assist students to run web servers on the internet even though they might be behind routers and firewalls because students might not be able to configure port forwarding on the routers they use and might not want to pay for dynamic Domain Name System (DNS) services. The use of ngrok as a hacking tool is therefore not its intended use. ngrok can be purchased, which gives permanent URLs, or used for free, which has the limitation that the URL changes with each use. However, when attackers use the free version of ngrok, there is no payment trail to disclose the attacker.

The ChessMaster cyber espionage campaign (Hsieh and Kohei, 2017) is partly based on a technique that can be demonstrated with the use of Koadic (Takhion, 2018). Koadic (available from zero-sum0x0's github page) is a Command and Control tool built for educational purposes. It is like the Metasploit and Empire frameworks except that it exploits a Microsoft Windows JavaScript engine, mstha.exe, rather than using a payload. A user just needs to be persuaded to click on a web page link to launch the attack. These attacks work by creating a reverse proxy from the victim back to the attacker and could in practice use common ports like port 80 (HTTP) or 53 (DNS) which might be open to provide internet access.

1.2.5. *Phishing emails*

Phishing emails are often regarded as spam, but the difference is that they are generally targeted and have malicious links to code on external websites. By clicking on one a user might be doing no more than effectively confirming their email address.

By looking at the yearly reports from Symantec and Sophos it is seen that spear-phishing attacks are currently the most common attack vector. According to Symantec:

> "*If you're going to be attacked, the chances are that initial compromise, the gap in the fence the attackers sneak through, is going to be created by social engineering rather than anything technically sophisticated such as exploit of a zero-day vulnerability. Spear-phishing emails are the number one*

means of attack we've seen used, meaning a well-crafted email, sent to an unsuspecting staff member is the most likely source of compromise and can be the trigger to a potentially serious security breach." (Symantec, 2018) 74% of attacks involved phishing emails (Symantec, 2018, p. 76).

From Trustwave's 2017 Security Report, targeted spear phishing attacks are the most common method to gain initial access (Trustwave, 2018).

To be successful in duping a victim, the emails used for the attacks must be convincing. This level of detail in spear-phishing emails, i.e. the use of familiar names, logos and style, is now becoming commonplace. Vigilance, the verification of email instructions by other means and good email filtering is paramount.

1.2.6. *Documents with embedded code and other attachments*

According to the Sophos Annual Report 2018 the two most common Office exploits in 2017 were CVE-2012-0158 and CVE-2017-0199 (Sophos, 2018). CVE-2012-0158 is the most exploited document vulnerability going back to 2012. Though patched it remains a popular exploit. This is a buffer overflow vulnerability in the ListView/TreeView ActiveX controls in the MSCOMCTL.OCX library (Janus, 2013). The CVE-2017-0199 vulnerability is exploited by malicious code that can be triggered by a specially crafted DOC or RTF file for Microsoft Office versions 2003, 2007 and 2010 (Jiang, 2017). This vulnerability allows a malicious actor to download and execute a Visual Basic script containing PowerShell commands when a user opens a document containing an embedded exploit.

1.2.7. *Business Email Compromise*

With so many email systems having web interfaces, improper use of webmail is not surprising, and the threat of Business Email Compromise (BEC) can easily be understood. The attack vector might be a link in an email, which leads a user to a clone website asking a user to change their password. The email looks legitimate and the website the user is directed to is a perfect clone of a web email service provider's website. Another scam is an email that requests users to log on and upgrade storage quotas (Ragan, 2017). Having gained access to a user's email, an attacker can gather information and look for an opportunity to intercept a future large transaction. An attacker will subsequently advise new bank details in relation to a payment at precisely the time the payment is expected. The sophistication can be extreme, and the sums defrauded in this way can be large. These attacks are targeted, customised and now extremely common. They are known as Business Email Compromise (BEC) and according to the FBI Internet Crime Complaint Center, BEC has been a bigger issue than ransomware since 2016 (FBI IC3, 2018). The FBI is therefore now tracking BEC as a single crime type (FBI IC3, 2017). The attack vector could be a shared computer in a hotel lobby that is set to record passwords.

1.2.8. *Emerging threats: Knock-Knock and Office 365*

Artificial Intelligence (AI) is seen as the concept that will make all our lives easier, although it can also be used as an attack tool. The Knock-Knock attack against Microsoft Office 365 servers is an example of this. Having determined an organisation to target, a company's email domain name is easily deduced from a company's website. The company's web site is then trawled for employee names, and the internet is searched for email addresses related to the company. Once one is found then the format of all others in the company is deduced. One of the flaws of Office365 is that the usernames are generally the email addresses. AI is used to try each email address with just two passwords, then move on to the next email address, which is how the attack gets its name. The attacking machine then goes to sleep or performs an attack on another company. It then returns and tries the email addresses again with another two passwords, then goes to sleep again and so on. Eventually an account is cracked, and a user's email is downloaded, which gives the attacker knowledge of everything a user is doing, including access to their calendar. Office365 accounts can be protected by the implementation of the Enterprise Security and Mobility Suite as this can be set to only allow registered devices to connect.

1.3. Exfiltration Methods

There are a couple of comprehensive reviews of data exfiltration methods, one published by Ullah *et al.* (2017), the other by Rashid *et al.* (2017); however, many of the methods discussed in Ullah *et al.* and Rashid *et al.* assume that an attacker has the necessary access rights to install malware. As mentioned earlier, locking down access rights, patching systems, restricting the ports that are enabled on firewalls and keeping antivirus systems up to date are normal practices on corporate networks, so this study will be limited to only the methods possible on such a system.

Rashid *et al.* highlights the concern that a growing number of attacks target remote users' home PCs as these are likely to be used to access targeted information elsewhere (Rashid *et al.*, 2017). Remote PCs are more likely not to have access rights set correctly and can be more easily targeted with phishing and cross-site scripting attacks. If a keylogger can be installed on a home worker's PC even though the PC may not hold any data of any value, credentials for an office system may be determined. The threat posed by remote workers, though, is not the focus of this study.

1.3.1. *Exfiltration using DNS aka DNS tunnelling*

DNS as a protocol is often allowed outbound even though DNS queries on a network should be resolved by internal DNS servers. Although DNS queries use UDP for speed the communication is 2-way in that a DNS response is expected. The DNS protocol only allows packets of 512 bytes, so to transfer any amount of data many queries need to be sent in the form of multiple packets to the same parent domain.

A DNS query will always find its way to the authoritative DNS server for the domain queried, see Fig. 1.1. The endpoint of the attack is therefore a server acting as an authoritative DNS server. DNS tunnelling is therefore a covert way of exfiltrating data and several toolkits are available with which to do this. To encode the communication, Base32/Base64 Binary encoding or Hex encoding

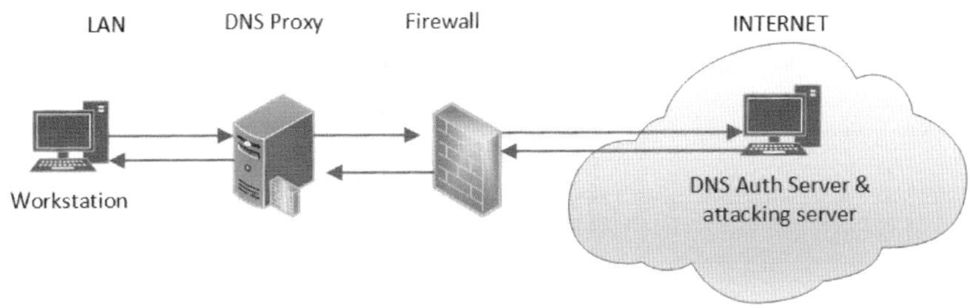

Fig. 1.1. Outbound DNS request followed by response.

is often used. The responses can either be CNAME (limited to 63 characters) or TXT (limited to 220 characters). EDNS can also be used to increase the payload.

1.3.2. *DNS tunnelling tools*

There are several tools available to effect DNS tunnelling. They are:

- DeNiSe — This is a Python script for DNS tunnelling.
- Dns2tcp — This exfiltrates data to an authoritative DNS server using UDP port 53.
- Dnscat2 (Dnscat, 2018) — This tool is specifically designed with Command and Control attacks in mind and is available as Windows and Linux binaries.
- Iodine — Iodine is a more recent tool that has client and server components. A VPN tunnel is effectively set up between the client and server using a different IP range to the physical IP addresses (Iodine, 2014).
- Meterpreter DNS Tunnel (K-Max, 2018) — Uses Kali as the attacking tool and a small payload on the compromised workstation.

Improvements to these existing tools are discussed by Revelli and Leidecker (2009).

Using varied name server queries and varied TXT responses, various tools have been developed, which has led to the development of NSTX (Name Server Transfer Protocol), another technique for exploiting DNS.

The tools Iodine and DNScat2, which are available for DNS tunnelling, require local administrative rights to install, and DNScat2 is detected by Sophos and AVG. Because having administrative rights on a workstation is not possible on a secured network, these tools are theoretically not a threat; however, this does not mean that the vulnerability is removed, as a new method using PowerShell could still work. A recent example of a DNS exfiltration tool is DNSExfiltrator (DNSExfiltrator, 2018), which has a JavaScript client that could be triggered by a cross-site script or rogue link.

1.3.3. *DNS tunnelling detection*

According to Zimba and Chishimba (2017) one of the greatest challenges in detecting DNS tunnelling is that most firewalls and IDS devices do not inspect DNS traffic. Mehmet and Ince (2016) highlight that if a workstation's configured DNS servers cannot resolve external DNS, DNScat2 can be configured to exfiltrate data using any DNS cache server that a workstation can communicate with.

DNS tunnels can be detected based on the entropy of requested hostnames (Butler and Grady, 2011). The number of DNS queries of a hostname for a given domain could also be an indicator.

Logging of DNS requests is therefore important as this provides evidence of DNS exfiltration and of the location where data is being exfiltrated to. An examination of the ownership of a domain name may provide some evidence of the attacker's identity should they have been careless enough not to use fake details. The obvious arguments against DNS logging are the sheer size of the logs that would be produced, and that these logs would need to be archived and managed.

Although DNS tunnelling might look complicated it is much safer an option for an attacker as DNS requests are less likely to be logged compared with HTTP/HTTPS requests which would be logged by a web proxy or outgoing SMTP email, which in turn would be logged by an email gateway.

DNS tunnelling is interesting in that although DNS is a layer 7 protocol, the object of DNS tunneling is to establish TCP communication (which would be layer 3 — the network layer) over DNS.

Netflow's FlowPro Defender is a tool that can be used to detect DNS tunnelling (Scott, 2016).

DNS logging allows one the opportunity of detecting requests to dynamic DNS hosts. Evidence of DNS tunnelling will be found in DNS Cache server logs. The requests will make use of the maximum DNS packet size which is 253 characters, with a maximum of 63 characters per label. This is defined in RFC1035 (Mockapetris, 1987) as x.y.z where y.z is a parent domain and x is (255 — length (y.z) – 63 – 63 – 63) characters (Dooley and Rooney, 2017).

DNS URLs over 52 characters are not normal, so in simple terms the first sign of something not being right is a long DNS frame (Guy, 2009). The next giveaway is the entropy of the first label. If a label is the first label of a DNS tunnel, it would be expected to be encoded with base32 giving a higher entropy (Butler and Grady, 2011).

DNSSEC may prevent DNS cache servers from DNS poisoning. However, as DNS exfiltration techniques use valid DNS packets, DNSSEC does little to prevent DNS tunneling. The reason for this is that DNSSEC is designed as a mechanism for a browser to check with a domain registrar that DNS records being returned by DNS Cache servers are consistent with the registrar's signature for those records. In other words, a rogue domain used for DNS exfiltration could still be protected by DNSSEC.

1.3.4. *Malware using DNS tunnelling*

A new trend is malware using DNS to send C&C commands (Khandelwal, 2017). DNSMessenger is an example of a Remote Access Trojan (RAT) that uses DNS queries to launch malicious PowerShell commands on compromised computers. Examples have been detected in sophisticated attacks launched from a VBA macro embedded in a Word document, which is used to execute a PowerShell script (Brumaghin and Grady, 2017). DNSMessenger is fileless as it does not write files to the targeted system, but uses DNS

TXT messages to fetch PowerShell commands stored remotely as DNS TXT records (Khandelwal, 2017). The method modifies the Windows Management Instrumentation (WMI) database to maintain persistence after reboots.

1.4. The Threat Posed by Web Storage and Web Exfiltration

Web-based exfiltration methods can either be covert or overt. Data can be transferred in the background using the web-based protocols HTTP or HTTPS, which use an organisation's proxy server, or by a rogue employee to a web storage account such as Dropbox, OneDrive, SpiderOak, etc. Microsoft OneDrive, Dropbox and SpiderOak are all examples of commonly used web storage accounts. Dropbox can be used with or without an agent, however, in order to use the agent, further TCP ports must be configured on a firewall, so using Dropbox in this mode would not be possible on a secure network. The OneDrive App is often installed with Microsoft Office and the App works quite happily over a web proxy. SpiderOak provides encrypted web storage and so is an example of a business system that could be exploited by an attacker who would be able to conceal the data stolen.

The threat of employees transferring data to web storage accounts is very real. OneDrive is ubiquitously installed on workstations and can easily be configured by users to steal data, then to be removed from a system. It is interesting to note that OneDrive is unusual as an application in that it does not require local administrative rights to install and often installs itself when Office is upgraded as access rights are automatically elevated by the operating system to install updates. OneDrive is also installed by default on many new machines. Microsoft OneDrive for Business is an application which is often unintentionally installed on systems when Microsoft Office is installed. Assuming OneDrive is installed on a workstation, all a user or an attacker needs to do is temporarily configure it to use a Microsoft account. Once data has been taken, OneDrive can then be reconfigured, leaving no obvious trace that it has been used to exfiltrate data.

Tracking browsing is difficult as one webpage might reference several others for content. Looking at proxy server logs can also be confusing as references to other sites can often imply that a user has knowingly navigated to these referenced sites.

Not surprisingly, removing general web browsing from networks is becoming more common. Proxy servers can be set to allow access to only the banking sites and business sites needed. This might sound extreme but is not as impractical as it sounds. If access is removed totally, any forms that need to be completed online can be done by machines in a DMZ, and the completed forms transferred up to internal systems by email or hot folders. This model is effectively that of cloud computing where internet access from the cloud is restricted but a user can access the web directly from the desktop. Done properly this is like the age-old model used by the military called Bell-LaPadula where information can be transferred up to more secure areas but not down.

1.4.1. *ICMP tunnelling*

Several utilities are available for establishing ICMP tunnels. The most popular tool is ptunnel (Stodal, 2005). The main reason for these utilities is to allow a notebook user to bypass a proxy server on a public WIFI system. Despite the use of these, a good firewall should detect this traffic; however, to remove the vulnerability, the organisation's firewall rules should not allow users to send the Ping message from workstations.

ICMP tunnelling tools were developed to provide a means to bypass a proxy server by creating an ICMP tunnel to an external web proxy server. However, it is easy to see how ICMP tunnelling can be exploited in a similar way to DNS tunnelling to create a covert channel by which data could be exfiltrated.

1.4.2. *NTP tunnelling*

Liska (2016) highlights that NTP is an old protocol with certain vulnerabilities in its design. NTP uses UDP port 123 and is required by servers to synchronise time. Workstations generally synchronise with domain controllers as part of a global policy. NTP or UDP 123 outbound is therefore not required from a workstation, however it can be used to generate several attacks internally and as an exfiltration method from a server configured as the network's internal time server. Hyper-V replication requires that time is synchronised on a network to within 5 minutes, else replication stops. Microsoft's Kerberos implementation requires time not to drift too much else machines have problems accessing network resources. Therefore, disrupting time on a network has serious consequences. Because an NTP query to the internet requires a response, NTP could also be used to establish a tunnel in a way similar to DNS tunnelling. The firewall rule allowing NTP outbound should therefore be restricted to genuine NTP time servers only. CVE-2015-7871 is a vulnerability that allows a server to accept a forged NTP packet from temporary peers (Liska, 2016). Safebreach, in their 2017 Security report, highlights that NTP is a sneaky method that hackers use to exfiltrate data (Safebreach, 2018).

1.4.3. *The threat posed by email*

Tracking email is quite straightforward, as each email generally has one source and one recipient. So, if email is exfiltrated by email, seeing what has happened is straightforward assuming an email gateway such as the Trustwave Secure Email Gateway or Mimecast has been used. Any rogue insider with a little knowledge would be aware that using email as a method to exfiltrate data is likely to leave a trail.

1.4.4. *Steganography*

This is the practice of hiding a message within a picture. The most popular method is to use the least significant bit of a pixel to hide data, as changing this causes no visible change to the appearance of a picture. Steghide, Stegosuite, Jsteg, Openpuff, JPHide and JPSeek are just some of the tools available with which to do this (Hegarty, 2018). Another technique is to merely append code to the end of a file; however, this is more likely to get detected.

Several leaks have used steganographic means to exfiltrate data; however, looking at this from a practical perspective, an attacker needs to find image files on a system in which sensitive data can be hidden. If a large amount of data is to be stolen, then it goes without saying that the amount of data to be exfiltrated using steganographic means will become significant, causing a bottleneck for the attacker. The volume of network traffic generated by using this method would provide easily detectible evidence, especially for any traffic monitoring systems such as Darktrace or Bro. An attacker would also need to be transmitting different pictures for the transfer not to look odd. The automation of the process of sending out data via varying pictures so that the hidden data can easily be extracted is perhaps a bit unlikely, though this method is not to be overlooked as a way of exfiltrating small amounts of data. The main threat from steganography is as an attack vector to deliver payload hidden in a picture. eBay and Facebook now re-render images uploaded to their platforms, which corrupts any steganographic content. Software tools like Stegohunt have been developed to detect the presence of hidden data and payloads in images (Whetstone, 2018), though real-time detection using antivirus programs is not standard.

1.4.5. *Dealing with a cyber attack*

After an incident, the key element that one looks at is logs. Logs hold tangible evidence of events. After an incident, a timeline must be drawn up showing what happened where and when. If clocks are not synchronised, this becomes not only very difficult but extremely confusing and provides ammunition for contesting any breach report. The time synchronisation of a system to a single reference time source is a requirement of ISO27001:2013(A.12.4.4).

Response plans need to be in place to address likely risks and recovery plans need to be designed to meet organisational recovery objectives in the event of system interruption or failure. Recovery plans need to be tested according to the "Plan, Do, Check" model of continual improvement described in BS 22301 (2014).

Whilst systems can be made resilient by deploying virtual servers on clusters using storage array networks and implementing server replication, the threat from ransomware is that unauthorised changes to data are also replicated to replica servers. For this reason, offline backups are vital. The downside of offline backups is the time taken to restore them and the loss of any data that may have been added or changed since the backup was taken. It is important where recovery time objectives are low to create an environment whereby as many risks as possible to system uptime are eradicated.

Should an incident occur, affected systems must be isolated immediately. The measures deployed will depend on budget and the organisation's risk appetite.

1.5. Remediation of Security Breaches

In theory one has a CERT (Cyber Emergency Response Team) or a BERT (Business Emergency Response Team) on standby should an incident occur. A BERT is an inhouse version of a CERT, so would be familiar with company procedures and will have no conflicts of interest in terms of the confidentiality of the data or services being restored. A CERT, however, being a community response, poses lots of issues in terms of GDPR processor agreements, confidentiality etc.

Should external assistance be part of the recovery plan then a CERT will need to comply with the company's vetting policy and suitable NDAs will need to be signed. Though a company might not see Computer Forensics as its business, inevitably HR will have to hire for a Computer Forensics department when internal investigations are required. When this happens, it is important to follow the advice of the UK Association of Chief Police Officers and the guidance provided by ENISA (ACPO, 2012). In Computer Forensics, there are four basic rules (Schou and Hernandez, 2014).

1. Investigators must not take on work that is beyond their skill.
2. A log must be kept of how the evidence is preserved from point of collection to court. This is called a Chain of Custody.

3. Evidence must not be degraded. This is called Preservation.
4. Every step of an investigation must be recorded.

Should personal data be put at risk as a resultant incident then the organisation's GDPR breach reporting procedures will need to be followed and the appropriate supervisory authority notified without undue delay, and not later than 72 hours after the organisation becomes aware of the breach. Article 33 of the GDPR also requires that if the breach is likely to result in a high risk of certain individuals' rights and freedoms being adversely affected, those individuals must be informed without undue delay, and that the cause of the breach must be identified, and that measures must be put in place to contain the breach and prevent any repetition of the incident. Seeking the advice of the Information Commissioner's Office when reporting a breach to confirm the response is correct is accepted as expected practice.

Event logs are crucial for determining the cause of a breach. ISO27001 specifies that logs should be maintained for months, as does COBIT 5. Logs can be unmanageable and even a small organisation with a few virtual servers will produce many logs. A SIEM (System Information Event Management) solution that collates logs solves this problem. Splunk goes further and is a SIEM solution that analyses logs in real time for unusual behaviour (Splunk, 2018).

1.5.1. *Detecting attacks using honeypots*

Honeypots are a terrific way of detecting that something is not right on a network. The idea is that should an attacker get in then the first thing they would want to do is to scan the network for vulnerabilities. This would normally be a scan of all the IP addresses in the local area network's IP range and either all the ports or the most likely ports which the attacker can use to hop onto a server. A honeypot will sit on one IP address on the network and will be listening on all ports. Should another device try to connect to the honeypot, an alarm will be triggered and an alert will be sent. Thinkst Canary is a honeypot that can simulate a Windows server or a Web server, and is designed to entice an attacker to investigate further before triggering an alert (Thinkst Canary, 2018).

1.5.2. *Detecting attacks by network monitoring*

Darktrace and Snort, which monitor network traffic, are great tools with which to detect anomalies. Traffic monitoring is expensive, though, as the idea of traffic monitoring is to detect anything abnormal on a network. In practice, the setting up of new workstations where large amounts of programs and data move round the network and even Windows updates are good examples of false positives that can trigger an alert, so this method is not without its drawbacks.

1.6. Detection of Security Breaches — Overview

One of the issues in comparing security products is that there is no comprehensive dataset to be used for data exfiltration testing, and no generic framework for testing. This is an issue highlighted by Ullah *et al.* (2017).

Al-Bataineh and White (2017) describe how botnets can be used to exfiltrate data using encrypted channels. Interestingly they make the point that rather than providing a problem, encryption can give the attacker away, as a large transfer using encryption could be identified as an anomaly. Zeus is the most common botnet which allows an attacker to manage the botnet remotely to log key strokes and take screen shots. It can even add fields to forms to enable the collection of more information than a form would normally need, and if applied to a banking site might even ask for a social security number or a credit card PIN. Al-Bataineh and White observed that HTTP traffic exchanged by botnets has normal headers; however, the content of POST responses is often random which could assist with detection. Although encryption hides what an attacker is doing, Al-Bataineh and White propose that one should “consider encryption as an opportunity for detection rather than a limitation because if encryption is detected where it is not expected it should be considered an anomaly".

In an encrypted message the frequency of a byte in a message should be the same for every byte. This is known as Shannon's Entropy. To maintain throughput when inspecting traffic flows, a manufacturer may decide, having identified a file type upon examining the start of a file, that it is not necessary to examine the rest of the data stream (Shannon and Weaver, 1949).

Deep packet inspection (DPI) of HTTPS packets is another technique that is emerging on some firewalls. This works by decrypting encrypted channels at a firewall then re-encrypting them before they reach the user.

On anything but a small corporate network a proxy server would be expected. This is now a requirement in PCI DSS questionnaire C and the UK Cyber Essentials scheme. Proxy servers are designed to inspect and log data downloaded but not necessarily to detect data uploaded so it is important to ascertain how good they are at detecting and recording data being uploaded. From an attacker's perspective exfiltrating data using web-based services might appear a risky strategy because requests are likely to be logged but even if access to websites and users and downloads may be logged it does not follow that data being uploaded is being logged.

Anomaly detection can either be host-based or network-based, the first looking for anomalies on the host, the latter looking for anomalies in network traffic. An example of suspicious network traffic would be web use where the upload traffic volume is higher than the download volume. An example of a host-based anomaly could be high levels of network traffic at an unusual time of day (e.g. at night) (Darktrace, 2018).

1.6.1. *Black hat, white hat and grey hat hacking*

To check whether vulnerabilities can be exploited, ethical hackers or penetration testers are often employed. They then try to find and exploit vulnerabilities on the basis of some knowledge (grey hat), no knowledge (black hat) or a lot of knowledge (white hat) of the system being tested. It is important that a reputable company is used for this, and, when systems are being tested, that system administrators are on hand should any services hang as a result. Attempting to hack a system without authorisation is a criminal offence, so penetration testing companies must be certain that they have the proper authorisation and that any undesirable consequences are understood before attempting to see if any vulnerabilities can be exploited.

1.6.2. *Open-sourcing of security tools*

Many security tools are available open source for Linux. Bro is another tool for network analysis and security monitoring (Bro, 2018). Snort is an open source intrusion prevention system capable of real-time traffic analysis and packet logging. Pfsense is an increasingly popular open source firewall (Pfsense, 2018).

1.7. Methods and Models for Security and Privacy

From Ullah *et al.* (2017) it is apparent that many of the methods proposed in academic studies for detecting and preventing data loss have not been trialed by real companies and remain academic ideas and that the practicalities of implementing some of the ideas have been overlooked.

The data classification model chosen will depend on the types of data an organisation holds. For many organisations this is just confidential, personal data, and unclassified data. In a military context, top secret data would be on a need-to-know basis, so a higher-ranking officer might not have access to some data that lower ranks working on projects might have. “Need to Know” or “Least Privilege” are security practices that are common in many organisations.

Document management systems like iManage (iManage, 2018) and Laserfiche are good ways to protect documents as, with these systems, documents are stored in a repository rather than on file shares, thus adding another layer of security. Further access permissions are then set with the document management system providing a further layer of protection.

1.7.1. *Methods for security reengineering*

Email is the lifeblood of many organisations, however when it comes to agreeing to contracts with other parties it is soon seen how inefficient it becomes. Multiple versions of draft documents which are stored by all parties do not just clog up email systems but file storage and message archives too. Several products that make this experience better are portal-based. Some also provide the ability to compare documents online and this means that the whole collaborative experience can be achieved online. Examples of this are Objective-Connect, iDeals data rooms and Workshare. SharePoint can also be configured to provide this functionality.

Products like iDeals, Workshare, and Objective-Connect provide secure online virtual data rooms where companies can share documents with other parties. These systems provide a more efficient way for companies to collaborate when compared to email. The use of portals has become common for large companies, councils and universities, removing the need to send large attachments by email. Some of the products available to provide this functionality are Objective Connect (Objective, 2017), which allows users to share and version documents with others in its portal, iDeals which features document sharing with very restrictive viewing, and DeltaView's Workshare which provides document comparison within its portal.

Blackberry UEM is an alternative approach to providing mobile access to an Exchange Server. This is a full MDM solution which can provide connectivity with mobile devices and devices running Blackberry's iOS or Android app. It uses outbound ports only, thus eliminating the threats that go with having inbound ports configured (Blackberry, 2018).

1.7.2. *Privacy-enhancing technologies and trustworthy information systems*

A common technique is to tag documents with keywords, then use an AV tool such as ClamAV to generate signatures. The signature can then be added to a proxy server such as Squid to block these from leaving the organization (Rashid *et al.*, 2017).

Boldon James provides tools to add metadata tags to documents (Boldon James, 2018). These can work with Data Loss Prevention systems such as Forcepoint, Intel Security and Symantec DLP.

Tukan's GREENmod (TukanIT, 2018) is another tool. This integrates with McAfee Threat Intelligence Exchange/Data eXchange Layer (TIE/DXL), and McAfee DLP (McAfee, 2017), also to prevent data exfiltration.

Safetica is an example of a Data Leak Prevention product which deploys agents on workstations (Safetica Endpoint Client) which communicate with a Safetica Management Server. This is an example of perhaps what will be a suite of new products to protect against data loss. Data can be tagged depending on folder location or file type and using DLP rules, which look at tags and file contents. Sensitive data can be prevented from being attached to emails or transferred to web storage, and even screenshots of sensitive data can be prevented. Safetica also provides the ability to see an overview of all web browsing, all sent email, all file activity and all printing by a user.

1.8. What Kinds of Products Are There to Prevent Data Theft?

The approaches to detecting and preventing data exfiltration fall into 5 categories:

1. Block data being exfiltrated at a firewall. Several firewall manufacturers now offer a DLP bolt-on which uses deep packet inspection to provide protection against data loss. The protection is based on rules that have been set to detect phrases and number patterns.
2. Use an agent that applies centrally managed policies and blocks leaks at the endpoint. This approach enables a great deal of flexibility in terms of integration with Active Directory, file tagging, reporting and alerting a user that they are doing something which is not permitted. Safetica is an example of a system that deploys a workstation agent.

3. Use of a proxy server that has built-in data-loss detection and prevention capabilities. The Trustwave Secure Web Gateway (SWG) is a good example of this.
4. Next generation firewalls that are both firewall and web proxies.
5. Traffic monitoring. Based on an analysis of normal network traffic, AI is used to detect abnormal network traffic. This is the principle used by Darktrace.

We will discuss these three approaches and some of the products using these approaches, and test them accordingly.

1.9. Detect and Block Using a Firewall

It is important to configure firewalls in the right arrangement from day one as the architecture of a network is hard to change later without service disruption and risk.

It is interesting to note that the separation of the internal network from the DMZ and the internet by 2 firewalls, as in Fig. 1.2, is now a requirement by some banks under PCI DSS questionnaire D. The three-legged firewall, as in Fig. 1.3, which has been a cost-saving option for smaller companies for several years, is therefore falling foul of security standards. If multiple firewalls are used, a DLP solution would normally be required on the internal firewall only.

Quality switches like the CISCO SG500 series now have access control lists either based on a MAC address or an IP address. These switches are effectively firewalls. Complex rules can now be set on many network switches and unused ports can be shut down. 'Sticky

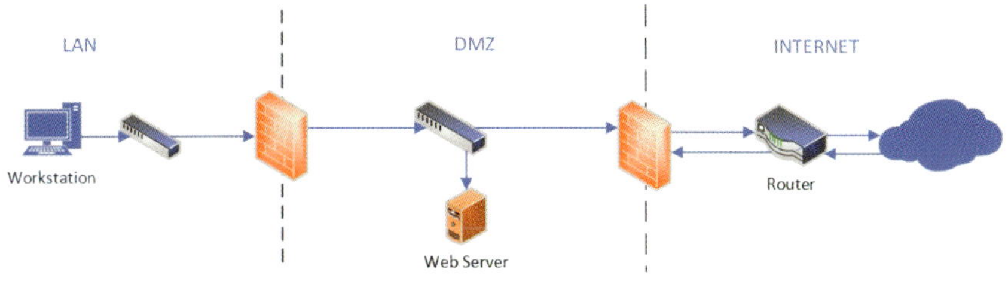

Fig. 1.2. Traditional network diagram.

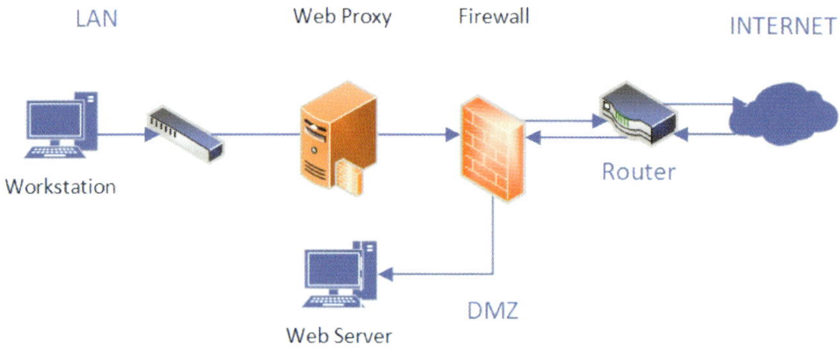

Fig. 1.3. The three-legged firewall.

Macs' is a feature whereby a switch learns and remembers connected MAC addresses and should an MAC address violation occur the affected port can be automatically shut down.

1.9.1. *Detect and block using an agent or app at the endpoint*

Safetica and Infoblox are full data loss prevention solutions which defend against planned or accidental data leaks and malicious insider actions by deploying a centrally managed agent on workstations. By using an agent on each workstation documents are tagged according to sensitivity which then allows access controls determining whether the documents may be copied, printed or emailed. Safetica can also prevent screen shots or clips of sensitive documents (Safetica, 2018; Infoblox, 2018).

McAfee DLP is a utility that can scan, identify and classify data without user intervention. Policies can be defined around how it alerts users to policy violations (MacAfee, 2017). The attraction here is not having to classify data every time data is saved.

Symantec DLP is another utility that can scan and automatically detect sensitive documents and images. Network Prevent for Web can be deployed at network egress points and integrates with proxy servers using the Internet Content Application Protocol (ICAP, 2018). Symantec DLP can monitor the use of sensitive data and goes as far as digitally shredding documents (Symantec, 2018). McAfee, Sophos, Trend Micro, Kaspersky, and Symantec all follow the ICAP standard. They all provide real-time content filtering, though it is not necessarily implemented in any of their products. It must be noted that the ICAP protocol and feeds are also legitimately used for advertising as well as virus checking and language translation (ICAP 2018).

SonicWall Capture Client is a workstation agent designed to detect ransomware by Sentinel One. Should an attack happen it can roll back the attack (SonicWall, 2017).

1.9.2. *Detect and block using a proxy*

Trustwave Secure Web Gateway (SWG) is Trustwave's 'Zero-Malware' web-proxy solution (Trustwave, n.d.). Because the secure web gateway uses its own DNS settings, a gateway firewall can be configured such that DNS outbound on UDP port 53 is only possible from the Secure Web Gateway device.

1.9.3. *Detect and block using a next-generation firewall*

Sophos XG UTMs and Zyxel USG UTMs are examples of all-in-one firewalls, web proxy, and network monitoring solutions. These are ideal for very small organisations.

1.9.4. *Detect and alert using network traffic analysis*

Darktrace and Snort are network-based anomaly detection systems which identify unusual network traffic. These were discussed in Section 1.5.2.

1.9.5. *Detecting sensitive data*

Many of the tools that are designed to assist with data classification are designed with large companies in mind. An example is Spirion (formerly IdentityFinder) which is a tool that can be used to search file shares for sensitive data (Spirion, 2018).

Unlike traditional security systems (e.g. IDS, IPS and firewalls), which are supposed to act when an attacker enters the enterprise, data exfiltration countermeasures are expected to work when an attacker is on the way out with sensitive data (Ullah *et al.*, 2017). Firewalls are generally designed to keep attackers from getting in, not from getting out when they are inside. This is very similar to what Houdini did; he exploited the fact that locks at the time were designed to prevent people from entering areas, not from getting out of them.

GlobalVelocity (GlobalVelocity, n.d.) is a DLP solution for protecting data in the cloud. The challenge for companies using cloud providers is not knowing the level of protection in place and having limited control over how DLP products might be configured.

Microsoft Intune is an example of a cloud-based DLP solution whereby the configuration is done by the company whose systems are being hosted rather than by the cloud provider. The Office365 Enhanced Protection and Mobility Suite offers several security mechanisms to protect data. Rules can be set up in Office365 to detect the exfiltration of credit card data and social security and national insurance numbers. The DLP rules can be set for all country formats or specific countries, thus catering for various formats of national insurance numbers. However, setting countries unnecessarily in the rules could obviously increase the rate of false positives.

1.10. Recommendations to Protect Against Data Theft

The following recommendations should be considered to protect against data theft:

- Uninstall Microsoft OneDrive using a group policy (GPO) if it is not required in an organization.
- Use a proxy server that can block web storage websites.
- Instant messaging systems should be blocked by the organisation's web proxy.
- Consider blocking Ping (ICMP) and NTP outbound from workstations.

- Companies should consider a default deny on a proxy server for website browsing and only websites needed for business purposes should be added as needed.
- Primary and secondary internal DNS servers should not be configured to resolve external DNS names, as good web proxy servers can be configured to use external DNS cache servers. This not only improves security, it also reduces the load on the internal DNS servers. For WSUS and AV to get updates, a dedicated DNS server should be used.
- Limiting the size of email attachments and the number of attachments that can be attached to an email are practical steps to restrict the amount of data that can be stolen by email.

Supply chain vulnerabilities must also be considered. To quote the National Cyber Security Centre's annual report:

> *"2017 saw some significant examples of supply chain attacks, including the compromise of a large number of managed service providers (MSPs), enabling access to commercially sensitive data from them and their clients. At least two software companies had their products (MeDoc and CCleaner) compromised at source, resulting in their customers being infected with malware when downloading the software/updates."* (NCSC, 2018)

Minimizing the amount of sensitive information that an organisation holds clearly minimizes any impact from a data leak. This principle is at the heart of information governance and GDPR strategies with respect to personal data. The same principle must apply to all confidential and sensitive information, that regardless of the measures that are put in place to protect data, unnecessary data should not be collected as this increases the impact of any breach.

The deployment of end-to-end encryption systems such as GalaxKey or WhatsApp on a system makes it very difficult for monitoring systems to identify data in an email or text message as the monitoring system will have no way of decrypting the data it is trying to monitor. However, the use of these systems for specific occasions where a high level of confidentiality is required makes perfect sense.

To quote Rashid *et al.*: "Due to the diversity of attack vectors no single security control provides protection against all of these vectors. Multiple detection mechanisms must be used together in a multi-layered approach" (Rashid *et al.*, 2017). The result is often referred to as defence in depth, but as any practitioner knows, this leads to unintended conflicts between products. Antivirus updates can be blocked by firewalls and one-time links which are often used for password resets are claimed by proxy servers, to name just a couple of the possible issues. Setting exclusions and resolving conflicts has become a regular part of an IT system manager's day.

One interesting approach to reducing the impact of data leaks is the concept of Zero Trust, where everything is untrusted (Vijayan, 2018). The concept is that any threat is limited to the data on one desktop; however, this means that the reporting and monitoring of devices becomes difficult. Microsoft has addressed this issue for a user of Office365 with the Enterprise Security and Mobility suite, which does cater for this, as Microsoft Intune registers and validates that connecting devices are patched and safe to connect to. For companies not using Office365, Centrify provides a similar Zero Trust framework (Centrify, 2018). In an office environment where all services are cloud services, the use of Zero Core clients that have a Citrix or terminal server that is imbedded in firmware is a strategy that removes the threat from viruses at the endpoints.

Due to the plethora of approaches there is no standard implementation, meaning staff with experience in one organization cannot transfer their knowledge procedures to another company, as the systems, methods and procedures in addressing the security of sensitive data will differ. This poses real challenges for companies that rely on contract staff.

1.11. The Future — STIX, TAXII and Cyber Threat Intelligence

To aid the sharing of the security information protocols that have been developed, the computer language known as Structured Threat Information Expression (STIX, 2018) and the protocol known as Trusted Automated Exchange of Intelligence Information (TAXII, 2018) are designed to share CTI (Cyber Threat Intelligence) information. One would expect that a good firewall with DLP would interface with external live CTI databases and that it would automatically update itself using these databases.

Data Classification system vendors need to integrate their systems with gateway firewalls and web proxies to protect against data leakage. With so many solutions available it is important that products adopt the ICAP (ICAP, 2018) standard for transferring information.

1.12. Conclusion on How to Guard Against Attacks and Prevent Data Theft

Although the above technical exploits are perhaps emerging threats, an analysis of high profile historic exploits has shown that, generally, less sophisticated methods have caused many of the greatest leaks. It is also apparent that security standards like PCI DSS have yet to address some of the emerging methods that can be used for data exfiltration. This will no doubt happen as the standards continue to evolve. In the breaches reviewed, the auditing of systems has often not been as robust as it should have been, as is seen in the cases where patches and SQL injection were the causes of leaks. Other breaches have involved deception from insiders. Since 2017, however, it is apparent that attacks are getting more sophisticated. Based on the attack vectors discussed, security auditing will need to become more robust, standards will need to evolve faster, and the assessment of emerging risks will need to be a regular item on a corporate board's agenda.

Packet inspection creates a huge overhead on a firewall's performance; however, if firewalls are going to be fit for purpose they will need to do more. With so-called next-generation firewalls, manufacturers are rising to the challenge. This is perhaps evident in the recent fast-rising costs of the latest next-generation firewalls, which have increasingly faster processors. Firewalls have sophisticated features that take time to develop and, due to the long testing processes required, this unfortunately means that the detection methods deployed are not necessarily aligned with the detection of emerging threats.

Companies need to assess the risks of storing data on mobiles and desktops. This data can be exfiltrated using apps that may be able to read data on the devices. Security standards will need to become much more adaptive to changes in the usage of technology. Firms that claim compliance should be required to regularly requalify. Banks and other payment providers have required retailers to reassess their PCI DSS compliance on an annual basis, and companies that do not comply have fines applied to their credit card accounts which are automatically paid from a retailer's bank account. The fines are relatively small but are automatically applied as a way of making sure firms address their need to be compliant. The UK's Cyber Essentials scheme may need to follow similar strategies.

This reflects how quickly the use of technology changes and how slowly several security standards have evolved to deal with emerging threats. It is notable that the PCI DSS has reacted quickly to change with annual updates, unlike the ISO27001 standard that has only had 3 revisions since 2013. As stated previously, it is surprising that ISO27001:2013 does not mention data loss prevention other than the physical measures taken to prevent data loss which are detailed in Section A.11.2. However, one could argue that ISO27001, COBIT 5 and NIST embrace the need for rapid change in their concept of risk, and that they emphasise an organisation's responsibility to assess risks, mitigate risks, and remove risks. ISO27001 Section A.12.6.1 states *"Information about technical vulnerabilities of information systems being used shall be obtained in a timely fashion, the organization's exposure to such vulnerabilities evaluated and appropriate measures taken to address the associated risk."* ISO 27005:2011 12.1 highlights the responsibility of an organisation to re-assess risks based on *"new threats that could be active both outside and inside the organisation and that have not been assessed."* Risk managers must therefore research and assess the risks from emerging threats. These threats may not only apply to a company's systems but may also have adverse effects on the rights and freedom of others.

Sadly, security standards have often failed to remove the threat from insiders. It is important that employees are vetted and understand the motivations for the implementation of systems that monitor their behavior. IT departments must work closely with management and HR departments to not only monitor staff but also to develop a positive culture in an organisation whereby information security is the concern of every employee. Culture, and the ability of companies to implement new policies and get staff to grasp the importance of adhering to them, are essential to improving security and preventing data loss.

Web exfiltration is by far the greatest threat. DNS exfiltration is possible but can be dealt with by not allowing a workstation to resolve external DNS URLs. NTP and ICMP are not required outbound from a workstation so these ports do not need to be enabled though a firewall from a workstation.

Glossary

APT	Advanced Persistent Threat
BEC	Business Email Compromise
BERT	Business Emergency Response Team
CERT	Cyber Emergency Response Team
CTI	Cyber Threat Intelligence
CVE	Common Vulnerabilities and Exposures database maintained by the Mitre Corporation and funded by the US Government
CVV	Card Verification Value
DLP	Data Loss Prevention
DoS	Denial of Service
EMS	Endpoint Management System
GDPR	General Data Protection Regulation
GeoIP	Geographic IP address
GPO	Group Policy Objects
HTTP	Hypertext Transfer Protocol
HTTPS	Hypertext Transfer Protocol Secure
ICAP	Internet Content Application Protocol

ICMP	Internet Control Message Protocol
IDS	Intrusion Detection System
ISACA	The non-profit organization responsible for Cobit 5
IPS	Intrusion Prevention System
NSTX	Name Server Transfer Protocol
PCI DSS	Payment Card Industry Data Security Standard
PUA	Potentially unwanted application
SMB	Small Message Block
SQL	Structured Query Language
STIX	Structured Threat Information Expression
TAXII	Trusted Automated Exchange of Intelligence Information
TCP	Transmission Control Protocol
UDP	User Datagram Protocol
UTM	Unified Threat Management
WSUS	Windows Server Update Services
XSS	Cross Site Scripting
Zero-Day Exploit	Malware for which a signature is yet to be determined

References

1. Abelson, R. and Goldstein, M. (2015). *Anthem Hacking Points to Security Vulnerability of Health Care Industry* [Online]. Available at: https://www.nytimes.com/2015/02/06/business/experts-suspect-lax-security-left-anthem-vulnerable-to-hackers.html (Accessed: 11 August 2018).
2. Al-Bataineh, A. and White, G. (2017). *Analysis and Detection of Malicious Data Exfiltration in Web Traffic* [Online]. Available at: https://ieeexplore.ieee.org/document/6461004/ (Accessed: 22 May 2018).
3. Appleby. (2018). *Appleby, Guardian News and Media Limited and the BBC Settle Paradise Papers Dispute* [Online]. Available at: https://www.applebyglobal.com/media-statements/appleby-guardian-news-and-media-limited-and-the-bbc-settle-paradise-papers-dispute.aspx (Accessed: 1 July 2018).
4. Armerding, T. (2018). *The 17 Biggest Data Breaches of the 21st Century* [Online]. Available at: https://www.csoonline.com/article/2130877/data-breach/the-biggest-data-breaches-of-the-21st-century.html (Accessed: 18 August 2018).

5. Association of Chief Police Officers (ACPO). (2012). [Online]. *ACPO Good Practice for Digital Evidence* [Online]. Available at: https://www.digital-detective.net/digital-forensics-documents/ACPO_Good_Practice_Guide_for_Digital_Evidence_v5.pdf (Accessed: 24 September 2018).
6. BBC. (2015). *Sony Pays up to $8 m Over Employees' Hacked Data* [Online]. Available at: https://www.bbc.com/news/business-34589710 (Accessed: 11 August 2018).
7. Blackberry. (2018). *A Single Platform for Securing the Enterprise of Things* [Online]. Available at: https://www.blackberry.com/en (Accessed: 3 October 2018).
8. Boldonjames. (2018). *File Classifier: Apply Metadata Labels to Any Files in Windows File Store For Greater Control of Your Data* [Online]. Available at: https://www.boldonjames.com/products/file-classifier/ (Accessed: 1 October 2018).
9. Bro. (2018). *The Bro Network Security Monitor* [Online]. Available at: https://www.bro.org/ (Accessed: 1 September 2018).
10. Brumaghin, E. and Grady, C. (2017). *Covert Channels and Poor Decisions: The Tale of DNSMessenger* [Online]. Available at: https://blog.talosintelligence.com/2017/03/dnsmessenger.html (Accessed: 19 August 2018).
11. Bupa. (2017). *Bupa Hacked* [Online]. Available at: https://reader.elsevier.com/reader/sd/C1AE7C93AD4ABF9E62D285829B471450DC86596D5240BADCD4BAE691B0842C60CED2B9155637E80CC129A65E3B6149FB (Accessed: 28 June 2018).
12. Bupa. (2015). *BUPA: Our Vacancies: Information Risk and Governance Officer* [Online]. Available at: http://jobsearch.bupaglobal.com/jobs/job/Information-Risk-Governance-Officer/123 (Accessed: 17 August 2018).
13. Butler, P., Xu, K. and Danfeng D. (2011). *Quantitatively Analyzing Stealthy Communication Channels.* [Online]. Available at: http://people.cs.vt.edu/danfeng/papers/ACNS-DNS-CC.pdf (Accessed: 18 August 2018).
14. Cappelli, D., Moore, A. and Trzeciak, R. (2012). *The CERT Guide to Insider Threats: How to Prevent, Detect, and Respond to Information Technology Crimes.* Upper Saddle River, NJ, USA: Addison-Wesley Professional.
15. Cellan-Jones, R. (2011). *Sony's PlayStation Data Warning After Hacker Attack* [Online]. Available at: https://www.bbc.com/news/av/technology-

13206754/sony-s-playstation-data-warning-after-hacker-attack (Accessed: 11 July 2018).

16. Cellan-Jones, R. (2018). *Dixons Carphone Says Data Breach Affected 10 Million* [Online]. Available at: https://www.bbc.co.uk/news/business-45016906 (Accessed: 1 October 2018).
17. Centrify. (2018). *Rethink Security for Zero Trust* [Online]. Available at: https://www.centrify.com/zero-trust-security/ (Accessed: 19 August 2018).
18. Darktrace. (2018). *The World Leader in Cyber AI* [Online]. Available at: https://www.darktrace.com/ (Accessed: 29 September 2018).
19. Daileda, C. (2017). *Someone Reportedly Hacked Deloitte Through an Account Without Two-Step Verification* [Online]. Available at: https://mashable.com/2017/09/25/deloitte-hack/#1Gdrw_yg1OqC (Accessed: 2 August 2018).
20. DNSCat. (2018). *Welcome to DNSCat2, a DNS Tunnel That WON'T Make You Sick and Kill You!* [Online]. Available at: https://github.com/iagox86/dnscat2 (Accessed: 1 October 2018).
21. DNSExfiltrator. (2018). *DNSExfiltrator* [Online]. Available at: https://github.com/Arno0x/DNSExfiltrator (Accessed: 2 Oct. 2018).
22. Dooley, M. and Rooney, T. (2017). *DNS Security Management.* Hoboken, Canada: Wiley IEEE Press.
23. Ducklin, P. (2017). *Apache Struts "Serialisation" Vulnerability — What You Need to Know* [Online]. Available at: https://nakedsecurity.sophos.com/2017/09/06/apache-struts-serialisation-vulnerability-what-you-need-to-know/ (Accessed: 2 August 2018).
24. Economist. (2015). *What Lies Behind the JPMorgan Chase Cyber-Attack* [Online]. Available at: https://www.businessinsider.com/ebay-hack-2014-5 (Accessed: 11 August 2018).
25. Farivar, C. (2018). *Yahoo Hacker Whose Work Compromised 500M Accounts Sentenced to 5 Years* [Online]. Available at: https://arstechnica.com/tech-policy/2018/05/yahoo-hacker-whose-work-compromised-500m-accounts-sentenced-to-5-years/ (Accessed: 11 July 2018).
26. FCA. (2018). *FCA Fines Tesco Bank £16.4 m for Failures in 2016 Cyber Attack* [Online]. Available at: https://www.fca.org.uk/news/press-releases/fca-fines-tesco-bank-failures-2016-cyber-attack (Accessed: 1 October 2018).
27. Federal Bureau of Investigation (FBI IC3). (2018). *Federal Bureau of Investigation, Internet Crime Compliant Center, 2017 Internet Crime Report* [Online]. Available at: https://pdf.ic3.gov/2017_IC3Report.pdf (Accessed: 29 September 2018).

28. Federal Bureau of Investigation Internet Compliance Center (FBI IC3). (2017). *2017 Internet Crime Report* [Online]. Available at: https://www.ic3.gov/media/2017/170504.aspx (Accessed: 28 September 2018).
29. Finkle, J. (2014). *It Took eBay Three Months to Figure Out 145 Million User Accounts Were Hacked* [Online]. Available at: https://www.businessinsider.com/ebay-hack-2014-5 (Accessed: 11 August 2018).
30. FT. (2018). *British Airways Vows to Compensate Passengers After Data Breach* [Online]. Available at: https://www.ft.com/content/5eddd118-b27e-11e8-99ca-68cf89602132 (Accessed: 7 September 2018).
31. Globalvelocity. (n.d.). *Securio Cloud for MSPs, ISPs, and SaaS Vendors* [Online]. Available at: http://www.globalvelocity.com/products/securio-cloud-for-msps (Accessed: 1 October 2018).
32. Guy, J. (2009). *DNS Part II: Visualization.* [Online]. Available at: http://armatum.com/blog/2009/dns-part-ii/ (Accessed: 12 September 2018).
33. Hackersgrid. (2018). *Koadic Outside LAN Exploit Windows PC* [Online]. Available at: http://hackersgrid.com/2018/05/koadic-outside-lan.html (Accessed: 9 September 2018).
34. Hegarty, M. (2018). *Steganography, The World of Secret Communications.* Scotts Valley, CA, USA: Createspace Independent Publishing Platform.
35. Hern, A. and Pegg, D. (2018). *Facebook Fined for Data Breaches in Cambridge Analytica Scandal* [Online]. Available at: https://www.theguardian.com/technology/2018/jul/11/facebook-fined-for-data-breaches-in-cambridge-analytica-scandal (Accessed: 1 October 2018).
36. ICAP. (2018). *Internet Content Application Protocol* [Online]. Available at: http://www.icap-forum.org/ (Accessed: 1 September 2018).
37. ICO. (2016). *TalkTalk Cyber Attack — How the ICO's Investigation Unfolded* [Online]. Available at: https://ico.org.uk/about-the-ico/news-and-events/talktalk-cyber-attack-how-the-ico-investigation-unfolded/ (Accessed 10 August 2018).
38. iManage. (2018). *Document and Email Management* [Online]. Available at: https://imanage.com/product/document-email-management/ (Accessed: 29 September 2018).
39. Ince, M. (2016). *Data Exfiltration (Tunneling) Attacks Against Corporate Network* [Online]. Available at: https://pentest.blog/data-exfiltration-tunneling-attacks-against-corporate-network/ (Accessed: 17 August 2018).
40. Infoblox. (2018). *Infoblox Advanced DNS Protection* [Online]. Available at: https://www.infoblox.com/wp-content/uploads/infoblox-datasheet-infoblox-advanced-dns-protection.pdf (Accessed: 18 June 2018).

41. Iodine. (2014). *Iodine* [Online]. Available at: http://code.kryo.se/iodine/ (Accessed: 1 Oct. 2018).
42. K-Max V. (2018). *Meterpreter DNS Tunnel* [Online]. Available at: http://asintsov.blogspot.com/2017/12/data-exfiltration-in-metasploit.html (Accessed: 18 August 2018).
43. Kaspersky Labs. (2014). *Global Corporate IT Security Risks* [Online]. Available at: http://media.kaspersky.com/en/business-security/kaspersky_ global_IT_security_risks_survey_report_eng_final.pdf (Accessed: 1 October 2018).
44. Khandelwal, S. (2017). *New Fileless Malware Uses DNS Queries to Receive PowerShell Commands* [Online]. Available at: https://thehackernews.com/2017/03/powershell-dns-malware.html (Accessed: 19 August 2018).
45. Kitten, T. (2011). *Citi Card Data Breached Again* [Online]. Available at: https://www.bankinfosecurity.com/citi-card-data-breached-again-a-3933 (Accessed: 2 August 2018).
46. Liska, A. (2016). *NTP Security*. Alphen aan den Rijn, the Netherlands: Apress Printforce.
47. Matsacis, L. and Lapowsky, I. (2018). Everything We Know About Facebook's Massive Security Breach [Online]. Available at: https://www.wired.com/story/facebook-security-breach-50-million-accounts/ (Accessed: 2 October 2018).
48. Maurer, T. (2018). *Cyber Mercenaries: The State, Hackers, and Power.* Cambridge, UK: Cambridge University Press.
49. McAfee. (2017). *McAfee Total Protection for Data Loss Prevention* [Online]. Available at: https://www.mcafee.com/enterprise/en-us/assets/solution-briefs/sb-total-protection-for-dlp.pdf (Accessed: 1 September 2018).
50. McGlasson, L. (2009). *Heartland Payment Systems, Forcht Bank Discover Data Breaches* [Online]. Available at: https://www.bankinfosecurity.com/heartland-payment-systems-forcht-bank-discover-data-breaches-a-1168 (Accessed: 18 August 2018).
51. Mockapetris, P. (1987). *Request for Comments: 1035 — Domain Names — Implementation And Specification* [Online]. Available at: https://www.ietf.org/rfc/rfc1035.txt (Accessed: 15 September 2018).
52. Nakashima, E. (2013). *Chinese Hackers Who Breached Google Gained Access to Sensitive Data, U.S. Officials Say* [Online]. Available at: https://www.washingtonpost.com/world/national-security/chinese-hackers-who-breached-google-gained-access-to-sensitive-data-us-officials-say/2013/05/20/51330428-be34-11e2-89c9-3be8095fe767_story.html?utm_term=.26c70b21f1f8 (Accessed: 11 August 2018).

53. NCSC. (2018). *The Cyber Threat to UK Business 2017–2018 Report* [Online]. Available at: https://www.ncsc.gov.uk/cyberthreat (Accessed: 5 October 2018).
54. NGROK. (2018). *Spend More Time Programming. One Command for an Instant, Secure URL to Your Localhost Server Through Any NAT or Firewall* [Online]. Available at: https://ngrok.com/ (Accessed: 1 October 2018).
55. Objective. (2017). *Secure External Collaboration* [Online]. Available at: http://www.objectiveconnect.com/ (Accessed: 1 October 2018).
56. OPM. (n.d.). *Cybersecurity Resource Center* [Online]. Available at: https://www.opm.gov/cybersecurity/ (Accessed: 18 August 2018).
57. Packard, A. (2013). *Digital Media Law.* Chichester, UK: Wiley Blackwell.
58. PCI DSS. (2018). *Payment Card Industry PCI Data Security Standard Self-Assessment Questionnaire D and Attestation for Merchants* [Online]. Available at: https://www.pcisecuritystandards.org/documents/SAQ_D_v3_Merchant.pdf (Accessed: 17 August 2018).
59. Pfsense. (2018). *Open Source Security Tools* [Online]. Available at: https://www.pfsense.org/ (Accessed: 3 October 2018).
60. Ragan, S. (2017). *Office 365 Phishing Attacks* [Online]. Available at: https://www.csoonline.com/article/3225469/security/office-365-phishing-attacks-create-a-sustained-insider-nightmare-for-it.html (Accessed: 29 September 2018).
61. Rashid, A., Ramidhany, R., Edwards, M., Kibirige, S. M., Babar, A., Hutchinson, D. and Chitchyan, R. (2017). *Detecting and Preventing Data Exfiltration* [Online]. Available at http://www.security-centre.lancs.ac.uk/data-exfiltration (Accessed: 15 May 2018).
62. Revelli, A. and Leidecker, N. (2009). *Playing With Heyoka: Spoofed Tunnels, Undetectable Data Exfiltration and More Fun With DNS Packets* [Online]. Available at: http://heyoka.sourceforge.net/heyoka-shakacon2009.pdf (Accessed: 1 Oct. 2018).
63. Safebreach. (2018). *Safebreach Hacker Playbook Q3/2017* [Online]. Available at: https://go.safebreach.com/rs/535-IXZ-934/images/Hacker_Playbook_3rd_Edition.pdf (Accessed: 1 October 2018).
64. Safetica. (2018). *Your Data Is Your Most Important Asset. Keep It Safe With Safetica* [Online]. Available at: https://www.safetica.com/ (Accessed: 5 September 2018).
65. Schou, C. and Hernandez, S. (2015). *Information Assurance Handbook: Effective Computer Security and Risk Management Strategies.* London, UK: McGraw-Hill Education.

66. Scott. (2016). *What is DNS Tunneling?* [Online]. Available at: https://www.plixer.com/blog/network-security-forensics/what-is-dns-tunneling/ (Accessed: 18 August 2018).
67. Shannon, C.E. and Weaver, W. (1949). A Mathematical Theory of Communication. *Bell System Technical Journal,* **27**, pp. 397–423.
68. Smith, C. (2014). *It Turns Out Target Could Have Easily Prevented Its Massive Security Breach* [Online]. Available at: https://bgr.com/2014/03/13/target-data-hack-how-it-happened/ (Accessed: 18 August 2018).
69. Sonicwall. (2018). *Sonicwall Capture Client* [Online]. Available at: https://www.sonicwall.com/SonicWall.com/files/56/568260a9-8210-4726-a3ee-41b84a575c62.pdf (Accessed: 25 September 2018).
70. Spirion. (2018). *Free Trial* [Online]. Available at: https://www.spirion.com/freetrial/ (Accessed: 4 July 2018).
71. Splunk. (2018). *Splunk Next. Work the Way Your Data Works* [Online]. Available at: https://www.splunk.com (Accessed: 3 October 2018).
72. STIX. (2018). *Introduction to STIX* [Online]. Available at: https://oasis-open.github.io/cti-documentation/stix/intro (Accessed: 14 August 2018).
73. Stodal, D. (2005). *Ping Tunnel* [Online]. Available at http://www.mit.edu/afs.new/sipb/user/golem/tmp/ptunnel-0.61.orig/web/ (Accessed: 18 September 2018).
74. Storm, D. (2016). *Biggest Hack of 2016: 412 Million FriendFinder Networks Accounts Exposed* [Online]. Available at: https://www.computerworld.com/article/3141290/security/biggest-hack-of-2016-412-million-friendfinder-network-accounts-exposed.html (Accessed: 18 August 2018).
75. Sweet, K. and Liedtke, M. (2017). *Equifax Traced the Source of Its Massive Hack to a Preventable Software Flaw* [Online]. Available at: https://www.businessinsider.com/how-did-equifax-get-hacked-2017-9 (Accessed: 2 August 2018).
76. Symantec. (2017). *Internet Security and Threat Report: Living Off the Land and Fileless Attack Techniques* [Online]. Available at: https://www.symantec.com/content/dam/symantec/docs/security-center/white-papers/istr-living-off-the-land-and-fileless-attack-techniques-en.pdf (Accessed: 6 April 2018).
77. Symantec. (2018). *Symantec Data Loss Prevention* [Online]. Available at: https://www.symantec.com/products/data-loss-prevention (Accessed: 1 September 2018).
78. Takhion. (2018). *Use the Kaodic Command & Control Remote Access Toolkit for Windows Post-Exploitation* [Online]. Available at: https://null-byte.

wonderhowto.com/how-to/use-koadic-com-mand-control-remote-access (Accessed: 3 October 2018).

79. TalkTalk. (2016). *Boy, 17, Admits TalkTalk Hacking Offences* [Online]. Available at: https://www.bbc.com/news/uk-37990246 (Accessed: 15 July 2018).
80. Taxii. (2018). *Introduction to Taxii* [Online]. Available at: https://oasis-open.github.io/cti-documentation/taxii/intro.html (Accessed: 14 August 2018).
81. Thinkstcanary. (2018). *Know When It Matters* [Online]. Available at: https://canary.tools/ (Accessed: 3 October 2018).
82. Trustwave. (2018). *Trustwave Annual Cyber Report* [Online]. Available at: https://www2.trustwave.com/GlobalSecurityReport.html (Accessed: 4 April 2018).
83. Trustwave. (n.d.). *Trustwave Secure Web Gateway* [Online]. Available at: https://www.trustwave.com/Products/Content-Security/Secure-Web-Gateway/ (Accessed: 4 August 2018).
84. TukanIT. (2018). *Effective Data Loss Prevention* [Online]. Available at: http://en.tukanit.pl/ (Accessed: 1 October 2018).
85. Ullah, F., Edwards, M., Ramidhany, R., Chitchyan, R. and Babar, A. (2017). *Data Exfiltration: A Review of External Attack Vectors and Countermeasures* [Online]. Available at: http://eprints.lancs.ac.uk/88549/ (Accessed: 15 May 2018).
86. Vaas, L. (2018). *Hackers Sentenced for SQL Injections That Cost $300 Million* [Online]. Available at: https://nakedsecurity.sophos.com/2018/02/19/hackers-sentenced-for-sql-injections-that-cost-300-million/ (Accessed: 18 August 2018).
87. Verizon. (2017). *2017 Data Breach Investigations Report* [Online]. Available at: https://www.ictsecuritymagazine.com/wp-content/uploads/2017-Data-Breach-Investigations-Report.pdf (Accessed: 23 July 2018).
88. Vijayan, J. (2018). *What It Takes to Build a Zero Trust Network* [Online]. Available at: https://www.csoonline.com/article/3287057/network-security/what-it-takes-to-build-a-zero-trust-network.html (Accessed: 18 August 2018).
89. Wetstone. (2018). *Stegohunt Suite* [Online]. Available at: https://www.wetstonetech.com/pdf/11-28-17%20Datasheet%20(StegoHunt).pdf (Accessed: 5 October 2018).
90. Whittaker, Z. (2018). *Air Canada Confirms Mobile App Data Breach* [Online]. Available at: https://techcrunch.com/2018/08/29/air-canada-confirms-mobile-app-data-breach/?guccounter=1 (Accessed: 8 September 2018).

91. Williams, M. (2017). *Inside the Russian Hack of Yahoo: How They Did It* [Online]. Available at: https://www.csoonline.com/article/3180762/data-breach/inside-the-russian-hack-of-yahoo-how-they-did-it.html (Accessed: 1 October 2018).
92. Wilson, D. (2011). *Citibank Was Hacked by Altering URLs* [Online]. Available at: https://www.theinquirer.net/inquirer/news/2079431/citibank-hacked-altering-urls (Accessed: 12 August 2018).
93. Wired. (2016). *The Security Flaws at the Heart of the Panama Papers* [Online]. Available at: http://www.wired.co.uk/article/panama-papers-mossack-fonseca-website-security-problems (Accessed: 2 July 2018).
94. Wired. (2018). *The Ticketmaster Hack is a Perfect Storm of Bad IT and Bad Comms* [Online]. Available at: https://www.wired.co.uk/article/ticketmaster-data-breach-monzo-inbenta (Accessed: 30 September 2018).
95. Wong, J. C. (2017). *Uber Concealed Massive Hack That Exposed Data of 57 m Users and Drivers* [Online]. Available at: https://www.theguardian.com/technology/2017/nov/21/uber-data-hack-cyber-attack (Accessed: 11 August 2018).
96. Zimba, A. and Chishimba, M. (2017). *Exploitation of DNS Tunneling for Optimization of Data Exfiltration in Malware-free APT Intrusions* [Online]. Available at: https://www.researchgate.net/publication/323202936_Exploitation_of_DNS_Tunneling_for_Optimization_of_Data_Exfiltration_in_Malware-free_APT_Intrusions (Accessed: 9 September 2018).

Chapter 2

Management of a Cyber Attack

Thomas Welsh

Northumbria University London, UK
twelsh37@gmail.com

ABSTRACT

This article will look at the ways an organisation can prepare for, deal with and then recover from a cyber attack against it. There are multiple possible scenarios that can be attributed to a cyber attack. This paper looks at the creation of security policies, cyber incident response plans and organizational risk and cyber insurance.

Keywords: cyber attack, management, cyber warfare, IDS, firewall, governance policy, security policy, cyber incident response, risk, cyber insurance

2.1. Introduction

We live in interesting times. Almost daily, we see reports or news of yet another cyber attack. The stories of breaches come out so regularly nowadays that cyber security issues are getting a lot of visibility in the boardrooms up and down the country (Rothrock, Kaplan and Van Der Oord, 2018).

To give a flavour of what has been happening over the past year or so I have included four noticeable breaches that made the mainstream news in the United Kingdom. These are by no means the biggest or the most destructive of the breaches that have occured over the past few years. This is just a taste of what we will discuss in this chapter.

Morrisons: In 2017, Morrisons, the UK Supermarket chain, was sued by current and former employees after a member of staff stole data on over 100,000 employees. The member of staff in question was fired and subsequently went to jail for 8 years. (BBC News, 2017)

Tesco Bank: In 2016, Tesco Bank, the online finance arm of the Tesco Supermarket chain, admitted that over 40,000 accounts of its customers had been accessed. 9,000 of those accounts had money removed before Tesco Bank froze the online transactions (Jill Treanor and Jones, 2016).

BA: In 2018, BA announced that it had been hacked and that its web site and mobile applications had been breached. The cyber criminals got away with financial information on over 380,000 of BA's customers. BA are looking at fines from the regulator, the Information Commissioner's Office (ICO), in the region of £500 million (Calder, 2018).

Facebook: In 2018, Facebook was fined £500,000 by the ICO. This was for their part in the Cambridge Analytica scandal. The fine was for two breaches of the Data Protection Act. The ICO concluded that Facebook failed to safeguard its users' information and that it failed to be transparent about how that data was harvested by others (Hern and Pegg, 2018).

If you have been paying attention to the security news over the past couple of years you will notice that I have not included the major ransomware outbreaks like Wannacry and NotPetya or any breaches of Industrial Control Systems like the Ukrainian power plants (Park, Summers and Walstrom, 2017).

This article will focus on a practitioners' view of cyber security. Specifically, it addresses the management of a cyber attack.

In Section 2.1, the introduction, we run through some statistics regarding cyber attacks and cyber crime. We define what we mean by a cyber attack.

Section 2.2 looks at security incident response and covers areas such as security policies and cyber incident response, then walks the reader through an example of how to handle a ransomware incident using a runbook.

Section 2.3 examines organisational risk and the use of tools like cyber insurance to mitigate some of these risks. There are tables in this section that look at the insurance marketplace of 2017 and show the state of the cyber insurance playing field. GDPR fines and their insurability are also discussed.

Section 2.4 is the conclusion and is a brief wrap-up of the chapter.

2.1.1. *What is a cyber attack?*

Depending on which information sources you consult, you can find various definitions of a cyber attack. In the military, a cyber attack may present itself completely differently from a cyber attack against a civilian organisation. Hathaway *et al.* (2012) state that there can be multiple definitions of a cyber attack depending on your viewpoint.

Most of these definitions fall into a few categories.

- Cyber attacks — An entity takes an action that impairs the function of a computer or computer network
- Cyber crime — An action that is carried out by non-state entities, executed from a computer system, that breaks criminal law
- Cyber warfare — A cyberattack that damages property or results in physical injury that is similar to normal warfare

If one was to examine each of the above definitions for a cyber attack, the meaning of the term could be distilled down to the following: a cyber attack is an unauthorised action carried out with the goal of subverting a security control or policy. This is in keeping with Hathaway *et al.*'s (2012) definitions.

Examples of these kinds of attacks are:

- An adversary launches a Distributed Denial-of-Service (DDoS) attack against an organisation's website. The outcome of this is that the organisation's website is no longer available. The impact of this could be a loss of revenue that would have been generated in sales. Reputational damage could be one other impact of such an attack. It can be an embarrassment for a major organisation to lose control of its website, and it can be a breach of regulation or legislation for a regulated business to lose control of its website.

- A database is compromised, and the data in it is changed. This can lead to the loss of integrity of the data held in the database. This attack can be caused by the actions of an insider. The insider in question may be someone manipulating pricing for financial gain, a disgruntled employee, an errant process or database call, etc.
- A targeted attack is made against a military objective with the aim of evaluating the defenders' response to such an attack. Multiple such incursions into a network/device can be used to footprint the organisation and from this, insights into how a defender may react to specific sets of circumstances may be gleaned.

2.1.2. *Some cyber attack statistics*

If you look at a newspaper today, you can probably find at least one article pointing to the rise in cyber attacks globally. Table 2.1, taken from Lewis (2018), shows the estimated daily activity for several different types of cyber crime.

As you can see there are significant numbers of threats found each day. Some of the malicious scans can be attributed to things like Shodan, Google bots or other automatic scanning software. The

Table 2.1. Estimated daily cyber crime activity (Lewis, 2018).

Cyber Crime	Estimated Daily Activity
Malicious Scans	$80 Billion
New Malware	$300,000
Phishing	$33,000
Ransomware	$4,000
Records Lost to Hacking	$780,000

Table 2.2. Regional distribution of cyber crime in 2017 (Lewis, 2018).

Region (World Bank)	Region, GDP (USD Trillions)	Cyber Crime Cost (USD Billions)	Cyber Crime Loss (% GDP)
North America	20.2	140 to 175	0.69 to 0.87
Europe and Central Asia	20.3	160 to 180	0.79 to 0.89
East Asia & The Pacific	22.5	120 to 200	0.53 to 0.89
South Asia	2.9	7 to 15	0.24 to 0.52
Latin America & The Caribbean	5.3	15 to 30	0.28 to 0.57
Sub-Saharan Africa	1.5	1 to 3	0.07 to 0.20
Middle East & North Africa	3.1	2 to 5	0.06 to 0.16
World	75.8	445 to 608	0.59 to 0.80

large amount of phishing and ransomware activity seen daily is more interesting.

The cost of cyber crime is not insignificant. Lewis (2018) breaks the estimated costs down in the "Economic Impact of Cyber Crime — No Slowing Down" report. The results of this report are shown in Table 2.2.

The costs indicated in Table 2.2 for the world lie in the range of \$445 to \$608 billion dollars. This is a huge amount of money and clearly indicates that cyber crime does indeed pay.

Organisations trying to thwart this kind of ongoing onslaught need to invest heavily in cyber defences. These defences should be a combination of physical, technical and policy-based controls. Examples of these controls could be, but are not limited to, the ones on the following list:

- Access control systems
- Firewalls/intrusion detection systems (IDSs)
- Policy documents, e.g. acceptable use policies
- Awareness training

Without controls in place it can be very hard to gain any security traction in an organisation. A security practitioner needs to know what the organisational security stance looks like before they can put in place a relevant security plan. With a plan you can gauge your security maturity against a set of standards. Some examples of these standards follow:

- UK Cyber Essentials/Cyber Essentials Plus
- CIS Top 20
- ISO27000/27001

Adhering to a security standard also allows an organisation to gauge itself against its peers in their industry. This can sometimes be good as it allows you to see how well you are doing against the competition. It should be remembered, though, that each company is different and they all have their own unique challenges.

2.2. Security Incident Response from an Organisation's Viewpoint

Whenever an organisation comes under sustained or targeted cyber attack, it is the responsibility of the security team, working in conjunction with other operational or business teams, to mitigate the attack to the best of their abilities. Sometimes this will entail little input from other teams in the organisation; sometimes it may entail operational teams in the business working with other external third-party companies/agencies.

To enable the security team, and the organisation in general, to deal with cyber attacks successfully, there should be effective policies, procedures and guidelines in place that enable the employees in an organisation to be aware of what a cyber security incident is and what their actions should be when they detect a breach of policy or observe a suspicious event.

Procedures put in place by a security team are there to enable the security team or an operational team to better handle specific types of cyber attack, be they phishing campaigns against specific individuals in an organisation or virus/ransomware outbreaks right through to Distributed Denial-of-Service (DDoS) attacks against an organisation's internet-facing services.

This section will concern itself with policies and procedures that should be in place in an organisation that will enable it to react to and manage to a logical conclusion a cyber attack aimed at an organisation.

2.2.1. *Creating effective security policies*

Security policies are at the heart of an organisation's security posture. Having effective and pertinent security policies defined for an organisation is the first port of call for any new security department.

Policies are in themselves security controls. A breach in a security policy by an employee could trigger a human-resources (HR) incident whereby the employee may have to take part in some sort of HR review process. In the worst-case scenarios, a breach of a security policy could lead to the termination of an employee.

Whenever a new employee starts with an organisation, as part of the induction process into the organisation, the new employee should acknowledge that they have read the relevant policies applicable to them. This then puts the onus on the employee to adhere to the policy and report breaches of the policy to the relevant party.

Security policies should be based on a standard template for the organisation. This ensures consistency of approach from the company and is also a good practice from an auditors' point of view. If an auditor were to look at 20–30 policies from a company and they all had different layouts, then this may suggest to the auditor that there is no "joined up plan" in respect to the company's policies. Conversely, if an auditor were to look at 20 policies and see that they all maintained a standard layout with a consistent approach, then that makes it easier for the auditor to audit and it also makes it much easier for an employee wishing to get to the heart of the policy statement itself.

2.2.1.1. *Format and layout of a policy*

The thought of creating a policy from scratch can be quite daunting. It was for the author when he had to create a new policy for the first time. What he soon realised though is that there are a lot of reference policies available freely on the internet. Though these may not fit your organization exactly as you would like, reading other policies gives you a general overview of what a policy is, and what it comprises. SANS Institute, for example, have multiple security policy templates. You just need to fill in the organisation's name and you will have a working policy.

When creating policies from another person's/organisation's policy, it is important that you consider the wording of the policy. Does it "fit" with what you want your policy to say? If not, what can be changed to make it more applicable?

The wording of a policy is also important. The writer of the policy does not need to be a wordsmith, but word usage in policy is important. The word "SHOULD" is ambiguous in policy. You are telling someone that they should do something, but that it's ok if they don't. Replacing "SHOULD" with "MUST" changes the reading of the sentence and its applicability.

Consider the following control statement:

> All company assets SHOULD be patched on a regular basis.

Reading this statement, the reader can take away two meanings. The first of these is that it is not mandatory that systems are patched regularly, and the second of these is that all assets are patched regularly.

If we rewrite the control statement as follows, it is much clearer:

> All company assets MUST be patched on a regular basis.

Reading this, the only thing a reader can take away is that all systems MUST be patched regularly. You could argue that regularly is also ambiguous as it could mean weekly or annually since both are regular. Other wording in the policy could help you get around this ambiguity.

Brander (1997) in his RFC 2119 "Key words for use in RFCs to Indicate Requirement Levels" sets out to define the use of the above keywords and several others as they should be used in RFC documents.

Such clarity is sometimes achievable in a good policy and it assists both the reader and the writer in the definition of the policy. The RFC states:

> "The key words "MUST", "MUST NOT", "REQUIRED", "SHALL", "SHALL NOT", "SHOULD", "SHOULD NOT", "RECOMMENDED", "MAY", and "OPTIONAL" in this document are to be interpreted as described in RFC 2119"

A good policy document is as succinct as it can possibly be, but it should at least incorporate the following sections.

2.2.1.2. *Preparing a security policy*

The actual writing of a security policy is relatively simple when you have pulled together the layout and content of what you wish to incorporate in the policy.

As a "rule of thumb", you should have sections similar to the sections denoted in Table 2.3.

Always aim to write a policy in as succinct a manner as possible. Being too "wordy" can often complicate the policy and allows ambiguity and interpretation to slip into the wording. This is not a good thing as it can derail the policy.

The policy statement tells the reader what is defined in the policy. Table 2.4 is a section of a WIFI acceptable-use policy that the author wrote. Using the SANS (2014) Wireless Communications policy as a starting point the author created the security policy control statements in Table 2.4.

After the policy statement had been written, it was then run through the legal team to ensure it complied with local laws and regulations. Bear in mind that if you are an international company then it may require several revisions to have an overarching policy that is compliant with all regions in which the organisation conducts business. It may be necessary to have an overarching policy and then certain region-specific mini policies to cope with local laws and regulations.

As can be seen from Table 2.4, there are 6 policy control statements. Each one is well bounded with what control it is putting in

Table 2.3. The main sections of a policy document.

Section	Contents
Versioning/ Document Control	This section records the following. The policy owner Who approved the policy How often it is reviewed Next review date
Review Schedule	This section lays out what would trigger a review of the policy
Overview	What the policy is aiming to cover
Objective	What the objective of the policy is
Scope	The scope of the policy and any limits put on it
Policy	This section lays out the policy statements
Compliance with policy/Handling exceptions to policy	This section is used to inform users of how policy compliance will be measured, how to deal with an Exception to Policy (ETP), and how to deal with breaches to policy.

Table 2.4. An example of control statements in a security policy.

Security Policy Control Statements
"The Company" provides free WIFI access to the internet for employees, contractors and visitors to the "The Company'" business premises.
Employees, contractors and visitors must not use the "The Company" WIFI connection to:
Upload, download, use or reuse any material which violates any applicable copyright laws or which violates the rights of any individual or entity;
Access defamatory, obscene, indecent, abusive, offensive, harassing, violent, hateful, inflammatory, or otherwise inappropriate material or content;
Visit sites that could be deemed inappropriate, offensive, pornographic, or that contain material of an obscene nature;
Use peer-to-peer software on their own personal devices, for the collection or dissemination of copyrighted material for which they are not the copyright holder;
Attempt to bypass any security controls put in place to monitor or restrict access to the "The Company" WIFI; and
Introduce any viruses, trojan horses, worms, logic bombs, or other software or material which is malicious or technologically harmful.

Table 2.5. Liability clause.

Liability Clause
"The Company" is not responsible for the accuracy, validity, legality or usefulness of information available, or any viruses and software designed to damage equipment and networks, which you may encounter while connected to "The Company" WIFI
"The Company" is not responsible for damage caused by connecting personal devices to the "The Company" WIFI.
"The Company" is not responsible for any use or transactions carried out using the "The Company" WIFI service. Responsibility for the security of such transactions rests with the user and "The Company" cannot accept responsibility or liability for any loss or damages arising from such use of its WIFI services.

place. This will assist the Security Team in monitoring the policy for compliance and will assist the business in dealing with breaches of the policy.

Table 2.5 is the final part of the policy and defines what the company is not responsible for on the WIFI policy. Specifically, the policy states that it is not responsible for incorrect information, damage to property attached to the WIFI network and for the security of any connections carried out over the WIFI network.

2.2.1.3. *Exceptions to policy*

An Exception to Policy (ETP) should not be confused with a policy breach.

A policy breach is when a security incident has occurred that has broken one of the policy statements. An ETP is an outlier in an organisation who is not able to comply with a policy statement at a particular time. This may be for technical, business, or financial reasons.

Exceptions to Policy should be logged somewhere in an organisation and should be reviewed on a regular basis to see if the ETP has been rectified or if an extension to the ETP is required. It would be prudent for the person/people reviewing the ETPs to do this on at least a 6-monthly basis. Any longer and the ETP almost becomes irrelevant, as the ETP, instead of being an Exception to Policy, is supporting a policy breach.

Security policies are an important part of the security practitioner's toolset. Well-maintained and well-reviewed policies help a company to protect its information assets as well as the organisation as a whole.

2.2.2. *Cyber incident response plan*

The Cyber Incident Response Plan (CIRP) is the "go to" document in a business arsenal that defines how a cyber incident is handled.

2.2.2.1. *Security procedures*

Having defined a robust policy document, the next task for security practitioners is to lay out the procedures to be followed when handling a security incident.

Procedures differ from policy in that they are the methods by which breaches of policy can be followed up. These are well-defined and include such things as:

- When a procedure should be instigated.
- Who will control information flow whilst the procedure is being executed.
- What tasks need to be completed at the end of an incident.
- Any other follow-up tasks.

There is no such thing as an overarching procedure that governs all others. Procedures backed up by policy are fluid documents. They mature over time and are never really finished. They are often referred to in business circles as "living documents"

When defining procedures, it is advisable to have a methodology already planned. This methodology will lay out the different phases of the procedure and allow the writer to assign tasks to the specific phase. Figure 2.1 shows the phases of an incident response process. This process may not fit every procedure or playbook but it does give a high level view of the procedures that will be defined.

Fig. 2.1. High level incident response process.

Fig. 2.2. Ransomware incident response process.

Each of these phases logically flows into the next and this provides for a structured process. This process, however, is fluid. It may be necessary to modify the process so that it fits with a particular security incident playbook. For instance, upon discovery of a data breach under the European General Data Protection Regulation (GDPR) you must inform the regulator, which is the Information Commissioner's Office (ICO) if you are in the United Kingdom, of the breach within 72 hours of the breach occurring (Marotta *et al.*, 2017). Note that the 72 hours is linear and does not honour working hours. If you discover a breach or a reportable event at 12pm on a Thursday, you are duty bound by the auspices of the GDPR to report the breach or reportable event to the regulator by 12PM on the Saturday.

Figure 2.2 shows the process defined in Fig. 2.1, modified to fit a ransomware playbook.

The individual phases in the ransomware process which are defined in Fig. 2.2 will now be discussed.

2.2.2.2. *Identification*

When a device is initially infected with ransomware there are several potential Indicators of Compromise (IOCs)

- If the user was completely unaware, then the first indicator a user would receive would be a message telling them that their files had been encrypted and that in order to recover their files a ransom would need to be paid.

- If a user is more familiar with the work patterns of their computer then they may in the first instance notice that the computer is more sluggish than usual. This is because the ransomware is consuming CPU cycles and disk IO bandwidth encrypting the user's data.

When the user has identified that they have been a victim of ransomware then they will escalate the incident to the respective incident handling process.

Initially, when the incident responders conduct their triage of the computer, they should note the ransomware details and any ransomware payment demands. The incident responders should note which resources have been affected by the ransomware and whether any shared resources were affected, e.g. corporate file shares.

2.2.2.3. *Initial containment*

It is important to treat a potential ransomware incident with the gravity it deserves. Ransomware can pose a significant risk to normal business operations. Take a look at the news and press articles surrounding the WannaCry ransomware outbreak and how it disrupted the National Health Service (NHS) in the UK. The NHS was severely crippled due to the scale of this outbreak.

Ransomware poses a substantial risk to an organisation's normal operations. In the event of a ransomware outbreak, the initial response should be swift and sharp. This will help limit the effects of the outbreak and help prevent further impact to the normal business operations of the company.

Where containment efforts may lead to the interruption of normal business operations, the business owners of that process should be involved in the decision process.

2.2.2.4. *Notification*

The initial notification of an incident is usually one of the shortest phases of the whole incident response process, although there should be ongoing notification throughout the lifecycle of the incident.

Without a doubt, ransomware will have an effect on normal business operations. To this end there will be multiple notifications that may need to be sent out to both internal and external third parties.

Employees need to understand what has happened and what is being done about it.

External parties may include the regulator, law enforcement, insurance companies if the company has cyber insurance, and any other regulatory or legislative body that local regulations mandate should be informed.

2.2.2.5. *Analysis*

The majority of ransomware breaches normally originate from a user clicking on a link in a malicious email, or from a drive-by download on a user's computer. It is of the utmost importance that this evidence is captured so that a root cause analysis can be carried out to identify the malicious file. This evidence will be on the initially infected computer that executed the ransomware program. It will not be on file shares encrypted by the ransomware. The collection and preservation of this evidence is paramount.

Once a particular user's computer has been identified as the initial infection point, this computer should be isolated from the network. The easiest way to do this is to remove its network connection. The computer should not be powered down until a memory dump has been taken. This ensures that whatever malicious code was being executed can be captured in memory.

If the normal business operation is to then format/rebuild the computer, a disk image of the hard disk/disks should be taken. Bear in mind that if full disk encryption is used then the decryption keys for the disk should also be saved. It is ultimately preferable to keep the whole machine quarantined until the investigation is over. If this is not possible, then the hard disk should be retained, as this is also a better chain of evidence than a disk image taken by an employee. The running of anti-virus scans prior to disk imaging should be prevented as this can taint the evidence.

Analysis is used to confirm the initial infection vectors and to confirm what the capabilities of the ransomware are. With this information it may be possible to identify the ransomware type/family. All disk-based analysis should be taken on a disk image and not on the original disk itself. This will protect the integrity of the evidence.

Analysis of the malware may require third party support from incident responders if there is no in-house expertise in malware analysis.

2.2.2.6. *Containment*

Although there are similarities between the containment and initial containment stages the main differentiator is the criticality. The initial containment actions are reactionary and possibly temporary in nature. They are put in place to contain the initial outbreak. In the containment phase the actions are carried out in a planned and methodical manner. They are implemented to manage the full scope of the incident.

When the initial infection vector is identified, further containment actions will need to be carried out. If IOCs are identified as URLs, IP addresses, email addresses, etc., then blocks/alerts can be put in place to inform the incident responders of further infections on the organisation's infrastructure. These blocks/alerts help mitigate the threat and prevent it from reoccurring. It should be borne in mind that malware authors change up their malware regularly and that an IOC for the current outbreak may not work for a future outbreak.

If any further IOCs are discovered on the organisation's infrastructure, then these systems should be isolated from the network, and memory and disk images taken to preserve evidence.

2.2.2.7. *Eradication*

During the eradication phase, the organisation removes the threats and elements identified as part of the contamination from its infrastructure. Having contained the infection, eradication follows closely behind.

The eradication phase is when the organisation removes all indications of the infection from its systems and the systems are put back into service. It is hoped that systems placed back in service have had service restored to a state similar to the state before the ransomware was detected.

2.2.2.8. *Recovery*

The recovery phase is when the organisation's systems return to normal operations. In this phase it is assumed that the ransomware threat has been neutralised to such an extent that no further impact of the ransomware can occur.

The recovery phase can only commence when all containment and eradication actions have been completed. This should have included blocking the attackers' website and patching or mitigating the vulnerable software or services on the organisation's infrastructure. During this phase, files may be retrieved from backup and the rebuilding of computers from verified known good media may have commenced.

In the event that some parts of the business may require some files or information retrieved as a matter of priority, further steps must be taken. Even before all the eradication steps have been completed, it is of the utmost importance that these restored resources are properly secured from re-infection. The organisation should limit what files can be restored to reduce the work needed. Files restored should have the least amount of access privileges possible in order to enable operation but prevent re-infection. It is not unheard of for restored files to be re-encrypted when a successful containment and eradication process fails.

2.2.2.9. *Post-incident actions*

Having reached a state of normalcy after the ransomware infection it is imperative that the organisation carry out a post-incident review (PIR). The PIR is carried out to ensure that all lessons learned are captured and fed back into the process. The ultimate aim is to ensure that similar incidents do not occur again, and if they do, then any previous incident experience is captured and distilled down into knowledge which is captured in the organisation's appropriate playbooks.

In the PIR meeting all the parties that were involved in the incident should have representation. It is important to have this meeting chaired by a person of sufficient authority that can guide the meeting along. PIR meetings are not a forum to deride other teams for their performance or lack thereof. This is not constructive but will put them on the defensive and will therefore prevent valuable lessons from being documented from the previous incident.

The PIR should consider what went well and what went badly. It should identify areas of improvement and minute any actions to be reported back to the review in a timely manner. Areas to consider may include any of the following:

- Policies
- Patch Management
- Vulnerability Monitoring
- Alerting
- Firewalls and blocking software
- Employee training
- Preparatory tasks that may help in the future

Finally, organisations need to ensure they have sent out any additional notifications that are required both internally and externally. Nothing enrages employees more than lack of communication. If you do not put out notifications to update the organisation's employees, then they will fill this communication void with hearsay and conjecture. This can ultimately derail all the good work carried out by the incident responders. Organisations and individuals also have to bear in mind their reporting requirements in relation to any relevant legislation and regulation that their organisations may work under.

2.3. Business Risk and Cyber Insurance — Its Place in Your Cyber Response Toolkit

It seems like almost every day we hear about a new system that has been exploited or a news story on how some organisation has had a data breach (BBC, 2017; BBC, 2018). As more and more of these breaches and exploits become available, more boards of companies are beginning to wake up to the risks posed to their organisations.

The management of an organization can no longer ignore these threats. On their part, governments and regulators have set up new laws and regulation to try and create a consistent framework and consistent breach reporting mechanisms across regions. In fact it could be argued that the relatively new European Union General Data Protection Regulation (GDPR) is already shaking up certain parts of business risk. Albrecht (2016) posits that businesses were already pointing to GDPR as a major risk and that it was being looked at as a key management task for an organisation.

Not all organisations are taking the responsibility for GDPR regulation as seriously as others. Addis and Kutar (2018) point out that a large number of organisations may not have been compliant with the GDPR regulation by the time it was implemented in May 2018. In fact, if you look around you will see that larger organisations have implemented GDPR programs in their organisations and are actively pursuing them. Conversely, a lot of smaller companies are not aware of their responsibilities under GDPR and are woefully unprepared for any actions that may be taken against them (Addis and Kutar, 2018).

One recent article by Page, Kaur and Waters (2017) looks at directors' liability and the growing concern as to what it means in the industry. The authors point out that cyber attacks and data loss are two of the biggest concerns facing companies. Because of regulation in certain sectors of industry directors are having more and more regulation and legislation heaped on them. Directors now must look at ways to mitigate this risk against their personal liability whilst discharging their duties efficiently.

2.3.1. *What is risk management?*

Marotta *et al.* (2017) state that "Risk is the possibility of suffering a loss or harm". Looking at this statement we can divine that risk is the outcome of several factors.

- Incident — The occurrence of a risk
- Threat — A cause of the risk
- Vulnerability — A weakness that can be exploited to create an incident
- Impact — The direct and indirect consequences of the actions of a threat on a vulnerability

The management of the above four items is called risk management. It is all about identifying risks in an organisation and then putting plans in place to handle or mitigate risks.

Risk management is made up of two distinct parts.

- Risk identification — Involves listing the elements of risk: threats, vulnerabilities and impact.
- Risk analysis — Involves carrying out the analysis of risks, focusing on the probability of a risk happening and the impact that risk would have on the organisation.

The World Economic Forum defines the above as a simple calculation.

Risk = probability × impact

Having carried out your risk analysis you can then move on to define a risk treatment. This allows you to define the measures you wish to implement to handle the identified risks (Taylor *et al.*, 2016).

There are only four ways to handle risk.

- Accept — A company may accept the risk of an outcome happening if there is deemed to be a low likelihood of the risk materialising.
- Reduce — A company may put controls in place to reduce the impact or likelihood of a risk materialising.
- Transfer/Share — This is where an organisation may look to transfer the risk to another party, e.g. buying insurance policies to cover the risk.
- Avoid — Some risks are just not worth taking on and a business may choose to avoid them, e.g. choosing not to entering a new market where the risks are not fully understood.

The next section of this chapter discusses how you could transfer/share the risk with a third party in the form of a cyber insurance policy.

2.3.2 *Cyber insurance*

It could be said that cyber insurance first started to appear around the 1970s. A company could purchase insurance to cover them for computer crime (Marotta *et al.*, 2017). From those early days specialist insurance has sprung up to assist companies in attempting to mitigate the risk of a cyber event. Property and liability insurance policies will not, in general, cover a cyber event (Biener, Eling and Wirfs, 2015).

When an organisation looks to procure a cyber insurance policy it is useful to have some terms of reference to put to the insurance organisations. This allows the organisation to easily judge each company on the same basis. A useful term of reference could be using the same taxonomy for the discussions with the insurers, so that the organisation is discussing similar products on a similar footing.

Table 2.6 lays out a taxonomy of operational cyber security risks. It was developed by Cebula, Young and Popeck (2014). This is version two of the taxonomy and it was updated from the original, dated 2010.

As can be seen, Table 2.6 lays out four classes, each with its own sub-categories. These sub-categories each have elements that apply to that class. The table can be used to do a detailed risk analysis of actions inside each of the classes. Cebula, Young and Popeck (2014) point out that a risk in one category can possibly create a risk in other categories. An example of such is below.

"...a software failure due to improper security settings could be caused by any of the elements of inadvertent or deliberate actions of people" (Cebula, Young and Popeck, 2014).

As mentioned previously, GDPR is a boardroom issue in companies that are aware of it. One of the major risks of GDPR are the fines the regulator can impose. In the United Kingdom prior to GDPR the maximum fine the Information Commissioner's Office could hand out to a company was £500,000 (Information

Table 2.6. Categories of cyber risk, derived from Cebula, Young and Popeck (2014).

Category	Description	Elements
Actions of People		
1.1 Inadvertent	Unintentional actions taken without malicious or harmful intent	Mistakes, errors, omissions
1.2 Deliberate	Actions taken intentionally and with intent to do harm	Fraud, sabotage, theft and vandalism
1.3 Inaction	Lack of action or failure to act in a given scenario and lack of availability of personnel to take action	Lack of appropriate skills, knowledge, guidance, availability
Systems and Technology Failures		
2.1 Hardware	Risks traceable to failures in physical equipment	Failure due to capacity, performance, maintenance and obsolescence
2.2 Software	Risks stemming from software assets of all types, including programs, applications and operating systems	Compatibility, configuration management, change control, security settings, coding practices and testing
2.3 Systems	Failures of integrated systems to perform as expected	Design, specifications, integration and complexity
Failed Internal Process		
3.1 Process design and/or execution	Failures of processes to achieve their desired outcomes due to poor process design or execution	Process flow, process documentation, roles and responsibilities, notifications and alerts, information flow, escalation of issues, service-level agreements, and task hand-off
3.2 Process Controls	Inadequate controls on the operation of the controls	Status monitoring, metrics, periodic review and process ownership

Table 2.6. (*Continued*)

Category	Description	Elements
3.3 Supporting Processes	Failure of organisational supporting processes to deliver the appropriate resources	Staffing, accounting, training and development, and procurement
External Events		
4.1 Catastrophes	Events, both natural and of human origin, over which the organisation has no control and that can occur without notice	Weather event, fire, flood, earthquake, unrest
4.2 Legal Issues	Risk arising from legal issues	Regulatory compliance, legislation and litigation
4.3 Business Issues	Risks arising from changes in the business environment of the organisation	Supplier failure, market conditions and economic conditions
4.4 Service Dependencies	Risks arising from the organisation's dependence on external parties	Utilities, emergency services, fuel and transportation

Commisioner's Office, 1998). Now with the GDPR being in effect the fines are much heavier. A breach of the GDPR could leave an organisation liable for a fine of €20 million or 4% of global turnover, whichever is greatest (Marsh, 2016).

One of the major sticking points of cyber insurance is that the coverage of regulatory fines is a grey area. Aon and DLA Piper (2018) and Marsh (2018) both agree that your insurability for GDPR fines is really dependent on where you are located in Europe (Fig. 2.3). Basically, if you are in a highly regulated environment then you will be unlikely to get insurance to cover GDPR fines without any stipulations on a policy.

Now that we have covered the insurability of GDPR fines it will be worth looking at what other risks can be covered by a cyber insurance policy.

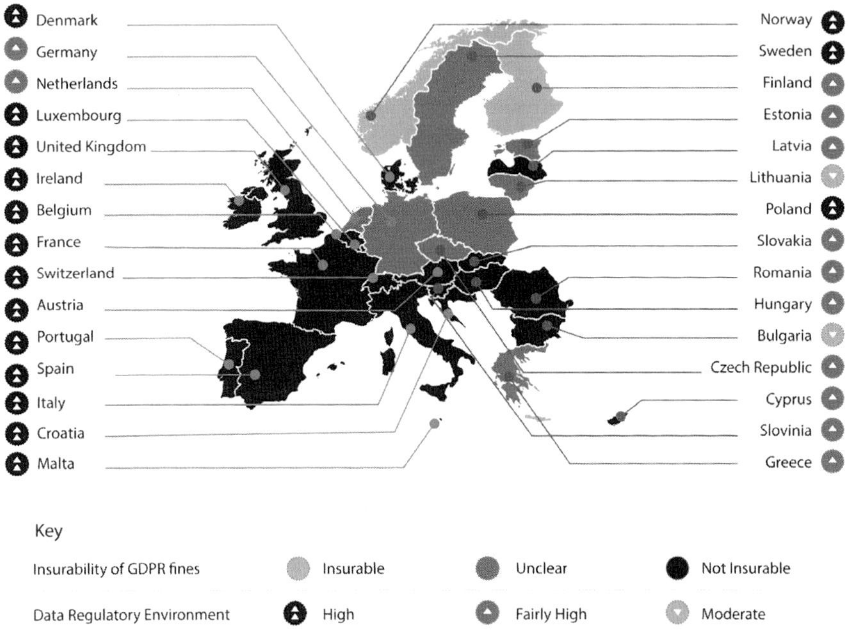

Fig. 2.3. Insurability by country, Aon and DLA Piper (2018).

Typically, an organisation will have a level of risk they are willing to accept. This is usually set by senior management and will be cascaded down through functions like operational risk or a risk management function. Sometimes these functions are carried out by a single person, sometimes by teams, depending on the size of the organisation.

Table 2.7 by Marotta *et al.* (2017) shows a quick view of what levels of cover an insurance company may be willing to provide. It should be noted that when dealing with insurance companies the organisation may be better suited to using an insurance broker who has experience in the area of cyber risk and cyber insurance (Shackelford, 2012).

As Shackelford (2012) points out, organisations should not rely completely on cyber insurance policies to mitigate their cyber risk.

Table 2.7. Coverage of several existing insurance policies derived from Marotta *et al.* (2017).

	Coverage	Allianz	QBE	AEGIS	CNA	InsureTrust	CDRM LLC	Travelers	Zurich	ACE	Hiscox	Insureon	Marsh	Chub	AIG
First-party	Loss or damage to digital assets	X	X	X	X	X		X	X	X	X	X	X	X	X
	Business interruption	X	X	X	X	X	X	X	X	X	X	X	X	X	X
	Cyber extortion	X	X	X	X	X	X	X	X			X	X		X
	Theft of money and digital assets	X	X		X		X	X	X	X	X	X	X	X	
Third-party	Security and privacy breaches	X	X	X	X	X	X	X	X	X	X	X	X	X	X
	Computer forensics investigation	X	X	X	X	X	X			X		X			X
	Customer notification/PR expenses	X	X		X	X	X	X	X	X		X		X	X
	Multi-media liability	X	X	X		X		X	X	X					X
	Loss of third-party data	X		X	X	X	X	X	X	X	X	X	X	X	
	Third-party contractual indemnification		X			X			X	X				X	

Kopp, Kaffenberger and Wilson (2017), in their working paper for the International Monetary Fund, point out that 90% of the costs of a cyber incident can be attributed to indirect factors.

This is broken down into four phases with examples of both direct and indirect costs shown in Table 2.8.

The four phases can be broken down as the following:

- **Prevention** — These are the normal day-to-day running costs of a business taking care of its regulatory and business requirements.

Table 2.8. Costs of cyber events (Kopp, Kaffenberger and Wilson, 2017).

Phase	Direct Costs	Indirect Costs
Prevention (continuous)	Cyber security costs (preventative safeguarding of systems and data) Regulatory compliance cost	Opportunity cost
Reaction (immediate)	Technical investigation Stop intrusion and initiate recovery of systems Customer notification	Cost of operational disruption Opportunity costs Loss in revenue Loss in equity value
Impact management (short-term)	Adjustment to infrastructure and processes System and data recovery Damage reduction Post-breach customer protection Initiation of cyber audit Attorney and litigation cost	Opportunity costs Loss in revenue Loss in equity value Customer loss (turnover)
Business recovery and remediation (medium- to long-term)		Increased funding costs Lower future demand for breached firm's services Redesign of business processes and systems Rebuilding relationships, reputation and brand value Investment in better security systems and preparedness capabilities

- **Reaction** — This is when the initial breach takes place and how the company reacts to it. This could entail incident response, forensics, and communications to both internal and external parties.
- **Impact Management** — This is when an organisation checks on its security controls and infrastructure configurations. It is about managing the direct impact of a breach.
- **Business Recovery and Remediation** — These are the costs of repairing the breach and putting in controls that will assist in preventing a similar breach in future. As part of this phase the organisation should start to rebuild reputation and customer goodwill.

An effective and well understood cyber strategy should underpin any organisation no matter how big or small they are. Cyber security is the melding of people, process and technology, sometimes termed the Three Pillars of Cyber Security (IT Governance, 2018).

2.4. Conclusion

As can be seen from this paper, to be in a position to manage a cyber attack effectively takes time and resources.

From the introduction to this article, we explained the definition of a cyber attack and how this can change depending on the viewpoint of the practitioner. We distilled these meanings down to a single definition that in our opinion covers all three areas.

Looking at the statistics of cyber attacks we can see that the cost and frequency of attacks are continuing to grow, and that cyber attackers are here for the long haul.

We discussed how to create security policies which can be put in place to manage the expectations of users using tailored policy control statements. Running through policies brought us naturally to cyber incident response plans.

We walked through a ransomware runbook and saw how, using our cyber incident response framework, we can work through an incident to reach a logical conclusion. We also carried out post-incident actions.

This is when we can use what we have learned in the investigation to update our controls so they are always improving.

Looking at business risk, we covered some of the language used in the risk arena. This took us on to the section on cyber insurance. It can be said that there really is no single policy that will address the risks borne by every organization. Not everything can be insured. We pointed out that for some companies cyber insurance will not indemnify an organisation against regulatory breaches or fines. This is an important point as GDPR fines of €20 million or 4% of global turnover far outstrip the maximum fine of £500,000 under the UK's Data Protection Act 1998.

Preparing for and defending against cyber attacks at an organisational level is a complicated task. Hopefully some of the information in this article will be useful to other practitioners in the field.

References

1. Addis, M. C. and Kutar, M. (2018). *The General Data Protection Regulation (GDPR), Emerging Technologies and UK Organisations: Awareness, Implementation and Readiness* [Online]. Available at: https://www.ukais.org/resources/Documents/ukais 2018 proceedings papers/paper_39.pdf (Accessed: 1 October 2018).
2. Albrecht, J. (2016). How the GDPR Will Change the World. *European Data Protection Law Review*, **2**(3), pp. 287–289. doi: https://doi.org/10.21552/EDPL/2016/3/4.
3. Aon and DLA Piper. (2018). *The Price of Data Security: A Guide to the Insurability of GDPR Fines Across Europe* [Online]. Available at: http://www.aon.com/attachments/risk-services/Aon_DLA-Piper-GDPR-Fines-Guide_Final_May2018.pdf (Accessed: 1 October 2018).
4. BBC. (2017). *NHS Cyber-Attack: GPs and Hospitals Hit by Ransomware* [Online]. Available at: http://www.bbc.co.uk/news/health-39899646 (Accessed: 28 November 2017).
5. BBC. (2018). *Equifax Finds More Victims of 2017 Breach* [Online]. Available at: https://www.bbc.co.uk/news/technology-43241939 (Accessed: 24 July 2018)
6. BBC. (2017). *Supermarket Morrisons Sued by Staff Over Personal Data Leak* [Online]. Available at: https://www.bbc.co.uk/news/uk-england-41552911 (Accessed: 12 October 2018).

7. Biener, C., Eling, M. and Wirfs, J. H. (2015). Insurability of Cyber Risk: An Empirical Analysis. *The Geneva Papers on Risk and Insurance–Issues and Practice*, **40**(1), pp. 131–158.
8. Brander, S. (1997). *Key Words for Use in RFCs to Indicate Requirement Levels* [Online]. Available at: https://tools.ietf.org/pdf/rfc2119.pdf (Accessed: 10 June 2018).
9. Calder, S. (2018) *BA Data Breach: What Does the British Airways Hack Mean for Customers?* [Online] Available at: https://www.independent.co.uk/travel/news-and-advice/british-airways-flights-ba-hacked-data-theft-customers-a8526516.html (Accessed: 12 August 2018).
10. Cebula, J. J., Young, L. R. and Popeck, M. E. (2014). *A Taxonomy of Operational Cyber Security Risks Version 2* (Report No. CMU/SEI-2014-TN-006). Pittsburgh, PA, USA: Software Engineering Institute, Carnegie Mellon University. doi: 10.1007/978-1-4419-7133-3.
11. Hathaway, O. A., Crootof, R., Perdue, W. and Levitz, P. (2012). The Law of Cyber-Attack. *California Law Review*, **100**(4), pp. 817–886. doi: 10.15779/Z38CR6N.
12. Hern, A. and Pegg, D. (2018). *Facebook Fined for Data Breaches in Cambridge Analytica Scandal* [Online]. Available at: https://www.theguardian.com/technology/2018/jul/11/facebook-fined-for-data-breaches-in-cambridge-analytica-scandal (Accessed: 25 September 2018).
13. Information Commisioner's Office. (1998). *Data Protection Act 1998, s. 55C(1)*. Available at: https://www.legislation.gov.uk/ukpga/1998/29 (Accessed: 30 September 2018).
14. IT Governance. (2018). *What is Cyber Security?* [Online] Available at: https://www.itgovernance.co.uk/what-is-cybersecurity (Accessed: 9 November 2018).
15. Kopp, E., Kaffenberger, L. and Wilson, C. (2017). Cyber Risk, Market Failures, and Financial Stability [Online]. *IMF Working Papers*, **17**(185), pp. 1–36. Available at: https://www.imf.org/en/Publications/WP/Issues/2017/08/07/Cyber-Risk-Market-Failures-and-Financial-Stability-45104. doi: 10.5089/9781484313787.001 (Accessed: 30 September 2018).
16. Marotta, A., Martinelli, F., Nanni, S., Orlando, A. and Yautsiukhin, A. (2017). Cyber-Insurance Survey. *Computer Science Review*, **24**, pp. 35–61. doi: 10.1016/j.cosrev.2017.01.001.
17. Marsh. (2016). *UK Cyber Risk Survey Report : 2016* [Online]. Available at: https://www.marsh.com/content/dam/marsh/Documents/PDF/UK-en/UK Cyber Risk Survey Report 2016.pdf Survey Report 2016.pdf (Accessed: 27 July 2018).

18. Marsh. (2018). *GDPR Fines and Penalties : Insurability Will Vary by Location, Policy Details, and More* [Online]. Available at: http://mouillere.com/universconvergents/wp-content/uploads/2018/09/Marsh-Cyber-Insurability-Report-UK.pdf (Accessed: 27 August 2018).
19. Page, J., Kaur, M. and Waters, E. (2017). Directors' Liability Survey: Cyber Attacks and Data Loss — A Growing Concern. *Journal of Data Protection & Privacy*, **1**(2), pp. 173–182.
20. Park, D., Summers, J. and Walstrom, M. (2017). *Cyberattack on Critical Infrastructure: Russia and the Ukrainian Power Grid Attacks.* Available at: https://jsis.washington.edu/news/cyberattack-critical-infrastructure-russia-ukrainian-power-grid-attacks/#_ftnref1 (Accessed: 11 July 2018).
21. Rothrock, R. A., Kaplan, J. and Van Der Oord, F. (2018). The Board's Role in Managing Cybersecurity Risks. *MIT Sloan Management Review*, **59**(2).
22. Sans Institute. (2015). Wireless Communication Policy. Available at: https://www.sans.org/security-resources/policies/network-security/pdf/wireless-communication-policy (Accessed: 14 September 2018).
23. Shackelford, S. J. (2012). Should Your Firm Invest in Cyber Risk Insurance? *Business Horizons*, **55**(4), pp. 349–356. doi: 10.1016/j.bushor.2012.02.004.
24. Taylor, A., Alexander, D., Finch, A. and Sutton, D. (2016). *Information Security Management Principles* (2nd ed.). Swindon, UK: BCS learning and Development.
25. Treanor, J. and Jones, R. (2016). *Tesco Bank Freezes Transactions After Cash Taken From 20,000 Accounts* [Online]. Available at: https://www.theguardian.com/business/2016/nov/07/tesco-bank-freezes-transactions-online-attack (Accessed: 24 July 2018).

Chapter 3

Practical Cyber Security for Digital Trains

George Copeland

Northumbria University London, UK
george.copeland@outlook.com

ABSTRACT

On-train networks have moved from being a set of isolated engineering solutions to becoming integrated cyber-physical systems, creating 'Digital Trains'. The interconnectivity between Digital Train systems is generally driven by operational efficiency and cost rather than security. It is asserted that the architectural standards which define on-train networks have not kept pace with the developments in the industry or with cyber security, and that the combination of ICT and ICS networks introduces potential risks that are not fully understood by decision makers. Inclusion of both the Digital Railway and Digital Trains in the scope of Critical National Infrastructure CPNI (2108) and therefore the NIS Directive (Directive (EU) (2016/1148) should help in this respect but that may not be soon enough to prevent an incident. Following these recently introduced regulatory requirements, consideration is required as to which is the most appropriate security standard with which to provide appropriate assurance given the mix of technologies.

Keywords: digital train, digital railway, critical national infrastructure, NIS, IACS, cyber-physical

3.1. Introduction

The current drive for digitisation in automation and control is often referred to as 'Industry 4.0', or the fourth industrial revolution. "While Industry 3.0 focused on the automation of single machines and processes, Industry 4.0 focuses on the end-to-end digitisation of all physical assets and integration into digital ecosystems with value chain partners" (PWC, 2016). In the UK, the railway is part of the transition to digitalisation, but because of the way that it is currently structured, the approach has been fragmented and disparate, not least between Digital Trains and the Digital Railway. In the UK, trains are owned by Rolling Stock Leasing Companies (ROSCOs), and operated by Train Operating Companies (TOCs), mostly delivering fixed term franchise agreements let by DfT. TOCs generally include major investments, including train upgrades and purchases, in their franchise bids, returning assets to the ROSCOs at the end of the franchise. The trains run on the infrastructure provided by Network Rail, which is a nationalised organisation. Digital Trains are one of the major investments being made by TOCs, and the Digital Railway is being developed by Network Rail without much synergy. This is not the only reason for current concerns about how the railway is operating but has contributed towards the need for a "review to look at the structure of the whole rail industry, including increasing integration between track and train" (DfT, 2018). This research focuses on Digital Train development with a view to defining a practical way to deal with the "new operational risk for smart manufacturers and digital supply networks: cyber" (Deloitte, 2017).

On-board train networks have moved from being a set of isolated engineering solutions to becoming integrated cyber-physical systems. The extent of on-board systems ranges from the provision of public wifi to operational controls, creating a 'multi-agent' architecture, described by Yagdereli *et al.* (2015) as comprising multiple sub-systems or being systems of systems. Although it is recognised that segregation is desirable the interconnectivity between on-board systems is often driven by operational efficiency and cost rather than security. It is asserted that the standards which define on-train networks have not kept pace with the developments in the industry or with cyber security and the potential risks are not fully understood by decision makers. In the UK the inclusion of the railway in the scope of Critical National Infrastructure CPNI (2108) and therefore the NIS Directive (Directive (EU) (2016/1148) may help in this respect but early indications appear to set compliance at a low level.

The Digital Railway includes the infrastructure used to support railway signalling and other safety systems. In the UK this is managed by Network Rail. The Digital Railway's footprint on trains is largely confined to the driver's cab where it delivers safety systems designed to alert the driver to unexpected events and in some cases override train controls to stop the train. These systems currently include ATP (Automatic train protection), AWS (Automatic warning system) and TPWS (Train protection and warning system). All of these systems are delivered through a dedicated communications network called GSM-R (Global System for Mobile communications — Railway). Network Rail is in the process of delivering a strategy to upgrade the Digital Railway, deploying systems that provide in-cab signalling, traffic management and a connected driver advisory system. This will use the same (and upgraded) GSM-R to implement the following: ETCS (European Train Control System) to allow trains to run closer together and to travel at their best speeds while maintaining safe braking distances, CDAS (Connected Driver Advisory Systems) and ATO (Automatic Train Operation) which provide decision support to drivers in the cab so that they have the information they need at the right time to boost performance and safety, and TM (Traffic Management) to optimise performance as trains flow across the network, maximising the throughput that existing track can support and adapting in real-time as network conditions change to aid rapid recovery (NR, 2018). ETCS is an advanced form of ATP and the combination of ETCS and GSM-R is referred to as ERTMS (European Railway Traffic Management System) (EU, 2018).

Digital Train includes the remaining on-board systems that deliver services such as RCM (remote condition monitoring), PIS (passenger information systems), SRS (seat reservation systems) and public wifi. These systems do not have access to GSM-R and use a separate MCG (Mobile Communications Gateway) to enable internet access using data sims procured from commercial MNOs (Mobile Network Operators).

From a rolling stock perspective, the Digital Railway includes the Train Control Systems that are safety-critical, whereas Digital Train includes Train Management Systems, which may be operational or business-critical and are less regulated. Ideally the Digital Railway and Digital Train systems remain segregated, but for operational efficiency and cost management new trains are being delivered with more and more systems being interconnected.

Train Communications Networks (TCN) were originally based on industrial field-buses. They lacked performance and were not designed for trains. As there was no standard, proprietary designs emerged which resulted in a lack of interoperability between vehicles. Schafers and Hans (2000) describe the development of IEC 61375-1 and its publication as an international standard in October 1999. The initial standard included only a Multifunctional Vehicle Bus (MVB) which connects equipment on and between vehicles and a Wire Train Bus (WTB) which interconnects vehicles via jumper cables or automatic couplers.

The IEC 61375 standard, as shown in Fig. 3.1, has since been supplemented to elaborate on the protocols for the bus networks and:

i. in 2012 to add the CAN-Open protocol based on ISO 11898 much like that used in road vehicles, and
ii. in 2015 to add the Ethernet Train Backbone (ETB) and introduction of the concept of an Ethernet Consist Network (ECN)

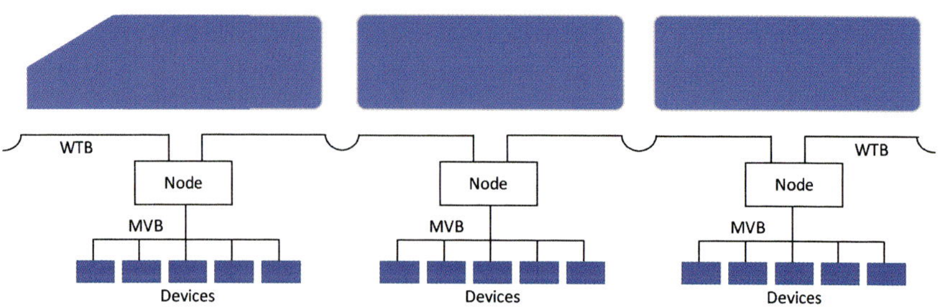

Fig. 3.1. IEC 61375 architecture.

The components of IEC 61375 are shown below in Fig. 3.2:

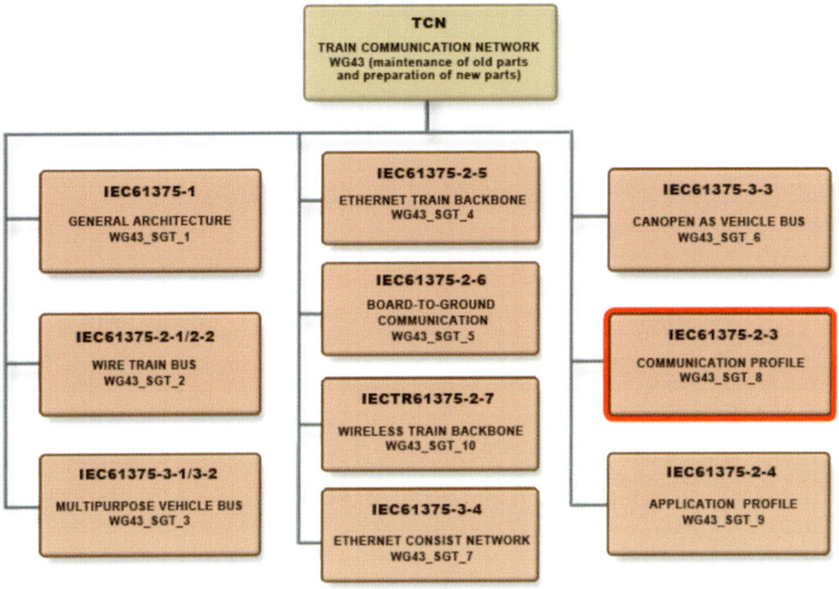

Fig. 3.2. IEC 61375 series of standards.

An ECN is the network that serves a single Consist: "A Consist can be a train set or unit, a rake of coaches, it is a single vehicle or a group of vehicles which are not separated during normal operation. A Consist contains one, several or no Consist networks," IEC 61375-2-6:2016 (Draft). This is illustrated in Fig. 3.3.

Using an ETB to connect the train means that communication between ECNs can exploit ethernet performance, currently up to 10 Gb/s (10000BASE-T). An example is shown in Fig. 3.4 below. This enables greater flexibility in train reconfiguration. To avoid IP conflicts, whenever two or more Consists are reformed to make a train there is a process of Inauguration, which gives all nodes of the ETB their IP address and controls how they relate to all the other nodes on the same backbone.

The draft IEC 61375-2-6:2016 is entitled 'On-board to ground communication'. This document introduces a Mobile Connectivity Gateway (MCG) onto the ETB to enable connectivity to shore-based systems.

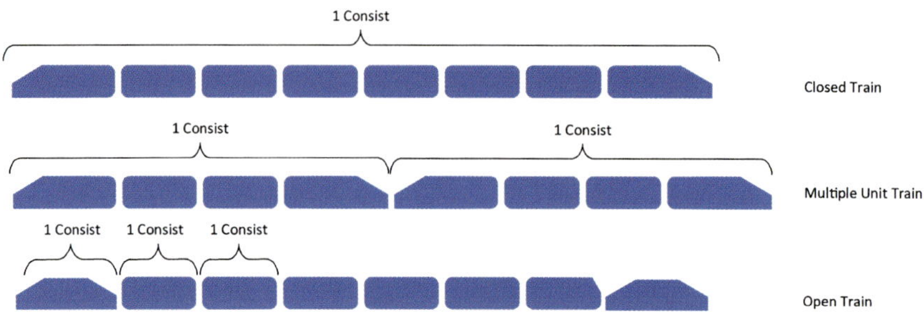

Fig. 3.3. Train consists.

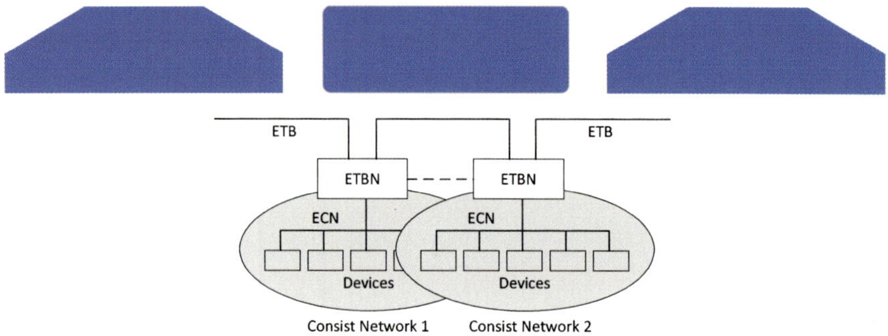

Fig. 3.4. Consist networks.

The introduction of an Ethernet network onto the train and its use to interconnect the MVB, WTB and CAN-bus transforms the network into a LAN, and the connectivity provided by the MCG gives the LAN a WAN connection. The IEC 61375 standard offers little cyber security direction; only the as yet unpublished IEC 61375-2-6 refers to IEC 62443 for guidance on risk assessment and mitigation.

As well as its multi-agent nature there are a number of characteristics that make the Digital Train LAN/WAN distinctive:

i) WAN connectivity is usually via 4G which is unreliable across the railway network;
ii) There are approximately 20,000 passenger vehicles distributed across the country according to DfT (2017);

iii) Each train generally has 1 or 2 company representatives on-board, and maybe several hundred customers, some of whom are using the on-board network to access the internet; and
iv) Trains move, sometimes at high speed.

This is not the same cyber security problem, with the same risks, that exists with land-based networks.

Ethernet Backbones have been included in the new train design and build since the IEC 61375 standard was extended in 2015 to include the ETB, but with public WiFi having become a hygiene factor in the customer experience, and with governmental influence on the rail industry, legacy fleets are also being fitted with 'Ethernet Backbones' and an MCG to provide internet connectivity to deliver public WiFi and 'Infotainment'. Where this network is used only for public services there is no issue but once the network is available the temptation for train engineers to use it to connect other systems is difficult to resist. Although some industry bodies have published guidelines, there are few firm design principles, and any that there are have been constrained through limitations on power, space and cost when retrofitting aged vehicles.

Referring to retrofitted systems, RSSB (2016) alludes to the problems that have arisen due to the ad hoc nature of on-board network implementation and attributes these to the poor standard of network awareness and uncoordinated commercial influences. RSSB advocated separate train networks but recognises the drivers towards integration and warns that "the integrity needs to be robust and provided with security and privacy controls". To elaborate, connectivity to on-board systems started with individual system upgrades introducing 4G receivers for a single device. This enables systems such as seat reservations displays to be updated remotely. Similarly, some condition-based monitoring systems were updated to enable data to be offloaded, again using a 4G connection. It was the introduction of public wifi on trains that prompted the retrofitting of ETBs, albeit with a simpler architecture than that defined in IEC 61375. It was recognised in some quarters that network segregation and security controls

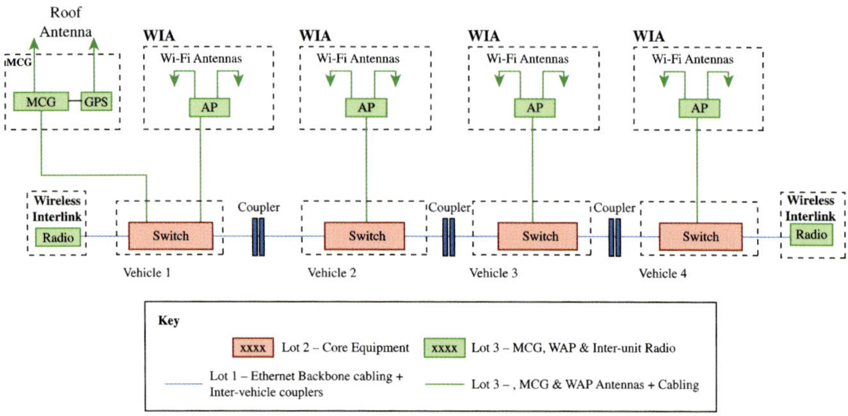

Fig. 3.5. Basic retrofit architecture.

were a necessary consideration and early publications such as Tonks (2016) raised awareness regarding the emerging requirements.

The need to segregate networks was initially envisaged as a physical exercise and dual backbone designs were originally proposed but the cost of duplicating switches, the lack of on-board space to accommodate additional equipment and in many cases the lack of sufficient power has guided suppliers towards single backbones such as the one shown in Fig. 3.5 above, reproduced from Duffy (2018), which shows a typical implementation solely to provide public wifi.

From the same source, Duffy (2018), a more complex design to accommodate a wider range of connected on-board systems is shown in Fig. 3.6 below.

Neither the 61375 standard nor the solutions advertised by the rail supply chain make much reference to cyber security, yet it is clear that such advances in integrated solutions have an impact on both threats and vulnerabilities. Previously, all on-board systems stood alone and required specialist knowledge to access, but large-scale integration expands the attack surface available. The use of ethernet as a link layer protocol extends the source of threats as it brings the means to attack it into the capability of a far wider group of actors. In the corporate world it would be inconceivable to allow such a scenario to be unprotected and yet industries such as rail have been slow to react, with requirements generally being driven by regulation rather than corporate risk management.

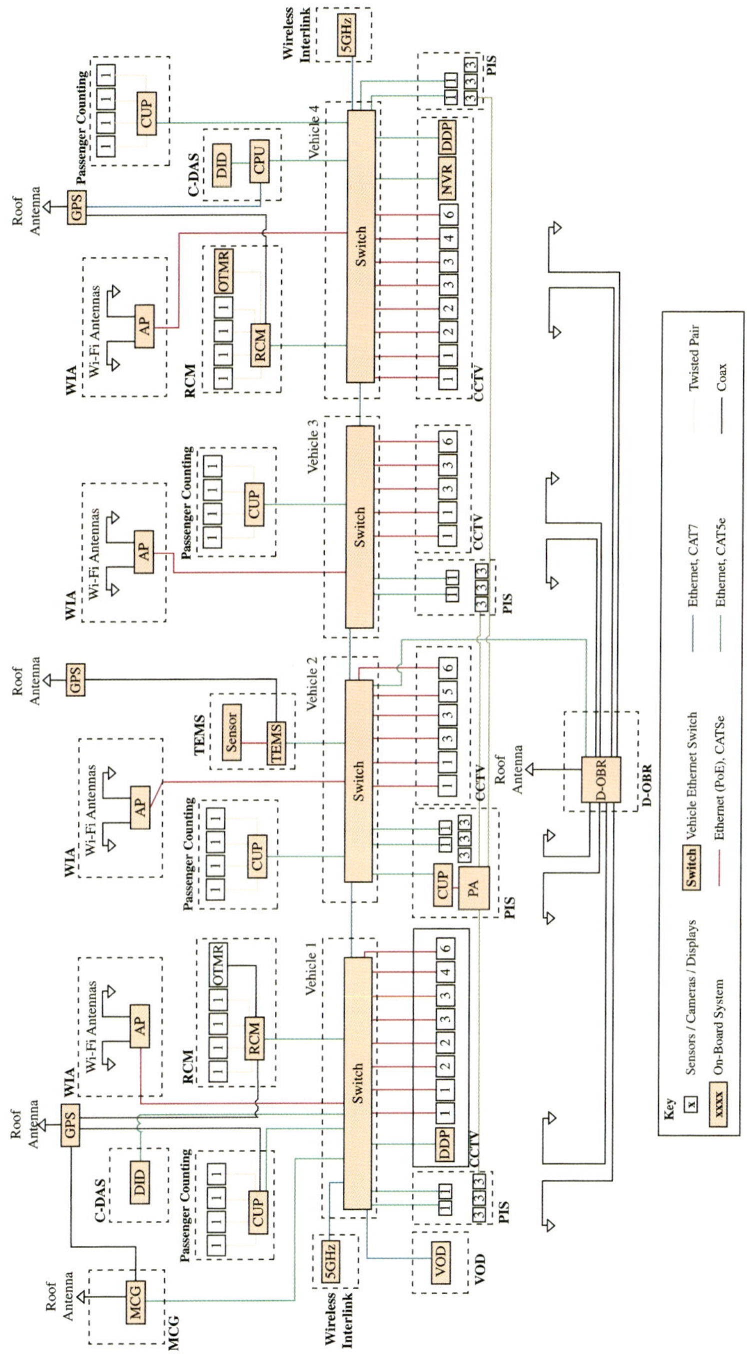

Fig. 3.6. Complex retrofit architecture.

3.2. In Search of Solutions

Many international standards are adopted by peer organisations around the world and renamed to identify the local standard authority's approval. For instance, ISO 27001 is also known as BS EN ISO/IEC 27001 in the UK and AS/NZS ISO/IEC 27001 in Australasia. In Germany the DIN (Deutsches Institut für Normung e.V. (German Institute for Standardization) organisation has published DIN EN ISO/IEC 27001 and so on around the world. Standard referencing requires that standards are cited as 'authorising organisation and year', e.g. 27001 would be cited as BSI (2013), but BSI published many standards in that year, including other standards referenced in this document. For that reason, and for readability, this document will use the basic nomenclature, without any prefix, when referring to a standard and will include the nomenclature where it is cited. The reference will identify a BSI standard if one is available or will refer to the standard originator, e.g. IEC, if there is not, which will also clarify which version of the standard is being used, e.g. 27001 will be cited as (BSI, 2013) 27001 and referred to as 27001 and IEC 62443-1-1 which at the time of writing has yet to be included in BSI's library, will be cited as (IEC, 2009) 62443-1-1 and referred to as 62443-1-1.

There are multiple sources of guidance to industry from both government and non-partisan industry organisations including NCSC (National Cyber Security Centre), DfT (Department for Transport), DCMS (Department for Digital, Culture, Media and Sport), HSE (Health and Safety Executive), RDG (Rail Delivery Group) and RSSB (Rail Safety and Standards Board).

RDG (2017), the Rail Cyber Security Strategy, is published by the Rail Delivery Group, which is an industry body designed to represent the interests of the rail Train Operating Companies (TOCs). The document references various standards, including (BSI, 2013) 27001 and the NIST Cyber security Framework (NIST, 2018) although in 2017 it referenced the 2017 version, which in turn references (BSI, 2011) 62443 (but as the ISA version dated 2009) and other security standards.

In the UK, 'Transport' is part of the critical national infrastructure (CPNI, 2018). The government has identified DfT as the 'Competent Authority' for Transport and DfT have included TOCs under the sub-sector 'Rail Transport' (DfT, 2018) in the scope of the NIS Directive, (Directive (EU), 2016/1148). It therefore follows that the sensible option is to follow standards that will deliver the most cost-effective route to NIS compliance. NCSC (2018a) gives some guidance on this, also helpfully pointing towards both the 27000 and 62443 series of standards.

Whichever is the most appropriate security standard for this environment is far from clear. The diagram shown in Fig. 3.7 below shows some of the material that is available to the industry and how they interact.

As Fig. 3.7 shows, there is plenty of guidance relating to IACS and also to trains in particular but it is generally vague and simply offers possibilities. This is not just a problem in the rail industry. For example Leszczyna (2018) in a survey of standards appropriate to smart grids observed "the situation that operators may find it difficult to orientate themselves in this plethora of literature".

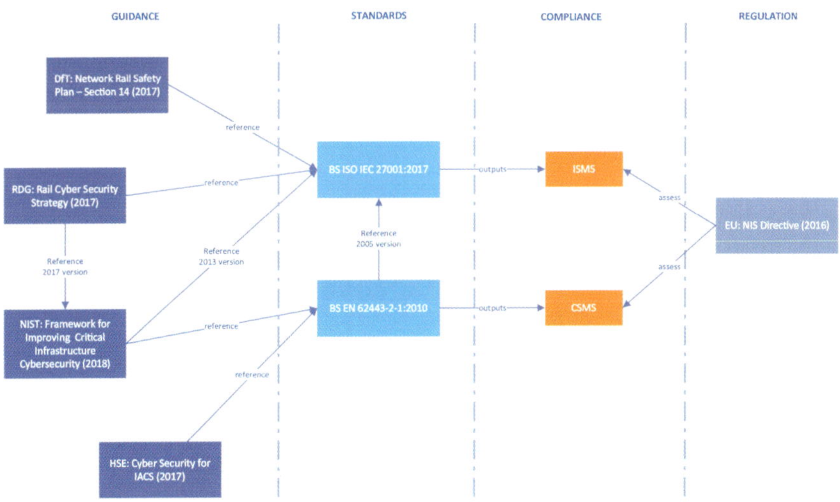

Fig. 3.7. Industry guidance.

The common theme of industry guidance documents is that they recommend the development of a management system driven by one of the requirement standards relating to cyber security. NIST (2018) is very helpful in this respect as it includes references to a variety of standards that satisfy the requirements of each subcategory in the framework it defines. This is possibly due to NIST providing a voluntary framework as opposed to a regulatory directive like NIS. RDG (2017) references both NIST (2017) (NIST is updated every year and so RDG referenced the version current at the time of its own publication) and (BSI, 2013) 27001. In turn NIST (2017) includes both (BSI, 2013) 27001 and a number of the 62443 standards (as IEC publications) in the standards it references. The question remains: which standard is most appropriate for Digital Trains and, importantly, will satisfy the requirements of NIS?

In a lecture at Stanford University, Weiss (2011) described the fundamental differences between IT security and the security requirements of IACS (he called it ICS). Much of what he said is still true today and illustrates why 62443 is different to 27001. The objectives of Information Security are often stated in terms of the triad CIA (Confidentiality, Integrity and Availability), listed in that order of criticality. Additionally, non-repudiation and other factors are considered as well but CIA is the baseline. In IACS the emphasis changes because the systems are concerned with making things happen rather than protecting intellectual property.

CIA	IT Objectives	IACS Objectives
C	Confidentiality is the priority for IT as it is protecting information that is private to an individual or organisation either of which has entrusted it to the system. The responsibility for protecting this information is enforced through GDPR.	Confidentiality is generally unimportant to IACS. There may be proprietary information involved but largely data is in the form of control signals that are created and then consumed. Safety is the prime directive.

(*Continued*)

CIA	IT Objectives	IACS Objectives
I	Integrity is important to IT as it is either storing or processing information and needs the confidence of its users that it can replay the information without corruption.	Integrity is also important to IACS as the system must be sure that the command received is the same as the one that was sent as corruption could have physically disastrous consequences resulting in injury or loss of life.
A	Availability in IT is about enabling access to information for the right user at the right time. Time criticality is not usually a factor. Business processes generally include a fair amount of latitude. Rebooting is the panacea for desktop support.	Availability in IACS is paramount as system failure could result in immediate and catastrophic consequences. A delay to allow for a reboot is unacceptable. If a valve is not opened or a brake applied at the right time then, as with integrity, it could be catastrophic. Time-criticality is also much more important especially where 'real-time' systems are involved.
N-R	Non-repudiation is probably equally important in IT as IACS. Where in IT it is important to know the source of information, so it is in IACS, and in both cases the source could easily be a user or a system component.	

Safety does not feature in 27001, yet in IACS it is even more important than either confidentiality, availability or integrity. In a cyber-physical environment the consequences of a system failure could result in loss of life or limb, which is why safety standards are part of industrial culture whereas security is not.

However, as Humphreys (2016) states, the ISO 27000 range of standards provides well-tried and well-tested processes that are well-established in over 100 countries. The first issue of BS ISO/IEC 27001 was in 2005 with the subtitle BS 7799-2:2005 in recognition of its development from that British Standard. As the guidance in BSI (2015) describes, 27001 was completely restructured in 2013 with changes that included alignment with BS ISO 31000:2009 for risk management and to strengthen management involvement in leadership and review. As BSI (2013) 27001 itself states, the standard defines the requirements for an Information Security Management System (ISMS) with the objective of preserving the triad of Confidentiality, Integrity and Availability. The ISMS is intended to be tailored to the organisation; the standard is generic and intended to apply to all types of organisation irrespective of their size or nature.

As an alternative, the emerging set of standards under the 62433 heading illustrated in Fig. 3.8 below doesn't appear to offer such a stable platform.

A large part of the standard set is still unpublished and, oddly, although BSI has issued 62443-2-1 as a BS EN standard at the time of writing it has not done the same with 62443-1-1, which includes the terminology, concepts and models that underpin the rest of the set.

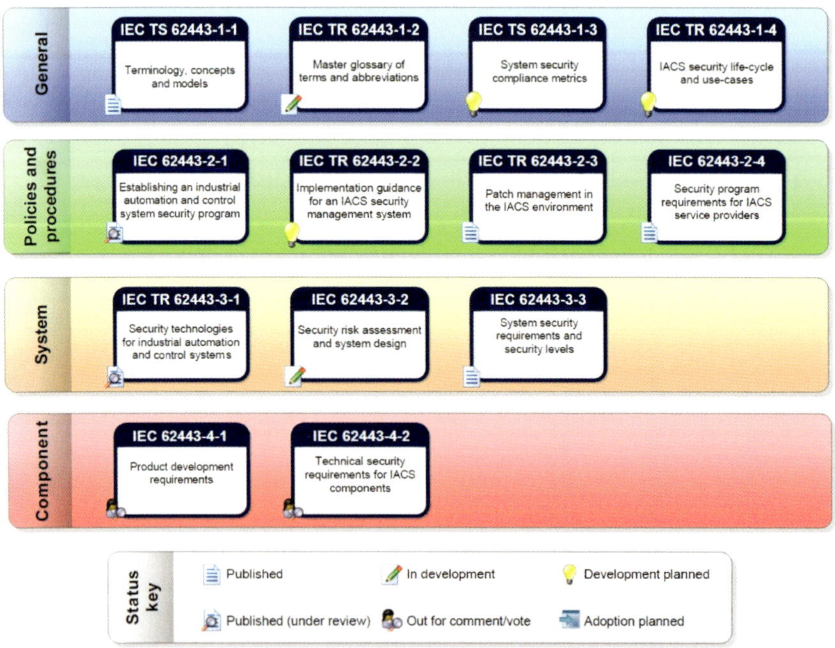

Fig. 3.8. The 62443 series of standards.

There seems also to be some recognition from the authors of 62443-2-1 that it should have been more closely aligned to 27001 as it includes the note "The revision of this international standard will be initiated shortly after this standard is published. The next revision will be aligned more closely with ISO/IEC 27001, which addresses many of the same issues but without consideration of the specialized requirements for continuous operation and safety that are common in the industrial automation and control systems environment" (BSI, 2010) 62443-2-1. It is unfortunate that the statement was made such a long time ago especially as 62443-2-1 cross references the 2005 version of 27001.

Those observations aside, 62443 is making some headway towards establishing itself, particularly in industries where safety is the 'prime directive' and where the IEC version of the standard is placed alongside IEC 61508 and IEC 61511 which address functional safety. Sieber and Hildenbrandt (2016) note that "the IEC 61511 (safety) and IEC 62443 (security) standards coincide on the demand for independent layers of protection". EN 50129 is the railway specific standard that includes IEC 61508 general requirements and so when IEC 61508 is referenced it can be assumed that for railways EN 50129 applies.

The diagram shown in Fig. 3.9 below shows the relationship between the safety standards and the published 62443 standards:

Note that 62443-4-1 and 2 were both published in 2018 in February and August respectively and that although 62443-4-1 has been adopted by BSI, 62443-4-2 has yet to be.

62443-2-1 defines the requirements for a Cyber Security Management System (CSMS) and although it has used a different term, in its first paragraph, BSI (2010) 62443-2-1 refers to the output of 27001 as a CSMS. The 62443 CSMS however, reverses the information security triad and precedes it with safety, to become Safety, Availability, Integrity and Confidentiality, in recognition of the HSE implications of cyber security in an industrial environment. In the same way as 27001, it requires the implementation of risk management and review processes that support the CSMS lifecycle.

The fundamental differences in approach between 27001 and 62443 become more apparent in 62443-3-3 (although some of the content in this part of the standard is destined for inclusion in

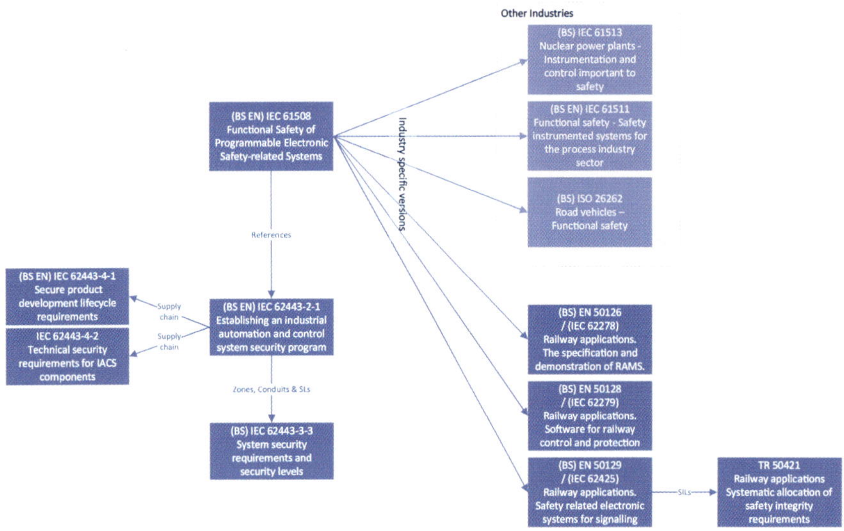

Fig 3.9. Associated safety and security standards.

62443-1-1 as the standard develops) which describes the use of security vectors, a term credited to Gilsinn and Schierholz (2010). A parallel is drawn between SLs (Security Levels) and SILs (Safety Integrity Levels), the latter being the measure applied in 61508, and supporting standards, which include 61511.

SLs are determined during the 62443 risk assessment process; as part of the network segregation controls, the IACS network is divided into zones, each zone grouping system components that require the same level of protection. An SL-T (Target Security Level) is assigned to the zone according to the level of protection required, i.e.

- SL 0: No specific requirements or security protection necessary
- SL 1: Protection against casual or coincidental violation
- SL 2: Protection against intentional violation using simple means with low resources, generic skills and low motivation
- SL 3: Protection against intentional violation using sophisticated means with moderate resources, IACS-specific skills and moderate motivation
- SL 4: Protection against intentional violation using sophisticated means with extended resources, IACS-specific skills and high motivation

Each system component is then assessed against security requirements defined in the standard to assess its SL-C (Security Level Capability). If the SL-C is greater than or equal to the zone's SL-T then no further controls are required, but if it is of a lower value then either the residual risk must be formally accepted or further controls are required. It is likely that there will be a mix of SL-Cs for the systems in any particular zone, in which case it is the lower value SL-Cs that must be addressed to achieve the SL-T.

For verification, the system can be inspected, audited or otherwise security tested and an SL-A (Actual Service Level) determined by the inspector. Risks are managed using these three values: ST-T, SL-C and SL-A.

62443-2-1 intends that SLs will ultimately provide a quantitative approach to addressing security for a system or a component part of it. This is presumably a long-term aspiration, not to be realised until more data becomes available through wider adoption of the standard. It is also intended to deliver a repeatable model and be applicable to both devices and countermeasures.

The safety risk analysis process defined by 50129 is concerned with safety hazards and how often they occur rather than security threats. It explores the consequence of any failure in terms of accidents, near-misses or 'safe failures' and whether the outcome is acceptable in safety terms. It uses SILs as "a means of matching the qualitative approaches (to avoid systematic failures) with the quantitative approach (to control random failures), as it is not feasible to quantify systematic failures" ((BSI, 2003) 50129). Systematic failures are those introduced by human error at some point during the system lifecycle, and are managed by process, e.g. quality management. Random failures result from the reliability of hardware components, which can be calculated from known failure rates and expressed as a THR (Tolerable Hazard Rate). The safety level requirement expressed by the SIL is a combination of process and an acceptable THR.

Adopting the use of SLs and assuming similarity to SILs and SLs could be misleading in that the two measures are somewhat dissimilar. As Braband (2016) advocates, the probabilistic approach applied to SILs does not really apply to SLs and IT security as it is not possible to rely on statistical data or experience as the threat landscape can change immediately and without warning.

The similarities and the differences between safety and security risk assessment are explored in some depth by Braband and Schäbe (2016) who assert that the risk assessment processes for safety and security are very similar and that it would be logical to apply the same process for each. The article goes on to identify that safety risk assessments defined by international safety standards are based on 'probability' whereas security risk assessments are based on 'likelihood'. ISO (2009) defines these two different words respectively as "a measure of the chance of occurrence expressed as a number between 0 and one, where 0 is impossibility and one is absolute certainty" and "the chance of an event happening". Safety standards are based on the concept that there is a probability that a dangerous failure will occur at some point in time and that the chance of it happening can be measured. The failures could be systematic or random; the occurrence of random failures can be calculated and for systematic failures there is a commonly agreed upon set of countermeasures that is generally accepted across the industry. Likelihood is far less precise and relies far more on subjective opinion. The reason that safety can deliver more objectivity is that the safety environment is slow to change and much can be learned from past experience. Security is far more volatile and can change from day to day. This can frequently be observed in information technology as new vulnerabilities emerge and the threat landscape changes. A good example of the latter can be observed on the NCSC's Alerts and Advisory web pages (NCSC, 2018b):

Advisory: Russian state-sponsored cyber actors targeting network infrastructure devices

16 Apr 2018 **Topics:** Cyber threats, The NCSC

Advisory: Hostile state actors compromising UK organisations with focus on engineering and industrial control companies

05 Apr 2018 **Topics:** Cyber threats, Cyber attacks

State actors are likely to be the most capable and resourceful attackers, which could raise the SL-T requirement of any potential target to SL 4 to give it any possible chance of being able to withstand an attack.

Kriaa *et al.* (2015) take a similar stance to Braband and Schäbe, recognising that safety hazards are relatively stable over time and feedback from analysts on previous accidents is reliable, whilst security attributes are less predictable. This situation makes it more difficult for security analysts to assess and particularly, quantify, potential scenarios. It is observed that the use of quantitative approaches is more widely adopted in the field of safety but is not so readily accepted within security disciplines.

Nevertheless, the development of the 62443 series continues and 2018 has seen the publication of two more standards: 62443-4-1 in February and 62443-4-2 in August, both addressing supply chain factors. Figure 3.10 shows their relationship with the rest of the set.

62443-4-2 is a particularly helpful step forward as it defines how product suppliers in the IACS supply chain can achieve an SL-C for a system component. Where there is confidence that a claimed SL-C has been verified, e.g. by certification, this supports the system integrators and operators in their overall risk assessment and mitigation. Even though 62443-4-2 was only published towards the end of Q3 in 2018, there is already evidence that suppliers are recognising compliance with the standard as a valuable marketing tool. In a white paper pub-

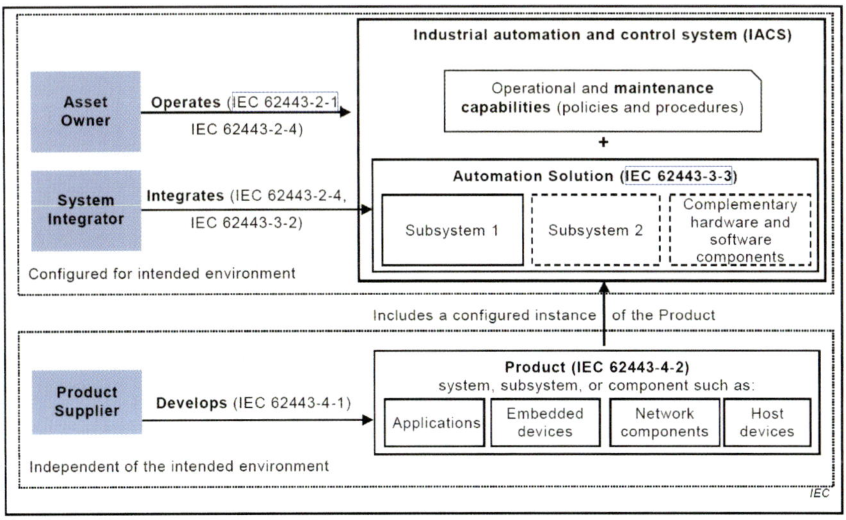

Fig 3.10. 62443 for product suppliers (BSI, 2018) 62443-4-1.

lished by a major supplier of IACS (including railway) network switches, Chen (2018) announced firmware upgrades to make their equipment compliant to the 62443-4-2 standard "to ensure the integrity of data and the network from known security leaks and unknown attacks".

3.3. Critical Infrastructure

As Digital Trains are within the scope of NIS, compliance is obviously a requirement. In its first year of operation it is clear that Competent Authorities (CAs) are setting the bar fairly low in order to allow industry to become compliant without undue pressure. NIS is only interested in systems that support or deliver critical services; it does not address scenarios where organisations can suffer other impacts such as financial loss, or loss of reputation. The current criteria for requiring a cyber security incident to be reported to NCSC are for a significant proportion of a TOC's services being cancelled. This makes it clear that NIS is focused on the impact on the country rather than the TOC. TOCs that only address NIS compliance and do not apply good cyber security practice to all of their services are only addressing part of the cyber security problem.

In its guidance on how to comply with the directive, NCSC offers a number of guidance sources. The 27000 and 62443 series of standards are well represented in these sources but it is interesting to note that in some cases NCSC offers guidance from its own website instead even when the standards clearly cover that topic. Risk management, for instance, is covered in depth in 27001, 27005 and 62443-2-1 but NCSC prefers to offer more general guidance of its own. This is possibly because the systems that support critical services are both corporate and operational, and although 62443 recommends that its requirements apply to the whole business, in many cases it will be used to complement an existing 27001 ISMS and organisations are unlikely to re-work their existing processes when they are connecting control systems to their corporate ones. Until 62443 is updated to achieve its stated aspiration to be more closely aligned to 27001 there will be gaps between the standards that need to be dealt with in other ways, either by filling the gaps or

Principle	27000	62443	NCSC	Other
Objective A. Managing Security Risk				
A1. Governance	✓	✓	✓	
A2. Risk Management			✓	
A3. Asset management	✓			✓
A4. Supply chain			✓	
Objective B. Defending systems against cyber attack				
B1. Service protection policies and processes	✓	✓		✓
B2. Identity and access control	✓	✓	✓	✓
B3. Data Security	✓	✓	✓	
B4. System security	✓	✓	✓	
B5. Resilient Networks & Systems	✓	✓		✓*
B6. Staff Awareness & Training			✓	✓
Objective C. Detecting cyber security events				
C1. Security Monitoring	✓	✓	✓	✓
C2. Proactive Security Event Discovery			✓	
Objective D. Minimising the impact of cyber security incidents				
D1. Response and Recovery Planning	✓		✓	✓
D2. Improvements	✓		✓	

*including 27019

Fig 3.11. Standards referenced in NIS guidance (NCSC, 2018a).

securing the border between the two environments. This is illustrated in Fig. 3.11 above which is a consolidated view of the references NCSC provides.

3.4. Conclusion

Fraga-Lamas *et al.* (2017) state, "Rail operators have to comply with a set of international industry and government standards on the topic of security (e.g., ISO 27001, NIST SP800-53, ISA/IEC 62443 or APTA)". This is simply not true; although the article is otherwise generally a well-informed one and differentiates between Train

Control Systems and Train Management Systems, there is certainly no such requirement on TOCs. In its overview, the article also lists cyber security as a requirement only for Train Control Systems, although why it takes that position is unclear. Cyber security must apply to the complete Digital Train both to protect all operational systems and to minimise attack vectors for safety-related systems.

In another seemingly well-informed article Valdivia *et al.* (2018) correctly state that neither 61508 or 50129 safety standards cover security issues. They go on to claim that the standards mention intentional malicious activity and propose the use of 62443 to deal with this, which is not strictly true; only 61508-1 makes any such recommendation, whereas the railway standard, 50129, which can be used in isolation from 61508, does not. One might expect both of the above claims to be correct but this does not make them so. It does however highlight the safety standards' presumption that safety incidents are the result of accidents and security ones are malicious whereas the logical view is that "the only difference between a malicious attack and an accident is the motivation of those involved" (Weiss, 2011).

Although 50129 doesn't consider security, it isn't ignored by the safety community altogether. The NRSP (National Rail Safety Plan) in its Section 14 widens the scope to include risk to assets, reputation, operation as well as putting lives at risk. But the NRSP is only concerned with safety-critical systems, it is not concerned with operational or business systems that also exist on trains.

What is clear is that safety is paramount on the railway, where safety processes are embedded in the culture. Cyber security represents a safety hazard but this is largely unrecognised by the safety standards. It is probably true to say that a system cannot be safe unless it is secure but it can be secure without being safe, but that doesn't help either discipline very much. However, 62443 takes safety into account whereas 27001 doesn't.

62443 approaches security with a similar process to 61508 but the skill set is different and the results aren't equivalent. There are similarities in the process though which could be used to create synergies and exploited to develop opportunities to improve security acceptance.

62443 would appear to be the better fit for the industrial parts of rail but business systems are in many cases already 27001 compliant. However, not many are certified. Given the current demands on security resources it would not be sensible to rework the existing ISMS into a CSMS. 62443 states the intention to align more closely with 27001 in future versions so the suggested approach is to take it at its word and implement the CSMS as an extension to the ISMS, supplementing the ISMS with any additional policies that are required, but following the 62443-2-1 approach for its delivery. This would enable the engineering functions to gain the benefit of supply chain compliance, with standards such as 62443-4-2.

The 27001 and 62443 approaches are not that dissimilar. For instance, both recommend network segregation as a fundamental control. The difference is that 27001 offers it as a recommendation but 62443 provides a step by step approach for delivery, with a process that engineers will recognise.

A key part of any solution will be to recognise that many components in an IACS have no inbuilt security whatsoever and so if there is a security requirement it will need to be applied as a supplementary control. Hardening of network zones and conduits is likely to be a key feature. Hardening the complete network will have an impact on cost and so the identification of 62443 SLs will inform the prioritisation of that process.

Glossary

4G	Fourth generation of mobile telecommunications technology
ATO	Automatic Train Operation
ATP	Automatic Train Protection
AWS	Automatic Warning System
BS	British Standards
BS EN	UK version of a European harmonised standard
BSI	British Standards Institute
CA	Competent Authority
CAF	Cybersecurity Assessment Framework
CAN	Controller Area Network

CDAS	Connected Driver Advisory Systems
CIA	Confidentiality, Integrity and Availability
CPNI	Centre for Protection of National Infrastructure
CPS	Cyber Physical System
CSF	Cyber Security Framework
CSMS	Cyber Security Management System
DCMS	Department for Digital, Culture, Media and Sport
DfT	Department for Transport
DIN	German Institute for Standardization
ECN	Ethernet Consist Network
ERTMS	European Railway Traffic Management System
ETCS	European Train Control System
ETB	Ethernet Train Backbone
ETBN	Ethernet Train Backbone Node
EU	European Union
Gb/s	Gigabits per Second
GDPR	General Data Protection Regulation (EU Directive)
GSM-R	Global System for Mobile communications — Railway
HSE	Health and Safety Executive
IACS	Industrial Automation and Control System
ICS	Industrial Control System
IDS	Intrusion Detection System
IEC	International Electrotechnical Commission
IP	Internet Protocol
ISA	International Society of Automation
ISO	International Organisation for Standardisation
IT	Information Technology
ISMS	Information Security Management System
LAN	Local Area Network
MAC	Media Access Control
MCG	Mobile Connectivity Gateway
MNO	Mobile Network Operator
MVB	Multi Vehicle Bus
NCSC	National Cyber Security Centre
NIS	Network and Information Systems (EU Directive)

NIST	National Institute of Standards and Technology
OGC	Office of Government Computing
OT	Operational Technology
PIS	Passenger Information System
RCM	Remote Condition Monitoring
RDG	Rail Delivery Group
ROSCO	Rolling Stock Leasing Company
RSSB	Rail Safety and Standards Board
SIL	Safety Integrity Level
SL	Security Level
SL-A	Actual Security Level
SL-C	Capability Security Level
SL-T	Target Security Level
SRS	Seat Reservation System
TCN	Train Communications Network
THR	Tolerable Hazard Rate
TM	Traffic Management
TOC	Train Operating Company
TPWS	Train Protection and Warning System
UK	United Kingdom
WAN	Wide Area Network
WTB	Wire Train Bus

References

1. Braband, J. and Schäbe, H. (2016). Probability and Security — Pitfalls and Chances. *Safety and Reliability*, **36**(1), pp. 3–12. DOI: 10.1080/09617353.2016.1148920.
2. Braband, J. (2016). What's Security Level Got to Do With Safety Integrity Level? [Online] In *Proceedings of the 8th European Congress on Embedded Real Time Software and Systems (ERTS 2016), Toulouse, France, January 27–29.* Available at: https://hal.archives-ouvertes.fr/hal-01289437 (Accessed: 21 October 2018)
3. Braband, J. (2017). *Towards an IT Security Risk Assessment Framework for Railway Automation* [Online]. Available at: https://arxiv.org/abs/1704.01175 (Accessed: 21 October 2018).

4. BSI. (2003). *BS EN 50129: Railway Applications — Communication, Signalling and Processing Systems — Safety Related Electronic Systems for Signalling*. London, UK: The British Standards Institution.
5. BSI. (2010). *BS IEC 62443-2-1: Industrial Communication Networks — Network and System Security — Establishing an Industrial Automation and Control System Security Program*. London, UK: The British Standards Institution.
6. BSI. (2013). *BS IEC 62443-3-3: Industrial Communication Networks — Network and System Security — System Security Requirements and Security Levels*. London, UK: The British Standards Institution.
7. BSI. (2013). *BS ISO/IEC 27001, Information Technology — Security Techniques — Code* of *Practice for Information Security Control* (2nd ed.). London, UK: The British Standards Institution.
8. BSI. (2018). *BS EN IEC 62443-4-1: Industrial Communication Networks — Network and System Security — Secure Product Development Lifecycle Requirements*. London, UK: The British Standards Institution.
9. Chaput, B. (2017). NIST Cybersecurity Framework Offers Both Integration and Customization. *Health Management Technology*, **38**(11), p. 24.
10. Chen, V. (2018). *Securing Network Devices With the IEC 62443-4-2 Standard: What You Should Know* [Online]. Available at: https://www.moxa.com/doc/white_papers/Moxa_White_Paper--Cybersecurity_Standard_IEC_62443-4-2.pdf (Accessed: 27 October 2018).
11. CPNI. (2018). *Critical National Infrastructure* [Online]. Available at: https://www.cpni.gov.uk/critical-national-infrastructure-0 (Accessed: 31 May 2018).
12. DEKRA. (2016). *New EU Directive on Protection Against Hacking* [Online]. Available at: https://www.dekra-certification.com/en/press_release?p_p_lifecycle=0&p_p_id=ArticleDisplay_WAR_ArticleDisplay&_ArticleDisplay_WAR_ArticleDisplay_articleID=61456751 (Accessed: 1st September 2018).
13. DfT. (2018). *Implementation of the NIS Directive, DfT Guidance version 1.0.* London, UK: Department for Transport.
14. DfT. (2017) *Rolling Stock Perspective* (3rd ed.). London, UK: Department for Transport.
15. EU. (2016). *Directive 2016/1148: Directive on Security of Network and Information Systems*. Brussels, Belgium: The European Union.
16. EU. (2016). *Directive 2016/680: General Data Protection Regulation*. Brussels, Belgium: The European Union.
17. Gilsinn, J. D. and Schierholz, R. (2010). *NIST Publication 906330: Security Assurance Levels: A Vector Approach to* Describing *Security*

Requirements. Gaithersburg, MD, USA: National Institute of Standards and Technology.
18. Gmiden, M. *et al.* (2016). An Intrusion Detection Method for Securing In-Vehicle CAN Bus. In *Proceedings of the 17th International Conference on Sciences and Techniques of Automatic Control and Computer Engineering (STA), Sousse, Tunisia, December 19–21*, pp. 176–180.
19. IEC. (2018). *IEC 62443-4-2: Industrial Communication Networks — Network and System Security — Part 4–2: Technical Security Requirements for IACS Components*. Geneva, Switzerland: International Electrotechnical Commission.
20. ISO. (2009). *ISO Guide 73: Risk Management — Vocabulary*. Geneva, Switzerland: International Organization for Standardization.
21. Knowles, W. *et al.* (2015). A Survey of Cyber Security Management in Industrial Control Systems. *International Journal of Critical Infrastructure Protection*, **9**(C), pp. 52–80.
22. Kriaa, S. *et al.* (2015). A Survey of Approaches Combining Safety and Security for Industrial Control Systems. *Reliability Engineering and System Safety*, **139**, pp. 156–178.
23. Leszczyna, R. (2018). A Review of Standards With Cybersecurity Requirements for Smart Grid. Computers & Security, 77, 262–276.
24. Nazir, S, *et al.* (2017) Assessing and Augmenting SCADA Cyber Security: A Survey of Techniques. *Computers and Security*, **70**, pp. 436–454.
25. NCSC. (2018a). *Table View of Principles and Related Guidance* [Online]. Available at: https://www.ncsc.gov.uk/guidance/table-view-principles-and-related-guidance (Accessed: 29th October 2018).
26. NCSC. (2018b). *Alerts and Advisories* [Online]. Available at: https://www.ncsc.gov.uk/index/alerts-and-advisories?f%5B0%5D=field_topics%253Aname%3ACyber%20threats (Accessed: 21 October 2018).
27. NCSC. (2018c). *Indicators of Good Practice* [Online]. Available at: https://www.ncsc.gov.uk/guidance/indicators-good-practice (Accessed: 7 November 2018).
28. NIST. (2018). *Framework for Improving Critical Infrastructure Cybersecurity, v1.1*. Gaithersburg, MD, USA: National Institute of Standards and Technology.
29. RDG. (2017). *Rail Cyber Security Strategy V1.1* [Online]. Available at: https://www.raildeliverygroup.com/about-us/publications.html?task=file.download&id=469772253 (Accessed: 31 May 2018).
30. Sieber, P. and Hildenbrandt, P. (2016, July 1). Plant Functional Safety Requires IT Security. *Chemical Engineering*, pp. 42–46.
31. Ye, X. *et al.* (2015). Quantitative Vulnerability Assessment of Cyber Security for Distribution Automation Systems. *Energies*, **8**(6), pp. 5266–5286.

Chapter 4

An Approach to Identify Risk-Based Human Behaviour Profiling Within an Office Environment

Jon Cosson*, Haider M. al-Khateeb† and Stephen Sampana‡

**JM FINN, London, UK*
jon.cosson@jmfinn.com

†University of Wolverhampton, UK
H.Al-Khateeb@wlv.ac.uk

‡Refinitiv (previously Thomson Reuters)
steve.sampana@refinitiv.com

ABSTRACT

Documented cases involving Edward Snowden (Greenwald *et al.*, 2018) and Chelsea Manning (Lewis, 2018) highlight the need for an effective employee risk mitigation process.

Mitigation has generally focused on system and network access controls to determine the risk level and where possible neutralise the threat. However, these controls rely on access to a computer network before behaviour analysis can determine the threat potential.

Determining the threat posed by individuals is a challenging concept as human behaviour can be unpredictable as there may be an exponential number of factors that can influence movement patterns. There are also environmental considerations that may have a direct impact on the movement of an individual.

To address this threat, an algorithm has been developed that attempts to identify anomalous human behaviour patterns within a controlled physical environment. The algorithm incorporates multi-dimensional factors such as office entry points, trajectories, time analysis and the physical attributes of the environment. The algorithm also incorporates categorical (qualitative) and continuous (quantitative) attributes within the detection process.

The algorithm was embedded within a threat detection application that was designed to be independent of the monitoring solution providing the source data. It achieved this through a data restructure process to ensure it met the criteria of the anomaly detection process.

The algorithm was evaluated within a real-life scenario, leveraging data from a Bluetooth proximity human monitoring solution installed within a financial services institution located within the City of London. The data tracked the movement patterns of 50 contractors working for the target organisation. This then fed into the algorithm to determine the potential threat posed by trusted contract employees operating within a multi-storey, open plan office building.

Keywords: darktrace, human behaviour, risk, insider threat

4.1. Background

In recent years the computer security industry has seen a rapid growth in network-based behaviour systems. Technologies such as Dark Trace Enterprise (Darktrace.com, 2018) and NUIX Adaptive Security (Nuix.com, 2018) have made significant strides in incorporating behaviour patterns into their threat detection matrix. Vendors have identified weaknesses in traditional intrusion detection design, incorporating machine learning techniques and advanced algorithms to enhance the ability to determine subtle variations in usage patterns.

Advanced behaviour analysis is now used in a plethora of security products, some providing out-of-the-box solutions that claim to detect the slightest nuances in usage patterns that can determine a threat to an organisation. As an example, Dark Trace Enterprise uses world-leading machine learning and Artificial Intelligence (AI) to detect, classify and visualise cyber-threats that evade other defences from within the enterprise (Darktrace.com, 2018). These solutions all rely on a steady stream of data extracted from network traffic, system logs or end-point applications. Using the same behavioural principles, the researcher aims to analyse data based on human movement patterns within a controlled business environment and to determine if the target represents a risk to the business.

In its simplest form the process of analysing human movement has similar attributes to behaviour-based network threat detection. They both process data through an algorithm, attempting to identify anomalies and ultimately reduce risk. The algorithm could therefore be considered the key component when constructing a threat detection model. This paper will detail the methodology undertaken to construct an algorithm based on theoretical research and live data collected through a proximity location system deployed at the target organisation.

4.1.1. *The target organisation*

For the purposes of this research paper, the target organisation will be referred to as Dakota.

Dakota is a UK-based investment management company employing 500 staff operating from 5 UK offices. Dakota's primary business focus is high net worth individuals, and it offers a bespoke service to meet its clients' financial requirements.

Dakota's head office is located within the City of London where 400 London staff occupy 5 floors of a low-rise modern office building.

Like many organisations operating within the highly regulated UK financial services sector, Dakota are risk-averse. This posture has been reinforced by the impending Senior Management Regime (SMR), which comes into force in 2019 (FCA, 2018).

Dakota have identified insider threat, specifically that posed by 3rd party contractors, as a significant risk to the business. All Dakota staff are screened before they are employed by the organisation. The screening process can take a month to complete and includes rigorous background checks, including a criminal records search. Dakota do not own their offices, they lease from a corporate landlord who employs a management agency to facilitate and maintain the building. Dakota must therefore rely on numerous 3rd party contractors working predominantly under the control of the managing agents to maintain the nine-storey office building they share with four other corporate tenants.

As their 3rd party contractors predominantly fall under the direct control of the building management company, Dakota have little control over the screening process and employment of the contractors employed to maintain the building. Dakota senior management have identified this as a risk to the business, which will require additional mitigation controls.

Due to the nature of the role, external contractors may require access to sensitive areas of the business. These occurrences may be unsupervised and outside of normal operational hours.

Regulation dictates that financial institutions within the UK must ensure its permanent and fixed-term contract staff undergo pre-screening prior to employment (fca.org.uk, 2017).

Contractors employed through 3rd parties may not be subject to the same rigorous screening regime that is enforced throughout Dakota. Organisations may have little choice but to rely on the integrity and due diligence of an external party.

Whilst 3rd party agreements can arguably address some of the risk, the quality of external contract staff may never be fully verified especially given the highly sensitive, unmonitored access that may be required by some roles.

4.2. Security Architecture

As Dakota's London headquarters is located within a shared office complex, a communal entrance is in place. The reception is staffed continuously by security guards employed by the managing agents and forms the first layer of defence at the building perimeter.

All visitors are required to sign a register before being issued with a pass, which must be displayed at all times. Visitors may only access Dakota's private reception area on the 1st floor, as a building-wide access control solution prevents non-authorised individuals accessing other floors occupied by Dakota.

The building access control solution used by tenants is based on Radio Frequency Identification (RFID) technology. RFID is classified as a wireless identification and data capture technology (Barjis *et al.*, 2010). Dakota's access control system is deliberately separate from the building's solution, as this provides an additional layer of control and assurance. To ensure seamless conformity between the landlord's and Dakota's access control solutions, a technology standard was agreed on to ensure a single access pass could be programmed to operate between areas controlled by the landlord and those controlled by Dakota.

An access control pass is only assigned to permanent staff, or contractors requiring access to floors other than the Dakota reception area. Whilst access control can arguably provide some security assurance through the prevention of unauthorised individuals entering private areas where there are physical controls such as a door, the technology could be deemed weak if deployed as the sole line of defence against unauthorised physical access.

Dakota addressed the perceived limitations of the RFID technology by implementing a proximity-based monitoring solution. The proximity solution is based on Bluetooth technology and works in parallel with the RFID access control system, adding advanced real-time monitoring features that can be analysed by security staff. The proximity system forms an integral part of Dakota's access control solution, combining a door entry system that incorporates elevator access and Closed-Circuit Television (CCTV).

Dakota was chosen for the experiment because the researcher had full access to the security technology and the data. The organisation was also considered a typical example of an open plan modern office environment.

4.2.1. *Proximity technology*

There is currently a broad range of access control solutions on the market, providing a wealth of security features and functionality. Many of these solutions rely on the physical attributes of a building such as internal partitioned walls to separate operational units or specific areas of a business. Whilst it could be argued that these traditional access control systems are able to secure physically separated areas, they still rely on human observation to prevent tailgating and unauthorised access.

To mitigate the risk of tailgating, organisations can consider deploying a proximity monitoring solution that incorporates access control functionality whilst providing location-specific visibility. Dakota decided to implement a proximity monitoring solution based on Bluetooth technology (Bluetooth.com, 2018), which leveraged a series of beacons, strategically deployed throughout the building. Each Bluetooth beacon is powered and linked through a structured Power over Ethernet (PoE) network. The beacons communicate with, and are controlled by, a virtualised communications server hosted locally.

Figure 4.1 depicts how the proximity solution can be deployed within a typical working environment. Whilst access control can determine who has access to a specific room, it has inherent weaknesses within an open plan environment.

Open plan environments have become very popular in recent history as many organisations believe an open plan office encourages openness and enhanced productivity (Joseph, 2018).

This can be challenging for security personnel and traditional access control solutions that rely on physical separation to enforce security controls.

If proximity zoning technologies are incorporated, it is possible to visually determine the location of staff within an open plan environment and potentially alert security personnel to unauthorised access. The ability to identify and locate employees within a controlled environment can prove useful for health & safety purposes. However, it is reasonable to assume such data could be superfluous if the target has legitimate operational reasons to be at that location.

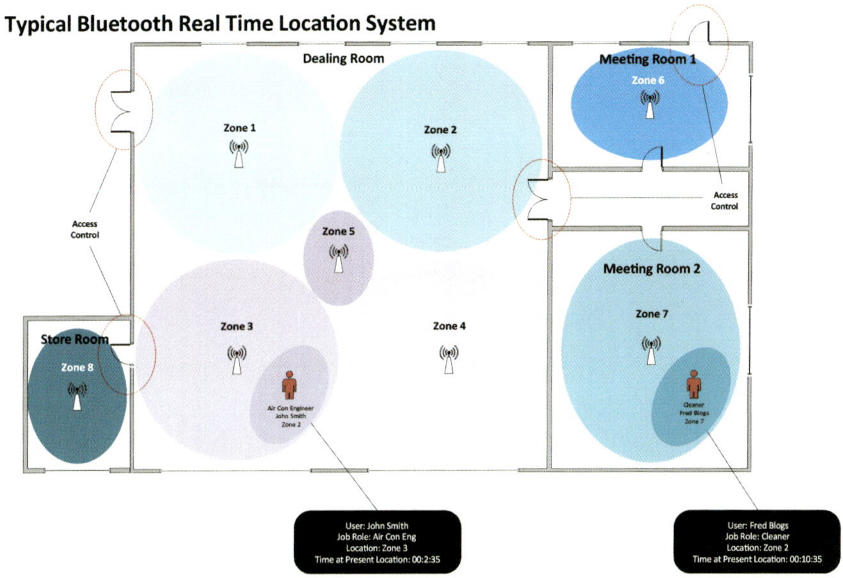

Fig. 4.1. Typical real-time location system.

Simply identifying an individual within an area at a specific time may not provide sufficient data to prove the target is acting suspiciously, or poses a threat to the business. The deployment strategy of the Bluetooth beacons can be considered important and is dependent upon the physical attributes of the office design. Beacon deployment should be carefully planned and installed at strategic areas of the office or where the radio frequency dictates (Zonith, 2018). The open plan characteristics of Dakota's London headquarters are typical of the financial sector. To accommodate this design the beacons are configured to facilitate virtual zoning within an open office space.

Figure 4.2 depicts Dakota's beacon deployment on one of the floors within their London office. The beacons are located at strategic locations based on the physical attributes of the floor space and the criticality of the desks. It is important to note the receiving variance of each beacon can be independently controlled. This is considered important when designing specific zones, particularly if the zone is deemed sensitive and requires precise detection.

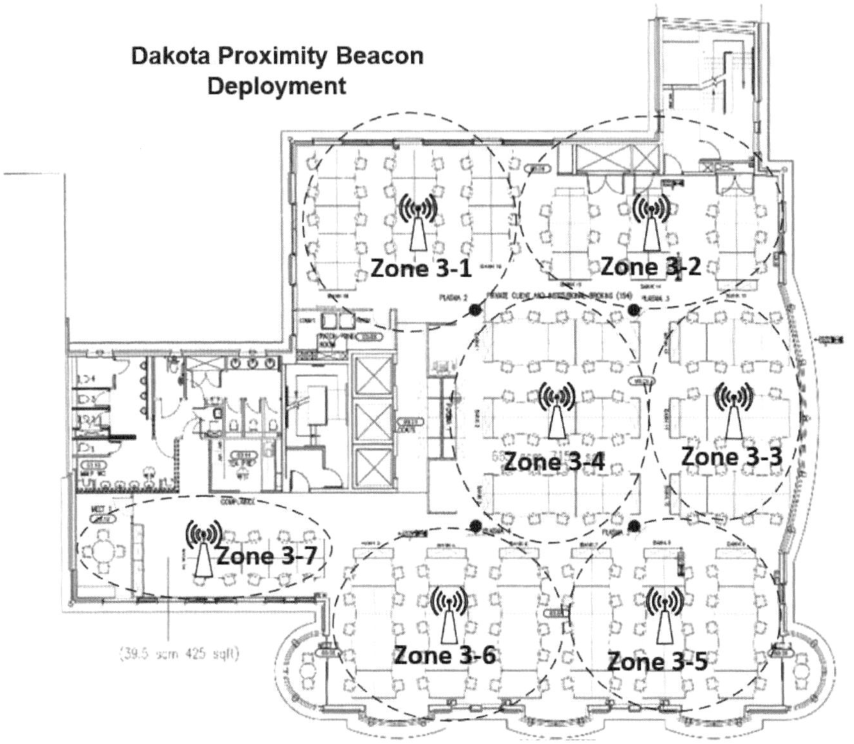

Fig. 4.2. Dakota 3rd floor beacon locations.

The power and sensitivity of each beacon is controlled through the communications server. This allows authorised staff to manipulate the monitoring environment to meet the needs of the security personnel or if the layout of the office changes.

4.2.2. *Data source*

The research data has been sourced directly through Dakota's proximity solution and stored within a proprietary database that is located on the same server as the application software that controls the proximity security system.

It is evident that this research project is critically dependant on the source and accuracy of the data. Care has been taken to ensure

Table 4.1. Raw data from proximity solution.

Date	Time	ID MAC Code	Beacon MAC Code	Entry	Exit
13/02/18	13:46:20	001e9c012578	00:07:80:ab:ee:58	13:46:20	13:46:25
13/02/18	13:46:25	001e9c012578	00:07:80:b3:aa:18	13:46:25	13:47:00
13/02/18	13:47:00	001e9c012578	00:07:80:ab:ee:2f	13:47:00	13:47:30
13/02/18	13:47:30	001e9c012578	00:07:80:ab:ee:3d	13:47:30	13:48:35
13/02/18	13:48:35	001e9c012578	00:07:80:ab:ee:31	13:48:35	13:52:45
13/02/18	13:52:45	001e9c012578	00:07:80:ab:ee:74	13:52:45	13:53:20

source: Dakota

that the data source accurately reflects the movement of staff and that the security personnel had adopted sufficient procedures to ensure the correct pass was issued to the contractors.

Once the pass has been issued and activated, human movement data is transmitted from the security pass into the Bluetooth beacons. The data is then sent via the ethernet structured cabling into the security database, which forms an integral part of the control server.

The raw data stream supplied by the Bluetooth proximity solution provides limited information. Whilst this is sufficient to monitor the position of an individual, it was not considered to contain enough detail to construct an effective mechanism to detect movement patterns.

The database contains data streams that are sent by each Bluetooth pass as it is initially detected within each zone. Table 4.1 depicts each field within a typical data stream.

Each cell plays a pivotal role when determining the pattern of movement and the time spent within each specified zone. There is no personal data transmitted within the data streams; the 'User ID' field determines which Bluetooth pass is being used.

The fields within the stream are constructed as follows:

REC ID: Contains a specific record identification value. This is important as it identifies each data stream, which allows the time spent within each zone to be calculated

Date: Date the signal is received.

Time Stamp: Time the signal is received.

User ID: Identifies the unique identifier of the Bluetooth ID badge holder. This is cross-referenced in the security database to identify the individual.

Entry/Exit Flag: As the Bluetooth badge is identified by a specific beacon a '1' is applied to the data field. Once the Bluetooth badge leaves the zone covered by the beacon a '0' (zero) identifier is applied.

Enter ID: To determine the time spent within a zone the application must determine an entry point for reference. For example, using the data within Table 4.2, 'Record ID 1' refers to the entry point and 'Record ID 2' refers to the exit point. The 'Enter ID' field (within 'Record ID 2') must therefore reference the entry point which was identified in 'Record ID 1'.

Zone: This field depicts the specific zone the Bluetooth ID card has connected with.

Timing: The Timing field displays the time spent within each zone. A calculation is made between the 'Time Stamp', the 'Entry/Exit' flag and the 'Enter ID' fields.

Table 4.2. Proximity data stream.

REC ID	Date	Time Stamp	User ID	Entry/ Exit Flag	Enter ID	Zone	Timing
1	13/02/18	13:46:20	22	1	—	3-1	00:00:00
2	13/02/18	13:46:25	22	0	1	3-1	00:00:05
3	13/02/18	13:46:25	22	1	—	3-2	00:00:00
4	13/02/18	13:47:00	22	0	3	3-2	00:00:35
5	13/02/18	13:47:00	22	1	—	3-3	00:00:00
6	13/02/18	13:47:30	22	0	5	3-3	00:00:30
7	13/02/18	13:47:30	22	1	—	3-4	00:00:00
8	13/02/18	13:48:35	22	0	7	3-4	00:01:05
9	13/02/18	13:48:35	22	1	—	3-5	00:00:00
10	13/02/18	13:52:45	22	0	9	3-5	00:04:10
11	13/02/18	13:52:45	22	1	—	3-7	00:00:00
12	13/02/18	13:53:20	22	0	11	3-7	00:00:35

As the Bluetooth security card passes through each zone, a new data stream is created. This will provide the digital footprint of the individual as they move through the controlled environment.

Along with the recorded data stream, a live depiction of the current location of the individual is displayed through a security monitoring application that is used by security staff. This can provide valuable real-time data that can be used by trained security professionals to potentially determine a threat to the business or a potential health and safety issue.

This chapter has focused on the physical security architecture and the data stream as it is evident that these attributes are an important factor when designing a suitable and effective threat detection model. This data will be used when constructing the algorithm that will form the nucleus of the research project.

4.2.3. *Design approach*

Whilst there has been a significant amount of research pertaining to video and network surveillance, there appears to be limited work within the public domain in reference to threat detection through proximity sensors.

Determining human movement within an area can present specific challenges and the outcome depends on the methods used to monitor movement patterns. Fong *et al.* (2007) argue that the detection of suspicious patterns in physical environments, using multiple reference points to detect human movement patterns, can provide an increased threat detection method within a business environment.

It is evident that the physical environment can play a pivotal role when determining movement patterns. As an example, an area with natural barriers such as an office space with multiple meeting rooms, or a doctor's practice with private consultancy surgeries, can provide reference points and natural transient areas.

Conventional access control and monitoring systems can leverage the design of a building, incorporating monitoring points at key access areas. Fong *et al.* (2007) define a logical security model based on an access-controlled door-entry system, which can log entry and exit metrics to determine movement patterns.

Whilst it can be argued that this type of design is able to provide movement detection metrics through control points, it does not address the inherent risk of tailgating. There can also be an apparent lack of controls attributed to a one-dimensional access control solution, which can be easily circumvented, intentionally or not.

A key aspect of any anomaly detection technique is the nature of the input data. Input is generally a collection of data instances (also referred to as object, record, point, vector, pattern, event, case, sample, observation, or entity) (see Tan *et al.*, 2005).

Assuming movement is monitored through access control logs, determining anomalies based on entry and exit times may prove challenging. Fong *et al.* (2007) describe 'known penetration scenarios', which are essentially sequences of actions that are able to identify human movement as it shifts from a normal to a compromised state. By detailing an anomaly detection model, one can detect threats based on the data mined from a generic access control database.

One of the primary objectives of the research project is to identify anomalous behaviour patterns using data derived from a generic data source. However, as the target organisation (Dakota) operates an open plan environment, the technology adopted for the research project will be based on proximity sensors.

The researcher has taken a holistic approach to anomaly detection, creating an algorithm that is adaptive by design. This decision is based on the apparent lack of controls through a one-dimensional access control solution.

As an example, processing access control data requires a physical device, with sensors on each side of the door to detect entry into and exit from the controlled zone. This method has an intrinsic risk of tailgating as a door opened by one member of staff can allow access to others without the need for those others to be authenticated. As staff enter a door in groups only one card is registered on the access log, which can distort the data when those individuals leave the controlled zones using their access cards.

Leveraging data derived from the location tracking technology that is seamless with respect to the individual being monitored can be considered important, particularly in an open space environment that does not have access-controlled entry/exit points.

The data is therefore key to the algorithm and its attributes should be understood before the security model is constructed. Data attributes can be described as binary, categorical (qualitative), or continuous (quantitative). Each data instance might consist of only one attribute (univariate) or multiple attributes (multivariate). In the case of multivariate data instances, all attributes might be of the same type or might be a mixture of different data types (see Chandola *et al.*, 2009).

The nature of the data attributes determines the anomalous detection method applied. Input data can also be categorized based on the relationship present among data instances (see Tan *et al.*, 2005). The algorithm will require multiple data instances measuring time, duration and date, etc. These can be described as continuous and will be associated with the individual and the location (categorical).

The attributes used within the algorithm are depicted in Fig. 4.3.

Murenin *et al.* (2017) explore human movement and interaction patterns between employees within an office environment. This may provide a valuable insight when determining natural human movement patterns within an office environment. Murenin *et al.* (2017) extracted data from various entry points within a typical office building and analysed access control logs within controlled zones. Leveraging employee data, including job function and sector location, and cross-referencing this against the specific physical characteristics of the building, a threat model was created.

Whilst this research focuses on anomalous employee behaviour within an office building using proximity monitoring data, there are other threat detection solutions, based on a variety of different technologies, that may also be considered.

4.2.4. *Insider threat*

An insider can be described as a person who possesses some combination of knowledge and access that distinguishes his or her

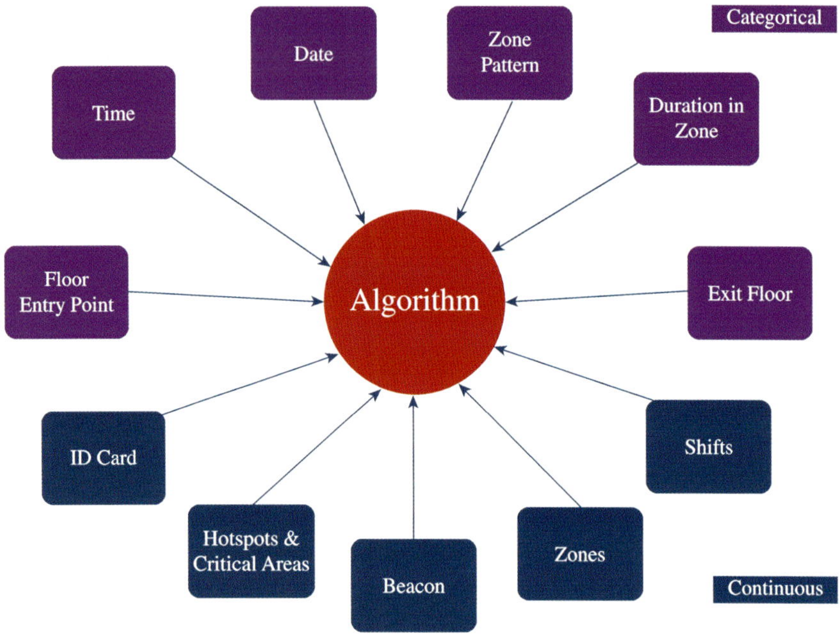

Fig. 4.3. Algorithm attributes.

relationship within the organisation from that of the people that are outside (see Gelles, 2016). One of the core objectives of this research paper is to recognise and address the risk that an insider poses to an organisation. The Centre for the Protection of National Infrastructure (CPNI) describes an insider as a person who exploits, or has the intention to exploit, their legitimate access to an organisation's assets for unauthorised purposes (cpni.gov.uk, 2018), see Appendix D.

Employee disgruntlement has been identified as a recurring factor in insider compromises, particularly in cases of insider IT sabotage. An insider's disgruntlement can be caused by a single event or multiple factors, these can include:

- inadequate salary increases or derisory bonuses
- company resource restrictions
- diminished responsibilities
- perception of unfair working practises
- co-worker bullying or intimidation

These factors can play a vital role when determining if a trusted worker becomes a threat to an organisation (resources.sei.cmu.edu, 2018).

4.3. Behaviour Traits

Behaviour traits can be considered an important factor when determining the potential threat of an insider and can provide valuable insight when designing a security model. It is important to establish what constitutes normal behaviour so a baseline can be constructed and used to identify suspicious activities.

Baseline construction would involve active monitoring of normal operational activity. This needs to be carefully carried out to ensure the accuracy of the data. It may not be sufficient to only deploy the proximity solution and analyse the movement data before one builds a robust baseline; it is possible that this approach may not be thorough enough. The researcher therefore decided to actively monitor staff, covertly, to ensure there was no contamination of the results.

This was achieved through a passive time and motion process for each job role. Over a period of two months (December 2017–Jan 2018), a clear picture of the working practises was constructed to reinforce the data being collected by the proximity monitoring solution.

Understanding and identifying adverse behaviour traits using human movement patterns can be considered difficult as one is dealing with a quantitative process. Building in qualitative elements may be subjective as the emotive state of the target may not be quantifiable.

The research here closely monitored each of the targets, identifying common behaviour patterns and routines.

This included such criteria as:

- How they entered the floor
    - o Elevator or stairs
- If elevator, which entry point
    - o Left or right

- Did they have a regular pattern
- Did they take a toilet break
  - What route did they take
  - How long did they spend in the toilet
- Did they take a tea or coffee break
  - What route did they take
  - How long did they stay in the break area
- Did they spend an unusual amount of time in any particular area or desk group
- Were there any unusual events that should be considered when building the baseline

The data was cross-referenced against the data collected by the proximity monitoring solution to ensure accuracy. The findings were conclusive. The proximity monitoring solution data matched the observation data exactly, with no exceptions.

The data did not produce any surprise results except for the amount of time the contractor spent in some areas. This data is considered important as it needs to be incorporated into the algorithm.

Human interaction with staff was also observed as this may impact the movement patterns and the time spent within each area.

Through the exploration of the potential employee interaction patterns, it is possible to produce heat maps that may identify potential human gathering points or hotspots. This can provide valuable data when determining deviations in movement patterns that may denote anomalous behaviour (see Murenin *et al.*, 2017).

4.4. Threat Detection Methodology

Employees can have an in-depth operational knowledge of an organisation, how it functions and its inherent weaknesses. Whilst this can be considered an asset, if those employees have malicious intentions they can represent a significant risk to the business.

Since the collapse of Enron (royce.house.gov, 2018) and post the 2008 financial crisis, organisations have been under renewed scrutiny and are increasingly becoming risk-focussed. Businesses now face heavy penalties if they fail to address the threat of a data breach. A Gartner report (gartner.com, 2018) suggests organisations are making significant capital investments to mitigate the likelihood of a successful cyberattack, including new technologies designed to identify spurious or unusual network or system activity.

Whilst it could be argued that new security solutions have significantly reduced the risk of a technically-based attack, the threat of a data breach instigated by an insider with malicious intent represents an unacceptable level of risk to many businesses.

The threat of a data breach was Dakota's primary business driver when implementing an enhanced proximity monitoring solution. Senior management believed the level of risk relating to the insider threat was unacceptable and agreed to implement an enhanced security solution to reduce the risk.

Due to data protection and privacy laws, specifically the General Data Protection Regulation (GDPR) that was enforced on the 25th May 2018, organisations wishing to monitor staff movement must carefully consider the legalities relating to staff monitoring (see regulation and privacy laws) (ico.org, 2018).

Dakota decided that the highest risk relating to the insider threat came from 3rd party contractors and therefore decided to address this specific area. This is contrary to the findings of the Centre for the Protection of National Infrastructure (CPNI) (2013) paper 'Insider Data Collection Study' that revealed the majority of malicious insider activity was undertaken by permanent staff (88%), with only 7% of cases involving contractors, and 5% involving temporary staff (cpni.gov.uk, 2018), see Appendix D.

4.4.1. *Roles and relationships*

The core objective of this research paper is the creation of a robust threat detection model that will incorporate an effective algorithm that could be applied directly to the movement of contract staff within a controlled business environment.

Prior to the construction of the security model, the researcher needed to identify and analyse the targets and their function.

To facilitate the maintenance of a modern building, numerous external specialist personnel are required. These individuals may require constant access to an organisation's office space and dependent on the role, are potentially unsupervised.

Within the target organisation the roles have been identified as follows:

- 8 × cleaning staff
- 4 × electricians
- 4 × air conditioning maintenance engineers
- 6 × catering staff
- 8 × building maintenance staff
- 4 × structured cabling specialists
- 6 × outsourced IT staff (peripherals)
- 4 × waste engineers
- 2 × datacentre maintenance staff
- 4 × security

Each of the 50 contractors will have specific and potentially unique characteristics that need to be analysed and incorporated into the threat detection model.

These roles may be focused around a singular function or task; however, some roles may be multi-functional, which presents a complex challenge when designing an effective algorithm to detect a threat to the organisation.

The researcher observed that simply understanding each job function was insufficient when constructing a threat model. The building and specific office characteristics are unique to the organisation and this may have a significant impact on the working practices of the contract staff.

As an example, air conditioning engineers would require access to all levels of the building; however, the air conditioning fans and coils are only contained within specific zones in the office. Therefore, it would be acceptable if an air conditioning maintenance engineer was detected for a period of time within that specific zone. However, an additional layer of complexity is introduced as the monitoring of the ambient temperature of the office may require access to other zones within the office environment.

Other considerations must be incorporated into the model, such as the location of toilets and beverage areas that have the potential to become 'hot-zones' where staff congregate. The researcher observed that the natural human movement of staff will have an impact on roles within an organisation. These form part of the normal human interactions and therefore must be understood and incorporated into the model to limit false positives (see the section on human interaction patterns).

4.4.2. *Zoning*

To ensure the algorithm was able to effectively detect potential threats to the organisation, the proximity data needed to be cross-referenced to specific locations within the office. It was therefore considered important to understand the key business areas and the physical attributes of the building position. This data could be used to position the Bluetooth beacons at optimal locations.

The researcher needed to work with Dakota to understand the key operational areas of the business and specific infrastructure elements that, if compromised, posed a specific threat to the organisation.

4.4.3. *Infrastructure features*

Working with Dakota's Facilities Management team, the researcher was able to identify the building's critical infrastructure. This included structured cabling wiring closets, electrical cupboards with fuse arrays, air conditioning control units and CCTV locations.

4.4.4. *Business areas*

Along with the critical infrastructure, key business locations were identified. Dakota based its teams and departments on specific desks. This policy was adopted to assist staff who could consequently locate a team's resources in one area when they needed to access them. When the team or department was too large to be positioned on one group of desks, additional desk groups were assigned. This policy made it easier when identifying key locations within the office space.

As an example, Dakota are a financial organisation and employ a team of traders to purchase and sell stocks, shares and bonds from various global trading locations. It is therefore evident that these locations are important to the organisation and should be identified as a key business area.

4.4.5. *Locating beacons and aligning with risk areas*

Once the key infrastructure and business areas were identified the Bluetooth beacons could be located in the most effective location, and tuned accordingly.

A key requirement of the threat detection model is the ability to detect a threat based on the proximity, the time and the movement pattern of a contractor. To effectively build the algorithm that can detect potential threats, the researcher had to see the zoning process and the identification of critical areas associated with specific zones as an important element of the research project. Figure 4.4 depicts the critical areas within Dakota's 3rd floor; these are outlined in red. The Dealing area beacon also encompasses the structured cabling wiring closet (although this room is separately secured via RFID access control and CCTV).

The other areas include the electrical riser cupboard, which controls the power to the entire floor, and the Compliance department. The Compliance department contains sensitive client and staff data, which the business has identified as a key area of risk.

A similar process of critical area identification has been undertaken by the researcher to ensure the movement profiling within the security model can prioritise selective areas of importance and assist when detecting anomalies. Table 4.3 details the key business departments, their locations and any specific security controls.

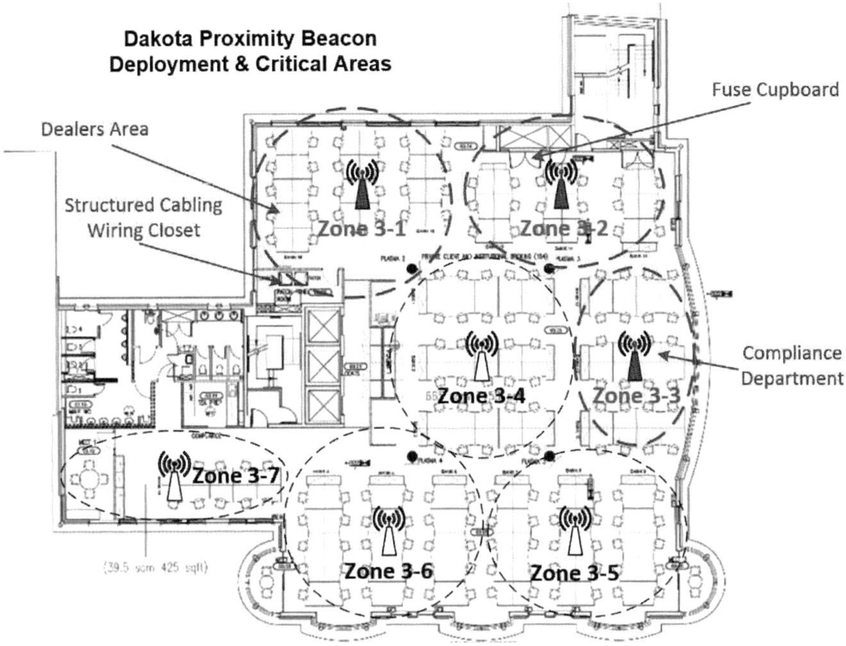

Fig. 4.4. Dakota proximity beacon deployment and critical areas.

Table 4.3. Business critical operational areas.

Area/Department	Zone(s)	Floor(s)	Secure Areas	Secure Areas with Access Control
Compliance	3-3	3	No	open plan office
Dealing	3-1	3	No	open plan office
Datacentre	LG-3	LG	Yes	2 factor access control/CCTV
Wiring closets	G-4, 1-4, 2-4, 3-1	G,1,2,3	Yes	RFID access control/CCTV
Finance	2-3	2	No	open plan
HR	2-4	2	Yes	RFID access control
CEO	2-4	2	Yes	RFID access control
IT	LG-5	LG	Yes	RFID access control

Understanding these critical areas is considered important, as is understanding the associated adjacent zones. Doing so can assist in the movement pattern analysis that can be used to determine a potential threat. This can be considered pertinent in an open plan office area, which has limited physical barriers.

The example depicted in Fig. 4.4 features a typical floor layout adopted by Dakota and highlights critical areas that represent the highest risk to the business.

4.4.6. *Mapping roles*

Once the physical attributes of a controlled office space were identified and the critical areas analysed, the researcher focused on the roles of the targets.

There are 50 contractors that are either directly or indirectly employed to service Dakota's head office. Each is employed through various 3rd party contracts; each performs a specific function within the business and requires differing degrees of access to the building. Table 4.4 provides a detailed breakdown of each contractor role. This includes the floors where access is required, the zones within each floor and the standard operating hours for each specific role. Additional information relates to secondary zone data and whether the contractor will be supervised by security or a permanent member of Dakota staff.

As Dakota operates an open plan environment, contractors may stray from their assigned allocated zone. This needs to be incorporated within the algorithm to limit the chance of a false positive.

Table 4.4 also highlights high risk zones, which may contain sensitive information or key utilities, and identifies whether the contractor operates within a hotspot zone.

Hotspots are areas of the office where staff congregate, such as the water cooler or coffee machine. Murenin *et al.* (2017) explore the impact of interaction between employees within organisations and the importance of staff movement patterns when designing a security model. This is explored in more depth in the section on human interaction patterns.

Table 4.4. Dakota contractor roles, floors, zones & working practices.

Roles	Floor(s)	Primary Zones	Secondary Zones	Hours of operation	Days of operation	Supervised	High Risk Zones	Hotspots
Cleaners	All	All	N/A	5am-7am 12pm-2pm 5pm-8pm	Mon-Sun	No	All	G4
Electricians	All	3-2, 2-4 1-4 G-4, LG-4	None	24/7	All	No	3-2 2-4 1-4 G-4 LG-4	G4 LG4
Air conditioning maintenance	All	All	N/A	24/7	All	Yes	All	All
Building maintenance	All	All	N/A	24/7	All	No	All	All
Catering	1, LG	1-1, 1-2 1-3, 1-4 3-6, 2-2 G-4 LG-1 LG-3, LG-4	LG-2 LG-5	7am-6pm	Mon-Friday	No	LG-4	All
Waste disposal		3-1, 3-2 3-5, 3-6 2-2, 2-4 G-2, G-3 LG-3, LG-4	None	6am-10pm	All	No	3-1, 3-2 LG-3 LG-4	LG-3
Structured cabling engineers	All	All	N/A	24/7	All	No	All	All
External IT support staff	All	All	N/A	7am-6pm	Mon-Friday	No	All	All
Security	All	All	N/A	24/7	All	No	All	All
Datacentre maintenance	LG	LG-5	LG-4	24/7	All	Yes	LG-4 LG-5	LG-4

4.4.7. *Human interaction patterns*

The spatiotemporal patterns of employees and the interactions between them can be considered important when designing a threat detection security model. To fully understand the significance of these patterns and their ultimate impact on the design of the algorithm, the researcher decided to monitor staff movement within the organisation and particularly the interaction between departments. Specific personnel who traverse teams and floors within the building were also identified as this could impact the natural movement pattern of staff.

Whilst the primary resource of this research paper is the data derived through the proximity monitoring solution, to ensure the data can be interpreted effectively it is considered important that the data derived from the natural movement patterns of permanent members of staff that are not under the scope of the proximity monitoring solution must be taken into consideration. Contractors may interact with permanent staff. This is human nature and does not necessarily indicate a threat to the business.

As a wealth management organisation, the relationship between investment management and investment administration staff is considered an important business characteristic.

Investment management and administration staff also regularly converse with 'middle office' departments such as HR, Finance and IT. This was also considered important when constructing the security model.

Through the analysis of the access control sensor logs (derived through each employee's RFID pass) a picture of human movement patterns between departments located on separate floors was identified.

Murenin *et al.* (2017) have observed that using such data to analyse a set of moving points or trajectories could sufficiently increase the understanding of the existing work patterns.

Constructing behaviour patterns from trajectories could also make it possible to detect anomalies through the observed data set.

Whilst it can be argued that the data derived through the access control sensors is limited, it can provide a useful insight on how permanent staff exit the building and what floors they visit throughout the course of the day.

Access control sensor logs were analysed for all contractors and permanent members of staff and characterised as follows:

- Floor entry points
  - Elevator access
  - Primary stairwell access
  - Secondary stairwell access
- Alternative floor access

Access control sensors are only used when entering the office space located on each of the floors within the building. Therefore, there is no sensor data available when exiting any of the 5 floors Dakota occupies. This policy has been enforced to satisfy health and safety concerns.

Whilst the data appears limited, it can indicate movement patterns between floors and departments. It may also provide valuable entrance-derived data that could identify hotspots, or access points for tailgating.

Figure 4.5 depicts a typical floor layout at Dakota, identifying all the controlled access points into the office.

Using the data taken from these access points and cross-referencing them with job roles, the researcher is able to construct a heat map of popular entry points and to determine how staff interact between floors.

There are obvious limitations as the data will only depict basic movement between floors. This may not be granular enough to determine the specific team or department visited but could be incorporated into the algorithm as it will indicate potential hotspots that may impact the threat detection model.

4.4.8. *Hotspots*

Exploiting the data derived from the access control system, the researcher was able to extract some interesting results.

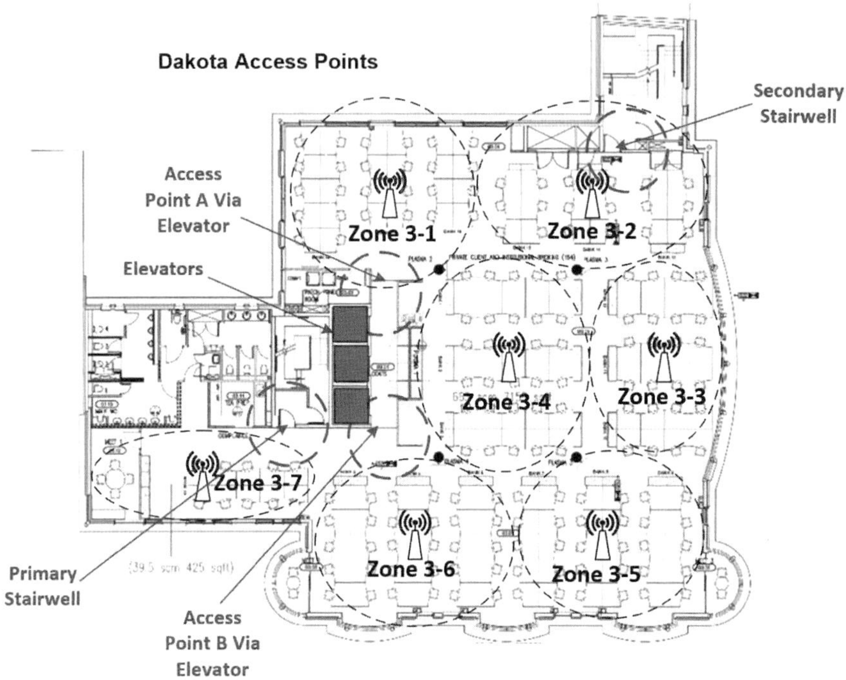

Fig. 4.5. Dakota access points.

The key findings of the sensor log analysis do provide some interesting statistics that can enhance the security model. Using the data analysed from the 3rd floor it is evident that the majority of staff used the elevator and access point B (to the right of the elevator shaft). This is irrelevant of the position of their desk and in relation to the nearest entry point.

Further analysis identified that staff were more likely to visit the toilets or the communal kitchenette area that contained a water cooler and hot beverages. Those staff using the stairwell also chose the access point nearest the toilets and the kitchen area. However, as this is the primary stairwell, the data is not so conclusive.

Figure 4.6 depicts the hotspot entrance areas observed by the access control sensor logs. This data has been used to determine a hotspot zone (3-7) that will be incorporated into the algorithm.

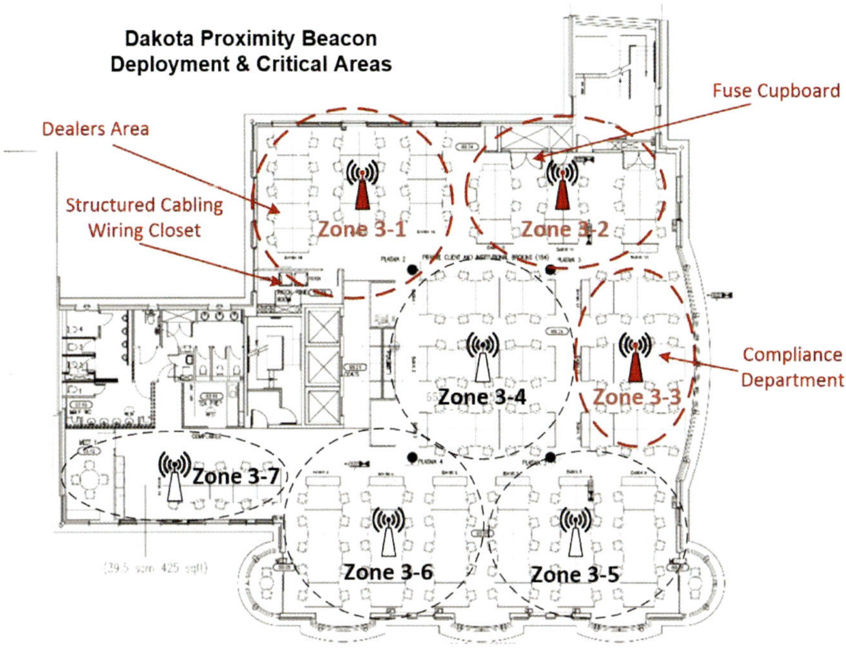

Fig. 4.6. Dakota hotspots and critical areas.

4.5. Anomaly Detection

Anomaly detection can refer to the problem of finding patterns in data that do not conform to expected behaviour (Chandola *et al.*, 2009). Nonconforming patterns can be described as anomalies, peculiarities or exceptions. Anomaly detection is used in a variety of applications such as credit card & banking fraud, insurance claims and security surveillance.

The detection of an anomaly within a dataset has been studied as early as the 19th century (Edgeworth, 1887). This has led to numerous research studies carried out to analyse a variety of anomaly techniques that have been developed for specific applications.

Anomaly detection can be described as the translation of data into categories based on specific criteria. For example, spurious data travelling through a computer network could be considered an anomaly that has been caused by a malicious intruder, malware or a software bug. This event may subsequently trigger an alert or initiate a workflow dependent on the activity and how it is categorised. Anomalies in credit card transaction data could indicate credit card or identity theft (Aleskerov *et al.*, 1997), or anomalous readings from a space craft sensor could signify a fault in some component of the space craft (Fujimaki *et al.*, 2005).

4.5.1. *Data noise*

Rousseeuw *et al.* (1987) and Teng *et al.* (1990) both describe the relevance of data noise when determining anomalies. Noise can be defined as a phenomenon in data that is of no interest and which becomes an impediment when analysing data. Noise removal is driven by the need to remove the unwanted objects before any data analysis is performed. Noise accommodation refers to immunising a statistical model estimation against anomalous observations (Huber, 1974).

Within Dakota, data noise can be described as crossover zones that contractors enter on their way to their destination. The intersection of zones could also be identified as data noise that should be eliminated from the detection algorithm. The data derived from the crossover area between two zones has been identified within the dataset. This can be observed as flickering between two zones over a prolonged period.

To eliminate the crossover effect and data retrieved when contractors are in transit between zones, a minimal time period has been incorporated into the security model. As an example, the researcher identified the time taken by contractors when walking between zones by analysing the time they entered and exited fields within the data stream. To improve accuracy the researcher also physically monitored human movement patterns within the Dakota environment to cross-reference the Bluetooth data with observation data (see the section on physical monitoring).

It was evident from the data retrieved from the proximity monitoring solution, in addition to the observation data, that a 10-second limit should be set within any zone to eliminate data noise.

4.5.2. *Detecting anomalies*

At an abstract level, an anomaly is defined as a pattern that does not conform to expected normal behaviour (Chandola *et al.*, 2009). Therefore, in its basic form, anomaly detection can be described as the identification of normal behaviour, and, within a specific environment, observing any changes that are different from the normal pattern.

The anomaly identification process can be very challenging as there are many factors that need to be taken into consideration:

- Understanding normal behaviour and identifying the nuances of how humans integrate with others within a working environment.
- Determining the boundaries between normal and abnormal behaviour may not be an exact science. There are potentially an infinite number of contributing factors that may alter the perceived normal behaviour pattern.
- Individuals with malicious intentions can adapt and attempt to disguise their actions to look normal.
- As what is defined as normal behaviour will potentially evolve over time, continuous realignment will be required to prevent false positives.
- The definition of an anomaly may be different depending on the role and even the specific individual within an organisation.
- Noise within the data can alter the perception of the threat and trigger an alert. The environment will need to be explored and superfluous data ignored.

4.5.3. *Classification*

The primary purpose of this research paper is to construct a security model that incorporates an algorithm that will detect a potential threat through an anomaly detection process. An important aspect of the detection process is the classification of an anomaly once the anomaly is detected.

The research has classified the anomalies into the following groups, classes or sets.

4.5.4. *Point-based anomalies*

Based on data collected over a period of time, an individual whose movement patterns are considered anomalous in relation to the baseline data would represent an anomaly. Chandola *et al.* (2009) describe anomaly detection as the problem of finding patterns in data that do not conform to expected behaviour. They define the term anomaly as identifiable patterns in data that do not conform to a well-defined notion of normal within a two-dimensional dataset.

This can be visualised in Fig. 4.7 which depicts a typical point-based anomaly approach.

N1 and N2 represent the baseline data areas that have been identified as normal behaviour. T1, T2, T3 and T4 are classed as anomalies (potential threats) as they fall outside of the boundaries of the baseline areas denoted by N1 and N2.

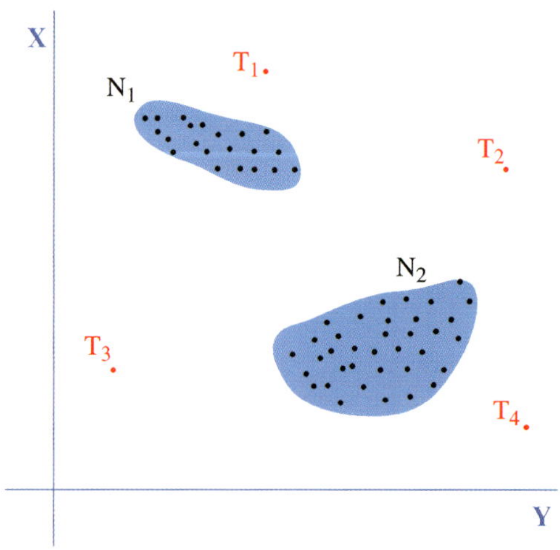

Fig. 4.7. Point-based anomaly approach (source: Chandola *et al.* (2009)).

A simple example of a point-based anomaly could be a bank account, where N1 and N2 represent normal spending patterns. T1, T2, T3 and T4 represent abnormally high spending patterns, or spending outside of normal geographical locations.

Whilst this could be considered a simple example, it does demonstrate how pattern analysis can be used to detect spurious patterns and how it has real-life applications. The detection of anomalies in credit card transaction data could indicate credit card or identity theft (Aleskerov *et al.*, 1997). The anomalous patterns within an MRI image may indicate the presence of malignant tumours (Spence *et al.*, 2001).

4.5.5. *Contextual-based anomalies*

Contextual or conditional (Song *et al.*, 2007) data is anomalous but only in a specific context. In other ways the data may conform to normal behaviour. The contextual attribute of the data will determine if it represents abnormal or normal behaviour.

Contextual anomalies are defined through two attributes:

- Contextual
  - Determines the context or location of that instance. As an example, in geospatial data, latitude and longitude could be used as contextual attributes.
- Behavioural
  - The behavioural attributes of a data set could be defined as the non-contextual characteristics of each specific instance. As an example, in a spatial data set representing global average temperatures, the temperature of a city would be considered behavioural.

Figure 4.8 depicts a graph demonstrating contextual abnormality within a temperature time period.

The temperature (data) is the same in T1 and T2; the context of that data within the different time periods has an impact when

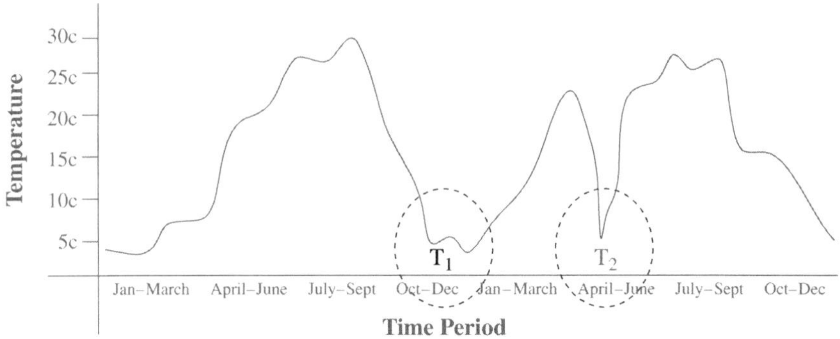

Fig. 4.8. Contextual anomaly approach.

determining if the data is abnormal for the season. T1 is normal but T2 can be seen as an anomaly for the time of year.

4.5.6. *Collective anomalies*

If a collection of related data instances is anomalous with respect to the entire data set, it is termed a collective anomaly. The individual data instances in a collective anomaly may not be anomalies by themselves, but their occurrence together as a collection is anomalous (Chandola *et al.*, 2009). This does not imply that individual data sets are anomalies, but that their occurrence collectively with other data sets can be classified as an anomaly.

As an example, during August 2017, Dakota's access control logs displayed an unusual increase in staff located on the 3rd floor visiting other floors, and in particular the floor directly below. The data was analysed and the entry point used by the vast majority of staff was to the right of the elevator. Under closer inspection the log data also appeared to only affect male members of staff.

The issue was quickly identified. The male toilets on the 3rd floor were unavailable for 24 hours so staff had to use the facilities on other floors. The toilet was also located to the right of the elevator, so staff used this access point.

A single observation (member of staff) visiting another floor is not unusual, but a collective data set (multiple staff) could be considered anomalous and can be classed as a collective anomaly.

4.6. Threat Model and Algorithm

The primary objective of this research paper is to reduce the risk posed by an insider through the development of a robust threat detection model which incorporates an effective and tested algorithm.

Dakota's recently implemented proximity monitoring solution provides a constant stream of human movement data that is interpreted and processed within a dedicated security server.

Whilst Dakota security personnel are able to selectively monitor movement of the Bluetooth security badges, Dakota senior management believe it is not cost-effective to deploy a team of dedicated security staff to permanently monitor the movement of 50 separate individual contractors. It is also believed impractical for security personnel to understand the regular movement patterns of contract staff, their working practises and the specific zones in which they operate.

Leveraging data obtained from the Bluetooth proximity monitoring solution, a purpose-built application has been constructed to process the data using an algorithm that determines the threat posture of each individual contractor.

4.6.1. *Extracting the data*

The proximity solution is provided by Zonith, a Danish-based security solution provider who specialises in security, alarm handling and notification solutions (Zonith, 2018). Zonith's proximity solution is based around generic hardware components that are not vendor-specific.

The Zonith solution comprises adapted Bluetooth Beacons, Bluetooth enabled devices (including Bluetooth security badges) and the Zonith application. The Zonith application is known as the Real Time Location Solution (RTLS), and incorporates customised schematics of the client office space. Dakota have preloaded a plan for each of the floors it occupies within its London headquarters.

RTLS is hosted on a single dedicated security server, running Windows 2016. The front-end application is delivered through an

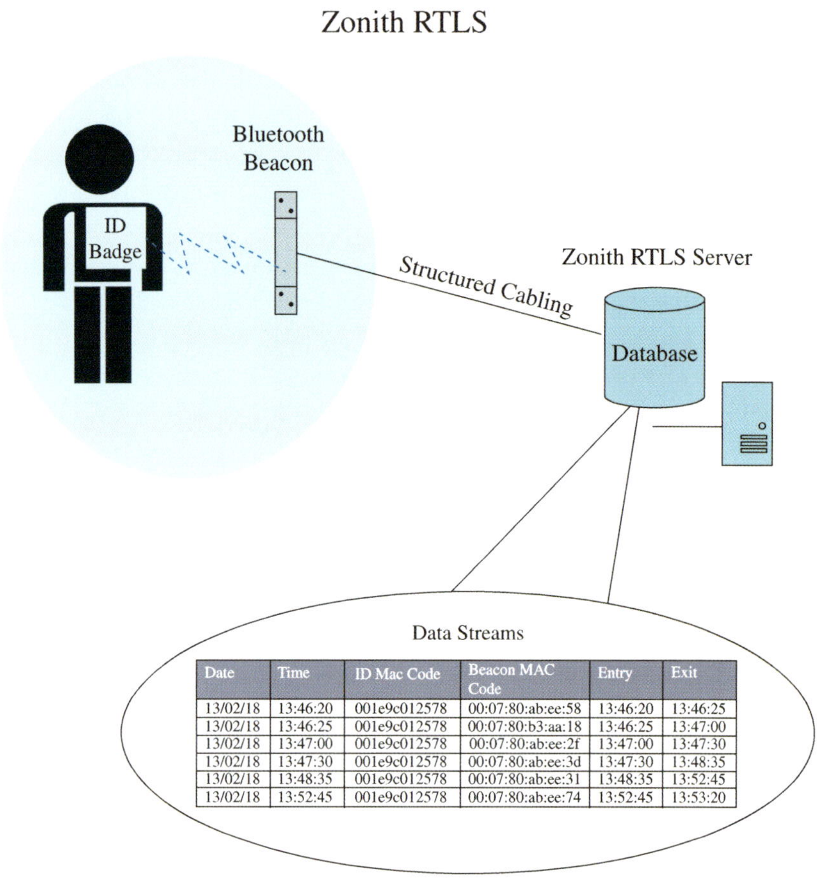

Date	Time	ID Mac Code	Beacon MAC Code	Entry	Exit
13/02/18	13:46:20	001e9c012578	00:07:80:ab:ee:58	13:46:20	13:46:25
13/02/18	13:46:25	001e9c012578	00:07:80:b3:aa:18	13:46:25	13:47:00
13/02/18	13:47:00	001e9c012578	00:07:80:ab:ee:2f	13:47:00	13:47:30
13/02/18	13:47:30	001e9c012578	00:07:80:ab:ee:3d	13:47:30	13:48:35
13/02/18	13:48:35	001e9c012578	00:07:80:ab:ee:31	13:48:35	13:52:45
13/02/18	13:52:45	001e9c012578	00:07:80:ab:ee:74	13:52:45	13:53:20

Fig. 4.9. Zonith RTLS.

Internet browser environment using an Apache Tomcat server. The data is stored on a dedicated proprietary database, which is located on the same server (Project, 2018).

Data is fed from the Bluetooth-enabled ID badge to the beacon. This is then sent to the RTLS server and stored onto the embedded database. Figure 4.9 outlines this process.

After analysis of the data provided by the RTLS system, it was discovered that in its native format the data was not sufficient to construct time analysis. Additionally, the native data set did not provide the sequence number that would be required for time calculation or movement profiling.

Sufficient data from all the job roles was therefore required to provide a baseline for the algorithm. To achieve this an extraction of two months' historic data was analysed to determine recognised movement patterns and anomalies within the data set.

The data was reassembled, and a sequence number was added at the beginning of each data set. To reduce the length of the data processed, a unique User ID field was also added. This associated the Media Access Control (MAC) address of the Bluetooth proximity ID pass with a simple, much smaller numerical value. An entry and exit flag was then included as this would indicate if the Bluetooth ID pass entered or exited a zone.

To identify the time spent in each zone, two data sets were required for the calculation, one made up of instances when the Bluetooth ID badge entered a zone (or beacon) and one made up of instances when it left a zone. By default, each beacon sends a signal when the Bluetooth ID badge enters a zone and a second signal when it leaves a zone. To connect these two data sets together an Enter ID flag was inserted. As the Bluetooth ID badge enters a zone, a null value is added to the data set, but when the badge leaves the zone, the Enter ID flag is set to the sequence number associated with entering that zone. Table 4.5 depicts how the two fields and data sets are connected, thus identifying the time spent within each zone.

By calculating the difference between the entry and exit time stamp fields (connected by the entry/exit flag and the enter ID field), the time spent in each location was calculated and displayed within the Timing field.

Using Fig. 4.9 as an example, the individual entered the zone and generated the REC ID '1' at 13:46:20 (time stamp), the entry/exit

Table 4.5. Typical data set manipulated for the algorithm.

REC ID	Date	Time Stamp	User ID	Entry/ Exit Flag	Enter ID	Zone	Timing
①	13/02/18	13:46:20	22	1	—	3/1	00:00:00
2	13/02/18	13:46:25	22	0	①	3/1	00:00:05
3	13/02/18	13:46:25	22	1	—	3/2	00:00:00
4	13/02/18	13:47:00	22	0	3	3/2	00:00:35

flag was set to '1' (denoting an entry) and the enter ID field was set to null (no connection with another data set). When the individual left the zone, a second data set was created, sequence no '2' (within the rec ID field) at 13:46:25.

The entry/exit flag was set to '0' (exit indicator) and the enter ID was set to '1' as this refers to the sequence number depicted in the rec ID field.

4.6.2. *Threat detection application*

To build a threat detection system that could identify anomalies from movement data retrieved via the RTLS system, a threat detection application was created, named Shadow Guard.

Shadow Guard was written as a progressive web based application using Hypertext Mark-up Language (HTML), Cascading Style Sheets (CSS) and PHP: Hypertext Pre-processor (PHP). A MySQL database was embedded within the threat detection server to store and process the data.

Figure 4.10 depicts how movement data is detected and passed from the ID badge to the beacon (using Bluetooth) and then into the RTLS server through an Ethernet connection.

Once the data was written into the Zonith proprietary database, a trigger was created (within RTLS) that copies data from the RTLS database into the Shadow Guard server where the data is reconstructed and stored in the new format.

4.6.3. *Baseline behaviour*

Once the data collection method was constructed and the data sorted into a readable format within the Shadow Cloud application a series of baselines was constructed to determine the normal working patterns of Dakota's contractors.

Extensive testing was undertaken by the researcher, who was assisted by Dakota's facilities staff. Each security pass was checked to ensure each of the beacons was able to detect the badges and the zoning was correct with minimal bleedover.

Referencing the job roles outlined in Table 4.5, Dakota's security personnel staff were engaged and each of the Bluetooth access cards

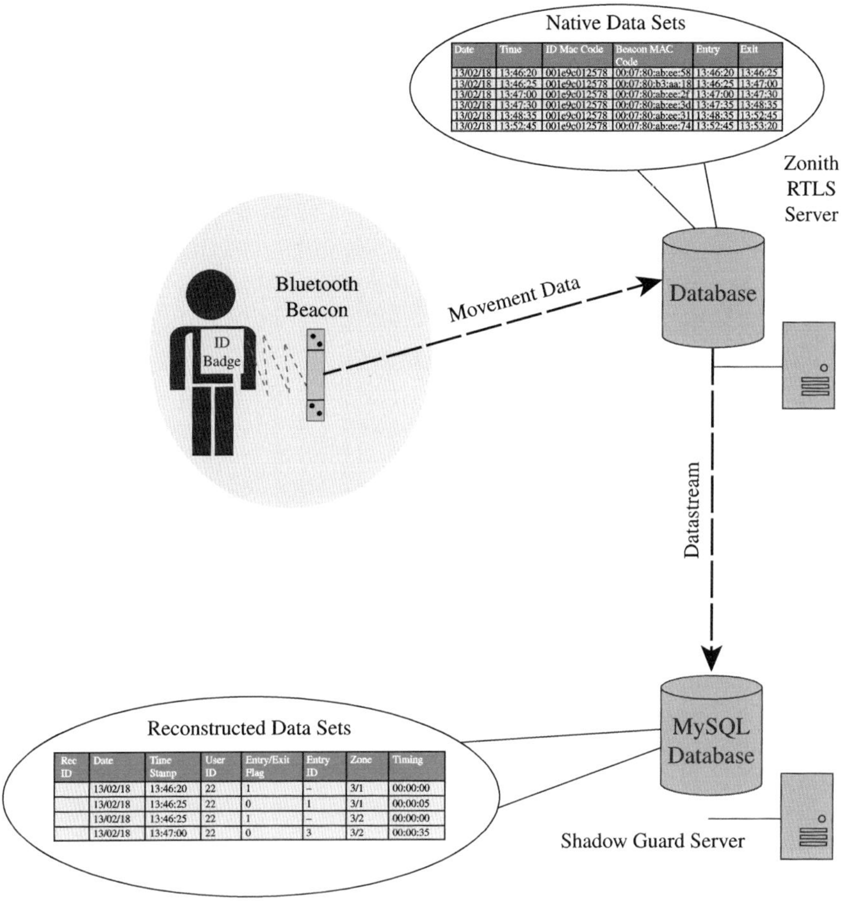

Fig. 4.10. Data stream between RTLS and Shadow Guard.

was activated and handed to each of the contractors working within the office area of Dakota's head office in London.

The 3rd party contracts were scrutinised by lawyers to ensure the advanced monitoring required for anomaly-based threat detection did not breach any privacy laws or contractual concerns.

Each of the Bluetooth badges was charged and permanently attached to the building RFID access control card (see Appendix B).

To ensure sufficent data was collected to provide an effective baseline, an initial two-month collection period was implemented. As the amount of data collected would be dependent on the specific job role, the researcher decided to concentrate the analysis on one specific role within the organisation.

Using the data contained in Table 4.5, which outlines the access required by each of the contractor roles and the standard operating times, it was evident that the cleaners would provide the level of data required to build a baseline. Whilst data from all contract staff was collected, the initial baseline analysis was concentrated on the 9 cleaning contractors employed by Dakota.

Data was collected from November 2017 until January 2018; this included the Christmas holiday period. The data was then reconstructed into the new format that included a unique sequence number, user ID (to replace the ID badge MAC code), entry/exit flag, zone (based on the beacon MAC code) and the timing field, see Fig. 4.10.

4.6.4. *Analysing data*

Once sufficient data was collected the analysis process could take place. The data was separated into individual floors. To detect abnormal behaviour patterns it was evident that there could be multiple determining factors that indicate potential malicious intentions. To understand and analyse the risk factor, the data was separated into different sections.

4.6.5. *Entry points*

As each floor had its own unique characteristics, including specific hotzones, critical areas and entry/exit points. It was considered important to analyse each floor's entry point as this could indicate an anomaly.

As an example Dakota's 3rd floor has four separate entry points, these are as follows:

- Elevator A
- Elevator B
- Stairwell A
- Stairwell B (fire escape)

As the three elevators that service each of the floors are communal, there was a risk of unauthorised access to Dakota's private floorspace. To reduce this risk Dakota installed two glass doors on either side of the exit/entry path from the elevators.

Figure 4.11 depicts Dakota's 3rd floor layout, incorporating two security doors. Note that each access point requires RFID access

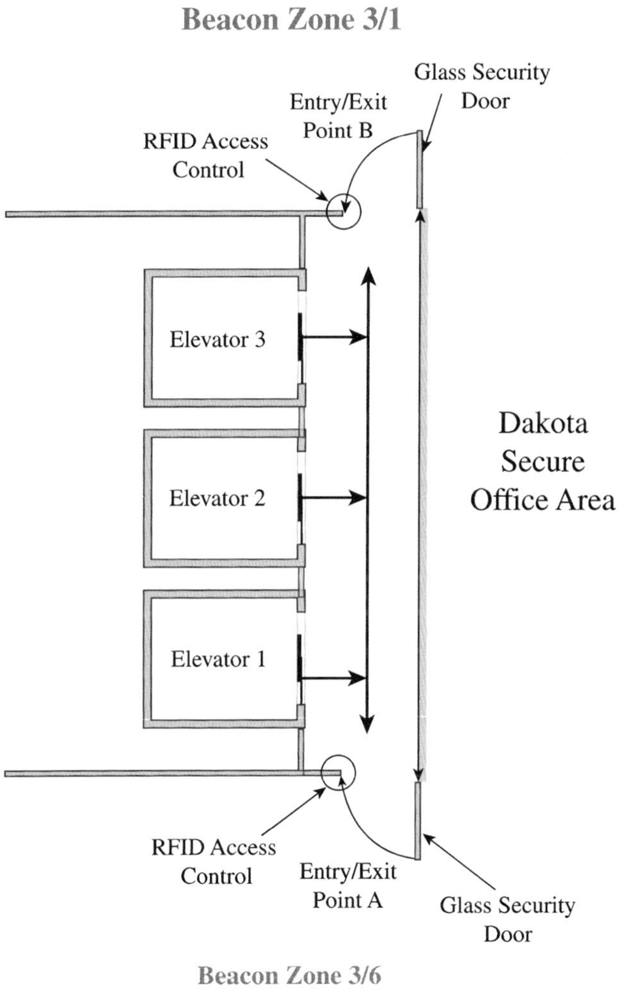

Fig. 4.11. Typical Dakota office access point.

control to enter and triggers separate beacons (zones) at each entry point.

Two stairwells also service the 3rd floor and are located at separate areas of the open plan office. These extry/exit points also require access control and trigger separate Bluetooth beacons.

As the contractors must enter the zone using their respective RFID access control cards (which are attached to the Bluetooth badges), they will be picked up by a beacon as they enter the office area.

Although the specific entry point may be considered less important when determining the threat level, it can still represent anomalous behaviour that may impact the threat detection algorithm.

A key aspect of any anomaly detection technique is the nature of the input data (Chandola *et al.*, 2018). It can therefore be considered important to determine the relevance of the data collected and its importance when defining the algorithm.

As an example, based on the data collected over the two-month baseline period, it was clearly evident that the cleaners accessed the floor through the same entry point 90% of the time. This can be explained using the chart in Fig. 4.12.

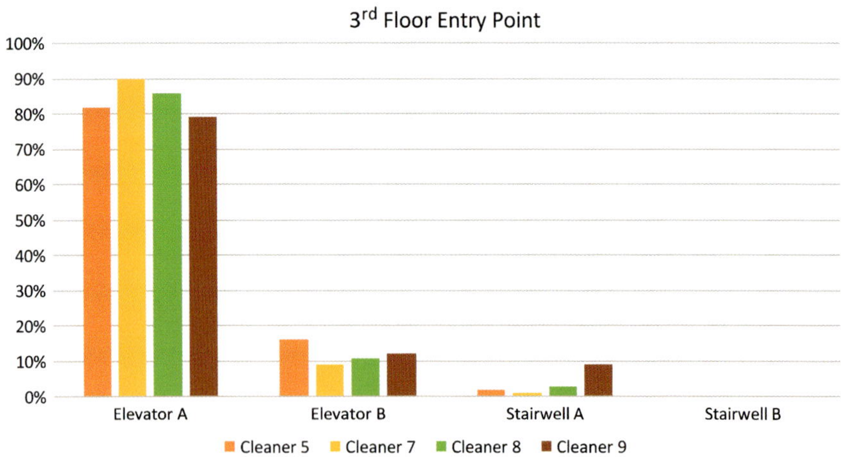

Fig. 4.12. Entry point statistics for the 3rd floor.

These results were cross-referenced and verified using RFID access control data. Whilst there may be legitimate reasons to use different access points, the evidence indicates a clear pattern forming.

The rationale for using the elevator access point A is also clear, as the cleaners regularly start their shift at the small kitchenette area, which is located nearest to the elevator access point A.

As an additional layer of assurance and based on the times each cleaner visited the 3rd floor, the researcher was able to verify the theory that the kitchenette and potentially the toilet (which is located adjacent to the kitchenette) were the targets of the cleaners each time they visited the 3rd floor.

4.6.6. *Time of day*

Using the data acquired through the access control logs and the Bluetooth beacon data, the next process to be measured was the specified time the cleaner accessed the floor.

Using the data within Table 4.2, it is straightforward to calculate the time of entry against the contractual agreements. The data can be verified and cross-referenced using the access control and beacon logs.

It is worth noting that whilst an individual can gain access to a floor using tailgating techniques, it would be considerably more difficult to prevent the beacon detecting the Bluetooth ID badge.

Dakota's cleaners' specific operating hours are regimented and are mostly based outside of normal business hours.

As Dakota are a financial services organisation, their operational hours are based on the London Stock Exchange's (LSE) trading hours. The cleaners visit the office from 5am–7am, 12–2pm and 5pm–7pm from Monday to Friday.

There may be specific occasions where cleaning staff are authorised to work over the weekend and lunchtime, but this is for specific tasks that are not included in their regular duties. The extra hours worked are not considered normal working hours.

It is evident that the identification of anomolous activity requires careful consideration and analysis of 3rd party contracts and historical data collected by the proximity monitoring solution. This element of the overall anomaly detection process could be considered subjective and dependent on the role of the people being tracked.

As an example, cleaners usually work contracted hours that may be specific to the business, so it is easier to measure and detect discrepancies in their working patterns. The working patterns of electricians or specific maintenance staff who may have sporadic working patterns, on the other hand, could prove challenging to analyse.

4.6.7. *Time spent in a zone*

Once an individual has entered a secure area that has no further access control barriers, zone analysis must then be incorporated into the anomaly algorithm. Using historic movement data, it is possible to detect routes taken within an open plan office based on the sequence of zones the proximity sensor has entered. However, routes are subjective and may be difficult to quantify.

Using baseline data, specific patterns can be detected based on the time spent within each zone. Using the cleaners' data as an example, Fig. 4.13 depicts the data collected over the baseline period for a single zone.

The cleaners are assigned specific areas and supported by other cleaners where necessary. Cleaners are also expected to cover an alternate floor when another cleaner falls sick or goes on holiday. As an example, Cleaner 8 is the primary cleaner for the 3rd floor. However, other cleaners will provide support where necessary. For example, they might help to collect the refuse once the individual desk bins have been emptied.

Using a point-based anomaly approach, Fig. 4.13 analyses the cleaners' access data for Zone 1 on the 3rd floor (over the baseline period).

The data highlights an interesting pattern: The regular cleaner (Cleaner 8), spends more time in the zone and visits the zone more frequently.

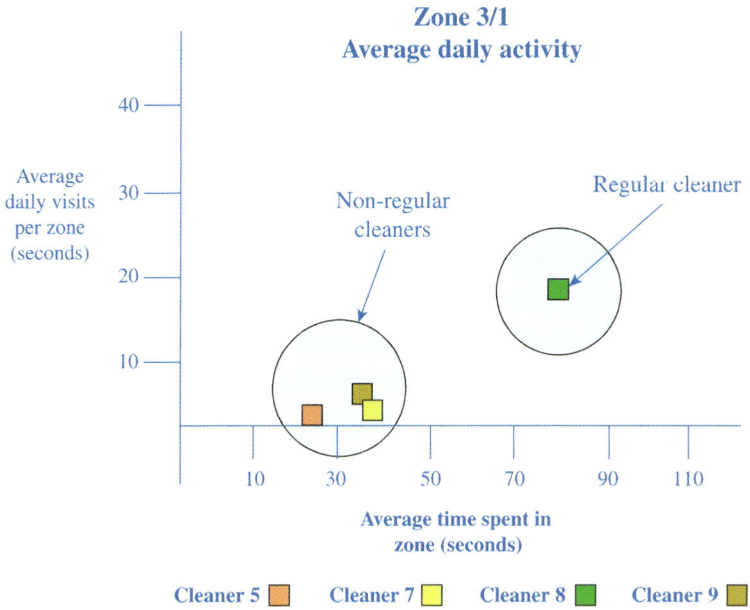

Fig. 4.13. Average daily activity in a single zone.

The non-regular cleaners' data is clearly grouped, they collectively spend a shorter period of time within the zone under analysis.

This pattern is reflected across the entire floor, showing the primary cleaner spending considerably more time within each zone, whilst the supporting cleaners enter the zones less frequently and for a shorter period. Based on the working practices of the job role this could be considered normal behaviour.

Using the same point-based anomaly approach, a single zone was analysed over a 7-day period. The purpose was to identify normal and abnormal activity.

Figure 4.14 uses a point-based anomaly approach, detailing the time each cleaner spent within a typical zone.

Using the data provided, there is a clear demarcation point between standard and unusual activity.

This data set is typical across all the zones, except when a cleaner was at a hotspot. In that case, the time spent within that area increased.

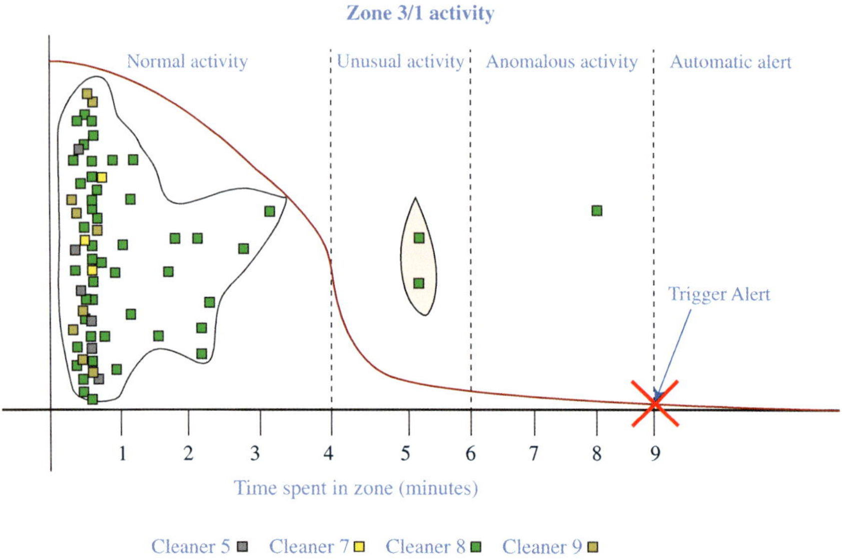

Fig. 4.14. Typical zone activity.

When determining threat metrics, it is important to understand the thresholds for normal, unusual and anomalous behaviour.

Figure 4.15 references the demarcation point as a percentage of normal operating activity that includes a margin of error based on the data collected. The chart includes a detailed breakdown of user activity within one zone over a 7-day period.

Activity has been correlated into three bands — normal, unusual and abnormal activity. It is evident that the normal time spent within this specific zone by one job role accounts for 95.5% of all activity. It can therefore be assumed that this data group represents normal activity.

The data defines a much smaller grouping that can be identified as unusual behaviour (3.5%). The last recorded data point for this zone was between 7–8 minutes (1.5%) and this has been designated as abnormal.

Data recorded beyond this demarcation point would be considered a potential threat and an alert would be generated.

The snapshot of data detected within Zone 3/1 is typical of other zones within the target organisation. Whilst each zone may

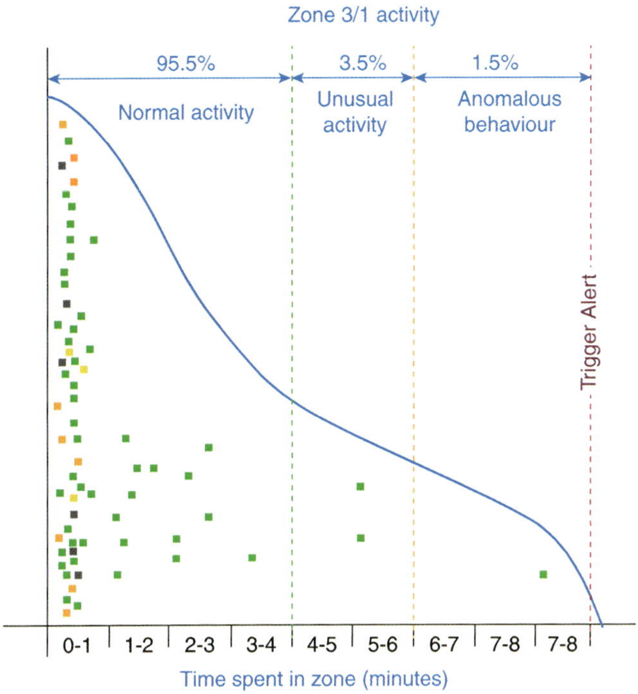

Time	Visits
0-1 Minute	51
1-2 Minutes	7
2-3 Minutes	5
3-4 Minutes	1
4-5 Minutes	0
5-6 Minutes	2
6-7 Minutes	0
7-8 Minutes	0
8-9 Minutes	1

Fig. 4.15. Point-based anomaly chart detailing user activity (source: Dakota).

have differing time values, which can be dependent on the specific zone or the job role, the percentages stay constant.

Novikova and Murenin observe that making note of the duration each employee stays in the controlled zone allows one to identify anomalies and potential malicious behaviour (Novikova and Murenin, 2017).

4.6.8. *Zone metrics*

Once the individual leaves a specific floor, their activity can be analysed and appropriate metrics applied through the algorithm. When the individual leaves a controlled zone, it can be detected as the data set will have no corresponding data set on that floor, see Table 4.6.

Figure 4.16 depicts zone data extracted from the proximity solution and confirms the working practices of selected job functions. Using Fig. 4.16 as a reference, it is possible to determine in which floors a cleaner predominately operates.

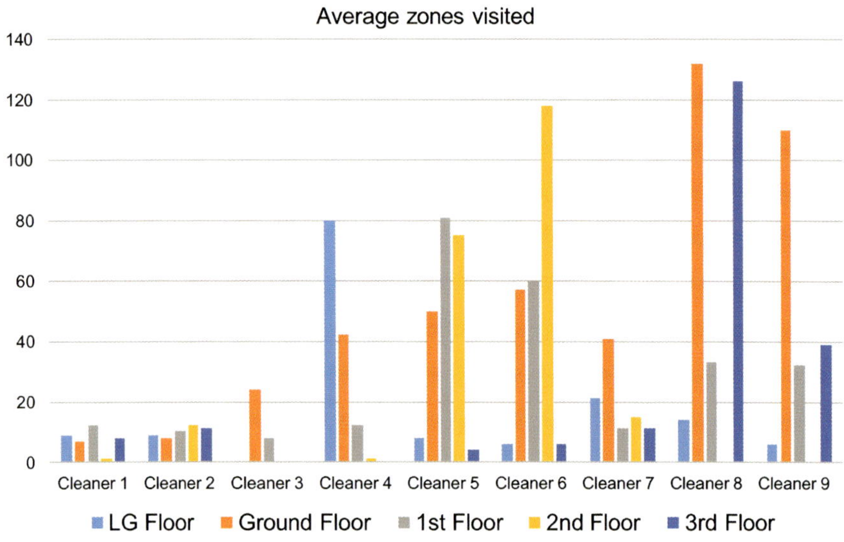

Fig. 4.16. Average zones visited.

This can provide a baseline metric to highlight significant changes to the work patterns that might indicate unusual behaviour. Determining thresholds can be challenging as it may be necessary to temporarily reassign staff to different floors.

Working on the same metrics used when determining anomalies within zone activity, a similar threshold can be applied when determining significant pattern changes.

Using a single individual as an example, Fig. 4.16 details the average number of zones visited by Cleaner 5. The metrics are taken from the proximity monitoring solution and confirm the floors in which the cleaner is a regular visitor.

Data was collected and processed over a two-month period and used to construct a baseline; however, once the Shadow Cloud application is fully deployed this metric will be updated in real-time.

Using the 2nd Floor as an example within Fig. 4.17, one can see that Cleaner 5 has a daily average of 75 zone hits. Using the same margin-of-error metric previously employed when measuring the zone activity, behaviour is considered unusual if the number of visits in a particular day ≥50% of the average day's zone visits.

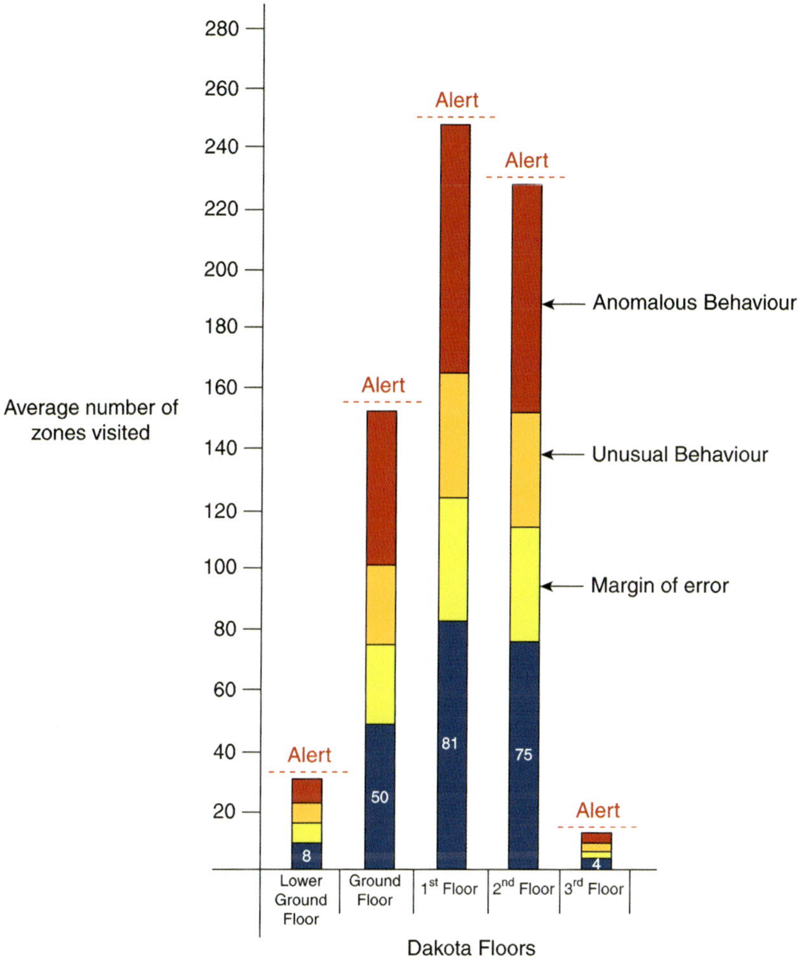

Fig. 4.17. Zones visited by Cleaner 5.

Again, using the same methodology, behaviour can be considered an anomaly when the threshold reaches ≥100%. If daily zone visits are ≥200% then an immediate alert is triggered.

4.6.9. *Pattern triggers*

The final analysis phase of the anomaly detection process could be considered the most complex. Movement analysis through an open plan office, with limited physical controls, can be challenging.

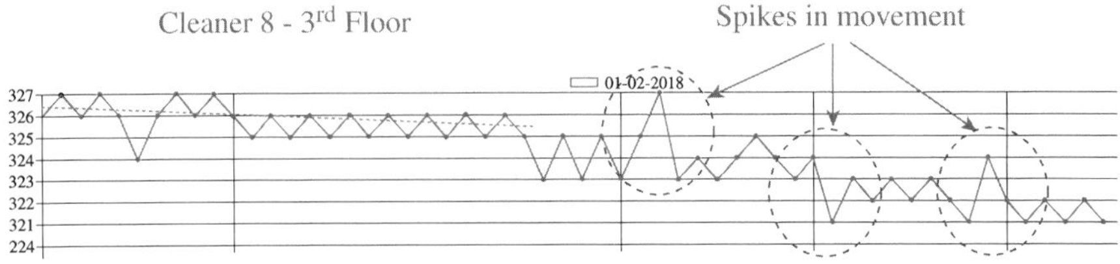

Fig. 4.18. Movement patterns of Cleaner 8 through multiple zones.

Data recorded by the proximity monitoring solution movement was analysed over a period of two months to identify specific patterns based on the job role and other mitigating factors such as hotspots or desk configurations.

The cleaners were used as an example as they provide a regular stream of data that can be analysed over the baseline period. Figure 4.18 details an extract of data recorded on the proximity monitoring solution over a period of an hour. Movement patterns appear to be controlled, following a predictable path. The cleaner entered the floor at the expected entry point and stayed within adjacent zones until the three spikes in the movement pattern were identified and highlighted. Cross referencing these zones with the floor map can provide some clarity and explains the slight deviations in movement. These do not represent and may not indicate anomalous behaviour.

Using historic pattern analysis, one can detect anomalies that can affect the baseline data. However, subtle changes need to be accommodated so that the risk of false positives is reduced. Historic pattern analysis may not be possible for some roles as the data may not be available due to the nature of the task.

As an example, a plumber may not visit the premises regularly, potentially only when an emergency occurs. They may also require access to all areas within the building to address a water leak.

As part of the experiment, where there was sufficient data available to construct a baseline pattern of movement analysis, data was analysed in an attempt to identify a standard pattern for each role on each floor. Figure 4.19 depicts the movements within three separate days at the same time. It is evident the movement pattern was too random for accurate pattern analysis and could cause too many

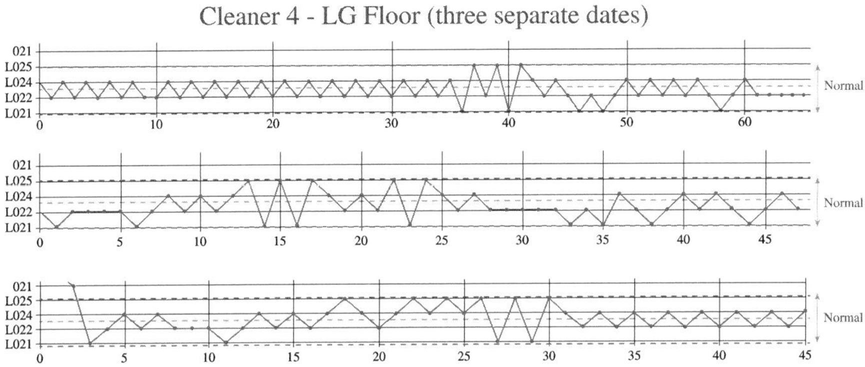

Fig. 4.19. Pattern analysis over three separate dates.

false positives as there were potentially too many variables to consider when constructing an effective threat model. This was evident when analysing the cleaners, whose movement can be erratic and who may have a legitimate excuse to move freely around an open plan office area.

However, it is possible to construct triggers based on historic pattern analysis when analysing other job functions whose movement is dictated by the task. As an example, air conditioning engineers will operate in or around the airflow extractor fans on each floor. These are located at specific locations within an office, so a trigger could be incorporated if they moved to other areas without legitimate reason.

Figure 4.20 outlines data captured over two days of tracking the same individual. This allows one to visualise how movement patterns can be completely different on a daily basis and illustrates how an anomaly can be detected within a complex movement pattern.

A single event may not indicate anomalous behaviour and could cause false positives. The threat anomaly solution is not based solely on a single method to detect anomalous behaviour. It relies on multiple factors and processes. Each has the potential to raise an alert or increase the risk counter until a combination of events triggers an alert. Murenin *et al.* (2017) describes how anomalous behaviour can be detected through the analysis of human movement trajectories and anomalies in routes using uncommon controlled zones.

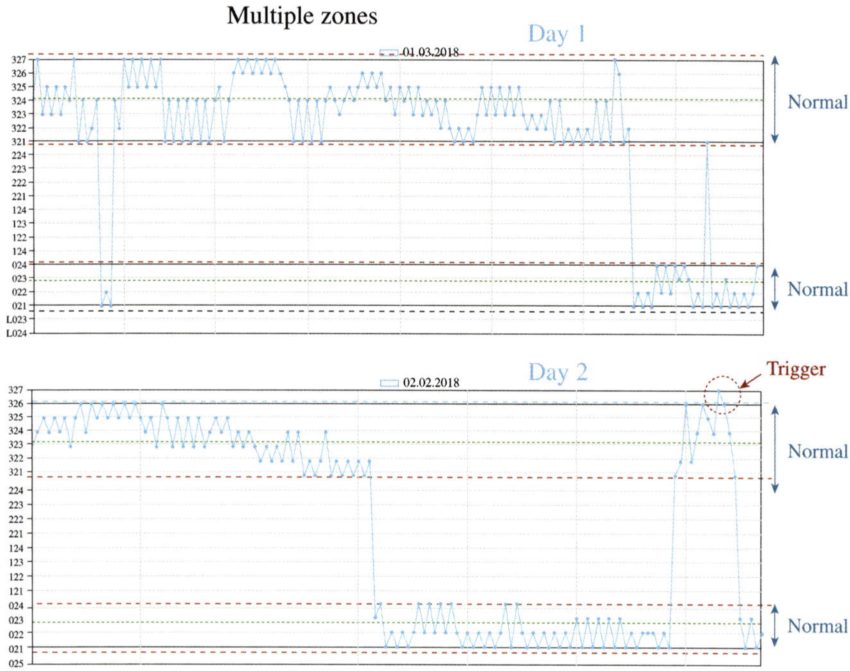

Fig. 4.20. Movement patterns that incorporate a trigger.

4.7. The Algorithm

One of the primary objectives of this research paper is the construction of a robust and effective algorithm that leverages data retrieved from the recently deployed proximity monitoring solution. The algorithm is an integral part of the Shadow Cloud application that was created for this research project. The algorithm is constructed from active elements, each with the ability to alert and increase a running threat counter. As the contractor enters Dakota's controlled office space a counter is reset to '0' (zero).

The main elements of the algorithm are as follows:

- Entry point
- Date
- Time of day

- Time spent in each zone
- Number of zones entered
- Zone pattern anomaly

Figure 4.21 depicts the algorithm as a process flow.

4.7.1. Verification process

Once the proximity solution had been fully integrated within the working practices of Dakota and its 3rd party contractors, a verification process was initiated. With the assistance of the facilities department and the security staff, the algorithm, which formed part of the Shadow Cloud application, was tested to determine any anomalies and false positives.

Triggers were configured at each stage of the algorithm and triggers were analysed to ensure the metrics fell within an acceptable margin of error.

Figure 4.22 depicts each stage of the algorithm and the average percentage of triggers within each stage over a two-month period. As an example, the time spent by each cleaner within each zone was within the permitted parameters 95% of the time. This is visualised in Fig. 4.15, which can be seen as indicative of normal behaviour.

The algorithm has been designed to incorporate some false positives. These would allow a margin of error to be incorporated. As an example, the threat threshold for Dakota has been set to '3'. This is based on the analysis of the targets and the data collected. The threshold for another organisation may be higher or lower depending on the risk appetite, the job functions or the physical attributes of the building.

4.7.2. False positives

The initial testing phase of the threat model produced some false positives that needed to be addressed. Detailed analysis was undertaken at each stage of the algorithm process to ensure the appropriate controls were incorporated into the design.

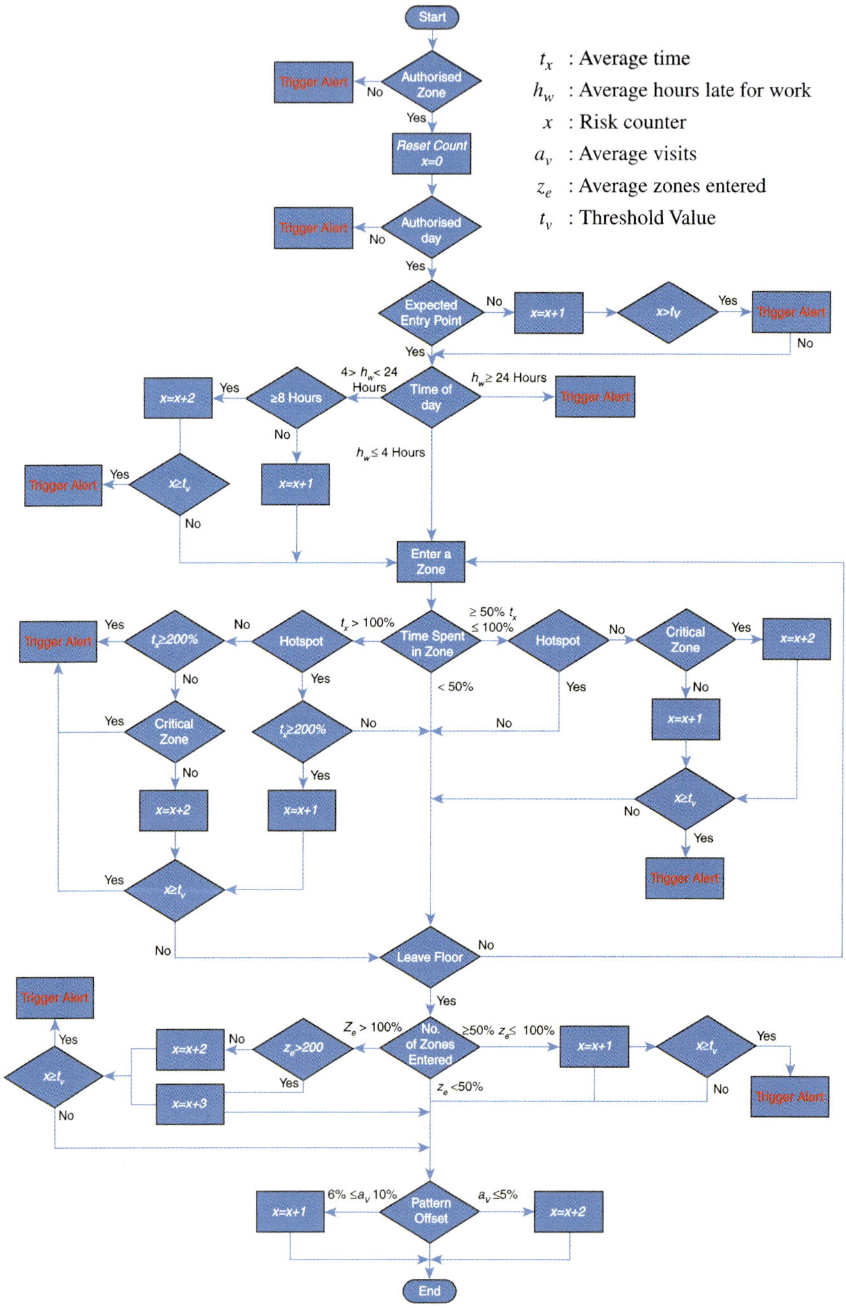

Fig. 4.21. The algorithm as a process.

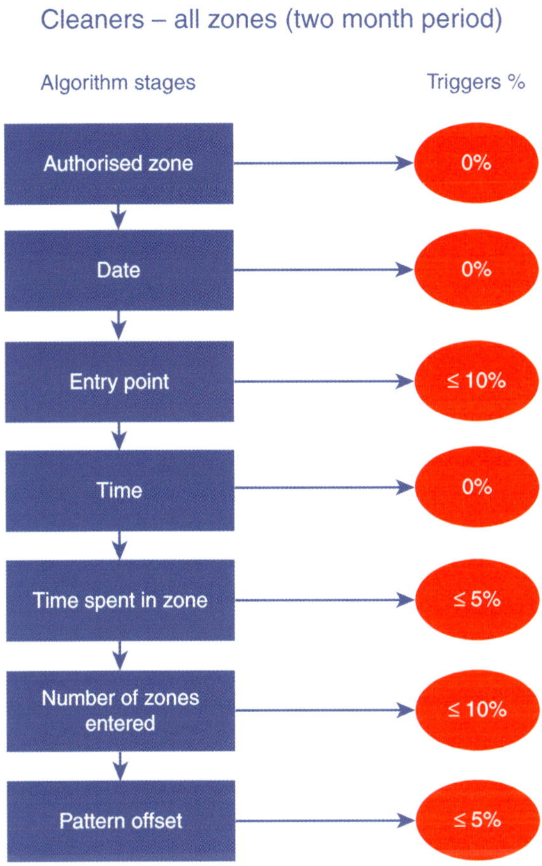

Fig. 4.22. Algorithm triggers.

Focussing on the 8 cleaners, Fig. 4.22 depicts the number of triggers as a percentage over the two-month baseline period and through the various phases of the algorithm. Table 4.6 details the number of instances when each specific cleaner activated a trigger over the baseline period.

Each trigger was investigated to ensure the threshold values were sufficient to prevent unnecessary false positives within the overall algorithm. To ensure the experiment did not create false working patterns the data subjects were not directly approached. Facilities and security were questioned to ensure the cleaners' activity was

Table 4.6. False positive triggers over a two-month baseline period from December 2017 to January 2018.

Contractor	Authorised Zone	Unexpected Date	Unexpected Entry Point	Unexpected Entry Time	Unexpected Time Spent in Zone	Unexpected Number of Zones Entered	Pattern Offset – Zones Breached	Total False Positives
Cleaner 1	0	0	0	0	2	0	0	2
Cleaner 2	0	0	7	0	2	1	0	10
Cleaner 3	0	0	0	0	1	1	1	3
Cleaner 4	0	0	3	0	3	3	2	11
Cleaner 5	0	0	2	0	4	10	1	17
Cleaner 6	0	0	5	0	5	2	2	14
Cleaner 7	0	0	7	0	8	7	1	23
Cleaner 8	0	0	8	0	3	3	1	15
Percentage of false positives	0%	0%	9%	0%	5%	10%	4%	13.5%

normal. There were two methods that could be used to set the threshold levels. One of these could be carried out at the algorithmic function stage and the other required changes to be made to the overall threat detection level. To provide the most flexibility, each stage of the algorithm was adjusted to allow a margin of error based on the false detection rate.

4.7.3. *Experiment validation*

Whilst it can be argued that historic data analysis can determine trigger thresholds, an independent test of the parameters can provide additional assurance. Dakota regularly engages independent cyber and physical security specialists to conduct social engineering tests against the organisation. Once the proximity solution was implemented and Shadow Cloud configured to accept data, a physical penetration test was conducted against Dakota's London headquarters. A team of two ethical social engineers gained access to Dakota's London office using social engineering techniques. They posed as sensitive waste disposal contractors, using bogus identification to gain access. They obtained two security passes, with Bluetooth tracking embedded. They gained access to three of the five floors within Dakota's private office space, as sensitive waste disposal contract staff are only permitted to access selected floors within the building. Due to the time they arrived, tailgating was not an option as no staff were present. The social engineers gained access to the three floors where sensitive waste bins were located, as their access passes permitted them to do.

Figure 4.23 details the expected floor entry point and the zones visited. It also depicts the actual entry points and the floors visited by the social engineers.

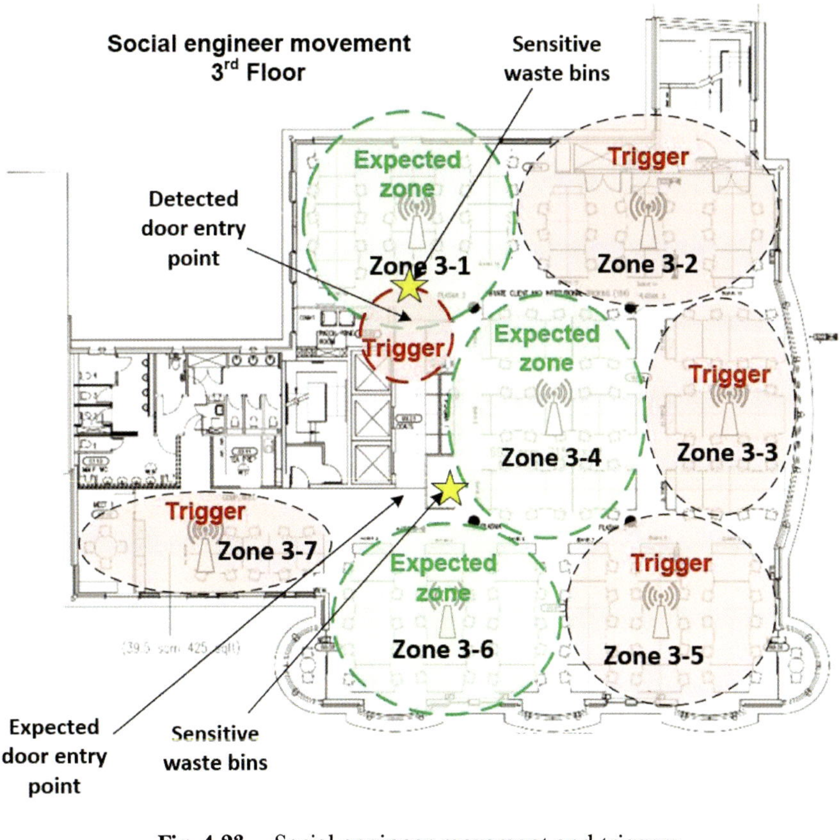

Fig. 4.23. Social engineer movement and triggers.

Table 4.7. Social engineer proximity data.

Action	Expected	Actual	Result	x value
enter floor	Access point A	Access point B	x = x + 1	1
zone 3-1	120 seconds	185 seconds	x = x + 1	2
zone 3-2	No	unexpected zone	a_v increased	2
zone 3-3	No	unexpected zone	a_v increased	2
zone 3-5	No	unexpected zone	a_v increased	2
zone 3-4	120 seconds	100 seconds	No change	2
zone 3-6	60 seconds	115 seconds	x = x + 2	4
zone 3-7	No	unexpected zone	a_v increased	4
zone 3-6	60 seconds	30 seconds	no change	4
leave zone				
zones visited	3	7	z_e > 200% x = x + 3	7
pattern offset	>=90%	<=5%	x = x + 2	9

Source: Dakota

The algorithm triggered numerous times during the period the social engineers visited the 3rd floor. Table 4.7 outlines the data collected and the specific triggers.

The threshold value for Dakota was set to ≥3. The social engineers triggered an alert due to the zones they visited and the time spent within those zones. This was prior to the 'zones visited' and 'pattern offset' elements being processed. Whilst this could be considered an extreme example as social engineers were used, it validates the algorithm based on the thresholds set using baseline data.

4.8. Regulations and Legal Considerations

4.8.1. *GDPR*

The General Data Protection Regulation (GDPR), which comes into effect on 25th May 2018, will impact all EU organisations that collect, store and process personal or sensitive data (Ico.org.uk, 2017). To provide an effective threat mitigation solution, Shadow Cloud will record and process human movement data that is not anonymised. As part of its GDPR preparation process Dakota enhanced its privacy and data protection policies, seeking legal advice to ensure the data recorded was lawful and met the ICO's regulatory requirements.

4.8.2. *Privacy laws*

Bruce Schneier (Schneier, 2016) describes surveillance as a technical and a legal problem. A key project deliverable is the identification of threats based on data collected on human behavior patterns.

As Shadow Cloud requires the tracking of individuals it will inevitably pose privacy questions. Whilst it could be argued that analysing data to prevent threats is ethically acceptable, using the data to target individuals for other purposes, which may include discriminating against the target, could breach privacy and human rights law.

To ensure Dakota comply to privacy regulation a clear and concise agreement with all 3rd party organisations was reviewed by the Data Protection Officer and the organisation's legal representative to ensure the enhanced proximity monitoring process did not infringe on the individual rights of its contract staff. Law professor Eben Moglen once wrote 'if people are doing nothing wrong then they have the right to maintain a balance between the individual and the power that is monitoring'.

4.9. Conclusions and Recommendations

This research project has explored the relationship between human movement patterns and the potential threat posed by an insider with malicious intentions. The real challenge perhaps is to understand how employees navigate a specific environment, how they process physical obstacles and how they interact with co-workers.

Whilst it can be argued that humans have distinctive movement traits, such as using the same entry point, it is evident that trajectories within an open plan office environment can be influenced by a complex set of variables.

Understanding the characteristics of the building and including areas where staff congregate, such as the water cooler, were considered integral when designing a threat model.

The primary focus of the project was the creation of an algorithm that would form part of an overall threat detection solution. The algorithm would initially leverage the data supplied from the target organisation but could be adaptive and used by other human monitoring solutions.

As the target data was analysed it was evident that the algorithm could not rely on a single trigger as this would produce too many false positives. It was clear that a multi-dimensional approach measuring a set of contrasting variables was required.

The algorithm was dissected into seven components, each able to process the specific characteristics of the targets, analysing the time, the date and their movement patterns. The research had intended to identify specific movement patterns that were evident within other research papers that focused on door entry data.

The data provided from the proximity monitoring solution highlighted the complexity of the human decision-making process. When a binary decision had to be made between different access points, the targets would invariably choose the same option; this was evident when entering a floor, as 90% chose the same entry point. However, when presented with multiple options the patterns were far less predictable.

This is why the algorithm could not rely on one measurement metric and incorporated a variety of data sets to determine an anomaly, ultimately reducing the risk of false positives.

References

1. Agrawal, S. and Agrawal, J. (2015). Survey on Anomaly Detection using Data Mining Techniques. In *Proceedings of the 19th International Conference on Knowledge-Based and Intelligent Information and Engineering Systems, Singapore, September 7–9. Procedia Computer Science* **60**, pp. 708–713.
2. Aleskerov, E., Freisleben, B. and Rao, B. (1997). Cardwatch: A Neural Network-Based Database Mining System for Credit Card Fraud

Detection. In *Proceedings of the IEEE Conference on Computational Intelligence for Financial Engineering, New York City, NY, USA, March 24–25*, pp. 220–226.
3. Barjis, J. and Fosso Wamba, S. (2010). Organizational and Business Impacts of RFID Technology. *Business Process Management Journal*, **16**(6), pp. 897–903.
4. Bluetooth Technology. (2018). *Radio Versions* [Online]. Available at: https://www.bluetooth.com/bluetooth-technology/radio-versions (Accessed 5 May 2018).
5. Chandola, V., Banerjee, A. and Kumar, V. (2009). Anomaly Detection: A Survey. *ACM Computing Surveys*, **41**(3), Article 15.
6. CPNI. (2018). *CPNI Insider Data Collection Study: Report of Main Findings* [Online]. Available at: https://www.cpni.gov.uk/system/files/documents/63/29/insider-data-collection-study-report-of-main-findings.pdf (Accessed 22 April 2018).
7. Darktrace. (2018). *Technology* [Online]. Available at: https://www.darktrace.com/technology/#darktrace-threat-visualizer (Accessed 5 May 2018).
8. Edgeworth, F. Y. (1887). On Discordant Observations. *The London, Edinburgh, and Dublin Philosophical Magazine and Journal of Science*, **23**(5), pp. 364–375.
9. Esling, P. and Agon, C. (2012). Time-Series Data Mining. *ACM Computing Surveys*, **45**(1), Article 12.
10. FCA. (2018). *Senior Managers and Certification Regime: Banking* [Online]. Available at: https://www.fca.org.uk/firms/senior-managers-certification-regime/banking (Accessed 3 May 2018).
11. Fong, S. (2011). Integrating RFID Technology in Internet Applications. *Communications in Computer and Information Science*, **162**, pp. 207–216.
12. Fong, S. and Zhuang, Y. (2007). A Security Model for Detecting Suspicious Patterns in Physical Environments. In *Proceedings of the Third International Symposium on Information Assurance and Security, Manchester, UK, August 29–3*, pp. 221–226.
13. Fujimaki, R., Yairi, T. and Machida, K. (2005). An Approach to Spacecraft Anomaly Detection Problem Using Kernel Feature Space. In *Proceedings of the 11th ACM SIGKDD International Conference on Knowledge Discovery in Data Mining, Chicago, IL, USA, August 21–24*. ACM Press, pp. 401–410.
14. Gartner. (2018). *Gartner Forecasts Worldwide Security Spending Will Reach $96 Billion in 2018, Up 8 Percent from 2017* [Online]. Available at:

https://www.gartner.com/newsroom/id/3836563 (Accessed 5 May 2018).
15. Gelles, M. (2016). *Insider Threat* (1st ed.). Oxford, UK: Butterworth-Heinemann.
16. Greenwald, G., MacAskill, E. and Poitras, L. (2018). *Edward Snowden: The Whistleblower Behind the NSA Surveillance Revelations* [Online]. Available at: https://www.theguardian.com/world/2013/jun/09/edward-snowden-nsa-whistleblower-surveillance (Accessed 23 April 2018).
17. Huber, P. (1974). *Robust Statistics.* New York City, NY, USA: Wiley.
18. ICO. (2017). *Overview of the General Data Protection Regulation (GDPR)* [Online]. Available at: https://ico.org.uk/for-organisations/data-protection-reform/overview-of-the-gdpr/ (Accessed 2 September 2017).
19. Joseph, J. (2018). *Do Open/Collaborative Work Environments* [Online]. Available at: https://digitalcommons.ilr.cornell.edu/cgi/viewcontent.cgi?article=1098&context=student (Accessed 14 May 2018).
20. Lewis, P. (2018). *Bradley Manning Given 35-year Prison Term for Passing Files to WikiLeaks* [Online]. Available at: https://www.theguardian.com/ world/2013/aug/21/bradley-manning-35-years-prison-wikileaks-sentence (Accessed 23 April 2018).
21. Murenin, I. N., Novikova, E. S. and Volkov, A. A. (2017). Uncovering Interaction Patterns Between Employees of the Organization. In *Proceedings of the 2017 XX IEEE International Conference on Soft Computing and Measurements (SCM), St. Petersburg, Russia, May 24–26,* pp. 746–749.
22. Novikova, E. S., Murenin, I. N. and Shorov, A. V. Visualizing Anomalous Activity in the Movement of Critical Infrastructure Employees. In *Proceedings of the 2017 IEEE Conference of Russian Young Researchers in Electrical and Electronic Engineering (EIConRus), St. Petersburg, Russia, February 1–3,* pp. 504–509.
23. Nuix. (2018). *Nuix Adaptive Security* [Online]. Available at: https://www.nuix.com/products/nuix-adaptive-security (Accessed 5 May 2018).
24. Project, A. (2018). *Apache Tomcat® — Welcome!* [Online] Available at: http://tomcat.apache.org/ (Accessed 28 April 2018).
25. Rousseeuw, P. J. and Leroy, A. M. (1987). *Robust Regression and Outlier Detection.* Hoboken, NJ, USA: John Wiley & Sons.
26. Schneier, B. (2016). *Data and Goliath: The Hidden Battles to Collect Your Data and Control Your World.* New York City, NY, USA: W. W. Norton and Company.

27. Software Engineering Institute, Carnegie Mellon University. (2018). *Common Sense Guide to Mitigating Insider Threats* [Online]. Available at: https:// resources.sei.cmu.edu/asset_files/TechnicalReport/2016_005_001_484758. pdf (Accessed 12 May 2018).
28. Spence, C., Parra, L. and Sajda, P. (2001). Detection, Synthesis and Compression in Mammographic Image Analysis with a Hierarchical Image Probability Model. In *Proceedings of the IEEE Workshop on Mathematical Methods in Biomedical Image Analysis, Kauai, HI, USA, December 9–10*, pp. 3–10.
29. Tan, P. N., Steinbach, M. and Kumar, V. (2005). *Introduction to Data Mining*. Boston, MA, USA: Addison-Wesley Longman Publishing Co.
30. Teng, H., Chen, K. and Lu, S. (1990). Adaptive Real-Time Anomaly Detection Using Inductively Generated Sequential Patterns. In *Proceedings of the IEEE Computer Society Symposium on Research in Security and Privacy, Oakland, CA, USA, May 7–9*. IEEE Computer Society Press, pp. 278–284.
31. United States House of Representatives. (2018). *The Enron Collapse* [Online]. Available at: https://royce.house.gov/uploadedfiles/rs21135.pdf (Accessed 12 May 2018).
32. Zonith. (2018). *Safety and Security Solutions* [Online]. Available at: https://zonith.com/ (Accessed 26 April 2018).

Chapter 5

Ransomware

Usman Javed Butt* and Arvind Kumar†

**Brunel University, London, UK*
usman.butt@brunel.ac.uk

†Northumbria University, London, UK
arvind.kumar@northumbria.ac.uk

ABSTRACT

In this modern era, malware has emerged as a malicious cyber threat to critical information and communication infrastructure. Ransomware is a type of malware which holds the victim's computer hostage by encrypting the data available on it, which makes the data unusable and inaccessible to its legitimate user. The attacker demands that the user pay before the decryption key is released to reverse the attack. This chapter explains about ransomware and its classification, how it impacts different platforms, the severity of ransomware, the methodology used by ransomware to penetrate target machines, the attack vectors used, the latest ransomware attacks, the most common targets of ransomware attacks, how to prevent ransomware attacks, and ways to recover.

Keywords: malware, ransomware, botnets, cryptography, bitcoins, crypto-lockers, attack vectors, exploit kits, RSA public key, MD5 algorithm, AES, symmetric key, WannaCry, Petya, SimpleLocker, TeslaCrypt, NotPetya, IoT

5.1. Introduction

According to Kapersky, as computers evolved from floppy-disk bootable machines into more sophisticated workstation devices such as laptops and smartphones, malicious software technology or ***malware*** as it is most commonly known evolved along with them (Kaspersky, 2018a). Kaspersky also suggests that malware was existent from information technology's infancy but that the use of malware only bloomed when personal computers began to be accessible to everyone. The first malware was called the **"Elk Cloner Virus"** (Tasril *et al.*, 2017). Examining the features of the Elk Cloner Virus, we see that this malicious technology, which once used simple motifs and techniques, has become more sophisticated and now does more serious damage to computer devices. The Elk Cloner Virus was formed as a "prank" and did not do much harm. Its self-spreading feature relied on social engineering techniques such as floppy-disk insertions (Touchette, 2016). Cyber criminals built upon these foundations until they formed the cyber crime industry as it exists today.

Cyber crime, which has cost industries approximately 100 billion USD, is classified according to the types of malware that the industry produces. Research done by Kapersky has identified the types of malware in a diagram in Fig. 5.1 called the "Malware Classification Tree" (Kaspersky, 2018b).

According to the same report, the classified malwares are considered "specific function" malwares, which means that these malwares are only capable of designated damage and do not produce a complex effect on devices. In contrast, cyber criminals have devised

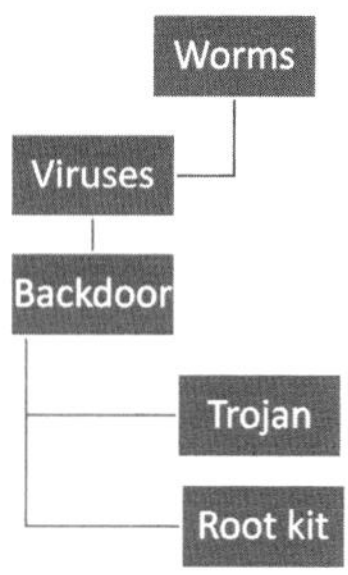

Fig. 5.1. Malware classification tree.

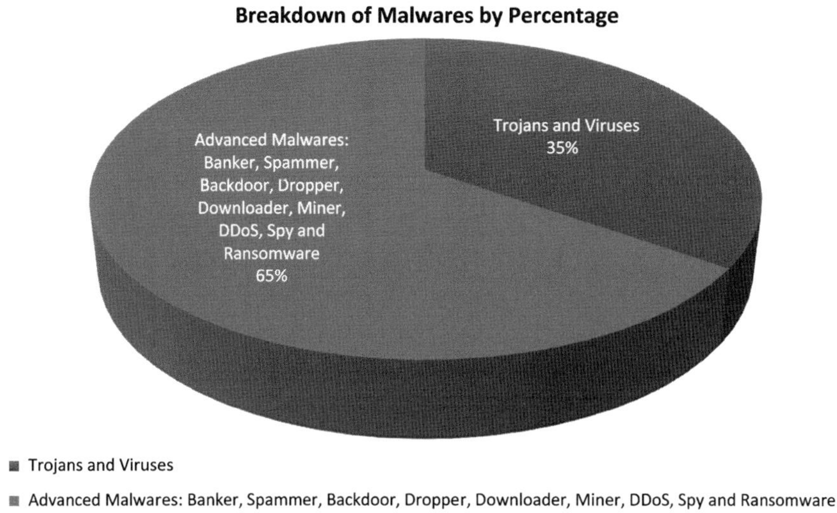

Fig. 5.2. Pie chart of multi-functional malware vs. single-function malware (Trojans).

multi-dimensional and multi-functioning malwares. 65.32% of these are *botnets* which affect devices worldwide, and 34.68% of these are a combination of trojans and worms as shown in Fig. 5.2 (Soni, 2018).

Cisco has classified these versatile malwares as "Advanced Malwares" and has identified the most prominent advanced malwares as the following: riskware, spyware, adware and ransomware with *ransomware* being the deadliest due to its capabilities (Cisco, 2018). Esset defines riskware as a type of malware which increases security risk by using encryption methods to identify user procedures and diverting the procedures into digital transactions (e.g. using a credit card) without the user's permission (Esset, 2018). Spywares are types of malware which, as can be deduced from their name, collect data about a device, encrypt the information and send the data back to the origin of the malware. These data are used illegally to blackmail the people from whom the data is collected (Stavrou *et al.*, 2010). Avast, an anti-virus company, adds that spywares are usually accompanied by adwares, which bombard the user with inappropriate and unwanted pop-ups or advertisements which are harmful to the device (Avast, 2018). Finally, when these features are combined and tailored for a bigger purpose, ***ransomware*** is produced.

An observation can be made that most of the advanced malwares were enhanced by the development of encryption and of new ways to cipher text. The field of **cryptovirology** was developed when researchers realised how these cryptographic techniques could be used to develop malware (Young, 2017).

5.2. Ransomware and How It Impacts Different Platforms

Ransomware has affected several companies worldwide by making it necessary for them to pay a large amount of money to their attackers without actually gaining anything beneficial. For instance, Arran Brewery, a brewing company in Scotland, recently paid 2 Bitcoins worth 9,600 GBP to a group of anonymous hackers just to restore the company's system after all the computers of the company had been locked down (BBC, 2018). A similar incident also happened to the United States government when the Pennsylvania Senate Democratic Caucus had to pay Microsoft to reconstruct the senate's IT Framework after it was breached on March 3, 2017 (Cimpanu, 2019). The same report states that hackers were demanding 28 Bitcoins as payment, which comes up to 30,000 USD, but instead the government decided to reconstruct for the hefty price of 700,000 USD in order to discourage future attacks to government offices. As these incidents start to increase, attacks are reportedly getting worse.

Ransomware is a type of advanced malware where the victim is held at ransom for infected files or documents. The files will not be made available to the victim unless payment is given to the attacker, at which point the attacker will remove the malware from the system (Young, 2017). Ransomware is believed to be one of the most effective malwares for the year 2017, with a total amount of more than 12 million malware counts. The number of malware counts increased by 36% in the last quarter of 2017 (McAfee, 2017). The fact that ransomware accounted for 5 billion US dollars lost globally in the year 2017 led Europol to conclude that ransomware was the most dangerous malware threat, and to say so at their conference entitled "Internet Organised Crime Threat Assessment (IOCTA) 2018" (Walker, 2018).

As ransomware has turned into a booming business, ransomware authors have devised two types of ransomwares: *locker ransomware* and *crypto ransomware* (Deloitte, 2016).

Locker ransomwares are the types of ransomwares which do less damage since these ransomwares do not encrypt the files of the victim. Locker ransomware is used to terrorise the victim by prompting the victim to pay for a fine charged for misusing the internet (i.e. watching pornography or downloading illegal programs from torrents). These ransomwares usually come with an interface credible enough for the victim to believe that the warrant is legitimate. Attackers may include the targeted user's sensitive data, such as their IP address and their last viewed malicious website, to make the warrant more convincing (Deloitte, 2016).

Crypto ransomwares (crypto-locker ransomwares) are the types of ransomwares which do more damage to the device and to the financial stability of the victim. Crypto-lockers are a type of ransomware which infects a device and ***encrypts*** the victim's files until the ransom has been paid. Some of these crypto-lockers even delete the back-up from the system, making it harder to recover the victim's files (Richet, 2016).

5.3. Methodology of Ransomware

The word ransomware comes from the words "ransom" and "malware". One could define the word ransom as a payment or acquiescence to certain demands in exchange for the release of a hostage or of something held hostage (Merriam-Webster, 2018). So, understanding the criticality of a malware capable of holding virtual platforms to ransom and how the procedure is undertaken is deemed essential.

Much research related to ransomware has pointed out that different ransomwares can have different approaches of propagation, but all ransomwares follow a pattern of propagation that has five phases beginning from the point when the victim's system is compromised. The five phases are as follows (Brewer, 2016):

1. ***First Phase: Acquisition, Utilisation and Infection***

The process of acquiring ransomware is similar to the process of acquiring any other type of malware (Ali, 2017). Norton by Symantec suggests that ransomware and other forms of malware can be categorised into five types depending on how they are acquired, and these are as follows (Norton, 2018):

- Software-integrated malwares: This is when a user downloads a software which is tagged as "free" but which actually comes with the hefty price of having one's system infected by malware.
- Peer-to-peer virtual sharing: This is when a user shares files electronically by using BitTorrent, uTorrent etc. This does not only refer to file sharing between familiar peers but also refers to the ***illegal*** download of applications via anonymous uploads.
- Removable media: This is the most common method of malware acquisition. Malware is transferred to the victim via electronic devices such as USBs, CDs, External HDDs, etc.
- Network acquisition: This happens when a device connected to the internet comes across a website which has malicious cookies or pop-ups and the victim falls into the trap by exploring the links integrated into these digital platforms.
- General lack of protection: This happens when a device is not kept secure by software which offers protection from malwares.

Attack Vectors of Ransomware

Although there are plenty of ways to be infected by malwares, researchers have identified that ***fortunately***, there are only a few ways of acquiring ransomware. These vectors could be divided into those which are acquired through virtual means and those which are acquired through physical means.

Virtual Means of Ransomware Acquisition:

a) **Emails** are the main source of ransomware attacks. Statistics show that there are approximately 354.5 billion emails delivered daily worldwide and 85.35 percent of these emails are spam, which means only 14.64 percent of emails are legitimate (Cisco Talos,

2018). IBM estimates that there was a 350 percent increase in spam mails from January 2015 to December 2016 and, alarmingly, despite the fact that not all spam mails contain malwares, the total malware content in spam mails by percentage is increasing. Malware-containing spam mails made up approximately 10 percent of 100 percent of spam mails sent in January 2015. By 2016, spam mails had increased by 450 percent, and malware-containing spam mails made up 210 percent of the 450 percent (IBM, 2016) as shown in Fig. 5.3.

Symantec suggests that these malwares are spreading largely due to a botnet named Necrus which was established just to send out spam mails worldwide (O'Brien, 2017). Symantec also states that ransomware, if acquired through email, can be activated through one of the following steps (O'Brien, 2017):

- Malicious attachments being opened
- Malicious attachments initiating third party JavaScript or PowerShell commands
- Malicious attachments initiating the download of **exploit kits**

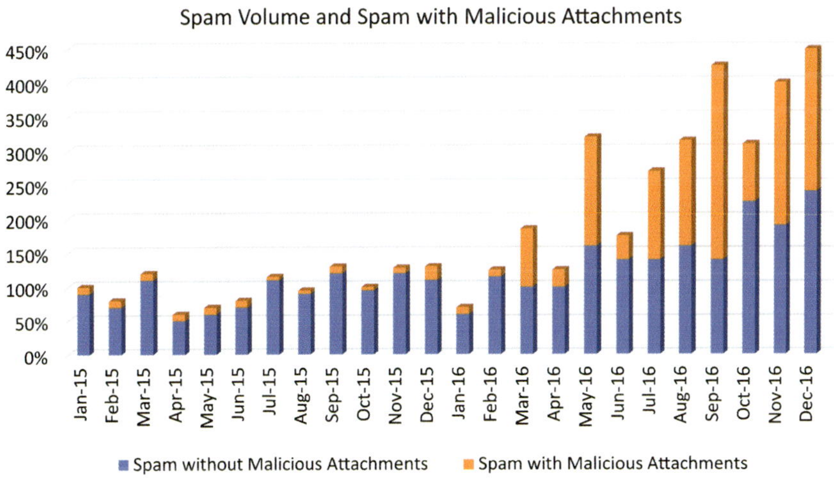

Fig. 5.3. Volumes of malicious and non-malicious spam.

b) **Exploit Kits** literally exploit the vulnerabilities of a computer. Exploit kits are used to take advantage of a particular device's weaknesses via web browsers, programs or operating systems. Most exploit kits are integrated into websites, and once a user visits that particular site, the kit is activated in the user's device. The kit will then scan for vulnerabilities in the device used to navigate the website and, subsequently, it will implement the malware into the device in question. The infected website is not necessarily a malicious website since legitimate websites like BBC or Yahoo could be infested through advertisements as well (Monrose *et al.*, 2015). According to a study done by Malwarebytes, as shown in Fig. 5.4, 61 percent of all exploit kits contain exploit payloads for ransomware (Malwarebytes Labs, 2016).

Physical Means of Ransomware Acquisition

Social Engineering is used as a sure but risky way to spread malware. Social Engineering is the manipulation of human psychology in order to persuade a person to perform a behaviour which may have a devastating effect on that person, another person or a group of individuals. Researchers may refer to it as "hacking" a human for an intended purpose (Mann, 2008).

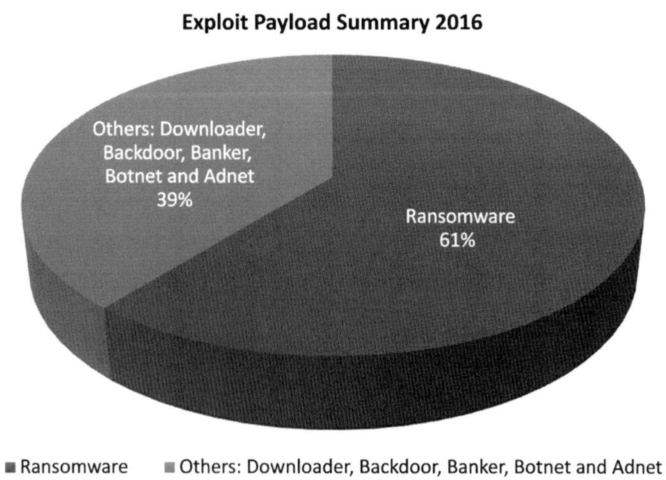

Fig. 5.4. Exploit payload summary.

Kevin Mitnick's Proposed Social Engineering Methodology (Gallegos-Segovia, 2017):

- **Information Gathering:** This is the step where details of the victim are gathered by certain individuals.
- **Trust:** This is the step where the attacker establishes a deeper connection with the victim. By doing so, an appropriate attack vector could be identified by the attacker.
- **Exploitation:** This is where the attacker executes the plan of exploitation and the ransomware infects the device.
- **Reach:** This is where the system is finally compromised. Usually the attacker is not in contact with the victim at this point.

The *December 2015 Ukraine Power Grid Cyber Attack* is an example of how these methods have been used. Numerous reports suggest that the incident was a well-planned attack on Ukraine's power company named Ukrenergo (BBC, 2017). Most investigators were amazed by how well the information and trust gathering was executed and further blamed the Russians for devising a way into the Ukraine's SCADA system then manipulating the system through an infection caused by a USB (Zetter, 2016).

These proposed methods of social engineering can be further used to identify the different types of attacks that can be established. These are as follows (Gallegos-Segovia, 2017):

- **Ego Attacks:** The attacker tries to create a personal connection with the victim by offering help and proving the reliability of the attacker's intelligence to the victim. Once the victim falls for a transparent manipulation, the attacker executes the ransomware on the system.
- **Sympathy Attacks:** The attacker uses emotional means to create a connection with the victim. When the victim starts trusting the attacker, the attacker executes the ransomware on the system.
- **Bullying Attacks:** The attacker uses force, dominance or blackmailing to gather information. This is the most common and most effective type of social engineering attack.

2. ***Second Phase: Consignment and Implementation***

The next step is the process of installing the malware on the system, encrypting the ransomware program inside the device and further establishing a secure platform for the **upcoming** command and control network.

The ransomware uses a simple RSA asymmetric public key (Emsisoft, 2018) that will call a **GET** or **POST** request at some point (Securonix, 2018). The **GET** or **POST** request would consist of the following parameters to be collected (Emsisoft, 2018; Securonix, 2018):

- computer name
- processor information
- volume serial
- operating system
- active drives
- Public IP in a pattern of: { ipv4bot[.]whatismyipaddress[.] com}
- disk space

Researchers (Emsisoft, 2018) have identified the reasons why ransomware developers use RSA public keys in coding ransomwares and these are the following:

- They take up lesser space in memory and can be easily transported.
- Third parties or malware analysts surveying the network would only see plain texts and scrambled encrypted network traffic.
- This gives the malware authors a chance to use their own server during the communication with the deployed ransomware.

After identifying the victim through their unique hashed identity (using the MD5 Algorithm), the ransomware would identify whether the process was running via **root or admin access** (Rajpal and Kotov, 2014). If the ransomware was running through either root or admin access, then further installation of the ransomware would take place through the following steps (Rajpal and Kotov, 2014):

As shown in the flowchart, the ransomware would unpack itself to the memory of the device or the hard disk and then would execute

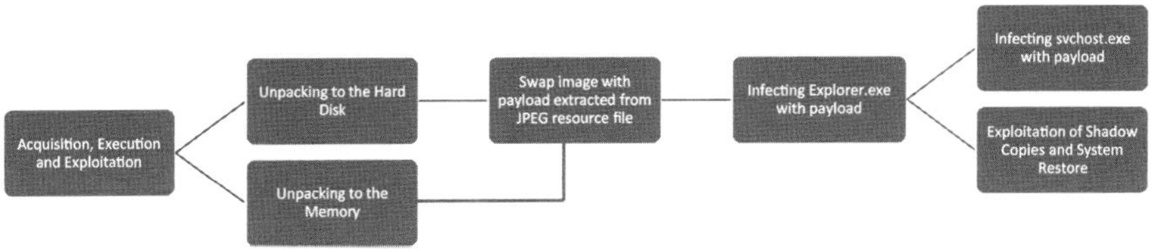

Fig. 5.5. Ransomware installation procedures.

itself. The software would then create multiple copies of a stage dropper and inject the payload into explorer.exe and svchost.exe. In the next *phases*, the ransomware would also delete all shadow copies and back-up files and finally disable the device's ability to restore the system.

These processes normally take only a few seconds to execute and usually are executed without the user's knowledge (Brewer, 2016), as shown in Fig. 5.5.

3. ***Third Phase: File Encryption and Command and Control (C2)***

Command and Control Establishment

This phase is the most important phase of a ransomware since, in this phase, a ransomware will do whatever it has been coded to do. After making sure that all packages of the ransomware have been successfully injected into the system, the ransomware platform in the device would now communicate to the command centre (host) via an RSA key pair (Brewer, 2016). A .bit namecoin would then be used to query .bit domain-friendly DNS servers through the code: {ns1.crop[.]corp-servers[.]ru; a[.]dsnpod[.] com}. Once the connection is established, this is where the information gathered via a **GET** or **POST** request would be sent to the host in the Base64 encoding format [31].

Researchers have (Rajpal and Kotov, 2014) identified that over the past few years, ransomware developers have shifted from using HTTP to using TOR and SSL during the communication phase of command and control establishment. The simplest reason is that it is more complex to decrypt TOR and SSL data in contrast to HTTP data. Data encrypted with RC4 encryption, which is the most commonly used method to encrypt HTTP data, can be decrypted and fingerprinted using the simple *mathematical expression* [a – z]\ = [z – z 0 – 9]+, also called *Regrex* (Kaspersky, 2016). TOR and SSL's full encryption makes it difficult for developers to code a network signature for initial stage detection; however, TOR is less used due to multiple network restrictions (Rajpal and Kotov, 2014).

File Encryption Process

The following files and folders are excluded from encryption:

- desktop.ini
- autorun.ini
- nuser.ini
- GDCB-DECRYPT.txt

These are excluded to allow the command server to connect to the device controlled (NJCCIC, 2018).

The encryption of files is done through a combination of RSA 2048bit (public key) and AES 256bit (victim data) encryption. After data encryption, the ransomware is expected to encrypt the files by assigning a public-private key for the randomly generated symmetric key. This process is shown in Fig. 5.6.

This type of encryption does not need any shared secret key, which makes it easier for the attacker to keep the ciphered text and only allow the victim access once ransom is paid (Emsisoft, 2018).

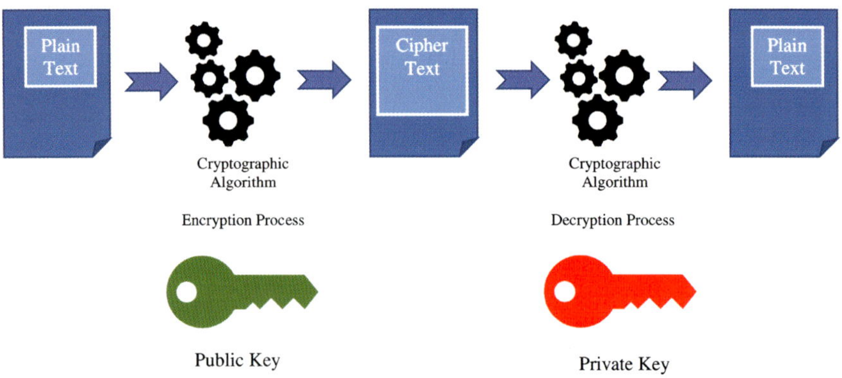

Fig. 5.6. Process of encryption used by ransomware.

In most ransomwares, Virlock is commonly used for encryption. Virlock consists of two layers of encryption in which the **first layer** is a combination of XOR and ROL encryption which is backed up by a **second layer** of XOR encryption (Lindskog and Zavarskya, 2016). All the encrypted files are converted into .GDCB or .KRAB files which then prompt a report back to the command centre using the same **GET** or **POST** request (Rajpal and Kotov, 2014).

4. ***Fourth Phase: Back-Up Corruption***

Unlike most malwares which are usually designed just to implement the infection that the program is designed to spread, most ransomwares are designed to delete the back-up of the victim's files or at least the back-up of the ransomware (Brewer, 2016).

Ransomwares usually end by deleting the shadow copies of the victim's files by either of two available methods: the VSSAdmin service or the WMI service. The two methods are identified in (Securonix, 2018), which also shows the exact code used by the ransomware to delete all the shadow copies. This code can be seen below.

5. ***Fifth Phase: User Detection, Payment and Clean-Up***

The FBI has claimed that the Barack Obama Blue Blackmail Virus has been one of the biggest issues faced by the USA. The virus resulted in numerous people logging in to their devices and suddenly seeing President Obama's face along with an FBI notice asking them to pay a certain fine (Osborne, 2018). This news is a perfect example of the aftermath of a ransomware attack. Attackers demand a certain amount of pecuniary reimbursement for the locked files, which should be paid within a certain period of time.

Due to the advancement of technology, most attackers require victims to pay using bitcoins but there are other viable means of payment like credit or debit card payments, etc. (Rajpal and Kotov, 2014).

Table 5.1 suggests that most ransomware attackers require victims to pay from a range of 100 USD to 500 USD or from 0.5 BTC (3,280 USD) to 0.8 BTC (5,250 USD).

Usually these instructions are saved in the hard drive with file names such as "HELP_DECRYPT" for CryptoWall V3 or

Table 5.1. Payment options.

Family	Payment Options	Price of Decrypting
TeslaCrypt	Bitcoin Payments are normally required but developers also accepted credit or debit card payments in the earlier variations.	500 USD — increased to 1000 USD if not paid within the time frame (Kaspersky, 2018c)
CryptoLocker	Started off with more options but eventually these options were narrowed down to Bitcoin	300 USD (Cannell, 2018)
Petya or NotPetya	At this point only Bitcoin is accepted by the criminals (Fruhlinger, 2017).	0.3–0.5 BTC
WannaCry	Payments must be made in Bitcoin	Between $300 (£228) and $600 (Gibbs, 2017)
SimpleLocker	Payments must be made via the Ukrainian MoneXy cash transfer system.	260 hryvnias ($22, £13) (NJCCIC, 2016)
GandCrab	Dash or Bitcoin	1200 USD — increased to 2400 USD if not paid within the time frame (Abrams, 2018)

"HELP_YOUR_FILES" for CryptoWall V4. Once payment is given to the attacker, the attacker will decrypt the files and the ransomware will clean up by itself (Brewer, 2016).

5.4. Latest and Most Prominent Ransomwares

As explained before, ransomware is an evolving business with malware developers as its vendors and cyber criminals as its customers. Due to this "booming" trend, many variations of ransomwares have become available in the market. The following are the top five strongest ransomwares in the last five years, as identified by an organisation of security decision makers called CSO.

Top Five Strongest Ransomwares (Fruhlinger, 2017):

1. **CryptoLocker**: considered the most generic variation of ransomware due to its ability to encrypt all the files inside the victim's device. These ransomwares use law enforcement-themed GUIs to

threaten the victim into paying the ransom, which they must do since decryption is near to impossible. All back-up files are deleted as soon as the infection starts (Cannell, 2018). CryptoLocker is usually called the "primitive ransomware" since the developers have not updated the features of the said ransomware (Fruhlinger, 2017).

2. **TeslaCrypt**: considered a subvariant of CryptoLocker; this ransomware started claiming victims in 2015. This ransomware used gaming websites to spread itself and to infect devices, which is why those affected by this ransomware were mostly gamers. This ransomware only encrypted files with a file size lower than 268 MB (Osborne, 2018). The developers of the ransomware have decided to shut down operations and upon doing so, the developers also posted the universal decryption key which helped infected devices to recover successfully (Koller, 2016).

   The final message of TeslaCrypt, which included the master decryption key, read as follows:

   "Project closed! Master key for decrypt: 440A241DD80FCC5664E861989DB 716E08CE627D8D40C7EA360AE855C727A49EE. Wait for other people make universal decrypt software. We are sorry!"

3. **SimpleLocker**: a ransomware effective on the Android platform which gathers the IMEI, the model number and the manufacturer details for the command and control centre. Encryption is done via the AES encryption method and the ransomware also accesses the camera to take a picture of the victim. This picture is used to further threaten the victim into paying the ransom (NJCCIC, 2016).
4. **WannaCry**: considered one of the deadliest ransomwares to be developed. This ransomware shut down multiple hospitals across the United Kingdom and Ukraine. The developers of WannaCry were able to detect vulnerabilities in Windows which were first discovered by the United States National Security Agency. Symantec later on began to suspect that the developers originated from a North Korean-linked group called Lazarus (Fruhlinger, 2017). This ransomware is also one of the latest. 6,912 appointments were cancelled and 19,000 affected when WannaCry affected NHS operations in the year 2017. This attack, despite being "unsophisticated" as Kingsley Manning suggests, became

so successful due to the fact that the different NHS offices were "intertwined" with each other, thus quickening the spread of the ransomware (BBC, 2017).

5. **Petya** and **NotPetya**: launched a week after the WannaCry outbreak, this ransomware is confirmation that a new age of ransomwares has begun (Fruhlinger, 2017). Petya or NotPetya was spread by attackers who sent a job application document via email in the PDF file format. When the PDF file was accessed by the company, the ransomware was unleashed. NotPetya is the very first ransomware which does not need any spam emails to be sent or social engineering to be carried out in order for infection to occur and administrative access to be gained. As long as there is a network connection in between two devices, Petya or NotPetya can move from one to the other (Fruhlinger, 2017).

Aside from these famous ransomware attacks, there are a few other ransomwares making their name in the market. One of the most prominent in recent years is GandCrab which just released their latest version, Version 4, in July 2018. GandCrab acts exactly like CryptoLocker and is also considered deadly since the ransomware converts files to .KRAB extension files once encrypted (Abram, 2018).

5.5. Platforms Affected by Ransomware Attacks

Malwares in general can affect multiple technological platforms, but recent studies have shown that ransomware has only affected three technological platforms so far. During the height of the *WannaCry* ransomware attacks, banks and bank users in India were falsely warned through circulating *Whatsapp* messages that the ransomware had actually breached ATM machines throughout the country. These allegations were proven to be hoaxes upon deeper investigation by one of the leading banks of India, called the Rural Bank of India (NDTV, 2017). Had this been true, ransomware could have been considered a deadly terrorism weapon by governments around the world.

Researchers have identified that ransomware has affected mobile platforms, computing platforms, and IoT and cloud computing platforms. Out of these three types of platform, it is most vital to keep IoT and cloud computing platforms secure.

a) **Computing Platform:** Computing platforms have always been those most affected by ransomwares. As previously discussed, ransomwares act on computers by infecting the system and encrypting the files in the system until a certain amount of ransom is paid. A large number of ransomware attacks on computing platforms — 86.87 percent of total ransomware attacks in 2016 — are directed at home users (Walton, 2017).
b) **Mobile Platform:** Due to people spending more time on their mobile phones, doctors have concluded that most people are suffering from mobile addiction (SC Magazine, 2017). Having this in mind, cyber criminals have taken advantage of people who are "addicted" to mobile phones.

   Android — This has been the biggest target of ransomware attacks on mobile platforms. This is mainly due to the "openness" of the Android platform. With mobile ransomware increasing by 137.8% from the first to the second quarter of 2017, SC Magazine predicted that there would be a spike in mobile ransomware in 2018 (Snow, 2016). However, in Android ransomware and in mobile ransomware overall, cryptolockers are less common since file encryption would be useless on mobile platforms due to the cloud backup feature that most mobile devices have. This is the reason why most Android ransomwares lock applications with a coded GUI which shows the details of the ransomware once the application is opened (Norton, 2018). The newest mobile ransomware, specifically dedicated for Android, is better implemented. This ransomware, which is tagged as *Android.Lockroid.E*, locks the whole mobile device instead of just locking the specific applications inside the mobile device. This way, the user's mobile device would be locked and unusable until the ransom had been paid (Savage *et al.*, 2015).

   iOS — According to a report released by Symantec, iOS devices are mostly secure due to Apple's Technological and Security Ecosystem Structure. The only way that an iPhone can be vulnerable to ransomware is when the mobile device in question has undergone the process called "jailbreaking" (Ismail, 2018). Despite all the protection that Apple offers for iOS phones, researchers suggest that Proton Remote Access Trojan (RAT) has affected plenty of iPhones worldwide (Snow, 2016).

c) **IoT and Cloud Computing Platforms**
As previously discussed, the invention of NotPetya paved the way for a type of ransomware which does not need third party connections like spam mails or social engineering to infect and gain administrative access to any device. This led developers and researchers to think of the next step that ransomware would become capable of. Although there has been no reported ransomware attack on any IoT or cloud computing platform, the implementation of this idea is not too far away, especially now that IoT is being plagued by DDoS attacks such as Mirai (Cobb, 2017). Since ransomware developers can now understand and create ransomwares which can multiply by themselves on a shared network, IoT technologies are not safe any more since all IoTs share a common network, that is, the cloud (Budd, 2016). Although speculation about Microsoft 365's cloud-based technology being attacked by a ransomware named CERBER or RANSOM_CERBER. CAD has not been fully proven, TrendMicro researchers have stated that the ransomware in question can encrypt 442 file types using AES 265 and RSA encryption techniques. However, it seems like the coding of cloud ransomware is just in its initial stages since the only command that the ransomware can successfully deliver is to play an audio message in a computer-generated (creepy) voice (Sneed, 2016). These incidents may actually hint at a growth of ransomware in the IoT and cloud industries.

d) **Industries**
Ransomwares are not only built for the sole purpose of affecting regular citizens but are also built for a larger cause. Since malware development can be used for money making and has already become a booming business, malware developers have concentrated attacks on industries where more benefit could be derived. A

report by Scientific American Magazine states that cyber criminals have been targeting and crippling important "institutions that everybody relies on" through different types of ransomware (Martin, 2017). According to a report by CSO, the three industries which have been most affected by ransomware attacks are the following: healthcare, government and education. Out of these, *healthcare* has been the most affected of all (Osborne, 2018). These industries are targeted more since they run 24/7 and thus need their updated files all the time. Serious threats can arise when institutional or organisational data from these industries is leaked or sold on the dark web. This is why these industries tend to pay for the ransom quicker than the other ransomware victims (Cylance, 2018).

Alarmingly, it has been made clear in a report by Cylance (called the 2017 Threat Report) that healthcare has obviously been targeted the most, and that law enforcement and/or ICT developers within the healthcare industry do not seem to have any methods to overcome these threats.

The pie charts below show the ransomware attacks performed on each type of industry over the span of a year (Kidron, 2017). Whilst there was a significant drop in the percentage of total ransomware attacks affecting almost every industry from 2016 to 2017, as shown in Fig. 5.7, the percentage of total ransomware attacks affecting the

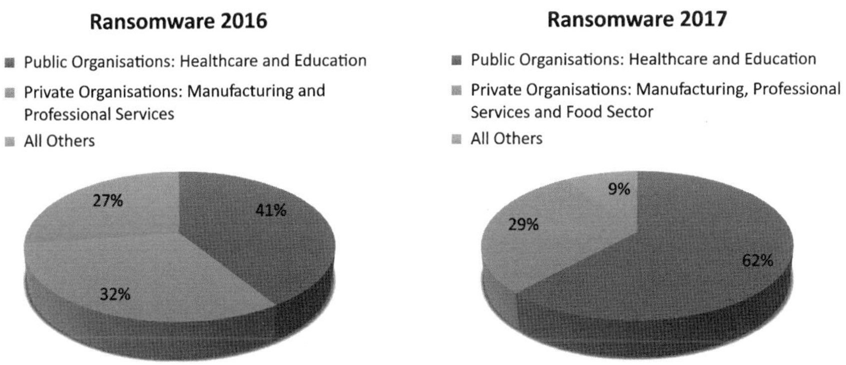

Fig. 5.7. Industries impacted by ransomware (Kidron, 2017).

healthcare and food industries increased (by 24 percent for the healthcare industry). Scientific American Magazine (Martin, 2017) has reported that, aside from the Pennsylvania Senate incident, police stations such as the Swansea Police Department (2013) and Fire Departments in Maryland (2015) have been struck by ransomwares due to the simple fact that these organisations hold sensitive and important data about citizens which is vital for the proper functioning of the government. The police department of Swansea had to pay 750 USD just to recover their files but the Fire Department of Maryland opted not to pay in order to discourage further attacks.

Scientific American Magazine's report (Martin, 2017), delivered a clear warning to those in charge of law enforcement and cyber security. These cyber attacks are happening to the health industry and the government now, but a day will come when these malicious attacks could become worse. Critical infrastructures such as dams, power grids or worse could be attacked. Supervisory Control And Data Acquisition (SCADA) systems, which must be frequent users of the internet in order to function, could also be attacked. A report suggests cyber criminals have coded a ransomware which is dedicated to infecting SCADA systems and this ransomware is named LogicLocker (Kidron, 2017). This ransomware uses socket APIs and manipulates weak credential-authentication mechanisms into infecting the workstation. After infection, the ransomware does not encrypt the files but instead deletes all current authentication passwords and lets the command and control centre change the password to one of the attacker's choice. This way, the company affected needs to pay the ransom for the new authentication details (Turpin and Harmsworth, 2001).

5.6. Preventing Ransomware Attacks

Different companies, different researchers and different anti-virus brands have different suggestions for preventing ransomware infection and spreading. Although different research studies have yielded different and sometimes opposing opinions on how to prevent ransomware, the general approach to preventing ransomware is always the same. Prevention can be done in two ways, which we call human prevention and advanced prevention.

a) **Human Prevention**

Information Dissemination: With the advancement of technology, people are now expected to gather information, be vigilant and ***educate*** themselves about the latest news in the digital society (Ali, 2017). Information about harmful software, not just *ransomware*, should be disseminated on different platforms so that they reach a wider audience. These platforms are as follows (Carbon Black, 2018):

- **Mail** (Physical Mail or Email)
- **Newsletters**
- **Company or educational briefings**
- **Websites**
- **Reports**
- **Conferences**
- **Workshops**
- **Other media** (Social Media etc.)

Although people can learn plenty from these sources, they should be wise enough to choose credible sources like the government or IEEE. Websites accessed for information regarding malwares should ideally be from anti-virus company blogs such as Kaspersky, Avast, Esset, etc.

b) **Technical Prevention:** A few technical but simple steps are suggested by multiple research studies in the field of malware. These steps are subcategorised by different digital vectors and most of these steps can be found online.

   Back-up, Back-up, Back-up! (Rajpal and Kotov, 2014):

- *Regularly Back-up Data*: Back-up could be done in two different ways. Since there is a minimal chance of being hit by ransomware on both your device as well as a selected cloud application, users are advised to use a cloud back-up for important and sensitive files. This is the same reason why mobile ransomware does not encrypt files inside the mobile device but just locks the whole system instead.

- *External Hard Disk Back-up:* An external hard disk can also be suggested as a back-up measure, but researchers suggest that after back-up, external hard disks should be unplugged from the computers (Ali, 2017).
- *Deploy User Account Control:* This will help limit the access of ransomwares since most ransomware procedures require administrative permissions.

Email Security (O'Brien, 2017):

- Prevent downloads of unknown attachment files.
- Do not open spam mails if the mail is sent by an unknown user.
- Install special email defender applications that have real-time link following.
- Disable macro scripts on the files received via emails (O'Brien, 2017).

Anti-Virus:

- Anti-virus software should always be updated (Ali, 2017).

Other Important Preventive Measures:

- Disable remote services if not in use.
- Disable Bluetooth services if not in use.
- Limit access to unreliable websites (i.e. porn sites).
- Limit clicking on links provided by colleagues; instead, type the full address into the link bar.

Prevention for Mobile Users (Ismail, 2018):

- Apps should only be installed from trusted application stores.
- Check the permissions of the application being downloaded to see if the permissions are appropriate for the use of the application.
- Try as much as possible not to jailbreak iOS platforms

c) Advanced Prevention

Multiple research studies online have given suggestions for different approaches that bigger companies can use in preventing ransomware attacks. A few of the most effective advanced prevention techniques are (Zetter, 2016):

- Key back-up
- Process monitoring on Android platforms
- Using a connection monitor and connection breaker
- Honeypot techniques

Ways to Recover from Ransomware Attacks

An incomplete ransom attack is when the user gets to know that there is a possible ransomware attack due to appearances of .KRAB and/or GDCB-DECRYPT.txt files but the files are not yet encrypted. In order to recover from an incomplete ransom attack, the user is advised to automatically run the anti-virus application, which will do a virus scan of the system. It is also suggested that all devices infected with the ransomware should be disconnected from the network to protect cloud based or external back-up files (Brewer, 2016).

It is much harder to recover from a **successful** ransom attack. Organisations and researchers always ask a common question: **To Pay or NOT To Pay?** There is a good reason why researchers and organisations ask the question and it all has to do with the rate of success of file recovery and the eradication of the ransomware. Even when the ransom has been paid and the files decrypted, the user can never be sure that there are no more residual files from the ransomware left in the system (Brewer, 2016). The ransomware residual files can actually hide in mailboxes or directories without the user knowing and these files can be triggered at any time that the user is logged in to the computer. If the user opts to pay for the ransom, as previously stated, the ransomware **should** delete itself and hostage files should be returned without any alterations. The article (Brewer, 2016) finally suggests that buying a newer device is wiser especially if files are backed up online since this would help reduce the likelihood that the ransomware developer will produce more ransomware applications.

5.7. Conclusion

Although ransomwares are ranked as only the sixth most prominent malware in most cyber crime reports, ransomware is still a deadly malware. This is due to the fact that ransomware has the capability to do damage by means of infecting a user's device and encrypting either all the files or the whole device. The damage will only stop when the victim has paid the ransom, and in most cases, the length of time given for the victim to pay the ransom is limited. If the deadline passes, multiple research studies have suggested that the victim would then be obliged to pay double the original ransom price. Multiple research studies also suggest that despite the victim being able to pay the ransom price, there is no guarantee of his files being returned and/or the ransomware being eradicated completely from the system.

Most of the prominent ransomwares such as WannaCry, CryptoLocker, TeslaCrypt, SimpleLocker, GandCrab, Petya and NotPetya use RSA 2048-bit encryption for the public key and AES 256-bit encryption to encrypt the victim's data. Ransomware's most prominent feature aside from encryption is the command and control feature which actually gave birth to a new type of malware. This step made Kaspersky predict that the new trend for 2018 is for a shift from ransomwares to ***cryptomining*** to occur. Cryptomining is a term that describes an attacker's use of better ransomware.

Human Involvement

Human involvement in an attack is key since ransomware as a simple hard-coded software is **useless.** Ransomware cannot spread and infect devices **on its own.** Human involvement actually gives life to ransomware and the way ransomware infects devices. Humans create the ransomware software and humans spread the virus. As previously stated, most acquisitions of ransomwares occur due to a human falling for the spam email trick set by hackers. Social engineering, which was previously discussed, also plays a vital part since social engineers use psychology to achieve illegal ends. Humans are also responsible for activating the malware since most ransomware activation happens when .exe files disguised as PDF or Word files are executed. Cyber criminals are also responsible for the encryption of files inside the victim's device. Finally, once the trap is set, humans are also responsible for choosing whether **to pay** or **not to pay.**

Human empowerment, along with the proper dissemination of information, is key, as it is important for the public to know what ransomwares are and how to fight the attacks. With proper education about this topic, humans can actually reduce the likelihood of these types of cyber attacks by means of early-stage prevention. Finally, ransomware attacks can only be prevented if the **humans** in the computing environment are willing to critically educate themselves about the digital advancements in different computing industries.

References

1. Abrams, L. (2018, 3 July). *GandCrab V4 Released With the New .KRAB Extension for Encrypted Files* [Online]. Available at: https://www.bleepingcomputer.com/news/security/gandcrab-v4-released-with-the-new-krab-extension-for-encrypted-files/ (Accessed: 11 October 2018).
2. Ali, A. (2017). Ransomware: A Research and a Personal Case Study of Dealing With This Nasty Malware. *Information Science Institute,* **14**(1), pp. 87–99.
3. Avast. (2018). *Adware* [Online]. Available at: https://www.avast.com/c-adware (Accessed: 2 October 2018).
4. BBC. (2017, 27 October). *NHS 'Could Have Prevented' WannaCry Ransomware Attack.* London: BBC.
5. BBC. (2017, 11 January). *Ukraine Power Cut 'Was Cyber-Attack'.* London: BBC.
6. BBC. (2018, 20 September). *Arran Brewery Hit by Ransomware Attack.* Scotland: BBC Scotland.
7. Brewer, R. (2016). Ransomware Attacks: Detection, Prevention and Cure. *Network Security,* **2016**(9), pp. 5–9.
8. Budd, C. (2016, 20 July). *Ransomware Infects the Cloud: What You Need to Know* [Online]. Available at: https://blog.trendmicro.com/ransomware-infects-the-cloud-what-you-need-to-know/ (Accessed: 11 October 2018).

9. Cannell, J. (2013, 8 October, last updated 21 February 2018). *Cryptolocker Ransomware: What You Need to Know* [Online]. Available at: https://blog.malwarebytes.com/101/2013/10/cryptolocker-ransomware-what-you-need-to-know/ (Accessed: 11 October 2018).
10. Carbon Black. (2018). *Advance Your Ransomware Defences: An Enterprise Guide to Hardening Your Endpoints Against Future Ransomware Attacks.* Waltham, MA, USA: Carbon Black.
11. Cimpanu, C. (2018, 24 September). *Pennsylvania Senate Democrats Paid $700,000 to Recover From Ransomware Attack* [Online]. Available at: https://www.zdnet.com/article/pennsylvania-senate-democrats-paid-700000-to-recover-from-ransomware-attack/ . (Accessed: October 2018).
12. Cisco. (2018). *What Is Malware?*[Online] Available at: https://www.cisco.com/c/en/us/products/security/advanced-malware-protection/what-is-malware.html (Accessed: 2 October 2018).
13. Cisco Talos. (2018). *Email and Spam Data* [Online]. Available at: https://www.talosintelligence.com/reputation_center/email_rep. (Accessed: October 2018).
14. Cobb, S. (2017). *RoT: Ransomware of Things* [Online]. Available at: https://cdn1.esetstatic.com/ESET/US/Newsroom/2017/03/ESET_Trends-and-Prediction_2017_Ransomware.pdf (Accessed: 11 October 2018).
15. Cylance. (2018). *2017 Threat Report* [Online]. Available at: https://www.cylance.com/content/dam/cylance/pdfs/reports/CylanceThreatReport2017.pdf . (Accessed: September 2018).
16. Deloitte. (2016). *Ransomware Holding Your Data Hostage.* London: Deloitte Threat Intelligence and Analytics.
17. Emsisoft. (2018). *Spotlight on Ransomware: Ransomware Encryption Methods* [Online]. Available at: https://blog.emsisoft.com/en/27649/ransomware-encryption-methods/ (Accessed: 9 October 2018).
18. Esset. (2018). *Viruses, Malware and Remote Attacks Defined* [Online]. Available at: https://support.eset.com/kb186/ (Accessed: 2 October 2018)
19. Fruhlinger, J. (2017, 17 October). *Petya Ransomware and NotPetya Malware: What You need to Know Now* [Online]. Available at: https://www.csoonline.com/article/3233210/ransomware/petya-ransomware-and-notpetya-malware-what-you-need-to-know-now.html (Accessed: 11 October 2018).
20. Fruhlinger, J. (2017, 1 August). *The 5 Biggest Ransomware Attacks of the Last 5 Years* [Online]. (CSO) Available at: https://www.csoonline.com/

article/3212260/ransomware/the-5-biggest-ransomware-attacks-of-the-last-5-years.html (Accessed: 11 October 2018).
21. Fruhlinger, J. (2018, 30 August). *What is WannaCry Ransomware, How Does it Infect, and Who was Responsible?* [Online] Available at: https://www.csoonline.com/article/3227906/ransomware/what-is-wannacry-ransomware-how-does-it-infect-and-who-was-responsible.html (Accessed: 11 October 2018).
22. Gallegos-Segovia, P., Bravo-Torres, J., Larios-Rosillo, V., Vintimilla-Tapia, P., Yuquilima-Albarado, I. and Jara-Saltos, J. (2017). *Social Engineering as an Attack Vector for Ransomware.* Pucon, Chile: IEEE.
23. Gibbs, S. (2017, 3 August). *WannaCry: Hackers Withdraw £108,000 of Bitcoin Ransom* [Online]. Available at: https://www.theguardian.com/technology/2017/aug/03/wannacry-hackers-withdraw-108000-pounds-bitcoin-ransom (Accessed: 11 October 2018).
24. IBM. (2016). *IBM X-Force Threat Intelligence Index.* Armonk, NY, USA: IBM.
25. Ismail, N. (2017, 21 December). *Ransomware of IoT Will Become a New Security Nightmare in 2018* [Online]. Available at: https://www.information-age.com/ransomware-iot-new-security-nightmare-123470151/ (Accessed: 11 October 2018).
26. Kaspersky. (2018). *History of Malicious Programs* [Online]. Available at: https://encyclopedia.kaspersky.com/knowledge/history-of-malicious-programs/ (Accessed: 29 September 2018).
27. Kaspersky. (2018). *TeslaCrypt Ransomware Attacks* [Online]. Available at: https://www.kaspersky.co.uk/resource-center/threats/teslacrypt (Accessed: 11 October 2018).
28. Kaspersky. (2018). *Types of Malware* [Online]. Available at: https://www.kaspersky.co.uk/resource-center/threats/malware-classifications (Accessed: 2 October 2018).
29. Kaspersky Lab. (2016). *KSN Report: PC Ransomware in 2014–2016.* Woburn, MA, USA: Kaspersky Lab.
30. Kidron, M. (2017, 22 February). *LogicLocker Brings Ransomware to SCADA Networks* [Online]. Available at: https://blog.skyboxsecurity.com/logiclocker-brings-ransomware-to-scada-networks/ (Accessed: 11 October 2018).
31. Koller, M. S. (2016, 20 May). *TeslaCrypt Ransomware Developers Retire, Release Master Decryption Key* [Online]. Available at: https://www.dataprivacymonitor.com/cybersecurity/teslacrypt-ransomware-developers-retire-release-master-decryption-key/ (Accessed: 11 October 2018).

32. Lindskog, D. and Zavarskya, M. P. (2016). Experimental Analysis of Ransomware on Windows and Android Platforms: Evolution and Characterization. *Procedia Computer Science,* **2016**(94), pp. 465–472.
33. Malwarebytes Labs. (2016). *Ransomware Dominates the Threat Landscape*[Online]. Available at: https://blog.malwarebytes.com/cybercrime/2016/06/ransomware-dominates-the-threat-landscape/ (Accessed: 8 October 2018).
34. Mann, I. (2008). *Hacking the Human: Social Engineering Techniques and Security Countermeasures* (1st ed.). London, UK: Routledge.
35. Martin, J. A. (2017, 14 July). *Who is a Target for Ransomware Attacks?* [Online] Available at: https://www.csoonline.com/article/3208111/security/who-is-a-target-for-ransomware-attacks.html (Accessed: 11 October 2018).
36. McAfee. (2017). *McAfee Labs Threat Report.* Santa Clara, CA, USA: McAfee.
37. Merriam-Webster. (2018). *Ransom* [Online]. Available at: https://www.merriam-webster.com/dictionary/ransom (Accessed: 6 October 2018).
38. Monrose, F., Jang, J., Hu, X., Wang, T., Taylor, T. and Stoecklin, M. (2015). *USA Patent No. US9723016B2.*
39. NDTV. (2017, 16 May). *ATMs Closed Due to WannaCry Ransomware? Experts Debunk WhatsApp Hoaxes* [Online]. Available at: https://gadgets.ndtv.com/internet/news/atm-closed-india-cyber-attack-whatsapp-wanna-cry-rumours-1694207 (Accessed: 11 October 2018).
40. NJCCIC. (2016, 5 July). *Simplelocker* [Online]. Available at: https://www.cyber.nj.gov/threat-profiles/ransomware-variants/simplelocker (Accessed: 11 October 2018).
41. NJCCIC. (2018, 31 January). *GandCrab* [Online]. Available at: https://www.cyber.nj.gov/threat-profiles/ransomware-variants/gandcrab (Accessed: 10 October 2018).
42. Norton. (2018). *Malware 101: How Do I Get Malware? Simple Attacks* [Online]. Available at: https://us.norton.com/internetsecurity-malware-malware-101-how-do-i-get-malware-simple-attacks.html (Accessed: 9 October 2018).
43. Norton. (2018). *New Variant of Android Ransomware Takes Advantage of the Lockscreen's User Interface* [Online]. Available at: https://us.norton.com/internetsecurity-emerging-threats-new-variant-of-android-ransomware-takes-advantage-of-the-lockscreen-user-interface.html (Accessed: 11 October 2018).
44. O'Brien, D. (2017). *ISTR: Internet Security Threat Report — Ransomware 2017.* Mountain View, CA, USA: Symantec.

45. Osborne, C. (2018, 1 May). *Healthcare Was a Top Target for Ransomware Families in 2017* [Online]. Available at: https://www.zdnet.com/article/ransomware-operators-select-the-healthcare-industry-as-a-top-target/ (Accessed: 11 October 2018).
46. Osborne, C. (2018). *Meet Ransomware Which Wears the Face of Former President Barack Obama* [Online]. Available at: https://www.zdnet.com/article/meet-ransomware-which-wears-the-face-of-former-president-barack-obama/. (Accessed: October 2018).
47. P. S. Foundation. (2012). *Regular Expression Operations* [Online]. Available at: https://docs.python.org/3.1/lbrary/re.html. (Accessed: November 2018).
48. Rajpal, M. S. and Kotov, V. (2014). *Understanding Crypto-Ransomware: In-Depth Analysis of the Most Popular Malware Families.* Cupertino, CA, USA: Bromium.
49. Richet, J.-L. (2016). Extortion on the Internet: The Rise of Crypto-Ransomware. *Harvard Researches*, **2**(1), pp. 2–6.
50. Savage, K., Coogan, P. and Lau, H. (2015, 6 August). The Evolution of Ransomware. Mountain View, CA, USA: Symantec.
51. SC Magazine. (2017). *Malware and the "Other" Platforms: Mac and Android Devices are Increasingly at Risk* [Online]. Available at: https://media.scmagazine.com/documents/314/malware_and_the_"other"_platfo_78268.pdf (Accessed: 11 October 2018).
52. Securonix Threat Research Team. (2018). *Grandcrab Ransomware Attack.* Addison, Texas, USA: Securonix .
53. Sneed, A. (2016). *The Most Vulnerable Ransomware Targets Are the Institutions We Rely On Most.* New York, NY, USA: Scientific American.
54. Snow, J. (2016, 29 June). *Ransomware on Mobile Devices: Knock-Knock-Block.* Available at: https://www.kaspersky.com/blog/mobile-ransomware-2016/12491/(Accessed: 11 October 2018).
55. Soni, V. (2018). *Multifunctional Malware Becoming Extensive in 2018, Finds Kaspersky Lab Report.* Available at: https://www.dailyhostnews.com/multifunctional-malware-becoming-extensive/ (Accessed: 2 October 2018).
56. Stavrou, A., Rhandi, M., Ghosh, A., Jajodia, S. and Andrianakis, C. (2010, 9 April). *USA Patent No. US8935773B2.*
57. Tasril, V., Ginting, M., Mardiana and Siahaan, A. (2017). Threats of Computer System and its Prevention. *IJSRST*, **3**(6), pp. 448–451.
58. Touchette, F. (2016). The Evolution of Malware. *Network Security*, **1**(1), pp. 11–14.

59. Turpin, S. and Harmsworth, S. (2001, July). *Creating an Effective Dissemination Strategy: An Expanded Interactive Workbook for Educational Development Projects* [Online]. Available at: https://ajpp-online.org/resources/downloads/06-CreatingAnEffectiveDisseminationStrategy-AnExpandedWorkbook.pdf (Accessed: 12 October 2018).
60. Walker, J. (2018). *Ransomware Remains Biggest Malware Threat in 2018, Says Europol* [Online]. Available at: https://portswigger.net/daily-swig/ransomware-remains-biggest-malware-threat-in-2018-says-europol (Accessed: 6 October 2018).
61. Walton, A. G. (2017, 11 December). *Phone Addiction Is Real — And So Are Its Mental Health Risks* [Online]. Available at: https://www.forbes.com/sites/alicegwalton/2017/12/11/phone-addiction-is-real-and-so-are-its-mental-health-risks/#527d531813df (Accessed: 11 October 2018).
62. Young, A. L. and Yung, M. (2017). Privacy and Security Cryptovirology: The Birth, Neglect, and Explosion of Ransomware. *Communications of the ACM*, **60**(7), pp. 24–26.
63. Zetter, K. (2016). *Inside The Cunning, Unprecedented Hack of Ukraine's Power Grid*. London, UK: Wired.

Chapter 6

Protecting and Securing Data Through Blockchain Across Industries

Stefan Kendzierskyj* and Hamid Jahankhani†

Northumbria University London, UK
**stefan.kendzierskyj@northumbria.ac.uk*
†Hamid.jahankhani@northumbria.ac.uk

ABSTRACT

Blockchain is being viewed as a mechanism that can further protect and enhance the security of data due to its properties of immutability, auditability and encryption, whilst providing transparency between parties who may not know each other and who therefore are operating in a trustless environment. It's true that blockchain has its roots in cryptocurrency applications and is still evolving for that purpose in the financial sector, but many other organisations across different industries are beginning to see the non-crypto use cases in which this mechanism can be used to record data that cannot be changed or reversed or as smart contracts (as a way to time-stamp transactions between parties). Consequently, blockchain is becoming extremely relevant and purposeful. Organisations have various options. They can run blockchain as permissionless (anyone can join), permissioned (invitations are required) or hybrid (like a consortium). They can also choose whether data should be held on-chain or off-chain in data lakes. With industry entering its fourth industrial revolution (Industry 4.0), the addition of blockchain as a complementary technology has its place; there are some industries very suited to the significant impact it may bring. Also, the advances made in areas such as Internet of Things and Machine Learning and Artificial Intelligence may have considerable impact on the amount of data we collect for analysis and the ways in which we store, manage and analyse it. They may also increase the likelihood of cyber attacks and the ripple effects they cause. This has also become complicated, as cyber attacks have become much more sophisticated in recent years. Cyber attacks come in different configurations, and various industry sectors have suffered from a range of these different attack vectors, resulting in some devastating outcomes. These cyber attacks have manifested in the shape of ransomware, malware, manipulation methods, phishing and spear-phishing. Whilst data breaches are a serious incident, there is a growing concern in most organisations regarding attacks that are designed to have a more destructive effect, such as the Ukraine cyber attack in 2015 that resulted in a shutdown of the power grid, or the WannaCry ransomware attack in 2017 that caused widespread chaos with healthcare institutions unable to carry out any tasks since access to data/systems was unavailable.

Keywords: blockchain, Industry 4.0, smart contracts, cyber attacks, IoT, AI, ML, WannaCry, immutability, auditability

6.1. Introduction

With the fast-growing development of cloud-based architecture, smart technology such as Internet of Things (IoT) and many other new developments of Artificial Intelligence (AI) and Machine Learning (ML) have caused a large increase in data volumes and more complexities to arise during the process of finding a more secure and efficient way to handle and manage the data. This is heightened by the increasing cyber attacks and the wide range of attack vectors. Cyber attacks have become a lucrative and more organised criminal behaviour with the availability of ransomware-as-a-service, as an example. It's becoming apparent that even with attention to the various business structures and methods to mitigate cyber security risks, such as continual review of policies/compliance, training, patching, deploying Intrusion Detection and Prevention Systems (IDPS), etc., the cyber security breach effect has not been lessened. In fact, more diverse types of cyber attacks are increasing and growing year on year at a faster and faster rate, particularly in the healthcare industry. Attacks on the healthcare industry account for more than 50% of all cyber attacks. From an organisational perspective, there are of course many advantages to having access to modern software and system developments, and to living in a 'data on demand' culture. Organisations will benefit in many ways, particularly with the more recent developments in Artificial Intelligence and Machine Learning. However, there is a feeling that data usage and access to data are not very strictly controlled. There are also concerns over the possible impact this may have. For instance, it may lead to criminal activity such as identity theft and victimisation.

With these points in mind, there is a growing motivation for industry to look at the benefits blockchain can offer in the shape of providing another layer of security and privacy to the organisation's data and allowing the option to control data permission and use. This can provide an added layer of security which can work in harmony with the traditional cloud security systems and allow for a more secure and transparent way to handle data. The synergy between cloud and blockchain might be useful, especially as putting all data on the blockchain may place too heavy a burden on the blockchain in terms of processing, performance and scalability. Also, one must take into account the requirement of GDPR that those whose data have been collected by the organization must have the right of erasure. This prohibits the storage of personal data on a blockchain level. It might be useful in some cases to handle data off-chain and use blockchain as an immutable mechanism to capture details in chronological order and to authenticate access to data held off-chain in data lakes.

6.2. What Is Blockchain?

Blockchain is said to be one of the most disruptive computing paradigms after the Internet (Swan, 2015). The technology has advanced such that it is now more than just a means of financial and economic trading. Recently, different arms of industry have started to harness the technology to take advantage of its benefits and the many ways it can be applied.

The concept of blockchain was first circulated as a white paper (Satoshi, 2008), and created under the pseudonym Satoshin Nakamoto. As it was originally developed for use with a cryptocurrency (Bitcoin), blockchain is often referred to as Blockchain 1.0 when it is used with cryptocurrencies (Swan, 2015, p. ix). Blockchain 2.0 refers to the blockchain technology underlying smart contracts which go beyond just cash transactions, and Blockchain 3.0 describes blockchain technology which can be used in healthcare, government, intellectual property, etc. The healthcare industry is a good example of an industry in which issues surrounding privacy, security and access collide. It is also under pressure in several different directions, as there is a growing global demand for medical services as the elderly population grows and the number of elderly patients increases, an increase in the amount of data to be stored, an increase in data breaches, and so on. Blockchain adoption in the healthcare community is becoming widely accepted, as some surveys by leading industry providers indicate.

A recent survey (carried out by the IBM Institute for Business Value in 2017) of 200 healthcare executives (a mix of payers and providers across 16 countries) found that 16% were expecting a blockchain solution for healthcare to be deployed soon. This survey suggests that the percentage of healthcare executives who expected a blockchain solution to be deployed in their industry in 2017 is much higher than the percentage of executives from other sectors such as banking/finance and commerce who expected a blockchain solution to be deployed in their industry in 2017. This is despite the fact that blockchain methodology has been established in these sectors longer than it has been established in healthcare. Figure 6.1 describes the early adopters in the healthcare industry as 'trailblazers' and compares

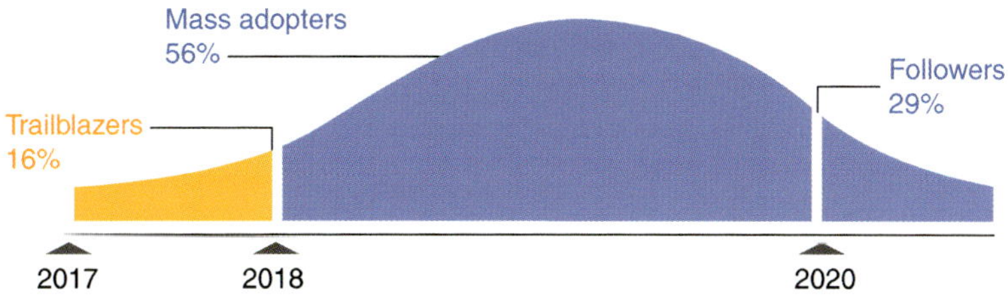

Fig. 6.1. Confidence with early adopters (IBM Institute of Business value, 2017).

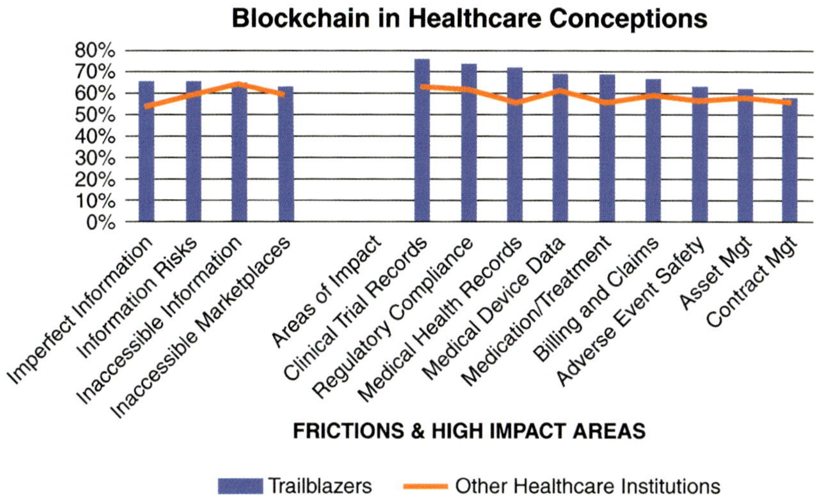

Fig. 6.2. Survey of 200 healthcare executives; source a mix of two data sets (IBM Institute of Business value, 2017).

them to other healthcare institutions. It also serves as a timeline of how the healthcare industry will react to adoption.

To understand the use cases, it is necessary to analyse the healthcare sector and how the development of electronic records has not improved the interoperability between different devices. Essentially, the electronic data is sitting in silos. The IBM survey (Fig. 6.2) shows the friction areas around inaccessible information (that is, the interoperability and security/privacy concerns regarding data). Both leading trailblazers and other healthcare institutions mostly agree that these friction areas exist. Also, both trailblazers and other

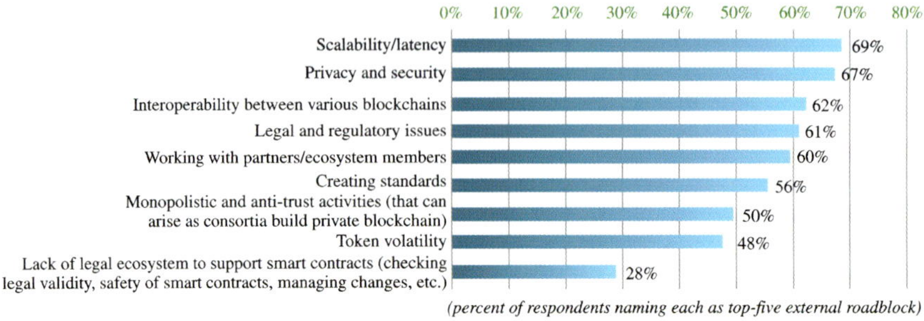

Fig. 6.3. Survey of 558 respondents proficient with blockchain in healthcare (Cognizant, 2017).

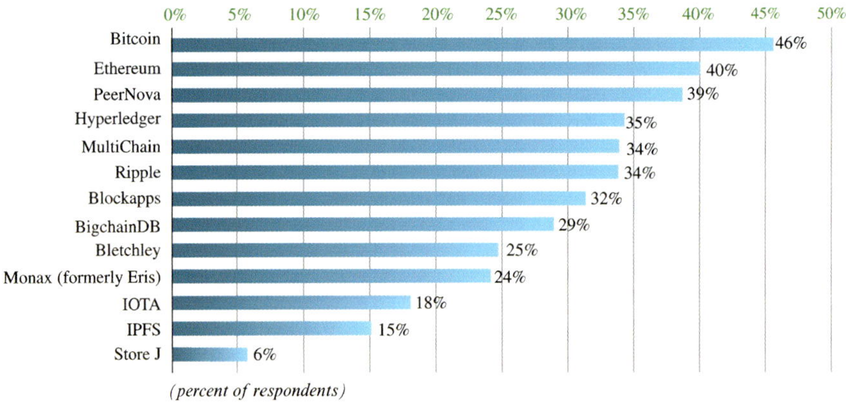

Fig. 6.4. Types of blockchain under evaluation in healthcare (Cognizant, 2017).

healthcare institutions agree that the top three impact areas are clinical trial records, medical health records and regulatory compliance.

Figure 6.3, a global survey of 558 respondents carried out by Cognizant (2017), shows a similar outlook with regards to issues of privacy, security, interoperability and regulation.

Figure 6.4 displays mostly the types of blockchain under consideration for use in healthcare, as an example.

6.2.1. *Blockchain overview: How does it work?*

Blockchain technology has allowed records to be 'shared by all network nodes, updated by miners, monitored by everyone, and owned and controlled by no one' (Swan, 2015, p.1).

Blockchain is based on a decentralised system — a distributed ledger database where identical copies of a sequential inventory of transactions are shared and maintained by numerous individuals over network nodes. Its qualities include being tamperproof, being immutable and being maintained by multiple parties through the use of a timestamped audit trail. The timestamp links to the previous record and is never removed, so becoming immutable. Cryptography is the key to the security used to link the chain of records. Multiple parties hold the consensus on the data and its validity rather than one individual (hence blockchain technology is decentralised; see Fig. 6.5 for an illustration). The exact

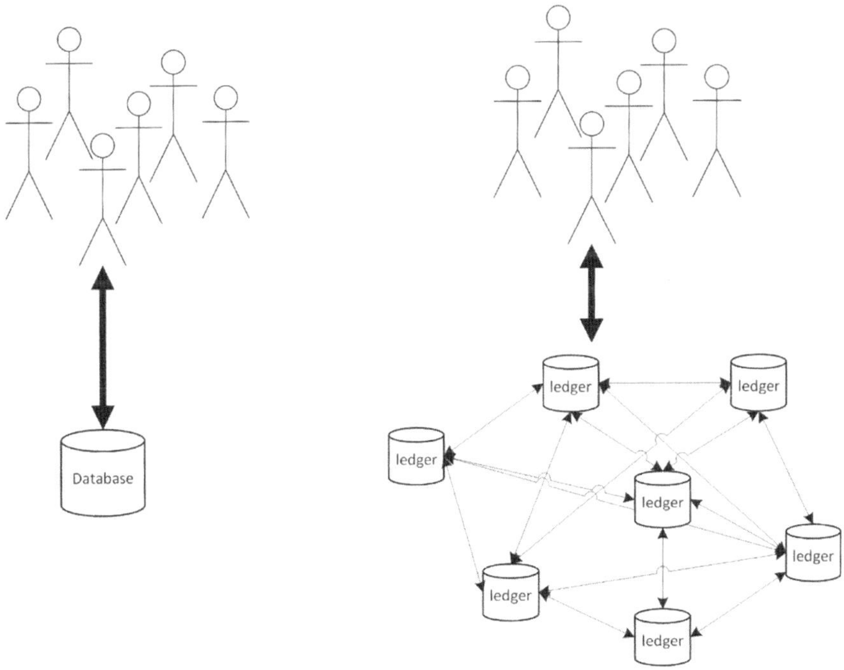

Fig. 6.5. Shift from central databases to distributed ledgers for information sharing (Ølnes *et al.*, 2017).

procedure depends on the type of blockchain, but miners, or persons who validate the new transactions, mostly follow the same general steps to reach a consensus. Miners will try to solve a cryptographic puzzle for each block of transactions by matching a hash (randomly generated numbers and letters) to its target. The miner who solves the puzzle broadcasts to the network. This is validated by other miners, who approve and add copy to the first miner's node. This method is usually referred to as 'proof of work'. If this were, for example, the Ethereum blockchain, then the miner would be awarded ether (a form of coin to support or power the Ethereum network). The hash value can be controlled by the network, so, if it takes too long to solve the puzzle (more than the usual 14 seconds on Ethereum), adjustments are made to the computational puzzle. However, a large amount of computing power is required so a potential miner should evaluate the likely profitability of bitcoin mining before investing in the necessary equipment. The hash value is used to encrypt the contents of the block of transactions.

In addition, when each transaction is made, a pair of keys is generated: a public key which can be accessed by all and a private key for the originator of the transaction. Only those with the private key can gain access to their cryptocurrency and authorise transactions. Also, one must rely on one's private key to decrypt a message authorising a transaction.

Cryptography also offers a protection against attack, since more than 51% of the blockchain network would need to be compromised for a successful attack to occur. Engelhardt (2017) summarizes this immutability, which is a key component of blockchain. As he says, each block in the chain contains exact information on the creation of the block, the cryptographic signature in the preceding block in the chain and the transaction data being recorded in the block. The signature — a hash which is a unique record identifier — has a cryptographic sequence of a particular length and is alphanumeric. This signature uniquely determines the digital entity. This is how one can identify if the blockchain has been compromised by someone changing a previous record — there would be a break in the chain. Records cannot be removed, only added. This must be done with the approval of all the miners, who must reach consensus. This is one way in which blockchain technologies have difficulty complying with GDPR's mandate that all users should have the 'right to be forgotten'. If the information associated with a transaction is immutable, it cannot be forgotten.

Auditability is another important aspect of the blockchain as transparency allows all stakeholders to see the data. Auditability might also help improve the transparency of clinical research data, as discussed in this research study. When new transactions take place between parties, they are broadcast to the network for all to see and the network miners will verify them. It's this collective verification that will only allow new blocks to be added. This is how the 'trustless' method works. It does not rely on a single entity to be the only authority to verify transactions, as with the centralised models. For various sectors of industry (Blockchain version 3.0), having additional data requirements such as smart contracts and flexibility in regulation makes sense, as this increases the trust people have in data.

6.2.2. *Public and private blockchains*

As there are different types of blockchain, the stakeholders need to decide who can enter a particular blockchain community. Each industry needs to be matched with the blockchain methods that are best suited to them. These methods can be either permissioned or permissionless. Understanding these two types of blockchain will help organisations decide what type of blockchain technology should be deployed for a particular data set and how they should allow permissions/authentication.

Permissionless Blockchains: Also referred to as public blockchains, these blockchains allow anyone to participate with no restrictions on the reading/submitting of transactions. Examples of these are Bitcoin and Ethereum. On the other hand, entry to public permissioned blockchains is restricted, but anyone can read/submit transactions.

Permissioned Blockchains: These private blockchains will restrict access to the network and control who may enter it. Transactions can only be validated by those recognised as authenticated on the ledger. Access to private permissioned blockchains is usually totally restricted. Examples of such blockchains include Bluemix by IBM or Rubix by Deloitte.

Consortium Blockchains: Approved entities validate transactions. A business ecosystem would find this type of blockchain more suitable since all parties have a say in deciding which data workflow process should be included, etc.

6.2.3. *Blockchain data storage*

A white paper that was selected as one of the winning papers from more than 70 submissions sent in for an ONC ideation challenge entitled The Use of Blockchain in Health IT and Health-Related Research (Deloitte, 2016) advises organisations on how they should evaluate the technical and confidentiality constraints of blockchain technology and how best to execute a particular model of blockchain technology depending on the type of data collected, the people who need access to that data, and how sensitive that data is. A compromise between speed/scalabilty and security may need to be made as storing large amounts of data off-chain presents potential difficulties with slow processing speeds and scaling. Security, however, is higher (Deloitte, 2016). The other option is providing encrypted links which direct a user to a separate centralised database when activated by the private key. It is also possible to store some standard data sets directly on the blockchain (this is beneficial for immediate permissioned access) and to otherwise rely on off-chain data links where appropriate.

For transaction purposes, blockchain can store data as two methods. These are summarized as follows:

On-chain: Data is stored on the blockchain structure. The advantage here is that the data would be immediately visible. However, storage size can be an issue and this method could prove to be much costlier than the other should file sizes become large. This method would generally be used for more standardised data in summary format.

Off-chain: This would suit larger data sets. In addition, data of any format can be stored, even data such as medical details, X-Ray images, MRI scans, etc. The access links are saved on blockchain and act as authenticated indicators to data stored in other centralised networks/databases. However, more integration and blended technology may be required if data is to be stored off-chain in data lakes. For instance, good management is required to ensure there is no data decay on the blockchain. Presumably though this is more likely to be a permissioned type blockchain and so management and governance would form part of the methodology.

6.2.4. *Benefits of blockchain*

Surveys mentioned earlier in this chapter indicate heavy support for blockchain in most industries. This is due to severe problems associated with interoperability, security, data integrity, and privacy issues in centralised networks, as well as other challenges faced by the users of these networks. As more people begin believing that blockchain will be part of their business in one shape or form, a few industry-leading white papers have emerged that voice a similar message.

The IBM Global Business Unit (2016) white paper, which was consulted by the government during their market research, states that 'blockchain promises to put privacy and control of data back in the hands of citizens'. Blockchain might also be a good way to save costs. Costs in healthcare, for example, have risen dramatically over the years, and for some countries the rising costs herald a crisis. Over the last 10 years there has been a 60% increase in health expenditure (The World Bank, 2015). This is compounded with the issue of an aging population in developed countries. In the healthcare sector, blockchain is looked upon as the technology that can provide a solution by making possible the re-use of huge masses of anonymised healthcare data for clinical research. It not only protects the privacy of patients, but removes expensive middle layers and escrow services, thus connecting all stakeholders without great expense (Engelhardt, 2017).

Another interesting benefit of blockchain is that, due to the nature of its decentralisation, it may offer better protection against certain types of cyber attacks, such as the WannaCry ransomware attacks in 2017. In order for such an attack to succeed, a blockchain would need to be simultaneously attacked by numerous sites (Mattei, 2017). It is important that users are better protected as there has been a recent rise in identity theft attacks by malicious outsiders. The data showing this is provided and analysed later in this chapter.

The section below gives similar use cases across many industry sectors. Healthcare is referenced in places as a specific industry example due to the many possible applications of blockchain within the health industry.

Interoperability, transparency and longitudinal healthcare records — The data collected by an organisation is often trapped in data silos, and therefore not integrated. This can make it difficult to analyse and places restrictions on how it can be used. Ideally, there should be interoperability between the different systems in which different data sets are stored. In addition, those in charge of each system should be held accountable for how the data within that system is collected, stored and used. Other issues in this category include the limited control an individual has over their data, and the occurrence of data breaches which might result in data loss, or perhaps even identity theft. Blockchain technology can help by eliminating data silos and providing a more coherent and seamlessly integrated data model. Access to the data would be controlled through cryptographic methods, but all the relevant parties would be allowed access. These changes could lead to innovations such as longitudinal healthcare records for patients, which could be analysed to improve health outcomes.

Privacy and Security — Confidentiality, integrity, availability and authenticity (CIAA) are four information security concepts that should ideally be adhered to when data is being dealt with. In reality, internal issues such as accidental data loss, and issues caused by external vectors such as targeted malicious behaviour for the purpose of identity and data theft, are widespread. As previously mentioned, industry is trying to tackle this by carrying out the day-to-day actions that will help mitigate risk and continually learning new methods to keep data secure. Blockchain can help by providing an additional layer of security with the use of encryption. The use of a decentralised and distributed ledger system would increase the integrity of the data. Data encryption, as well as more complex permission settings, will provide good controls for a securely authenticated data exchange.

Time stamping and chronological ordering — If records and data are held in silos, there is more chance of corruption, fraud, the abuse of traceability and so on. One of the benefits blockchain can offer is its undeniable immutability. Even if blockchain is used only for authentication, perhaps to allow data to be stored in a 'data lake' (a centralised data storage solution which can be created in the cloud), the fingerprints associated with this type of activity would be time-stamped and kept in chronological order (as with smart contracts). No one would be able to tamper with the records. Depending on the type of blockchain, parties can then make use of smart contracts to help provide greater efficiency and integration.

Procurement and Contract Process — Using the properties of blockchain that make it suitable for use in smart contracts will help relieve a lot of the complex processes, negotiations and supply chain issues currently faced. This will be done by streamlining the process to promote efficiency and reduce cost. It will then be possible to provide automated supplier contracts and analytics to maximise productivity and control.

6.2.5. *Potential security issues and limitations on blockchain*

Whilst support behind blockchain technology is growing, and whilst the benefits of blockchain technology to both clients and industry are becoming better known, one must not overlook the risk factors associated with blockchain technology. By knowing these risks and carrying out further research alongside blockchain use, one can contribute to the formation and development of alternative procedures that may make blockchain deployment safer or mitigate its risks.

Quantum Computing — It has been much debated whether quantum computing poses a future threat to cryptography. In order to do so, quantum computing would need to be large and reliable so that it can perform millions of quantum bits (qubits) to break current cryptographic algorithms (Aumasson, 2017). As Aumasson mentions, it's not yet known if quantum computing is scalable or fault-tolerant and general consensus believes it is not able to break current cryptographic algorithms yet. But it is good to know that cryptographers are looking at post-quantum cryptography (as the back-up plan for future-proofing).

Irretrievable Data — Blockchain data access will be facilitated with a key. This use of private key security will allow a user to control their own data, but if the key is lost, data will become irretrievable. However, solutions can be put in place. It is possible to introduce a 'back door' concept, but that potentially may replace one issue with another (Engelhardt, 2017).

Scalability and Performance — Further investigations must be carried out on the different types of blockchain and script execution. For example, the average transaction time on the Ethereum blockchain is approximately 14 seconds, while the average transaction time of Bitcoin is 10 minutes. It's well known in cryptography that speed and security have an inverse effect on each other. Time is required to achieve consensus over the blockchain network, and to do the computation needed to verify a transaction. This will probably not be a show stopper, however. Over time, technology will improve and so too will speed and computation time.

Malicious Attacks — Xu (2016) researched attacks (both malicious attacks and fraud) that one can be exposed to while using blockchain technology. He comments upon these attacks and recommends defensive and preventative measures.

Google DeepMind Scenarios — The Google DeepMind project is an example of the mismanagement of data. In that particular case, patient data was recorded through an app. In order for the app to be created, the NHS allowed Google to access large amounts of sensitive medical information, not only from users of the app, but from the records of nearly 1.6 million NHS patients. Controversially, it was claimed that 'implied consent' had been given for the information to be released. This seems to suggest a lack of transparency and has muddied privacy and security concerns.

6.3. Threats to Mission Critical Data: Vulnerabilities and Cyber Attacks

The previous section in this chapter gave a formalised appraisal of how blockchain works, including its methods and key attributes. This section highlights the increasing number of vulnerabilities and the increasing scale of various types of cyber attacks, in order that the complexity of these attacks and the extent of the devastation caused can be understood. A high percentage of cyber attacks occur because a malicious outsider attempts to commit identity theft. There can be many types of malicious outsiders, ranging from users of low level malware-for-hire to hacktivists to state-sponsored attackers.

For example, the 2015 cyber attack on Ukraine's power grid was initiated through phishing attacks, but it took six months for the cyber attackers to gather the security credentials they needed to compromise the SCADA network before the main thrust of the attack took place. Whilst 27 power distribution centres were knocked out of operation, the attack was made stronger by creating interference and inundating the call centres supporting the 225,000 customers that were affected with call traffic. During these chaotic types of attacks and potentially even during the build-up to the attacks, cyber attackers may be accessing core mission-critical data. This type of theft is masked by the chaotic nature of events. In essence, this also helps strengthen the case for blockchain, since it's clear there are good use cases for blockchain technology that can be applied to various industries. However, there should also be another layer of security that offers protection to mission-critical data, since it is likely that cyber attackers will attempt to breach it. At least then if a cyber attack is successful, the core data remains uncontaminated.

It has now become extremely important that every business should have a set of key information governance policies so that they can retain control of and ensure the safety of assets and information. It is also hoped that this will improve user confidence in how the assets are stored, protected and processed. Information governance is also an important part of an organisation's structure as it tells the Executive Board what the risk treatment plan should be. The risk treatment plan should match the business risk appetite. There are valuable benefits to managing risk in this way.

There are also various frameworks that contain good practices that an organisation can use to deliver IT service management such as ITIL. These frameworks complement policies like ISO 27001 or CMMi. They help in training staff, improving the quality of IT services and provide a backbone to help monitor risk and improvements. This is all designed to assist in identifying vulnerabilities and taking note of lessons learned so that everything about how the current landscape is changing can be documented. Based on this information, new strategies can be developed and followed. There are different types of cyber attacks and a wide range of cyber attacks within each type, and this variety can lead to a multitude of issues both with regard to the organisations affected by ransomware and the users of services provided by those organisations. The possible consequences are unknown, but it is likely that the users' data will be compromised in some way, as a cyber breach generally leads to a data breach. This is where the problems begin for the client.

Organisations can bring forth technical countermeasures to tighten security against attacks and highlight user awareness through education but all this still does not provide protection to the client once the cyber attack succeeds and data is taken. The awareness through education is needed to lessen the chance for an attack to succeed, but there is more thought being given to using blockchain as another added layer of security to protect the data. The data need not necessarily be held on-chain (as it can be stored off-chain) but the access and authentication would be initiated through blockchain and all fingerprint information would be stored on blockchain with all the attributes mentioned in earlier sections.

6.3.1. *Ransomware*

What is Ransomware?

There has been a significant increase in the volume and diversity of ransomware attacks over the last two years (see Fig. 6.6 for growth details). Attack formations have become more complicated, and the perpetrators of ransomware have progressed from script kiddies to crime-for-hire (ransomware-as-a-service) and sophisticated hackers. As Parent and Cushack (2016) mention, 'a new layer cake in cybercrime' has arisen. However, attack success relies on the victim acting as the catalyst to initiate the chain of events.

Ransomware is sophisticated and malicious software that blocks the victim's access to their files or that threatens to publish or make

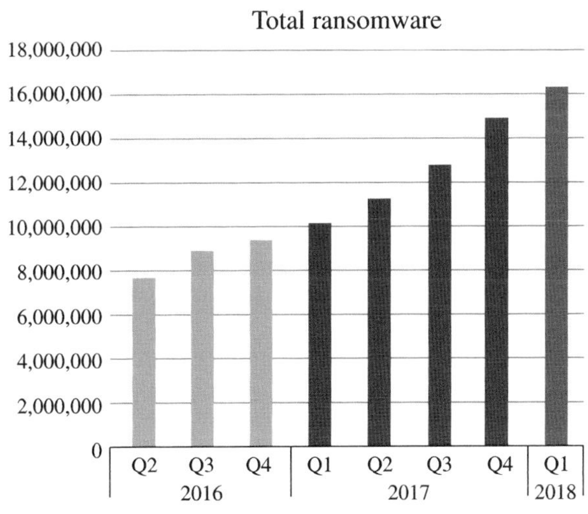

Fig. 6.6. Ransomware increases (McAfee Labs, 2018).

available the victim's data (based on cryptovirology). What usually happens next is the request for a ransom to be paid so that the victim can access their files again. Over the last five years the extent and complexity of ransomware has increased, and some organisations have taken to paying the ransoms through digital currencies such as Bitcoin. The victim dilemma is there is no sure way to know after paying a ransom whether the attacker will release the decryption key. There are some victims that have paid the ransom and were successful in accessing the data once again. Others have paid but the cyber attackers did not release the decryption keys. Yet others paid and received the decryption keys but they did not work. There is always the possibility as well that after the organisation pays the initial ransom, the cyber criminals may continue to ask for additional ransom.

Without doubt, attacks are on the increase. Just three years ago, GCHQ and the Ministry of Defence warned the government of a serious cyber attack and suggested that the National Cyber Security Centre (NCSC) was a step in the right direction (Hutchins, 2017). In this newspaper article (Hutchins, 2017), General Sir Richard Barrons also mentions that the NCSC is not as powerful or as integrated as the US Cybercom model.

How does Ransomware work?

The intrusions made by ransomware are usually carried out using a Trojan (to the user this seems a legitimate file but is the disguised malware). This can occur due to a vulnerability in the network or because the user opened the file (often as an email attachment). The attackers rely on the curiosity in human nature which often leads us to click on a link without thinking of the consequences, even when we are unsure of whom the sender is. This causes the payload to run a program that then either locks the system or appears to lock it (Scareware program). The consequences for the user depend upon the type of payload downloaded by the ransomware. The level of sophistication of the attack depends on the attacker's capabilities but there are many 'malware programs' for hire on the dark web (Tor/similar network) so even a moderately skilled attacker can cause a massive impact on single or multiple organisations. These malware businesses selling cryptovirology tools are collectively known as 'ransomware-as-a-service', as noted by Young and Yung (2017). The payloads can vary from simple applications that appear with fake warnings to top-end programs using strong encryption such that the only way to deactivate the malware is with the attacker's decryption key (cryptoviral). Young and Yung (2017) describe the explosion of cryptovirology and how formidable a threat it is, with victims that include individuals, hospitals, police precincts, universities, transportation systems and government offices making daily news.

How is it spread?

Social engineering is the key skill used by attackers to spread ransomware, as they know it is easy to trick a user into opening a malicious email attachment. The attackers use many ingenious ways to disguise the malware as fake PDF/Word files. The issue is that the victim may not know the sender of the email or the fake company but as the email is made to appear official, often will click the email attachment. Other methods include tricking the victim to confirm, for example, an online order. There may be ways the attacker can convince the victim to run an embedded program. As an example of the speed with which malware can spread, the WannaCry ransomware attack began on 12 May 2017 and in just a day had infected 230,000 computers in over 150 countries. This is covered in the article *Strategic Comments* (2017).

How can we prevent Ransomware?

With the increase in ransomware, various individuals and organisations have offered focused guidance on how to respond to incidents/ attacks. McGoogan (2017) lists a number of core rules to follow in the Telegraph newspaper shortly after the WannaCry attack. There are quite a few basic rules that will stop most attacks occurring and some that will make paying the ransomware unnecessary. It has become evident that ransomware appears to be the most profitable malware and that the amount of ransomware will not decrease soon

(Cisco, 2016). Organisations are starting to understand the risks and to take proactive measures such as those recommended by Kaspersky Lab and Intel Security. They have given advice on how to avoid attacks and on what to do if attacked. They have also shared actual known decryption keys with the public (No More Ransom, 2017).

The following are generally recommended for most organisations:

File backups — This should be part of any Business Continuity Plan (BCP) and set of Disaster Recovery (DR) procedures so that in case of an attack, if the system is taken down, at least the system can be recovered to the point before the attack.

Emails, attachments and websites — As part of their IT Policy, organisations will have guidelines which advise staff not to open any emails or attachments from unknown or suspicious senders. This can also be part of training/awareness programs. Alert reminders can also be created to warn staff. These alert reminders could be triggered when staff members log on to the system.

Patching and installing updates — This is a critical aspect of attack prevention that is the responsibility of the Information and Communications Technology (ICT) department. Patch vulnerability was one of the reasons that some of the NHS locations were exposed to WannaCry.

Incident Response Team and Preparation — For example, there should be Service Improvement Plans and tasks concerning fast identification and mitigation allocated to specific team members. The core incident team should practice their response to the situation like they do with BCP and DRP scenarios, but the scenarios should be specific to ransomware attacks.

Non-payment of ransom — Admittedly, this is easier said than done, as there will be great pressure on the victim to pay the ransom in order to retrieve the data. It is advisable not to pay the ransom as it is not guaranteed that the decipher process will be released. It may also lead to more requests for ransom or more concerted attacks.

Regular Training — This is vital. As Arndt (2017) mentions, "organizations that phish-exercise their staff at least four to eight times a year have dramatically better awareness than organizations that don't do it or that do it just once or twice a year."

The most complex part to contain or control in handling cyber security risks is the human element. No matter what amount of training or what training programme is used in organisations to heighten awareness of attacks made by malicious outsiders, it seems evident that social engineering attacks such as phishing will still increase due to human curiosity. Intrusion Detection and Prevention Systems (IDPSs) will help, but instead one could add an extra layer of security through blockchain. This would allow high value data (sensitive or personal data) to be protected so that even if attacks have succeeded there are other hurdles that require defeating encryption to overcome before a data breach occurs.

6.3.2. *Social engineering: Phishing and spear-phishing*

Phishing and spear-phishing techniques often contribute to the success of ransomware. As ransomware became sophisticated, so too has social engineering. Phishing has been around for some time and until users stop clicking on email from unknown senders or enabling programs in attachments, the attackers will still continue to succeed. In 2016, phishing attacks rose by 65% compared to in 2015, as mentioned by Sharma (2017), and are set to increase further again, with organisations more in the sights of the attackers than individuals. Social media may bring many benefits, but it also offers attackers a wealth of additional information that gives rise to more sophisticated phishing methods and increases the likelihood of a victim opening an infected email/program. Steer (2017) notes the existence of a more dangerous threat known as spear-phishing, where the email is targeted at specific individual employees. Attackers now search social media to make an email look convincingly genuine to mask the tracks of the ransomware. This 'familiarity' of appearance to a user makes this method a very dangerous entry point. The even newer dangers of malvertising include malwares that no longer require users to 'click' links to activate them.

Manipulation Methods: It is interesting to see the evolution/development of new attack methods, but successful entry to the victim's system relies on methods like phishing or spear-phishing that are activated because victims do not easily change their behavioural patterns. There are some more manipulative means of entry; attackers can use sub-domains, hidden URLs (links hidden under plain text), misspelt URLs (bought domains that look similar to the real site e.g. google.com) and IDN homograph attacks.

Script-Based Malware: A McAfee (2017) lab report indicates a rise in malware scripting techniques. JavaScript, VBScript, PHP, Powershell, etc, are used to distribute ransomware, and in some cases, are even used in the ransomware (e.g. Nemucod ransomware uses PHP and JavaScript). Attackers take this route because doing so allows them to evade detection. This is the reason why this newer technique has seen a sharp rise over the last two years (McAfee, 2017).

Internet of Things (IoT): Yaqoob *et al.* (2017) discuss how there are expected to be 26 billion sensors and IoT devices by 2020. These will be deployed across wearable devices, connected smart homes, cars, health, utility, etc. On the one hand, it is a great technological advancement, but as Yaqoob *et al.* (2017) have discovered, over 70% of IoT devices are vulnerable to attacks. With the growth of ransomware it is inevitable that IoT offers a vast surface attack area: see Fig. 6.7 as per Yaqoob *et al.* (2017). It is important that confidentiality, integrity and availability (CIA) should be preserved in tandem with technological advancement. Safe ways to protect IoT from malware should take priority.

Botnets and other IoT issues: Yaqoob *et al.* (2017) state that ransomware can also be penetrated using botnets inside IoT networks. These botnets are usually activated through phishing and may compromise the whole IoT network. The research goes on to say that attackers can inject ransomware-as-a-service into the cloud and the ransomware may appear as a 'legitimate service' to the user. More research shows the extent of the potential issues with IoT. Some possible attacks include thermostat hacking (turning the temperature up), Flocker ransomware (which locks the smart TV with malware embedded in a fake movie) and Android Simplocker (which affects

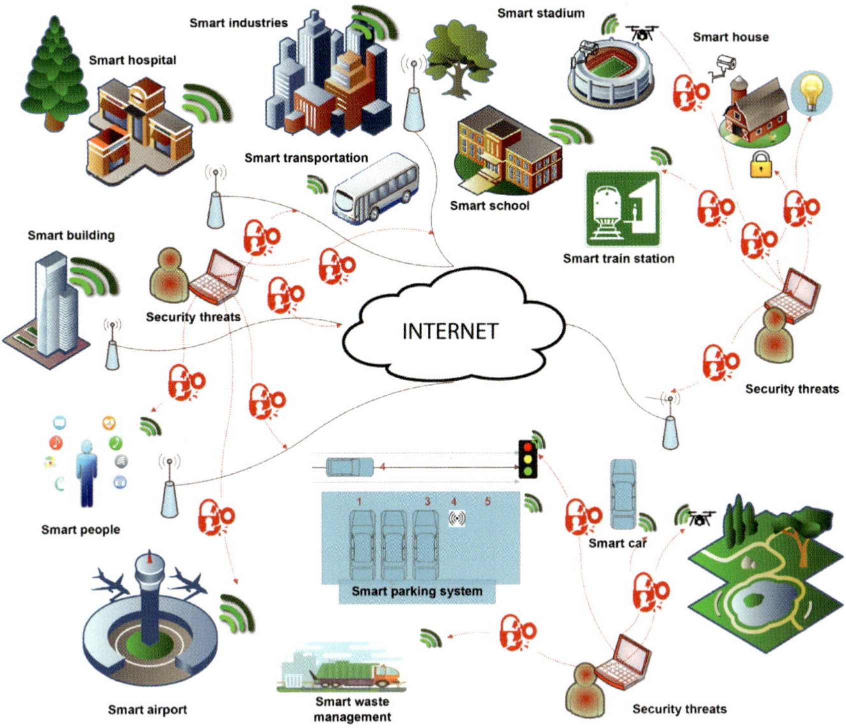

Fig. 6.7. Security concerns in IoT (Yaqoob *et al.*, 2017).

Android wearable devices). There have also been some tests on the practicality of ransomware used to attack smart bulbs.

Malvertising and Ransomware: There has been a sharp increase in the use of malvertising to propagate malware, specifically ransomware (RiskIQ Research, 2017). This new type of technique threatens the benefits from digital marketing many organisations have legitimately enjoyed. Now, users may block ads for fear that they have become attack vectors for deploying malware. Users need not even click on the malicious ads and can be infected just by visiting the website. This is in itself a new technique that provides infection without user interaction (e.g. the Astrum exploit using a vulnerability in Flash). Palmer (2017) reported that a few UK Universities were hit with this ransomware, but it is very hard to consolidate the extent of the attacks as many education and government-type organisations resist openly discussing attacks made on them for fear of negative publicity.

Future Type of Ransomware Attacks: Future ransomware attacks may come in new forms. For instance, Mansfield-Devine (2016) suggests that ransomware distributed through mobile devices and the cloud will become increasingly common. This can be quite a concern since a user can upload an infected file to the cloud and unknowingly disperse it to the rest of the community (as users might assume it's a legitimate 'safe' service to download). Also, more and more enterprises are seeking cloud- and SaaS-based models, believing them to be safer than on-premise models, even if this may not be the case. This is why a more thorough analysis of cloud security needs to be carried out. Educating humans not to click on unauthorised links or to be vigilant in checking the source of a link before clicking on it will be an ongoing process, and it still will not solve the problem of how to control data access and storage, or, in the event of a cyber breach, how to give the malicious attackers more hurdles to overcome by adding layers of security such as blockchain and encryption. Also, with blockchain there has been further research on using artificial intelligence (AI) to detect malicious outsider attacks and the patterns associated with them. This adds further levels of security so that the blockchain stays protected.

6.4. Cyber Breaches and Client Data Theft Concerns

It has already been highlighted that industry is under pressure from cyber threats which may result in data theft. Table 6.1 (breachlevelindex.com, 2018) shows the number of data breaches in each industry sector. Healthcare leads with the greatest number of breaches due to the value of the data. The data report and other extended reports on the site are provided by Gemalto, an organisation that collates and aggregates information about worldwide data breaches in various industries and that proactively monitors

Table 6.1. Cyber security breaches 2017 industry comparison (breachlevelindex.com, 2018).

Industry	2013	2014	2015	2016	2017
Healthcare	346	449	451	531	471
Financial Services	166	213	276	241	219
Retail	97	197	240	247	199
Education	36	174	166	166	199
Government	196	293	299	289	193
Technology	112	140	124	203	130
Professional Services	—	1	1	1	92
Other Industries	263	275	316	160	68
Industrial	—	—	—	32	60
Entertainment	—	—	5	31	46
Hospitality	1	1	2	35	36
Insurance	—	—	2	15	22
Non-Profit	—	—	—	28	21
Social Media	—	1	2	2	9
TOTALS	1,217	1,743	1,883	1,981	1,765

source: BREACHLEVELINDEX.COM

reports of data breaches worldwide through breachlevelindex.com. It can be assumed that the data collected is high-quality quantitative data. In their other reports, Gemalto measure a breach in terms of the data records lost/stolen, the type of breach, the source of the breach, how far the breach has affected the industry sectors in question and the risk factor of the breach. They have developed a scoring system to measure the risk factor of the breach, which is as follows:

1 – 2.9 (minimal)
3 – 4.9 (moderate)
5 – 6.9 (critical)
7 – 8.9 (severe)
9 – 10 (catastrophic)

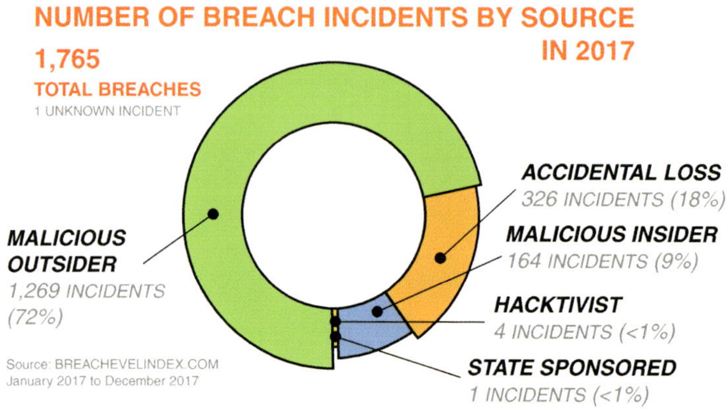

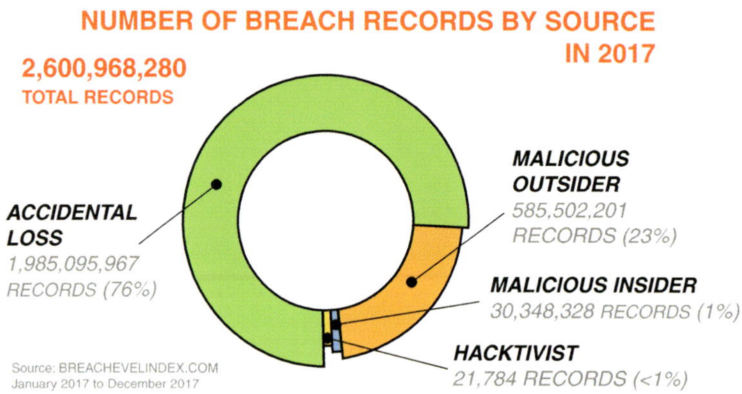

Fig. 6.8. Data taken from the breachlevelindex.com site.

BREACH SOURCE	2013	2014	2015	2016	2017
Malicious Outsider	2,081,285,434	674,544,208	274,762,361	1,057,189,069	585,502,201
Accidental Loss	15,068,756	309,823,689	265,209,847	292,246,026	1,985,095,967
Malicious Insider	10,371,810	185,738,742	64,791,635	13,963,040	30,348,328
Hacktivist	875,946	8,182,103	30,573,822	12,371,864	21,784
State Sponsored	165,053	509,928,563	108,076,636	10,797,581	0
Unknown	77,525	1,307	591	950,000	0
TOTALS	2,107,844,524	1,688,218,612	743,414,892	1,387,517,580	2,600,968,280

Fig. 6.9. Comparison showing the extent of the types of breaches (breachlevelindex.com, 2018).

6.4.1. *Cyber breach analysis*

Cyber-attack vectors can be categorised in the following way, which helps us define the type of breach and the source of the breach (breachlevelindex.com, 2018):

Type of Breach:

- Identity Theft
- Nuisance
- Account Access
- Existential Data
- Financial Access
- Financial Loss

Source of Breach:

- Accidental Loss
- Malicious Insider
- Malicious Outsider
- Hacktivist/State Espionage

From the Breachlevelindex analysis shown in Figs. 6.8 and 6.9, two factors stand out, that is, that the greatest number of records are lost due to accidental loss and that malicious outsiders committing identity theft have the next biggest impact. From these trends it seems that better training should be given to help mitigate the accidental loss and reduce the number of records lost. Staff members should also be vigilant to prevent malicious outsiders from committing identity theft. The Breachlevelindex analysis also discovered that there were fewer data breaches in which encryption was used.

6.4.2. *Deep web impacts to the client*

It is extremely unpleasant for a victim to discover that criminals have access to their identities and can use them to commit crimes because the organisation they have shared their data with has been breached by a malicious attacker. At least with GDPR in place, the authorities must be notified of data breaches within 72 hours or a penalty will be imposed. The consequences are worse when identity theft has occurred. A stolen credit card can be cancelled if the theft is discovered in time by the victim, but one's identity cannot be changed. It is possible to steal someone's identity with the aid of medical records accessed through an attack on a healthcare organisation. Medical records hold valuable data points that map a person's identity. If the data breach goes unannounced or is announced too late, the attacker might have enough time to plan how best to use the stolen data.

The large-scale WannaCry ransomware attack (BBC news, 2017) highlights the dangers of a large-scale data breach. In one of these, no one really knows how far the identity theft will go. On the deep web, the value of medical data is said to be ten times that of stolen credit card numbers (Sulleyman, 2017) and if big data sets are available they can go for large sums of money. As a result, it can be very lucrative to attack the healthcare industry. There likely is a much larger adverse effect on those that suffered from identity theft and criminal victimisation because of the data breach, as identity theft is a deep violation of the patient's privacy. The loss of data surrounding one's identity is of course a problem, but so too can be having one's sensitive medical history (e.g. HIV information) made public. Therefore the impact is far deeper and greater on the victim than a loss of credit card details would have been.

6.5. Is Blockchain the Answer Industry is Looking for Regarding Securing Data?

Many worldwide have considered how blockchain may fit into industry environments and into a number of different use cases. It is certain that a new technology such as blockchain has both risks and benefits, but more individuals and organisations are adopting and accepting the use of blockchain. This is probably because this technology provides a much better service than is otherwise available to its users and the organisations using it, whilst also offering higher levels of security. When we look at various industry sectors, it is possible to quickly understand these drivers, and also how blockchain facilitates securing data privacy.

- **Healthcare:** The healthcare industry suffers the most cyber attacks, and this is reason enough to find a way to better protect the core data. It is a well-known fact that healthcare data is worth 10 times the value of financial credit card data when offered by criminals on the dark net. In 2018, millions of records were breached, and consequently, more people have become aware of the impact of identity theft. Also, although medical records are now kept in electronic rather than in paper form, the main issue is that currently records are still mostly stored in silo environments. This causes major inefficiencies for providers and patients, and makes it difficult for a seamless healthcare data interchange to occur. If blockchain is applied, longitudinal medical histories can be generated from the data that used to be in various silos. Blockchain also puts the patient in control of their data, and also allows them to control who has access to it. Blockchain can also be used to store other types of sensitive data that are increasing in volume e.g. WBAN (wireless body area network) data that collects medical data through sensors and automatically syncs with storage systems. Since these storage systems contain sensitive data they are again of attraction to cyber attackers and so a great deal of attention needs to be paid to security.

  Another use case is drug traceability. As it stands, counterfeit drugs are estimated to account for 50% of all drugs in low-income countries, with a global market range of $200 billion (DrugPatentWatch, 2017). Counterfeit drugs may not cure the patient, or may kill them. Blockchain allows the creation of a supply chain in which one can record all transactions without anyone being able to tamper with the records. The result is a transparent method to secure the chain of custody and data.

- **Supply Chain:** In the world of manufacturing and logistics, there are no longer small networks or groups of organisations. Instead, there are large and wide ecosystems comprised of multiple parties, from those processing raw materials to manufacturers to wholesalers and distributors. Each entity has to manage its processes, data and systems. Again, interoperability is important here if one is to avoid having islands of data, or duplicating the data. Blockchain can help all the parties record data so that they have a permanent record of every transaction that is immutable. Products would be traceable and tracking through the chain of custody would be ensured. In the case of the food industry, keeping records of products and tracing them to their source is essential (Marr, 2018). An example is Walmart, which uses blockchain to keep track of its pork sourced from China. Among the types of data stored are the sources of the meat, where it's processed and stored, and its expiry date. In another example, De Beers utilises Blockchain for auditability and in order to track diamonds from the point where they are mined to the point where they are sold to consumers. They use their record as proof of their ethics and of the non-contamination of the diamonds they sell with conflict diamonds. Consequently, consumers are certain they are ethical and genuine (Marr, 2018). Smart contracts can also be deployed as part of the blockchain structure so that time-stamping can be used and payments or penalties can be triggered after transactions are recorded.

- **Identity Management:** With the world we live in as it is, online transactions that leave a digital footprint are unavoidable. Online transactions generally require that personal or financial details must be disclosed. The more online transactions one conducts, the more databases the information is stored on. Typically, the information will be cloned and might end up on numerous other databases (Pinto, 2018). The information in these datasets is accessed by other third party providers who in turn clone these datasets, usually without the owner of the data knowing. This takes ownership and control away from the individual concerned. Blockchain can give individuals the ability to deploy encrypted digital identities, making multiple passwords and identification names unnecessary. Estonia is one of the few countries that has adopted blockchain as an infrastructure to power the Estonia ID card that has replaced a number of other cards covering services such as (Thomson Reuters, 2018):

  - legal travel ID for Estonian citizens travelling within the EU
  - national health insurance
  - proof of identification when logging into bank accounts

- digital signatures
- i-Voting
- checking medical records, submit tax claims, etc.
- using e-Prescriptions

— **Critical National Infrastructure (CNI):** Critical National Infrastructure (CNI) can be the physical or virtual systems, assets, facilities, processes and networks that are needed for a country to operate. Cyber attacks on critical infrastructure are increasing in velocity and are caused by advanced threat actors (CERT-UK, 2016). The threat to CNI is very real as there have been a number of successful attacks over recent years. The computer systems underpinning CNI that, for example, hold sensitive data in healthcare facilities or Industrial Control Systems (ICS), or that operate, control and monitor physical structures such as nuclear power plants, electricity grids, and railway networks, may have a number of vulnerabilities that cyber attackers are drawn to (Logsdon, 2016). The Ukraine power grid attacks and WannaCry were explained earlier in the chapter, and it's possible these large-scale devastating attacks that leave systems in chaos have more sinister reasons for their occurrence than data theft. Currently there is research looking at how blockchain can support the cyber physical systems so that blockchain-distributed data storage, IoT sensing technology and cloud-based delivery systems work together harmoniously (Dong *et al.*, 2018).

— **Financial Aid Tracking and Transparency:** Blockchain is being used in the tracking of foreign aid as one of the biggest challenges here is transparency. The issue is that as the chain of custody passes through various middlemen (this is what generally happens before international aid is received by a particular country) the tracking of the distribution of funds becomes difficult (Hjønnevåg, 2018). The immutability, tracking and auditability of blockchain can minimize fraudulent activity. For example, there is no need for cash to exchange hands in the Zaatari refugee camp as the World Food Program uses biometric technology as well as blockchain technology. A retinal scanner controls the provision of food, and every refugee's identity is digitally stored in a biometric database. The point of sale verifies the buyer's identity through the retinal scanner. The sale is recorded on the World Food Program blockchain so that it can be tracked, and to acknowledge that the account has been settled. Greater accountability will allow us to raise funds more easily as one of the concerns of fund raising is that fraudulent activity will take place and funds will be misused. Blockchain technology will therefore improve the welfare of those who need it most.

— **Insurance and Claims Adjudication:** Insurance and claims organisations face fragmented IT systems and data held in silos. These often create inefficiencies, delays, higher than necessary costs and fraudulent activity. Data volumes are increasing, especially with the large amounts of data being generated by IoT that make it necessary to sift through large datasets. Through blockchain, the verification of claims/payments data from third parties can be automated, and insurance companies can easily verify transactions. As a result, the records will show only one version of the truth (Cummings, 2018). The security of blockchain can provide assurance that there is no duplication of data and smart contracts ensure a better customer engagement cycle.

— **Intellectual Property and Media:** Intellectual Property (IP) has faced many challenges, especially with the availability of digitalised content which can be shared with minimal hassle through avenues like the Internet. The cost of software piracy in the US in 2015 was reported at over $9 billion (manufacuring.net, 2016). If IP rights are registered with blockchain technology (in the case of patents, for example), it will be much easier to verify who owns them. Any infringement can be challenged, and doubts can be counteracted by the use of smart contracts in which terms of engagement are set out.

6.6. Conclusions

The benefits of blockchain look to be clear and straightforward; blockchain technology can help to secure and protect data in many industry sectors. The defined properties of blockchain include the enhanced security due to encryption, the immutability that prevents any tampering, the auditability which depends on the use of chronological time-stamping/smart contracts and the transparency that allows precise tracking. In this chapter, the importance of securing data, especially in the sectors under heavy cyber attack such as the healthcare or energy sector, was discussed.

If we consider blockchain a mechanism which works in harmony with other technologies then it has the potential to offer an additional layer of security to protect mission-critical data. This could be deployed in harmony with the practices of rolling out policies/compliance, training, keeping patching up to date, IDPS and so on. These are to further protect the privacy of an individual's data and enhance the security through methods of encryption which provide that added layer of security should traditional methods break down due to sophisticated cyber attacks and targeted methods used to obtain data and commit identity theft. Also, with the recent emergence of IoT and the value-add it brings to many organisations, it is important to consider how the huge increase in data should be handled and kept secure. The billions of additional smart wearable devices in use today may contain sensitive data on individuals which should be protected by a combination of traditional security methods and blockchain.

Blockchain security is itself interesting. More research in machine learning and algorithms may also help in protecting blockchain as machine learning and algorithms can detect intrusions from and recognise patterns in data collected through behavioural monitoring and profiling (Xu, 2016). This will help strengthen the defences against malicious attackers and prevent them from succeeding if the method is recognised by AI. The wider adoption of blockchain will also help protect users against malicious activity as more effort will be expanded on developing prevention systems. Certainly, blockchain has many applications, and can be made to work in synergy with traditional cyber security mechanisms. For the time being, blockchain is a formidable and strong security option. It is a useful mechanism which can provide support in many industries which collect sensitive and personal data, particularly in industry sectors which are most vulnerable to cyber attack.

References

1. Arndt, R. (2017). Frequent Employee Training Helps Stave Off Ransomware. *Modern Healthcare,* **47**(23), pp. 16–18.
2. Aumasson, J. (2017). The Impact of Quantum Computing on Cryptography. *Computer Fraud and Security,* **2017**(6), pp. 8–11. doi: 10.1016/S1361-3723(17)30051-9.
3. BBC News. (2017). *NHS 'Could Have Prevented' WannaCry Ransomware Attack* [Online]. Available at: http://www.bbc.co.uk/news/technology-41753022 (Accessed: 7 May 2018).
4. Breachlevelindex. (2018). *Data Breach Database* [Online]. Available at: https://breachlevelindex.com/data-breach-database# (Accessed: 3 June 2018).
5. CERT-UK. (2016). *Annual Report 2015/16* [Online]. Available at: https://www.ncsc.gov.uk/content/files/protected_files/report_files/CERT-UK-Annual-Report-2015-16.pdf (Accessed: 22 January 2019).
6. Cisco. (2016). *Midyear Cybersecurity Report* [Online]. Available at: https://www.cisco.com/c/dam/m/en_ca/never-better/assets/files/midyear-security-report-2016.pdf (Accessed: 20 April 2018).
7. Cognizant. (2017). *Healthcare: Blockchain's Curative Potential for Healthcare Efficiency and Quality* [Online]. Available at: https://www.cognizant.com/whitepapers/healthcare-blockchains-curative-potential-for-healthcare-efficiency-and-quality-codex2995.pdf (Accessed: 6 August 2018).
8. Cummings, R. (2018). *How Blockchain is Disrupting the Insurance Industry for the Better* [Online]. Available at: https://www.cio.com/article/3301163/blockchain/how-blockchain-is-disrupting-the-insurance-industry-for-the-better.html (Accessed: 22 January 2019).
9. Deloitte. (2016). *Blockchain: Opportunities for Health Care* [Online]. Available at: https://www2.deloitte.com/content/dam/Deloitte/us/Documents/public-sector/us-blockchain-opportunities-for-health-care.pdf (Accessed: 3 August 2018).
10. Dong, Z., Lou, F. and Liang, G. (2018). Blockchain: A Secure, Decentralized, Trusted Cyber Infrastructure Solution for Future Energy Systems. *Journal of Modern Power Systems and Clean Energy,* **6**(5), pp. 958–967. doi: https://doi.org/10.1007/s40565-018-0418-0
11. DrugPatentWatch. (2017). *Can Blockchain Technology Put an End to Counterfeit Drugs* [Online]. Available at: https://medium.com/drugpatentwatch/can-blockchain-technology-put-an-end-to-counterfeit-drugs-c4087e652fe0 (Accessed: 30 May 2018).

12. Engelhardt, M. (2017). Hitching Healthcare to the Chain: An Introduction to Blockchain Technology in the Healthcare Sector. *Technology Innovation Management Review*, **7**(10), pp. 22–34. doi: http://doi.org/10.22215/timreview/1111
13. Hjønnevåg, J. (2018). *How Blockchain is Revolutionising Foreign Aid Delivery* [Online]. Available at: https://hackernoon.com/how-blockchain-is-revolutionizing-foreign-aid-delivery-7674de0beb21 (Accessed: 22 January 2019).
14. Huchins, M. (2017, 16 May). Britain Knew the Risks, Says Ex-Military Chief. *The Times*, pp. 14–15.
15. IBM Global Business Services. (2016). *Blockchain: The Chain of Trust and Its Potential to Transform Healthcare* [Online]. Available at: https://www.healthit.gov/sites/default/files/8-31-blockchain-ibm_ideation-challenge_aug8.pdf (Accessed: 1 April 2018).
16. IBM Institute for Business Value. (2016). *Healthcare Rallies for Blockchains: Keeping Patients at the Center* [Online]. Available at: https://www-01.ibm.com/common/ssi/cgi-bin/ssialias?htmlfid=GBE03790USEN (Accessed 31 May 2018).
17. Logsdon, M. (2016). *Why Companies Using SCADA Systems Need to Wake Up to the Increased Threat of Cyber-Attacks* [Online]. Available at: https://www.scmagazineuk.com/why-companies-using-scada-systems-need-wake-increased-threat-cyber-attacks/article/1477598 (Accessed: 22 January 2019).
18. Mansfield-Devine, S. (2016). Ransomware: Taking Businesses Hostage. *Network Security*, **2016**(10), pp. 8–17. doi: https://doi.org/10.1016/S1353-4858(16)30096-4.
19. Manufacturing.net. (2016). *The Cost of Piracy Software* [Online]. Available at: https://www.manufacturing.net/data-focus/2016/07/cost-software-piracy (Accessed: 22 January 2019).
20. Marr, B. (2018). *How Blockchain Will Transform the Supply Chain and Logistics Industry* [Online]. Available at: https://www.forbes.com/sites/bernardmarr/2018/03/23/how-blockchain-will-transform-the-supply-chain-and-logistics-industry/ (Accessed: 22 January 2019).
21. Mattei, T. A. (2017). Privacy, Confidentiality, and Security of Health Care Information: Lessons From the Recent WannaCry Cyberattack. *World Neurosurgery*, **104**, pp. 972–974. doi: https://doi.org/10.1016/j.wneu.2017.06.104
22. McAfee. (2017). *McAfee Labs Threat Report* [Online]. Available at: https://www.mcafee.com/uk/resources/reports/rp-quarterly-threats-sept-2017.pdf (Accessed: 1 August 2018).

23. McGoogan, C. (2017, 16 May). *How to Protect Yourself From Ransomware* [Online]. Available at: http://www.telegraph.co.uk/technology/0/protect-ransomware/ (Accessed: 14 August 2017).
24. No More Ransom. (2017). *Unlocking Your Digital Life Without Paying Your Attackers* [Online]. Available at: https://www.nomoreransom.org/en/index.html (Accessed: 1 August 2018).
25. Ølnes, S., Ubacht, J. and Janssen, M. (2017). Blockchain in Government: Benefits and Implications of Distributed Ledger Technology for Information Sharing. *Government Information Quarterly*, **34**(3), pp. 355–364. doi: https://doi.org/10.1016/j.giq.2017.09.007.
26. Palmer, D. (2017). *This Malvertising Campaign Infected PCs With Ransomware Without Users Even Clicking a Link* [Online]. Available at: http://www.zdnet.com/article/this-malvertising-campaign-infected-pcs-with-ransomware-without-users-even-clicking-a-link/ (Accessed: 6 August 2018).
27. Parliamentary Office of Science and Technology. (2017). *Cyber Security of UK Infrastructure* [Online]. Available at: http://researchbriefings.files.parliament.uk/documents/POST-PN-0554/POST-PN-0554.pdf (Accessed: 6 August 2018).
28. Parent, M. and Cusack, B. (2016). Cybersecurity in 2016: People, Technology, and Processes. *Business Horizons*, **59**(6), pp. 567–569. doi: https://doi.org/10.1016/j.bushor.2016.08.005.
29. Pinto, R. (2018). *How Blockchain Can Solve Identity Management Problems* [Online]. Available at: https://www.forbes.com/sites/forbestechcouncil/2018/07/27/how-blockchain-can-solve-identity-management-problems/#1c63fa913f56 (Accessed: 22 January 2019).
30. RiskIQ Research. (2017). *Malvertising Rises 132% in 2016 Over 2015, Says RiskIQ Research* [Online]. Available at: http://www.businesswire.com/news/home/20170131005420/en/Malvertising-Rises-132-2016-2015-RiskIQ-Research (Accessed: 6 August 2018).
31. Satoshi, N. (2008). *Bitcoin: A Peer-to-Peer Electronic Cash System* [Online]. Available at: https://bitcoin.org/bitcoin.pdf. (Accessed: 6 August 2018).
32. Sharma, U. (2017). *Blockchain in Healthcare: Patient Benefits and More* [Online]. Available at: https://www.ibm.com/blogs/blockchain/2017/10/blockchain-in-healthcare-patient-benefits-and-more/ (Accessed: 25 July 2018).
33. Steer, S. (2017). Defending Against Spear-Phishing. *Computer Fraud and Security*, **2017**(8), pp. 18–20. doi: https://doi.org/10.1016/S1361-3723(17)30074-X.

34. Sulleyman, A. (2017, 12 May). *Medical Information Can Be Worth Ten Times More Than Credit Card Numbers on the Deep Web* [Online]. Available at: https://www.independent.co.uk/life-style/gadgets-and-tech/news/nhs-cyber-attack-medical-data-records-stolen-why-so-valuable-to-sell-financial-a7733171.html (Accessed: 27 June 2018).
35. Swan, M. (2015). *Blockchain: Blueprint for a New Economy*. Sebastopol, CA, USA: O'Reilly Media Inc.
36. The WannaCry Ransomware Attack. (2017). *Strategic Comments*, **23**(4), pp. vii–ix. doi: http://dx.doi.org/10.1080/13567888.2017.1335101.
37. Thomson Reuters. (2018). *e-Estonia: The Power and Potential of Digital Identity* [Online]. Available at: https://blogs.thomsonreuters.com/answerson/e-estonia-power-potential-digital-identity/ (Accessed: 22 January 2019).
38. World Bank. (2015). *World Development Indicators: Health Expenditure Per Capita (Current US$)* [Online]. Available at: https://data.worldbank.org/indicator/SH.XPD.PCAP (Accessed: 6 August 2018).
39. Xu, J. (2016). Are Blockchains Immune to All Malicious Attacks? *Financial Innovation*, **2**(1), p. 1. doi: https://doi.org/10.1186/s40854-016-0046-5.
40. Yaqoob, I. *et al.* (2017). The Rise of Ransomware and Emerging Security Challenges in the Internet of Things. *Computer Networks*, **129**(2), pp. 444–458. doi: https://doi.org/10.1016/j.comnet.2017.09.003.
41. Young, A. and Yung, M. (2017). Privacy and Security Cryptovirology: The Birth, Neglect, and Explosion of Ransomware. *Communications of the ACM*, **60**(7), pp. 24–26. doi: 10.1145/3097347

Chapter 7

Bring Your Own Device: GDPR Compliant or Headache? The Human Aspect in Security and Privacy

Jaime Ibarra Jimenez* and Hamid Jahankhani†

Northumbria University London, UK
**jaime.jimenez@northumbria.ac.uk*
†hamid.jahankhani@northumbria.ac.uk

ABSTRACT

The world is facing an era in which technology has a crucial impact on the growth of businesses. It is claimed that in 2020 20 billion devices will be connected to the internet, therefore, data is crucial for employees, customers and organisations. The implementation of the European General Data Protection Regulation (GDPR) gives the owner better control of their personal data. Consequently, organisations must be prepared to face cutting-edge threats to security in order to protect individuals against potential harm caused by unauthorized access to their data. Bring Your Own Device (BYOD) is a policy which provides some flexibility within organisations, and which results in better commitment in employees. This chapter analyses the impact of GDPR in BYOD architectures and proposes the integration of a multi-layer policy with an Information Governance Framework to ensure data privacy, focusing on the human factor when protecting personal devices.

Keywords: BYOD, GDPR, Blockchain, cyber security, mobile platforms, insider attack

7.1. Introduction

Since May of 2018, the European General Data Protection Regulation (GDPR) has been implemented, and organisations keep struggling to adapt their procedures and core functions to achieve regulatory compliance. A survey of over 1,000 companies in the UK, Germany, France, and Italy before its implementation discovered that 60% of these companies were not ready for GDPR, whilst 44% showed concern about whether their company could comply with it (Jltspecialty.com, 2018).

One of the biggest concerns for organisations currently is the BYOD policy. BYOD allows employees to bring their own devices to work and to use them for professional purposes. Most companies allow the use of personal devices within the premises because this saves money. Allowing users to purchase their own devices makes a simpler network infrastructure (commonly wireless-based) a possibility, reducing the stress of IT administrators regarding network and endpoint management (McKinney and Pickard, 2016). Employees feel more comfortable increasing the productivity of the organisation by having the most up-to-date mobile devices and are able to continue working outside of work hours. Years ago, organisations were adapted to the Use What You Are Told (UWYT) principle. Electronic devices were provided by the company and were also customized according to their requirements and organisational goals (Wainwright, 2018). However, nowadays the world is facing an era when "millennials" are modifying the business landscape by having their personal devices connected at any time and at any place. These days, students who are still in high school already have the most up-to-date mobile devices, which are linked to their social media accounts. Moreover, they say that they do not have any concerns about sharing their personal information on the Internet. However, this is worrying for security experts because of the risks associated with this mindset. Security experts aim to train people to reduce risks based on social engineering techniques that could compromise the organisation's productivity along with its prestige (Thomson, 2012). This is easily achieved in big organisations because they have the budget, governance frameworks, policies and controls to achieve compliance. However, this is not the case for SMEs, which often lack skilled cyber security personnel (McKinney and Pickard, 2016).

The BYOD policies implemented in most organisations are imprecise and immature in terms of security. This chapter analyses whether BYOD complies with the recently implemented GDPR, or whether it seems likely to cause trouble and concern for IT administrators and security experts, who need to ensure regulatory compliance. In addition, it shows the importance of the human factor when it comes to security and privacy. The rest of the chapter is divided as follows: Section 7.2 gives the reader a brief description of BYOD, along with the architecture commonly used in enterprise networks for personal devices, and the security concerns surrounding BYOD, Section 7.3 analyses the impact of GDPR on modern BYOD policies, Section 7.4 suggests practices and guidelines for achieving endpoint security in personal devices, Section 7.5 proposes a framework for the design, implementation and monitoring of a BYOD policy, and also discusses the importance of governance in achieving GDPR compliance regardless of the size of the organisation, and finally Section 7.6 concludes this chapter.

7.2. BYOD Architecture, Security Status and Challenges

BYOD started gaining popularity since 2009, and it is considered as a solution for business environments. It entails organisations allowing employees the use of their own personal devices for professional purposes. It is common nowadays that people interpret the phrase "personal devices" to refer to smartphones, laptops, tablets, etc. (Eslahi, 2014).

Years ago, before the massive growth of internet-based services, organisations used to provide personal devices to employees. This was known as *Use What You Are Told* (UWYT), and these devices were meant to be used only for professional duties. Computers were purchased and customized to help employees perform their duties and contribute to the accomplishment of the business's goals. Furthermore, taking these devices outside the organisation was not allowed, making it harder for malicious attackers to steal personal data, because Internet use was not as frequent at that time.

Nowadays, because of the Internet revolution, it is easy to appreciate the fact that employees purchase their own devices for both personal and professional motives. Organisations have limited budgets, and therefore the BYOD policy has been implemented, allowing employees to use personal devices that satisfy their tastes. Likewise, network administration became easier for IT admins because it only requires the creation of configured network points at employees' desks which adhere to the internal policies adopted by the organisation. In addition, more Access Points (APs) have been implemented in such a way that personnel can connect their wireless devices to the corporate network. Furthermore, these mobile devices are being used to perform professional duties during the commute between the organisation and any other destination and vice versa (Wainwright, 2018).

Figure 7.1 shows the general architecture for BYOD. It is also an overview of how personal devices get connected to a corporate network. The lower layer is the access network, where personal devices can access Internet services through Wi-Fi networks which can be personal or public networks. Likewise, personal devices can get Internet access using mobile networks. The transport network is

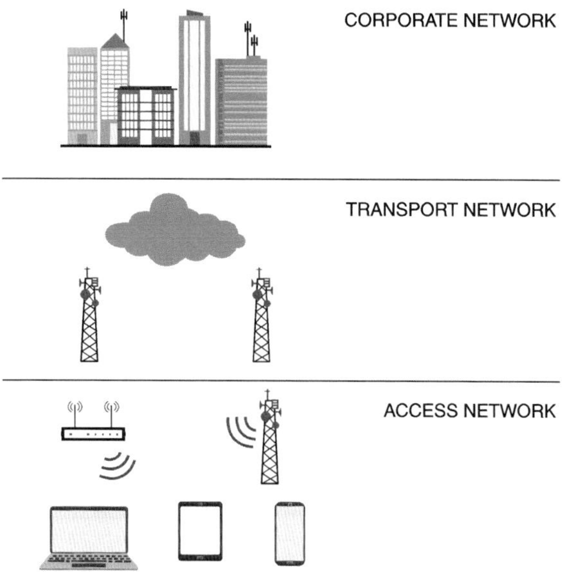

Fig. 7.1. Architecture of BYOD and connectivity to corporate networks.

known as the Internet, where ISPs control the traffic routing, and end users cannot take control of their information because in this layer the data is being transmitted. And finally, the corporate network is where the main servers are allocated and policies from organisations are enforced.

The implementation of a BYOD policy seen from the technical perspective simplifies the network architecture, infrastructure implementation and management. Moreover, business software comes along with this solution to ease the network management for IT administrators (e.g. Active Directory). Analysing BYOD from the Human Resource (HR) perspective, it has been noted that employees are more satisfied as this solution allows them to engage completely with their professional roles, reducing stress, increasing productivity and therefore improving the organisation's finances. Moreover, they do not have to budget for the purchase of devices that adhere to their internal policies (Ghosh *et al.*, 2013). When their personal devices are used at work, professional staff can perform their tasks outside the office as long as they have internet connectivity. In addition, allowing the use of personal devices within the organisation attracts applicants who enjoy the flexibility offered. Nowadays, the "millennial" generation are more engaged with smartphones and use the Internet more frequently. High school and college students who are not afraid to share their information on the Internet are looking for flexible job opportunities.

7.2.1. *Current security models*

There are currently some BYOD models which are applied for security purposes. These are *Mobile Device Management (MDM), Mobile Application Management (MAM)* and *Mobile Information Management (MIM)*. The models are described down below with more of a focus on MDM, which is better known in the commercial market (Kale, 2013). The benefits to organisations of implementing these solutions within BYOD environments are the presentation of a stronger security posture to customers based on the importance of protecting information, as well as the protection and satisfaction of their employees, who enjoy having a flexible workstation that enhances productivity. The details of the features of various security solutions to BYOD environments are shown in Table 7.1.

Table 7.1. Features to consider when implementing secure BYOD environments.

Governance	Identification and Access Control	Enforce Strong Passwords
		Auto Lock
		Device Lock
		Password Attempt Limit
	Authentication	Two Factor Authentication
		Biometric Authentication
		PIN, Password, Pattern Drawn
	Network Isolation	BYOD Specific Wi-Fi
	Data Protection	Data Encryption
		Storage Encryption
	Remote Management	Local Wipe
		Remote Wipe
		Selective Wipe
	Backup	
	Device Location	
	Application Security	Management Approval
		Third-Party Applications
		Marketplace Applications
		Whitelist, Blacklist
	Integrity Control	Anti-Malware
		Host-Based Firewall, IDS
		Virtual Private Networks
		Logging
	Compliance	Risk Management
		Internal Audit
		Law Enforcement
		Isolate Personal and Professional Information

7.2.1.1. *Mobile Device Management (MDM)*

Implementing MDM systems in an organisation allows the organisation to monitor in a remote manner the performance and functions of mobile devices. An MDM system is based in the client/server architecture, of which the main components are the agent and the server

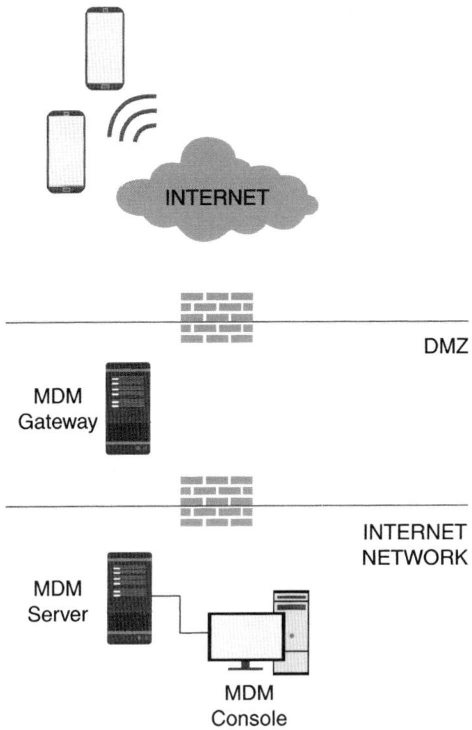

Fig. 7.2. MDM architecture.

respectively. Figure 7.2 shows the general architecture of such a system, where an MDM gateway (relay server) is configured within the DMZ to enable mobile devices to get access to the corporate network whilst the server is monitoring their performance. The MDM agent is installed in the mobile device, and it transmits information about the user account and the status of the device whilst the server enforces the policies implemented to comply with the internal regulations from the organisation (Vignesh and Asha, 2013).

7.2.1.2. *Mobile Application Management (MAM)*

IT administrators use this model to install, monitor, control, update, audit or remove customized applications created for the organisation in a remote manner. This feature allows IT administrators to take control of the applications allowed on each mobile device with the use of whitelists and blacklists (Kale, 2013). The main purpose of this solution is to control whether the applications installed on a mobile device fit with the policies of the organisation and to monitor in real time the performance of the customized applications. The solution balances three main features, which are performance, ease of use and security. In addition, customized applications and embedded systems are monitored to avoid exposing or compromising sensitive personal information from the current user/owner.

7.2.1.3. *Mobile Information Management (MIM)*

This model has great applicability in private cloud environments. The MIM system ensures the protection of and avoids any leakage of information, which is considered a crucial asset for the organisation. The model also demonstrates the limitations of installing trusted applications in mobile devices to control the data. The MIM solution comes across with the integration of MAM APIs into mobile devices, hence IT administrators can monitor whether information used by the user/owner is considered essential enough for the organisation to take the necessary measures to protect it. If the organisation protects the data, it will do so without getting involved with personal data.

7.2.2. *Security concerns*

Upon an analysis of the mind map shown in Fig. 7.3, it can be concluded that BYOD brings flexibility to organisations. This is accomplished thanks to the deployment of cloud environments, customized applications that can be installed on the endpoint devices, and the ability to allow employees to work remotely, saving them time. However, to reach the demanded levels of information assurance while avoiding any data leakage, strategic plans are required. These include resource optimisation and management, as well as the establishment of internal procedures and policies that can be controlled with suitable governance practices to keep the balance between flexibility, performance and security. As mentioned above, when BYOD is discussed, the use of wireless devices is also discussed,

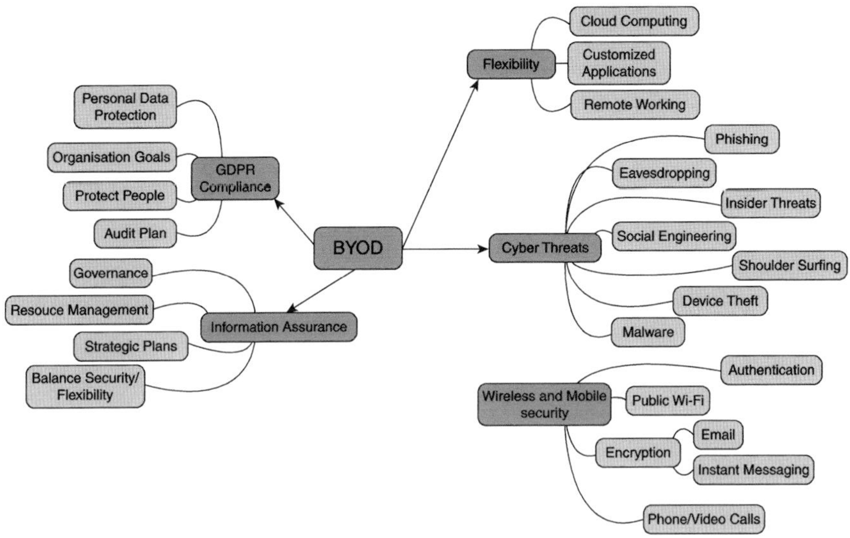

Fig. 7.3. Implications of BYOD.

and so is wireless and mobile security. The protection of devices when connecting to public Wi-Fi networks, the encryption of sensitive information, the protection of phone and video calls against *eavesdropping* or *man-in-the-middle* attacks (MITM), and the protection of email and SMS services are all essential to the organisation. The high use of wireless personal devices increases in parallel their exposure to the cyber risks which are mentioned below:

- *Social engineering* is when attackers take advantage of the lack of security awareness among employees to extract sensitive information.
- *Phishing* is sending emails with malicious links that could lead to credential harvesting or unauthorized malware downloading to users while pretending to be a known contact.
- *Spear-phishing* is the sending of phishing emails to a specific target (e.g. emails including the name of the owner).
- *Malware* is the abbreviated term for "malicious software". Such software can be installed in a device to take control of it, to steal information or to launch future cyber attacks (e.g. trojans, worms, rootkits, viruses, ransomware).

- *Device theft* is considered a risk to the organisation despite it being out of the control of the owner. This is due to all the information stored in the device.
- *Insider threats* can happen because of frustrated employees or can be performed by cyber crime organisations. They occur when a person gets unauthorized access to the main computers used by an organisation.
- *Man-in-the-middle attacks* happen when attackers intercept messages between client and server in order to eavesdrop on information or manipulate it.
- *Shoulder surfing* is when an attacker is able to see the user typing out their credentials and acknowledging personal information such as banking or contact information on their personal devices. Despite being simple, it can cause great harm to organisations.

7.2.3. *BYOD security challenges*

There has been significant growth in the development of mobile devices in the last few years. Nowadays smartphones have features comparable to those of laptops. These outstanding features have enhanced functionality, therefore the use of smartphones by employees for professional purposes has been accepted by many organisations. In addition, these devices have become more accepted in the workplace as they now come with stronger security applications and features. Unfortunately, technological organisations are competing fiercely for market share and therefore, when developing devices and software applications, they tend to focus on innovation and ease of use rather than on security and reliability (Eslahi *et al.*, 2014).

When talking about information security, it is necessary for cyber security practitioners, senior management and users in general to achieve security while maintaining performance and ease of use of computer systems in a professional environment. This is a complex endeavour. Following Fig 7.4, there are three components that must be appropriately balanced in computer systems, which are security, ease of use and performance. If software applications are developed to enhance business productivity and to improve organisational performance, their user interfaces must be easy to use, and during data processing they must follow the necessary protocols and functions to assure confidentiality, integrity and availability. For instance, if a system has more of the strongest security mechanisms, its performance is likely to degrade steadily, making the user interface less simple to use.

New electronic devices which can connect to *Internet of Things* (IoT) networks are being produced in great quantities. Mobile devices play a crucial role in managing these personal networks (e.g. autonomous cars, smart home devices). Currently, constrained devices on an IoT network tend to be in the form of hardware and are normally managed by smartphones using wireless communication (i.e., Bluetooth, ZigBee, Wi-Fi). However, this great technological advancement comes with minimal or no security features because of its electronical limitations, and thus, creates new opportunities for attackers to penetrate computer systems and succeed in causing personal identifiable information (PII) breaches, which in turn cause financial, technological and reputational damage to organisations. In addition, due to the increased use of mobile devices, organisations are dealing with the fact that confidential information is often delivered to devices that IT departments cannot manage properly, exposing the organisation to data leakage, theft and failure to achieve regulatory compliance. Attackers will try both simple and sophisticated tactics, techniques and procedures (TTPs) to achieve their malicious objectives. Mobile devices will still be exposed to simple threats such as keyloggers, malware infection and vulnerability exploitation

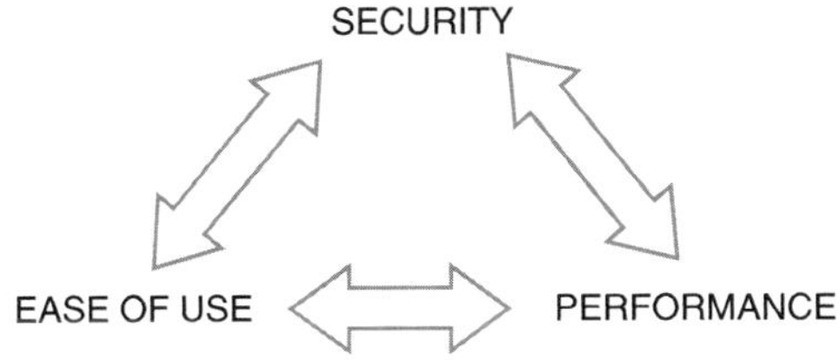

Fig. 7.4. Features that need to be balanced in computer systems.

methodologies that could lead to the attacker gaining unauthorized access, compromising the user, the supply chain of the organisation he / she works in, the reputation of the organisation and the customer's trust in the organisation. The next sections will discuss the impact of the European GDPR on BYOD environments, followed by guidelines aimed at teaching users how to protect their personal devices. Finally, a framework to enhance the security posture of organisations committed to the acceptance and use of mobile devices will be discussed.

7.3. Impact of GDPR on BYOD Architectures

The General Data Protection Regulation (GDPR) is designed to enable individuals to better control their personal data. It is hoped that these modernised and unified rules will allow businesses to make the most of the opportunities created by the Digital Single Market by reducing regulation and benefiting from reinforced consumer trust. Privacy and data protection are fundamental rights protected by EU law. Privacy refers to the part of our lives that we as individuals want to control and keep to ourselves. The right to privacy is an umbrella concept that contains many meanings; it protects our communications, homes, bodies, lives, dignity, freedom, liberty and autonomy so that we can develop intimate relationships with others and achieve personal prosperity and wellbeing.

In the EU Fundamental Rights of Privacy which are covered in Article 7 of the Charter Fundamental Rights of the European Union, the respect for private and family life, home and communications is emphasised. Today, when ICT is increasingly being used, data collection and processing has become an important factor and a way of life. The Right to Data Protection was therefore developed to protect individuals from potential harm due to data abuse and misuse. In the EU, the Right to Data Protection is covered by Article 8 of the Charter; this article states that everyone has the right to the protection of their personal data. The right to the protection of personal data is furthermore enshrined in Article 16 of the treaty on the functioning of the European Union. In the digital age, new technology has been widely deployed in all aspects of life and many of these new technologies can invade privacy if they are misused or abused. They may cause harm to individuals or society even without us knowing it. However, we have become more and more dependent on such privacy-invading technologies and on the ever-growing data processing. Of course, data ownership, transparency and auditability will be one of the major challenges for EU citizens. In this regard, it is important to clarify individual rights that citizens are entitled to under EU Law. For this very reason, the GDPR has provided us with a robust legal compliance system (Shu and Jahankhani, 2017).

The GDPR requires that personal data be securely processed. This is not a new obligation when it comes to data protection, of course. However, the GDPR's "appropriate technical and organisational measures", which have been previously addressed under the Data Protection Act of 1998 (the 1998 Act), provides more specifics on what you have to do to securely process data and how to assess information risk so that appropriate security measures can be put in place. This is an important element when it comes to BYOD as it is now a legal requirement.

Article 5(1)(f) of the GDPR is concerned with the "integrity and confidentiality" of personal data and explains that data should be "processed in a manner that ensures appropriate security of the personal data, including protection against unauthorised or unlawful processing and against accidental loss, destruction or damage, using appropriate technical or organisational measures".

Organisations are required to refer to the GDPR's "security principle", which is concerned with the broad concept of information security. The "security principle" requires that the appropriate security is put in place to prevent the personal data you hold being accidentally or deliberately compromised. This is important when it comes to BYODs. It is vital to know that whilst "information security" is sometimes interpreted to mean "cybersecurity", which involves the protection of networks and information systems from attacks, it also covers other aspects including physical and organisational security measures. Therefore, it is important to consider the "security principle" together with Article 32 of the GDPR, which discusses the specifics of the security of your processing. Article 32(1) states that; "taking into account the state of the art, the costs of implementation and the nature, scope, context and purposes of processing as well as the risk of varying likelihood and severity for the rights and freedoms of natural persons, the controller and the processor shall implement appropriate technical and organisational measures to ensure a level of security appropriate to the risk" (Shu and Jahankhani, 2017).

In addition to the six data protection principles, the GDPR Article 5(2) has "the principle of accountability". According to this principle, the controller shall be responsible for compliance with the principles listed in Article 5(1) of the GDPR and shall be able to demonstrate its compliance with them. With so many rights given to data subjects and so much accountability on data controllers under GDPR, organisations in the EU and organisations outside the EU which process the data of EU citizens are required to keep all the compliance boxes checked.

Further areas to look out for when implementing the GDPR are as follows:

- Incidents: The GDPR will now make it a legal duty to report any incidents to the ICO within 72 hours. This legislates similarly to current working arrangements of contacting the ICO in a similar time period.

The potential financial penalties could be very high for incidents in which the regulations were not adhered to. Article 83 states the general conditions for imposing administrative fines. Paragraphs 4 and 5 state the limits of administrative fines that potentially can be issued (this is dependent on member state approval of what the maximum fine will be). The maximum fines for failing to comply with the regulations could potentially be 20 million Euros or 4 % of the organisation's total worldwide annual turnover for the preceding financial year.

Data subjects must also have fair processing information made available to them "at the time when personal data are obtained"

(Article 13). Further to this, the fair processing information must include the following:

- "the contact details of the data protection officer"
- "the right to lodge a complaint with a supervisory authority"
- "the existence of automated decision-making, including profiling, referred to in Article 22(1) and (4) and, at least in those cases, meaningful information about the logic involved, as well as the significance and the envisaged consequences of such processing for the data subject"

Data subjects have the right to know what safeguards are in place for any personal data that is transferred to a "third country or an international organisation" (i.e. outside the UK). The applicable safeguards that can be used in international transfers are stated within Article 46.

Recital 47 states, in reference to the legitimate interests of a controller as a legal basis for processing a data subject's personal data, that "given that it is for the legislator to provide by law for the legal basis for public authorities to process personal data, that legal basis should not apply to the processing by public authorities in the performance of their tasks".

- Data Protection Impact Assessments (Article 35): Privacy Impact Assessments (PIAs) within the Act are named 'Data Protection Impact Assessments' (DPIAs).

There are limited differences between the two, except that the appointed Data Protection Officer's (DPO) advice (currently, the SIRO's advice) must be sought and, "where appropriate, the controller shall seek the views of data subjects or their representatives on the intended processing". Recital 84 states that "where a data-protection impact assessment indicates that processing operations involve a high risk which the controller cannot mitigate by appropriate measures in terms of available technology and costs of implementation, a consultation of the supervisory authority should take place prior to the processing". Article 25 states that data protection must not only be by default but must be by design. Privacy by design is a key element in BYOD implementation.

- Data Protection Officer Role (DPO): According to Article 37, Paragraph 1, the organisation must appoint a DPO.

The details of the appointed DPO must be published and submitted to the ICO. In some regards the DPO role has general similarities to the SIRO role. For example, all PIAs will need to have consultations with the DPO.

However, Article 38 states that "data subjects may contact the Data Protection Officer about all issues related to processing of their personal data". It is unclear from this whether tasks such as subject access requests can be delegated. As the ICO would be the supervisory body in this respect, advice should be sought from them.

Similarly, guidance issued by the Working Party (EU Joint Committee of Member States' Supervisory Authorities [ICOs]) about the role of the DPO is not clear. Guidance states that "the personal availability of a DPO is essential to ensure that data subjects will be able to contact the DPO" in Article 38, Paragraph 4, in regard to "all issues related to processing of their personal data and to the exercise of their rights under this Regulation". The levels of expertise, skill, knowledge, etc. that are relevant to the role are stated in Articles 37-39 and Recital 97. It is also given that the DPO must be available to communicate directly with data subjects and the Supervisory Board (Shu and Jahankhani, 2017).

- Subject Access: Article 12, Paragraph 3, states that Subject Access Requests or SARs (as stated under Article 13) need to be complied with 'without undue delay' and within a month of receipt of the request (Article 12 does not state whether this is 31 days, or if organisations have until the same day next month to comply, e.g. from the 15th of Jan to the 15th of Feb).

Article 12, Paragraph 5 states that there shall be no charge issued to the requestor in complying with their SAR, unless requests from a data subject are 'manifestly unfounded or excessive, in particular because of their repetitive character'. If a request is denied on these grounds, an unspecified fee may be charged (in relation to the administrative cost of dealing with the request). The request may be denied, but the controller must demonstrate that the request was excessive or manifestly unfounded.

The processes for providing the information to the applicant remain the same. When a large quantity of information on a data subject is being processed, the controller maintains the ability to ask the data subject to specify the information or processing activities to which the request relates. The fact that there can now be no charge for the first SAR made by a data subject has potentially large financial implications for an organisation.

- Processing Activities: Article 30 states that data controllers "shall maintain a record of processing activities under its responsibility". An organisation currently undertakes similar programmes of activity through their information governance policy requirements. If these are followed, all data-sharing agreements and contracts should in theory be recorded and logged, however, in reality this is not done comprehensively in a consolidated repository or format.
- Strategic work to undertake in partnership with other organisations and potential future work: Article 40, Paragraph 1 states that the drawing up of codes of conduct in keeping with the regulations should be encouraged. Paragraph 2 states that "bodies representing categories of controllers or processors" should help prepare the codes of conduct.

In relation to the above, Article 41 states that compliance with the code of conduct must be undertaken by an appropriate body which has an appropriate level of expertise (expertise in this case is decided by the regulatory body — the ICO).

Article 42 states that data protection certification mechanisms for demonstrating compliance with the GDPR should be created and complied with. It is currently unknown what form any certification will take, however, the task of deciding competency for a certification body shall lie with the supervisory authority (the ICO).

- Other Considerations: Current legislation maintains that only the data controller for information may be liable for non-compliance with the Data Protection Act. Article 82, Paragraph 2 states that "a processor shall be liable for the damage caused by processing only where it has not complied with obligations of this Regulation specifically directed to processors or where it has acted outside or contrary to lawful instructions of the controller" — in effect stating that a processor is now equally liable, or entirely liable if, as stated in Paragraph 3, the controller "proves that it is not in any way responsible for the event giving rise to the damage".

In such circumstances, Paragraph 4 states that either the controller or the processor will be held responsible for paying the entire fine, but Paragraph 5 gives recourse whereby the "controller or processor shall be entitled to claim back from the other controllers or processors involved in the same processing that part of the compensation corresponding to their part of responsibility for the damage".

In general, it is very clear that accountability for security will provide adequate support so that matters are not overlooked and as a result the organisation's overall security position will not become flawed or out of date.

An information security policy is an appropriate organisational measure to demonstrate what steps are required to comply with the "security principle". Further to policy, organisations do need to consider security and other related matters such as the co-ordination between key people within the organisation. For instance, the security manager will have to know about the commissioning and disposing of any IT equipment, physical access to premises, equipment given to anyone outside the organization including computer maintenance, etc.

All this of course brings in additional security considerations and may influence the business continuity arrangements. However, information security policies provide pointers on how the organization can protect and recover any personal data being held. A regular check needs to be done to ensure that security measures remain appropriate and up to date.

Although technical measures play a key role in the protection of personal data, it is often the case that security incidents occur due to theft or loss of equipment or incorrect disposal of equipment. Technical measures here include cyber security, which is complex and ever-evolving.

From a security point of view, it is best to assume that an organisation's systems are vulnerable and to constantly take steps to protect them through factors such as:

- The security of the network and information systems, including those which process personal data.
- The security of the data held within the organisation's systems, including BYOD systems. These can be secured by ensuring appropriate access controls and data security policies.
- Online security, including the security of the organisation's website and other online services, or of applications used by the organisation.
- Device security with a clear policy on BYOD.

All these need to link to the nature and practices of the business. For example, if the organisation is allowing staff to work from home, then measures must be introduced to ensure that this does not compromise the organization's security, and these measures must be appropriate to the nature of the personal data held and the harm that might result from any compromise. The Cyber Essentials Scheme is a good starting point as it provides a basic set of controls, however, risk analysis should be also be looked at in parallel.

7.3.1. *Threats to personal data security*

Organisations adopting BYOD architectures need to be aware that they are collecting personal information about employees, customers, advisors and third-party consultants. That information might be names, contact details (e.g., phone, email, address), date of birth, national insurance number and critical information such as service-level agreements and non-disclosure agreements. Furthermore, organisations may occasionally require the collection of certain types of personal data for legal compliance purposes. Regardless of how it is collected, recorded and used — for instance, it may be collected using a computer or recorded on other media, which include hard copy pages and pictures from a CCTV — all this personal information must be handled properly to ensure compliance with the European GDPR.

In the United Kingdom, organisations should comply with eight principles, which are summarised as follows:

- Personal data shall be processed fairly and lawfully
- Personal data shall be obtained or processed for specific lawful purposes
- Personal data must be adequate, relevant and not excessive
- Personal data must be accurate and kept up to date
- Personal data shall not be kept for longer than necessary
- Personal data shall be processed in accordance with the rights of the data subjects
- Personal data must be kept secure
- Personal data shall not be transferred outside the European Economic Area (EEA) unless there is adequate protection

The three major threats to data security are data tampering (integrity), data loss (availability), and unauthorized access or leakage (confidentiality). Considering these threats risk affecting data security, they must be treated as main priorities for organisations. There are two main types of threats (Garba *et al.*, 2015). Organisational threats occur when users abuse their privileges on computer systems and perform actions without authorization, or without having the legal rights to perform those actions. Systemic threats consist in the misuse of information by individuals who have legitimate access to it. These threats are also called insider threats when they occur in organisations.

7.4. Guidelines to Enhance Security Posture on Mobile Devices

The protection of mobile devices must be taken with the seriousness it deserves. This is because, nowadays, organisations along with their employees tend to use personal devices daily for professional purposes. Furthermore, new generations are becoming familiar with technology from an early age. For instance, children are using tablets and smartphones to play video games and download applications from marketplaces, exposing these devices to outsider threats and social engineering techniques. Malicious APIs uploaded on trusted and untrusted sources are likely to be the source of this threat. It is normal having meetings with stakeholders at places outside the organisation (e.g. cafeterias, restaurants) to create new partnerships between companies, and personal devices tend to get connected to public Wi-Fi networks. It is necessary for organisations to consider the protection of personal devices within their risk management framework, in light of the recently implemented European GDPR.

This section mentions security practices that protect mobile devices even when they are connected to mobile and public wireless networks. Regardless of the mobile operating system one uses (e.g. Android, Blackberry, Apple), these guidelines can be applied to any smart mobile device that has access to the internet and is used for both personal and professional purposes. It is important for the user to understand that using personal devices is commonly allowed in most organisations. Nevertheless, there are some exceptions (e.g., governments, federal agencies) where they work with UWYT policies because the sensitivity of the information they tend to manipulate requires higher levels of information assurance (Kale, 2013).

Now that the impact of the newly implemented GDPR mentioned above has been analysed and the benefits of implementing BYOD security architectures have been mentioned in Section 7.2, the implementation of the following security mechanisms and practices to protect mobile devices has been suggested.

7.4.1. *Strong passwords*

Nowadays it is very common that mobile devices which are used for professional purposes load default applications accessed by the user daily. For instance, users tend to immediately synchronize their smartphones to their e-mail and cloud-based accounts (e.g., Google Mail, OneDrive). Furthermore, most devices have a contract of access to 4G networks, with higher throughputs, allowing users to access internet-based services, download applications and documents, and upload files and folders to the cloud as well. The high rate of 4G devices acquired, and the high rate of cloud synchronizing that occurs, demands that the user have strong passwords. Despite having strong hashing algorithms and using salting techniques to strengthen passwords, if the mobile device is configured by the user to have passwords that are easy to guess/crack such as "Password" or "[Name][BirthYear]", attackers can apply old cracking techniques to retrieve passwords (e.g., John the Ripper, Hashcat).

Fortunately, on corporate networks there are software applications which are used to enforce strong password policies within an organisation (e.g., Active Directory). Nevertheless, as mentioned above, IT staff struggle to protect business data located in mobile devices. Strong passwords are recommended if personal services are going to be accessed on mobile phones. The UK National Cyber Security Centre (NCSC), along with various security consultancy organisations, recommend that passwords should be created according to the combination of three random words that users can remember without doubt. In addition to this combination, it is important to use numeric and symbolic characters for password configuration. Nowadays, there is password enforcer software which makes users set authentication credentials that have a minimum length of 15 characters. The longer the password is, the harder it will be for attackers to crack it.

7.4.2. *Anti-virus software*

Anti-viruses are used in computers and laptops within organisations for detective and corrective purposes. They can detect threats and risks which are reported on exploit databases and download the latest updates to counteract the threat posed by viruses and malware. Anti-virus software can be downloaded to smartphones from marketplaces (e.g., Google Play, Apple Store) because it is common for attackers to develop malicious software for smartphones which tricks users and injects payloads that run in the background and perform unauthorized procedures. Applications considered attractive to users are exposed to cyber risks executed by attackers, allowing them to trigger rootkits, trojans or any other kind of viruses which can in turn allow them to perform information theft, file navigation, eavesdropping, etc.

7.4.3. *Authentication mechanisms*

As mobile networks and devices improve in terms of their performance and the service they provide to users, they demand more sophisticated security mechanisms for their protection. One of these mechanisms is authentication. During the rise of mobile networks several years ago, security was not necessary because the wireless transmission channels used in mobile networks were based on analogical technology as it had greater coverage, and these were used only for phone calls. Later, with the rise of 2G networks, multimedia messaging services (MMS) and internet services at lower speeds (e.g., 56 kbps), authentication mechanisms began to be required. The first authentication mechanism of this sort was phone locking on mobile phones using a hardware-based button. The user could control how long the phone would have to lie idle before they got locked out. With the rise of Apple and Android devices, authentication mechanisms got more sophisticated. It became possible to set a specific pattern which would unlock the phone, allowing the user to access the main windows. The pattern unlocking systems required the user to draw a specific figure on a nine-button environment.

Mobile devices have different authentication mechanisms. The first one is based on "something you know", which, according to Fig. 7.5, can require the user to unlock the phone by: (a) drawing a pattern, (b) typing in a PIN number, or (c) inserting login credentials, in order to get access to the services the application offers. Login credentials are generally used to access services in BYOD environments. In addition, there is token-based authentication, which is commonly used for multi-factor authentication (MFA) purposes. For instance, some users receive a one-time passcode (OTP) via SMS, email or an application from the marketplace during the authentication process. This is called two-factor authentication (2FA) and is

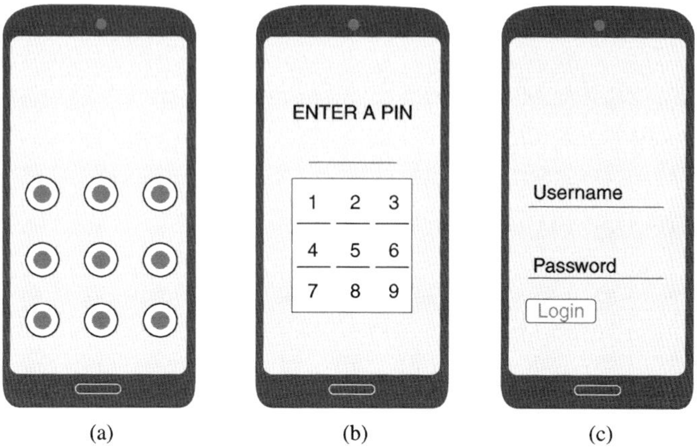

Fig. 7.5. Authentication mechanisms on smartphones. (a) Pattern, (b) PIN, (c) login credentials.

used to verify that the user legitimately owns the account they are logging in to. The latest authentication mechanism used nowadays on mobile devices is based on "something you are". For instance, the latest smartphones come with biometric authentication such as fingerprint reading, facial or iris recognition or voice-based authentication (Samaras *et al.*, 2014).

Upon analysing the authentication mechanisms, it can be concluded that the recommendation for mobile device users regardless of being connected or not to BYOD environments is to enable the latest authentication mechanism. Applications can also be purchased from the marketplace to add another layer of authentication to specific mobile applications. For instance, if a mobile device is hacked, the attacker would not be able to access a certain application or a certain piece of information if it is protected with another layer of authentication. This is because the attacker does not have the password, the temporary token, or even worse, the physical features of the owner that must be used for biometric authentication procedures.

7.4.4. *Remote control*

The implementation of BYOD security architecture and the MDM enables organisations to perform remote wipe or factory reset to mobile phones, but users can also take remote control of their mobile devices by registering them with the accounts associated with their respective marketplaces. For instance, to remotely protect Android devices, register the phone with a Google Account and use features such as *Find my Device*, which allows the user to locate the device through GPS services, play a sound remotely and remote wipe the phone to factory settings, deleting all the information on it, including any information in external storage.

7.4.5. *Importance of not rooting/jailbreaking the device*

Some years ago, the act of rooting mobile phones started gaining popularity, particularly in South American countries. This was because it gave users the freedom to customize their mobile phones to their tastes. One of the main reasons to root the device was to get access to applications from unknown sources for specific purposes, and to avoid paying for the benefits these applications provided. For Apple devices the process is called "jailbreaking", and it was commonly used to connect the phone to the mobile network and to get access to phone calls, SMS and internet services. However, attackers nowadays take advantage of rooted phones because they can escalate privileges on these phones easily, taking full control of the devices in order to perform actions such as installing rootkits, using the devices within a botnet to perform further attacks, especially DoS attacks, and performing crypto-mining in the background, thus consuming the phone's resources. Moreover, rooting the phone also voids the warranty given when the user purchased the device. This leads to the user losing certain benefits. For instance, the provider will no longer troubleshoot problems with the device, or repair the device for free, as they ordinarily would during the duration of the warranty. Even though the user will have to pay to download some applications if they do not root or jailbreak a device, it is still best not to root or jailbreak the device, as doing so will remove a layer of security and the provider will no longer have control over the device. Due to rooting and jailbreaking, mobile providers have also had to dedicate more resources to customer service (Vignesh and Asha, 2015).

7.4.6. *Virtual private networks*

In recent years, there has been steady growth in the deployment of public networks, especially in metropolitan cities where users can connect their mobile devices to Wi-Fi networks at many places. Attackers can take advantage of these facilities to perform attacks that could lead to information leakage, eavesdropping and MITM attacks including session hijacking, data tampering and extracting sensitive data that could be critical for organisations. Using a Virtual Private Network (VPN) service, one can establish an encrypted session between server and client to assure data privacy and confidentiality. A VPN service can be purchased in the marketplace, or a dedicated VPN service can be configured to allow users access to the corporate network.

7.4.7. *Download applications from trusted sources*

With the increased demand for smartphones and the tough competition in the market, especially between Android and Apple devices, users are always looking for applications that can improve their lifestyles, such as fitness apps, budgeting apps, etc. Attackers are always looking to gain unauthorized access to mobile phones, take control of them and steal information that could potentially harm users. For instance, this information could be used to perform fraudulent transactions or to impersonate a user during a transaction without their consent. One way to accomplish these objectives is by developing fake applications and uploading them in the marketplace, or uploading them to the internet so that users can download them and install them manually. For instance, attackers started developing mobile apps claiming to be the popular video game "Fortnite" in order to insert malicious software into mobile phones. This malware stole information from unencrypted HTTP sessions. This campaign was targeted at Android devices because of the decision made by the provider to make the software available for download from the official website.

7.4.8. *Update systems to latest patches*

One of the biggest implications of bringing innovative products to the competitive market is the lack of security or the presence of bugs in these products. Mobile devices are not the exception. Organisations should place as top priority the setting of appropriate patch management procedures pointing out which updates are critical to security. This is especially true if there are valid proofs of concept that the exploitation of bugs and vulnerabilities by attackers can cause significant damage to the user or the organisation in general. In BYOD environments, IT administrators cannot control the personal devices of members of the organisations unless they have installed dedicated software compatible with MDM architectures on those personal devices; however, users should take full responsibility for the security of their mobile systems. Users cannot blame organisations that develop mobile operating systems or applications for security bugs uncovered after the release of these operating systems or applications, because a culture of secure coding is already being encouraged, and besides, because of deadline constraints and marketing purposes, developers are focused on making their products innovative rather than providing built-in security. Therefore, users should be trained to always download kernel, operating system or application-level updates when they receive notifications about these updates.

7.5. Integration of a Multi-Layer Policy and the Information Governance Framework for a BYOD Security Framework

There are different security options for BYOD environments in various organisations, and each of them is designed for specific purposes. Most organisations, especially SMEs, are considered vague and unorganised according to security experts. This is because in SMEs cyber security is not fully considered due to financial issues or the lack of knowledge of personnel engaged with risk management procedures. Likewise, system administrators, who are commonly in charge of the security posture of the organisation, have frequently established few or no common policies and/or procedures to protect the personal data of employees, customers and third parties. Individuals should understand that cyber security does not only mean adding rigorous security technologies into the network infrastructure, it includes training employees to follow internal protocols to avoid risks caused by mistakes, internal threats and external attacks. Employees should be trained to respond properly to security breaches whilst assuring internal and regulatory compliance. The proposed BYOD security framework is based on the "Privacy by Design" principle, which considers the GDPR legislation along with the individual's rights. It consists of two core elements, a multi-layer security policy and the Information Governance (IG) Framework developed during previous research for England's National Health Service (NHS). The multi-layer security policy is formed by three layers of policies — Corporate Security, Application Security and Device Security policies — whilst this is supported by Information Governance according to Fig. 7.6.

Layer 1 — Corporate Security

Organisations must consider this layer in order to set the necessary terms and conditions with the employee prior to signing the respective policies regarding BYOD security. Policies and procedures are added to a checklist to be reviewed by executive management before they are implemented into the organisation. Implementation includes following protocols for internal compliance involving the protection of personal data during email usage, the usage of network services, communication privacy procedures and the usage of BYOD architectures. It is important to train users to back up their personal information and remove applications that could be considered a risk in the organisation. They should also be taught to avoid the usage of rooted or jailbroken devices and the consequences of policy violation should be explained to them.

The use of Access Control must be limited to a certain number of employees according to their roles and responsibilities, and it must be implemented in all the procedures established in the organisation

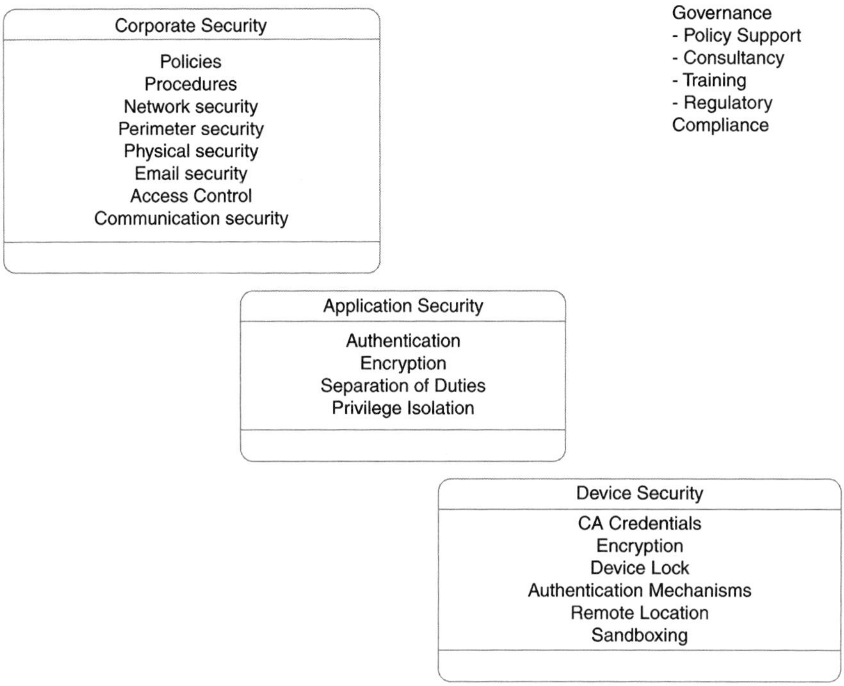

Fig. 7.6. BYOD security framework.

(e.g., Incident Response, Business Continuity, Forensic Investigation, System Administration). Devices must be registered within the organisation and must not have access to the main corporate network due to confidential reasons. For network security purposes it is suggested that the implementation of isolated networks takes place to ensure sandboxing, meaning the isolation between personal and professional information (Zahadat *et al.*, 2015). However, both personal and professional information can compromise the integrity of the organisation when involved in a breach. In addition, this layer suggests profiles which can be used to categorize employees in terms of privilege level:

- Standard User: A standard user is an employee at a junior level, who has spent little time working for the organisation. They may have undergone some training in terms of cyber security, but this training has not been extensive. They can bring their devices; however, they must sign a form stating that the devices will be used only for personal purposes, meaning no email synchronization or integration of corporate services or access limits within the enterprise network.

- Professional User: A professional user is one with experience and advanced security knowledge and expertise, commonly considered to be at a senior level or higher. Moreover, they are highly trusted and require the usage of personal devices in the workplace and at home. This is because they are likely to be sent to meetings with stakeholders and other organisations to establish partnerships, and meetings can be held at places where networks are not trusted by security experts. They use VPNs and cloud services to access confidential information.
- Guest User: A guest user is the new user in the network. Their devices do not have access to the corporate network. Organisations must also consider the configuration of guest wireless networks used only for web browsing purposes. These should have strong access controls, which can be established by rules at access points and proxies to prevent the leakage of network information that can expose the organisation.

Layer 2 — Application Security

This layer provides strong security for mobile devices such as smartphones through monitoring carried out by enterprise applications which assist the user in securing their devices. The application used for this purpose is the MDM, which has three main functions — control, monitoring and protection. Its main server can be configured and accessed from this application. The installation of the MDM allows for the implementation of various kinds of device control such as locking down, creating an SSL connection to the server, remote wipe, siren, data backup and policy enforcement on mobile devices. MAM is used to control specific applications on the device. It should be applied to control customised applications developed for the organisation, and should include patch management to correct coding bugs encountered by vulnerability testers and software developers. Furthermore, these customised applications must be developed properly to ensure GDPR compliance. To this end, the user must accept the terms and conditions set out by the application, which includes giving the application consent to run on their mobile device and accepting their responsibilities as a user. A good example of this is the use of cookies on websites. This is done in the name of regulatory compliance. MIM is the most important application, to be used when handling sensitive information. The installation of this application must be enforced mainly for professional users who have higher privileges within the organisation. The application must be implemented in smartphones, tablets and PDAs. In addition, customised applications should be developed with strong authentication mechanisms to validate legitimate users. The use of two-factor authentication, i.e., the generation of random tokens with every new session to avoid session hijacking, is suggested (Eslahi *et al.*, 2014).

There should be external encryption software installed to protect data from external storage media. This is because, when a user installs an application from a marketplace, the application generally asks for permission to access some features in mobile devices such as:

- Account details
- Application information
- Phone calls
- Camera, gallery
- Network communication
- Location
- Storage
- Messaging
- Synchronization settings
- System Tools
- Bookmarks and web browsing history

The abovementioned features and credentials are sensitive, and when some applications request access to this information, the device is made more vulnerable to attackers as it becomes easier for details of the devices to be exposed and leaked. The MDM should monitor and restrict the application being installed and label it as a high-risk application if it requests access to lots of sensitive information. This is because the application could contain malware, or devices could be used to form a botnet for further attacks, or data could be used for information theft and privilege escalation within a corporate network. Therefore, MDM must warn the user before they install a high-risk application on their mobile devices.

Layer 3 — Device Security

Most organisations leave device-level security to the owner and the manufacturer of the device. Previously, device-level security policies included the certificate authority, data encryption and multiuser and rooting events. Nowadays, every smartphone comes with preloaded trusted CAs, and the removal of one can result in the user working online in untrusted networks. If a digital certificate is hacked, the chances of accessing the device is higher, and if the organisation is using the same certificate, the attacker can gain access to critical systems. Therefore, the device must monitor the CA credentials. The latest smartphones come with inbuilt encryption applications, ciphering data such as accounts, settings and applications. Moreover, some smartphones make it possible to encrypt the SD card inserted. In countries like Australia, USA and the UK rooting is considered legal, hence organisations must prevent the usage of rooted devices in a BYOD environment.

Information Governance Framework

It is a legal requirement for organisations to implement an efficient and effective agreement for information governance. These requirements are set out in the Information Governance Framework.

Organisations adopting BYOD environments are the data controllers for the personal and confidential data under their custody. Therefore, they have a legal responsibility to comply with the information governance requirements associated with this design. To ensure their accountability regarding information governance, organisations should consider that professional users must have access to a range of core support services. The elements of the framework are detailed below:

- **Core Element 1 — IG policy support:** Must be in place for the production and maintenance of local IG policies and procedures. Provides advice and support on the approval, ratification and adoption of IG policies by organisations. These must include policies on confidentiality, consent procedures for the use of personal data, responsibilities and requirements, human rights with regard to privacy, information security (paper records, access control for computer systems, mobile computing risk management), incident management and reporting, staff training and needs assessments.
- **Core Element 2 — IG Consultancy and Support** — Advice and support by phone and/or email on IG issues, including operational processes and new business initiatives. Advice and guidance about access and laws (including GDPR advice for regulatory compliance).
- **Core Element 3 — IG Training** — Training staff regarding IG, which includes the development and provision of training materials to support IG as required and communication methodologies to enhance teamwork and better relationships between stakeholders, customers, employees and third-party providers so as to achieve personal data security.
- **Core Element 4 — Compliance Support** — Advice and guidance for IG compliance. When following the IG framework, compliance support allows organisations to ensure internal and regulatory compliance, including compliance with the new GDPR.
- **Core Element 5 — Incident Management and Investigations** — Advice and support during the investigation of possible cyber security incidents and data breaches. Advising on incident assessment and reporting the incident to regulatory authorities (e.g., ICO in the UK). The reporting should be done by the CISO, the DPO and the involved personnel. Advice on post-incident reviews and actions taken to protect the organisation's and individual's rights.

7.6. Conclusion

In this chapter, the impact of the European GDPR on "Bring Your Own Device" environments was analysed. BYOD environments are used by most organisations to save money while ensuring better commitment from employees. However, the increased demand for mobile device usage in professional workplaces has increased the risks of breaches and unauthorized access, as well as of insider threats, which could be accidental or intentional. The framework proposed involves the integration of a multi-layer security policy along with the Information Governance Framework, which enhances the security posture of organisations regarding the usage of personal mobile devices. Increasing communication between staff, stakeholders and third parties can aid in the implementation of preventive and corrective measures against data breaches. In addition, with the increased use of IoT devices, and the increase in the number of small devices connecting to the Internet, every organisation should train its employees so as to increase their awareness of threats and to impart basic skills in cyber security to them. This is especially unavoidable if the organisation chooses to offer flexibility by allowing the use of personal devices at work. Given the advances in technology, the adoption of policies, procedures, and guidelines which allow organisations to ensure regulatory compliance is recommended. The GDPR framework, for instance, is based on the "Privacy by Design" principle, and includes security guides to enhance mobile security and protect the rights of organisations and of individuals regarding their personal data. More generally, communication is essential if organisations are to respond properly to a security breach that could harm the individual. A quick and effective response to a cyber attack ensures business continuity, which is important in retaining customer trust.

References

1. Eslahi, M., Naseri, M. V., Hashim, H., Tahir, N. M. and Saad, E. H. M. (2014). BYOD: Current State and Security Challenges. In *Proceedings of the 2014 IEEE Symposium on Computer Applications and Industrial Electronics (ISCAIE), Penang, Malaysia, April 7–8,* pp. 189–192.

2. Garba, A. B., Armarego, J. and Murray, D. (2015). A Policy-Based Framework for Managing Information Security and Privacy Risks in BYOD Environments. *International Journal of Emerging Trends and Technology in Computer Science,* **4**(2), pp. 189–198.
3. Ghosh, A., Gajar, P. K. and Rai, S. (2013). Bring Your Own Device (BYOD): Security Risks and Mitigating Strategies. *Journal of Global Research in Computer Science,* **4**(4), pp. 62–70.
4. Jltspecialty.com. (2018). *Companies Continue to Struggle With GDPR Compliance* [Online]. Available at: https://www.jltspecialty.com/our-insights/publications/cyber-decoder/companies-continue-to-struggle-with-gdpr-compliance (Accessed: 13 September 2018).
5. Kale, A. (2013). *Mobile Application Management* [Online]. Available at: https://docplayer.net/2154194-Mobile-application-management-www-wipro-com-anand-kale-mobility-solutions-head-banking-financial-services-wipro-mobility-solutions.html (Accessed: 21 October 2018).
6. McKinney, J. S. and Pickard, J. L. (2016). *The Impact of Bring Your Own Device (BYOD) to the Architectural Development Process* [Online]. Available at: http://www.infosecwriters.com/Papers/jmckinney_BYOD.pdf. (Accessed: 15 August 2019).
7. Samaras, V., Daskapan, S., Ahmad, R. and Ray, S. K. (2014). An Enterprise Security Architecture for Accessing SaaS Cloud Services With BYOD. In *Proceedings of the 2014 Australasian Telecommunication Networks and Applications Conference (ATNAC), Melbourne, Australia, November 26–28,* pp. 129–134.
8. Shu, I. N. and Jahankhani, H. (2017). The Impact of the New European General Data Protection Regulation (GDPR) on the Information Governance Toolkit in Health and Social Care With Special Reference to Primary Care in England. In *Proceedings of the 2017 Cybersecurity and Cyberforensics Conference (CCC), London, UK, November 21–23,* pp. 31–37.
9. Thomson, G. (2012). BYOD: Enabling the Chaos. *Network Security,* **2012**(2), pp. 5–8.
10. Vignesh, U. and Asha, S. (2015). Modifying Security Policies Towards BYOD. *Procedia Computer Science,* **50**, pp. 511–516.
11. Wainwright, A. (2018). *7 Benefits of BYOD on Enterprise Wireless Networks* [Online]. Available at: https://www.securedgenetworks.com/blog/7-Benefits-of-BYOD-on-Enterprise-Wireless-Networks (Accessed: 13 September 2018).
12. Zahadat, N., Blessner, P., Blackburn, T. and Olson, B. A. (2015). BYOD Security Engineering: A Framework and Its Analysis. *Computers and Security,* **55**, pp. 81–99.

Chapter 8

GDPR Compliance: Incident Response and Breach Notification Challenges

Orret R. Grey* and Raymond Brown†

QA Higher Education & Northumbria University London, UK
**orret.grey@northumbria.ac.uk,*
†ray.brown@northumbria.ac.uk

ABSTRACT

Over the last decade, the prevalence of new computing devices with greater processing power and ubiquitous internet-ready devices helped to facilitate the creation and sharing of vast amounts of data. This has brought increased risks to personal data and rendered previous regulations on data privacy less effective in the new digital age. The GDPR regulation was introduced across EU states on the 25th of May 2018 and brought radical changes that govern activities around the processing and sharing of data and how the protection of personal data is administered by various organisations. GDPR necessitates the re-assessment of existing frameworks in order to meet new requirements outlined in the articles and recitals of the regulation. This research addresses the existing challenges of integrating GDPR into incident response and breach notification plans, and proposes a conceptual Decision Support System (DSS) to address the challenges identified. Existing industry standard frameworks such as ISO27001, NIST, and SANS were analysed alongside Focus Group interviews with subject matter experts to gather feedback on the relevance and applicability of a DSS to meet GDPR compliance requirements. The findings of the study reveal a number of compliance gaps in existing incident handling frameworks which could be mitigated by employing decision support techniques as proposed in the study.

Keywords: GDPR, incident response, data breach notification, decision support systems

8.1. Introduction

An incident response plan is a formal document that outlines a series of measures to promptly identify and neutralise security threats and mitigate the associated risks to personal and sensitive information. It is typically established through technical controls, policies, procedures, and designated response teams with specific responsibilities. The proliferation of cyber attacks and important changes in regulation warrants a radical re-assessment of existing governance frameworks and security policies, in order to gain full visibility of data that traverse the internal and external sphere of an organisation.

Articles 33 and 34 of GDPR explicitly outline requirements for reporting data breaches within a specific timeframe and for organisations to demonstrate reasonable steps have been taken to secure personal data (GDPR, 2016). GDPR promulgates the foundation for a risk-based approach to assess the risk to personal data, and for privacy protection measures to be introduced by default when collecting and processing personal data. This requires organisations who are either controllers or processors of personal data to assess the risks relating to the rights and freedom of data subjects and formulate appropriate policies and security measures to protect personal data (Garber, 2018). This indicates that complying with GDPR necessitates a clear and consistent approach towards interpreting and integrating the relevant articles and existing incident response and breach notification plans.

The aim of this research is to investigate compliance challenges by formulating the following questions:

1. What are the main challenges and enablers of implementing GDPR into an incident response and breach notification plan?
2. What decision support process or system could be developed to address the challenges identified?
3. What method could be adopted to assess the relevance and usability of the design for meeting the new requirements of incident response and breach notification challenges?

8.1.1. *Background*

In recent years, the upsurge in cyber attacks and data breach incidents has become a phenomenon that represents an existential threat for organisations who fail to formulate robust security policies and stringent measures to safeguard valuable data. Appropriate preparation plans are imperative for effectively responding to the evolving threats that could cause irreparable damage to business operations and reputation. This helped to precipitate a paradigm shift in recognising the value of personal and business information, as well as the importance of adapting to the changing legal and regulatory landscape.

Despite this recognition and various measures taken by organisations to implement security policies via existing incident handling frameworks, new requirements for breach notification and communication in GDPR have created potential gaps in compliance that need to be re-examined. Moreover, there are no specific recommendations in GDPR that organisations can check against to verify they are fully compliant. According to Hedley and Jacobs (2017), verifying compliance will be done through either external audits or a process of self-assessment by individual organisations who interpret and implement relevant areas of the regulation into their existing incident handling frameworks with policies and procedures.

This indicates that organisations will need to justify and demonstrate to their relevant supervisory authority that stringent security safeguards are in place for securing personal data. The research director of Gartner, Mark Horvath (2018), elaborated that, even if appropriate security policies are established, organisations could still be held accountable under GDPR if employees intentionally or accidentally precipitate serious data breach incidents.

In 2015, a reported cyber attack on telecommunications group Talk Talk precipitated several deleterious consequences that included a rapid decline in stock market value, a loss of revenue amounting to £80 million, and the alienation of many of the customers affected. The Information Commissioner's Office (ICO) conducted subsequent investigations and a £400,000 penalty was levied on the company for failing to adequately secure their customers' personal data (Ico.org.uk, 2018). Fowler (2016) noted that, under the stringent edicts outlined in the GDPR, the fines imposed could have amounted to approximately £70 million. The new mandatory 72-hour deadline outlined in Article 33 for reporting instances of data breach has left some organisations behind the curve in their efforts to establish appropriate frameworks and security measures for meeting compliance under GDPR (Mansfield-Devine, 2016).

The sophistication of new threats and the absence of appropriate response approaches and security policies can greatly increase the chances of a threat exploiting vulnerabilities in an information system with the result that personal data is compromised. Figure 8.1 illustrates a number of emerging threats that are contributing to the increased risks to personal and sensitive data.

8.1.2. *Aims*

The aims of this research are to examine the challenges that exist when interpreting and implementing GDPR through incident response plans, and to develop a structured process or decision support system to address the challenges identified. The research also aims to create an incident decision process flow to provide guidance for breach notification requirements. The objectives created for the research represent important building blocks for constructing and delivering the main goals of the research.

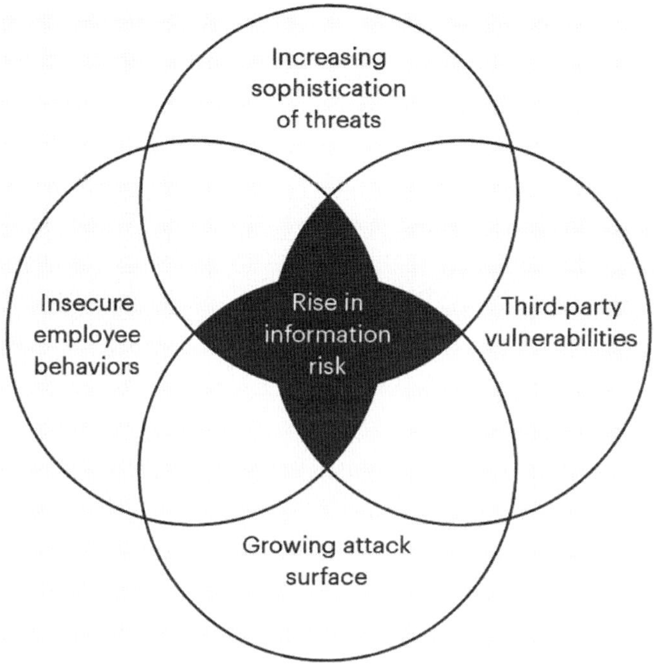

Fig. 8.1. Factors contributing to the increased risks to information (Hedley and Jacobs, 2017).

8.2. Literature Review

The contents of this section provide insights into scholarly articles and publications to help ascertain what has been done and what remains unaddressed in the subject domain. This will help clarify the context and relevance of the research and lead to a more in-depth understanding of the challenges that exist in integrating GDPR into incident response plans. In the initial step, we examine the GDPR publication to identify the new compliance requirements, and then we critically analyse techniques and methods employed in previous works completed within the body of literature.

8.2.1. *Changes in the legal and regulatory landscape*

The introduction of the GDPR denotes a significant inflection point in which a minimum tick box approach to compliance and a

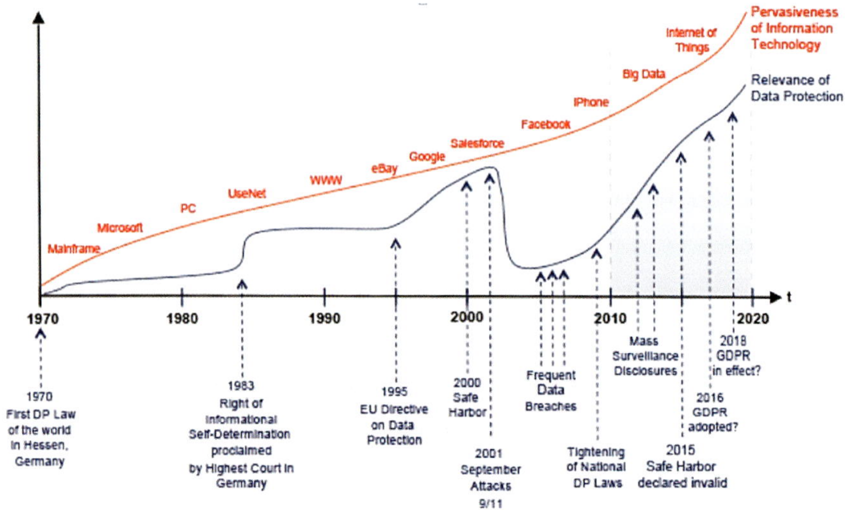

Fig. 8.2. An illustration of regulatory changes in data privacy.

self-regulation paradigm will no longer be sufficient for complying with the new requirements. Various emerging threats and new attack vectors being employed by disparate threat actors have contributed to the profusion of reported cyber attacks and increased data breach incidents. The implementation of GDPR across the EU in 2018 introduced a radical far-reaching approach that brings data protection laws in line with the dynamic and evolving way in which personal and sensitive data is collected and processed. The pervasiveness of internet-ready devices within a highly data-driven interconnected world has led to the generation of a vast amount of personal data that needs to be protected. Figure 8.2 illustrates important changes in data protection regulation over several decades.

8.2.2. *Exploration of a data breach and its wider impact*

The rise in reported data breach incidents has become a notable concern for businesses and consumers because of the deleterious impact it can have on a company's reputation as well as on the individuals who are affected by the data breach. To strengthen the privacy and security of personal data, GDPR regulations outlined important mandatory stipulations for data controllers and processors. Articles (24) and (31) outline the responsibility of the controller requiring the implementation of technical and organisational measures to demonstrate stringent measures to protect data and develop accountability (EU, GDPR, 2016). In recent years, numerous publications about data breaches have shown a litany of security failures that had contributed to vast amounts of data being compromised, and the trend shows no sign of abating.

The introduction of the GDPR could also have wider implications for the legal sector if the personal information of clients becomes compromised. Due to the business model and the sensitivity of a client's information, a serious breach of personal data could have ramifications that go beyond incurring substantial fines. The Solicitors Regulation Authority (SRA) recently highlighted information security as the foremost risk facing most law firms in the UK. The ICO data breach report in 2015/2016 indicates that 27% of security issues in the legal sector were attributed to theft of paper work and data being faxed or sent to the wrong recipient (Schwarz, 2016). Table 8.1 shows recent data breach incidents pre- and post-GDPR regulation. In 2016, a ransomware attack compromised personal data and

Table 8.1. Data breach incidents and associated fines.

Data Breach in Organisations	Number of Records	Date of Breach & Fines	Pre –GDPR	Under GDPR
Aggregate IQ Unlawful processing of user data		Sept 2018 Pending Appeal		✓
British Airways (BA)Personal data captured from web payment site and mobile app	380 K	Aug 2018 Pending Appeal		✓
Equifax Breach due to vulnerability in open source web creation platform.	145 m	Sept 2017 £500K	✓	
Yahoo Vulnerability exploited with cross-site scripting (XSS) via victim's email.	500 m	Sept 2016 £250K	✓	

rendered multinational law firm DLA Piper unable to access their client's data (Steiner, 2018). It is therefore imperative to assess the risk to personal data and to implement appropriate security measures to mitigate the impact of a subsequent data breach incident.

One of the biggest data breaches recorded in 2017 was a cyber attack on US-based credit card rating firm Equifax. It affected approximately 145 million users in several countries including the UK [24]. The company later revealed that the vulnerability, "CVE-2017-5638" in the open source software Apache Struts was exploited (Cobb, 2018). This security breach highlights the importance of establishing effective security controls and vulnerability management to counter various threats. Research by Luszcz (2018) provided further analysis of the technical and security gaps in the design and implementation of new systems that can create various security vulnerabilities.

While new technological innovations provide many opportunities, the increasing number of data breaches also highlights a discernable chasm between effective internal security practices and substandard system development strategies for new and existing systems being implemented within the information and communication infrastructures. Reding (2010), argued in favour of a balance between the benefit of new technology and the assessment of potential risks, that if materialised could cause a serious data breach incident. Figure 8.3 illustrates a collaborative process between decision makers for managing risks. Now that the GDPR is in effect, assessing various risks and strengthening privacy policies for personal data are crucial for meeting compliance.

8.2.3. *Privacy risks in IoT and third-party apps*

The increasing trend of privacy issues involving Internet of Things (IoT) and third-party applications highlights new risks to personal data and a number of ethical concerns. A case involving misuse of personal data and breach of privacy occurred in 2015, when Facebook allowed a third-party application created by Cambridge Analytica onto their platform. The app was configured to

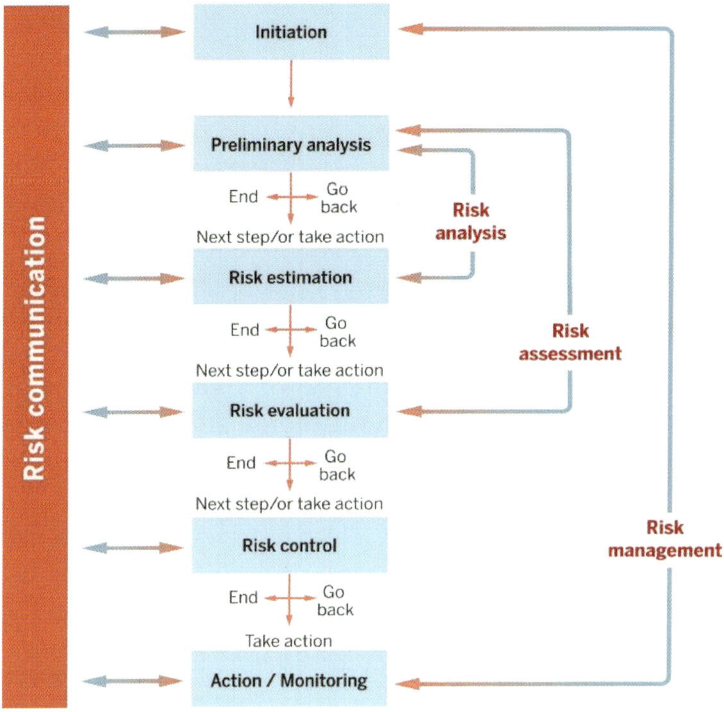

Fig. 8.3. Collaborative process between decision makers for managing risks (Fischhoff, 2015).

surreptitiously harvest the data of 87 million profiles from which information was used during a UK referendum and US election campaign. A subsequent investigation by the ICO identified major failures in data protection standards and a £500,000 penalty was levied on Facebook for violating data protection laws. The fine issued at the time was the maximum amount under the Data Protection Act 1998 (DPA), however, the penalties under the GDPR could have totalled 4% of global revenue amounting to circa £1.4 billion.

Wood (2015), examined the privacy risks and unintended consequences arising from various internet-ready devices with built-in cameras. He elaborated on potential legal issues, highlighting an instance where hackers exploited a vulnerability in a network that hosts connected baby monitoring systems and shouted obscenities in a nursery that was using one of the devices. While some manufacturers extol the enticing virtues of new systems, serious ramifications can arise when they are implemented with substandard security measures. Bowles (2018), focused on potential new patterns of abuse and ethical issues. This included instances where partners of victims of domestic abuse used mobile apps to deliberately change functions on devices such as thermostats, door locks, and security cameras to cause distress and exert control.

8.2.4. *Establishing privacy by design and default*

As previously highlighted, the absence of appropriate measures to assess security risks during the development and implementation of third-party systems can significantly increase the chances of data becoming compromised. Innovative systems design may enhance business functionalities; however, it also represents a substantial security risk. Unlike previous legislations under directive (95/46/EC), the GDPR contains specific provisions that address substandard system development practices, where security is only incorporated as an after-thought during the design phase of new systems.

The capricious nature and complexity of threats such as advanced persistence threats (APT) means organisations must engage in continuous assessment and refinement of their security strategies in order to counter emerging threats. Solterbeck (2006), postulates that decisions to invest in advanced technical tools such as Intrusion Detection Systems (IDS) and Security Information and Event Management Systems (SIEMS) will lead to the ability to analyse network anomalies and increase response capabilities. Conversely, Von Solms and Van Niekerk (2013), point out that these systems on their own will not prevent malicious attacks in all instances and argue that a more comprehensive approach incorporating people and processes will be required.

8.2.5. *Encryption and pseudonymisation*

Encryption and pseudonymisation techniques are among the measures that can be taken to secure personal data. They can be used to remove certain attributes from information that could be used to identify an individual. As discussed in Section 8.2.4, securing personal data and demonstrating robust security measures such as data protection by design and default are imperative in meeting compliance. The effectiveness of cryptographic technique was demonstrated in research by Bitar and Jakobsson (2017) who addressed data privacy requirements by utilising a hardware security model (HSM) as a cryptography method for anonymisation through encryption and access control.

A Delphi method was used to gather empirical data from subject experts to ascertain the most important aspects for meeting compliance within the GDPR. Bitar and Jakobsson (2017) demonstrated that access control, followed by data classification, was the most important aspect in securing personal data. These results were supported by Solterbeck (2006), who advocated that encryption methods can be adopted as an effective solution for protecting sensitive data. On balance, the strength of the findings provided insights for addressing relevant areas of GDPR such as Article 34 by employing the HSM encryption method. Nevertheless, the highly technical approach adopted for the research left other areas unaddressed, for example, the notification and communication of a data breach.

8.2.6. *Comparison of incident response frameworks*

A number of established industry frameworks are used by organisations as a blueprint for incident management; however, new regulations necessitate a reassessment of incident response phases in order to protect personal data and meet compliance. These include frameworks such as the National Institute of Standards and Technology (NIST), the International Organization for Standardization (ISO 27000/27001), and the Enisa Good Practice Guide for Incident Management. The National Institute of Standards and Technology (NIST) Special Publication 800-61 framework outlines guidance in three main areas: organisation capability, incident handling procedures and information sharing and communication as per Cichonski *et al.* (2012).

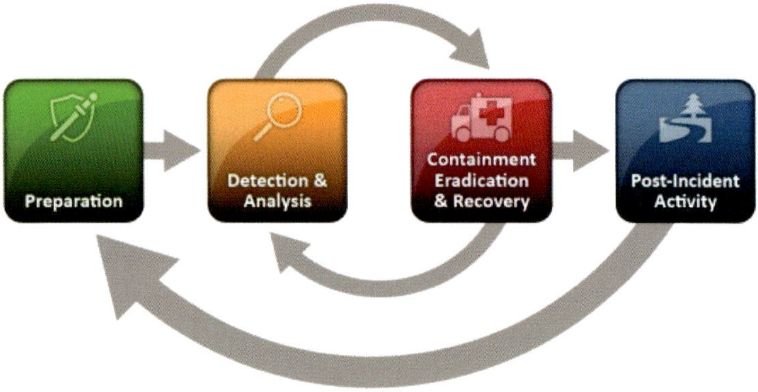

Fig. 8.4. Incident response life cycle outline by NIST.

NIST was primarily created for the federal government in the US and is responsible for developing guidelines and standards to address information security risks and incident management. Figure 8.4 illustrates four primary incident phases recommended by NIST for incident handling. The free publications are regularly updated and can be adopted for implementation within public or private organisations. Other frameworks such as the ISO/IEC 27001 are part of the ISO 27000 suite and are frequently revised. The information security framework is widely used in many organisations to establish, manage, and continually improve the information security management systems (Solterbeck, 2006).

The Enisa incident handling framework provides practical information management guidelines with the focus on incident handling techniques for incident response teams (Enisa.europa.eu, 2011). Although there are some overlaps within the response phases and the techniques adopted, there are notable gaps for the notification and communication of a data breach.

8.2.7. *Security culture and leadership within incident response programs*

As discussed in the previous section, the assessment of the human element plays an important role in the development of an effective

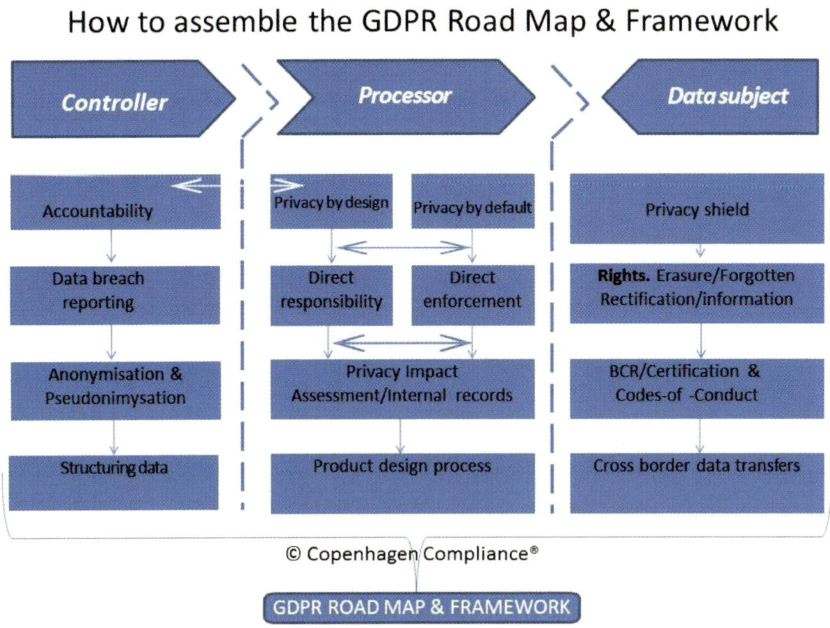

Fig. 8.5. Interactions between organisation and data subject under GDPR [13].

incident response plan to enable prompt response to security incidents. Buchler *et al.* (2018) explored the human element of cyber security by assessing leadership and coordination challenges within cyber defense teams using an Observational Scaled Assessment of Teamwork (OAT) to assess the qualitative aspect of teamwork. The OAT model by Buchler *et al.* (2018) in Fig. 8.5 measures two distinct factors: (1) communication and collaboration, and (2) strong leadership.

The main findings identified strong leadership and face to face interaction as key attributes for building resilient CSIRTs. However, Wood (2015) adopts a contrary view and argues that leadership and collaboration should be explored at both the individual level and within the collective organisational security culture in order to improve the effectiveness of incident response.

New requirements in GDPR legislation mean that the previous tick-box approach by organisations that only addressed minimum compliance will no longer be adequate. Organisations need to make strategic decisions to assess existing systems and encourage proactive responses to security incidents to effectively counter various security threats. A recent report by PWC (2018), examined the merits of security culture within organisations and discovered that defining the security culture was an efficacious way to change individual staff behaviours and could also help strengthen overall security within an organisation. This indicates that, rather than focusing disproportionately on enforcing security policies, organisations should run appropriate cyber awareness initiatives that include staff as part of the security solution as these contribute to better security.

8.2.8. *Summary of literature*

The methods and techniques explored in the literature provided insights into important works that had been previously completed and provided context for challenges that need to be addressed. The General Data Protection Regulation has been in effect since May 2018 and has introduced a new legal mandate for governing how data is collected and processed in the EU. Given the wider remit in the new legal mandate and the option for imposing substantial penalties, it is crucial that organisations reassess existing frameworks for gaps in compliance and establish robust policies and procedures for interpreting and integrating the GDPR.

The literature provided a myriad of useful techniques and approaches for addressing various regulatory challenges. The research by Mansfield-Devine (2016) provides insights into common challenges organisations encounter when interpreting and integrating the GDPR. Bitar and Jakobsson (2017) adopted a technical approach by developing an HSM encryption model for securing data, while Alawadhi and Udeaja (2018) explored the need for assessing the human element in incident response programs. Nevertheless, the new requirements in the GDPR that make it compulsory to report instances of data breach and their impact on data subjects are beyond the scope of existing incident-handling frameworks. This research aims to build on existing frameworks and to formulate a decision support system that can be used to meet compliance for incident response.

8.3. Development of Decision Support System

Prior to the introduction of the GDPR, some organisations were ambivalent about the level of impact they would incur if they reported serious data breaches. Consequently, they were reluctant to report some instances of data breach. While previous privacy legislation made implicit reference to this practice in order to deter it, the GDPR made explicit reference to the practice, asking for controllers and processors to demonstrate accountability and transparency. Article 5 (2) of the GDPR regulation explicitly outlines that controllers should be responsible for the development of appropriate frameworks and be able to demonstrate compliance with principles relating to the processing of personal data (PwC, 2018). This indicates that a demonstration of accountability goes beyond simply achieving the minimum compliance requirements outlined in the GDPR.

This research aims to address these challenges by formulating a conceptual decision support system for incident response and breach notification requirements. Research by Hevner *et al.* (2014), outlines principles within design science that can be employed in the development of artefacts, instead of verifying theories in research. Design science can be employed to guide the development of IT artefacts in a structured way and can include formal logic diagrams, software systems or rigorous mathematical-based design (Hevner *et al.*, 2014). Design science paradigms can be used to solve complex IT problems and provide defined processes that can be used in conceptual system designs.

8.3.1. *Pre-GDPR incident response frameworks*

An incident response framework can act as a blueprint for responding to security incidents. This is an important part of business continuity and provides specific instructions that can be implemented to quickly identify and neutralise security threats and minimise their impact on normal business functions. A number of widely used incident handling frameworks such as NIST, SANS and CERT can be employed by organisations of varying size to guide incident response activities.

The NIST incident handling guide comprises a standard four-phase incident response which shares several similarities with other models employed within incident response programs. Nevertheless, new requirements in the GDPR such as the reporting of a data breach within 72 hours and the notifying of data subjects must be considered in order to comply with the GDPR.

8.3.2. *Compliant GDPR framework design*

The design of the DSS was informed by challenges identified in the literature and the mandatory requirements for incident response and breach notification. Existing incident response frameworks were extended and relevant areas of the GDPR were integrated into policies and process to meet compliance. The European Data Protection Board (EDPB) provides guidance for consistent interpretation and implementation of GDPR articles, while the ENISA incident handling guide offers demonstrable and practical steps for establishing incident management procedures (Cichonski *et al.*, 2012).

The creation of the decision support framework aims to be flexible and adaptable and integrates a three-step approach. Firstly, the GDPR incident response dashboard provides an overview of additional response phases that are aligned with new requirements in the GDPR.

The subsequent steps include change restriction measures. These measures contain functionalities that can be leveraged to track and audit system changes and mitigate security incidents. In addition, these measures help to address the requirements in Article 32 that require organisations to demonstrate technical and organisational measures for protecting personal data. The final phase of the DSS presents a conceptual incident process flow that is structured using UML notations. The design of the DSS aims to extend the theoretical findings in the literature review by using a UML activity diagram to model breach notification processes and incorporate a technical element within the scope of the research.

The design included a distinct colour scheme and decision process flow to identify different levels of incidents such as minor, medium and major data breaches. The incident response dashboard expands existing frameworks by employing an eight-phase incident response cycle that incorporates the new requirements outlined in the GDPR such as the requirement to document the nature and extent of the data breach and the requirement to notify the ICO and data subjects within a specific timeframe.

The creation of incident scenarios forms part of a system design that provides practical steps for assessing security incidents and mitigates the adverse impacts and consequences of security incidents. The breach scenarios aim also to demonstrate the applicability of the DSS to aiding incident response activities and addressing various security incidents. This is complemented by the formulation of change restriction measures which include established tools and processes that can be leveraged to track and audit system changes, mitigate security incidents, and address the requirements in Article 32 of the GDPR that require organisations to demonstrate technical and organisational measures for protecting personal data. The change restriction measures can also be employed to govern access requests and ensure stringent measures are in place to protect personal data.

8.3.3. *Justification for component selection*

Design Science has been widely used in research to guide artifact development and solve problems identified in organisations as stated by Hevner *et al.* (2014). The organisational challenges identified in the literature provide a basis for the design of the artifact and accordingly Design Science provides proven principles to guide the development of the DSS. In order to formulate a comprehensive response approach, both the security and privacy characteristics of data need to be addressed.

The stipulation in Article 32, Paragraph (1) (b) outlines the need for robust security policies and procedures that continuously satisfy confidentiality, integrity and availability of personal data (EU, GDPR, 2016). Although there is no specific requirement to map the articles in the regulation, mapping the articles can be the first step towards meeting compliance with the GDPR. In order to simplify the design of the DSS, different elements of the decision support system provide the requisite functionalities to facilitate the consistent interpretation of GDPR articles to allow a prompt response to incidents.

This can be achieved by using diagrammatic modelling and categorisation of incident response processes to aid decision making. UML is an industry standard language with notations and methods for visualising conceptual system designs and it can represent the first step towards developing complex software systems (Fowler, 2016). The notation in UML was deemed suitable to enrich the design of the DSS and show interactions between different levels of data breach via a step-by-step decision process flow.

8.4. Focus Group

When assessing appropriate methods to employ in this research, the intent was to garner professional feedback on and in-depth insight into the design and usability of the decision support system. Focus group interviews are exploratory in nature and qualitative data can be gathered through feedback, opinions and attitudes (Kuada, 2012). To that end, a focus group interview was deemed suitable to achieve the objectives of the research. The design incorporated a two-step process: firstly, inferences drawn from the literature were used to inform the design of the DSS, then, focus groups with semi-structured interviews were conducted to gather feedback and analysis, and finally, the results were interpreted and analysed.

8.4.1. *Recruitment of participants*

The way in which participants are recruited can determine the success of the focus group. According to Kuada (2012), care should be taken to ensure participants possess the right attributes and experience to contribute to the discussions. The recruitment of participants was conducted using deliberate sampling, which was described by Hevner *et al.* (2014) as purposive sampling. Participants from different organisations and industry sectors with a minimum of 10 years' experience in their fields were selected to ensure they met the criteria and could fully participate in the discussions.

The data-gathering instruments included a notepad, an audio recorder and a video recorder; however, as one of the participants was ambivalent about the video recording, it was subsequently omitted from the sessions. The focus group sessions commenced with general questions being asked before narrowing down to specific probes to obtain appropriate feedback. The first set of questions was a general introduction to initiate the discourse on the overall design of the system. The second set of questions introduced several case studies and asked about the usability of the system design.

The final set of questions allowed participants to discuss and assess the overall strengths and weaknesses of the system and to recommend future improvements (Kuada, 2012). The importance of the researcher in facilitating the discussions and enabling an open atmosphere where everyone could contribute was highlighted. The researcher was the only moderator conducting the session; however, the interactions and responses were carefully monitored and recorded, and probing questions and prompts were used to keep the conversation going. This facilitated more in-depth discussions, which were instrumental in gathering the required feedback to meet the objectives of the study.

8.4.2. *Ethical consideration*

Whilst conducting this research, it was necessary to correspond and interact with human participants (listed in Table 8.2) to capture their opinions and feedback on the design of the system; however, this can present various ethical and professional concerns. Hevner *et al.* (2014) outlined the importance of addressing ethical neutrality in the collection and analysis of the data. Therefore, while conducting the focus group interview, it was necessary to consider the needs, values and the views of the participants. After processing and reporting on data gathered from the focus group session (shown in Table 8.3), participants

Table 8.2. Sample selections of participants in the group interview.

Current Position	Gender	Industry	Recent Degree	Years of Experience	Size of the Organisations
IT Data Protection Officer	M	Financial services	MSc	10	4000
IT Project Manager	M	Education	BSc	15	600
Information Security Analyst	M	Technology	MSc	12	2000
IT Audit Manager	F	Health	PhD	13	5000
IT Risk Manager	M	Technology	MSc	10	250
IT Change Request Manager	F	Retail	BSc	12	800

Table 8.3. Refined codes and key themes from the focus group session.

Themes Identified	Transcript Paragraph Ref.	Interview Question Ref.
Applicability of DSS for incident response and breach notification	P.1, P.2, P.3, P.4, P.5, P.6, P.7, P.8, P.9, P.10, P.11, P.12, P.13, P.14 , P.15, P.16, P.19, P.37, P.38, P.39	Q.1, Q.2, Q.3, Q.4, Q.6, Q.12
Usability of DSS for the comprehensive incident response approach	P.17, P.18, P.19, P.21, P.22, P.23, P.24, P.25, P.26, P.27, P.28, P.29, P.30, P.40, P.41, P.42, P.43, P.44	Q.5, Q.6, Q.7, Q.8, Q.9, Q.10, Q.11, Q.12
Employing DSS design for assessing 3rd party risks	P.31, P.32, P.33, P.34, P.35, P.36	Q.13, Q.14
Usability of DSS for addressing privacy by design and default	P.47, P.48, P.49, P.50, P.51, P.52, P.53	Q.14, Q.15, Q.16
Feedback and recommendation for improving design	P.54, P.55, P.56	Q.17, Q.18, Q.19
Feasibility of DSS for implementation	P.57, P.58, P.59, P.60	Q.19, Q.20

were given the opportunity to verify that their views were accurately represented.

8.5. Results and Analysis

The written and audio recordings were transcribed verbatim, after researchers continuously listened to the recording and made relevant notes.

Kuada (2012) emphasizes that focus group analysis differs from individual interviews, in that the data gathered will also come from observing participants' reaction patterns and the overall interpersonal dynamics. The data gathered from the focus was analysed using a structured approach to present a range of evidence on the design, usability and efficacy of the DSS.

8.5.1. *Results*

The applicability of the system design was assessed by subject experts with working knowledge of GDPR who provided feedback on the topic. Over the last few years, organisations have seen an increased trend in data breach incidents and sophisticated attack vectors (P.1, P.2, P.3, P.4, P.5, Q.1, Q.2). Some of the attacks became more targeted. Such attacks are probably motivated by financial gain.

8.5.2. *Usability of DSS for addressing privacy by design and default*

The design of the system employing the UML process flow provides an overview of processes that can aid decisions to address security incidents as well as breach notification and communication requirements (P.39, P.40, P.41, P.42, P.43, P.44, Q.12, Q.13). When assessing the usability of the system with reference to the incorporation of privacy by design and default, the participants noted the relevance of the change request diagram and the distinct colour scheme of the UML process flow to developing and integrating security safeguards for new hardware and software systems

(P.45, P.46, P.47, P.48, P.49, Q.14, Q.15). Further discussions on the mapping of articles against security controls noted the usability and relevance of the DSS mapping document for the interpretation and integration of the GDPR into the incident response plans (P.50, P.51, P.52, Q.16, Q.17).

8.5.3. *Feedback and recommendations for improving design*

The discussions and feedback provided by the focus group interviewees presented valuable professional insight into the GDPR implementation challenges and the use of a decision support system for addressing mandatory requirements. The feedback on the overall design described the system as having the relevant features for formulating GDPR incident response plans, however further improvements were recommended so that the system would have response procedures for incidents occurring outside of normal working hours. It was also recommended that the contacts of key personnel in the response teams be listed (P.53, P.54, P.55, Q.17, Q.18). Other recommendations for improvement in design included suggestions for the next phase iteration of the coding of the UML design into a software plugin.

8.5.4. *Feasibility of DSS for implementation*

After providing feedback and recommendations for future improvements of the DSS, the participants discussed the scope of the system design and its suitability for implementation within an organisation. Several implementation solutions were discussed and the DSS was assessed as appropriate for deployment along with existing systems as a guide for creating GDPR incident response plans. In addition, participants noted that business areas such as legal departments and change management departments would need to sanction the deployment of such systems in their organisation.

On balance, the recommendation for system implementation highlighted key functionalities of the system design that are appropriate for incident response and breach notification, however it was suggested that the DSS was suitable for implementation only as an annex to existing frameworks. In addition, further suggestions for improvements to and the refinement of the next phase of design included the development and testing of the DSS to automate some of the incident response phases (P.58, P.59, P.60, Q.20).

8.5.5. *Summary of results and analysis*

The feedback on the usability of the DSS design provided information on the relevance of the functionality of each component to addressing the challenges in implementing the GDPR. Discussions on the merits of the overall design of the DSS can facilitate the decision to establish a GDPR incident response and breach notification program within an organisation. Nevertheless, there were also recommendations for further improvements to the next phase of the DSS design, including recommendations to incorporate interactive response phases and to automate some of the functionalities of dashboards.

The development of the Decision Support System and the feedback provided by industry practitioners provided valuable insights into the viability of the design and its ability to meet incident response requirements. The participants suggested that the current design of the system could be implemented as an annex to existing systems integrating the GDPR. The feedback also confirmed some of the challenges found in the literature such as the need to have comprehensive incident response strategies and the issues associated with the ad-hoc and generic response approach for security incidents. The findings are further strengthened by the triangulation of the literature review, the analysis and the interpretation of qualitative data gathered from the feedback. Further insights into the context of the outcome can be obtained by evaluating the overall research approach and this is covered in the next chapter.

8.6. Evaluation of Research Process and Methods

Part of the objective in developing the system included contrasting different methods to garner feedback on the artefact design. Several distinct methods such as online surveys, one-to-one interviews and focus group interviews were critically assessed before semi-structured focus group interviews were adopted for the research. Focus group interviews are widely used in many disciplines, including the social sciences, to gather knowledge and opinions of a particular phenomenon. Hevner *et al.* (2014) demonstrated the use of a focus group for gathering feedback and the refinement of the artifact.

Although some computer-assisted qualitative data analysis software (CAQDAS) is available to help manage the data collected, due to the learning curve and the researchers' lack of familiarity with any of the software mentioned, MS Word and Excel were used to process transcripts from the focus group. Although transcribing and coding the data using this method required more time and effort, with the requisite skills and persistence it was accomplished satisfactorily.

8.6.1. *Research limitations*

The research is limited to computer security incident response and data breach notification, but there are other important considerations when securing a system, including environmental and physical security. However, this is beyond the remit of this research. During the interview sessions, participants provided personal knowledge acquired from many years of experience. However, they could perceive themselves as representing their respective organisations and may be reluctant to provide information that might portray weakness or failures in their respective organisations.

The recording and transcription of the focus group interviews was limited to a single researcher. Whilst the participants were culturally diverse and heterogeneous in experience and the industry sector, the sample feedback could be considered relatively little in comparison to the views of experts in various and wider industries. Moreover, another limitation of the feedback on DSS is that it did not include the implementation or period of maturation within an organisation. For the purpose of this research only a single session of focus group interviews was carried out. However, the research provides a firm basis for the design to be extended in further research.

8.7. Conclusion and Recommendation

The numbers of reported data breach incidents have been increasing over the last few years and this highlights the need for privacy legislation to be strengthened in accordance with changes in technology and the new ways in which data is created, shared and processed. The research started out by posing the following questions.

1. What are the main challenges in interpreting and integrating the GDPR into incident response and breach notification plans?
2. How can the development of a decision support process or system address the challenges identified?
3. What method can be employed to provide feedback on the design and usability of the formulated solution?

To address these questions, the literature review was used to identify existing challenges and to help to inform the design of the Decision Support System using Design Science and UML notation. Focus group interviews were adopted to provide feedback on the usability of the system for meeting GDPR compliance requirements. The feedback from these interviews and the literature showed that a comprehensive response strategy is crucial for managing complex threats as well as the risks associated with third party entities. The research findings also highlight the importance of establishing data privacy by design and default and the potential consequences of failing to notify the relevant supervisory authority and data subjects in the aftermath of a data breach.

The findings further showed that the data breach scenarios and change restriction measures within the DSS were useful for situational analysis and mitigating security risks to personal data. Overall feedback on the usability of DSS indicated it that it was relevant for addressing incident response and breach notification challenges associated with the GDPR. For example, the findings show that the mappings of relevant articles could help facilitate the interpretation and integration of the GDPR into incident response programs. The design of the DSS builds on previous research by assessing the impact of data breaches on data subjects and by incorporating new requirements in Articles 33 and 34 of the GDPR.

The design of the system also provides guidance that can be used by organisations to facilitate incident response decisions and protect personal data. Moreover, further rigor is provided by adopting a hybrid assessment for the development of the DSS by using principles in Design Science and feedback from focus group interview sessions.

8.7.1. *Recommendations for future work*

While conducting the research, several noteworthy discoveries were made for viable future work on and improvement of the DSS design. Part of the findings revealed that no formal auditing of security policies or agreement for immediate notice of data breach was established between some organisations and their associated third-party partners. Therefore further research is needed to develop an incident notification framework between data controllers or processors based inside of the EU jurisdiction. The recommendations drawn from the findings also suggested that the possible next stage improvements of the DSS design could generate codes from each of the UML process flows to develop a GDPR software system as a plug-in for integration with other systems.

References

1. Alawadhi, S. and Udeaja, C. (2018). Obstacles and Benefits in Implementation of Gold, Silver, and Bronze (GSB) Model in Emergency Response in the UAE. *Procedia Engineering*, **212**, pp. 427–434.
2. Bitar, H. and Jakobson, B. (2017). *GDPR: Securing Personal Data in Compliance with new EU-Regulations* [Online]. Available at http://www.diva-portal.org/smash/get/diva2:1113478/FULLTEXT01.pdf (Accessed: 6 October 2018).
3. Bowles, N. (2018). Thermostats, Locks and Lights: Digital Tools of Domestic Abuse [Online]. Available at: https://www.nytimes.com/2018/06/23/technology/smart-home-devices-domestic-abuse.html (Accessed: 29 September 2018).

4. Buchler, N., Rajivan, P., Marusich, L., Lightner, L. and Gonzalez, C. (2018). Sociometrics and Observational Assessment of Teaming and Leadership in a Cyber-Security Defence Competition. *Computers and Security*, **73**, pp. 114–136.
5. Cichonski, P., Millar, T., Grance, T. and Scarfone, K. (2012). Computer Security Incident Handling Guide [Online]. Available at: https://nvlpubs.nist.gov/nistpubs/SpecialPublications/NIST.SP.800-61r2.pdf (Accessed: 23 October 2018).
6. Cobb, M. (2018). Plugging the Skills Gap: The Vital Role That Women Should Play in Cyber-Security. *Computer Fraud and Security*, **2018**(1), pp. 5–8.
7. Enisa.europa.eu. (2011). Guidance on the Security Measures in Article 13a [Online]. Available at: https://resilience.enisa.europa.eu/article-13/guideline-for-minimum-security-measures/technical-guideline-for-minimum-security-measures-v1.0 (Accessed: 8 November 2018).
8. Fischhoff, B. (2015). *The Realities of Risk* — Cost-Benefit Analysis [Online]. Available at: http://science.sciencemag.org/content/350/6260/aaa6516 (Accessed: January 2019).
9. Fowler, K. (2016). *Data Breach Preparation and Response Network Security* [Online]. Available at: https://books.google.co.uk/books/about/ Data_Breach_Preparation_and_Response.html?id=m5SZBgAAQBAJ&printsec=frontcover&source=kp_read_button&redir_esc=y#v=onepage&q&f=fals (Accessed: 26 May 2018).
10. Garber, J. (2018). GDPR — Compliance Nightmare or Business Opportunity. *Computer Fraud and Security*, **2018**(6), pp. 14–15.
11. General Data Protection Regulation. (2016). *OJ L119/1, Regulation (EU) 2016/679 of the European Parliament and of the Council* [Online]. Available at: https://eur-lex.europa.eu/legal-content/EN/TXT/HTML/?uri=CELEX:32016R0679&from=EN (Accessed: 18 October 2018).
12. Hedley, D. and Jacobs, M. (2017). The Shape of Things to Come: The Equifax Breach, the GDPR and Open-Source Security. *Computer Fraud and Security*, **2017**(11), pp. 5–7.
13. Hevner, A. R., March, S. T., Park, J. and Ram, S. (2014). Design Science in Information Systems Research. *Management Information Systems Quarterly*, **28**(1), pp. 75–105.
14. Horvath, M. (2018). *EU Privacy Rules to Have Global Implications* [Online]. Available at: https://www.gartner.com/podcasts/eu-rivacy-rules-have-global-implications/ (Accessed: 6 June 2018).

15. Ico.org.uk. (2018). *TalkTalk Gets Record £400,000 Fine for Failing to Prevent October 2015 Attack* [Online]. Available at: https://ico.org.uk/about-the-ico/news-and-events/news-and-blogs/2016/10/talktalk-gets-record-400-000-fine-for-failing-to-prevent-october-2015-attack/ (Accessed: 12 September 2018).
16. ISO. (2018). *ISO/IEC 27001:2013: Information Technology — Security Techniques — Information Security Management Systems — Requirements* [Online]. Available at: https://www.iso.org/standard/54534.html. (Accessed: 28 October 2018).
17. Kothari, C. R. (2004). *Research Methodology: Methods and Techniques* (2nd ed.). New Delhi, India: New Age International Publishers.
18. Kuada, J. E. (2012). *Research Methodology — A Project Guide for University Students* (1st ed.). Frederiksberg, Denmark: Samfundslitteratur.
19. Luszcz, J. (2018). Apache Struts 2: How Technical and Development Gaps Caused the Equifax Breach. *Network Security*, **2018**(1), pp. 5–8.
20. Mansfield-Devine, S. (2016). Data Protection: Prepare Now or Risk Disaster. *Computer Fraud and Security*, **2016**(12), pp. 5–12.
21. PwC. (2018). Information Security Breaches Survey 2017: Redefining the Security Culture — A Better Way to Protect Your Business [Online]. Available at: https://www.pwc.be/en/news-publications/publications/2017/information-security-breaches-survey.html (Accessed: 9 October 2018).
22. Reding, V. (2010). The Upcoming Data Protection Reform for the European Union. *International Data Privacy Law*, **1**(1), pp. 3–5.
23. Schwarz, P. (2016). *Risk and High Risk: Walking the GDPR Tightrope* [Online]. Available at: https://iapp.org/news/a/risk-and-high-risk-walking-the-gdpr-tightrope/ (Accessed: 23 September 2018).
24. Solterbeck, A. (2006). Protecting Data at Rest and in Motion. *Network Security*, 2006(9), pp. 14–17.
25. Steiner, D. (2018). *Hackers Are Aggressively Targeting Law Firms' Data* [Online]. Available at: https://www.cio.com/article/3212829/cyber-attacks-espionage/ hackers-are-aggressively-targeting-law-firms-data.html (Accessed: 15 October 2018).
26. Von Solms, R. and van Niekerk, J. (2013). From Information Security to Cyber Security. *Computers and Security*, 38, pp. 97–102.
27. Wood, M. (2015). CES: Security Risks From the Smart Home [Online]. Available at: https://www.nytimes.com/2015/01/08/technology/personaltech/ces-security-risks-from-the-smart-home.html (Accessed: 29 September 2018).

Chapter 9

Evaluation of the Standardised Digital Forensic Investigation Process Model (SDFIPM)

Reza Montasari*, Richard Hill†, Victoria Carpenter‡ and Amin Hosseinian-Far§

**Department of Computer Science*
School of Computing and Engineering
The University of Huddersfield
r.montasari@hud.ac.uk

†Department of Computer Science
School of Computing and Engineering
The University of Huddersfield
r.hill@hud.ac.uk

‡Research Development Innovation and Enterprise Services
University of Bedfordshire
victoria.carpenter@beds.ac.uk

§Faculty of Business and Law
University of Northampton
amin.hosseinian-far@northampton.ac.uk

ABSTRACT

The existing digital forensic investigation process models (DFIPMs) have often been developed by digital forensic practitioners (DFPs) based on their own personal experience and on an ad-hoc basis, without attention to the establishment of standardisation within the field. This has prevented the institution of both scientific and generic processes that are urgently required within the different fields of law enforcement, commerce and incident response. Therefore, a novel model — the Standardised Digital Forensic Investigation Process Model (the SDFIPM) — was developed to address these shortcomings. Following the selected research methodology, Peffers *et al.*'s Design Science Research Process (DSRP), the SDFIPM was also subjected to both Demonstration and Evaluation activities to determine how well it would support the solution to the stated research problem. Therefore, this paper presents the results of the Demonstration and Evaluation activities applied to the proposed model. Our study makes three significant and novel contributions to the field of Digital Forensics (DF): First, it implements a process model, the design of which is inclusive of all the advantages of the previous models through their synthesis, harmonisation and extension. No such model previously existed in the literature. Second, the SDFIPM is generic in that it can be applied within the three fields of law enforcement, commerce and incident response. Third, unlike the majority of the previous models, the effectiveness of which is unknown due to the lack of an evaluation process, the SDFIPM's efficacy is demonstrated in relation to both components of 'utility' and 'usability'.

Keywords: SDFIPM, digital forensics, cloud forensics, chain of custody

9.1. Introduction

In order for digital evidence to be admissible, investigators need to demonstrate that they have specialized knowledge and that the evidence was acquired using reliable principles and methods (Montasari, 2018; Montasari, 2016a; Kessler, 2010). Careful notice is taken in court of the manner in which the digital investigative process (DIP) has been carried out (Montasari, 2016a; Kessler, 2010; Cohen, 2011; Mason, 2007). A DFP might discover significant and incriminating evidence, but if they cannot present the evidence in a coherent and understandable way to the lay audience (such as the judge and jury), the case may be lost (Sherman, 2006). The complexity of tools and methodologies used to perform a DIP requires investigators to be able to explain the process in a manner that a judge and jury can understand (Kessler, 2010). Nevertheless, the field of DF still lacks formal process models that courts can employ to determine the reliability of the digital evidence presented to them (Montasari, 2017; Montasari, 2016b; Montasari *et al.*, 2015; Valjarevic and Venter, 2015; Kohn *et al.*, 2013; US-CERT, 2012; Agarwal, 2011). The absence of agreements associated with DFIPMs has been widely acknowledged by many researchers in the field (Montasari, 2016c; Montasari, 2016d; Montasari, 2016e; Valjarevic and Venter, 2015; Kohn *et al.*, 2013; Agarwal *et al.*, 2011; Rogers *et al.*, 2006). Zainudin *et al.* (2011) state that one of the most significant problems encountered by DFPs is the absence of standardisation in the field of DF. Casey (2011) argues that the development of a formal process model enables a complete, rigorous investigation, ensures proper evidence handling and reduces the chances of mistakes created by preconceived theories, time pressures, and other potential pitfalls (Casey, 2011). Similarly, Valjarevic and Venter (2015) state that conducting a digital forensic investigation (DFI) requires a formalized process model, arguing, "There is currently neither an international standard nor a global, harmonized DFI process."

One reason for the absence of formal process models is the relatively recent addition of DF as a scientific discipline compared to traditional forensic science (Cohen, 2012). The latter has developed, together with its fundamental biological sciences, over several decades (Beebe and Clark, 2005; Palmer, 2001), whereas DF science is still being formed and therefore lags considerably behind the better-developed, underlying Computer Science (CS) (Montasari, 2016a; Beebe and Clark, 2005; Carrier and Spafford, 2003). The DF discipline has developed without any of the initial research required to provide an essential, thorough, scientific foundation (Valjarevic and Venter, 2015; US-CERT, 2012; Peisert *et al.*, 2008; Meyers and Rogers, 2004; Carrier, 2002). The United States Computer Emergency Readiness Team (US-CERT, 2012) notes, "Because computer forensics is a new discipline, there is little standardization and consistency across the courts and industry." Meyers and Rogers (2004) take an even stronger view, warning that DF is branded as a "junk science" because of the absence of certifications, standards or peer-reviewed methods (Meyers and Rogers, 2004). Similarly, Carrier (2002) highlights that issues are raised in considering DF as a science due to the absence of generally agreed-upon standards and procedures. A further cause of the lack of formal models for DIP is the 'ad-hoc' approach taken by the authors of these models, who have failed to employ scientific approaches when developing them (Montasari, 2017a; Montasari, 2016a; Montasari, 2016b; Montasari, 2016c; Montasari *et al.*, 2015; Agarwal *et al.*, 2011).

Previous models have often been developed by practitioners who are not necessarily scientists. These models are based on their personal experience and are developed on an ad-hoc basis (Montasari, 2016a; Montasari *et al.*, 2015; Valjarevic and Venter, 2015; Agarwal *et al.*, 2011; Montasari, 2016c). However, as also stated by Karyda and Mitrou (2007), using ad-hoc methods and tools for the extraction of digital evidence can undermine its reliability and credibility. Referring to the same issue, Reith *et al.* (2002) state, "This is a problem because evidence must be obtained using methods that are proven to reliably extract and analyse data without bias or modification." This is further supported by Beebe and Clark (2005), who argue that rigor in a DFIPM is achieved only through the use of "formal" and "scientific" approaches, and by Solomon *et al.* (2011), who argue that current procedures and tools should not be mistaken for a consistent investigative process. The latter authors contend, "Tools and procedures are developed from the experience of law enforcement and system administrators simply in an ad-hoc manner rather than coming from the scientific community where other traditional forensic sciences get their methodologies." (Solomon *et al.*, 2011).

Therefore, the adoption of ad-hoc approaches in developing previous models has led to a variety of process models with conflicting stages, activities and terminology, which in turn has prevented the establishment of the formal processes needed by courts and investigators alike (Montasari *et al.*, 2015; Agarwal *et al.*, 2011). As a result, many researchers have increasingly called for scientific approaches and formal methods for the DIP (Cohen, 2012; Carlton and Worthley, 2009; Garfinkel *et al.*, 2009; Pollitt, 2009; Leigland and Krings, 2004). A further issue with the existing models is their tendency to focus on one specific area of DF, neglecting other environments (Montasari, 2016a; Montasari, 2016b; Montasari *et al.*, 2015). Unlike in other domains of forensic practice, DFPs operate in various fields (Freiling and Schwittay, 2007; Beebe and Clark, 2005; Ciardhuáin, 2004; Carrier and Spafford, 2003). Therefore, as Carrier and Spafford (2003) argue, "A model must be abstract and apply to law enforcement investigations, corporate investigations, and incident response." However, instead of being generic, previous models have often focussed on only one specific area, such as law enforcement, commerce or incident response (Montasari, 2016a; Montasari, 2016b; Adams, 2012; Pollitt, 2009), therefore failing to consider the requirements of those operating in different domains. The result has been the hindering of the development of a generic model that can be applied in the various fields of DF (Montasari, 2016a; Montasari, 2016b; Montasari *et al.*, 2015).

A third significant concern associated with the previous models is that they are not comprehensive, failing to cover the entire DIP. Beebe and Clark (2005) argue that a more comprehensive and generally accepted framework is needed to enhance scientific rigor and facilitate education, application and research. Similarly, Ciardhuáin (2004) states, "A comprehensive model of cyber crime investigations is important for standardising terminology, defining requirements, and supporting the development of new techniques and tools for investigators."

9.1.1. *Research problem*

The foregoing considerations were formulated in Montasari's [3] study into the following research problem:

> *There does not exist a comprehensive model encompassing the entire digital investigative process that is formal, such that it can assist a court of law in determining the reliability of the investigative process followed, and that is generic, in that it can be applied in the different fields of law enforcement, commerce and incident response.*

To address the above research problem, Montasari (2016a) developed a comprehensive model, the Comprehensive Digital Forensic Investigation Process Model (the CDFIPM), which the Standardised Digital Forensic Investigation Process Model (the SDFIPM) forms the middle part of. The CDFIPM, which encompasses the entire DIP, is formal in that it synthesizes, harmonises and extends the existing models, and also generic in that it can be applied in the different fields of law enforcement, commerce and incident response. The focus of this study is only on the middle part of the CDFIPM, namely the proposed SDFIPM. To this end, we first introduce and discuss the SDFIPM prior to presenting the results of the Demonstration and Evaluation activities applied to the model.

9.1.2. *Structure of the paper*

The remainder of the paper is structured as follows: Section 9.2 presents a background summary to the previous DFIPMs. Section 9.3 discusses the research methodology, while Section 9.4 provides an overview of the proposed model. Section 9.5 discusses the Demonstration activity, whereby the SDFIPM is applied to a case study, and a walkthrough of the model is performed. Section 9.6 describes the Evaluation Process, through which the SDFIPM is subjected to an external, independent evaluation by leading experts within the three domains of law enforcement, commerce and incident response. Finally, in Section 9.7, the paper is concluded, the research contributions are outlined, and future work is discussed.

9.2. Background to the Previous DFIPMs

Prior to the design and development of the SDFIPM, we performed a critical review of the previous models followed by an assessment of each of the models against three different sets of assessment criteria (Montasari, 2016a), including: the Daubert Test (Farrell, 1993) Five-Point Requirement, the Carrier and Spafford (2003) Five-Point Requirement and the Beebe and Clark (2005) Four-Point Requirement. The aim of this critical analysis was to gain an in-depth insight into the previous models and also to determine which could contribute to the proposed model. Since law enforcement, commerce and incident response were the three environments on which our research focussed, previous models within those three domains which most closely met the assessment criteria were considered for their possible contributions to the new model. Adams (2012) has adopted a similar approach in which he assesses the previous DFIPMs against the Daubert Test and Carrier and Spafford Five-Point Requirements.

Our approach for assessing the previous DFIPMs was considered important (Kohn *et al.*, 2013; Cohen, 2012; Cohen, 2010) as any model institutionalized through subsequent intellectual discourse and practical use must take into account other researchers' perspectives, approaches and "vernacular". Having critically reviewed and assessed the previous models (Montasari, 2016a; Montasari, 2016c; Montasari, 2016e), our findings revealed that these models had often been developed by DFPs based on their own personal experience and on an ad hoc basis without any consideration of how standardization should be established within the field (Valjarevic and Venter, 2015). It was further revealed that this had prevented the establishment of formal processes that were urgently needed by courts of law (Montasari, 2016a; Montasari *et al.*, 2015). As Table 9.1 (Montasari *et al.*, 2015) clearly demonstrates, the previous DFIPMs display significant disparities in terms of the number of phases, the scope and the specific domains that they have been developed for. As a result, these models have often been criticised for being too specific (Carrier and Spafford, 2003; Reith *et al.*, 2002), too high level (Beebe and Clark, 2005), too broad (Rogers *et al.*, 2006), too technical (Venter, 2006) and too complex (Selamat *et al.*, 2008). Therefore, the proposed model was developed to address the shortcomings of the previous models. It was demonstrated that an implementation of our model would be of immediate value to both DFPs and courts of law.

9.3. Research Methodology

The Design Science Research (DSR) methodology, widely adopted in the domain of Information Systems (IS) (Hevner and Chatterjee,

2010; Peffers *et al.*, 2006; Hevner *et al.*, 2004; March and Smith, 1995; Walls *et al.*, 1992; Nunamaker *et al.*, 1990), was selected as the methodology to conduct this research. The main aim of DSR is to achieve or develop knowledge and understanding of a problem domain by building and applying a designed artefact (Van Aken, 2005; Hevner *et al.*, 2004). DSR involves the design of novel or innovative artefacts and the analysis of the performance or use of such artefacts (Watts *et al.*, 2009; Kuechler and Vaishnavi, 2008). The development and evaluation of artefacts form an important part in DSR (Hevner *et al.*, 2004; March and Storey, 2008). Artefacts include, amongst others: models, methods, constructs, instantiations and design theories (March and Storey, 2008; March and Smith, 1995), social innovations, and new or previously unknown properties of technical, social or informational resources (March and Storey, 2008). The artefact related to this research is a new model, the SDFIPM, which encompasses the middle part of the larger model, the CDFIPM. The organisational context associated with the research is that of law enforcement, commerce and incident response. Our research also addresses the hitherto unsolved problem that there does not exist a DFIPM that is formal in that it synthesizes, harmonises and extends the existing models, and that is generic in that it can be employed in the different fields of law enforcement, incident response and commerce. Our adoption of the DSR methodology as a research methodology in a DF study is informed by Adams (2012), who originally applied the DSR methodology to a study in DF.

The selection of the DSR methodology over other alternative methodologies such as the Grounded Theory (GT) methodology or Requirements Engineering (RE) methodology was due to its relevance to the task of design and the subsequent evaluation of a new process model. Hence, because this study also has at its focus the design, development and subsequent evaluation of the SDFIPM, the DSR methodology was considered to be the most appropriate choice. It is also preferable as it is more pragmatic than alternatives such as the Explanatory Science Research (ESR) methodology [46] and as it can be used to solve a problem for which no solution has already been found (Peffers *et al.*, 2006; Hevner *et al.*, 2004). Therefore, since this research is a problem-based study, again the DSR methodology was deemed the most appropriate methodology. Moreover, the DSR methodology uses both inductive and deductive processes. Since our original study, from which this paper is derived, is aimed at producing a new knowledge and literature (through the inductive process), as well as testing its two research hypotheses (through the deductive process), once again the DSR methodology was considered the most appropriate choice.

Various researchers both within and outside the IS domain have provided guidance to define the DSR and have described what goals should be followed in its production (Hevner and Chatterjee, 2010; Peffers *et al.*, 2006; Hevner *et al.*, 2004; Vaishnavi and Kuechler, 2004; Adams and Courtney, 2004; Rossi and Sein, 2003; March and Smith, 1995; Walls *et al.*, 1992; Eekels and Roozenburg, 1991; Nunamaker *et al.*, 1990; Takeda *et al.*, 1990; Archer, 1984). These researchers have often proposed various methods, processes or theoretical frameworks to rationalise the DSR studies. However, the design science research process (DSRP) model proposed by Peffers *et al.* (2006) was selected as the appropriate DSR methodology to conduct the research in this study. The rationale for doing so is due to the fact that it provides a graphical representation of the conceptual process for both carrying out and presenting the DSR. Such a mental model facilitates the application of the DSR and can also assist the authors in producing and presenting a high-quality DSR that would be accepted as valuable, rigorous and publishable within the field of digital forensics science (Montasari, 2018; Montasari, 2016a).

Peffers *et al.*'s (2006) DSRP consists of six components as shown in Fig. 9.1. The remainder of this section aims briefly to discuss the way in which we applied these six components to our study. For more details regarding the application of the DSRP to our research study, see Montasari's study (Montasari, 2016a).

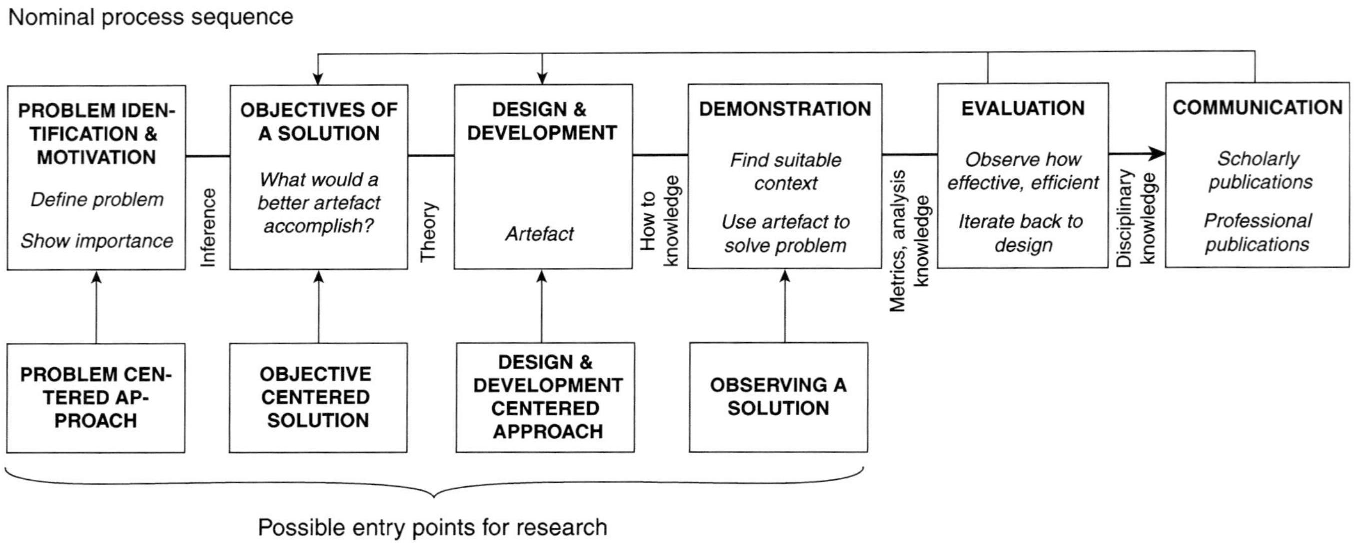

Fig. 9.1. The design science research process (DSRP) model after Peffers *et al.* (2006).

Activity 1 — Problem Identification and Motivation

A profound knowledge of the problem addressed by this research was acquired through a detailed analysis and assessment of the literature related to previous DFIPMs. Having drawn conclusions from the literature review, we were able to formulate the research problem that this study intends to address. Interactions with other experts and our own experience in the field of DF also provided insight into the stated problem.

Activity 2 — Objectives of a Solution

The research aim was formulated according to the definition of the problem. This approach is supported by Peffers *et al.* (2006), who state that objectives should be deduced rationally from the problem specification. Therefore, in order to formulate the stated aim, a deep knowledge was acquired of the state of the problem and its current solution in the form of previously proposed DFIPMs and their efficacy.

Activity 3 — Design and Development

Prior to designing and developing the SDFIPM, all previous DFIPMs were critically reviewed and assessed against three sets of assessment criteria to establish which could contribute to the new model. Law enforcement, commerce and incident response were the three environments on which this research focussed. Therefore, previous models within those three domains were considered for their possible contributions to the new model. Once the most reliable models were identified, their specific key contributions were determined for inclusion in the new model. Following this, the essential components necessary for the new model were identified from the specific key contributions. These formed the basic structure of the SDFIPM. The prevailing models were then built upon by the construction of a new set of domain-specific components. The components identified in the previous models contributed to the development of the new models, as did the new set of constructed components. The SDFIPM was graphically represented in the form of UML Activity Diagrams.

Having already applied the first three components of the DSRP to our research (Montasari, 2016a), in this chapter we focus on the remaining three components, namely Demonstration, Evaluation and Communication activities. The following sections describe how we intend to apply these elements to this study.

Activity 4 — Demonstration

Following the design and development of the SDFIPM, its implementation needs to be demonstrated within an appropriate environment based on the Demonstration Activity of the DSRP. Peffers *et al.* (2006) suggest the use of case studies as such an appropriate environment. Other researchers in the field (Valjarevic and Venter, 2015; Casey, 2011; Beebe and Clark, 2005; Carrier and Spafford, 2003; Ciardhuáin, 2004) have also used case studies as an appropriate environment to determine the applicability of their models. A case study pertaining to the different fields of law enforcement, commerce and incident response has been selected as an appropriate environment for testing the proposed model. Therefore, the SDFIPM will be applied to the selected case study in Section 9.5 in order to demonstrate its application and effectiveness within the three stated domains. We considered this activity important as it would enable us to address any shortcomings prior to the submission of the model to the external, independent experts for formal evaluation. Such an activity would also enable us to avoid impinging on the time of the external reviewers. The results of the Demonstration activity of the research will then determine whether the Design and Development stage needs to be repeated in order for certain alterations to be made.

Activity 5 — Demonstration

Based on the DSRP's requirements, the SDFIPM also needs to be evaluated to determine how well it supports the solution to the stated problem. This activity will compare the SDFIPM's application and effectiveness with the characteristics set out in the research problem. The Evaluation activity of this study, presented in Section 9.6, has involved the submission of the SDFIPM to DFPs within the three domains that are the focus of this research, namely law enforcement, commerce and incident response, and also to judges, barristers and researchers in academia. The aim of such an approach was to enable us to acquire insightful and reliable feedback as to the effectiveness of the SDFIPM from authoritative external reviewers. As with the Demonstration phase, once the evaluation has been carried out, we will be able to judge whether to repeat the Design and Development Phase of the SDFIPM in order to make improvements. Any such amendments will subsequently be introduced to the Design and Development Phase of the SDFIPM.

Activity 6 — Communication

Again, in accordance with the DSRP's requirements, the problem addressed by this research and its importance, its solution (the SDFIPM), its utility and novelty, the rigor of its design and implementation, and its effectiveness will all need to be communicated to the intended user community. The Communication activity of the DSRP in relation to this research has already been covered through publications in well-known and peer-reviewed journals and conferences, and also via our attendance at various conferences, Digital Forensic Expositions and Cyber Security Summits. In addition, we aim to continue with further publications and also to initiate direct interactions with a wide variety of experts, including DFPs, legal practitioners and experts in academia, to communicate the importance of our proposed model.

9.4. Overview of the SDFIPM

The SDFIPM was designed using a top-down approach in order to enable DFPs to gain a better insight into its compositional components, namely Processes, Phases and Sub-Phases. The model consists of seven Processes, each of which contains a different number of Phases. Each Process provides additional lower layers of details, i.e. Phases and Sub-Phases. Figures 9.2 and 9.3 represent the first instance of the formal representation of the SDFIPM, i.e. the UML Activity Diagrams, the combinations of which make up the entire

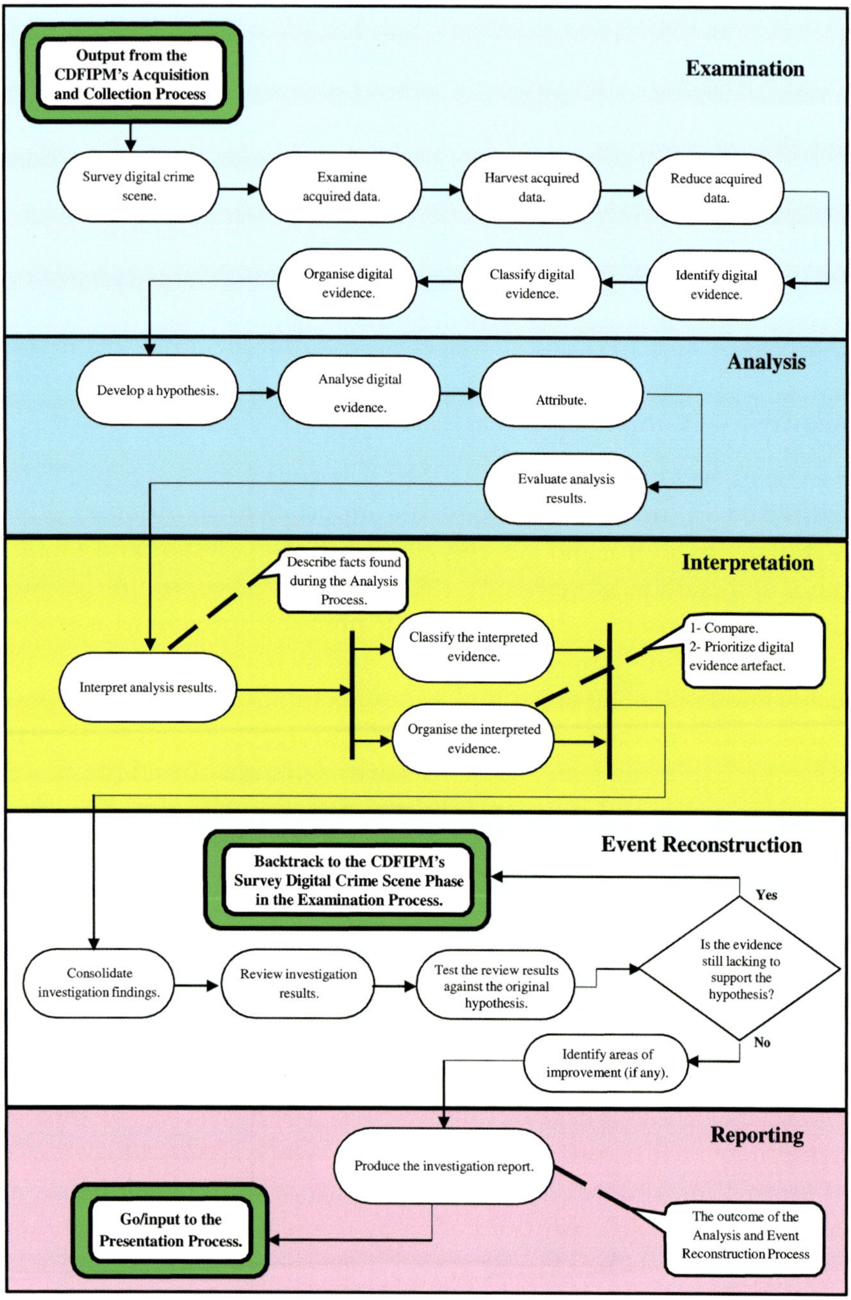

Fig. 9.2. The examination, analysis, interpretation, event reconstruction and reporting processes.

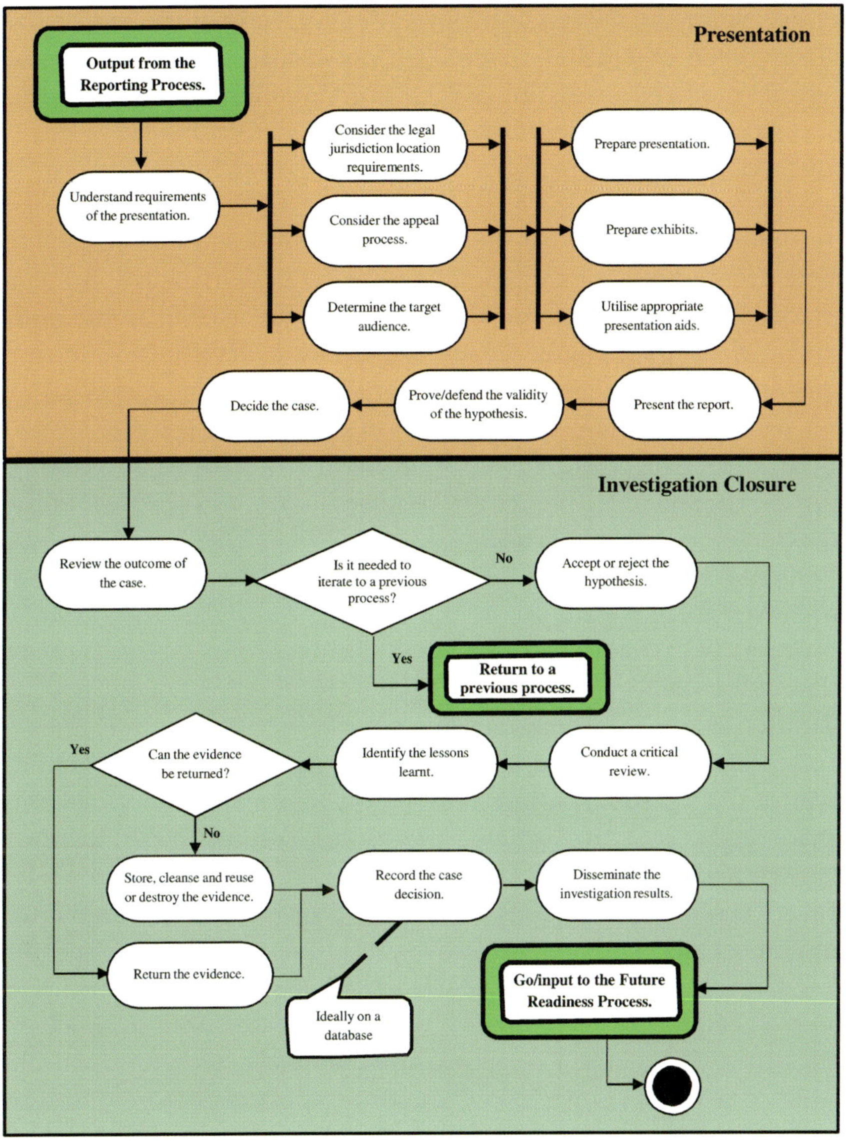

Fig. 9.3. The presentation, investigation closure and future readiness processes.

model. Since the Design and Development Phase of the model has already been extensively covered in Montasari (2016a), the following subsections provide only a brief overview of the model.

9.4.1. *Examination process*

During this Process, a large number of techniques should be used to access, find and extract the potential digital evidence into a human-readable format (Montasari, 2016a; Montasari, 2016b; Kohn *et al.*, 2013). The Survey Digital Crime Scene Phase enables DFPs to find apparent pieces of digital evidence for a particular category of crime in a swift manner. It also assists them in ascertaining the skill level of the suspect, which in turn will allow them to decide what examination and analysis techniques are required in the next process of the SDFIPM, the Analysis Process (discussed later). DFPs must survey the digital crime scene to locate potential evidence, possibly within unconventional locations on the system (Montasari and Peltola, 2015). It is preferable to perform this Phase in a digital forensic laboratory (DFL), using the image (working copy) of the system acquired during the Acquisition Process [8], as it provides a controlled environment and the results can be repeated with another copy of the system. In cases where DFPs might need to perform this phase also on a live system, they must conduct field searches (Montasari, 2016a; Montasari, 2016d) by booting the system into what Carrier and Spafford (2003) call a "trusted environment". DFPs must adapt their investigative techniques based on the specific category of crime to expedite the subsequent Analysis activities as there is often a large volume of data to deal with. For instance, in cases involving server intrusions, DFPs should search for apparent signs of a rootkit installation, examine application logs and also search for new configuration files. Another example (Carrier and Spafford, 2003) concerns analysing network traffic to learn more about an incident; the Survey Digital Crime Scene Phase might analyse traffic for the incident time frame and filter out certain ports and hosts. In other cases, as suggested in Montasari and Peltola (2015), the investigators should also analyse the "common" and "uncommon" locations on the system that might contain artefacts related to the suspect's browsing activities. Unallocated file system space must also be extracted and processed for deleted files, and a low-level timeline of file activity should be examined to trace the user's activities. Often, there are large volumes of data to be examined (Kohn *et al.*, 2013; Ciardhuáin, 2004), and automated techniques should be employed using tools such as FTK (AccessData, 2018) or EnCase (Guidance Software, 2018) in order to support the investigators. Furthermore, a large number of techniques might be performed to process the obfuscated data. For instance, deleted or hidden data can be processed by utilising sound digital forensic methods, as File Allocation tables or disk indexing might be deleted in some investigations. Therefore, this Phase will enable DFPs to ensure that files that have been partially deleted are recognized from the original evidence. DFPs can also reverse-engineer suspicious executables and examine encrypted files (Carrier and Spafford, 2003). It might also be necessary for DFPs to examine the contents of every cluster (physical search) or every file (logical search) (Casey, 2011).

After all data including partially discovered files and folders have been made visible, data then needs to be harvested by giving a logical structure to the entire data set. The file and folder structure should be indexed to provide structure to acquired data. Raw data will be shown as information, and the partially deleted files which were processed during the Examine Acquired Data Phase will become visible to the degree that they were rendered visible. The result of the Harvest Data Phase is the production of a logical structured data set (Kohn *et al.*, 2013) where the extracted raw data has now become structured information (Kohn *et al.*, 2013; Cohen, 2009). Therefore, the harvested information can now be displayed by the original file systems such as FAT or NTFS. The data examined during the course of a DFI can be very large and therefore must be reduced to expedite the Examination Process. Identifying known elements can enable DFPs to reduce data. Metadata and unique identifiers such as MD5 must be used to remove known system files and other application data (Casey, 2011; Cohen, 2009; Beebe and Clark, 2005). The data that remains will be modified data or data that could be uniquely attributed to the users of a specific computer system. This will result in the identification of the potential digital evidence from data that has been examined, harvested and reduced. DFPs should also group together digital evidence with similar identifying patterns by focusing on the incident type. Digital evidence also needs to be restructured so that the investigation can be conducted more appropriately. If similar types of incidents or crimes have taken place in the past and are known to DFPs, they should then use the known classification in order to compare the current digital forensic data to the similar past incidents or crimes. The output of the Examination Process becomes the input to the Analysis Process, discussed in the following subsection.

9.4.2. *Analysis process*

Based upon the results of the Examination Process, DFPs must now be able to define what the exact characteristics of the incident are and who is to be held accountable for the incident. The Analysis Process enables investigators to reconstruct fragments of data based on their significance and determine a possible root cause of the incident (Montasari, 2016a; Montasari *et al.*, 2015). Once DFPs have addressed what is possibly known from the digital evidence (Montasari *et al.*, 2015), they must now be able to formulate a hypothesis of how the incident took place. To do so, they need to reconstruct a sequence of events which has resulted in the current state of the system under investigation. Investigators must thoroughly analyse and test data that was organised in the Examination Process against the hypothesis that they have formulated. The legal validity of the possible digital evidence must also be questioned by considering issues such as relevance, admissibility and weight as discussed in Montasari (2017b), Montasari (2016a) and Kessler (2010). Digital evidence should then be linked and attributed to the root cause of the incident by correlating the results of the digital crime scene with physical evidence. For instance, DFPs might need to correlate data center access logs to logins, linking online chat activities found on the computer with the activity of an undercover officer, and correlating activity on a compromised server with activity on the suspect's home system and network activity recorded by an ISP. Subsequent to the attribution, investigators need to evaluate their findings to ensure that their hypothesis holds true. At this stage of the Investigative Process, backtracking from the Analysis Process to the Examination Process is often to be expected as the investigators acquire a better understanding of the root cause of the incident. The output of the Analysis Process becomes the input to the Interpretation Process, discussed in the next subsection.

9.4.3. *Interpretation process*

The main purpose of the Interpretation Process is to use scientifically proven methods to explain facts discovered throughout the Analysis Process within the context of the investigation (Montasari, 2016a; Montasari, 2016b; Palmer, 2001). During this process, investigators need to interpret the digital evidence to produce meaningful statements in the legal context for later reporting and presentation. They must be able to reconstruct the events associated with the digital investigation by using the results of the analysis techniques from the Analysis Process to put together the pieces of the digital puzzle so that an accurate reconstruction of events can be carried out. The interpretation of any evidence should depend on the available information regarding the circumstances surrounding the creation of that item of digital evidence (Valjarevic and Venter, 2015; ISO, 2015). DFPs must obtain information from individuals involved in the day-to-day operation of the system under investigation so that they can carry out a more effective interpretation of evidence. Moreover, investigators must consider information concerning the goal as well as the scope of the investigation. In cases where the contextual information changes, investigators might also need to change the interpretation so that it can reflect any such changes regarding the contextual information. DFPs must also utilise link analysis and timeline tools to assist them with the digital reconstruction. The interpreted evidence then needs to be classified and evaluated in order to ascertain the amount of trust that can be placed in it. The interpreted digital evidence should also be organised according to relevance in such a way that more important digital evidence can be differentiated from others. After completing this process, DFPs should now be able to determine how the digital evidence came into existence and what its presence denotes. The output of the Interpretation Process becomes the input to the Event Reconstruction Process, discussed in the next section.

9.4.4. *Event reconstruction process*

During this process DFPs need to reconstruct a possible event sequence which reflects the incident result as accurately as possible. In order to reconstruct the events, investigators must utilise the series of events that they have deduced from digital evidence. Event Reconstruction should not be established as factual; instead, DFPs should use this Process to explain how the incident might have taken place. During this Process, the investigation findings must be consolidated and refined prior to assessing the review results against the original hypothesis, which was formulated in the Analysis Process. This will be to determine whether the DFPs have acquired all the evidence required to support the original hypothesis. If all the evidence has not been captured, investigators will need to backtrack to the Examination Process, in which this Phase and subsequent Phases form a cycle that needs to be repeated until the DFPs can identify additional evidence and explain the incident. As an example, in cases where a server intrusion has taken place, this iteration involves DFPs linking the exploitation of a service that is open to attack with the installation of a rootkit and utilization of a network sniffer. If the source IP address of the network connections is investigated, this could result in the acquisition of additional digital evidence to examine. If there is no need to iterate to the Examination Process, DFPs must identify and address any areas of improvement. The output of the Event Reconstruction Process becomes the input to the Reporting Process, discussed in the next subsection.

9.4.5. *Reporting process*

DFPs need to compile, write and print out on paper a detailed and concise report during the Reporting Process. This report must contain conclusions that can be reproduced by independent third parties. Forensic reports that include opinions based on accurately documented digital sources are much more likely to withstand judicial scrutiny than opinions based on less reliable sources (Garrie, 2014). The report must contain the findings of the entire DIP in addition to the information about documentation, chain of custody, digital evidence preservation, authorisation and management. The report must be accurate, concise and clear and be restricted only to what is known (Beebe and Clark, 2005). Since a DFI might produce many incriminating items of digital evidence, investigators must ensure that all items of evidence are listed so that no valuable item of evidence is left out. The output of the Reporting Process becomes the input to the Presentation Process, discussed in the next subsection.

9.4.6. *Presentation process*

The output of the Reporting Process in the form of a well-written report must be presented to a wide variety of audiences such as courts, legal personnel, law enforcement, technical personnel and management. The report can be presented in the form of the expert testimony and can be accompanied by other formats such as the multimedia presentation and the deposition. During this Process, investigators need to prove their formulated hypothesis using supporting evidence. They must communicate their findings in such a way that facilitates future validation and that can be understood by both technical and non-technical audiences. In this regard, Beebe and Clark (2005) state that a presentation should be based on "careful consideration about how to best communicate information to various audiences". Moreover, the presentation must also include relevant documentation and processes conducted during the investigative process, as well as any relevant physical evidence that can further consolidate the case against the perpetrator. It is also vital for DFPs to prove that the investigation was conducted in a forensically sound manner (Mumba and Venter, 2014). Furthermore, since the judge and jury or other interested parties are often non-technical users, DFPs must ensure that in their presentation they avoid complex arguments, unless they also provide the audience with significant help so that they understand the technical points made. In cases where DFPs need to appear in court to give expert witness, they must ensure that they are fully aware of the jurisdictional legal requirements concerning the digital evidence. During the presentation, often the hypothesis is challenged by the defence lawyers through a contradicting hypothesis and supporting evidence. Thus, DFPs need to prove the credibility of their hypothesis and to be well-prepared to defend the hypothesis against criticism and challenge. In circumstances in which challenges are successful, investigators need to backtrack to the earlier stages to obtain and examine more evidence and develop a better hypothesis. If the decision is made in a court, it will be decided whether to convict the accused or to refute the allegations. If the decision is made in an organisational setting, it will be decided what disciplinary actions must be taken if the incident can be attributed to an individual. The output of the Presentation Process becomes the input to the Investigation Closure Process, discussed in the next subsection.

9.4.7. *Investigation closure process*

This process involves closing the investigation and applying the decision-making associated with it (Beebe and Clark, 2005). Lessons learnt must be captured, and the outcome of the investigation must be used to review the existing policies and procedures of the organisation. Moreover, relevant information concerning the entire investigation must be disseminated and communicated to all stakeholders. This includes communicating the need to return to a previous Process, deciding on the acceptance or rejection of the hypothesis or providing any reports or documents from the Presentation Process. The investigating organisation might decide to make some information available only within the organisation or they might decide to disseminate information more widely. The organisation's policies and procedures should determine the details in this regard (Ciardhuáin, 2004). The investigating organisation must also record the investigation results, the case decision and all the evidence items. Such information will have an impact on future investigations and might have an effect on the policies and procedures of the organisation.

Thus, the accumulation and preservation of this information is a key part of supporting the work of DFPs and might be a productive aspect for the development of innovative applications that integrate techniques such as data mining and expert systems. Hauck *et al.* (2002) provide a detailed example of the dissemination activity in which they define a system named Coplink that provides real-time support for law enforcement investigators through an analysis application on the basis of a large accumulation of information from past investigations. An additional example is provided by Harrison *et al.* (2002), whose system is not real-time but instead delivers an "archival function" database to support investigators. Finally, during this Process, a decision also needs to be made to determine whether or not digital and physical evidence should be returned to the proper owner and what criminal evidence must be removed. The jurisdiction in which the investigation takes place and the type of authorisation determine whether or not the evidence should be returned, cleansed and reused or destroyed or whether the evidence should be stored for a certain period of time before any of the three possibilities can be applied.

9.5. Demonstration of the SDFIPM

This section follows the Demonstration activity of Peffers *et al.*'s (2006) DSRP, used in this research, and discusses the method employed to demonstrate the potential deployment of the SDFIPM. The Demonstration activity of the DSRP requires a researcher to apply the artefact in an appropriate environment such as "experimentation" or a "case study" to solve the stated problem (Hevner and Chatterjee, 2010; Peffers *et al.*, 2006). Resources needed for the Demonstration activity include effective knowledge of how the artefact should be applied to solve the stated problem. In order to assess how the SDFIPM addresses the stated research problem, we adopt the case scenario approach whereby we apply the SDFIPM to a scenario and perform a walkthrough of the model. The approach followed is identified as being appropriate for evaluating "simulations" and "models" (Hevner *et al.*, 2010; Peffers *et al.*, 2006; Balci, 2004). The Demonstration activity was carried out prior to the model being submitted to the experts for independent evaluation (discussed in Section 9.6). A similar approach is adopted by other authors (Adams, 2012; Ciardhuáin, 2004; Beebe and Clark, 2005; Carrier and Spafford, 2003).

9.5.1. *Case study*

The following case study is based on an actual situation and is intended to demonstrate the potential deployment of the SDFIPM. It is modelled after Ciardhuáin's (2004) scenario, which pertains to the exploitation of a vulnerability found in an online service operated by a bank:

> This investigation started when Bank X in London (England) received an email claiming to have found a vulnerability in an online service operated by the bank. The email offered to provide details of the vulnerability in exchange for payment. On checking their logs, Bank X concluded that an unauthorised access had been made to their web server. The bank received further emails threatening to reveal the vulnerability to the press and public, including a link to a website which the suspect intended to use to disclose the vulnerability. Bank X reported the issue to the police in London who initiated the investigation. It became obvious that the compromised web server was located in Manchester (England) from Bank X's headquarters and that the source of the emails was in Cardiff (Wales). Therefore, another police force, namely SWP (the South Wales Police), took up the case to start the investigation.

Examination Process

- This activity initially occurs when the bank examines their log files. It also occurs when the police examine the log files, the emails and the working copy of both the hard drive and the RAM images of the suspect's system in the DFL. During the Examination Process, investigators process the deleted and hidden data to ensure that emails and log files are recognised from the evidence. Investigators also harvest data to provide structure to the data in which they are interested so that it can be mounted on the investigating machine. Since the suspect's system contains a large amount of data such as known system files, investigators use metadata and unique identifiers to reduce the data by removing known system files and data from other applications. The investigators are now left with the log files and the emails that the suspect sent to Bank X. Now, the emails can be uniquely attributed to the suspect who has been the user of that specific system.

Analysis Process

- This Process initially takes place when Bank X's system administrator, Mr. Thompson, and the incident response team, conclude from the log files that an unauthorised access has been made to their web server. Later on, this Process is conducted in a forensic laboratory by investigators who develop the initial hypothesis for the identity of the suspect and for the manner in which the incident has taken place.

Interpretation Process

- This Process occurs after investigators evaluate their findings in the Analysis Process and determine that their formulated hypothesis is true. During this Process, investigators interpret digital evidence to produce meaningful statements for later reporting and presentation regarding how the suspect made an unauthorised access to Bank X's web server. As part of this Process, investigators classify and organize the interpreted evidence such as log files and emails according to their relevance in order to distinguish which digital evidence items are more important than others.

Event Reconstruction Process

- This process occurs when investigators reconstruct the events which led to the identification of the suspect and the subsequent seizure of the suspect's computer. This entails the investigators iterating over the CDFIPM, and results in a more detailed hypothesis. Through this Process, investigators are able to explain how the suspect has carried out the intrusion to Bank X's web server. Investigators consolidate and review their findings prior to assessing the results of their review against the original hypothesis that they have formulated. Through this assessment, investigators ensure that they have gathered all relevant evidence related to that attack to support their hypothesis.

Reporting Process

- This Process takes place when investigators compile a report based on their findings to be presented in a court.

Presentation Process

- This Process occurs five times during the entire investigation. This includes: when the bank's IT Administrator presents the evidence to the management within the bank, when the bank approaches the MPS Police and presents their evidence to investigators, when the MPS Police passes the investigation to SWP, when evidence is presented to acquire a search warrant and when investigators present the evidence in court. The formality of the evidence increases as the investigation proceeds. Prior to presenting their findings to the court, investigators meet with the legal team to understand the presentation requirements. During the meeting, the target audience in the court is determined. Investigators also carry out the necessary preparation prior to attending court such as preparing expert testimony, exhibits and appropriate presentation aids.
- During the presentation in court, investigators are able to assist the judge and jury in understanding the technical points made by avoiding complex arguments and delivering their conclusion in a logical and structured manner. The presentation contains factual data that investigators have deduced. Moreover, investigators use the SDFIPM to enable the judge to comprehend the processes that they have followed during the investigation. In

the court, the investigators have to prove and to defend the validity of the hypothesis as it is challenged by the court and the defence lawyers. Since investigators have followed a formal model which enabled them to carry out the investigation in a forensically sound manner, the opposite hypothesis is refuted. The court decides that the suspect has made an unauthorised access to Bank X's web server and sentences him to prison.

Investigation Closure Process

- This Process takes place after a formal decision is reached by the court concerning the incident. During this Process, based on the outcome of the investigation, Bank X reviews its existing policies and procedures concerning its IT security. As there is no need to backtrack to the previous stages in the investigation, the bank management decides to accept the hypothesis. During this Process, the bank identifies the lessons learnt and the suspect's system is returned to his employer's company. The result of the case is recorded on the database for possible similar future cases.
- The final phase of this activity is Disseminate Investigation Results, where relevant information concerning this incident and its outcome are communicated to all stakeholders. The initial communication is carried out prior to the completion of the trial in order to remove the sensitive data from the disseminated information. The final phase, the Review Phase, discusses how the incident could have been handled better. One possible outcome is the installation of the central log server sooner than planned. The Review Phase includes a review of the investigation and identifies some new analysis techniques that are employed. The techniques are added to the official analysis procedures. During the analysis, new suspect files are identified, and they are added to the hash database so that they can be quickly found in future investigations.

This section followed the Demonstration activity of Peffers *et al.*'s DSRP (2006) and discussed the method employed to demonstrate the potential deployment of the SDFIPM. By using the selected method, we successfully applied the SDFIPM to a case scenario and performed a walkthrough of the model. This walkthrough mapped the model's components to the corresponding activities carried out by DFPs operating in the three fields of law enforcement, commerce and incident response. Having completed the Demonstration activity, the next stage in Peffers *et al.*'s DSRP [1] is the Evaluation activity, discussed in the following section.

9.6. Evaluation of the SDFIPM

This section follows the Evaluation activity of the Peffers *et al.*'s DSRP (2006), that requires the artifact to be validated in order to determine: (1) how well it supports the solution to the stated research problem, and (2) whether it is necessary to iterate back to the Design and Development stage to improve the effectiveness of the artefact. Thus, to assess how the SDFIPM addressed the stated research problem, we involved the participation of the SDFIPM's intended user community who could independently verify and validate the proposed model. This user community included DFPs operating within the three fields of relevance for this research, namely law enforcement, commerce and incident response, as well as experts in the domain of DF, legal practitioners and researchers in both academia and industry. Once the Evaluation Phase was completed, we were able to feed the results of the Evaluation activity back into the SDFIPM's Design and Development Phase and amend the model accordingly. Similar approaches that involve using such an evaluation activity have been adopted in previous studies, for instance by Adams (2012) and Ciardhuáin (2004). The remainder of this section provides a summary of results in relation to the Evaluation activities performed on the SDFIPM.

9.6.1. *Methods of validation*

A major component of any forensic research is to demonstrate the validity of the results. The DSR studies are prone to the same types of errors as are any other qualitative studies, so ensuring validity is important. Therefore, to assess our model's accuracy in meeting its intended outcomes, we employed a set of validation methods as opposed to relying on only one method. To ensure the credibility of the study results concerning the proposed model, we performed a triangulation technique to facilitate the validation of data. The triangulation consisted of combining five different methods to overcome the weaknesses or inherent biases and the problems that come from single-method, single-observer and single-theory studies. These methods enabling the validation of forensic artefacts included (Eddy *et al.*, 2012):

1. Internal Validity — the model's components are analysed and their accuracy is checked;
2. Cross Validity — results are compared with other models analysing the same problem;
3. External Validity — the model is used to simulate different scenarios;
4. Predictive Validity — the model results are compared with prospectively observed events; and
5. Face Validity — independent experts evaluate the model structure, its associated data and results.

In the context of this research, methods 1, 2 and 3 above have already been applied to the SDFIPM in the Design and Development stage of the SDFIPM, which is the middle part of the larger model, the CDFIPM, in Montasari's study (Montasari, 2016a). See Chapters 3 and 4 of Montasari's research study (Montasari, 2016a) for more comprehensive details about the results of methods 1, 2 and 3. For instance, in terms of the Internal Validity method, the model's components were analysed and justified in Chapter 3 (Design and Development), which addressed whether the model's components behaved as intended and whether it had been implemented correctly. In relation to the Cross-Validation method, the model was mapped and compared with the existing models, which involved determining the degree to which they calculated the same results. Concerning the External Validation method, similar to Section 9.5 of this paper, in Chapter 4 (Demonstration) of Montasari's research

(Montasari, 2016a), the model was applied to different scenarios and a walk-through of the model was performed to simulate different types of real life investigations. Method 4, Predictive Validity, has been excluded from this research on the basis that this validation method would need to be carried out over a long period of time, thus being outside the timing scope of this research.

Face Validity (method 5), which is considered to be the strongest form of the 5 stated validation methods (Law, 2014; Eddy *et al.*, 2012; Pace and Sheehan, 2002), is the topic of this section, where the external experts evaluate the model structure and its associated data, results and accuracy independently. This method is used to answer the following questions:

1. Does the model provide its users with both utility and usability?
2. Has the model been built right? and
3. Has the right model been built?

According to Pace and Sheehan (2002), the main validation method for models must include assessment by experts and peers. This argument is supported by other researchers in various scientific environments (Burgman *et al.*, 2011; Czembor and Vesk, 2009; Ludwig *et al.*, 2001). Moreover, in circumstances in which empirical data are scarce or unobtainable, expert knowledge and their input are often considered to be the best or only source of information (McBride and Burgman, 2012; Kuhnert, 2010; Sutherland, 2006). In these situations, experts can be requested to provide input for all the stages of the modelling process (Martin *et al.*, 2012; Cowling and Pressey, 2003; Pearce *et al.*, 2001). Thus, the remainder of this section draws upon the Face Validity method by recruiting external experts to answer the three questions above and to ultimately determine whether the SDFIPM has achieved both the 'utility' and 'usability' necessary for a model.

9.6.2. *Expert selection process*

Booker and McNamara (2004) define expert knowledge as the knowledge and expertise that qualified persons have acquired due to their technical practices, training and experience. Based on this definition, it is, therefore, reasonable to regard an individual as a 'domain expert' if he/she is familiar with the subject at hand and is accountable for the analysis of the issue and the provision of sound judgments. Moreover, according to McBride and Burgman (2012), the experts should be selected on the basis of explicit criteria in order to ensure transparency and establish that the results represent the full range of views in the expert field. The common metrics outlined in the literature for selecting experts include: experts' qualifications, employment, memberships in professional bodies, publication records, years of experience, peer nomination, and perceived standing in their community (Czembor and Vesk, 2009; Drescher *et al.*, 2008; Whitfield *et al.*, 2008). Additional considerations that need to be made include the availability and willingness of experts to participate, and the possibility of conflicts of interest (McBride and Burgman, 2012).

The appropriate number of experts should depend on (1) the scope of the research problem (see below) and (2) the available timing during which the research is expected to be completed (McBride and Burgman, 2012). However, the literature on expert selection strongly suggests the inclusion of as diverse a range of experts as possible (Armstrong, 2006; Clemen and Winkler, 1999) by recruiting multiple experts in order to reduce the impact of individual mistakes and biases and to pave the way for assessments that are representative of the entire expert community (Fisher, 2009; Hokstad *et al.*, 1998). In most scientific environments, as Martin *et al.* (2012) and Ludwig *et al.* (2001) point out, the breadth of research problems denotes that no one individual will be expert for all aspects of the problem. Hence, we identified and recruited a diverse group of experts with different skill sets for the Evaluation process. Therefore, since the intended applicability of the SDFIPM was aimed at three domains of law enforcement, commerce and incident response, we recruited experts operating within the stated fields to evaluate the model. This approach enabled us to ensure that the SDFIPM would undergo 'utility' and 'usability' testing by experts in relation to how 'useful' and 'relevant' the model would be to each of the experts' particular domains of practice. Therefore, to acquire the needed expert coverage, we recruited a diverse set of eminent experts who could provide expert review and feedback on the 'utility' and 'usability' aspects of the proposed model. We based our selection of experts upon the common metrics found in the literature such as those presented in Czembor and Vesk (2009), Drescher *et al.* (2008), and Whitfield *et al.* (2008). The following selection criteria were considered during the recruitment process:

- geographical operation — DFIs and legal practitioners needed to operate within the UK as the model's intended application would be aimed at the UK jurisdiction.
- period of experience and learning — the participants needed to have extensive knowledge and experience in the domain of DF for a period of at least 10 years.
- the manner in which the experience had been acquired — for instance, the experts' experience needed to have been attained through practice and theory to ensure that the expert panel would consist of both theorists and practitioners.
- qualifications — the participants needed to have appropriate qualifications in relation to DF, information security (IS) or computer science (CS).
- reputation — the experts needed to have a solid standing in their particular domains of practice.

Therefore, we deemed the use of the following diverse set of experts to be beneficial in increasing what McBride and Burgman (2012) term as "the acceptance or perceived validity of the elicitation process". This would ensure that different perspectives would be brought into the Evaluation Process. Experts (expert panel) who took part in the evaluation process were then categorized into three groups of (1) DFPs, (2) legal practitioners, and (3) researchers both in academia and industry. Experts from the panel were identified as representatives of their specific domains of practice based on their roles, responsibilities, experience and involvement within pertinent associations in the UK jurisdiction. The recruitment process for the expert panel was considered complete once numerous participants from each of the three fields covered by the research scope had consented to assist. The following are the profiles of the experts constituting the members of the three groups of the expert panel:

- A representative of law enforcement (MSc in Computing & Information Technology and EnCase Certified Examiner) with 25 years of experience as a police officer who manages the entire High-Tech/Cyber Crime team of the North West Regional Organised Crime Unit (TITAN), consisting of six police forces in Cumbria, Cheshire, Lancashire, Greater Manchester, Merseyside and North Wales;
- A representative of commercial practice with 18 years of experience as a Digital Forensic Investigator and a Forensic Triage Specialist who is the director of Digital Forensics for a large company;
- A representative of legal practice (LL.B) with 13 years of experience who is a self-employed barrister and who has worked on over 20 cases involving digital investigations;
- A Detective Sergeant of eForensics (BSc in Computing and Information Technology) who is a certified ENCE, a certified Security Incident Specialist, and a certified Forensic Investigation Analyst with 28 years of experience as a police officer who heads the Cheshire Police Headquarters (Cheshire Constabulary) High-Tech Crime Unit;
- A representative of commercial practice (MPhil in Operating System Anti-Malware/Security and an MSc in Internet Engineering);
- A Detective Constable of Digital Forensics at the South Wales Gwent Police High-Tech Crime Unit representative of law enforcement with 18 years of experience as a DFP;
- A Detective Constable of Digital Forensics at the South Wales Gwent Police High-Tech Crime Unit with 11 years of experience as a DFP;
- A representative of academia (PhD) who is a university professor and a prominent researcher with many publications on information security, biometrics and digital forensics. He has been the keynote speaker at reputable information security and digital forensics conferences;

- A representative of legal practice (LL.B) with 34 years' experience of practicing law who is a Deputy High Court Judge and a barrister based in Exchange Chambers within Manchester, Leeds and Liverpool and the Chairman of the Northern Chancery Bar Association and a Trustee of the North West Partnership;
- A representative of academia (PhD) who is a university professor and a well-known researcher with various publications on digital forensic practice.

9.6.3. *Feedback formats and analysis*

In the first instance, the experts participating in the Evaluation process were requested to assist in this research via email. Once the experts were identified and their confirmation for participation in the Evaluation process was obtained, then in line with the best practices outlined in the literature (Morgan and Henrion, 2010; Rothlisberger *et al.*, 2010; Cooke and Goossens, 2000), they were provided with relevant materials associated with the model that had been compiled into an appropriate, accessible form. These consisted of the UML Activity Diagrams of the model, the explanatory notes describing the model's components, a questionnaire (see Appendix B), background information such as the aim and objectives of the research, and also a description of what they were requested to undertake. These materials had already been carefully piloted to ensure that the documentation had been compiled properly. It was important to ensure that the Evaluation questions had been formulated appropriately to reflect the research problem, identify potential issues with biases or question phrasing, and elicit feedback about any potential ways to enhance the quality of the process and of the knowledge that was to be extracted. The pilot process was conducted with academic colleagues who checked the compiled documents prior to their submissions to the experts for review. Once piloted and compiled, the documents were sent to the participating experts via email so that they could have sufficient time to evaluate them, raise any potential concerns, comment on any aspect of the model, and volunteer relevant information. Having acquired the experts' feedback via e-mails, formal meetings were then held at the experts' workplaces at an arranged date and time to discuss their feedback with them and to elicit further expert knowledge that it was not possible to obtain via e-mails. These meetings took place following focus group and interview formats as such approaches are recommended in the literature based on their advantages as follows:

- The interview and focus group formats take full advantage of the experience and skills of those participating by being more open than a narrowly-focussed survey.
- Experts have a stronger understanding of the subject matter as they can ask questions concerning the research rather than simply replying to a fixed set of questions.
- Participants are able to express and discuss views that are not likely to be identified by a simple survey. Such issues can be analysed in some detail during the interview or focus group.
- Experts are left free to express their views in whatever manner they feel is most appropriate.

Once all the data was collected, the participants' responses were then subjectively analysed through a rigorous verification process and acted upon where necessary. In line with McBride and Burgman's (2012) and Cooke's (1991) suggestions, we checked for obvious errors or inconsistencies by comparing the expert's responses to those of others in the panel. In comparing an individual expert's responses with those of the rest of the panel, we looked for similarities, irregularities, biases, or strongly conflicting opinions in addition to varying interpretations of the information. When such irregularities or problematic responses were identified, we followed up on the conflicting feedback through further discussions with the experts. We then acted upon the acquired feedback which involved 'addition to', 'alteration to' and 'deletion from' the model. 'Addition' refers to a new component being added to the model, 'alteration' refers to the change in a component's naming or order and 'deletion' refers to the deletion of a component from the model. The aforementioned three terminologies that have been acted upon are represented on the model's UML Activity Diagrams using the following references:

1. Reference to Addition: 'REF: ADD #n', where 'n' represents the number of implemented 'additions'.
2. Reference to Alteration: 'REF: ALT #n', where 'n' represents the number of implemented 'changes'.
3. Reference to Deletion: 'REF: DEL #n', where 'n' represents the number of implemented 'deletions'.

Both generic and detailed feedback are presented below in the form of quotes together with our specific comments in response to the feedback. We first provide the positive comments followed by a discussion of the more detailed feedback.

9.6.4. *General feedback*

> *"I can see a lot of work has been put into this and you have covered everything I can think of, my only comment would be enabling your model to be interactive rather that a set procedure."* (Law enforcement DFP and Case Officer)

> *"The model is impressive in its detail and reasonably easy to understand and use. The author has clearly understood the practicalities of an effective and efficient digital investigation."* (Legal practitioner, barrister)

> *"With ACPO Guidelines, there is no defined structure to it, no defined path to it. What we need is that these methods have been validated scientifically. This is something you have worked out over long time. Your model has been peer reviewed both by practitioners and scientists even though we might choose it differently."* (Law enforcement DFP)

> *"This model is very timely and well-researched. It is my conclusion that you have gone deep enough into details of finding out what exactly is wrong with the existing models and what to do to improve them."* (University professor)

> *"This is sound standard for forensic service providers (FSPs). This is like UCAS was."* (Law enforcement DFP)

> *"Your model provides a concise guidance on the exact processes that examiners need to follow during any kind of digital investigation."* (Commercial DFP)

"It is necessary that the court understands the process that has been followed. Your model has done a great job as its processes are documented in a very rational way. A judge or barrister could pick up this model and work out what has been happening in a digital investigation." (Legal practitioner, judge)

"What you have presented is actually good. You have done a great job; I feel that the model you have presented would accelerate digital investigations because it gives a common order of processes and activities that a computer forensic investigation requires." (Law enforcement DFP and Case Officer)

"Your model is like modular plugin type for different fields." (Law enforcement DFP)

"There is much in your model that covers cybercrime and such attacks that are not covered in LE." (Law enforcement DFP)

"Sorry for the delay in replying. I have had a chance to look at your model and it is sound in its interpretation. How would you like my feedback?" (Commercial DFP)

"Your model reflects in part our Cheshire's existing model, and I do not intend changing to anything other in the near future as this model simply reflects what we already have." (Law enforcement DFP and Case Officer)

"I have had an initial look at your work and it looks interesting and a very comprehensive model." (Commercial DFP)

9.6.5. *Detailed feedback and responses*

Feedback E-3: "*Event Reconstruction is something we do not tend to practice as it is labour intensive. However, I would use this if the circumstances dictate.*"

- **Response:** Although Event Reconstruction might be labour intensive, it still must be part of any digital investigation so that it, together with the Analysis and Interpretation Processes, can enable DFPs to construct a full picture of the events that have taken place. If DFPs do not perform the Event Reconstruction Process, questions in relation to who, why, where, when and how will not be addressed properly. As a result, this can severely affect the outcome of the case in courts. However, in certain circumstances, Event Reconstruction might not be as necessary; for example, when the incident/crime is not classified as severe, and the investigation results are to be presented to the company management as opposed to a court. Thus, no further action will be taken in light of the above feedback.

Feedback E-21: "*Include team/investigation debrief in the investigation closure section.*"

- **Response:** This had already been covered under a different terminology 'Conduct a Critical Review' in the CDFIPM's Investigation Closure Process. Since it appears that DFPs are more accustomed to the term 'debriefing' as this was pointed out also by a number of different experts, the terminology 'Conduct a Critical Review' will now be changed to Conduct a Team/Investigation Debrief ("REF: ALT #4").

Feedback E-23: "*'Analysis' should come before 'developing hypothesis'. Although having analysis + hypothesis would be sufficient, you could always have a re-analysis in light of the hypothesis afterwards. In reality a competent investigator would always re-evaluate; so having a 're-analysis' component would simply acknowledge that (& perhaps encourage/ remind less competent investigators to do so!)*"

- **Response:** The above feedback is aimed at the Develop a Hypothesis and Analyse Digital Evidence Phases of the Analysis Process. The ordering of the two Phases will now be changed and a new Phase entitled 'Reanalyse Digital Evidence' will be included after the Develop a Hypothesis Phase in the Analysis Process ("REF: ALT #5") and ("REF: ADD #6").

Feedback E-24: "*What is meant by 'reduce acquired data'? Why?*"

- **Response:** The above question was posed by a legal practitioner in relation to the Reduce Acquired Data Phase of the Examination Process. The following is the response that we provided and the legal practitioner's further feedback.

The authors: "In terms of the 'Reduce Acquired Data' Phase, since a digital device can contain a large amount of data, most of which are not related to the case under investigation, investigators will therefore need to reduce data only to what they are interested in. Does this make sense?"

The legal practitioner: *"Yes, that makes sense. However, the fact that I (as a lay person) had to ask suggests it may be useful to provide a better explanation. An option would be to have a 'Glossary of Terms' at the end of the document — I think that would be really valuable, and I have seen them used a lot in other technical documents presented to the court."*

The above comment had already been addressed in the Appendix section of Montasari's (2016a) study.

Feedback E-25: *"There is no need to have 'Consolidate investigation findings' when you have 'review investigation results' immediately after it."*

- **Response:** The Consolidate Investigation Findings Phase will now be removed from the Event Reconstruction Process as it appears to be repetitive of its following Phase, namely Review Investigation Results ("REF: DEL #4").

Feedback E-26: *"After 'Identify areas of improvement', have a further action to act on any areas identified."*

- **Response:** A new Phase entitled 'Act upon Any Areas Identified' will be added after the Identify Areas of Improvement (If Any) Phase of the Event Reconstruction Process ("REF: ADD #7").

Feedback E-27: *"In the 'Presentation' section, why is there a requirement to consider the appeal process at this stage?"*

- **Response:** The Consider Appeal Process had been included in the Presentation Process in order to enable investigators to make contingency plans in advance to take account of possible case rejection by courts of law where they would need to launch an appeal. Therefore, this Phase will remain in the Presentation Process, and no further action will be taken.

Feedback E-28: *"Consider re-ordering 'Presentation' section as follows: Determine the target audience — Understand the require-*

ments of the presentation — Consider (and apply) the legal jurisdictional requirements — Consider the appeal process — Prepare exhibits — Use appropriate presentation aids — Present the report — Prove/ defend the validity of the hypothesis — Decide the case"

- **Response:** The ordering of the Phases in the Presentation Process will be amended as suggested above ("REF: ALT #6").

Feedback E-29: *"In 'Investigation Closure' section, 'Record the case decision' should come after accepting or rejecting the hypothesis and before the question of whether the evidence can be returned."*

- **Response:** The Record the Case Decision will now be placed immediately after the Accept or Reject the Hypothesis Phase as suggested in this feedback ("REF: ALT #7").

Feedback E-30: *"If the evidence cannot be returned, have separate actions for (a) store, cleanse and re-use the evidence, and for (b) destroying the evidence — ask a question the answer to which would identify which of these 2 options would be followed."*

- **Response:** The above comment refers to the management of evidence in the Investigation Closure Process. This is a very constructive piece of feedback which was brought to our attention as no explicit condition (question in the form of UML Activity Diagram notation) had previously been specified with regards to the sensitivity of digital evidence. Further clarification was needed in terms of the legal aspect of sensitive digital evidence. Therefore, further communication took place between us and the legal practitioner (judge) as follows:

  Authors: "Thank you very much for bringing such an important issue to my attention. I am going to create further conditions as suggested. So, they will be like this: 'Can the evidence be returned?' If the answer is 'yes', the evidence will be returned. If the answer is 'no', the investigator will be provided with another condition asking whether the evidence can be destroyed. If the answer to this question is 'yes', the investigator will need to destroy the evidence. If the answer is 'no', the investigator could cleanse and reuse the device. From a legal point of view, is this a sound approach? And is this similar to what you thought?"

Judge: *"Yes. I don't know whether you also need to include a more detailed guide for the investigator as to when each step would be appropriate. For example, presumably 'sensitive' information would not be returned, but would be destroyed. It may help investigators to have a finite list of which types of evidence would fall into each category; but I don't know if this goes beyond the remit of what you are trying to achieve here. Another, perhaps simpler way might be this:*

— *'Is the evidence sensitive?' (And / or other terms that would cover all scenarios which you would decide whether to return, destroy or cleanse & reuse evidence.)*
— *Yes — it cannot be returned — Can it be destroyed? .... (Cleanse and reuse, etc.)*
— *No — it can be returned.*

Based upon the above detailed feedback and further clarification, three new conditions have been developed that will be included in the Presentation Process to accommodate also for the 'sensitivity' of digital evidence ("REF: Add #8"). However, developing a fixed list of which types of evidence would fall into each category is outside the scope of this research and must be determined by the investigating organisations based on their own internal guidelines.

Feedback E-31: *"Consider swapping order of 'make recommendations' and 'develop a case study' in 'Future Readiness'".*

- **Response:** The ordering will be amended ("REF: ALT #8").

9.6.6. *Analysis of the results*

In relation to 'utility', this component of the Evaluation activity was intended to ensure that the proposed model had 'serviceability', 'applicability' and 'appropriateness' to the law enforcement, commerce, incident response and legal domains as stated in the research problem. The model was therefore subjected to an external, independent evaluation by the leading experts in its intended user community to ensure that it had been built right and that the right model had been built. The comments regarding the SDFIPM were very positive, and the feedback was both constructive and insightful. There were a total number of 31 detailed pieces of feedback in relation to the larger model, the CDFIPM, 11 of which related to the SDFIPM, including suggestions for new additions, amendments and deletions. Out of the 11 feedbacks for the SDFIPM, 2 new additions, 4 amendments and 1 deletion were made in and from the SDFIPM. Having made the new model subject to the experts' scrutiny, it became clear that there did not exist any aspects of the SDFIPM that were not representative of the processes as carried out in the fields covered by the research scope. Similarly, there were not any aspects of the processes as performed in the stated fields that were not covered in the SDFIPM. In response to the question of utility (see the questionnaire in Appendix B), "Please rate the model on the scale of 1 to 10, with 1 being not useful at all and 10 being the most useful.", experts provided the mean score of '9'. This suggests that the SDFIPM has achieved the intended component of utility required of a useful artefact. The following are some comments made by the experts in relation to the utility of the model:

- *"Much of your model covers most aspects in good detail of what is required but the order would change or be adopted to operational needs. But, all principles and processes are there in good details."* (Law enforcement DFP and manager)
- *"You have identified the relevant problems with the current models and have provided detailed analysis. I believe that your model has made a significantly novel contribution in its current length and presentation. Congratulations on accomplishing such a daunting task!"* (University professor)
- *"This model allows a smooth transition from one phase to another during a digital investigation. If I were to use it, it would certainly give me a detailed advice about what to do with the evidence."* (Commercial DFP)

- *"You have covered all avenues in different elements of digital investigations."* (Law enforcement DFP)
- *"It is absolutely practicable and structured. You would not go wrong."* (Commercial DFP)
- *"This model is very comprehensive; I can't see any loopholes. Some issues are raised about detaining a suspect, where there could be multiple persons in a property with none saying who the suspect is."* (Law enforcement DFP)
- *"I can say that your model provides transparency in acquiring produced result for each given process."* (Legal practitioner, Judge)
- *"Because of its level of details, your model will facilitate collecting high quality evidence in a fast manner."* (Law enforcement DFI)

With regards to the 'usability', this component of the Evaluation activity was intended to determine the ease with which experts in the law enforcement, commerce, incident response and legal domains can employ the SDFIPM to carry out those activities described by the model that relate to their practice. In response to the question of usability (see the questionnaire in Appendix B), "Please rate the model on the scale of 1 to 10, with 1 being very difficult to use and 10 being very easy to use", experts provided the mean score of '8.7'. This also indicates that the SDFIPM has achieved the intended component of usability required of a useful artefact. The following are some comments made by the experts in relation to the usability of the SDFIPM:

- *"This model is clear in its layout and the majority of its terms, which largely enables the user to understand the steps taken during the investigation without assistance. Where some of the terms are unclear or technical, the assistance of the explanation of a digital forensic investigator would overcome any difficulty in comprehension."* (Legal practitioner, barrister)
- *"It is important to have robust process behind the presentation of digital evidence because you have an adversarial system. Each seeks to undermine the evidence of the other if they can. Your model presents the forensic process very clearly; it is readily understandable to someone without technical expertise especially for jury."* (Legal practitioner, judge)

- *"Your model has a very clear layout that covers all aspects succinctly."* (Law enforcement DFI)
- *"I like the workflows as they are simple but effective."* (Law enforcement DFI)

The aim of this subsection was to evaluate the SDFIPM in order to determine whether the model had been built right and whether the right model had been built and consequently to establish whether the SDFIPM had achieved both the 'utility' and 'usability' components. To this end, the model was subjected to an independent, external evaluation by its intended user community. From the positive feedback received and its analysis, it has become clear that the model has been built right and the right model has been built. It has also become obvious that the SDFIPM has achieved both the utility and usability required from a forensic artefact.

9.6.7. *Alterations made to the SDFIPM*

This subsection presents the modifications that were made to the UML Activity Diagrams of the SDFIPM in response to the feedback provided by experts in subsection 9.6.5. Where a modification has been made, this is shaded and provided with its corresponding reference (addition, alteration or deletion) from the feedback in subsection 9.6.5. The idea to modify our model in such a way is adopted from Adams's (2012) study. The final version of the UML Activity Diagrams of the SDFIPM is presented in Appendix C.

9.7. Conclusion

9.7.1. *Research problem addressed*

Following the identification of three major issues with the previous DFIPMs, namely the lack of a model that has all three characteristics of being "comprehensive", "formal" and "generic", we formulated the following research question that we set out to address:

> There does not exist a comprehensive model encompassing the entire digital investigative process that is formal, such that it can

> assist a court of law in determining the reliability of the investigative process followed, and that is generic, in that it can be applied in the different fields of law enforcement, commerce and incident response.

Based upon Peffers *et al.*'s DSRP (2006), the acquisition of two resources was sought in order to define the "objectives of the solution". These included: "... knowledge of the state of the problem" and "current solutions and their efficacy, if any". The knowledge of the state of the problem for this research was covered in the Introduction section, where the research problem was defined and the value of its solution justified. However, to address the two resources fully, further knowledge of the state of the problem was required and current solutions, if any, had to be identified. In order to acquire the two stated resources, previous models were critically reviewed and assessed against three different sets of assessment criteria in Montasari's (2016a) research study, with the summary of this analysis being presented in this chapter. Through this assessment, the prevailing models that could contribute to the design and development of the proposed model were identified, and the necessary components that would constitute the basic structure of the new model were determined. Following the Design and Development activity of Peffers *et al.*'s DSRP (2006), the proposed model was designed and implemented based upon the information acquired through the critical analysis.

Once designed and developed, in accordance with the Demonstration activity of Peffers *et al.*'s DSRP (2006), we applied the model to a case study, thereby demonstrating the efficacy of the proposed model to solve the stated research problem. We then covered the Evaluation activity of Peffers *et al.*'s DSRP (2006), through which the model was subjected to a critical review and feedback process by the leading experts in its intended user community to determine how well the new model would support the solution to the stated research problem. To follow up on the feedback obtained from the experts, we returned to the Design and Development stage to make subsequent amendments, including new additions, alterations and deletions as shown in Figs. 9.4 and 9.5 in their amended

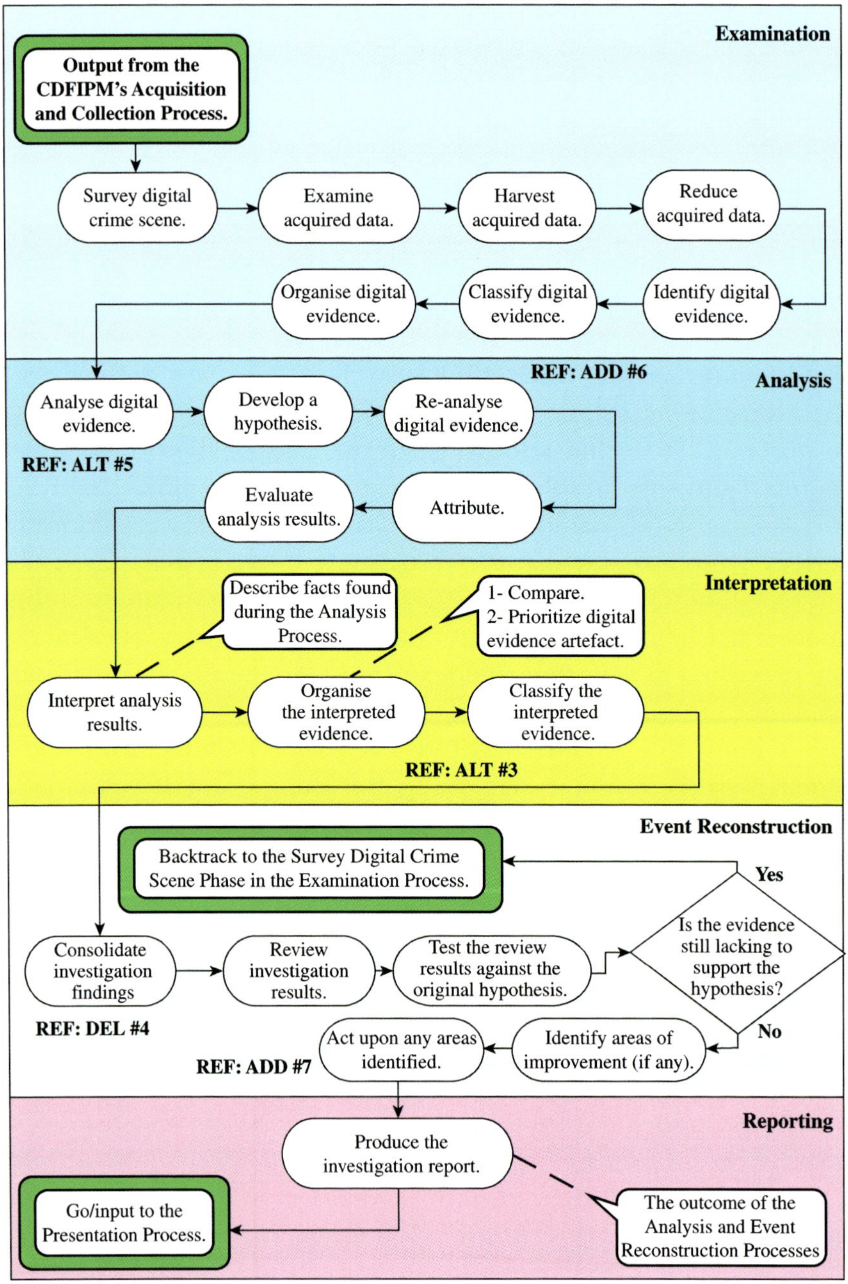

Fig. 9.4. Amendment to the SDIFPM for ADD #6 & #7, ALT #3 & #5 and DEL #4.

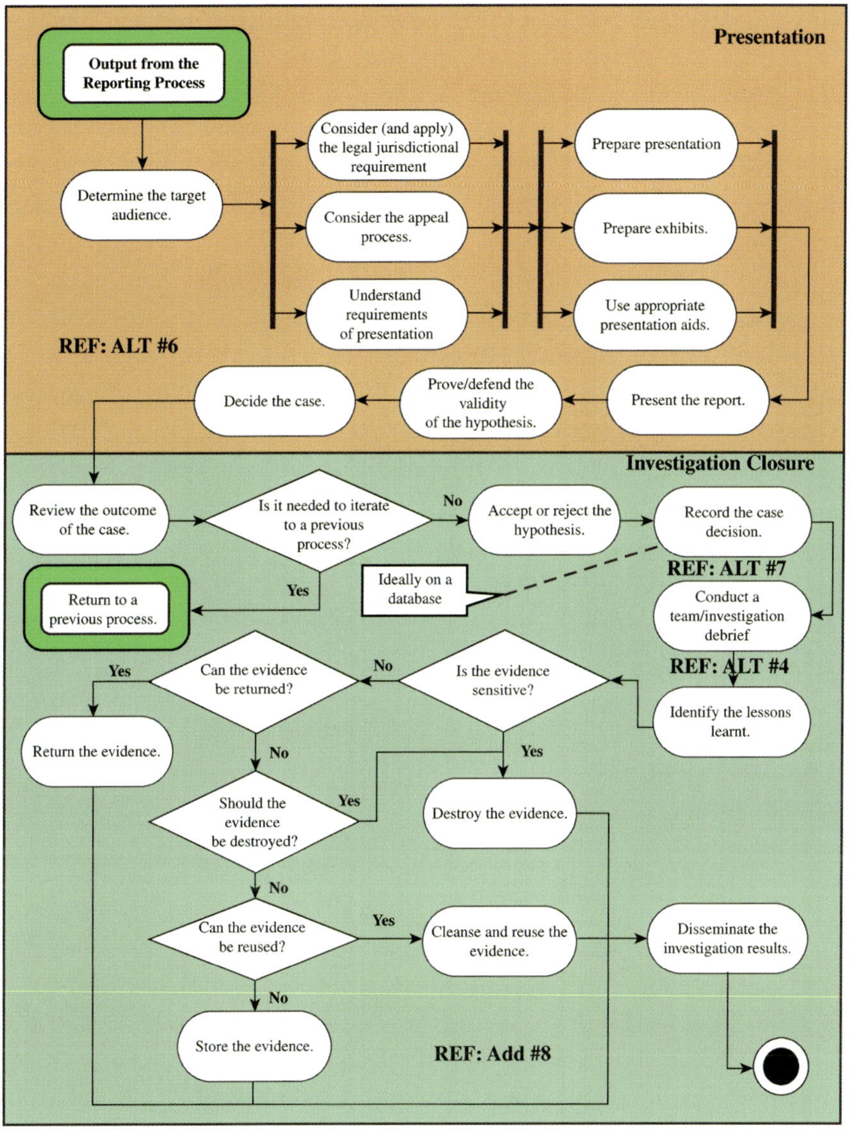

Fig. 9.5. Amendment to the SDIFPM for ALT #4, #6 & #7 and ADD #8.

form and in Appendix C in its final version. This was to address the two components of 'utility' and 'usability' further by finding the answers to the two following questions: 'has the model been built right?' and 'has the right model been built?'. All the acquired feedback was very positive, and there were no negative comments. When there was disagreement, we iterated back to the Design and Development Phase of the research, as stated, to make alterations based on the feedback in order to bring the model as close as possible (within the scope of the research) to its intended application. Having completed the formal evaluation of the model, we contend that 'the new model has been built right' and that 'the right model has been built' on the basis that its intended application has been observed, accepted and confirmed by the prominent experts in its intended user community. Therefore, the SDFIPM is complete, consistent, and accurate enough to fulfil the solution to the stated research problem, as defined in Section 9.1.

The last stage in Peffers *et al.*'s (2006) DSRP is the Communication activity, according to which the researcher needs to communicate the research problem and its importance, and also to explain the research artefact, its utility, usability and novelty, the rigor of its design, and its effectiveness to the intended user community. In relation to this research, we have made significant progress in this activity by attending various conferences, Forensic Expositions and Cyber Security Summits, and having extracts from our research study published in various peer-reviewed journals and conference proceedings.

9.7.2. *Research contribution*

This research has made a significant and novel contribution to the field of DF science by implementing a process model, the SDFIPM, that would assist DFPs in following a uniform approach. Our study has synthesized, harmonised and significantly built upon the existing models to produce the first process model that has all three characteristics of being comprehensive, formal and generic. No such model previously existed in the literature. The SDFIPM is scientifically rigorous as it assists courts in determining the reliability of the investigative process followed and generic in that it can be applied by DFPs operating in the three fields of law enforcement, commerce and incident response. The proposed model is inclusive of all the advantages of the previous models through their synthesis and harmonisation and contains purified terminology using the terms commonly agreed upon by DFPs. It is therefore argued that the SDFIPM would be a significant step towards the establishment of standards for the digital forensic investigative process. Every component in the model is well defined in terms of scope, functions and order. The model fully and thoroughly describes the flow of information in a digital investigation from the moment digital evidence is captured for examination until the investigation reaches its formal conclusion.

This study has also demonstrated how the digital investigative process can be represented through a proven formal notation, the Unified Modelling Language (UML). The representation of the SDFIPM via the UML Activity Diagrams will assist courts in properly understanding the digital investigative processes followed, a point acknowledged by the legal practitioners and judge who participated in the external evaluation of the model. Due to its level of detail and its step-by-step approach, the SDFIPM provides investigators with concise direction on the processes to be followed, enabling them to speed up the investigative process while minimising errors and negligence. Therefore, in the event of a challenge to the digital investigative process, there would be no doubt concerning the soundness of the processes followed. The proposed model also contains generic methods that DFPs can use to associate technology with non-technical observers. Importantly, the application of the SDFIPM could bring about the improved admissibility of digital evidence in courts, being a formal model with strong overriding principles resulting from rigorous scientific verification.

9.7.3. *Future work*

Although the SDFIPM is mainly aimed at the UK jurisdiction, it could easily be adapted to other jurisdictions. Without such modification, the model already has relevance to those jurisdictions which employ a similar legal basis for evaluating the digital investigative process. The SDFIPM focuses predominantly on Computer Forensics as opposed to other branches of DF. Although some much simpler models have claimed to be appropriate for various branches of DF, such a claim is not made in relation to the SDFIPM for accuracy purposes. However, it is argued that due to the SDFIPM's detailed and generic approach, it could easily be adapted to cover any branch of DF. Although an evaluation of the SDFIPM has been undertaken by the High-Tech Crime Units (HTCUs) of two different police forces in the UK, experts in corporate and incident response environments, legal practitioners and researchers in academia, they cannot be representative of all intended users. Future work could include a more comprehensive trial by DFPs, experts, legal practitioners and researchers as part of a wider study. Similarly, although the case scenarios to which the SDFIPM was applied represent each of the three fields of DF to which the model is relevant, the SDFIPM would benefit from further case studies to identify task hierarchies. This would improve task development efforts and facilitate scenario development, assisting its users, researchers and tool developers in understanding how to take advantage of and apply the model. Finally, as with the future work, the SDFIPM must be validated through the Method Validation under ISO 17025 accreditation to determine its compliance.

References

1. AccessData. (2018). *Forensic Toolkit (FTK)*. Available at: http://accessdata.com/products/computer-forensics/ftk (Accessed: 29 May 2018).
2. Adams, L. and Courtney, J. (2004). Achieving Relevance in IS Research Via the DAGS Framework. In *Proceedings of the 37th Hawaii International Conference on System Sciences, Big Island, HI, USA, January 5–8*, pp. 1–10.
3. Adams, R. (2012). *The Advanced Data Acquisition Model (ADAM): A Process Model for Digital Forensic Practice* (PhD thesis). Perth, WA, Australia, Murdoch University.
4. Agarwal, A., Gupta, M., Gupta, S. and Gupta, C. (2011). Systematic Digital Forensic Investigation Model. *International Journal of Computer Science and Security*, **5**(1), pp.118–130.
5. Archer, L. (1984). *Systematic Method for Designers*. London, UK: John Wiley.
6. Armstrong, C. and Armstrong, H. (2010). Modeling Forensic Evidence Systems Using Design Science. In *Proceedings of the International Federation for Information Processing Working Group 8.2/8.6 International Working Conference, Perth, WA, Australia, March 30–April 4*, pp. 282–300.

7. Armstrong, S. (2006). Findings From Evidence-Based Forecasting: Methods for Reducing Forecast Error. *International Journal of Forecasting*, **22**(3), pp. 583–598.
8. Beebe, N. and Clark, J. (2005). A Hierarchical, Objectives-Based Framework for the Digital Investigations Process. *Digital Investigation*, **2**(2), pp. 147–167.
9. Booker, J. and McNamara, L. (2004). Solving Black Box Computation Problems Using Expert Knowledge Theory and Methods. *Reliability Engineering and System Safety*, **85**(1), pp. 331–340.
10. Burgman, M., Carr, A., Godden, L., Gregory, R., McBride, M., Flander, L. and Maguire, L. (2011). Redefining Expertise and Improving Ecological Judgment. *Conservation Letters*, **4**(2), pp. 81–87.
11. Carlton, H. and Worthley, R. (2009). An Evaluation of Agreement and Conflict Among Computer Forensic Experts. In *Proceedings of the 42nd Hawaii International Conference on System Sciences, Big Island, HI, USA, January 5–8*, pp. 1–10.
12. Carrier, B. (2002). *Open Source Digital Forensics Tools: The Legal Argument* [Online]. Available at: http://citeseerx.ist.psu.edu/viewdoc/summary?doi=10.1.1.19.7899 (Accessed: 28 May 2018).
13. Carrier, B. and Spafford, E. (2003). Getting Physical with the Digital Investigation Process. *International Journal of Digital Evidence*, **2**(2), pp.1–20.
14. Casey, E. (2011). *Digital Evidence and Computer Crime: Forensic Science, Computers and the Internet* (3rd ed.). New York, NY, USA: Elsevier Academic Press.
15. Ciardhuáin, O. (2004). An Extended Model of Cybercrime Investigations. *International Journal of Digital Evidence*, **3**(1), pp. 1–22.
16. Clemen, R. and Winkler, R. (1999). Combining Probability Distributions from Experts in Risk Analysis. *Risk Analysis*, **19**(2), pp. 187–203.
17. Cohen, F. (2009). *Digital Forensic Evidence Examination* (2nd ed.). Livermore, CA, USA: Fred Cohen and Associates.
18. Cohen, F. (2010). Towards a Science of Digital Forensic Evidence Examination. In *Proceedings of the 6th International Federation for Information Processing Working Group 11.9 International Conference on Digital Forensics*, pp. 17–35.
19. Cohen, F. (2011). Putting the Science in Digital Forensics. *Journal of Digital Forensics, Security and Law*, **6**(1), pp. 7–14.
20. Cohen, F. (2012). Update on the State of the Science of Digital Evidence Examination, *Proceedings of the Annual ADFSL Conference on Digital Forensics, Security, and Law, Richmond, VA, USA, May 30–31*, pp. 7–18.

21. Cooke, R. (1991). *Experts in Uncertainty: Opinion and Subjective Probability in Science.* New York, NY, USA: Oxford University Press.
22. Cooke, R. and Goossens, L. (2000). Procedures Guide for Structural Expert Judgement in Accident Consequence Modelling. *Radiation Protection Dosimetry,* **90**(3), pp. 303–309.
23. Cowling, R. and Pressey, R. (2003). Introduction to Systematic Conservation Planning in the Cape Floristic Region, *Biological Conservation,* **112**(1), pp. 1–13.
24. Czembor, C. and Vesk, P. (2009). Incorporating Between-Expert Uncertainty Into State-and-Transition Simulation Models for Forest Restoration. *Forest Ecology and Management,* **259**(2), pp. 165–175.
25. Drescher, M., Perera A., Buse L., Ride, K. and Vasiliauskas, S. (2008). Uncertainty in Expert Knowledge of Forest Succession: A Case Study From Boreal Ontario. *The Forestry Chronicle,* **84**(2), pp. 194–209.
26. Eddy, D., Hollingworth, W., Caro, J., Tsevat, J., McDonald, K. and Wong, J. (2012). Model Transparency and Validation: A Report of the ISPOR-SMDM Modeling Good Research Practices Task Force–7, *Medical Decision Making,* **32**(5), pp. 733–743.
27. Eekels, J., and Roozenburg, N. (1991). A Methodological Comparison of the Structures of Scientific Research and Engineering Design: Their Similarities and Differences. *Design Studies,* **12**(4), pp. 197–203.
28. Farrell, M. (1993). Daubert v. Merrell Dow Pharmaceuticals, Inc.: Epistemology and Legal Process. *Cardozo Law Review,* **15**, p. 2183.
29. Fisher, L. (2009). *The Perfect Swarm: The Science of Complexity in Everyday Life.* New York: Basic Books.
30. Freiling, C. and Schwittay, B. (2007). A Common Process Model for Incident Response and Computer Forensics. In *Proceedings of the 3rd International Conference on IT-Incident Management & IT-Forensics, Stuttgart, Germany, September 11–13,* pp. 19–40.
31. Garfinkel, S., Farrell, P., Roussev, V. and Dinolt, G. (2009). Bringing Science to Digital Forensics With Standardized Forensic Corpora. *Digital Investigation,* **6**, pp. 2–11.
32. Garrie, D. (2014). Digital Forensic Evidence in the Courtroom: Understanding Content and Quality. *Northwestern Journal of Technology and Intellectual Property,* **12**(2), pp. [1]–128.
33. Guidance Software. (2018). *EnCase Forensics* [Online]. Available at: https://www.guidancesoftware.com/encase-forensic (Accessed: 29 May 2018).

34. Harrison, W., Heuston, G., Morrissey, M., Aucsmith, D., Mocas, S. and Russelle, S. (2002). A Lessons Learned Repository for Computer Forensics. *International Journal of Digital Evidence,* **1**(3), pp. 1–9.
35. Hauck, R., Atabakhsh, H., Ongvasith P., Gupta, H. and Chen, H. (2002). Using Coplink to Analyze Criminal- Justice Data. *IEEE Computer,* **35**(3), pp. 30–37.
36. Hevner A., March, S., Park, J. and Ram, S. (2004). Design Science in Information Systems Research. *MIS Quarterly,* **28**(1), pp. 75–105.
37. Hevner, A. and Chatterjee, S. (2010). *Design Research in Information Systems.* New York, NY, USA: Springer.
38. Hokstad, P., Oien, K. and Reinertsen, R. (1998). Recommendations on the Use of Expert Judgment in Safety and Reliability Engineering Studies: Two Offshore Case Studies. *Reliability Engineering and System Safety,* **61**(1), pp. 65–76.
39. International Organisation for Standardization. (2015). *ISO/IEC 27043:2015: Information Technology — Security techniques — Incident Investigation Principles and Processes.* Geneva, Switzerland: International Organization for Standardization.
40. Karyda, M. and Mitrou, L. (2007). Internet Forensics: Legal and Technical Issues. In *Proceedings of the 2nd International Workshop on Digital Forensics and Incident Analysis, Samos, Greece, August 27–28,* pp. 3–12.
41. Kessler, C. (2010). *Judges' Awareness, Understanding, and Application of Digital Evidence* (PhD thesis). Fort Lauderdale, FL, USA: Nova Southeastern University.
42. Kohn, M., Eloff, M. and Eloff, J. (2013). Integrated Digital Forensic Process Model. *Computers and Security,* **38**, pp. 103–115.
43. Kuechler, B. and Vaishnavi, V. (2008). On Theory Development in Design Science Research: Anatomy of A Research Project. *European Journal of Information Systems,* **17**(5), pp. 489–504.
44. Kuhnert, P., Martin, T. and Griffiths, S. (2010). A Guide to Eliciting and Using Expert Knowledge in Bayesian Ecological Models. *Ecology Letters,* **13**(7), pp. 900–914.
45. Law, A. (2014). *Simulation Modeling and Analysis* (5th ed.). New York, NY, USA:McGraw-Hill.
46. Leigland, L. and Krings, A. (2004). A Formalization of Digital Forensics. *International Journal of Digital Evidence,* **3**(2), pp. 1–32.
47. Ludwig, D., Mangel, M. and Haddad, B. (2001). Ecology, Conservation, and Public Policy. *Annual Review of Ecology and Systematics,* **32**, pp. 481–517.

48. March, S. and Smith, G. (1995). Design and Natural Science Research on Information Technology. *Decision Support Systems,* **15**(4), pp. 251–266.
49. March, S. and Storey, V. (2008). Design Science in the Information Systems Discipline: An Introduction to the Special Issue on Design Science Research. *MIS Quarterly,* **32**(4), pp. 725–730.
50. Martin, T., Burgman, M., Fidler, F., Kuhnert, P., Low-choy, S., McBride, M. and Mengersen, K. (2012). Eliciting Expert Knowledge in Conservation Science. *Conservation Biology,* **26**(1), pp. 29–38.
51. Mason, S. (2007). *Electronic Evidence: Disclosure, Discovery and Admissibility.* London, UK: LexisNexis Butterworths.
52. McBride, M. and Burgman, M. (2012). What Is Expert Knowledge, How Is Such Knowledge Gathered, and How Do We Use It to Address Questions in Landscape Ecology? In Perera, A., Drew, C. and Johnson, C. (eds.), *Expert Knowledge and Its Application in Landscape Ecology.* New York, NY, USA: Springer.
53. Meyers, M. and Rogers, M. (2004). Computer Forensics: The Need for Standardization and Certification. *International Journal of Digital Evidence,* **3**(2), pp. 1–11.
54. Montasari, R. (2016a). An Ad Hoc Detailed Review of Digital Forensic Investigation Process Models. *International Journal of Electronic Security and Digital Forensics (IJESDF),* **8**(3), pp. 205–223.
55. Montasari, R. (2016b). A Formal Two Stage Triage Process Model (FTSTPM) for Digital Forensics Practice. *International Journal of Computer Science and Security (IJCSS),* **10**(2), pp. 69–87.
56. Montasari, R. (2016). Review and Assessment of the Existing Digital Forensic Investigation Process Models. *International Journal of Computer Applications,* **147**(7), pp. 41–49.
57. Montasari, R. (2016a). *The Comprehensive Digital Forensic Investigation Process Model (CDFIPM) for Digital Forensic Practice* (PhD Thesis). Derby, UK: University of Derby.
58. Montasari, R. (2016b). A Comprehensive Digital Forensic Investigation Process Model. *International Journal of Electronic Security and Digital Forensics (IJESDF),* **8**(4), pp. 285–301.
59. Montasari, R. (2017). A Standardized Data Acquisition Process Model (SDAPM) for Digital Forensic Investigations. *International Journal of Information and Computer Security (IJICS),* **9**(3), pp. 229–249.
60. Montasari, R. (2017). Digital Evidence: Disclosure and Admissibility in the United Kingdom Jurisdiction. In *Proceedings of the International*

Conference on Global Security, Safety, and Sustainability, London, UK, January 18–20, pp. 42–52.

61. Montasari, R. (2018). Testing the Comprehensive Digital Forensic Investigation Process Model (the CDFIPM). In Dastbaz M., Arabnia H., Akhgar B. (eds.), *Technology for Smart Futures.* Cham, Switzerland: Springer.
62. Montasari, R. and Peltola, P. (2015). Computer Forensic Analysis of Private Browsing Modes. *Proceedings of the 10th International Conference on Global Security, Safety and Sustainability: Tomorrow's Challenges of Cyber Security, London, UK, September 15–17,* pp. 96–109.
63. Montasari, R., Peltola, P. and Evans, D. (2015). Integrated Computer Forensics Investigation Process Model (ICFIPM) for Computer Crime Investigations. *Proceedings of 10th International Conference on Global Security, Safety and Sustainability: Tomorrow's Challenges of Cyber Security, London, UK, September 15–17,* pp. 83–95.
64. Morgan, M. and Henrion, M. (2010). *Uncertainty: A Guide to Dealing with Uncertainty in Quantitative Risk and Policy Analysis.* New York, NY, USA: Cambridge University Press.
65. Mumba, E. and Venter, H. (2014). Testing and Evaluating the Harmonized Digital Forensic Investigation Process in Post Mortem Digital Investigations. In *Proceedings of the 9th ADFSL Conference on Digital Forensics, Security and Law, Richmond, VA, USA, May 28–29,* pp. 83–97.
66. Nunamaker, J., Chen, M. and Purdin, T. (1990). Systems Development in Information Systems Research. *Journal of Management Information Systems,* **7**(3), pp. 89–106.
67. Pace, D. K. and Sheehan, J. (2002). Subject Matter Expert (SME)/ Peer Use in M&S V&V, Paper presented at the Foundations for the V&V in the 21st Century workshop (Foundations 2002), pp. 1–34. Baltimore, MD, USA: John Hopkins University.
68. Palmer, G. (2001). A Road Map for Digital Forensic Research. In *Proceedings of the 1st Digital Forensic Research Workshop (DFRWS), Utica, NY, USA, August 7–8,* pp. 27–30.
69. Pearce, J., Cherry, K., Drielsma, M., Ferrier, S. and Whish, G. (2001), Incorporating Expert Opinion and Fine-Scale Vegetation Mapping Into Statistical Models of Faunal Distribution. *Journal of Applied Ecology,* **38**(2), pp. 412–424.
70. Peffers, K., Tuunanen, T., Gengler, C., Rossi, M., Hui, W., Virtanen, V. and Bragge, J. (2006). The Design Science Research Process: A Model for Producing and Presenting Information Systems Research. In

Proceedings of the 1st International Conference on Design Science Research in Information Systems and Technology, Claremont, CA, USA, February 24–25, pp. 83–106.
71. Peisert, S., Bishop, M. and Marzullo, M. (2008). Computer Forensics in Forensics. In *Proceedings of the Third International Workshop on Systematic Approaches to Digital Forensic Engineering, Berkeley, CA, USA, May 22,* pp. 102–122.
72. Pollitt, M. (2009). The Good, the Bad, the Unaddressed. *Journal of Digital Forensic Practice,* **2**(4), pp. 172–174.
73. Reith, M., Carr, C. and Gunsch, G. (2002). An Examination of Digital Forensic Models. *International Journal of Digital Evidence,* **1**(3), pp. 1–12.
74. Rogers, M., Goldman, J., Mislan, R., Wedge, T. and Debrota, S. (2006). Computer Forensics Field Triage Process Model. In *Proceedings of the 1st Conference on Digital Forensics, Security and Law, Las Vegas, NV, USA, April 20–21,* pp. 27–40.
75. Rossi, M. and Sein, M. (2003). Design Research Workshop: A Proactive Research Approach. In *Proceedings of the 26th Information Systems Research Seminar in Scandinavia, Porvoo, Finland, August 9–12,* pp. 9–12.
76. Rothlisberger, J., Lodge, D., Cooke, R. and Finnoff, D. (2010). Future Declines of the Binational Laurentian Great Lakes Fisheries: The Importance of Environmental and Cultural Change. *Frontiers in Ecology and the Environment,* **8**(5), pp. 239–244.
77. Selamat, S., Yusof, R. and Sahib, S. (2008). Mapping Process of Digital Forensic Investigation Framework. *International Journal of Computer Science and Network Security,* **8**(10), pp. 163–169.
78. Sherman, S. (2006). A Digital Forensic Practitioner's Guide to Giving Evidence in a Court of Law. In *Proceedings of the 4th Australian Digital Forensics Conference, Joondalup, WA, Australia, December 4th,* pp. 1–7.
79. Solomon, M., Rudolph, K., Tittel, E., Broom, N. and Barrett, D. (2011). *Computer Forensics JumpStart* (2nd ed.). Indianapolis, IN, USA: Wiley Publishing.
80. Sutherland, W. (2006). Predicting the Ecological Consequences of Environmental Change: A Review of the Methods. *Journal of Applied Ecology,* **43**(4), pp. 599–616.
81. Takeda, H., Veerkamp, P., Tomiyama, T. and Yoshikawa, H. (1990). Modeling Design Processes. *AI Magazine,* **11**(4), pp. 37–48.
82. US-CERT. (2012). *Computer Forensics* [Online]. Available at: https://www.us-cert.gov/security-publications/computer-forensics (Accessed: 30 November 2018).

83. Vaishnavi, V. and Kuechler, B. (2004). *Design Research in Information Systems* [Online]. Available at: http://www.desrist.org/design-research-in-information-systems (Accessed: 29 May 2018).
84. Valjarevic, A. and Venter, H. (2015). A Comprehensive and Harmonized Digital Forensic Investigation Process Model. *Journal of Forensic Sciences,* **60**(6), pp. 1467–1483.
85. Van Aken, J. E. (2005). Management Research as a Design Science: Articulating the Research Products of Mode 2 Knowledge Production in Management. *British Journal of Management,* **16**(1), pp. 19–36.
86. Venter, J. (2006). *Process Flow for Cyber Forensics Training and Operations* [Online]. Available at: http://researchspace.csir.co.za/dspace/handle/10204/1073 (Accessed: 29 May 2018).
87. Walls, J., Widmeyer, G. and El Sawy, O. (1992). Building an Information System Design Theory for Vigilant EIS. *Information Systems Research,* **3**(1), pp. 36–59.
88. Watts, S., Shankaranarayanan, G. and Even, A. (2009). Data Quality Assessment in Context: A Cognitive Perspective. *Decision Support Systems,* **48**(1), pp. 202–211.
89. Whitfield, P., Ruddock, M., Bullman, R. (2008). 'Expert Opinion as a Tool for Quantifying Bird Tolerance to Human Disturbance. *Biological Conservation,* **141**(11), pp. 2708–2717.
90. Zainudin, N., Merabti, M. and Llewellyn-Jones, D. (2011). Online Social Networks as Supporting Evidence: A Digital Forensic Investigation Model and Its Application Design. In *Proceedings of the International Conference on Research and Innovation in Information Systems, Kuala Lumpur, Malaysia, November 23–24,* pp. 1–6.

Appendix A

Table 9.1. Analysis of the previous DFIPMs as presented in Montasari *et al.* (2015).

No	Authors	Year	Digital Investigation Process Model	Readiness	Identification	Detection	Preservation	Evidence Collection	Examination	Analysis	Evidence Acquisition	Preparation	Approach Strategy	Forensic Duplication	Recovery	Survey
1	Polliu	1995	Computer forensics: an Approach to Evidence in Cyberspace		✓						✓					
2	Casey	2000	Digital Evidence and Computer Crime				✓									
3	Lee et al.	2001	Model of Scientific Crime Scene Investigation		✓		✓	✓								
4	Palmer et al.	2001	DFRWS – Investigative Process for Digital Forensic Science		✓	✓	✓	✓	✓	✓						
5	Reith et al.	2002	An Abstract Digital Forensics Model		✓		✓	✓	✓	✓		✓	✓			
6	Mandia et al.	2003	Incident Response & Computer Forensics					✓		✓					✓	✓
7	Carrier et al.	2003	An Integrated Digital Investigation Process	✓		✓										✓
8	Stephenson	2003	End-to-end Digital Investigation Process				✓	✓							✓	
9	Ciardhuain	2004	An Extended Model of Cybercrime Investigations					✓	✓				✓			
10	Casey et al.	2004	Digital Evidence and Computer Crime		✓		✓			✓	✓				✓	
11	Baryamureeba et al.	2004	The Enhanced Digital Investigation Process Model	✓		✓	✓	✓		✓						✓
12	Carrier et al.	2004	An Even-Based Digital Forensic Investigation Framework													
13	Beebe et al.	2005	A Hierarchical, Objectives-Based Framework for the Digital Investigation Process			✓	✓	✓	✓	✓		✓	✓		✓	✓
14	Kohn et al.	2006	Framework for a Digital Forensic Investigation		✓			✓	✓	✓			✓			
15	Kent et al.	2006	Guide to Integrating Forensic Techniques into Incident Response		✓		✓	✓	✓	✓	✓					
16	Ieong R	2006	FORZA – Digital Forensics Investigation Framework That Incorporates Legal Issues				✓				✓					✓
17	Freiling, F	2007	A Common Process Model for Computer Forensics and Incident Response	✓		✓				✓			✓	✓	✓	
18	Groble et al.	2010	A Multi-Component View of Digital Forensics	✓	✓			✓		✓	✓					
19	Zainudin et al.	2010	A Digital Forensic Investigation Model for Online Social Networking		✓			✓								✓
20	Alharbi et al.	2011	The Proactive and Reactive Digital Investigation Process: A Systematic Literature Review		✓		✓	✓			✓					
21	Yusoff et al.	2011	Common Phases of Computer Forensics Investigations Models				✓	✓		✓	✓					
22	Cosie et al.	2011	Chain of Digital Evidence-Based Model of Digital Investigation Process		✓			✓	✓			✓				
23	Agarwal et al.	2012	Systematic Digital Investigation Process Model				✓	✓	✓	✓						✓
24	Roger et al.	2012	Multi-Perspective Cybercrime Investigation Process Modeling		✓	✓	✓	✓			✓					
25	Valgarevic et al.	2012	Harmonised Digital Investigation Process Model			✓	✓	✓		✓		✓				
26	Saleem et al.	2014	Extended Abstract Digital Forensics Model with Preservation and Protection as Umbrella Principles				✓	✓	✓	✓		✓				

No	Interview	Deployment	Approved Methods	Authorisation	Harvesting	Organisation	Classification	Sampling	Seizure	Data Reduction	Compression	Presentation	Documentation	Live Data Collection	Trace Back	Dynamite	Decision/Resolution	Returning Evidence	Physical Crieme Scene Investigation	Digital Crieme Scene Investigation
1																				
2							✓				✓		✓							
3											✓	✓	✓							
4			✓	✓				✓		✓	✓	✓	✓				✓			
5												✓						✓		
6				✓																
7		✓		✓								✓	✓						✓	✓
8			✓	✓				✓		✓	✓									
9				✓								✓								
10			✓	✓					✓	✓										
11		✓										✓	✓		✓	✓			✓	✓
12													✓						✓	✓
13												✓								
14												✓	✓							
15																				
16	✓								✓				✓		✓					
17					✓	✓				✓		✓					✓			
18									✓			✓	✓						✓	✓
19												✓								
20																				
21												✓								
22				✓																
23												✓	✓	✓			✓			
24												✓		✓					✓	✓
25				✓								✓	✓							
26												✓						✓		

No	Review	Operational Readiness	Infrastructure Readiness	Notification	Evidence Search	Event Reconstruction	Awareness/Report	Hypothesis	Proff & Defence	Confirm	Record	Package	Transport	Store	Communication	Incident Response	System Restoration	Evaluation	Incident Closure	Dissemination
1																		✓		
2						✓														
3						✓												✓		
4																				
5																				
6																				
7	✓	✓	✓	✓	✓	✓				✓										
8																				
9				✓	✓		✓	✓	✓				✓	✓						✓
10					✓															
11	✓			✓	✓	✓				✓					✓					
12						✓														
13						✓	✓			✓		✓	✓	✓		✓			✓	
14				✓	✓								✓	✓						
15											✓	✓								
16																				
17																✓				
18					✓	✓				✓						✓	✓		✓	
19	✓			✓	✓			✓	✓				✓	✓						
20																				
21													✓	✓						
22						✓							✓	✓					✓	
23	✓																			
24																			✓	
25													✓	✓		✓				
26																				

Appendix B

The Comprehensive Digital Forensic Investigation Process Model (CDFIPM)

Please notice: any personal information provided will be kept confidential and will be deleted once the comments and feedback have been reviewed and analysed.

Prior proceeding to the questions, please state:

Your full name: ______________________________

The institution you work/ have worked for: ______________________________

Your job titles related to domain of digital forensics: ______________________________

Your period of learning and experience: ______________________________

The condition in which the experience has been gained: ______________________________

In reviewing / evaluating the model:

1. Please identify any aspects of the model that are not representative of the processes as carried out in your field of practice (utility).
2. Please identify any aspects of the processes carried out in your field of practice that are not covered in this model (utility).
3. Did you think that the model adequately represented the structure of investigations in your organisation (utility)?
4. Please describe which activities in the model most closely relate to your field of practice and your own experience (utility).
5. Please describe what aspects, if any, of the model you felt could be improved (utility).
6. Please rate the model on the scale of 1 to 10 with 1 not being useful at all and 10 being the most useful (utility).
7. Please rate the model on the scale of 1 to 10 with 1 being very difficult to use and 10 being very easy to use (usability).
8. Please provide any additional comments that you might have on the model attached.

(Please provide your answers/feedbacks/comments on a separate sheet of paper.)

Fig. 9.6. Evaluation questionnaire.

Appendix C

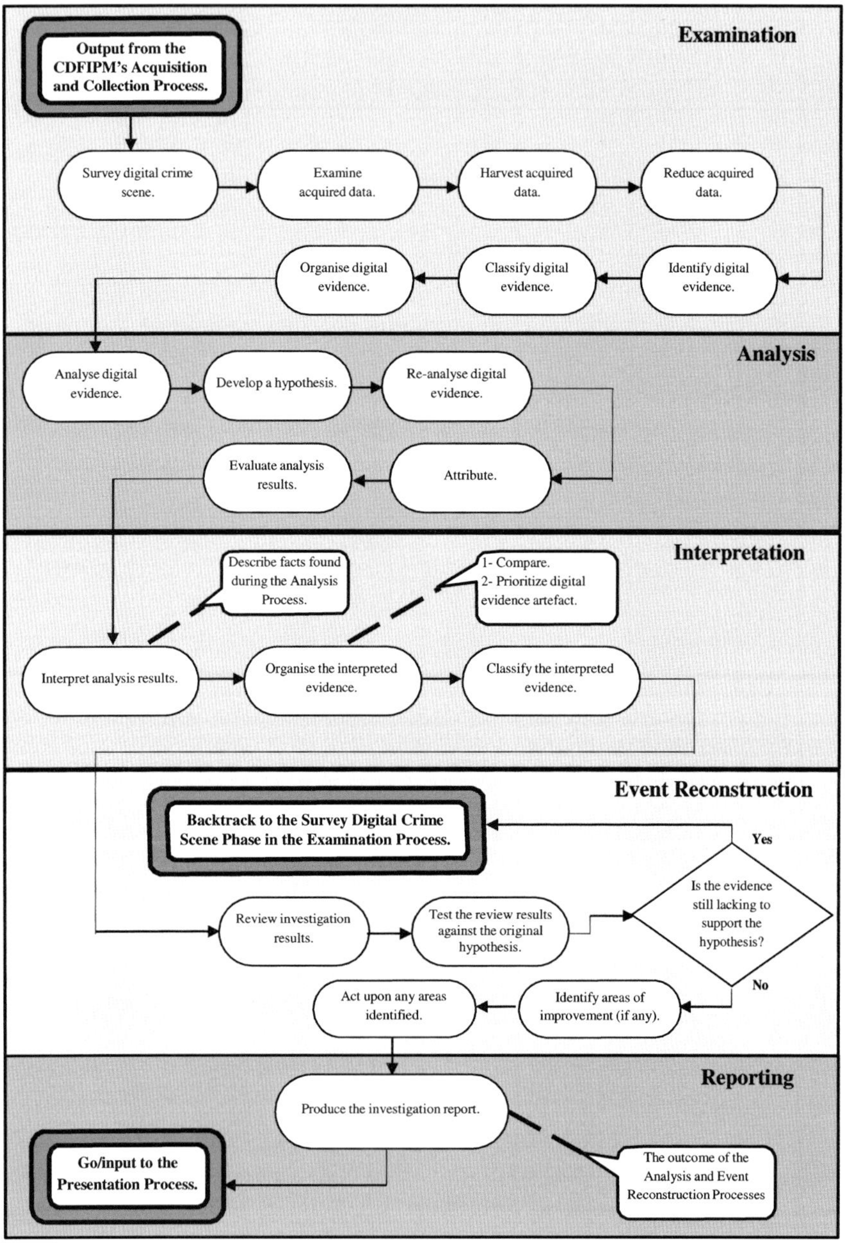

Fig. 9.7. Final version of the Examination, Analysis, Interpretation, Event Reconstruction and Reporting Processes.

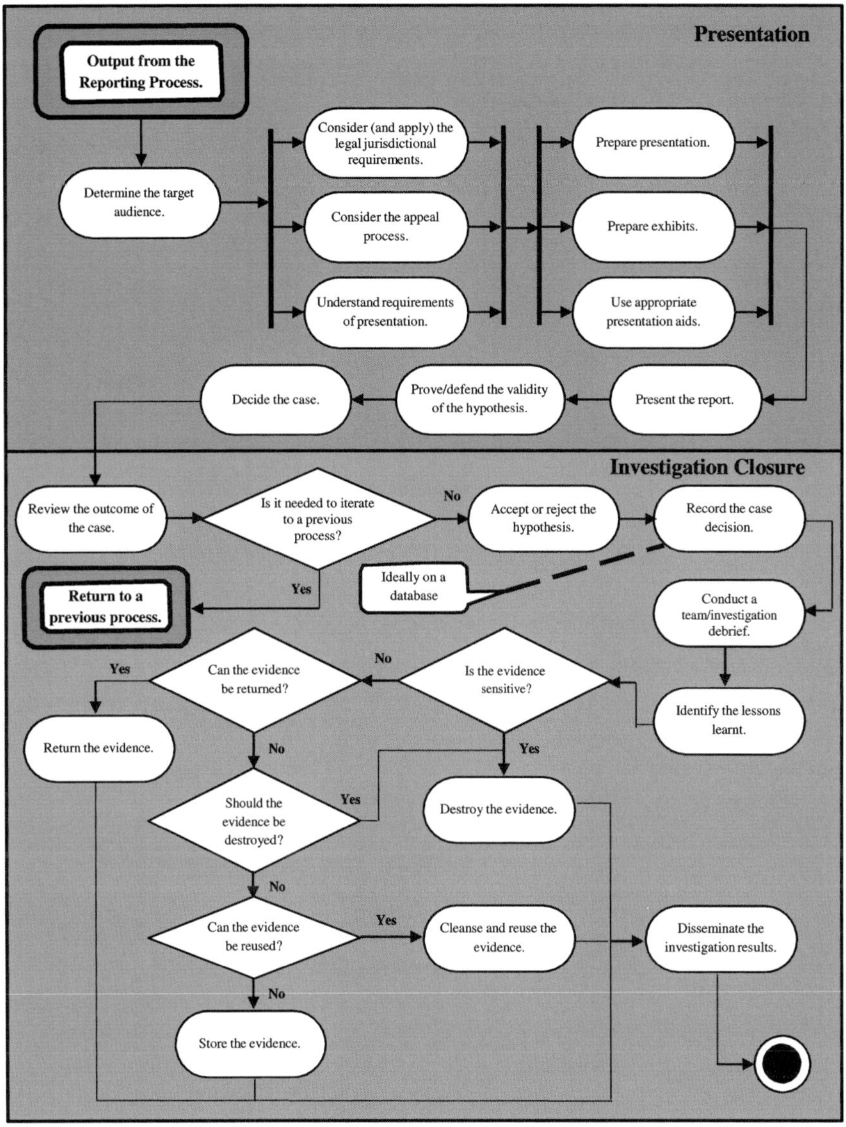

Fig. 9.8. Final version of the presentation and investigation closure processes.

Chapter 10

Blockchain of Custody, BoC

Ian Mitchell*,†, Sukhvinder Hara*,‡, Hamid Jahankhani¶ and David Neilson*,§

*Middlesex University, Dept. Computer Science, London, UK
†i.mitchell@mdx.ac.uk
‡s.hara@mdx.ac.uk
§d.neilson@mdx.ac.uk

¶Northumbria University,
Dept. Computer & Information Sciences, London, UK
h.jahankhani@northumbria.ac.uk

ABSTRACT

Ensuring continuity of evidence in any investigation is problematic, even more so when multiple agencies are involved. Ensuring there is consistency between paperwork concerning the seizure of artefacts is difficult, and can often be scrutinized in court. The development of this prototype blockchain is for the recording of the transfer of evidence during an investigation, with the aim of providing a guarantee for the continuity of evidence. The implementation of the blockchain is completed using Hyperledger and is referred to in this paper as Blockchain of Custody, or BoC. To test BoC two simple mock investigations are carried out and then evaluated. The evaluation includes querying the evidence, access control, development, security, and auditing. The implementation of BoC is considered a success and the future improvements, disadvantages and advantages are discussed.

Keywords: Bitcoin, HyperLedger, blockchain, chain of custody, timestamp, legal assurance

10.1. Introduction

Over recent years the hyperbole surrounding Decentralised Applications (DApps) and Blockchain has distracted researchers from their rationales by making them consider new developments. Is the technology pushing change, or is change pushing the technology? Here we have taken the opportunity to investigate how blockchain technology can be implemented for the seizure and transfer of evidence, or, put simply, how a blockchain of custody would work. This proposal considers the development, the implementation, the benefits, the issues and finally the impact on Forensic Science in general.

There are many issues with how a current chain of custody for the collection of evidence is completed. In particular, there is one issue about safeguarding from tampering (ISO, 2017 (Section 7.11)). Chain of custody automation software is almost standard for accredited labs and is recommended in ISO (2017, 2013). However, there is room for improvement when it comes to transferring evidence to third parties and ensuring that the chain of custody is immutable and irreversible. This is the main motivation for this paper, to investigate the blockchain software development lifecycle facilitating the chain of custody procedures.

Blockchain of Custody (BoC) is a decentralisation application that provides an immutable and irreversible record of the chain of custody for evidence collected after any incident. It does not intend to replace evidence management software that provides much of industry standard and structure to generate reports and manage staff and facilities, e.g., Foreman (Lowman, 2018). Instead BoC intends to work with this software and improve the capability, value and quality of evidential-related material regarding the chain of custody.

10.2. Background

Whilst many marvel at the value Bitcoin, B, has bought to cryptocurrency, the biggest contribution to software engineering that Bitcoin has provided us with is decentralised applications or blockchain.

Bitcoin (Nakamoto, 2008; Antonopoulos, 2017) and blockchain are inseparable; without blockchain technologies, Bitcoin would be unable to operate. Blockchain and consensus engineering are side products of Bitcoin. The blockchain is transparent, public, immutable, irreversible, secure, asynchronous, self-regulating and international. Briefly, Bitcoin users have a wallet, with which they can make transactions to other wallets securely using Public Key Infrastructures (PKI) encryption; this is facilitated by a distributed ledger, known as a blockchain. The blockchain is stored on multiple nodes in a network, each storing every transaction made between wallets. The confirmation of each transaction comes from the nodes, which check the validity of the transaction and then verify the transaction to all the other nodes in the network. The similarities between BoC and Bitcoin are as follows:

— Transactions: a transaction in Bitcoin represents the transfer of funds between two parties. Once this transaction has been verified it is added to the blockchain. BoC has transactions which record the transfer of artefacts between two parties and the blockchain can easily be modified to accommodate this type of transaction, see Greenspan (2015).
— Irrefutable: the motivation behind the validation of Bitcoin transactions is to ascertain that the spending party has the funds, and that there is no double-spending. Essentially, the motivation for validation comes down to financial accuracy. The motivation for the validation of BoC transactions are to ensure the integrity of the chain of custody.
— Longevity: in Bitcoin ledgers, the transactions are stored for the lifetime of Bitcoin itself. For BoC, all transactions of the chain of custody would also last for the duration of BoC, well beyond the time required for case information to be preserved. There is some concern over personal data being stored on BoC since it cannot be removed.
— Privacy: Bitcoin is public, so the ledgers can be seen by participants and non-participants of Bitcoin. BoC would be a private blockchain (Greenspan, 2015), often referred to as a permission blockchain, and would thus allow only authorised access.
— Data: Bitcoin transactions contain the users, the amount transferred, the timestamp and other meta-data. BoC transactions

would differ and typically contain the receiver, submitter, manager, evidence ID, investigation ID and timestamp.

— Latency: the latency of blockchain verification in Bitcoin is such that it can take up to 10 minutes for Bitcoin to be mined and for this to be verified by a network of nodes; this latency is too long for the BoC application. This latency can be reduced to 10-20 secs, which is acceptable on a private blockchain, see Greenspan (2015) and Hyperledger Architecture Working Group (2017).

— Incentivisation: the incentive to set up a Bitcoin node is a reward of some value, albeit in the form of a digital crypto-currency. There is no value or reward in this BoC, however, typically there would be an incentive amongst regulators, e.g., FSR (Forensic Science Regulator, 2017), and accredited labs. If this was to be a national incentive, the nodes would be run independently by the regulators. This provides private transparency and the ability to see the chain of custody for each item of evidence.

— Disintermediation (Gaur *et al.*, 2018): Many business and organisations rely on intermediaries, e.g. businesses rely on banks to complete transactions. It is necessary to trust one's intermediaries. BitCoin overcomes this via consensus engineering and therefore removes the reliance on intermediaries. BoC would benefit from disintermediation, or not relying on intermediaries such as regulators or auditors. However, unlike the absence of regulators such as banks in the Bitcoin system, regulators would be integrated into the BoC system.

In summary, BoC is a system proposed, that, once updated, is immutable and irreversible. The system is implemented with blockchain technology, which is based on the Bitcoin technology. Its main contribution is ensuring that the chain of custody is immutable and irreversible and will add significant benefits to the integrity of all artefacts seized as items of evidence, both physical and digital, and therefore improve the overall quality of Evidence Management.

10.3. Blockchain of Custody, BoC

Evidential Continuity is part of evidence management and included in ISO17025 (ISO, 2017 (Section 7.11)). This means that to be an

ISO17025 accredited forensic laboratory it is required, amongst other things, to have a secure information system that records, deletes, reports failures, ensures data integrity and has appropriate authorised access. ISO17025 compliance is an issue for all forensic laboratories handling evidence and allows the transparent audit of evidential continuity. These are usually only examined after the disclosure for a court case or audit. During the design and implementation of BoC the following are considered.

10.3.1. *Scope*

The scope of this evidence management system involves all stakeholders, but the system only records when evidence has been transferred between submitter and receiver. The details will include the unambiguous unique identifiers of submitter, receiver, investigation ID and artefact ID. The Business model involves the following stakeholders:

Law Enforcement Agencies: Police; Forensic Labs; Military; Security Agencies; Internal Quality Assurance Mechanisms; National Security Agencies; Expert Witnesses, and other government agencies.

Legal Representation: Prosecutors; Defence; Para-Legals; Internal Quality Assurance Mechanisms; Legal Mediator Assistants, and other business-related representatives.

Audit Agencies: Forensic Science Regulators; Independent Police Watchdogs; Legal Assurance Agencies, and other external agencies related to Law Enforcement and Legal.

10.3.2. *Transactions*

A DBMS has transactions to change the database from one consistent state to another. Partial transactions cannot occur, and transactions have to be committed. The transactions log, in a DBMS, is often used in backup instances or failures. Transactions have to pass the ACID test: Atomicity, Consistency, Isolation and Durability (Haerder and Reuter, 1983). Some years later came OLTP and OLAP, which now dominate the data warehousing and data mining activities of organisations. Brewer (2000) highlighted these same issues with GraphDB. The problem was paradoxical, and the large databases could not address all three issues simultaneously. Much research has happened since 2000, and Brewer (2017) went on to elaborate on the advances in technology.

Transactions in blockchain and distributed ledgers are defined as the recording of the transaction inputs, transaction outputs, and amounts spent. A transaction does change the data in the blockchain. However, little is known about how consistency is applied to the blockchain. Whilst blockchain is decentralised under certain circumstances it can pass the ACID test (Verdian *et al.*, 2018). This is important for such an application as BoC, in which consistency is required.

10.3.3. *No Wi-Fi, no reception*

Areas without Wi-Fi are common to crime scenes, e.g., underground. There are also issues with privacy on open networks, which are overcome by the encryption of the data submitted. In cases where there is no Wi-Fi access, the reliance on good old-fashioned forensics and physical paperwork will suffice and accompany evidence until a designated place with Wi-Fi access is reached and the blockchain can be updated. This is not unlike operations today, where internet access is prohibited due to network unavailability.

10.3.4. *Incentives*

The biggest implementation of blockchain is Bitcoin (Nakamoto, 2008). It is permissionless and secure; however, there are weaknesses. Sompolinsky and Zohar (2018) have discussed the arms race for 'proof-of-work', the updating of the blockchain and the rewards received. Such incentives yield an uneven playing field created by nodes investing heavily in ASIC hardware to complete 'proof-of-work' and can lead to centralisation. As pointed out by Sompolinsky and Zohar, this will even out when the reward for block creation is withdrawn, and the focus is on transaction rewards. This does not affect permissioned blockchains, whereby control can be exerted over the network through consensus engineering. In permissioned blockchain applications where there are no tokens or coins, this is not a threat since there are no incentives for block creation and no reward for transactions.

10.3.5. *Permissioned blockchain*

The idea and advantages of permissioned blockchain (aka private blockchain) are discussed in Greenspan (2015). Permissioned blockchain (aka public blockchain) only allows authorised access, in other words, it is not permissionless. For BoC, permissioned blockchain is advantageous for the following reasons:

— It allows one to maintain control over transactions and how they are completed.
— The blockchain is only accessible by approved, trained and certified personnel.
— The blockchain has low latency. Permissionless blockchains, e.g., Bitcoin, have some latency between the timestamp of the transaction and the creation of the blockchain. This is to prevent node domination and is the result of the consensus algorithm, 'proof-of-work'. With a permissioned blockchain, one can have control over the nodes, so competitive consensus algorithms are not required. Whilst consensus is required, the ability of a member of the blockchain to engage in node domination can be controlled.
— The members of the blockchain can be vetted. Vetting is an important process that is difficult in permissionless blockchains since anyone can join. In permissioned blockchain, members can be vetted and the issuance of keys can be controlled and managed.

10.3.6. *Tokens*

Blockchain is often incorrectly used synonymously with Bitcoin and therefore it is assumed that upon a transaction made on the blockchain an exchange of coins, or tokens, is required. Blockchain development can be completed without tokens; the question is, does the BoC application require them? Having a clear breakdown is not only important for designers and programmers, but also important for training purposes and ensuring that users follow procedures for updating the blockchain.

Typically, tokens are used in decentralised applications to prevent DoS attacks on nodes from disgruntled employees who have permissions to update multiple times. This could also apply to device breach, but this is unlikely since this would normally be reported and addresses associated with the device blocked. Tokens provide an additional level of security; however, the issuance of tokens would have to be centralised and updated accordingly. Re-distribution, re-use and the possible disposal of tokens is a concern, e.g. evidence store managers will have a surplus of tokens, whereas FRT members will have less, see Fig. 3.6. In order to perform a transaction, one would have to have a token of the minimum/smallest value. The value of the tokens can be controlled at issuance.

Figure 10.1 illustrates the exchange of tokens between actors when exchanging evidence. For example, the path between vertexes 3 and 1 is directed and shows a flow of 10 tokens. Figure 10.1 indicates that there is a possibility of uneven token distribution. The distribution and issuance of tokens would have to be governed and

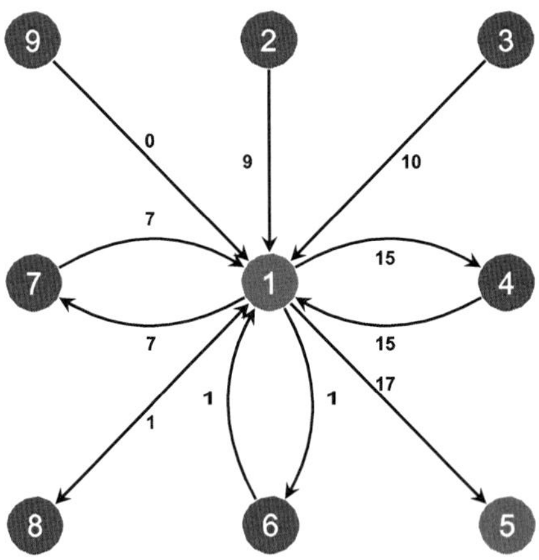

Node	Description
1	Custodian
2	Investigator
3	LEA
4	Staff
5	Manager
6	Legal
7	Third Parties
8	Specialist
9	Regulator

Path	Description	tokens
2-1	Investigators submitting 9 artefacts	9
3-1	LEA submitting 10 artefacts	10
4-1-4	Forensics receiving & returning 15 artefacts for examination	15
1-5	Disposal or repatriation of 17 artefacts	17
6-1-6	LMA receiving & returning 1 artefact for examination	1
8-1	Specialist Inspection	1
7-1-7	Third Parties receiving & returning 7 artefacts	7
9-1	Regulatory Inspection	0

Fig. 10.1. Uneven token distribution: Where the evidence life-cycle ends, due to disposal or returns, there is an accumulation of tokens, represented by highlighted nodes in red.

completed by a central authority. This could lead to operational issues, e.g., the inability to submit evidence due to a token deficit. The issuance of tokens is also problematic and might have to be resolved by organisational restructuring, e.g., all Forensic Scientists might have to spend a day collecting tokens as a Custodian in the evidence store. It may seem possible to incorporate such measures into a BoC system, but these measures may be disagreeable to organisations in which the role of the user is less inter-disciplinary or in high demand.

Due to the problems outlined above, tokens will not be used in BoC. BoC is a not-for-profit permissioned blockchain application to assist in the recording of artefacts at investigations. Blockchain has a formula for cost, where *(Value created by blockchain – network operation costs > 0)* (Gaur *et al.*, 2018 (Chapter 10)). However, when not-for-profit or public funds are used to cover costs the need and value of tokens diminish. When designing a blockchain application the need for tokens has to be considered and the important factors that play a role in this decision are as follows:

1. value of the token — is there any real value to the token;
2. purpose/funding of blockchain application — is the blockchain funded by the value of the tokens;
3. token issuance — how are tokens redistributed across all actors in the network;
4. uneven token distribution — does a particular type of user tend to accumulate tokens; and
5. organisational restructure — is organisational restructure required to redistribute your tokens.

10.3.7. *Hyperledger*

Participants, assets, transactions and events are the main components in a business network (Gaur *et al.*, 2018 (Chapter 6)). These components can be described as follows:

Participants: Participants are the actors playing various roles in the business network, e.g., in BoC the actors are investigators, custodians, etc. These roles need defining and Use Case Diagrams are particularly important for identifying the participants. As pointed out in Chapter 6 of Gaur *et al.* (2018) there are three types of participants: individual, organisational and system.

Assets: Assets are the items of value to the network that are securely exchanged and recorded between participants. These assets need to be kept confidential, protected and secure. Much like data structures in databases, assets have properties and relationships, e.g., the ownership of an asset is a property of the asset.

Transactions: Transaction records change. Essentially, this is the asset lifecycle and the changing of properties, relationships and ownership are recorded and updated on the blockchain. In addition, the user that made the transaction is recorded, along with the timestamp when the transaction was made and finally, a unique hash code.

Events: Events represent a transition in the business network, e.g., when an artefact reaches a certain location.

10.4. Design

The design and development of blockchain applications is in its embryonic stages. There is no standard approach and it is proposed that using a modelling technique based on UML will help to provide a structured approach during design. The following sections explain the proposal and are centred around four aspects of blockchain: user modelling (Section 10.4.1), data modelling (Section 10.4.2), access control (Section 10.4.3) and operational logic (Section 10.4.4).

10.4.1. *User modelling*

The use case diagram in Fig. 10.2 identifies the roles of individuals and key processes required for the operation of a chain of custody, which is an important aspect of Access Control (as explained in Section 10.4.3). The actors in the use case are generic and include a wide range of people in different organisations, e.g. Expert Witnesses are not included as a specific role, but can be accommodated in

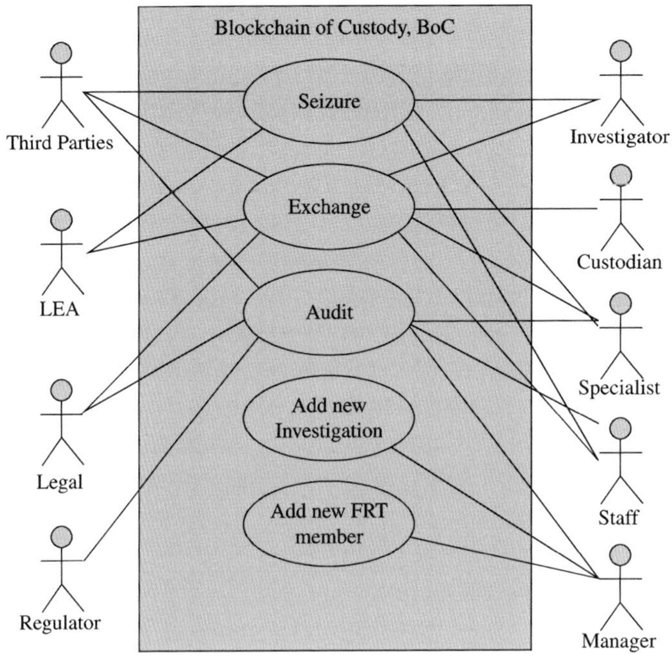

Fig. 10.2. Use case diagram for BoC. Internal actors on right, external actors on left.

either Third Parties or Specialists. The issue here is that the attributes, which would be processed at run-time, allow a specific role certain access. The transactions carried out in the use cases have a direct relation to the transactions required in the blockchain, with the exception of Audit. In summary, the use case diagram helps a designer identify actors and transactions to add to the system.

Figure 10.2 identifies five key use cases required: 'Add new Investigation'; 'Add new FRT member'; 'Seizure'; 'Exchange'; and, 'Audit'. With the exception of 'Audit', each of these use cases requires a bespoke transaction and a flowchart detailing the sequence of events. 'Audit' is an exception, since it is querying the process and merely monitoring the blockchain, and since this is something that Hyperledger already provides. Of course, this is only a prototype. Future modifications may require updates to the blockchain when auditors view data, thus enabling an audit on the auditors.

10.4.2. *Data modelling*

Figure 10.3 illustrates the data requirements for this system. The class diagram does not include data attributes or methods since they are stored separately, the former on the blockchain and the latter in the system. It simply outlines the components required for the system and their relationships. Of particular importance is the generalised inheritence of the class 'Person', which has relationships with the classes 'Custody' and 'Case' (later defined as Investigation). The classes highlighted as external are entities outside the organisation; however, they are not external to BoC. The purpose of highlighting them as external is to demonstrate the exploitation of vendor-neutral representations with blockchain technology. Whilst each external organisation may have a different

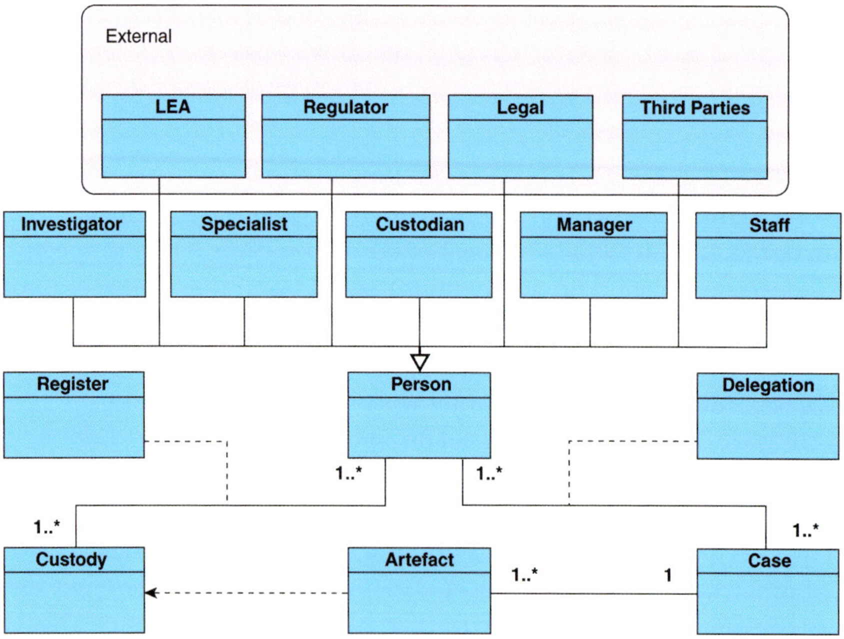

Fig. 10.3. Class diagram for BoC. The system includes external classes, which are accredited organisations that will have access to the permissioned blockchain. However, they have limited access. Access is controlled by an access policy at a policy enforcement point.

Management Information System, blockchain technology supplies a reliable, irrefutable and secure communication between any two organisations. This would be a significant challenge in system development and technology infrastructure. In summary, the classes identify the differences between assets, participants, transactions and information stored on the blockchain.

10.4.3. *Access control*

Access control provides participants with secure and authorised access to assets. During the embryonic development of access control, Role-Based Access Control (RBAC) (Ferraiolo *et al.*, 2001) played an important part in authorising groups of users. Over time, these groups of users became dynamic and included attributes that informed authorisation. For example, a user may only be authorised whilst at work, or, whilst they have been delegated a task by a manager. Typically, more roles were added, which eventually led to a role explosion and complexity (Kuhn *et al.*, 2010).

Many Access Control Models (ACM) have been proposed since Karp *et al.* (2009), however, spending some time finding the appropriate ACM for your system is worthwhile. This can often be dictated by the environment you are using, and in some cases, where there are no dynamic roles, RBAC would be perfectly adequate. This is not the case with BoC, as the roles are dynamic, e.g., the seizure of artefacts has to be delegated to the First Response Team, no one else can make the seizure since they are not clearly present. This has a dynamic role and access is dependent on the attributes of the participant and particular assets. It is these attributes that form an important part of the access control process. They are the reason why Attribute-Based Access Control (ABAC) (Hu *et al.*, 2014) has been chosen.

Essentially, there are three types of attributes when designing BoC, which are as follows:

1. Asset Attributes: These are referred to as object attributes in ABAC. In BoC there is only one asset, which is the artefact. The policy aims to protect artefacts from being accessed by unauthorised participants.

2. Participant Attributes: These are referred to as subject attributes in ABAC. In BoC there are many types of participants and their roles are dynamic. Initially, it is assumed that all participants are denied access to assets — this is a Hyperledger default. The attributes of each participant vary, and therefore, participants with the same credentials could have different authorisation. For example, consider two investigators, say A and B, and two cases, say 1 and 2. Investigator A has been assigned to manage Case 1 and, likewise, Investigator B has been assigned to manage Case 2. Investigator A can view the blockchain for artefacts submitted for Case 1, but not for Case 2. Conversely, the same applies to Investigator B.
3. Environment Attributes: These are attributes independent of the Asset and Participant Attributes, such as time, geo-location and threat level.

Use cases are recommended in Hu *et al.* (2014) to help in the development of Natural Language Policies. Figure 10.2 shows the use case and various access points. Access can be denied or permitted with the following privileges: read, write, update, delete and all.

Conflict of Rules: Access control lists have to be carefully implemented with consideration made to any demands in the transaction. By default, all participants have privileges denied. So, the access control list changes this default. However, care needs to be taken since privileges can contradict transactional access requirements. For example, consider artefact transfer. It is a key operation in the chain of custody and records the time of the exchange of the artefact. There are two definitions: the submitter, who, pre-exchange, is the current custodian of the artefact; and, the *receiver*, who, post-exchange, is the new custodian of the artefact. It requires a few rules, as follows:

1. The submitter can only read themselves.
2. The submitter of the artefact can initiate the exchange, no one else can do this on the submitter's behalf.
3. The receiver has to exist.
4. The artefact has to exist.
5. The receiver becomes the new Custodian after the exchange.

Rule 1 is initially provided for privacy, and all submitters can only view themselves on the system. This puts a restriction on the access of the current user. The dynamic situation means that the receiver inherits new privileges upon becoming the new custodian of the object, e.g. the receiver can now exchange that artefact with someone else. Unlike relational databases, blockchain does not enforce referential integrity, therefore it is possible to exchange an artefact with a receiver that does not exist. To prevent this the transactional code will check two things: i) if the current participant is the custodian of the artefact that is to be exchanged; and, ii) if the receiver exists in the participant registry. The second of the two checks will always fail, since rule 1 in the list above only allows the current participant to read themselves, and therefore when access to the participant registry is requested, only the current user is included in it. Therefore, even if the receiver exists, rule 1 prevents them from being identified and the exchange will be denied (under these rules the exchange does allow the submitter to exchange the artefact with themselves).

Deconfliction of access control rules often needs to occur to allow some transactions to be completed correctly. There is a compromise, which is unusual for security and which could potentially create vulnerability. When a user accesses the system, it would be unusual to allow read privileges to other users.

Modelling access control is problematic due to the dynamic process, however, all possibilities still have to be considered when designing a blockchain application. Here we have opted for flowcharts and demonstrate access control by providing a single role example.

Flowcharts are often overlooked as simplistic, but many are used in proposing standard operating procedures (SOP), e.g., Mitchell *et al.* (2018), and these can provide a sequence of instructions that are followed. Of course, there are many criticisms of such a simplistic method; however, here the aim is to provide a sequence of events for each transaction identified in the system. Normally, this would be identified in UML by sequence diagrams; however, this would be misleading and incorrect since the methods and data are not encapsulated in a class. In the physical implementation they are separated.

10.4.4. *Operational Logic*

Figure 10.2 identified four transactions, which are discussed in more detail below.

Adding a New Investigation: Only managers can add a new investigation.[1] Managers cannot add a new investigation on behalf of others. Therefore, the current participant has to be a manager and can only add themselves as manager to the new investigation. Finally, the Investigation ID provided has to be unique and only then can the blockchain be updated. This procedure is illustrated in a flowchart in Fig. 10.4 (left) which shows a single update to the blockchain before the entire procedure terminates. Strictly, the access control list is less dynamic and more role-based for this procedure.

During the procedure for adding an investigation ID, the ID is checked to see if it already exists in the system. This test of the integrity

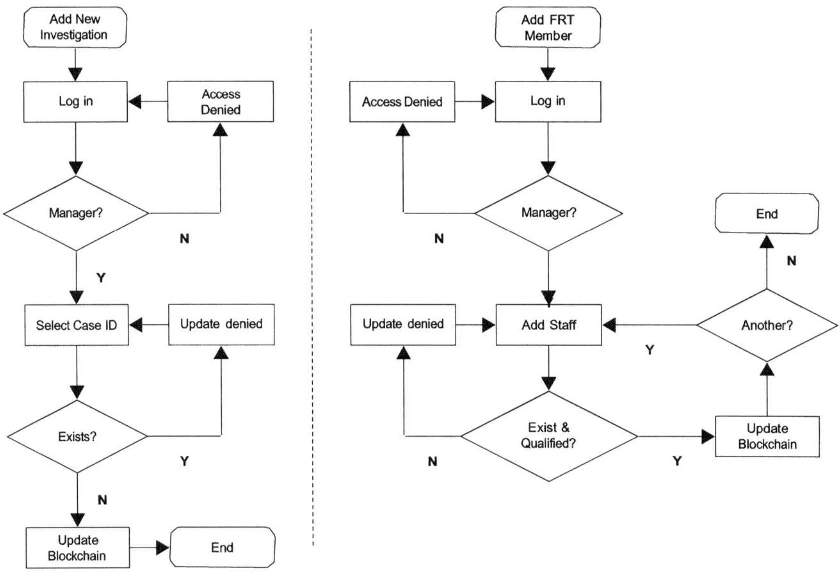

Fig. 10.4. Flowcharts for Adding a New Investigation (left) and Adding a Member of Staff to the FRT (right).

[1] Due to *case* being a reserved word, *investigation* is used instead

of the data is unusual since in most data modelling techniques it is accepted that such items would be validated by the system, e.g., referential integrity provided by RDBMS. Hyperledger does this, however, it is worthwhile to remember that the data on the blockchain is just that, and the processes, functions and methods controlling that data are driven by the business logic provided by the designer and stored elsewhere. So, the final test in the flowchart in Fig. 10.4 accesses all the investigations from the asset registries and searches to see if the ID provided is unique. For the implementation in Hyperledger, this is included in the system since each investigation asset is unambiguously and uniquely identified, and therefore duplicate investigations are prevented. However, it is included here to emphasise the point of the separation of data and methods and is not akin to the object-oriented or relational database methods the designers may be used to.

Adding a Member of Staff to the FRT: Again, only managers of the Investigation can add members of staff to the FRT. Here the access control is a little more dynamic, and the update can only be executed by the manager of the investigation to which staff are going to be added. This prevents managers from updating the FRT via proxy and links authority to responsibility. Remember, once updated on the blockchain, this information is immutable and therefore it is important to get this accurate. The procedure is for the manager to log in and add members of staff by providing the investigation ID and staff ID. Firstly, a check to see if the manager is the manager of the investigation ID is completed. Secondly, a check to see if the member of staff selected exists and is qualified is carried out. If the first and second checks are compliant, then the blockchain is updated. Finally, the second stage can be repeated many times to add further staff. The updates are not completed in batch mode; each individual added to the FRT is updated as an individual on the blockchain. The blockchain is updated at the first opportunity possible and not left to batch mode, i.e., information is not stored for a given length of time before all the updates are made at once. This procedure is illustrated in the flowchart in Fig. 10.4, which shows possible multiple updates to the blockchain before the procedure ends. Access here is dynamic and dependent on user type and membership.

As in the subsection on 'Adding a New Investigation', there is a check to see if the current user is the manager. The ID of the user is checked against the IDs on an access control list. Those classified as managers in the list are given update, read and write privileges with regard to the Investigation asset on the blockchain. There is no referential integrity and this needs encoding, so a further check is carried out to see if the ID of the person provided exists in the appropriate registry. An update to the Investigation asset and the blockchain is completed. This can then be repeated for further FRT members. Each blockchain has a unique transaction code. The ID of the manager submitting a timestamp and the unique transaction code are used to identify the transaction during later audits.

Seizure: Only members of the FRT can seize an artefact. The access control has to be dynamic. Potentially all users could seize an item, as long as they are a member of the FRT for the identified case. Figure 10.5 (left) illustrates the three stages of the seizure process. Each user would have their own device that would require some authentication

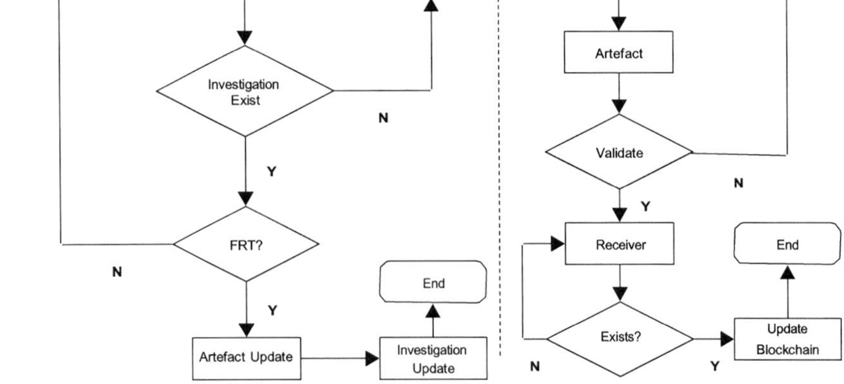

Fig. 10.5. Flowchart for Seizure (left) and Exchange (right).

and log in, e.g., a physical fingerprint and passphrase. Once logged in, the user can see the artefacts that they are the custodian of, other members of staff and the cases they have been assigned to. There is one additional piece of information that would show the users that they are a member of the FRT. When entering the case number there are two stages: i) due to human error if the wrong investigation ID is provided then access is denied and the user is required to enter the correct investigation ID; ii) if the user does not belong to the FRT of a particular case, then access to that case is denied and the user cannot seize any artefacts for that case. If the correct information is provided at stages i) and ii), the user can then update the artefact and the investigation and become the new custodian.

Exchange: Finally, we look at the exchange of an artefact between submitter and receiver. Figure 10.5 (right) illustrates the procedure the user has to go through to exchange an item. The submitter has to log in to their device and is only allowed to exchange items they are the custodian of. This is recorded as the user submitting to the blockchain, so there is no need to repeat this information in the transactional data. The submitter provides details of the Investigation and Artefact they are going to exchange. If these are validated as correct and belonging to the user, then further details of the receiver are provided and the update to the blockchain is completed. If the receiver does not exist then the submitter reenters the data. This update has additional information recorded by the system that includes: a timestamp (including the date), a unique identification (hash code) and the user who completed the transaction (in this case the submitter).

10.4.5. *Summary*

Data Modelling and Access Control lists are modelled above using a combination of class diagrams, use cases and flowcharts. The data modelling is abstract and the Blockchain application developed above does not enforce referential integrity, nor does it explicitly allow composite keys — not without some complications. This places some restrictions on the implementation of the blockchain.

It is also why class diagrams are better abstraction tools than ERDs, which are typically used to model many of the databases that blockchain aims to be integrated with or even to replace. If an implementation is of a simple register of a manager assigning staff to an FRT, then there are some simple rules that are taken for granted in databases but that need consideration in blockchain. The manager would have privileges to add and remove members of the FRT. Submission of evidence can only be done by these members of the FRT since no one else has authorisation. There would have to be a check of whether the staff member existed and then it would have to be possible to add them to the group via a simple update. Only existing group members can be removed from the group. All these rules sound obvious and simplistic but need consideration and coding. As a result, there is a danger of data duplication, something that databases strive to prevent. Such duplication not only results in an increase in the amount of effort required but also in inconsistencies in data if not approached properly.

The design of the operational logic for the transactions is modelled using flowcharts. Having a clear breakdown is not only important for designers and programmers, but also important for training purposes and ensuring that users follow the correct procedures for updating the blockchain. The procedures followed by programmers are the same as the procedures followed by users. This provides some consistency and gives the additional benefit of allowing users to concentrate on the investigation instead of having to bear a cognitive burden when completing the form.

10.5. Results

The implementation of BoC was completed using Hyperledger Composer-Playground and Hyperledger Fabric. The programming language for data modelling was completed in CTO, the access control was completed in Access Control Language and the operational logic was completed in Node.js. The operating system was Ubuntu 16.04 LTS (64-bit).

Two mock investigations were carried out. These were small digital investigations in which between 2 and 10 artefacts were

Table 10.1. Case C111 & C222. Information about the cases.

Key	Value	Key	Value
Date Time Location ID	28-AUG-2018 15:40hrs NW44BT C111	Date Time Location ID	04-SEP-2018 10:30hrs MK401DH C222

seized. The two mock incident scenes were conducted using BoC and the output is extracted from the blockchain and in JSON format. The details of the incident are included in Table 10.1.

From the results below the implementation of BoC was a success; however, problems were encountered. The first problem was using class diagrams to model the investigations, as typically the encapsulation of both data and methods is not possible with blockchain. The data, stored in registries, is on the blockchain, but methods such as transactions are not. This is why no data or methods are displayed in the class diagram in Fig. 10.3. However, other alternatives are also restrictive, e.g., ERDs are more restrictive with relationships. Class diagrams also allow the modelling to be more abstract from the physical representation.

A further problem that arose during the implementation was that a polymorphic method was required to capture the participant type at runtime. This would be required to access the correct and associated registries at runtime. In the design there is a separate registry for each specific role. This was necessary to implement restrictions on access, e.g., members of the legal profession can access the blockchain to inspect all transactions for the case, but are not allowed to exchange artefacts. Polymorphism is not possible, so an enumerator type was passed as a parameter in transaction-related methods in order to provide an indication of the registries required for inspection. This was considered a better solution than returning all the registries, which was the alternative but which had the issue of being inefficient.

As aforementioned, at least four transactions are required to make BoC possible. These are: the creation of a new Investigation; the addition of a new Member to the FRT; the seizure of an artefact; and the exchange of an artefact. These are discussed in the subsections below.

10.5.1. *Creating a new investigation*

Figure 10.6 shows the content of the blockchain after two investigations have been submitted. The transactions occur between lines 1-6 and 7-12 for investigation C111 and C222, respectively. These have been extracted from the blockchain and are in JSON format. The transactions on lines 3 and 9 show the unique ID for C111 and C222, respectively. The transaction ID generated by the system is on line 4 for C111 and the timestamp for C111 is on line 5. Likewise, the transaction ID and the timestamp for C222 are on lines 10 and 11, respectively. The two transactions are successes and can easily be retrieved from the blockchain. There is no record of who completed the transaction; this information was stored when the transaction was made and is also available from the investigation assets. From the transaction it can be seen that Information Managers 'P111116' and 'P100001' submitted Investigations 'C111' and 'C222', respectively. From the investigation assets the information for the Investigation ID, 'C222', and the Manager of Investigation (MoI), 'P100001', are shown on lines 2 and 3 respectively in Fig. 10.8 and are correct.

10.5.2. *Adding a new member to the First Response Team (FRT)*

Figure 10.7 shows the content of the blockchain after two transactions were made in order to add a new member to the FRT. The transactions for adding 'P111110' and 'P211112' to the FRT occur between lines 1-11 and 12-22, respectively. These have been extracted from the blockchain and it can be seen that both members have been added to the same investigation, 'C222'. Again, the transaction ID and timestamps for each of these transactions are shown on lines


```
1  {
2  "$class": "org.boc.net.addInvestigation",
3  "ID": "C111",
4  "transactionId": "ae86b543-54a4-444c-8aeb-28268cf02ff5",
5  "timestamp": "2018-08-28T15:57:21.212Z"
6  }
7  {
8  "$class": "org.boc.net.addInvestigation",
9  "ID": "C222",
10 "transactionId": "c8b05472-9299-4579-9c34-2788b4a731d7",
11 "timestamp": "2018-09-04T09:53:00.558Z"
12 }
```


Fig. 10.6. Blockchain record for the transaction of Creating an Investigation

```
1  {
2   "$class": "org.boc.net.newMemberFRT",
3   "currentInvestigation": "resource:org.boc.net.Investigation#C222",
4   "newMember": {
5    "$class": "org.boc.net.Person",
6    "PIN": "P111110"
7   },
8   "mtl": "Staff",
9   "transactionId": "6e621b4c-342f-4424-a7b7-1ed6aa8a9e0f",
10  "timestamp": "2018-09-04T09:53:46.149Z"
11 }
12 {
13  "$class": "org.boc.net.newMemberFRT",
14  "currentInvestigation": "resource:org.boc.net.Investigation#C222",
15  "newMember": {
16   "$class": "org.boc.net.Person",
17   "PIN": "P211112"
18  },
19  "mtl": "LEA",
20  "transactionId": "b4a0786f-b048-4a41-bb5b-38c477e7db5e",
21  "timestamp": "2018-09-04T09:57:12.531Z"
22 }
```

Fig. 10.7. Blockchain record for the transaction of Adding a Member of Staff to the First Response Team (FRT).

9-10 and 20-21, respectively. The two personnel added are from different roles and this is indicated by lines 8 and 19, which show that the first member belongs to the role, 'Staff', and the second member belongs to the role, 'LEA'. This is the aforementioned parameter to extract the relevant Participant Registry at runtime.

There is no record of who completed the transaction, for this information was stored when the transaction was made and is also available from the investigation assets. From the transaction information which Manager 'P100001' submitted and from the investigation assets, the FRT membership is shown between lines 5-17 in Fig. 10.8 and includes the personnel submitted in Fig. 10.7.

10.5.3. *Seizure*

Figure 10.8 shows the data stored in the asset registry on the blockchain for the investigation assets after the completion of the seizure of all the artefacts.

Figure 10.9 indicates an individual seizure transaction (lines 1-16) and the resulting entry in the artefact asset registry (lines 17-26). This may raise some concern amongst readers since there is no time or date in the investigation registry or the artefact. However, Fig. 10.9 does not show the full picture; the blockchain is updated with each individual seizure, and only the individual records and not

```
1  {"$class": "org.boc.net.Investigation",
2    "InvestigationID": "C222",
3    "MoI": "resource:org.boc.net.Manager#P100001",
4    "FRT": [
5      {"$class": "org.boc.net.Person",
6        "PIN": "P111110"
7          },
8          {"$class": "org.boc.net.Person",
9        "PIN": "P111113"
10         },
11         {"$class": "org.boc.net.Person",
12       "PIN": "P111112"
13     },
14     {"$class": "org.boc.net.Person",
15       "PIN": "P211112"
16     }
17   ],
18   "ArtefactList": [
19     { "$class": "org.boc.net.Artefact",
20       "ArtefactID": "4695",
21       "description": "",
22       "custodian": {
23         "$class": "org.boc.net.LEA",
24         "PIN": "P211112"
25     }},
26   { "$class": "org.boc.net.Artefact",
27       "ArtefactID": "1636",
28       "description": "",
29       "custodian": {
30         "$class": "org.boc.net.Specialist",
31         "PIN": "P111113"
32       }},
33         :
34         :
35         { "$class": "org.boc.net.Artefact",
36       "ArtefactID": "6856",
37       "description": "",
38       "custodian": {
39         "$class": "org.boc.net.Staff",
40         "PIN": "P111112"
41       }}
42   ]}
```

Fig. 10.8. The investigation asset registry for the item with Investigation ID 'C222'. Note that all custodians are members of the FRT. This changes when exchanges occur. Nevertheless, when a seizure transaction is made, only members of the appropriate FRT can be custodians of artefacts. Some artefacts have been removed to improve clarity.

the transactions are viewed in the Investigation and Artefact Registry. Further explanation is required.

In the seizure transaction in Fig. 10.9 (line 11) the custodian is identified with the PIN code '0950'. This does not match the committed code in the final output and furthermore the person identified by the code does not exist as a person in the system. This is not a mistake. The user is logged in via their business network card, which is issued by the system and uniquely identifies them. In this particular case the business network card is for 'S23', identified by 'P111113'. It is these values that are passed to the asset registries. If 'P111113' is a member of the FRT (clearly seen from Fig. 10.8, lines 8-9), then the update occurs to both registries. This explains

```
1   {========= SEIZURE TRANSACTION ==========}
2   {
3    "$class": "org.boc.net.seizure",
4    "currentInvestigation": "resource:org.boc.net.Investigation#C222",
5    "evidence": {
6     "$class": "org.boc.net.Artefact",
7     "ArtefactID": "1636",
8     "description": "",
9     "custodian": {
10     "$class": "org.boc.net.Person",
11     "PIN": "0950"
12    }
13   },
14   "transactionId": "dc94ace6-95af-4e78-8361-da67caf8eca3",
15   "timestamp": "2018-09-04T10:03:05.455Z"
16  }
17  {========= ARTEFACT ==========}
18  {
19    "$class": "org.boc.net.Artefact",
20    "ArtefactID": "1636",
21    "description": "",
22    "custodian": {
23     "$class": "org.boc.net.Person",
24     "PIN": "P111113"
25    }
26  }
```

Fig. 10.9. Individual seizure transaction and corresponding artefact.

the difference between the information in Figs. 10.8 and 10.9. Users cannot seize artefacts on behalf of other users.

Figure 10.9 does show when the transaction was committed to the blockchain. In the example, line 15 shows that the artefact '1636' was seized at '2018-09-04T10:03:05.455Z'. So, all the information about the seizure of this item can be retrieved for internal or external audits. Simple generic queries can be set up to recall and organise all artefacts seized for an investigation.

There is also the issue of integration of systems across LEAs. Figure 10.8 (lines 18-24) shows an example whereby an external person is included in the FRT and demonstrates that they are able to seize artefacts, as shown by person 'P211112' submitting artefact '4695'. The subject of the integration of systems is discussed in the final section but raised here to show a plausible solution.

10.5.4. *Exchange of artefact*

After the exchange, the investigation and artefact asset registry are updated. Figure 10.11 illustrates the data stored in the investigation asset registry for the investigation ID 'C222'. It is managed by 'P100001' (line 4), has four FRT members (lines 5-17) and has one artefact, '1636', with custodian 'P111115'.

```
1  {
2   "$class": "org.boc.net.exchange",
3   "receiver": {
4    "$class": "org.boc.net.Person",
5    "PIN": "P111115"
6   },
7   "mtl": "Custodian",
8   "evidence": "resource:org.boc.net.Artefact#1636",
9   "caseID": "C222",
10  "transactionId": "72b76ac8-e421-40b7-8258-767dc98fa56e",
11  "timestamp": "2018-09-04T11:30:03.572Z"
12 }
```

Fig. 10.10. Blockchain recovery. Inspection of the blockchain.

```
{
  "$class": "org.boc.net.Investigation",
  "InvestigationID": "C222",
  "MoI": "resource:org.boc.net.Manager#P100001",
  "FRT": [ {
      "$class": "org.boc.net.Person",
      "PIN": "P111110"
    },{
      "$class": "org.boc.net.Person",
      "PIN": "P111113"
    },{
      "$class": "org.boc.net.Person",
      "PIN": "P111112"
    },{
      "$class": "org.boc.net.Person",
      "PIN": "P211112"
    } ],
  "ArtefactList": [....
    {
      "$class": "org.boc.net.Artefact",
      "ArtefactID": "1636",
      "description": "",
      "custodian": {
        "$class": "org.boc.net.Person",
        "PIN": "P111115"
      }
    }.... ]
}
```

Fig. 10.11. Listing of Investigation Registry from the blockchain. Some artefacts have been removed to improve clarity.

Only FRT members are allowed to seize an artefact; however, a keen eye will note that the custodian for the artefact, '1636', is 'P111115' and is not a member of the FRT. Figure 10.10 shows who the *current* custodian is for each artefact, as does each artefact asset registry. Artefact '1636' has been exchanged and the seizure of the artefact is recorded by the seizure transaction explained in the previous subsection.

Figure 10.10 shows the exchange when the user, 'P111115' (line 5), received the artefact. In the exchange transaction only the receiver is recorded, since only the current custodian can exchange an artefact, an artefact cannot be exchanged on behalf of someone else. Figure 10.10 (line 11) shows that the artefact was exchanged at '2018-09-04T11:30:03.572Z' and includes the transaction ID.

Looking at the system, it can be seen that the transaction ID was completed by the user, 'P111113'. By combining all the transactions for this artefact, a chain of custody can be reconstructed, i.e., by combining transactions in Fig. 10.9 and Fig. 10.10. Of course, this can be completed using a query on the blockchain to retrieve all the seizures and transactions for the artefact '1636' belonging to the investigation 'C222' and displaying them in chronological order. Auditors can have read access to the blockchain and they can retrieve such queries.

10.6. Conclusions

The main contribution of this paper is twofold: i) blockchain engineering/modelling, and ii) prototype development of a decentralised application for evidence management. The two are entwined; however, it looks likely that the proliferation of decentralised applications is going to expand exponentially, and therefore methods are needed that can integrate and interact with all stakeholders.

Relying on UML-based design is problematic for decentralised applications, since whilst the implementation languages are object-based, the application is not. Our method has looked at use case diagrams and class diagrams to model the actors and data. The class diagrams are very abstract and do not include methods, but help identify attributes of the transactions, assets and participants. The transactions are then identified for the decentralised application and the sequence of events is modelled by flowcharts. Overall the design and implementation was a success. This has been proven by the completion of two investigations.

10.6.1. *Recommendations*

The gratuitous use of technology and the hyperbole surrounding BitCoin are not to be confused with blockchain development. However, blockchain has problems with disassociating itself from BitCoin. Excluding cost, new technologies should always bring improvements. BoC is an integrated system between all parties of an irreversible and immutable chain of custody for evidence management. In the process of designing and developing this blockchain application we have come up with several recommendations, which are as follows:

Permanent Data: ISO17025 (and GDPR to some extent) recommend that personal data be deleted. Of course, in legal cases, this is not permissible; however, once time spent has been completed, or acquittal been provided by courts or if information has simply not led to a court case, then there is the possibility of the disposal or return of evidence and the documentation related to it. Blockchain, by its very nature, does not allow the deletion of data — it is possible to delete data from the blockchain, however, there will be a record of this deletion and the previous blocks will contain secure, private and confidential data. It is the recommendation that personal data, e.g., the victim's identity, is not stored on the blockchain in case a request is made for it to be deleted.

Permissioned blockchain: The auditing of organisations is integral to good evidence management. As shown from the results, auditors can access and view cases and view the records regarding the transfer of artefacts and evidence management. This can all be completed with transparency and low latency. Whilst there is more to internal audits than evidence transfer, this does allow instant updates of an important role in evidence management.

Many LEA will have their own DB for recording evidence management. From personal discussions, these can be different within the Departments of LEA, e.g., digital forensics may use a different DB to Forensics. If personal discussions are not enough proof, look at the wide range of software available: EvidenceOnQ, EvidenceGuard (CaseGuard, 2018), Forman (Lowman, 2018), Evidence Traq, Oracle's Digital Evidence Management System (Oracle, 2017) and many more. BoC has an immutable and irreversible blockchain, and these are properties that databases do not have by default. That is the focus of the development of BoC. These databases are permissioned and require authentication and log in details. BoC is no different; it is permissioned, and under no circumstances should it be implemented as a permissionless blockchain application.

Modelling: Flowcharts display important interactions entered into by the users of the system. It is recommended that these be integrated into the training of individuals when implementing transactions.

Audits: BoC provides transparency, whereby an auditor can access all the transactions for a case without delay. It is recommended that auditors only have read access at all times.

Tokenisation: Not every blockchain application has to involve tokens or coins. The distribution, issuance and management of the tokens has to be considered. Finally, there is the value of the token. As discussed in Section 10.3.6, if the network operating costs outweigh the value generated by the blockchain then the cost of the network outweighs the benefit. The exception to this rule is when not-for-profit organisations are funding the blockchain; here, tokens become almost irrelevant as in the case of BoC.

NPE: Non-person entities have not been modelled; however, it is possible that NPEs could be necessary. NPEs are not associated with physical people, they are generated by the system, usually for administration purposes. In this case, there is a demand for NPEs, which could easily be added as another participant registry representing that role. Consider the issue of custody. Custodians are not always assigned 24/7 to artefacts; quite often artefacts are left in secure storage with no custodian. In such cases, there would be a problem with the current system. The principle of updating the blockchain every time an exchange is made may seem maddening. It may seem like quality overload is taking place without any value being delivered. This is not so. In evidence stores there are loopholes whereby persons who are not the custodian can exchange the artefact, leading to problems later on and thus devaluing the system. Here all artefacts have a unique custodian, and each time the Evidence Store Manager changes, so do the blockchain and the custodian for each item stored. This means only the custodian can exchange the artefact — it is a fundamental tenet of the system. So, going back to unmanned evidence stores, this would be where an NPE would be introduced. NPEs of evidence stores would not be allowed to update the blockchain except when an expected end-of-shift occurs. At this point, the NPE will be allowed to complete a special transaction that would allow all the items in the evidence store to change custody from the designated NPE to the designated Evidence Store Manager (now the custodian). This adds a further level of logical security. Whilst it cannot stop a physical breach, the blockchain will make it logically infeasible to exchange artefacts whilst the NPE is the custodian.

Rescinding: People make mistakes. If the seizure of an artefact goes wrong, can it be altered? Yes, it can be altered by giving the manager of the investigation delete privileges. An immediate request can be made, the manager can delete the request and all can get back to work. These errors are still recorded on the blockchain as transactions. The key here is transparency. BoC is about maintaining the auditability of actions, thus ensuring best practice. Therefore, the deletion of data records is not of concern, but when the deletion occurred or by whom the data records were deleted may be.

10.6.2. *Future work*

This paper covers the development of a prototype blockchain application using Hyperledger for a case study on evidence management. It is a beginning and, upon reflection, there are many improvements that can be made.

Firstly, the disintermediatory nature of blockchain allows multiple enterprise integration, or *interprise*. This has not been approached by this project, however, it is conceivable that international agencies could record transactions using multiple blockchains.

Secondly, combined with IoT and RFIDs, the tracking of evidence could become automated. This would require using different access control models, e.g., Xu *et al.* (2018), and could improve the automated control of events.

Thirdly, there is also a wider application of BoC to society in general. Where there are important transfers of artefacts between parties, and where no transfer of monetary value takes place, this model could be used. For example, BoC could be applied to conveyancy law, felony records, inmate records, or any other situation whereby documents are exchanged and a record of the change that has been updated by authorized personnel is required.

10.6.3. *Summary*

At the beginning of this chapter, it was judged that change was pushing technology, or that the tail was wagging the dog. In the past, the gratuitous use of technology to solve problems often proved to add little or no value, for example, online emergency services were used when a phone call was effective enough. Blockchain still has a long way to go to prove itself, however, in scenarios where there is a need to provide strict controls over the access to data, to provide a transparent and effective audit trail and to be secure, blockchain is a technology that should be considered.

References

1. Antonopoulos, A. M. (2017).*Mastering Bitcoin* (2nd ed.). Springfield, MO, USA:O'Reilly
2. Brewer, E. (2017). *Spanner, Truetime and the Cap Theorem* [Online]. Available at: https://research.google. com/pubs/pub45855.html . (Accessed: July 2018).
3. Brewer, E. A. (2000). Towards Robust Distributed Systems. In *Proceedings of the 19th Annual ACM Symposium on Principles on Distributed Computing (PODC), Portland, OR, USA, July 16–19, p. 7.*
4. CaseGuard. (2018). *EvidenceGuard* [Online]. Available at: https://caseguard.com/evidenceguard . (Accessed: July 2018).
5. Ferraiolo, D. F., Sandhu, R., Gavrila, S., Kuhn, D. R. and Chandramouli, R. (2001).Proposed NIST Standard for Role-Based Access Control. *ACM Transactions on Information and System Security (TISSEC)*, **4**(3), pp. 224–274.
6. Forensic Science Regulator (FSR). (2017). *Codes of Practice and Conduct for Forensic Science Providers and Practitioners in the Criminal Justice System.* Birmingham, UK: UK Government.
7. Gaur, N., Desrosiers, L., Novotny, P., Ramakrishna, V., O'Dowd, A. and Baset, S. A. (2018). *Hands-on Blockchain with Hyperledger: Building Decentralised Applications with Hyperledger Fabric and Composer.* Birmingham, UK:Packt.

8. Greenspan, G. (2015). *MultiChain Private Blockchain — White Paper* [Online]. Available at: https://www.multichain.com/download/MultiChain-White-Paper.pdf, 2015 (Accessed: Feb 2018).
9. Haerder, T. and Reuter, A. (1983). Principles of Transaction-Oriented Database Recovery. *ACM Computing Surveys (CSUR)*, **15**(4), pp. 287–317.
10. Hu, V. C., Ferraiolo, D., Kuhn, R. Schnitzer, A., Sandlin, K., Miller, R. and Scarfone, K. (2014).*Guide to Attribute-Based Access Control (ABAC) Definition and considerations* [Online]. Available at: https://nvlpubs.nist.gov/nistpubs/specialpublications/NIST.sp.800-162.pdf. (Accessed: July 2018).
11. Hyperledger Architecture Working Group. (2017). *Hyperledger Architecture, Volume 1* [Online]. Available at: https://www.hyperledger.org/wp-content/uploads/2017/08/HyperLedgerArchWGPaper1 Consensus.pdf (Accessed: July 2018).
12. ISO. (2017). *ISO17025:2017: General Requirements for the Competence of Testing and Calibrating Laboratories.* Geneva, Switzerland: International Organisation for Standardization.
13. ISO. (2013). *ISO27001:2013: Information Technology — Security Techniques — Information Security Management Systems — Requirements.* Geneva, Switzerland: International Organisation for Standardization.
14. Karp, A. H., Haury, H. and Davis, M. H. (2009). *From ABAC to ZBAC: The Evolution of Access Control Models.* Palo Alto, CA, USA: Hewlett-Packard Development Company.
15. Kuhn, D. R., Coyne, E. J. and Weil, T. R. (2010). Adding Attributes to Role-Based Access Control. *Computer*, **43**(6), pp. 79–81.
16. Lowman, S. (2018). *Foreman: Forensic Case Management Framework.* [Online]. Available at https://foremanforensics.wordpress.com. (Accessed: September 2019).
17. Mitchell, I., Ferriera, J., Anandaraja, T. and Hara, S. (2018). DaP∀: Deconstruct and Preserve for All: A Procedure for the Preservation of Digital Evidence on Solid State Drives and Traditional Storage Media. In Jahankhani, H. (ed.), *Cyber Criminology.* Basel, Switzerland: Springer Nature Switzerland AG.
18. Nakamoto, S. (2008). *Bitcoin: A Peer-to-Peer Electronic Cash System* [Online]. Available at: https://bitcoin.org/bitcoin.pdf. (Accessed: September 2019).
19. Oracle. (2017). *Digital Evidence Management for Police* [Online]. Available at: http://www.oracle.com/us/products/applications/ds-digital-evidence-management-3864416.pdf (Accessed: June 2018).

20. Sompolinsky, Y. and Zohar, A. (2018). Bitcoin's Underlying Incentives. *Communications of the ACM (CACM)*, **61**(3), pp. 46–53.
21. Verdian, G., Tasca, P., Paterson, C. and Mondelli, G. (2018). *Quant Overledger* [Online]. Available at: https://www.quant.network (Accessed: March 2018).
22. Xu, R., Chen, Y., Blasch, E. and Chen, G. (2018). *BlendCAC: A Blockchain-Enabled Decentralized Capability-Based Access Control for Iots* [Online]. Available at: *arXiv:1804.09267.* (Accessed: September 2019).

Chapter 11

New Issues in Cyber Security Forensics

Firas Hazzaa* and Sufian Yousef†

Anglia Ruskin University, UK
**firas.hazzaa@pgr.anglia.ac.uk,*
†Sufian.Yousef@anglia.ac.uk

ABSTRACT

Cyber security is the term used to describe the processes and technologies designed to protect computers, networks, data and programs from unauthorized access, damage or attack. Many businesses pay lots of attention to security concerns. For these reasons this research has been undertaken. Ad-hoc networks are crucial enablers of next-generation communications. Such networks can be formed and reconfigured dynamically and they can be mobile, standalone or internetworked with other networks. Mobile Ad-hoc Networks (MANETs) are established by a group of autonomous nodes that communicate with each other by establishing a multi-hop radio network and maintaining connectivity in an infrastructure-less manner. The security of the connections between devices and networks is crucial. The important challenges of supporting multimedia applications in an ad-hoc network are the security issues. In this chapter, a new and efficient media-aware security framework will be designed for facilitating various multimedia applications in ad-hoc networks over the Internet.

Keywords: cyber security, cyber crime, mobile devices, MANET, wireless network, DoS attack, forensics

11.1. Introduction

11.1.1. *Computer networks*

A **computer network** is a set of **computers** connected together for the purpose of sharing resources. In computer networks, computing devices exchange data with each other using connections between nodes. One example of a computer network is the internet, which has been developed over the last 45 years (Thomas and Robertazzi, 2017).

11.1.1.1. *Networks types and topology*

There are two types of network:

- **Wired Network**: A wired network is a set of PCs connected through wired links. Most of the wired networks use Ethernet cables to transfer data between connected PCs. One can use either routers or switches to organize the network, depending on its size (Cisco, 2016).
- **Wireless Network**: A wireless network is a set of connected devices that are not connected by cables of any kind. These networks use access points to get access to the network or use some wireless techniques such as ad-hoc and Bluetooth (Zheng *et al.*, 2013). These networks usually are cost effective and easily deployed.

  Also, there are two kinds of topology which can connect the networks. The two kinds of networks are infrastructure and infrastructure-less networks.
  - **Ad-hoc Network**: An ad-hoc network is an infrastructure-less network. It is a crucial enabler of next-generation communications. Such networks can be formed and reconfigured dynamically and they can be mobile, standalone or internetworked with other networks (Panaousis, 2012). For instance,

the Mobile Ad-hoc Network (MANET) is the most important one of these networks.

- **Mobile Ad-Hoc network (MANET)**: A mobile ad-hoc network is a set of mobile nodes that communicate with radio links. MANET network infrastructure is not defined and there is no centralized administration that controls the other activities (Aarti and Tyagi, 2013). MANETs are established by a group of autonomous nodes that communicate with each other by establishing a multi-hop radio network and maintaining connectivity in an infrastructure-less manner. They allow data, voice and video communications over a wireless channel (Thomas *et al.*, 2010). The main role of MANETs is to enable wireless and mobile communication services without using the expensive service-provider network and without having a previously set-up infrastructure.

There are several uses of these networks in real life; for example, they are used in disaster and emergency operations.

The security requirements of wireless ad-hoc networks are very important. One of MANET's big issues is that it is not a centrally-controlled network. Many applications on a network such as MANET need to be built with more care because the attacks on them may be internal or external. For example, connected vehicles currently connect to each other wirelessly with the Vehicular Ad-hoc Network (VANET). VANET is a wireless communication system that uses mobile cars as communication nodes to determine positioning and movement for the connected vehicles. Wireless networks like VANET validate every message circulating in their network without assessing the source's quality or the content's accuracy. As a result, VANET is inherently vulnerable to false messages being spread in the network by message-spoofing and denial-of-service (DoS) attacks (Sharma *et al.*, 2017). So security concerns should be given further attention.

11.2. Cyber Security on Mobile Devices

It is expected that, in 2020, more than 50 billion devices will connect to the Internet (Hammi *et al.*, 2017). Most of these devices should be wireless. 5G networks will make global life incredible, because they will enable the ICT to be faster, more reliable and more easily deployed. 5G networks consist of many types of networks. The significant parts of 5G networks are the wireless networks, such as mobile ad-hoc networks and wireless sensor networks. Houses, doors and windows are connected to the network; fridges, light systems and even personal coats are wirelessly connected to the network as well. For example, the sensor chip fixed inside a coat can automatically send the health information of a patient to the hospital if his situation is critical. Also, CCTV cameras and self-driving cars use wireless technology to connect with the network.

All of the above technologies will not be useful without security. Sometimes the absence of security may be a life or death matter. For instance, self-driving cars should be strongly protected against hackers, because any malicious breach would cause a disaster. According to Morgan (2017), the cost of cyber security reached $84 billion in 2015, and it is expected to reach $170 billion in 2020. So most businesses are paying lots of attention to security concerns. For these reasons we are undertaking this research.

Cyber security is the term used to describe the processes and technologies designed to protect computers, networks, data and programs from unauthorized access, damage or attack. According to the Telegraph, the cost of cyber attacks to UK businesses in 2017 reached $34 billion. To ensure cyber security, the corresponding efforts need to be made throughout an information system. The main elements of cyber security include applications security, information security, network security, disaster recovery and end-user education.

Unfortunately, conventional multimedia traffic management algorithms are developed mainly to guarantee delay while usually neglecting security requirements. A security-critical VoIP and multimedia service architecture is proposed, which jointly considers traffic analysis, security requirements, and traffic scheduling for multimedia applications. Many previous researchers (Nagendra and Sekhar, 2014; Ali *et al.*, 2014; Binod and Hyuk, 2010) adopted security algorithms that were weak enough to deal with the constraints of the quality of service (QoS) in such a way as to make the delay within limits. Also, using multiple keys for encryption and decryption will make the probability of the encrypted data being decrypted by a hacker very low, because even if the hacker knows what the first key is, it is not likely that he also knows what the other keys are.

Matesanz *et al.* (2012) shows the most common threats to ad-hoc networks and reviews several proposals that attempt to minimize some of these threats, showing their ability to protect these networks in light of their vulnerabilities and the threats that might arise. Some of these threats are described below.

Address Spoofing: This attack occurs when the malicious node intentionally selects an allocated or a free IP address. In the first case, the node takes an IP address which has been allocated to the victim, and once it has done so, hijacks the victim's traffic. In the other case, the node allocates the free IP address to itself so that it can join the network. Once in the network, the node collects important information which can be used to execute some attacks, like denial of service attacks.

Address Space Consumption: This attack occurs when the attacker consumes the address space by demanding a huge number of IP addresses. The attacker could request the assignment of IP addresses to fake nodes so as to prevent other nodes from being configured and connecting to the mobile ad-hoc networks.

Address Conflict Threat: This attack occurs when the malicious node assigns an additional address to a client which is already in use. This would produce many problems in the mobile ad-hoc networks and lead to an address conflict (Sandoval and García, 2012).

Denial of Service Threat: This threat occurs when, in an auto-configuration process, the attacker acts as a requester and sends AREQ messages to several nodes simultaneously, causing an overload of traffic.

Multiple Identities (Sybil): This kind of attack is possible when a repudiation system exists to state the legality of nodes in the network. The attacker could cause the isolation of valid nodes by creating messages to blacklist those nodes. Blackmail is a type of Sybil attack.

Layer	**Attacks**
Application Layer	data corruption, viruses and worms
Transport Layer	TCP/UDP SYN flood
Network Layer	hello flood, black-hole
Data Link Layer	monitoring, traffic analysis
Physical Layer	eavesdropping, active interference

Pietro *et al.* (2014) have surveyed emerging and established wireless ad-hoc technologies and highlighted their security/privacy features and deficiencies. They also identified open research issues and technology challenges for each surveyed technology.

Binod and Hyuk (2010) took the advantages of multipath routing which are useful for reliable MANET, and they proposed a basis for sending secure real-time streaming data over a multipath mobile ad-hoc network. Multipath routing can offers security for wireless ad-hoc routing and multimedia transfer. They considered digital signatures and encryption techniques. Their results show the good performance of the multipath mobile ad-hoc network. They also suggest the using of multicast, which is important in many video applications, in the future.

Emmanouis and Christos (2012) suggested a secure model for autonomous networks like mobile ad-hoc networks to create real-time communication in disaster rescue operations. Secure P2PSIP, intrusion detection and secure routing methods are vital parts of any secure model. The aforementioned concerns in the realm of emergency ad-hoc networks have been discussed. Emmanouis and Christos (2012) presented two additions to the IETF drafts and analysed them in relation to security power and scalability. The design of these extensions helps to meet the requirements of a mission-critical MANET within which rescuers can create links to communicate with each other by using lightweight devices such as PDAs. The situation concerning adaptive routing protocols and the use of IPsec to make them more secure has also been discussed.

These research studies have addressed some security issues for real-time traffic in MANET. However, they have not addressed the cryptographic issues in this network.

Sehgal *et al.* (2011) proposed an architecture in their research paper which states that self-organized distributed security could be provided by a five-layer security model, as well as authenticated and security-aware routing. After they carried out the simulation, they found that it provided security with negligible overhead.

A layered architecture can provide such advantages as modularity, simplicity, flexibility, and the standardization of protocols. The five-layer security architecture for MANETs incorporates the following layers: the Trust Relationship Security Layer, the Node-To-Node Security Layer, the Routing Level Security Layer, the Network Level Security Layer and the Application Level Layer. They expect this security architecture can be used as a framework when designing system security for ad-hoc networks.

Many previous research studies have also been conducted to address cryptographic issues related to real-time traffic. They could develop some algorithms to deal with real-time limitation issues, like delays.

Hu *et al.* (2009) propose a relay encryption scheme based on the threshold secret-sharing algorithm to enhance the data confidentiality, reliability and integrity in MANET. The basic idea is to distribute the whole encryption task to all the nodes along the route. Every node completes part of the encryption task instead of the single source node encrypting all of the data. They found that the encryption scheme can effectively alleviate the burden of the source node and reduce the transmission delay, besides, it improves the reliability of MANET.

Mohammed and Rohiem (2009) have introduced a Variable Mapping S-box technique with AES (VMS-AES) for the Voice over Internet Protocol (VoIP). A key is used to generate a parameter that is used to shift (remap) the substitution of the S-box randomly to another location depending on the initial key and the derived subkeys data. The results of this work could maximize nonlinearity so as to provide more resistance against linear attacks and to solve the fixed structure of the substitution function. They could also increase the overall security. Mohammed and Rohiem (2009) have also shown that seven rounds of encryption consume less power and execution time without affecting the security level. However, their findings have been criticised a long time ago, by Ferguson *et al.* (2001) and Daernen and Rijrnen (2002) who explained the possibility of saturation attacks on six and seven rounds of AES. They state that a seven-round attack can be mounted by adding one round before the distinguisher and two rounds after it. For these reasons their work is still unsuitable for the security requirements of wireless networks.

Another study on the topic has been published by Rahma and Yaco (2012). They proposed a symmetric dual key dynamic block algorithm (SDD) for digital video, which is a type of partial encryption technology. This algorithm meets the requirements of real time by combining a high level of complexity and a considerable speed. The proposed encryption algorithm SDD achieves better results than AES. It is faster by a factor of 13 times for encryption and faster by a factor of 9 times for decryption. It also has a high resistance to brute-force attack because two keys were used in the encryption process; however, it encrypts only selected parts of the data, which is considered a risk factor for a security breach. Also, in spite of the new features which have been achieved in their paper, there is still a lack of security analysis, which could have helped to prove its strength.

11.2.1. *Security and information protection*

1. Every wireless LAN implementation within UCSF must be done in accordance with a security plan. This plan must address the following issues at least:
    1. Make sure that only authorized people can use it.
    2. Prevent unauthorized users from being able to see confidential data appearing on the network, particularly UCSF passwords (Silver, 2017).
2. The Security Incident Response should include a wireless security response procedure.
3. Vendor default settings such as encryption keys and SNMP passwords must be changed regularly.
4. Wireless access point owners and managers are responsible for updating software.
5. Wireless networks which provide access to the UCSF campus network must limit usage to authorized users (Silver, 2017).
    1. As of July 1st 2010 this option is mandatory for wireless networks comprised of three (3) or more access points.

   2. As of July 1st 2010 this option is restricted to wireless networks comprised of two (2) or fewer access points.
   3. Legacy host-based authorization systems utilizing the machine address code (MAC) may continue to be used until June 30th 2010. In the interim it is strongly recommended that the vpn@UCSF system be used to protect the communications of the wireless network user.

6. Encryption and Data Protection:

   1. WPA2/AES-CCMP as defined by 802.11i is strongly recommended for departments that deal with highly sensitive information such as patient and HR/staff information. WPA2/AES-CCMP provides a higher degree of encryption protection for sensitive data being transmitted wirelessly.
   2. WPA and WPA2 (RSN) as defined by 802.11i are the standard protocols for UCSF wireless security.
   3. WEP on existing wireless access points must be updated to WPA or phased out by June 1, 2010. In the interim it is strongly recommended that the vpn@UCSF system be used to protect the communications of the access point users.

7. Wireless networks which do not support encryption and authentication:

   1. Until June 30th 2010 it is strongly recommended that the vpn@UCSF system be utilized to protect communications to provide user authentication as well as data protection.
   2. Starting July 1st, 2010 unencrypted wireless networks must restrict user access to the following:

      1. Informational pages regarding network access, local service or customer support and helpdesk.
      2. Access to vpn@UCSF or an ITS-approved authentication portal.
      3. Access to a specific system or service for which the wireless network has been created so long as that system or service contains no restricted or private data.

11.2.2. *Voice over wireless networks*

The voice requirements in wireless networks are different from those in wired networks. In the wireless networks we must carefully investigate and analyse the problems associated with this integration. The transmission of a voice is a real-time application that is sensitive to requirements in term of delay. For example, in phone call conversations, the voice should reach the destination quickly and efficiently. If the voice is delayed, the quality of the call will be affected. This quality of the call will also be affected if security rules are applied. Furthermore, this problem will become worse in wireless networks because of the nature of wireless networks. Many researchers have paid close attention to real-time application in wireless networks. They have tried to address some of the issues concerning security and delay. For instance, Binod and Hyuk (2010) and Emmanouis and Christos (2012) suggested a secure model for autonomous networks like mobile ad-hoc networks to create real-time communication during disaster rescue operations. Secure P2PSIP, intrusion detection and secure routing methods are a vital part of any secure model. The design of these extensions helps to meet the requirements of a mission-critical MANET where rescuers can create links to communicate with each other by using lightweight devices such as PDAs. Liang and Han (2011) designed a new security framework to enable different multimedia services in an IoT environment. Also, they presented a novel media-aware traffic security style based on the proposed traffic classification to enable the supply of various multimedia services to customers anywhere at any time. Furthermore, they proposed the scheme's basis and approach, that is, to perform a good trade-off between system flexibility and efficiency.

However, there are still some flaws in the real-time application of security and cryptography schemes. So, the question is: how does one transmit a voice securely over a wireless network without affecting its quality? As previously mentioned, the voice needs to be transmitted with speed and security at the same time, and this should be addressed in this research.

11.3. Wi-Fi Vulnerabilities

Wireless Fidelity (Wi-Fi) is the most widely-used network in the information technology field. It can be used indoors and outdoors, and it follows the IEEE 802.11 standard. There are two possible topologies that could form this network. The two resulting types of network are the ad-hoc network and the infrastructure network.

"**Vulnerability** is a cyber security term that refers to a flaw in a system that can leave it open to attack. A vulnerability may also refer to any type of weakness in a computer system itself, in a set of procedures, or in anything that leaves information security exposed to a threat." (Wolfram, 2018)

"Security researchers[1] have discovered a major vulnerability in Wi-Fi Protected Access 2 (WPA2). WPA2 is a type of encryption used to secure the vast majority of Wi-Fi networks. A WPA2 network provides unique encryption keys for each wireless client that connects to it.

Think of encryption as a secret code that can only be deciphered if you have the "key," and a vital technology that helps keep digital data away from intruders and identity thieves.

The vulnerability, dubbed 'KRACKs' (Key Reinstallation Attacks), is actually a group of multiple vulnerabilities that when successfully exploited, could allow attackers to intercept and steal data transmitted across a Wi-Fi network. Digital personal information that is transmitted over the Internet or stored on your connected devices — such as your driver's license number, Social Security number, credit card numbers, and more — could be vulnerable." (Norton, 2017)

11.3.1. *Threats and attacks*

- **Routing Attacks**: The routing signal is modified by unauthorized nodes and rerouted through an incorrect route in order to provide unauthorized data access to the attacker. Such attacks include breaking the neighbour, black hole, routing table poisoning, worm hole, and replay attacks.
- **Eavesdropping**: This is an unidentifiable, passive attack with no impact on normal system processing. The attacker aims to passively

intercept data by breaking encryption, without altering the normal routing protocol (Goodrich and Tamassia, 2011).

- **Denial of Service (DoS)**: This attack aims to disrupt routing in order to prevent the network from functioning and providing normal service. The attacker sends a massive volume of simultaneous requests to overwhelm the server and hamper its response time by jamming its mechanisms, ideally halting the complete system.
- **Sybil Attack**: Fake identities are deployed (i.e. in nodes) to gain access to wireless sensor networks in these attacks (Suriya and Rajamani, 2015).
- **Masquerading**: Similar to a Sybil attack, masquerading nodes (presenting themselves as legitimate nodes) intercept data during the neighbour acquisition process, and they either modify or replay these messages.
- **Alteration**: These attacks involve unauthorized alterations to data and codes, falsifying the system integrity.

11.3.2. *Wireless sensor networks*

Nowadays, the world is rapidly moving toward becoming a wireless environment. In 2020 most devices will connect wirelessly. The most significant part of this technology is wireless sensor networks (WSNs). According to Matin and Islam (2012), a WSN can be defined as "a self-configured and infrastructure-less wireless network to monitor physical or environmental conditions, such as temperature, sound, vibration, pressure, motion or pollutants and to cooperatively pass their data through the network to a main location or sink where the data can be observed and analysed".

Currently, many researchers are focusing on real-time Wireless Multimedia Sensor Networks (WMSNs), because they support many application layer services in order to solve real life concerns, such as health monitoring, transport management, weather forecasting and safety and security investigation (Elhoseny and Hassanien, 2018; Ehsan and Hamdaoui, 2012). A traditional WMSN consists of a variety of sensor nodes, including both simple and multimedia sensor nodes, and a Base Station (BS), as shown in Fig. 11.1.

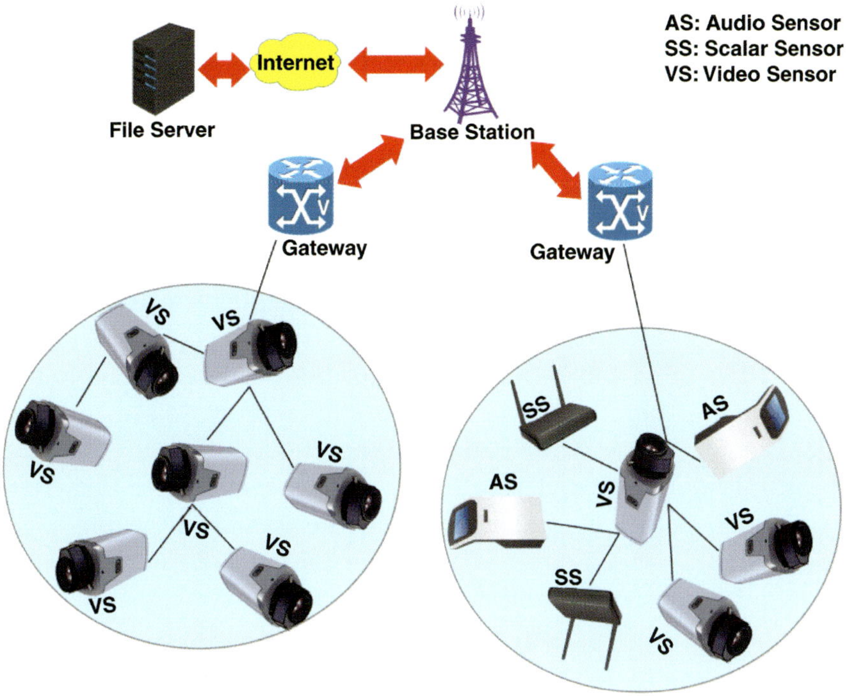

Fig. 11.1. Traditional wireless multimedia sensor network (Usman *et al.*, 2018).

WMSNs support the practical applications of advanced technologies for remote control, including IPv6 over Low power Wireless Personal Area Networks (6LowPAN), and for surveillance, within the Internet of Things (IoT) (Usman *et al.*, 2018). WSNs, like MANETs, have major security issues. The fundamental problem is that there is a trade-off between security and performance. WSNs face the issue of node sizes undermining network functional effectiveness, particularly with complex data such as voice messages used in communication, as discussed in detail below. Extensive research is required to improve technology in this area, particularly given the importance of the applications of WSNs. The applications of WSNs include, but are not limited to, environmental monitoring, industrial machine monitoring, surveillance systems, and military target tracking (Yick *et al.*, 2008). Each application differs in its features and requirements. To support this diversity of applications, the development of new communication protocols, algorithms, designs, and services are needed.

11.4. Security and Privacy Adaptation

11.4.1. *Network security challenges*

The recent increase in wireless portable users and data usage has placed a greater load on networks. Real-time applications over wireless networks often suffer from jitter, delay and packet loss. In future smart cities there will be a dense deployment of WSN with applications ranging from reserving water to public safety. As Hu and Cao (2017) said, "These WSNs and the Internet of Things (IoT) should be seamlessly integrated with future 5G networks. In cellular networks such as 3G, 4G and LTE, mobile devices are served by Base Stations (BSs) which cover a large area (about 1–2 miles). Due to many practical deployment issues, some areas have good coverage while other areas may not. As a result, the wireless signal strength of a mobile device varies based on its location". IoT devices are an attractive attack target for cyber criminals: they often employ weak security measures, and their compromise can lead to privacy breaches and safety threats in the real world. Recently, several malware families were found to target vulnerable IoT devices (e.g., routers, IP cameras, and CCTVs) and to use them to form botnets for DDoS. It is estimated that some IoT botnets comprise more than one million infected devices. In October 2016, a botnet attacked the DynDNS service provider, taking down a large portion of websites in North America, including GitHub, Twitter, Netflix, and so on (Cheng *et al.*, 2017). Also, the privacy of information that has been transferred into the network is repeatedly threatened by hackers. For example, man-in-the-middle attacks can reveal secure information by deceiving the users of the network.

Unfortunately, conventional multimedia traffic management algorithms have been developed mainly to guarantee delay while usually neglecting security requirements. According to Zhou (2010) and Zhao *et al.* (2009) applications and users can be sources of security threats.

Liang and Chao (2011) claim that it is very important to adopt a security strategy to protect critical voice and multimedia applications.

AES (Advanced Encryption Standard) is the best cryptography algorithm used in computing to protect the confidentiality of data. There have been no successful attacks against AES since 2004. The United States Government announced in June 2003 that the block cipher AES (Advanced Encryption Standard) algorithm for a key with a length of 128 bits can be used to protect SECRET information, while TOP SECRET information could be protected with the same algorithm for keys with lengths of 192 and 256 bits. Many previous researchers (Nagendra and Sekhar, 2014; Nada, 2014; Binod and Hyuk, 2010) adopted security algorithms that were weak enough to deal with the constraints of the quality of service (QoS) in a way that keeps the delay within limits. Also, using multiple keys for encryption and decryption will make the probability of breaking the encryption on the data very low, because even if the hacker knows what the first key is, it is improbable that they will also know what the other keys are.

11.5. Security in Mobile Operating Environments

The **operating environment** consists of a user interface provided by an applications manager and usually an application programming interface (API) for the applications manager.

A recent study by Forrester (2011) predicted that by 2015, mobile banking will reach one in five adults in the United States, and for many customers, mobile banking will become the preferred channel for basic banking transactions. In Europe, mobile banking trends are similar to those in the United States — as many as 12% of European Net users do some mobile banking.

"But the growth in mobile devices has also driven the incidence of fraud targeting these devices. Whether simple rogue text messages, fictitious billing scams, or more malicious attacks using malware installed on the device, the number of attacks are now increasing alarmingly — by one account mobile malware increased by more than 45% in 2010. And with less education about mobile threats, users seem more inclined to fall victim to them." (Byrnes, 2017)

11.5.1. *Mobile security vulnerabilities*

Mobile security involves several layers:

- Device operating system
- Browser
- Cloud
- Extended cyber enterprise (secure access to third-party apps such as Salesforce.com)
- App store

When we conducted the survey and in-depth telephone interviews late in 2011 for our "Leaders in Mobility Strategies" report, we found that 49 percent of the respondents had not yet developed a formal security policy on mobile devices and technologies — even though most of them were already on the mobility path and had adopted a bring-your-own-device (BYOD) model.

As illustrated in Fig. 11.2, mobile devices have unique security vulnerabilities that do not exist in other enterprise communication end points such as desktops or laptops (Rangaswami, 2012).

11.5.2. *Power in wireless devices*

Wireless networks have been a hot topic for many years. Their potential was first realized with the deployment of cellular networks for use with mobile telephones in the late 1970s. Since this time, many other wireless wide area networks (WWANs) have begun to emerge, along with the introduction of Wireless Metropolitan Area Networks (WMANs), Wireless Local Area Networks (WLANs), and Wireless Personal Area Networks (WPANs). The power consumed by individual nodes in each of these networks needs to be managed efficiently. Researchers have given significant consideration to energy-efficient schemes. These energy-efficient schemes, which are also referred to as "Green Computing", are the products of one of the most essential areas of research these days.

However, there are still some flaws in energy consumption when it is applied to security and cryptography schemes. According

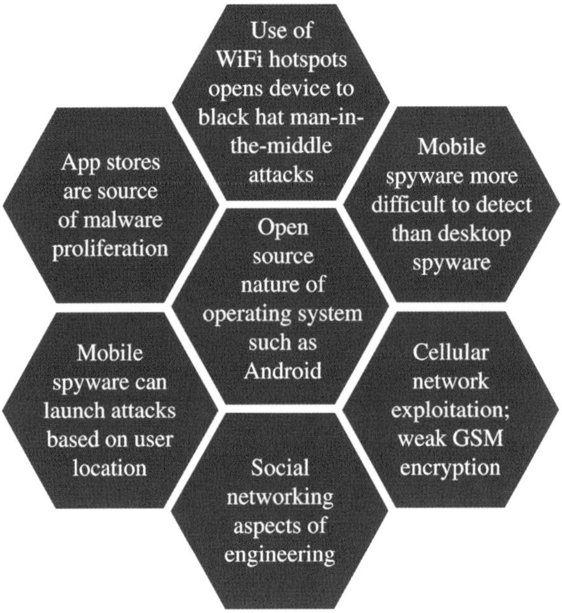

Fig. 11.2. Security risks and threats unique to mobile devices.

Note: The open source nature of mobile device operating systems is not necessarily a security threat. For example, Linux systems (which are open source) have proved to be pretty secure. However, device manufacturers could make insecure extensions to an operating system, which can open up new security vulnerabilities.

to Masoud *et al.* (2015), the performance evaluation of a symmetric encryption algorithm like DES, Bluefish, RC6 or AES showed that the cost of implementing these encryption algorithms in smartphones is high. They state that high power consumption may prevent developers from employing cryptographic algorithms in the communication applications they have developed for smartphones. Also, they reveal the requirements of new power-saving 'Green' encryption algorithms. For these reasons, encryption algorithms are not only about security; power consumption should be taken into account when designing these algorithms for smartphones.

So, the question is, how does one secure the data in wireless networks without affecting the power of the nodes? As mentioned, the wireless nodes need to keep their power for as long as possible when implementing security enforcement. This issue should be addressed in this chapter.

11.5.3. *Limitations caused by energy consumption in encryption*

A data encryption algorithm would not be of much use if it is secure but slow in performance, especially because it is a common practice to embed encryption algorithms in other applications such as e-commerce, banking, and online transaction processing applications (Nadeem and Javed, 2005). The wireless device is limited in resources such as processing power, memory and power supply (from a battery). Battery technology is improving at a slower rate than other technologies. This causes a "battery gap". This indicates that mobile devices normally operate on an economical power budget, and therefore, computationally intensive encryption/decryption algorithms and their related security parameters may not be supported. The key issue is that the processing in encryption algorithms consumes remarkable amounts of computing resources. This leads to battery power draining fast. That is the problem for mobile devices (Jiehong and Detchenkov, 2016). We also note that there are several applications such as wireless sensor networks in which the battery power limitation is extreme and recharging or changing drained batteries may be impossible.

Furthermore, there is a relationship between security and the power consumption. For instance, a higher number of rounds in AES encryption processes produces higher levels of security at the cost of additional power consumption. Figure 11.3 shows a general trend in the trade-off between vulnerability and power consumption with varying numbers of encryption rounds. Therefore, in order to design power-efficient encryption algorithms for wireless networks there is an **inherent need to understand the relationships between power consumption and encryption parameters**. Only then is it possible to optimize power consumption with respect to a security requirement.

Traditional cryptography deals generally with ensuring the security of the encrypted data. Several designs focus on security objectives

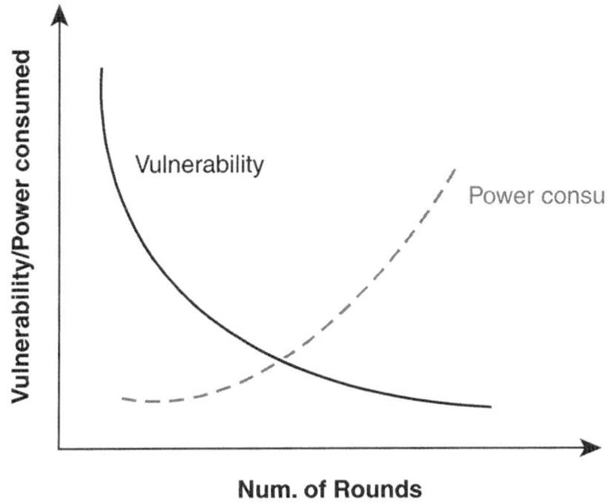

Fig. 11.3. Trade-off between vulnerability and power consumption.

while neglecting the QoS requirement. One main point is that the crypto-algorithms based on these designs usually do not account for physical constraints such as limited battery power (Chandramouli *et al.*, 2006). It may not be possible to support a security requirement given the power budget. Then, the key questions are twofold: how does one optimize crypto-parameters for a given power budget? Therefore, the primary challenge in providing security in low-power mobile wireless devices lies in the conflicting aims of minimizing power consumption and maximizing security. In general, we can safely assume that by doing more computations one can achieve a higher amount of security.

Many previous studies have addressed the issue of energy consumption in encryption processes. Khan *et al.* (2017) proposed a mechanism to reduce the cost of network coding by reducing the size of the data used for permutation. The basic idea is that the source permutes only global encoding vectors (GEVs) without permuting all the symbols in the message. This would significantly reduce the complexity and transmission cost over the network. Also, they suggest an algorithm for key generation and random permutation confusion key calculation. The proposed scheme achieves better performance in throughput, encryption time, and energy consumption. Zhang and

Lin (2014), introduced a permutation coding scheme, called P Coding, which is a lightweight encryption method.

Also, there are some hardware solutions to address the high power consumption in encryption processing. However, Hamalainen *et al.* (2006) declare that a loop-unrolled and pipelined hardware implies a large area and high power consumption. Furthermore, these architectures cannot be fully exploited in feedback modes of operation. The hardware implementation has many limitations as well. Bansod *et al.* (2015) stated that the standard algorithms such as DES & AES have vast memory requirements and it would not be possible to implement them in the embedded system. So many research studies tried to use lightweight encryption algorithms such as PRESENT which should be more efficient in devices connected to wireless networks. However, there are many claims by other authors which suggest that these algorithms are weak against cryptanalysis (Lee, 2014; Faghihi *et al.*, 2015) Several full-round attacks using biclique cryptanalysis have been introduced on PRESENT. According to Ramesh and Umarani (2012), "The last performance comparison point is the changing different key sizes for AES and UR5. In case of AES, we consider the three different key sizes possible, i.e., 128 bit, 192 bit and 256 bit keys. The simulation results are shown in Figure.... In the case of AES it can be seen that higher key size leads to clear change in the battery and time consumption. It can be seen that going from a 128 bit key to a 192 bit key causes an increase in power and time consumption of about 9% and going to a 256 bit key causes an increase of 17%. Also in the case of UR5, we consider the three different key sizes possible i.e., 128 bit, 192 bit and 256 bit keys." The encryption and decryption processes consume a significant amount of computing resources such as CPU time, throughput, and battery power (Jiehong and Detchenkov, 2016; Ramesh and Umarani, 2012). Figure 11.4, for instance, shows the time taken to encrypt different images.

These research studies have addressed some issues regarding wireless networks; however there are still some clear gaps in their research. For example, the proposed mechanism to reduce the cost of the network may not provide sufficient security. As only part of the message will be encrypted, this might affect the security level.

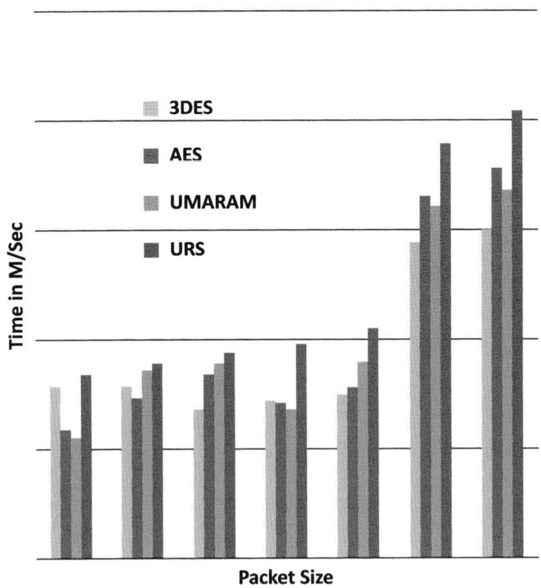

Fig. 11.4. The amount of time needed to encrypt different images (Ramesh and Umarani, 2012; Zhang *et al.*, 2014; Scarfone *et al.*, 2007).

Researchers have tried modifying the transmission protocol using AES encryption, but they have not tried to modify the AES algorithm itself to make it cost-effective. For these reasons we are going to develop the current AES algorithm to make it cost-effective by keeping its power consumption low and its security at a high level.

11.5.4. *Current state of security*

Security for a mobile environment today is much like it was in the early days of laptops. There is a sea of emerging mobile security solutions from both startups and more established software companies; we've published articles about several of these solutions on SandHill.com in the past few months. Organizations are trying to sort through the hype and figure out which products to use.

As companies learned over the years with laptops and desktops, a good mobile security strategy should be comprised of multiple solutions to provide in-depth security for the mobile device.

11.5.5. *Secure access to applications*

The security and management strategies for supporting a BYOD policy include an access-only approach to applications. This tactic prevents employees from downloading and storing any information on their mobile devices.

In addition, most of the CIOs we interviewed said their companies were looking at ways to separate corporate and personal data by implementing "container" structures on the devices. There are now several software companies with products enabling containment.

A **virtual desktop** is another structure which is used to contain information. This strategy eliminates the need for a BYOD policy and reduces device support costs while maintaining security and control. Currently software vendors such as VMware and Citrix and others are making virtual desktops more secure and therefore more organizations are following this strategy.

Using this strategy, a desktop in an employee's home becomes the means of mobility. The employee accesses corporate applications virtually, and the company maintains control over the applications' security. When the desktop shuts down, the connection to the applications is discontinued and no corporate data remains on the desktop.

"Smartphones and tablets are not yet powerful enough to handle this like desktops, but they will get there," stated a CIO we interviewed in the study. "I believe the adoption of the virtual desktop strategy will rapidly increase as this technology and wireless technologies mature."

However, a virtual desktop strategy has drawbacks even if mobile devices become powerful enough to handle it. It assumes continuous online availability, which is not assured in many locations, even in major metropolitan cities like New York City.

11.5.6. *Social media sites*

Allowing employees to access social media sites such as Facebook and Twitter from the company network is also a security risk. The challenge when employees go from an enterprise environment/network to another Internet site is that the company's policies get replaced by the security vulnerabilities and lowest-common-denominator approach used by those sites.

Organizations need to make sure their company's code of conduct for employee behaviour covers policies regarding accessing social media networks and websites through the enterprise mobile environment/network. Requiring employees to sign a code of conduct when hired is a common practice at many organizations (Paganini, 2012).

Companies and governments must be aware of the risks related to the careless use of powerful instruments. For instance, sensitive information could be exposed if the owners do not take the necessary precautions. The true revolution in the information technology world is the development and deployment of mobile systems, machines characterized by a processing capacity equal to that of a common desktop. This corresponds to a rise in smartphone ownership in certain countries, as seen in Fig. 11.5. People know our

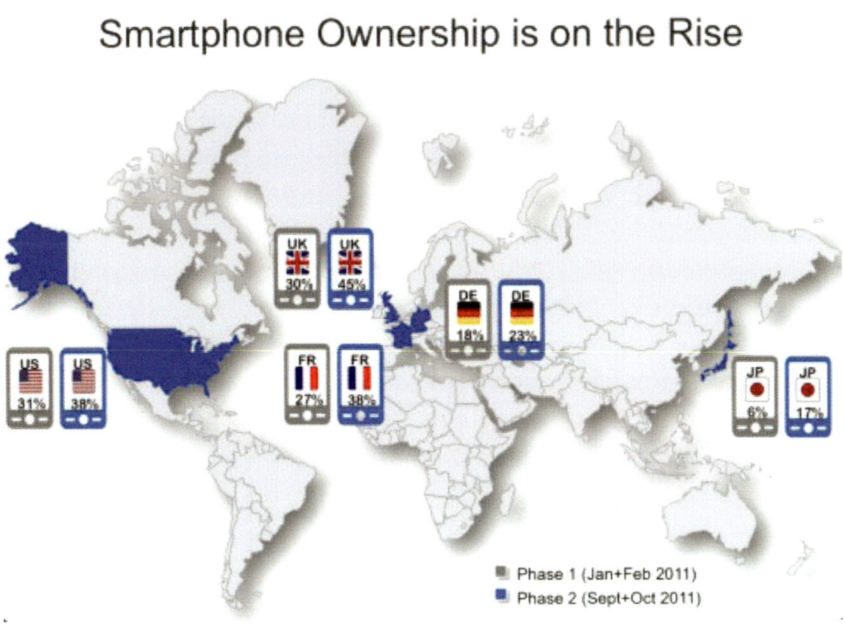

Fig. 11.5. Smartphone ownership rises in the USA, the UK, France, Germany, and Japan.

contacts (email, phone numbers) and manage our appointments, and when we surf on the web through these devices we indirectly provide them with information on our customs and traditions. A study reveals that Android-based smartphones suffered from more cyber criminal attacks due to their increased exposure to cyber threats. Due to how convenient they are, smartphones and tablets are becoming the preferred tools for browsing the Internet. The percentage of connections to the network from these mobile devices has increased significantly. This trend was evident in all countries, with the UK showing the largest increase in smartphone usage from 30 to 45% of the total population.

We have observed the increased attention of cyber criminals to the mobile sector. Cyber criminals often exploit security vulnerabilities in legitimate mobile apps, making data extraction and information gathering easier. The purpose is to steal information that is sensitive to the users such as banking credentials, but this is not the only purpose. Cyber espionage is another phenomenon that has exploded recently. Cyber criminals and government spies have discovered that it is really comfortable to spy on an individual by simply controlling his/her mobile device. Cyber criminals and government agencies are aware of the importance of information gained from mobile devices and are therefore showing high interest in the field. Hacker groups like Anonymous which target companies and individuals for various political reasons will pose a bigger threat to organizations that protect highly sensitive data. We have registered an exponential growth of malware designed to attack mobile systems and steal sensitive information which can be used to commit fraud. Don't forget that hacktivism is considered one of the most serious threats by all the governments of the world.

11.6. Cross Border Security

Wireless security is the prevention of unauthorized access or damage to computers using **wireless** networks. The most common types of **wireless security** are Wired Equivalent Privacy (WEP) and Wi-Fi Protected Access (WPA). WEP is a notoriously weak **security standard**.

"The Government has set out a series of minimum cyber security standards which will now be incorporated into the Government Functional Standard for Security, obliging government departments and suppliers to comply. The Standards comprise 10 sections, covering five broad categories: Identify, Protect, Detect, Respond and Recover, and also set expectations for governance, such as obliging government departments to create "clear lines of responsibility and accountability to named individuals for the security of sensitive information and key operational services" (Mayne, June 2018).

One of the consequences of the rise of cloud computing — which in simple terms refers to using scalable computing resources as a service via the Internet — is that computer data are increasingly stored remotely ('in the cloud') instead of on users' devices. This has significant implications for criminal investigation, particularly in cases where digital evidence is sought. Local search and seizure by the police will yield less and less evidence as users use cloud services such as webmail and remote data storage (Koops and Goodwin, 2014). This reinforces the existing challenges of cyber investigation, which not only has to deal with swift evidence-gathering due to the vulnerability of data loss, but which also has to find ways of remotely getting access to data, such as remote online searches or production orders directed at service providers. One particular challenge in cyber investigation is that such remote evidence-gathering powers may well extend beyond national borders. As remote access to computer data through remote cross-border searches and directly ordering foreign service providers to produce data are currently not allowed (Koops and Goodwin, 2014), states must resort to traditional procedures of mutual legal assistance, which tend to be relatively slow and not well-suited to securing digital evidence.

References

1. Aarti and Tyagi, S. S. (2013). Study of MANET: Characteristics, Challenges, Application and Security Attacks. *International Journal of Advanced Research in Computer Science and Software Engineering*, **3**(5), pp. 252–257.

2. Ali, N. M., Rahma, A. S. and Jaber, A. M. (2014). Random Key Permutation Stream Algorithm Based on Modified Functions in AES Algorithm. *International Journal of Engineering and Technology*, **4**(6), pp. 367–373.
3. Al-Khafaji, N. H. M. A., Rahma, A. M. S., Jaber, A. M. and Yousef, S. (2014). Random Key Permutation Stream Algorithm Based on Modified Functions in AES Algorithm. *International Journal of Engineering & Technology*, **4**(6), pp. 367–373.
4. Bansod, G., Raval, N. and Pisharo, N. (2015). Implementation of a New Lightweight Encryption Design for Embedded Security. *IEEE Transactions on Information Forensics and Security*, **10**(1), pp. 142–151.
5. Byrnes, M. (2017). *The Mobile Environment: Challenges and Opportunities for Secure Banking* [Online]. Available at: https://www.bankinfosecurity.com/webinars/mobile-environment-challenges-opportunities-for-secure-banking-w-216 (Accessed: September 2019).
6. Chandramouli, R., Bapatla, S. and Subbalakshmi, K. P. (2006). Battery Power-Aware Encryption. *ACM Transactions in Information and System Security*, **9**(2), pp. 162–180.
7. Cheng, S., Chen, P. and Lin, C. (2017). Traffic-Aware Patching for Cyber Security in Mobile IoT. *IEEE Communications Magazine*, **55**(7), pp. 29–35.
8. Cisco. (2016). *What Is a Wireless Network vs. a Wired Network?* [Online] Available at: https://www.cisco.com/c/en/us/solutions/small-business/resource-center/work-anywhere/wireless-network.html (Accessed: September 2019).
9. Daernen, J. and Rijrnen, V. (2002). *The Design of Rijndael*. Germany: Springer.
10. Dhamodharan, U. S. R. K. and Vayanaperumal, R. (2015). Detecting and Preventing Sybil Attacks in Wireless Sensor Networks Using Message Authentication and Passing Method. *The Scientific World Journal*, **2015**, Article ID: 841267, 7 pages.
11. Di Pietro, R., Guarino, S. and Verde, N. V. (2014). Security in Wireless Ad-Hoc Networks. *Elsevier — Computer Communications*, **51**, pp. 1–20.
12. Ehsan, S. and Hamdaoui, B. (2012). A Survey on Energy-Efficient Routing Techniques With QoS Assurances for Wireless Multimedia Sensor Networks. *IEEE Communications Surveys and Tutorials*, **14**(2), pp. 265–278.
13. Elhoseny, M. and Hassanien, A. E. (2018). *Dynamic Wireless Sensor Networks* (1st ed.). Studies in Systems, Decision and Control. Switzerland: Springer International Publishing AG.

14. Faghihi, S., Hossein, M. and Dakhilalian, M. (2015). Biclique Cryptanalysis of MIBS-80 and PRESENT-80 Block Ciphers. *Security and Communication Networks,* **9**(1), pp. 27–33.
15. Ferguson, N., Kelsey, J., Lucks, S. and Schneier, B. (2001). Improved Cryptanalysis of Rijndael. In Schneier, E. B. (ed.), *Fast Software Encryption.* New York, USA: Springer-Verlag.
16. Goodrich, M. and Tamassia, R. (2011). *Introduction to Computer Security* (1st ed.). USA: Pearson.
17. Hamalainen, P., Alho, T., Hannikainen, M. and Hamalainen, T. D. (2006). Design and Implementation of Low-Area and Low-Power AES Hardware Core. In *Proceedings of the 9th EUROMICRO Conference on Digital System Design, Dubrovnik, Croatia, August 30–September 1,* pp. 577–583.
18. Hammi, B., Khatoun, R. and Zeadaly, S. (2017). IoT Technologies for Smart Cities. *IET Networks,* **7**(1), pp. 1–13.
19. Hu, D., Wang, F. and Huang, C. (2009). A Novel Relay Encryption Scheme for Mobile Ad Hoc Networks. In *Proceedings of the 2009 Symposia and Workshops on Ubiquitous, Autonomic and Trusted Computing, Brisbane, QLD, Australia, July 7–9,* pp. 417–422.
20. Hu, W. and Cao, G. (2017). Quality-Aware Traffic Offloading in Wireless Networks. *IEEE Transactions on Mobile Computing,* **16**(11), pp. 3182–3195.
21. Jiehong, W., Detchenkov, I. and Cao, Y. (2016). A Study on the Power Consumption of Using Cryptography Algorithms in Mobile Devices. In *Proceedings of the 7th IEEE International Conference on Software Engineering and Service Science (ICSESS), Beijing, China, August 26–28,* pp. 957–959.
22. Khan, A., Sun, Q. T., Mahmood, Z. and Ghafoor, A. U. (2017). Energy Efficient Partial Permutation Encryption on Network Coded MANETs. *Journal of Electrical and Computer Engineering,* **2017**, Article ID: 4657831, 10 pages.
23. Koops, B. and Goodwin, M. (2014). *Cyberspace, the Cloud, and Cross-Border Criminal Investigation.* Netherlands: Tilburg Institute for Law, Technology, and Society.
24. Lee, C. (2014). Biclique Cryptanalysis of PRESENT-80 and PRESENT-128. *The Journal of Supercomputing,* **70**(1), pp. 95–103 doi:10.1007/s11227-014-1103-3.
25. Liang, Z. and Chao, H.-C. (2011). Multimedia Traffic Security Architecture for the Internet of Things. *IEEE Network,* **25**(3), pp. 35–40.
26. Masoud, M., Jannoud, I., Ahmad, A. and Al-Shobaky, H. (2015). The Power Consumption Cost of Data Encryption in Smartphones. In *Proceedings of the 1st International Conference on Open Source Software Computing (OSSCOM), Amman, Jordan, September 10,* pp. 1–6.

27. Matesanz, J. G., Orozco, A. L. and Villalba, L. J. (2012). Security Issues in Mobile Ad Hoc Networks. *International Journal of Distributed Sensor Networks,* **2012**(1), pp. 1–6.
28. Matin, M. A. and Islam, M. M. (2012). Overview of Wireless Sensor Network. In Matin, M. A. (ed.), *Wireless Sensor Networks.* London, UK: IntechOpen.
29. Mayne, M. (2018, 28 June). *UK Government Issues Minimum Cyber-Security Standards* [Online]. Available at: https://www.scmagazineuk.com/uk-government-issues-minimum-cyber-security-standards/article/1486651 (Accessed: September 2019).
30. Mohammed, F. Y., Rohiem, A. E. and Elbayoumy, A. D. (2009). A Novel S-Box of AES Algorithm using Variable Mapping Technique. In *Proceedings of the 13th International Conference on Aerospace Sciences and Aviation Technology, Cairo, Egypt, May 26–28,* pp. 1–10.
31. Morgan, S. (2017). *Cyber Security Cost* [Online]. Available at: https://www.forbes.com/sites/stevemorgan (Accessed: September 2019).
32. Nadeem, A. and Javed, M. Y. (2005). A Performance Comparison of Data Encryption Algorithms. In *Proceedings of the 2005 International Conference on Information and Communication Technologies, Karachi, Pakistan, August 27–28,* pp. 84–89.
33. Norton. (2017). *What You Need to Do About the WPA2 Wi-Fi Network Vulnerability* [Online]. Available at: https://us.norton.com/internetsecurity-emerging-threats-what-to-do-about-krack-vulnerability.html (Accessed: September 2019).
34. Orozco, A. L. S., Matesanz, J. G., Villalba, J. G., Díaz, J. D. M. and Kim, T.-H. (2012). Security Issues in Mobile Ad Hoc Networks. *International Journal of Distributed Sensor Networks,* **8**(11), pp. 1–6.
35. Paganini, P. (2012). *Cyber Threats in Mobile Environment* [Online]. Available at: https://securityaffairs.co/wordpress/4560/cyber-crime/cyber-threats-in-mobile-environment.html (Accessed: September 2019).
36. Panaousis, E. A. (2012). *Security for Mobile Ad-Hoc Networks* (PhD Thesis). London, UK: Kingston University London.
37. Panaousis, E. A., Politis, C., Birkos, K., Papageorgiou, C. and Dagiuklas, T. (2012). Security Model for Emergency Real-Time Communications in Autonomous Networks. *Information Systems Frontiers,* **14**(3), pp. 541–553.
38. Purevpn. (2017). *Here's How You Can Secure Your Wireless Network* [Online]. Available at: https://www.purevpn.com/blog/securing-wireless-network-guide/ (Accessed: September 2019).

39. Rahma, A. S. and Yaco, B. Z. (2012). Real-Time Partial Encryption of Digital Video Using Symmetric Dynamic Dual Keys Algorithm. *Engineering and Technology Journal*, **30**(5), pp. 710–728.
40. Ramesh, G. and Umarani, R. (2012). Performance Analysis of Most Common Symmetrical Encryption Algorithms. *International Journal of Power Control Signal and Computation (IJPCSC)*, **13**(1), pp. 42–45.
41. Rangaswami, M. C.-F. (2012). *Security and Privacy Considerations for a Mobile Environment* [Online]. Available at: http://sandhill.com/article/security-and-privacy-considerations-for-a-mobile-environment/.
42. Robertazzi, T. G. (2017). *Introduction to Computer Networking* (1st ed.). Switzerland: Springer International Publishing AG.
43. Scarfone, K. A., Souppaya, M. P. and Sexton, M. (2007). *Guide to Storage Encryption Technologies for End User Devices.* Gaithersburg, MA, USA: National Institute of Standards and Technology.
44. Sehgal, A., Ahuja, R. and Kumari, S. (2011). Security Architecture for Mobile Ad Hoc Networks. In *Proceedings of the 2011 International Conference on Science and Engineering (ICSE 2011), Rohtak, Haryana, India, January 21–23,* pp. 255–260.
45. Sharma, P., Liu, H., Wang, H. and Zhang, S. (2017). Securing Wireless Communications of Connected Vehicles With Artificial Intelligence. In *Proceedings of the 2017 IEEE International Symposium on Technologies for Homeland Security (HST), Waltham, MA, USA, April 25–26,* pp. 1–7.
46. Silver, E. (2017). *Wireless Networking and Security Standards* [Online]. Available at: https://it.ucsf.edu/policies/wireless-networking-and-security-standards (Accessed: September 2019).
47. Thomas, L., Pantelis, A. and Loukas, G. (2010). *Wireless Network Traffic and Quality of Service Support: Trends and Standards* (1st ed.). USA: Engineering Science Reference.
48. UK.gov. (2018). *UK Defence and Security Export Statistics for 2017.* UK: Gov.UK/Department of International Trade.
49. Usman, M., Yang, N. and Jan, M. (2018). A Joint Framework for QoS and QoE for Video Transmission over Wireless Multimedia Sensor Networks. *IEEE Transactions on Mobile Computing,* **17**(4), pp. 746–759.
50. Vaidya, B., Rodrigues, J. J. P. C. and Lim, H. (2010). Secure Multimedia Streaming Over Multipath Wireless Ad Hoc Network: Design and Implementation. In Nishi, K. (ed.), *Multimedia.* London, UK: IntechOpen.

51. Wolfram, W. (2018). *Vulnerability* [Online]. Available at: https://www.techopedia.com/definition/13484/vulnerability (Accessed: September 2019).
52. Yick, J., Mukherjee, B. and Ghosal, D. (2008). Wireless Sensor Network Survey. *Computer Networks,* **52**, pp. 2292–2330.
53. Zhang, P. and Lin, C. (2014). A Lightweight Encryption Scheme for Network-Coded Mobile Ad Hoc Networks. *IEEE Transactions on Parallel and Distributed Systems,* **25**(9), pp. 2211–2221.
54. Zhang, P., Lin, C., Jiang, Y., Fan, Y. and Shen, X. (2014). A Lightweight Encryption Scheme for Network-Coded Mobile Ad Hoc Networks. *IEEE Transactions On Parallel And Distributed Systems,* **25**(9), pp. 2211–2220.
55. Zhao, H. V., Lin, W. S. and Liu, K. (2009). A Case Study in Multimedia Fingerprinting: Behaviour Modelling and Forensics for Multimedia Social Networks. *IEEE Signal Processing Magazine,* **26**(1), pp. 118–39.
56. Zheng, Z., Cai, L. X. and Shen, X. (2013). *Sustainable Wireless Networks* (1st ed.) Switzerland: Springer International Publishing AG.
57. Zhou, L. (2010). Distributed Scheduling Scheme for Video Streaming Over Multi-Channel Multi-Radio Multi-Hop Wireless Networks. *IEEE Journal on Selected Areas in Communications,* **28**, pp. 409–419.

Chapter 12

Ethical Considerations and a Proposed Support Process When Employing People With Autistic Spectrum Disorder in Cyber Security Roles

John Goldie and Hamid Jahankhani*

Northumbria University London, UK
**Hamid.jahankhani@northumbria.ac.uk*

ABSTRACT

There is an acknowledged global shortage in qualified and skilled cyber security practitioners, so much so that governments, employers and educational establishments are developing new routes and opportunities to encourage interest and applications from demographics that would not normally apply for cyber security roles. These demographics include women, young children and people on the autistic spectrum. The potential employment of people from this last demographic — people on the Autistic Spectrum — in cyber security roles will be the focus of this research. Two areas are of interest, the ethical considerations in employing people on the Autistic Spectrum and the identification of a strategy to support the employee and employer relationship. Both are discussed here. In Europe the shortfall is expected to be in the region of 350,000 employees by the year 2020 and in the United States the number is expected to be 1.2 million by the same date. This research looks at how specific autistic traits and strengths can be matched to cyber security vacancies and discusses ethical considerations and a potential support process. A qualitative research methodology was used to identify suitable traits and potential cyber security vacancies. Ethical principles and a proposed support process are put forward to allow potential employers and autistic employees to engage in equitable employment opportunities. The autistic demographic does indeed offer skilled and capable resources to help fill cyber security vacancies; however, work is needed to allow both sides to benefit from the opportunities.

Keywords: Autistic Spectrum Disorder, ASD, ethics, cyber security, training, employment opportunities, special needs, traits

12.1. Literature Review

Employers are competing against each other to attract potential employees who have the necessary qualifications, skills or aptitude to succeed in cyber security roles. This is due to shortages in the United States, where approximately 1.8 million vacancies are expected by 2020 (Frost and Sullivan Executive Brief, 2017), and in the European Union, where the expectation is that there will be unfilled vacancies totalling 350,000 until 2020 (Ashford, 2017). This means that employment opportunities in cyber security are excellent with benefits that include high salaries, work-life balance packages and further incentives.

Baker states, "It has been firmly established that the nation's cyber workforce is lacking in numbers and in talented individuals needed to effectively operate in cyberspace. There is also undeniable evidence that the U.S. is trailing behind other countries in preparedness and sophistication in the cyber domain. While several directives, frameworks, programs, and initiatives exist that are designed to grow, train, and retain a skilled cyber security workforce, there are some gap areas where further focus could contribute to attaining measurable success." (Baker, 2013)

Given the budgetary constraints that the government of the United Kingdom is currently experiencing due to the existing austerity measures, attracting qualified and skilled cyber security professionals could prove difficult. To alleviate this, various government departments have been and are running a number of initiatives aimed at identifying and encouraging potential employees. These initiatives include Cyber First (NCSC, 2018), Cyber Summer Schools (GCHQ, 2018) and Cyber Discovery (DCMS, 2017).

The cyber security industry is also conducting research aimed at identifying expertise within its own community to encourage professional development within the workforce.

Fontenele states, "One of the major challenges in current cyber security initiatives is to place skilled people wherever needed whilst reducing the overall knowledge gap. Thus, in order to orchestrate roles in such a complex and dynamic environment, a novel approach *to discover talent within the cyber security community is required.*" (Fontenele, 2017)

The Center for Cyber Safety and Education has recently completed a research paper *"Women in Cyber Security"*, which identified that 11% of the cyber security workforce are women. The paper concluded that women are underrepresented in cyber security roles and organisations needed to "take swift and considerable actions to engage, develop and retain women in the field or the global workforce gap will continue to grow year over year" (Frost & Sullivan, 2017).

Another demographic that is under consideration for providing potential cyber security employees is that of people with Autistic Spectrum Disorder.

The Israeli Defence Forces have used people on the Autistic Spectrum to good effect in intelligence analyst roles. Most notably, Unit 9900, one of Israel's military intelligence units, has deployed male and female soldiers who have Autistic Spectrum Disorder in analysis roles where specific useful traits can be utilised to good effect (AIPAC, 2016).

Various United Kingdom government departments that have traditional information technology security and security service taskings are working with the National Autistic Society with the intention of identifying and developing opportunities for employing people on the Autistic Spectrum in cyber security roles within their organisations. The Cyber Security Challenge UK is a good example of this. It brings together the Information Assurance Advisory Council, CREST and the National Autistic Society to sponsor, develop and run "a series of national competitions, learning programmes, and networking initiatives designed to identify, inspire, and enable more people to become cyber security professionals. Established to bolster the national pool of cyber skills, it offers a unique programme of activities to introduce sufficient numbers of appropriately skilled individuals to learning and career opportunities in the profession." (IAAC, 2017)

Evidently there is a potential resource available with people on the autistic spectrum. Research indicates that there are traits that may be suitable for use in fulfilling the requirements of cyber security roles. The following sections will identify these traits and potential opportunities.

12.1.1. *Autistic Spectrum Disorder*

12.1.1.1. *Basic brain anatomy*

Research shows that there are anatomical differences between neurotypical and non-neurotypical brains. The reasons and causes are not fully understood.

Autism may be the result of abnormal or damaged neurons (neural networks) in the brain. These neurons may be unable to establish synaptic connections or achieve neural synchronisation. A neuron is a nerve cell that specialises in sending signals or nerve impulses from one part of the brain to another or from the brain stem to the nervous system. This disruption may cause the cognitive, social and sensory issues exhibited by autistic people. Research to support this idea comes from anatomical (Courchesne *et al.*, 2007), genetic (Geschwind and Levitt, 2007) and neuroimaging (Minshew and Keller, 2010) studies. Further research indicates that there may be much more densely folded grey matter in the rear regions of the brain, namely the left precuneus, left lateral occipital cortex and right temporal-occipital cortex (see Figs. 12.1 and 12.2).

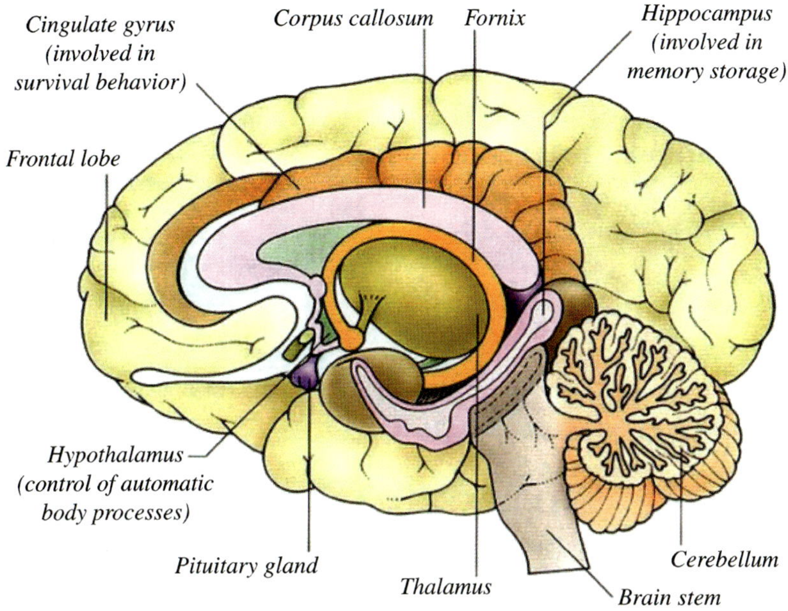

Fig. 12.1. Neurotypical brain (Lal Mali, 2014).

People on the Autistic Spectrum and those with Asperger's Syndrome have a range of potential issues (Section 12.1.2), that could be exploited, either intentionally or unwittingly, by employer organisations or their employees. There are relevant laws, as documented below, that should protect autistic employees but unless there is an advocate or the autists themselves raise an issue, these laws may not protect the vulnerable employee. How likely it is that autists would raise any issues is not a matter that will be dealt with in this paper.

It should be noted that ethical research into autistic people tends to be conducted through parents, guardians or court-appointed deputies of the autistic person and is generally concerned with children (Mukaetova-Ladinska *et al.*, 2012). Some autistic authors have highlighted this as an issue and suggest that more weight should be given to autonomy for autistic people, particularly when they have high-functioning autistic spectrum disorder.

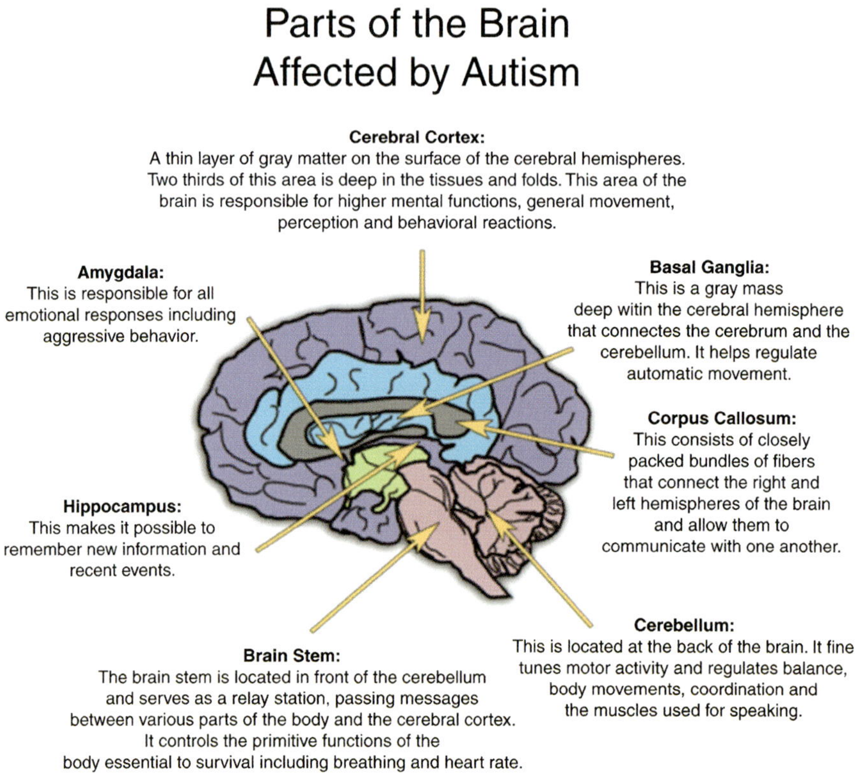

Fig. 12.2. Areas affected by autism in a human brain (Haydn, 2013).

12.1.1.2. *Support processes*

There are potential issues associated with employing autistic people but there has been extensive work carried out by researchers, clinicians and charitable organisations in discovering and developing support processes and assistive technology tools. Some of these support processes are described and referenced here.

There are no official statistics in the UK relating to employment rates for autistic people, although the National Autistic Society has produced some estimates from surveys of autistic people. They are summarised in a report entitled *"The autism employment gap: Too Much Information in the workplace"* (National Autistic Society, 2018).

"The Government wants to halve the disability employment gap. This would mean that 64% of disabled people would be in work.

60% of employers would worry about getting support for an autistic employee wrong.

60% of employers say they do not know where to go for support or advice about employing an autistic person." (NAS, 2017)

Employment offers social, psychological and financial benefits to all, including autistic people — for whom the psychological benefits may have a greater positive impact. Not least of these is the increased self-worth and autonomy that having a job can bring, which can lead to a feeling of contributing positively to society. There is also a decrease in the reliance on social and welfare benefits. There may be some issues associated with anxiety around integrating into the workplace and creating a new social network, although this can lead to psychological benefits once the initial anxiety and acceptance of change is recognised (Roux *et al.*, 2013).

Gaining employment is seen as a rite of passage from childhood into adulthood and gives a huge psychological boost to everyone, including autistic people (Bennett and Dukes, 2013; Wilczynski *et al.*, 2013).

It can be seen then, that there are improvements in quality of life, psychological and physical health, social standing and independence (both financial and social) associated with successful employment (Fleming *et al.*, 2013).

Another issue is the interview process. There is evidence that interviews can be a cause for concern for autistic people. Researchers have identified that social difficulties can mean that the job interview can represent an intense challenge (Smith *et al.*, 2014). This can lead to poor interview performance which results in a rejection; even in cases where the autistic person has the capability to perform the job.

The National Autistic Society, in the UK, advises organisations to make adjustments to their interview process and to consider using the following steps:

- *"Keep job description in simple English and focused.*
- *Weigh the qualities to indicate the main focus of the role.*

- *Be absolutely sure about what is essential and what is desirable.*
- *State that applications from autistic people and other under-represented people are welcomed.*
- *Avoid overblown statements about the company and the ideal applicant."*

(National Autistic Society, 2017)

By implementing the suggested adjustments to the interview process, organisations may see an improvement in applications from autistic people and may then benefit from the skills and capabilities that they could bring to the role.

Socialisation is important, so it is seen as vital that both employers and colleagues of autistic people are willing to interact with them and develop support processes to ensure successful employment. López and Keenan (2014) conducted a survey that demonstrated that *"lack of appropriate understanding from employers and co-workers"* is one of the biggest barriers to successful employment.

Research in the United States has identified that socialisation issues can be a serious barrier to employment for autistic people (Chiang *et al.*, 2013).

These socialisation issues can have a detrimental effect on work relationships when autistic traits and behaviours are exhibited (Test *et al.*, 2014). These barriers may be ritualised and focused behaviour, inattention to duties, hyperactivity, irritability and shouting, all of which are unacceptable in the workplace and could lead to dismissal. These behaviours can, however, be triggered by misunderstandings in the workplace. Triggers could be sensory overload, misinterpretation in communications and unexpected changes to the work schedule or office infrastructure and facilities (Hurlbutt and Chalmers, 2004).

The lack of secondary school educational qualifications and work experience could have a negative impact on employment prospects for autistic people and even if a job is offered there could well be a mismatch between a person's qualifications and abilities and the duties required by the role (Holwerda *et al.*, 2012).

This is indicative of a lack of understanding from employers as to the capabilities of autistic people and supports the findings expressed in the National Autistic Society's employment survey.

Prospects improve after a university education, whether the qualifications earned are undergraduate or postgraduate qualifications. This is predominantly true where extra transitional support or autistic mentors have been provided by the university or government agencies (Migliore *et al.*, 2014).

This does not mean that a university education will guarantee improved employment prospects. Reports indicate that there are still high levels of under-employment and unemployment for graduates with autistic spectrum disorder, with some researchers finding that nearly 50% of autistic people were overeducated for the jobs they hold (Baldwin *et al.*, 2014).

Studies show that having mentors during summer school periods can greatly enhance achievement for autistic students in their academic pursuits; especially when the student is encouraged to act as a mentor in the following summer school intake (Hotez *et al.*, 2018).

Continuing support from vocational service providers could improve employment success. Indeed, research shows that there are definite benefits when provision is consistent (Howlin, 2013). Occupational therapists could provide the necessary vocational training and help to prepare autistic people to transfer into employment through a combination of support and advice to potential employers about any workplace adaptations. However, there is an issue with the lack of availability of qualified and experienced vocational OTs in the UK at present.

Support workers are employed to provide continuous support to severely disabled people in either voluntary or employed positions. Evidence suggests that having a support worker provides enough specific and intensive support to be of benefit to people on the autistic spectrum despite the initial increased costs. The support worker delivers long term benefits to the employee, employer and the government (in reduced benefits payments) (Howlin *et al.*, 2005).

Support services have been shown to raise employment retention rates to nearly 90% for those autistic people who have access to them. This chapter will look at two approaches: TEACCH and Project SEARCH.

12.1.2. *TEACCH (Treatment and Education of Autistic and related Communication-handicapped Children)*

Mesibov and Shea (2010) state *TEACCH* "is a clinical service and professional training program, based at the University of North Carolina at Chapel Hill, that has incorporated and contributed to the evidence base of autism interventions". The late Eric Schopler, Ph.D., started the programme in 1972. The TEACCH approach is called "Structured Teaching." Structured Teaching is based on evidence and the observation that individuals with autism share a pattern of neuropsychological deficits and strengths that we call the 'Culture of Autism', which includes the following characteristics:

1. *Relative strength in and preference for processing visual information (compared to difficulties with auditory processing, particularly of language).*
2. *Heightened attention to details but difficulty with sequencing, integrating, connecting, or deriving meaning from them*
3. *Enormous variability in attention (individuals can be very distractible at times, and at other times intensely focused, with difficulties shifting attention efficiently).*
4. *Communication problems, which vary by developmental level, but always include impairments in the initiation and social use of language (pragmatics).*
5. *Difficulty with concepts of time including moving through activities too quickly or too slowly and having problems recognizing the beginning or end of an activity, how long the activity will last, and when it will be finished.*
6. *Tendency to become attached to routines and the settings where they are established, so that activities may be difficult to transfer or generalize from the original learning situation, and disruptions in routines can be uncomfortable, confusing, or upsetting.*
7. *Very intense interests and impulses to engage in favored activities and difficulties disengaging once engaged.*
8. *Marked sensory preferences and aversions."* (Mesibov and Shea, 2010)

The support generated from this approach is aimed at the individual and involves the management of time, environment and sequences of events in order to facilitate clearer learning and making activities easier to perform.

The TEACCH program has proven to be effective and relatively easy to implement and has gained international support. In the UK, the National Autistic Society promotes its use and highlights that "*the TEACCH approach tries to respond to the needs of autistic people using the best available approaches and methods known so far, for educating and teaching autonomy. It is not a single method and can be used alongside other approaches. Our support uses techniques from the TEACCH approach, and we provide TEACCH training to professionals.*"

TEACCH values consist of the following:

***T**eaching — sharing autism knowledge and increasing the skill level of professionals and practitioners.*

***E**xpanding — increasing own knowledge to provide high-quality services to people on the autism spectrum and their families.*

***A**ppreciating — appreciating the strengths and uniqueness of autistic culture.*

***C**ollaborating and **C**ooperating with colleagues, other professionals, people on the autism spectrum and their families.*

***H**olistic — adopting a holistic approach, looking at the person, their family and community.*

Some of the TEACCH Autism Programme priorities are:

- *focussing on the person, their skills, interests and needs*
- *understanding the 'culture of autism' and identifying differences based on individualised assessments*
- *using visual structures to organise the environment and tasks when teaching skills*
- *being broad-based, i.e. support people at work, teach skills but also ensure that people are supported during leisure and/or social activities*
- *being flexible and teaching flexibility.*

The TEACCH principles and techniques may always need to be in place for someone, but they may look very different at different stages of the person's life." (NAS, 2018)

12.1.3. *Project SEARCH*

Project SEARCH is a transition programme developed to help youths with disabilities. It has been adapted to provide support to help young people with ASD to transition into employment and further education.

"Key Project SEARCH programme components include setting a goal for employment, providing successive intensive internships in a community business, and assuring collaboration between school and adult services staff. Supports specific to students with ASD include providing intensive instruction in social, communication, and job skills; visual supports; and work routine and structure", (Wehman *et al.*, 2012).

The high retention rates in employment for autistic people, identified through research, tend to indicate that providing support services is beneficial from a social, psychological and financial (both for the employee and the government — through a reduction in overall costs) viewpoint.

12.1.4. *Transition*

Transitioning from secondary school to further education and employment is recognised as a major milestone for autistic people in socially advanced countries around the world (Westbrook *et al.*, 2015).The outcome is that autistic people achieve independence and employment.

It is recommended that these outcome-oriented transition services are made available as early as possible, with some researchers suggesting provision from the age of 14. This allows for longer individual preparation and could help to identify areas where further specific support is needed (Cimera *et al.*, 2013). This research highlighted the increased wages and lowered costs for people who got early access to transition services.

12.1.5. *Assistive technology*

In recent years there has been an exponential growth in technology that can aid autistic people in improving life skills. These technologies include picture guiding, audio assistance, video modelling, virtual reality and robotics. Each of these technologies has been utilised in training autistic people to improve their social skills (DiGennaro Reed *et al.*, 2011; Hopkins *et al.*, 2011).

Internet-based training has proven effective in improving social skills relevant to employment, e.g. job searches and interviews. There is a programme that uses virtual reality to allow autistic youths to practice interview techniques. This has proven to be significantly effective (Strickland *et al.*, 2013).

The use of technology to help people with disabilities has been proven across a range of physical and cognitive issues. Support can comprise of calendar entries to remind them of appointments or tasks that need to be completed. Communication can be improved through socialisation apps that ease misinterpretation between colleagues. Programs can be loaded onto tablets that allow for relaxation or rest when a situation is becoming stressful.

12.1.6. *Cyber security*

From the author's perspective, the term cyber security refers to the security controls and countermeasures deployed at ingress/egress points in a network (or where network traffic passes a boundary) and where a resource requires greater protection. These security controls and countermeasures can be policies, processes, tools, software, hardware and firmware.

As such, these security controls and countermeasures are incapable of making ethical decisions and it is the human individual that has the responsibility of deciding whether any activity is ethically acceptable and should therefore proceed.

The advent of machine learning and artificial intelligence may render this stance as untenable in the future but at present both machine learning and artificial intelligence are driven by sophisticated algorithms and are not yet capable of making ethical choices.

"The definition of computer ethics has various interpretations. One of the most oft-cited definitions is from James Moor: "A typical problem in

computer ethics arises because there is a policy vacuum about how computer technology should be used. Computers provide us with new capabilities and these in turn give us new choices for action. Often, either no policies for conduct in these situations exist or existing policies seem inadequate. A central task of computer ethics is to determine what we should do in such cases — that is, to formulate policies to guide our actions." (Dittrich, *et al.*, 2011)

The authors have been unable to find evidence of any prior research or published articles that specifically discuss ethics and cyber security in relation to security controls and countermeasures, although there is research available that examines how people use programs and malware to conduct attacks against targets. There is also a growing library examining ethics and cyber warfare.

To illustrate the point about cyber security elements being incapable of ethical decisions Stuxnet will be reviewed.

Langner states that Stuxnet *"marked a turning point in the history of cyber security — the arrival of the first cyber warfare weapon ever, known as Stuxnet. Not only was Stuxnet much more complex than any other piece of malware seen before, it also followed a completely new approach that's no longer aligned with conventional confidentiality, integrity, and availability thinking. Contrary to initial belief, Stuxnet wasn't about industrial espionage: it didn't steal, manipulate, or erase information. Rather, Stuxnet's goal was to physically destroy a military target — not just metaphorically, but literally."* (Langner, 2011)

Here we have a software program specifically written to attack a given target. In and of itself the program is incapable of determining the ethical correctness of its purpose. The responsibility lies solely with those people that authorised its development and use.

Some commentators view Stuxnet as the first ethically developed cyber weapon in that it was designed to attack a given target with no collateral damage expected (Lucas, 2017).

There are various threat actors driving attacks against target organisations or individuals. Target organisations are constituent parts in the following fields: government, financial services, utilities, manufacturing, technical, military, security services, etc.

Threat actors can include sovereign states (Gutmann, 2010), intelligence organisations, hacktivists (Warren and Leitch, 2016), organised crime, hackers, etc.

Drivers for attacks from these disparate groups could be state espionage, corporate espionage, financial gain, political gain, publicity, fun, challenge, etc.

Each threat actor will have a different ethical stance or rationalisation for their activities. Each ethical decision will be made by a responsible individual and not by the tool employed to conduct the attack.

Ethics in cyber security has gained a greater meaning due to the diverse nature of the internet and the difficulties faced by any government in trying to prosecute threat actors based in another country, particularly when the threat actors may be part of the host nation's intelligence services, and especially when the two nations may be geopolitically or ideologically opposed.

In 2015, the Office of Personnel Management, the US federal government's human resources organisation, discovered it had been hacked and that 22 million records had been stolen; allegedly by Unit 61398, part of China's People's Liberation Army's cyber espionage division (Koerner, 2016). To date, no evidence is available that the stolen data has been used maliciously. Which begs the question, "Why was the data stolen?" Could it be that the attack was a proof of ability or a warning from the Chinese to the Americans or an act of state cyber bullying?

Spoofing also presents issues in identifying a threat actor. If the attacker is able to effectively disguise the source of the attack or implicate another person or organisation, then innocent entities could be accused. This spoofing also allows states, organisations and individuals to claim innocence due to being framed. Plausible deniability, as Americans say.

In the case of the alleged attack on Sony Pictures by North Korea in 2014, Reuters reported *that "the results of a linguistic analysis of communications from the suspected hackers suggest they were more likely from Russia than North Korea"* (Hosenball and Finkle, 2014). In either case, neither country is likely to admit responsibility or extradite any potential suspects, due to the aforementioned geopolitical and ideological differences.

Sovereign states do not, technically, commit crimes, although their agents can be ordered to conduct activities that harm other states, organisations or individuals.

If one accepts that the points made above are correct, how can the perpetrators of these attacks be held legally or ethically accountable in the future? It is apparent that an international agreement is necessary.

There has been an attempt to implement an International Agreement to set acceptable parameters of cyber attacks. This followed the 2009 DDoS attacks against the Estonian government. This became known as the Tallinn Manual (named after the Estonian capital city where the Agreement was drafted, (NATO CCDCOE, 2013).

The manual was drafted by member states of NATO and had a US and Western European bias. This led to the proposals in the manual being rejected by China, Russia and Middle Eastern states.

Lucas (2017) states that *'emergent moral norms' sufficient to guide and govern the choices and actions of moral agents offer a hopeful prospect for obtaining some greater cooperation and constraint of activities as these choices and actions unfold in the cyber domain. One must be cautioned, however, that if the desired end is the governance of the cyber domain by means of an authentic moral point of view that is internalised, self-imposed and widely shared then we are still confronted with a profound obstacle. The prospects for attaining anything like an authentic morality or common ethos may prove all but unattainable in so diffuse, diverse and divided an environment as the cyber domain represents."*

This leads one to the assumption that only a truly international and non-geopolitical and ideologically neutral conference will be in a position to develop a globally acceptable set of laws or ethics pertaining to cyber security matters.

Given the identified issues relating to cyber security-based international laws and ethics, how then can organisations implement effective moral codes to ensure that their staff use cyber security tools and treat their colleagues, stakeholders and customers in an equitable manner?

Interested organisations are holding workshops specifically aimed at cyber security ethics. ACM SIGCOMM's "Cyber-security Research Ethics Dialogue & Strategy Workshop" in May 2013 is one example. The "workshop" embraced the theme of "ethics-by-design", and aimed to:

- *"Educate participants about underlying ethics principles and applications;*
- *Discuss ethical frameworks and how they are applied across the various stakeholders and respective communities who are involved;*
- *Impart recommendations about how ethical frameworks can be used to inform policymakers in evaluating the ethical underpinning of critical policy decisions;*
- *Explore cyber security research ethics techniques, tools, standards and practices so researchers can apply ethical principles within their research methodologies; and*
- *Discuss specific case vignettes and explore the ethical implications of common research acts and omissions."* (Kenneally and Bailey, 2014)

The IEEE Standards Association is running "IEEE Project: 7000 — Model Process for Addressing Ethical Concerns During System Design"

The IEEE website has the following quote: *"Engineers, technologists and other project stakeholders need a methodology for identifying, analyzing and reconciling ethical concerns of end users at the beginning of systems and software life cycles. The purpose of this standard is to enable the pragmatic application of this type of Value-Based System Design methodology which demonstrates that conceptual analysis of values and an extensive feasibility analysis can help to refine ethical system requirements in systems and software life cycles."* (IEEE SA, 2018)

Whilst the quote does not specify that such a methodology is needed in the field of cyber security, there is an obvious connection between security programming and ensuring that adequate security controls are embedded in systems during the development of software life cycles.

These workshops and projects indicate that interested global organisations are taking steps to develop and implement ethical processes. However, it is likely that these processes may take some time to be accepted and embedded into national and international organisations.

Another approach to embedding ethics which has been adopted by international and national organisations is for entities to publish "Codes of Conduct". These are particularly deployed by vocational organisations that provide certification and training in Information Security.

These Codes of Ethics are high level aims that set out the organisation's expectations of how their members/employees should act in relation to ethics — congruent to how organisations implement Tier 1 policies. If organisations combine these ethics codes with Corporate Responsibility processes and deliver training at induction and as part of an employee's annual professional and personal development requirements, this should mean that ethical processes become part of the organisational culture.

To this point, the focus has been on implementing ethics as cyber security software, tools and processes are used. When teaching people ethical hacking, educational establishments demonstrate how offensive tools can be used to attack a target device or network. Then descriptions are given as to what "white-hat, black-hat and grey-hat" hackers are. The skills are already "out of the bag" so to speak. Surely there is a need to teach ethics before the tools and skills are made available, particularly when the student is a young child or an immature youth/adult or a non-neurotypical person, as in the case of autistic people.

Obviously, some organisations have a duty to conduct offensive hacking as part of their role (such as intelligence analysts). This would be made clear in contracts and terms of engagement and it is likely that crown immunity would apply. However, there is still a need to make students and employees aware of ethical guidelines.

Training people in ethics in advance of teaching the use of offensive tools will not necessarily deter criminal activity or those hacking for the challenge or the fun of it but it should give an ethical baseline to students and employees.

12.1.7. *Laws and ethics*

12.1.7.1. *Relevant UK laws*

Interestingly there are not many laws specific to cognitive and physical disabilities in the UK. The major law is the rather catchall Equalities Act 2010 (Equality and Human Rights Commission, 2010) wherein peoples' rights to equality are guaranteed across the United Kingdom. Exceptionally, there is a law specific to autism in England. The Autism Act 2009 (UK Government, 2009) is the only condition-specific law within the United Kingdom and demonstrates the level of importance that Parliament attaches to protecting the rights of people on the autistic spectrum. In Scotland, the Scottish Strategy for Autism was developed (Scottish Government, 2011).

In 2010 an Adult Autism Strategy "Fulfilling and Rewarding Lives" (NAS, 2010) was published. This was then superseded by "Think Autism" in April 2014 (NAS, 2014).

There are two further laws for consideration. The Children and Families Act 2014 "*supports young people in preparing for adulthood*" (UK Government, 2014) and The Care Act 2014 "*places a strong emphasis on preventing and delaying needs for care and support, making sure that there is appropriate information and advice for people, support for carers, and promoting integration between social care and health care services. It also places a duty on local authorities to promote a person's well-being when carrying out any of their care and support functions in respect of that person.*" (UK Government, 2014)

12.1.7.2. *Ethics*

Ethics is a branch of philosophy that takes years of study to master and covers many different aspects from meta-ethics to normative ethics, which consists of areas such as virtue ethics, deontology, hedonism and consequentialism, to applied ethics consisting of areas such as bioethics, machine ethics and military ethics to moral psychology and descriptive ethics.

Clearly this section does not have sufficient space to deal with this level of philosophical ethics. Rather the section deals with ethics in a pragmatic way and looks at how policies and codes of conduct can provide support and guidance for organisations that are looking to employ autistic people in cyber security roles.

Embedding ethical and supportive governance processes into the business strategy may encourage relevant business units and employees to acknowledge and commit to the correct treatment of and engagement with their non-neurotypical workmates, thus establishing a set of guiding ethical principles for the organisation and workforce. This can also be considered as forming part of the governance processes established in an organisation. As such this would indicate that the Board and the executives of an organisation have responsibility for ensuring that ethical processes are embedded into the organisation's culture.

Valentine and Godkin state that introducing ethical policies and continuing ethical training (specific to an employee's role) by developing and implementing Corporate Social Responsibility processes will produce positive practices in the workforce and lead to higher retention rates and employee satisfaction (Valentine and Godkin, 2016).

Implementing policies and codes of conduct in a given field or organisation will provide guidance as to how organisations expect their staff to work in an ethical or moral way. However, this does not mean that the ethical requirements have been fully met if the relevant philosophers or experts have not thoroughly debated and proven the various aspects.

The approach of implementing codes of conduct in a given field or environment also ignores potential issues due to geopolitical or ideological differences on the international scene.

When considering a code of conduct for autistic people and their employers working in the field of cyber security one needs to consider autonomy and whether the participants fully understand the ethical requirements they are agreeing to. There needs to be an element of responsibility that will remain with those who authorise the activity. After all it has been established, in this research, that it is not possible to attach ethical considerations to the security controls and countermeasures that constitute cyber security.

It is likely that many of the autistic people who apply to work in cyber security roles will be high-functioning autists and will have the capacity to legally agree to adhere to a code of conduct but there may well be some people with special isolated skills or perceptual peaks that are able to carry out specific duties in a role, especially when it is an area that the autistic person enjoys and is focussed on, who may not have the capacity to make the required ethical declaration.

The codes of ethics published by ISACA (ISACA, 2018) and ISC^2 (ISC2, 2018) are excellent exemplars for information security and cyber security-based organisations but they do not provide adequate guidance when one considers that some of the people employed in the industry may be non-neurotypical and may not have the capacity to legally agree to requirements.

This section does not aim to address ethics from a philosophical perspective but from a layman's viewpoint to try to determine how ethical considerations can support autistic people in finding employment in cyber security roles and how employers can engage equitably with potential new employees who are on the autistic spectrum.

Ethics is similar to the Hippocratic Oath requirements that physicians are constrained by — do no harm, respect the individual or group and act in an ethical way.

When ethics is considered from a practical standpoint the situation becomes more complicated; many differing arguments are put forward by interested stakeholders leading to complex issues that should be addressed by each individual stakeholder. Researchers have identified four specific categories of ethics that may pertain to autists and their social and employment interactions — personal, professional, regulatory and tangible (Brosnan *et al.*, 2013).

The complexity of ethics could mean that organisations and their employees will pay lip service to ethical requirements and proceed with a nod towards laws and perceived morals, that is, trying to do the right thing. Whilst they may be well-intentioned, the potential for exploitation is apparent.

Stahl *et al.* (2013) identify different levels of ethical thinking. *"At the most basic level there is moral intuition which informs individuals with regard to what they perceive to be right or wrong. Where such moral intuition becomes problematic or contested, the second level, explicit morality, is needed so that clear statements can be made with regard to what is right or wrong. Ethical theory, the third level, seeks to justify such explicit morality. The fourth and most abstract level is meta-ethics, where ethical theories are reflected."* (Stahl *et al.*, 2013)

Embedding ethical policies and encouraging social responsibility may lead to employees taking the moral high road in working with both autistic people and cyber security tools.

Lucas (2017) states *"there are two possible strategies for the constructive role of moral considerations. The first involves exploring the relative advantages of morality as a form of self-governance in contrast to the constraints imposed by law. The second follows from the first and requires us to inquire more deeply into just what "ethics" represents as a kind of social institution and how it can plausibly claim to provide universal guidance for human conduct and the exercise of human (moral) agency. Both are important considerations in justifying claims for the efficacy of morality"*.

12.2. Methodology

12.2.1. *Qualitive review*

A qualitative research method was used to review secondary source information from peer-reviewed, respected journals, the Wellcome Collection Museum and Library and the National Autistic Society Library.

12.2.2. *Questionnaires*

Two questionnaires were developed, which continues the qualitative research methodology. Both consisted of open questions designed to elicit as much information as possible to detail what organisations were already doing with respect to autistic people and further to identify any ethical processes currently being followed and what support was under consideration or in place.

The open nature of the questions produced responses that were meaningful and salient to the responders and were therefore explanatory and rich in nature.

The questionnaires were also used to identify or confirm traits and strengths and potential cyber security vacancies at the employer organisations.

The first questionnaire was developed to gather information from The National Autistic Society.

The second questionnaire was developed to gather information from potential employer organisations.

12.2.3. *Case studies*

Finally, the case studies complete the qualitive research approach.

To ensure confidentiality and that data protection requirements are adhered to the name of the person discussed in this case study will not be divulged and random letters will be used to represent the individual in question. The letters JC will be used to identify the individual. The bespoke Managed Security Supplier (MSS) will not be identified.

Whilst attending an ethical hacking course in July 2017 an employee of a bespoke MSS met another attendee who had excellent programming, cyber security, vulnerability assessment and penetration testing skills but who had issues with communicating with the tutor and their classmates.

Through discussions during training modules and break periods it became apparent that JC was on the Autistic Spectrum. The MSS employee was able to encourage a tentative relationship to the point where JC accepted a business card and agreed to arrange a meeting between JC, his parents, a court-appointed deputy and the MSS.

The meeting established a willingness by all parties to enter into a short-term contract of employment for JC as a penetration tester. The initial, short length of the contract was to allow a sensible break if the agreement was unsuitable to either party.

It is noteworthy that JC was keen to have a level of autonomy in his role, although there was a legal requirement to agree to contractual and financial matters with the court-appointed deputy. All parties agreed to JC taking a lead in activities provided any legal issues were confirmed and agreed to with the firm of solicitors acting as JC's legal deputy. This process took several months to sort out, mainly due to delays from the Court of Protection having to sanction parts of the contract.

JC received the same equipment, pay and terms and conditions as the other penetration testers at the company and where necessary adjustments were made to facilitate JC's needs.

The role was home-based with occasional trips into the office to discuss requirements, adjustments or issues from JC's perspective.

Initially JC was invited to visit the office so that he could be introduced to the environment and meet with some of the people he could be interacting with. During the initial meetings JC struck up a relationship with one of the team managers and it was agreed that JC would report to that particular team manager.

All the MSS's clients were in the financial services domain so there was not any requirement to obtain security clearance — which could be an issue for anyone on the spectrum wanting to work on roles supporting government departments.

JC successfully provided vulnerability assessment and penetration testing services to the MSS and its clients for two years. One notable capability of JC's was that they could look at a screenful of coding and almost immediately spot issues with either syntax, spacing or numerical errors. When asked how he was able to spot the mistake so quickly he said that the colours were different.

On a number of occasions support was required from the MSS in the form of report writing or accompanied attendance at meetings requested by the end client. There were two episodes of unusual interaction with colleagues; both of which were the result of misunderstandings — one employee was given training in how to interact with an autistic person and JC had an unexplained tantrum.

On the whole the relationship was successful and rewarding for both JC and the MSS.

Due to recent changes in ownership at the MSS, JC decided to leave his employment and move on to other activities. He was offered a continuation by the new owners, under the same terms and conditions that he had worked under for the preceding two years, but he was unwilling to stay.

At his leaving interview, JC stated that he had enjoyed the work and found that as he interacted more with his colleagues he noticed that his social skills improved so that he was more able to communicate with colleagues.

From an employer's perspective the MSS was extremely satisfied with the quality of work that JC produced. Issues around reporting of findings were overcome when a team manager was able to build a good working relationship with JC. Some small adjustments had to be made to working practices but the benefits outweighed the costs.

The fact that JC was supported by a court-appointed deputy was an added complication but the only real negative was due to the time required to liaise with the deputy and the Court of Protection.

The role being home-based was a positive, as JC did not have to worry about unscheduled changes to the environment, workforce or duties which could have created an issue as change is recognised as a stress point for some autistic people.

Introducing JC to the office and keeping him informed of changes in personnel was a useful way of integrating him into the workforce and meant that any changes were forewarned and did not have a greater impact than they could have had.

Whether this approach would be acceptable in a government department or with a service management supplier in a central government contract, where security clearance is a requirement, is debatable as the processes around ensuring equivalency from a secure technical infrastructure in the home are complex and risk management of this will be a continuous task.

12.2.4. *Autistic savantism*

Professor Temple Grandin is a well-known scientist at Colorado State University, who works at reducing suffering in livestock. She is an accomplished author and gives speeches on autism and animal

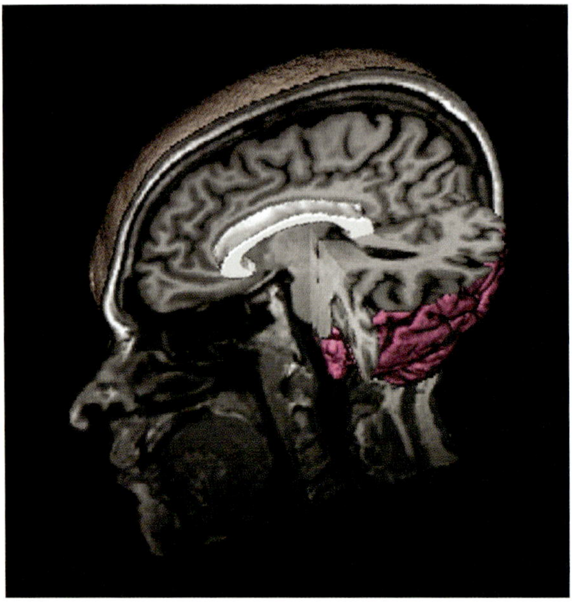

Fig. 12.3. MRI image of Grandin's left medial temporal lobe (McGowan, 2013). Taken by Jason Cooperrider, University of Utah.

behaviour. She has Asperger's Syndrome. She states that she thinks in pictures. She is considered to be a savant.

Grandin's left medial temporal lobe — involved in memory — appears in pink in this MRI, shown in Fig. 12.3. The white crescent is her corpus collosum, a bundle of fibres that connects the two hemispheres of her brain.

Jason Cooperrider, who is one of a team of neuroimaging experts at the University of Utah who study brain changes in autism, carried out research on Professor Temple Grandin's brain and reported that her brain is remarkable. The team scanned Grandin's brain using three different methods:

- High-resolution magnetic resonance imaging (MRI), which captures the structure of the brain;
- Diffusion tensor imaging (DTI), a method to trace the connections between brain regions;
- Functional MRI, which indicates brain activity.

The images revealed an unusual neural landscape that reflects Grandin's deficits and talents.

Overall, the right side of her brain dominates. One theory of autistic savantism suggests that during foetal development or early in life, some developmental abnormality affects the brain's left side, resulting in the difficulties that many autistic people have with words and social interaction, functions typically processed by the left hemisphere.

As can be viewed in Fig. 12.4, "*If brain tissue is damaged or does not develop fully, the ventricles — vessels filled with cerebrospinal fluid, shown in blue in this image based on neuroimaging work — expand to fill the space. Temple Grandin's enlarged left ventricle is a sign of abnormalities in her left hemisphere, which typically handles language, and may account for the difficulties she has with processing words. To make up for this, the right hemisphere sometimes overcompensates, which can lead to special abilities in music, art, and visual memory. Savantism is not well-understood, but between a tenth and a third of people with autism may have some of these abilities. Cooperrider's team also discovered that Grandin's amygdala, the almond-shaped organ said to play an important role in emotional processing, is larger than normal. This was not a surprising finding because among other functions, this region processes fear and anxiety, affective states often affected by autism. Her fusiform gyrus is smaller than normal — also not a surprise, since this region is*

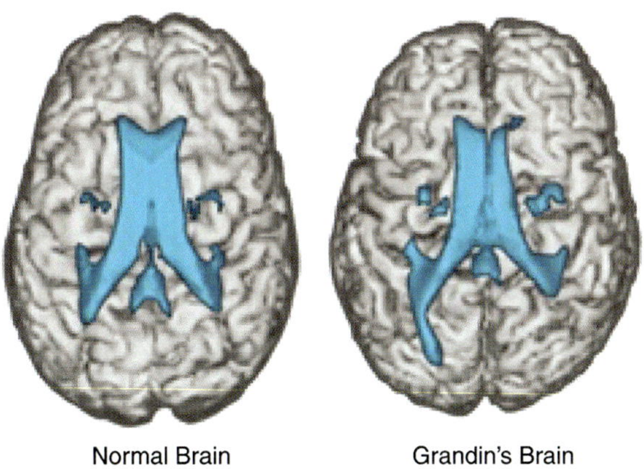

Fig. 12.4. Comparison of left ventricles in a control brain and Grandin's brain. Source (McGowan, 2013) from Roen Kelly, Discover Magazine (2013), by Jason Cooperrider, University of Utah.

involved in recognizing faces, a social skill that autism may disrupt." (McGowan, 2013)

The two case studies seem to indicate that there are anatomical differences in brain structure in autistic people when compared to neurotypical brains as can be seen in the comparative brain scans shown in Fig. 12.4 above. Grandin's brain scan shows marked differences in anatomical structure from the so-called normal brain. These differences could be caused by much more densely packed neurons in the highlighted area in Grandin's brain scan. As the neurons are responsible for passing electrical impulses, this extra density may indicate that the electrical impulses occur faster and so allow for increased ability in particular areas. This can be called savantism, special isolated skills or perceptual peaks.

Also, the two subjects report that they experience their environment differently from how most people would experience it.

These differences could be advantageous in cyber security roles in that issues may be picked up more quickly. This may be particularly useful in combating an ongoing attack or in completing a forensic examination. Business-as-usual processes could also be more efficient and effective if the analyst was able to instantaneously spot errors or code in a particularly fast way.

If the supposition documented by McGowan (2013), "*Savantism is not well-understood, but between a tenth and a third of people with autism may have some of these abilities*", is correct, then there could be between 70,000 and 235,000 autistic people in the UK with savant skills that may be useful in cyber security roles. Obviously not all will be useful in cyber security roles but this could indicate that there is a sizeable relevant skill set waiting to be identified and utilised in the autistic demographic.

12.3. Analysis and Critical Discussion

12.3.1. *Matching traits with opportunities*

The National Autistic Society provides support, information and services for autistic people (including those people with Asperger's Syndrome), and their relatives and guardians in the United Kingdom. It is a leading charity that campaigns for a better world for autistic people. The Society describes autism as "*a lifelong, developmental disability that affects how a person communicates with and relates to other people, and how they experience the world around them.*" (National Autistic Society, 2017)

The Society has been working with interested organisations, educational establishments and potential employees to identify specific traits that can be utilised in the workplace or act as a base for further education and training.

12.3.1.1. *Traits and strengths*

Listed below are some of the traits and strengths exhibited by autists (National Autistic Society, 2016):

- Attention to detail
- Methodical approach
- Good memory for factual information
- Strong problem-solving skills
- Strong numerical skills
- Neuro-diverse thinking
- Pattern recognition
- Reliable
- Resourceful

These traits and skills have been recognised as a good fit for roles in cyber security, intelligence analysis or information security. There are many cyber security organisations including United Kingdom government departments that are actively assessing and recruiting autists to fill vacancies in these domains (IAAC, 2017).

Organisations that have expressed an interest in employing autists include, but are not limited to, NCSC, Microsoft, SAP, IBM, BAe, QinetiQ, NCC Group, Northrop Grumman and Thales.

12.3.1.2. *Opportunities*

Questionnaires were sent to the National Autistic Society and various interested employer organisations to try to ascertain requirements from the perspectives of support and employer functions. Results from the employer questionnaires seem to indicate that there are specific roles where autists are under consideration as potential employees. These roles include:

- Penetration testers
- Vulnerability assessors
- Cyber forensic analysts
- Network security analysts
- Firewall engineers
- Threat intelligence analysts
- Security Information Event Management (SIEM) analysts
- Security programmers

These roles all require a methodical approach, a good attention to detail and a level of tenacity to keep working at a mentally tiring exercise. Numerical and problem-solving skills are key to each of the roles, whilst pattern recognition and lateral thinking would be a distinct advantage.

Other roles were identified in the questionnaires but as they fall outside of the cyber security field they will not be documented here.

Note: As the majority of the questionnaire respondents are involved in activities that require security clearance, an undertaking (in the form of non-disclosure agreements) was given not to identify which roles are directly associated with individual organisations. In compliance with this undertaking, specific questionnaire responses will not be attached to this document.

A comparison of the traits and strengths and roles listed above does seem to indicate a useful correlation that could, with the implementation of appropriate support processes, lead to meaningful employment and mutually beneficial work relationships for both autistic people and employer organisations.

12.3.2. *Potential issues*

There are a number of traits that are exhibited by people on the Spectrum that should be considered by employer organisations to ensure an equitable relationship.

The National Autistic Society states "*Autistic people see, hear and feel the world differently to other people. If you are autistic, you are autistic for life; autism is not an illness or disease and cannot be 'cured'. Often people feel being autistic is a fundamental aspect of their identity.*

Autism is a spectrum condition. All autistic people share certain difficulties but being autistic will affect them in different ways. Some autistic people also have learning disabilities, mental health issues or other conditions, meaning people need different levels of support. All people on the autistic spectrum learn and develop. With the right sort of support, all can be helped to live a more fulfilling life of their own choosing." (National Autistic Society, 2017)

These potential issues could be seen as reasons to avoid employing autistic people but the research documented in this paper indicates that with some reasonable adjustments in the work environment and how communication is handled between the autistic employee and the organisation, a mutually beneficial working relationship is possible.

12.3.2.1. *Social communication*

Autists may be unable to process verbal or non-verbal language such as tone of voice, gestures and facial expressions. They can take as literal anything that is said to them, as some do not understand sarcasm or jokes. This processing of verbal and non-verbal language is a skill that most of us learn as we interact with each other and we can pick up on the different nuances that escape autists.

Some autists have problems with the spoken language but can express themselves very clearly in other ways, for example by using sign language or visual symbology.

The case study relating to JC shows that it is possible to implement communication strategies to enhance and support communication for the autistic person, the employer and their clients. Each individual is different so it is important that time is taken to identify the most appropriate strategy for that person.

12.3.2.2. *Social interaction*

Autists can find it difficult to form friendships and often have trouble reading others, that is, recognising feelings, emotions and intentions.

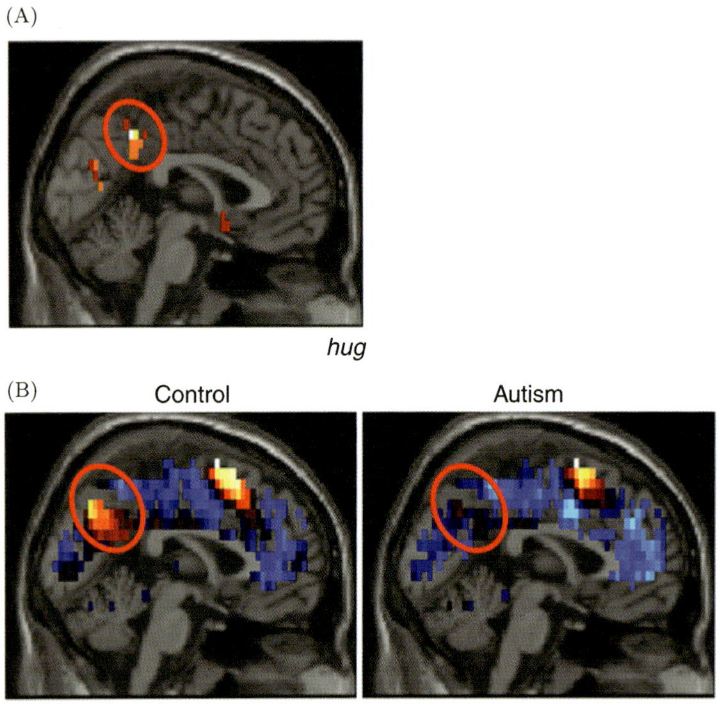

Fig. 12.5. MRI image detailing responses to the word 'hug' in a neurotypical and non-neurotypical brain. Image.

Source: Journal Plos.org.

This can lead to socially awkward events such as perceived strange behaviour, deliberate avoidance of groups (the desire to be alone) and the appearance of insensitivity and aloofness.

This is probably the most identifiable situation and is easily addressed by considering the work environment and letting relationships develop over time. Figure 12.5 shows how just hearing the word "hug" can have such a different impact on a neurotypical brain and a non-neurotypical brain (Ajakab *et al.*, 2013). Image A identifies the region of the brain that deals with social touching. Image B is the neurotypical control brain. Image C is the non-neurotypical brain (Journal Plos.org).

The images in Fig. 12.5 indicate very different responses in brain activity to the word "hug". The autistic brain shows much less activity, indicating potential issues in social interaction, than does the control brain. This difference in activity has been shown to be replicated in other areas of the brain under stimuli in further brain scans, supporting conclusions that the autistic brain works in different ways to neurotypical brains.

12.3.2.3. *Honesty*

The often uncompromising truthfulness of autistic people could be a barrier to developing equitable social relationships.

Internally this situation can be supported by providing coaching and training for all employees although a strategy should be developed to mitigate any issues that may arise with client organisations who are not aware of the relevant circumstances.

12.3.2.4. *Routines and repetitive behaviour*

Autists can view the world as a confusing and very unpredictable place. To manage this some may adopt routines such as always arranging belongings in a particular way, or adopting rules to ensure they follow the 'correct' way to do things, particularly if they have been introduced to something new. As change can be an issue, repetitive behaviour can be a coping mechanism.

This repetitive behaviour could have advantages in a cyber security role that requires continuous monitoring or tool calibration.

12.3.2.5. *Focussed interests*

People on the Spectrum can develop focussed and often intense interests across a wide range of topics — anything from art, computers, history, politics to zoology. Some of these interests will be of interest to potential employers but the narrow focus could prove to be an issue.

Some autists have reported that these activities are fundamental to who they are and to their holistic well-being.

Managing focussed interests carefully could mean a beneficial increase in throughput or production but care will need to be taken to ensure there is no detrimental effect on the autistic employee.

12.3.2.6. *Sensory perception*

Autistic people can have a heightened or lowered perception associated with their senses (vision, hearing, smell, taste, touch), temperature and pain. Responses to these stimuli could be anxiety, panic attacks or hyper-focus.

Obviously, any extreme responses will be upsetting to all involved but simple measures may help to control external stimuli.

Heightened sensory perception could manifest as special isolated skills or perception peaks, which in turn may provide advantages in cyber security roles.

12.3.3. ***Questionnaire response analysis***

12.3.3.1. *National Autistic Society questionnaire*

The NAS questionnaire identified autistic traits and strengths that could be useful in a wide range of roles including cyber security. NAS identified a wide range of roles, highlighting industries from the arts, libraries, administration, property management, information technology and horticulture.

Support strategies were identified and these strategies form part of the proposed support strategy proffered here.

From a law and ethics perspective the NAS discussed existing laws and policy requirements. Ethics related more to research ethics when clinical and social researchers were conducting autism studies.

The questionnaire identified a number of employer organisations that had worked with NAS in encouraging and assessing potential in cyber security work. These organisations include GCHQ, NCSC, BAe, NCC Group, Thales, Northrop Grumman, QinetiQ and UK government departments. This list informed which organisations received the Employer Questionnaire.

The National Autistic Society is a charitable institution that works specifically towards supporting autistic people. As such, there may be a natural bias in some of the responses received. As it is a single organisation, their views may not be wholly representative in the autistic environment.

12.3.3.2. *Employer questionnaire*

Eight employer organisations, from a total of ten, responded to the questionnaire; as the majority of them requested that available opportunities are not linked to their organisation and as some of the roles are associated with providing security-cleared services it was necessary to complete non-disclosure agreements to access the information. A decision has been made to retain confidentiality for all responding organisations.

The number of employer organisations which participated is small and may not be representative of the wider employment opportunities available. However, all those approached work in the cyber security domain and had previously expressed an interest in employing autistic people. The results could be improved by approaching more organisations for responses.

Potential vacancies are identified below. To maintain confidentiality the organisations will be identified using the numbers 1–8 in the following charts.

Figure 12.6 clearly shows there is great interest in employing autistic people in cyber security roles in the organisations that responded to the survey. Given the small survey size this may mean that the results are not representative across the industry. A larger employer survey is recommended to ascertain a more representative view.

Figure 12.7 indicates how the eight employer organisations are considering deploying autistic employees. Location is a consideration when employing autistic people as a changing environment could cause anxiety and lead to angry outbursts. If the correct support processes are put in place to mitigate this situation then any issues can be mitigated.

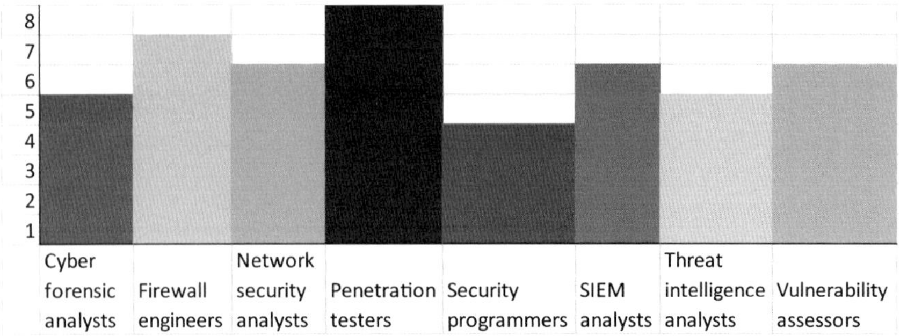

Fig. 12.6. Company-reported interest by cyber security role.

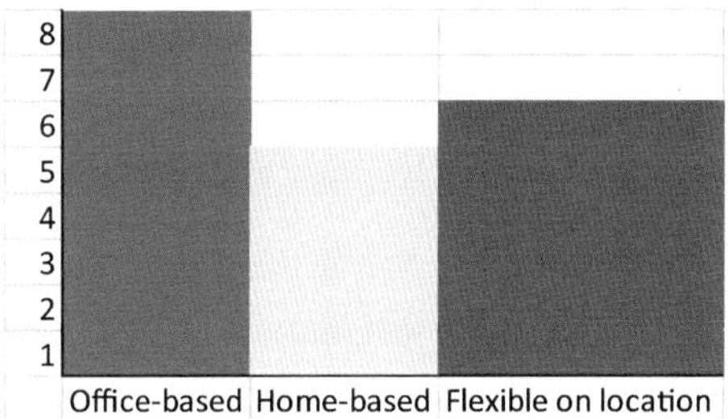

Fig. 12.7. Location preferences as expressed by employer organisations.

Where an autistic person is located could depend on the employer's or their end clients' requirements and this is something that needs to be taken into consideration.

The responses do indicate that employer organisations are considering some flexibility on deployment location.

Figure 12.8 represents whether the employer organisations have considered the different ethical options associated with employing autistic people.

The results seem to indicate that the organisations will rely upon existing relevant laws and their own policy document sets. The majority of the organisations highlighted their own Corporate Social Responsibility activities as being relevant. Only 25% reported that they had looked into ethical requirements, however, they did not stipulate how this was undertaken or what the results were. Less than half indicated that they were considering a mentorship scheme.

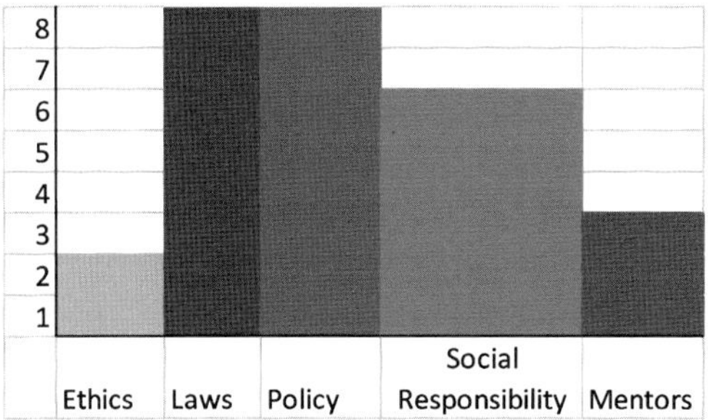

Fig. 12.8. What ethical considerations were discussed internally?

It should be noted that the responses recorded in Fig. 12.8 may represent the respondents' own views or their knowledge of what support processes may be deployed within their organisation and may not represent what actually would occur if an autistic person were to be employed by the organisation.

Overall, the small survey responses indicate that there are cyber security roles potentially available to autistic people.

Further consideration by the employer organisations needs to be given to ethical considerations on how the organisation will support the effective introduction of autistic people into the workforce and what adjustments need to be made.

Research shows that providing mentors is a positive step, particularly when mentors are themselves autistic and have been involved with a previous iteration of mentorship.

Change can be an issue and the employer organisations have indicated a willingness to allow flexibility in location. Combining this with effective communication on any planned changes in personnel, office environment or duties should lead to an effective business relationship for all parties.

12.3.4. *Autistic brain structural anomalies*

While basic brain anatomy has been discussed in previous sections, Fig. 12.9 in this section details the differences between a "normal" brain and an autistic brain.

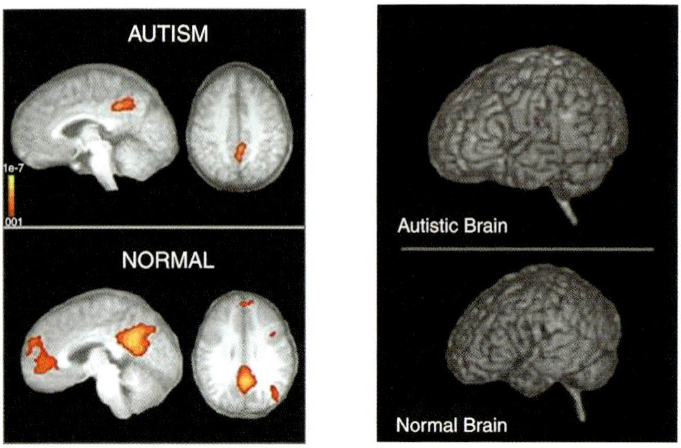

fMRI autism vs. healthy control activation pattern

MRI autism vs. healthy control volume comparision

Fig. 12.9. Anomalies in brain activity and anatomy — Autistic brain vs. control brain (Yamada *et al.*, 2016).

Research indicates that an autistic brain may have more densely grouped regions at the cerebral cortex and the cerebellum. This extra density can manifest itself in more folds in these regions. These folds can increase the surface area of the brain and bring neurons into closer proximity to each other.

"The insular cortex comprises multiple functionally differentiated sub-regions, each of which has different patterns of connectivity with other brain regions. Such diverse connectivity patterns are thought to underlie a wide range of insular functions, including cognitive, affective, and sensorimotor processing, many of which are abnormal in autism spectrum disorder (ASD)." (Yamada *et al.*, 2016)

The extra surface area and the close proximity of neurons could mean that neurological signals pass more effectively and efficiently in the areas that have anatomical abnormalities. This could then mean that the autistic person can utilise these differences in more focussed ways, leading to peak performances in, for instance, identifying patterns useful in checking network security baselines, penetration testing, configuring SIEM tools, writing software codes, etc.

Neurons process and transmit electrical-chemical signals throughout the nervous system and can be found in the brain, spinal column and peripheral nerves. The potential cognitive phenomena exhibited by autistic people can manifest across a range of subjects or areas, such as mathematics, exceptional memory, increased perceptual capacity, visual acuity, languages, music and art.

Mathematics can be directly associated with cyber security skills when one considers elements such as logic, cryptoanalysis, statistics, algorithms and computation. Similarly, memory skills, perceptual capacity — where there is an ability to process large amounts of information — and visual acuity can also be utilised in cyber security roles.

12.4. Conclusions

As evidenced in this research, there are traits and strengths exhibited by people on the Autistic Spectrum that can be utilised effectively by cyber security industry employer organisations.

There are some potential issues that should be taken into consideration to ensure an equitable relationship. There is the potential for anxiety and disruption for the new employee, the existing employees and the employer.

Although unlikely, there is the potential for either deliberate or accidental exploitation of the individual, particularly when cyber security tools are deployed in furtherance of national interests. The natural inclinations of some autists could also mean that they become focussed on discovering vulnerabilities in a given system or network and will keep at it regardless of the time it takes or the effect it could be having on them personally.

By developing ethical policies and support processes, these issues can be avoided or mitigated. There are existing laws that provide a level of protection but adopting ethical and support functionality will mean that both sides will understand their responsibilities and build an effective and fair working relationship.

The anatomical differences in brain structure and the denser collection of neurons in the rear of the brain (which function by passing electrical impulses) seem to indicate that in certain circumstances it is possible for the autistic person to exhibit special isolated skills, perceptual peaks or savant capabilities. These abilities can then produce some remarkable skills that can be effectively utilised in cyber security roles.

References

1. AIPAC. (2016). *YouTube–PC 2016–Unit 9900 Moment* [Online]. Available at:https://www.youtube.com/watch?v=TFMgo3pBm7I (Accessed: 5 December 2017).
2. Ashford, W. (2017). *Europe Faces Shortage of 350,000 Cyber Security Professionals by 2022* [Online]. Available at: http://www.computerweekly.com/news/450420193/Europe-faces-shortage-of-350000-cyber-security-professionals-by-2022 (Accessed: 6 December 2017).
3. Baker, M. (2013). *State of Cyber Workforce Development* [Online]. Available at: http://www.sei.cmu.edu (Accessed: 19 May 2018).
4. Baldwin, S., Costley, D. and Warren, A. (2014). Employment Activities and Experiences of Adults With High-Functioning Autism and Asperger's Disorder. *Journal of Autism and Developmental Disorders*, **44**(10), pp. 2440–2449.
5. Bennett, K. and Dukes, C. (2013). Employment Instruction for Secondary Students With Autism Spectrum Disorder. *Education and Training in Autism and Developmental Disabilities*, **48**(1), pp. 67–75.
6. Brosnan, C., Cribb, A. and Wainwright, S. P. A. W. C. (2013). Neuroscientists' Everyday Experiences of Ethics: The Interplay of Regulatory, Professional, Personal and Tangible Ethical Spheres. *Sociology of Health and Illness*, **35**(8), pp. 1133–1148.
7. Chiang, H., Cheung, Y., Li, H. and Tsai, L. (2013). Factors Associated With Participation in Employment for High School Leavers With Autism. *Journal of Autism and Developmental Disorders*, **43**(8), pp. 1832–1842.
8. Cimera, R., Burgess, S. and Wiley, A. (2013). Does Providing Transition Services Early Enable Students With ASD to Achieve Better Vocational Outcomes as Adults? *Research and Practice for Persons with Severe Disabilities*, **38**(2), pp. 88–93.
9. Cooperrider, J. R., Lainhart, J. E. and Taylor, J. S. (2013). Spectroscopic Brain Imaging in Autism. In Casanova, M. F., El-Baz, A. S. and Suri, J.

S. (eds.), *Imaging the Brain in Autism.* New York, NY, USA: Springer Science + Business Media.

10. Courchesne, E. *et al.* (2007). Mapping Early Brain Development in Autism. *Neuron,* **56**(2), pp. 399–413.
11. Cyber Security Challenge UK. (2016). *Autism and Careers in Cyber Security: A Short Guide for Employers* [Online]. Available at: https://www.cybersecuritychallenge.org.uk/app/uploads/2017/01/MCN-1423-A4-Cyber-Autism-and-careers-in-cyber-security-FINAL1.pdf (Accessed: 6 December 2017).
12. DCMS. (2017). *Cyber Discovery* [Online]. Available at: https://www.joincyberdiscovery.com/ (Accessed: 14 May 2018).
13. DiGennaro Reed, F. D., Hyman, S. and Hirst, J. (2011). Applications of Technology to Teach Social Skills to Children With Autism. *Research in Autism Spectrum Disorders,* **5**(3), pp. 1003–1010.
14. Dittrich, D., Bailey, M. and Dietrich, S. (2011). Building an Active Computer Security Community. *IEEE Security and Privacy,* **9**(4), pp. 32–40.
15. Elsevier. (2017). *ScienceDirect* [Online]. Available at: https://www.elsevier.com/solutions/sciencedirect (Accessed: 13 December 2017).
16. Equality and Human Rights Commission. (2010). *Equality Act 2010: Guidance* [Online]. Available at: https://www.gov.uk/guidance/equality-act-2010-guidance (Accessed: 7 December 2017).
17. Fleming, A., Fairweather, J. and Leahy, M. (2013). Quality of Life as a Potential Rehabilitation Service Outcome: The Relationship Between Employment, Quality of Life and Other Life Areas. *Rehabilitation Conselling Bulletin,* **57**(1), pp. 9–22.
18. Fontenele, M. P. (2017). *Designing a Method of Discovery Expertise in Cyber Security Communities: An Ontological Approach* [Online]. Available at: http://ethos.bl.uk/OrderDetails.do?uin=uk.bl.ethos.720046 (Accessed: 8 December 2017).
19. Frost and Sullivan Executive Brief. (2017). *Global Information Security Workforce Study Benchmarking Workforce Capacity and Response to Cyber Risk* [Online]. Available at: https://iamcybersafe.org/wp-content/uploads/2017/07/N-America-GISWS-Report.pdf (Accessed: 27 March 2018).
20. Frost and Sullivan. (2017). *Women in Cyber Security* [Online]. Available at: https://iamcybersafe.org/wp-content/uploads/2017/03/WomensReport.pdf (Accessed: 25 March 2018).
21. Furnell, S., Fischer, P. and Finch, A. (2017). Can't Get the Staff? The Growing Need for Cyber-Security Skills. *Computer Fraud and Security,* **2017**(2), pp. 5–10.

22. GCHQ. (2015). *CyberFirst Scheme Launched to Develop the UK's Next Generation of Cyber Security Experts* [Online]. Available at: https://www.gchq.gov.uk/news-article/cyberfirst-scheme-launched-develop-uks-next-generation-cyber-security-experts (Accessed: 5 December 2017).
23. GCHQ. (2016). *GCHQ launches Cyber Insiders Summer School* [Online]. Available at: https://www.gchq.gov.uk/press-release/gchq-launches-cyber-insiders-summer-school (Accessed: 5 December 2017).
24. GCHQ. (2018). *Students* [Online]. Available at: https://www.gchq-careers.co.uk/early-careers/students.html (Accessed: 15 May 2018).
25. Geschwind, D. H. and Levitt, P. (2007). Autism Spectrum Disorders: Developmental Disconnection Syndromes. *Current Opinion in Neurobiology*, **17**(1), pp. 103–111.
26. Grandin, T. and Panek, R. (2013). *The Autistic Brain: Thinking Across the Spectrum*. Boston, MA, USA: Houghton Mifflin Harcourt .
27. Gutmann, E. (2010). Hacker Nation: China's Cyber Assault. *World Affairs*, **173**(1), pp. 70–79.
28. Haydn, A. (2013). *Areas Affected by Autism in a Human Brain* [Online]. Available at: http://hayden26.blogspot.com/2013/10/autism-effects-of-brain-people-with.html (Accessed: 6 January 2018).
29. Holwerda, A., Klink, J., Groothoff, J. and Brouwer, S. (2012). Predictors for Work Participation in Individuals With an Autism Spectrum Disorder: A Systematic Review. *Journal of Occupational Rehabilitation*, **22**(3), pp. 333–352.
30. Hopkins, I. *et al.* (2011). Avatar Assistant: Improving Social Skills in Students With an ASD Through Computer-Based Intervention. *Journal of Autism and Developmental Disorders*, **41**(11), pp. 1543–1555.
31. Hosenball, M. and Finkle, J. (2014). *U.S. Suspects North Korea Had Help Attacking Sony Pictures* [Online]. Available at: https://www.reuters.com/article/us-northkorea-cyberattack/u-s-suspects-north-korea-had-help-attacking-sony-pictures-source-idUSKBN0K71FK20141230 (Accessed: 1 June 2018).
32. Hotez, E. *et al.* (2018). Designing a Summer Transition Plan for Incoming and Current Students on the Autism Spectrum: A Participatory Approach. *Frontiers in Psychology*, **9**(46), pp. 1–16.
33. Howlin, P. (2013). Social Disadvantage and Exclusion: Adults With Autism Lag Far Behind in Employment Prospects. *Journal of the American Academy of Child and Adolescent Psychiatry*, **52**(9), pp. 897–899.
34. Howlin, P., Alcock, J. and Burkin, C. (2005). An 8-Year Follow-Up of Specialist Supported Employment Service for High-Ability Adults With Autism or Asperger Syndrome. *Autism*, **9**(5), pp. 533–549.

35. Hurlbutt, K. and Chalmers, L. (2004). Employment and Adults With Asperger Syndrome. *Focus on Autism and Other Developmental Disabilities*, **19**(4), pp. 215–222.
36. IAAC. (2017). *Cyber Security Challenge* [Online]. Available at: https://www.cybersecuritychallenge.org.uk/ (Accessed: 3 April 2018).
37. IEEE SA. (2018). *IEEE Project 7000 — Model Process for Addressing Ethical Concerns During System Design* [Online]. Available at: https://standards.ieee.org/develop/project/7000.html (Accessed: 28 May 2018).
38. IEEE. (2018). *IEEE Code of Ethics* [Online]. Available at: https://www.ieee.org/about/corporate/governance/p7-8.html (Accessed: 18 May 2018).
39. ISACA. (2018). *Code of Professional Ethics* [Online]. Available at: https://www.isaca.org/Certification/Code-of-Professional-Ethics/Pages/default.aspx (Accessed: 18 May 2018).
40. ISC2. (2017). *Information Security Journal* [Online]. Available at: https://www.isc2.org/Member-Resources/Journal (Accessed: 13 December 2017).
41. ISC2. (2018). *Code of Ethics* [Online]. Available at: https://www.isc2.org/Ethics# (Accessed: 18 June 2018).
42. Jakab, A. *et al.* (2013). Autistic Traits in Neurotypical Adults: Correlates of Graph Theoretical Functional Network Topology and White Matter Anisotropy Patterns. *PLoS ONE*, **8**(4), e60982.
43. Jones, D. J. (2012). *Understanding Decision Making Relating to Out of Authority Placements for Pupils With Autism Spectrum Conditions* [Online]. Available at: http://ethos.bl.uk/OrderDetails.do?uin=uk.bl.ethos.564328 (Accessed: 9 December 2017).
44. Just, M. A. *et al.* (2014). Identifying Autism from Neural Representations of Social Interactions: Neurocognitive Markers of Autism. *PLoS ONE*, **9**(12), e113879.
45. Kenneally, E. and Bailey, M. (2014). Cyber-Security Research Ethics Dialogue and Strategy Workshop. *ACM SIGCOMM*, **44**(2), pp. 76–79.
46. Koerner, B. I. (2016). *Inside the Cyberattack That Shocked the US Government* [Online]. Available at: https://www.wired.com/2016/10/inside-cyber-attack-shocked-us-government/ (Accessed: 27 May 2018).
47. Lal Mali, B. (2014). *Neurotypical Brain* [Online]. Available at: http://human-diagrams.blogspot.com/2014/01/human-brain-diagram.html#.W-HJM5P7RPY (Accessed 16 December 2017).
48. Langner, R. (2011). Stuxnet: Dissecting a Cyberwarfare Weapon. *IEEE Security and Privacy*, **9**(3), pp. 49–51.
49. Libicki, M. C. (2014). *Shortage of Cybersecurity Professionals Poses Risk to National Security* [Online]. Available at: https://www.rand.org/news/press/2014/06/18.html (Accessed: 7 December 2017).

50. Lopez, B. and Kennan, L. (2014). *Barriers to Employment in Autism: Future Challenges to Implementing the Adult Autism Strategy* [Online]. Available at: http://www.autismrpphub.org/sites/default/files/articles/employment_report.pdf (Accessed: 31 May 2018).
51. Lucas, G. R. (2017). International Law Applicable to Stuxnet. In *Ethics and Cyber Warfare: The Quest for Responsible Security in the Age of Digital Warfare.* New York: Oxford University Press.
52. Lucas, G. R. (2017). The Advantages of Taking the "Moral Point of View". In *Ethics and Cyber Warfare: The Quest for Responsible Security in the Age of Digital Warfare.* New York: Oxford University Press.
53. Lucas, G. R. (2017). The Origins of Universal Moral Norms. In: *Ethics and Cyber Warfare: The Quest for Responsible Security in the Age of Digital Warfare.* New York: Oxford University Press.
54. McGowan, K. (2013). Exploring Temple Grandin's Brain. *Discover,* April 2013, pp. 542–543.
55. Meilleur, A.-A. S., Jelenic, P. and Mottron, L. (2015). Prevalence of Clinically and Empirically Defined Talents and Strengths in Autism. *Journal of Autism and Developmental Disorders,* **45**(5), pp. 1354–1367.
56. Mesibov, G. B. and Shea, V. (2010). The TEACCH Program in the Era of Evidence-Based Practice. *Journal of Autism and Developmental Disorders,* **40**, pp. 570–579.
57. Migliore, A., Butterworth, J. and Zalewska, A. (2014). Trends in Vocational Rehabilitation Services and Outcomes of Youth With Autism: 2006–2010. *Rehabilitation Counselling Bulletin,* **57**(2), pp. 80–89.
58. Minshew, N. and Keller, T. (2010). The Nature of Brain Dysfunction in Autism: Functional Brain Imaging Studies. *Current Opinions in Neurology,* **23**, pp. 124–130.
59. Mittelstadt, B. D. (2013). *On the Ethical Implications of Personal Health Monitoring* [Online]. Available at: http://ethos.bl.uk/OrderDetails.do?uin=uk.bl.ethos.613549 (Accessed: 10 December 2017).
60. Mukaetova-Ladinska, E., Perry, E. and Baron, M. (2012). Ageing in People With Autistic Spectrum Disorder. *International Journal of Geriatric Psychiatry,* **27**(2), pp. 109–118.
61. NAS. (2010). *Fulfilling and Rewarding Lives* [Online]. Available at: http://www.autism.org.uk/about/strategy/2010-strategy.aspx (Accessed: 26 March 2018).
62. NAS. (2014). *Think Autism* [Online]. Available at: http://www.autism.org.uk/about/strategy/2014-strategy.aspx (Accessed: 27 March 2018).
63. NAS. (2017). *The Autism Employment Gap* [Online]. Available at: http://www.autism.org.uk/get-involved/tmi/employment (Accessed: 5 June 2018).

64. NAS. (2018). *How Common Is Autism?* [Online] Available at: https://www.autism.org.uk/about/what-is/asd.aspx (Accessed: 18 June 2018).
65. NAS. (2018). *TEACCH* [Online]. Available at: http://www.autism.org.uk/about/strategies/teacch.aspx# (Accessed: 31 May 2018).
66. NAS. (2016). *Autism and Careers in Cyber Security*. London, UK: National Autistic Society.
67. NAS. (2017). *Information for Employers* [Online]. Available at: http://www.autism.org.uk/professionals/employers/information-for-employers.aspx# (Accessed: 6 December 2017).
68. NAS. (2017). *What Is Autism?* [Online] Available at: http://www.autism.org.uk/about/what-is.aspx (Accessed: 6 December 2017).
69. NAS. (2018). *The Autism Employment Gap. Too Much Information in the Workplace* [Online]. Available at: http://www.autism.org.uk/get-involved/tmi/employment (Accessed: 3 June 2018).
70. NATO CCDCOE. (2013). *Tallinn Manual* [Online]. Available at: https://ccdcoe.org/tallinn-manual.html (Accessed: 27 May 2018).
71. NCSC. (2018). *CyberFirst Nurturing Young Talent* [Online]. Available at: https://www.cyberfirst.ncsc.gov.uk/ (Accessed: 16 May 2018).
72. Roux, A. *et al.* (2013). Postsecondary Employment Experiences Among Young Adults With an Autism Spectrum Disorder. *Journal of the American Academy of Child and Adolescent Psychiatry*, **52**(9), pp. 931–939.
73. SAGE Publications. (2017). *Autism Journal* [Online]. Available at: https://uk.sagepub.com/en-gb/eur/journal/autism (Accessed: 13 December 2017).
74. Samra, S. H. (2016). *A Narrative Exploration of Sense-Making, Self and Identity in Young People Diagnosed With an Autism Spectrum Condition* [Online]. Available at: http://ethos.bl.uk/OrderDetails.do?uin=uk.bl.ethos.687497 (Accessed: 10 December 2017).
75. Scottish Government. (2011). *Scottish Strategy for Autism* [Online]. Available at: http://www.gov.scot/Publications/2011/11/01120340/0 (Accessed: May 2018).
76. Smith, M. *et al.* (2014). Virtual Reality Job Interview Training in Adults With Autism Spectrum Disorder. *Journal of Autism and Developmental Disorders*, **44**(10), pp. 2450–2463.
77. Stahl, B. C., Doherty, N. F., Shaw, M. and Janicke, H. (2013). Critical Theory as an Approach to the Ethics of Information Security. *Science and Engineering Ethics*, **20**(3), pp. 675–699.
78. Strickland, D., Coles, C. and Southern, L. (2013). JobTIPS: A Transition to Employment Program for Individuals With Autism Spectrum Disorders. *Journal of Autism and Developmental Disorders*, **43**(10), pp. 2472–2483.

79. Test, D., Smith, L. and Carter, E. (2014). Equipping Youth With Autism Spectrum Disorders for Adulthood: Promoting Rigor, Relevance and Relationships. *Remedial and Special Education,* **35**(2), pp. 80–90.
80. UK Government. (2009). *The Autism Act* [Online]. Available at: https://www.legislation.gov.uk/ukpga/2009/15/pdfs/ukpga_20090015_en.pdf (Accessed: 14 May 2018).
81. UK Government. (2014). *The Care Act* [Online]. Available at: http://www.legislation.gov.uk/ukpga/2014/23/pdfs/ukpga_20140023_en.pdf (Accessed: 29 March 2018).
82. UK Government. (2014). *The Children and Families Act* [Online]. Available at: http://www.legislation.gov.uk/ukpga/2014/6/pdfs/ukpga_20140006_en.pdf (Accessed: 28 March 2018).
83. Valentine, S. and Godkin, L. (2016). Ethics Policies, Perceived Social Responsibility, and Positive Work Attitude. *Irish Journal of Management,* **35**(2), pp. 114–128.
84. Warren, M. and Leitch, S. (2016). The Syrian Electronic Army — A Hacktivist Group. *Journal of Information, Communication and Ethics in Society,* **14**(2), pp. 200–212.
85. Wehman, P. *et al.* (2012). Project SEARCH for Youth with Autism Spectrum Disorders: Increasing Competitive Employment on Transition to High School. *Journal of Positive Behavior Interventions,* **15**(3), pp. 144–155.
86. Westbrook, J. *et al.* (2015). Transition Services for Youth With Autism: A Systematic Review. *Research on Social Work Practice,* **25**(1), pp. 10–20.
87. Wilczynski, S., Trammell, B. and Clarke, L. (2013). Improving Employment Outcomes Among Adolescents and Adults on the Autism Spectrum. *Psychology in the Schools,* **50**(9), pp. 876–887.
88. Yadron, D. (2015). *Iranian Hackers Infiltrated New York Dam in 2013* [Online]. Available at: https://www.wsj.com/articles/iranian-hackers-infiltrated-new-york-dam-in-2013-1450662559 (Accessed: 1 June 2018).
89. Yamada, T. *et al.* (2016). Altered Functional Organization Within the Insular Cortex in Adult Males With Highfunctioning Autism Spectrum Disorder: Evidence from Connectivity-Based Parcellation. *Molecular Autism,* **7**(41), pp. 1–15.

Chapter 13

An Ethical Approach to Understanding Cyber Security

Ojo Emmanuel Ademola

Northumbria University London, UK
emmanuel.ademola@northumbria.ac.uk

ABSTRACT

The study of ethics in cyber security often raises more questions than it answers. A student may ask the question, "Why should I study ethics in cyber security?" As research becomes specialized and technical skill sets appreciate in value, ethical questions become more important to ask.

This chapter reviews the ethical aspects of cyber security. Ethics, in general, underscores various studies in which right is distinct from wrong. The understanding of these delineations evokes various ethical issues in cyber security, such as the morality of human behavior, policies, laws, and social structures. Considering theories of consequentialism and deontology, ethical analyses of cyber security, information privacy and ethics, and privacy issues in the digital age are performed through the use of relevant ethically-driven cyber security case studies.

Keywords: ethics, digital age, cyber security

13.1. Introduction

An ethical approach to the understanding of cyber security in this digital age requires adaptability and continuous commitment as top priorities. A working definition of ethics that includes both consequentialist and deontological approaches to understanding the subject is emphasized. This definition also encompasses the introductory concepts that accentuate the issue of ethics in cyber security. Overall, the chapter provides a brief which is substantive enough to last the whole hour that a dedicated reader would commit to such an endeavour.

Retaining the highlighted comments about ethics or morals throughout this chapter, it is important to note other works that may provide help in understanding the ethical aspects of cyber security. The section titles in this chapter include:

- A Working Definition of Ethics
- Computer and Ethics in Cyber Security
- The Ethical Significance of Cyber Security
- The Undermining Ethical Issues in Cyber Security
- Cyber and Information Conflict
- Ethical View of the GDPR's Cyber Security
- Ethical Issues and Data Privacy
- Ethics and Research in Cybersecurity

Significantly enmeshed in the literature of ethics, data protection, computer ethics, and privacy, as well as GDPR, this chapter provides a real, hands-on understanding of cyber security and its ethical implications for both scholars and practitioners.

13.2. A Working Definition of Ethics

As we transition and adjust to the cyber age, the use of data and its associated evaluation relates to the ethics of data use. The moral ecology of application systems that engage with data occurs across innumerable situations within any given cyber-algorithmic context or condition.

Abel (2010) acknowledges the connection between cyber security, global migration, populace conduct, and change, which underscores Edwards and Veale's (2017) notion of ethical evaluation. These intertwined assessments illustrate approaches to moral views that relate to public sector engagement with machine learning, ambient intelligence (AmI), as well as variations in similar fields. Such connections underpin the ethical synergy of studying cyber security, which continues to gain traction globally.

Moreover, as deliberation and strategy continue, for example, in the United Kingdom (NCSS, 2016; see also Shafqat and Masood, 2016), the Netherlands (Kool, Timmer and Van Est, 2015), and France (CNIL, 2016), various positions on what constitutes "ethics" or "morals" of conduct emerge. Ethically, the simple thought of checking on "change" for instance, as a starting point, suggests above all else that something is "new." Secondly, it could indicate that similarities are still present, and might also suggest the reasons, both noteworthy and immaterial, why more change has not occurred. It is a challenge to depict the physical and causal needs underlying the process of change.

Bühlmann and Hovestadt (2013) encourage the activity of singling out an instance and asking which ICT or IoT venture has addressed its brief most fittingly. This approach includes quantitative estimations that evaluate significance through the minimum number of standardized examples. Meanwhile, Schwab (2017) depicts the scene as a challenge when managing social change, the estimation of the mass, and the peripheral connections with subjective judgments. It is an evaluation of contrasts that can prompt moralistic declarations, which on a fundamental level, could present an opportunity for a distinctive notion of ethics. It looks to embed and actualize a network of actions, either socially or politically, as ethics remain an issue (Arendt, 1958).

Ethics on this note characterize a term by Gieryn (1983), "boundary work." It originates from the Greek term *ethos*, as signifying "ongoing character and mien" in the plural, "behaviour," and alludes to a person's, community's, or organisation's exercises and lead. Conversely, the word "moral" originates from the Latin expression *moralis*, alluding to the best possible conduct of a person in a network or culture. Given the near and integrative vector of morals (which aims to extract from ethics and make them perfect), we discuss ethical issues in cybersecurity to address the level of society in which professionals engage with the subject of cybersecurity. We view this as constitutively pluralist and furthermore employ subjective methods for systematizing ethics as proposed in the literature (Benveniste, 1969; see also Lambert, 2001 and Lewallen, 2013).

There are numerous angles from which to consider the appropriate use of these two terms. One that appears to be critical to us is that, concerning cyber security, ethics or morals has less to do with something surely known. It might engage with the finding of a shared conviction or the insistence on not being entirely agreeable in professional circumstances. Such types of challenging requests we call "types of direct," which can be encoded and deciphered in different behavioural contexts. Thus, there is space for interpretation about types of direct. In that sense, sets of principles give "focal points" through which we can consider the formalized ideas adopted as standards and measures. At the point when codes of behaviours are established, they are ordinarily rendered in wording that then claims a global legitimacy in the form of benchmarks, rules, and so on.

Such procedures of speculation are, apparently, extraordinary because of the gauges that result from those standards. The refinements with which we work include the following: A measure can constitute a framework (as in IT guidelines), whereas a rule comes from a full structure, or from a projective, perfect frame. These refinements are critical because, in cyber security and additionally in ICT, we have systems that are insufficient when viewed as frameworks.

"Frameworks" is a term suggesting rationales (components and sayings), whereas "systems" is a term suggesting coordination (particles, hubs, and dispersions). This distinction has significant ramifications for how we reason, survey, and assess frameworks and systems. "Implicit rules," as we comprehend them, open up interrogative spaces in which to practice — either those that are endorsed normatively or those that are plainly obvious or "characteristic," as propensities, traditions, or customs. Sets of conventional rules are consequently held on to because of the inconvenience that stems from "cyber-coding" such conduct to fit open spaces, where one's custom is only one of the numerous conceivable ways to act. Haraway (2008) underscores that in spaces where coding or algorithms exist, an ethical view could be a propensity. Inherently, such a view could seem inconvenient when outlining an opening in order to understand an assertion. We should be cognizant, and give spaces a shape, keeping in mind the end goal.

Bühlmann and Hovestadt (2013) portray conventional rules as the state of probability for deciphering various practices without forcing a resolute pecking order. The paradigm moves crosswise over social laws because of the algorithmic conditions in cybersecurity that presently sort out life. In this manner, something beyond speed and frame-prescient apparatuses with which to quantify and study regulating methods of "quantitative institutionalization" is required. All things considered, Sharp *et al.* (2017) argue that it is not exclusively to represent moves in the association hypothesis, but in addition to having proper strategies, that emotionally supportive networks that draw in information must be consolidated into all choices. In this way, Harasim (2017) proposes an essential inquiry for morals in the working condition that discusses e-wellbeing, the populace, movement, security, correspondences, training, and research opt-in. It might be an analysis of how we create, utilize, and assess choice in emotionally supportive networks that draw in with information. The following inquiry might emerge: How can one turn the subject of cyber security into one with a reasonable response to ethics or morals?

13.3. Computers and Ethics in Cyber Security

Computers, cyberspace, and ethical analysis present a new infosphere when compared with any other utility. Considering the scope of this subject, "cyber" refers to computers and networks, focussing on the Internet, online, and web contexts as well as related technologies. Additionally, PCs, data morals, and different fields of connected ethics require ethical theories that soundly bring together deontological and consequentialist notions of ethics. Moor (1999) considers the hypothesis of just consequentialism as an underlying result of approaches inside the imperatives of equity, which makes just consequentialism a reasonable and hypothetically stable way to deal with the ethical aspect of cyber security. It is fundamentally a black box and could be unexplainable, especially when ethical issues reach a wrong conclusion. Considering ethical problems associated with computers and information ethics, ethical approaches are essential frameworks to justify the right outcome in general.

13.3.1. *Information governance and policy vacuum*

The flexibility of computers enables them to be utilized in novel and unexpected ways. The propulsion of computer innovation in the digital age leaves policy vacuums in its wake, and when necessary mechanisms do exist, they are regularly outdated and unable to be adapted. Fundamental objectives of cyber security include recognizing the need for appropriate governance and policy frameworks, illuminating related and reasonable perplexities, planning proper governance approaches, and standardizing appropriate ethics to justify applications.

Policies are standards ranging from formal laws to casual, verifiable rules for activity. Strategies suggest sorts of events that are at times dependent upon various circumstances. "Log out or switch off your system when you are done" is a command with less significant ethical value. "Try not to steal assets" is a phrase with clearer ethical substance. "Don't eavesdrop on conversations" could be a policy with less immediate ethical consequences. Notwithstanding, when systems are extensions of strategies, they can assist with regulations to make the use of computers good for society. We can better understand a situation and respond appropriately. For instance, if an eatery has the policy of using guest information to calculate the quantities of incoming telephone calls, we have the ability to decide whether we would prefer not to have our telephone number known by the eatery and can choose to protect our identity or go to another eatery. The central discourse focuses on governances and policies that have a moral effect and considers how to assess them legitimately.

Giving due diligence to ethical issues in cyberspace regarding policies is critical. Strategies have the appropriate level of complete statement to evaluate the profound quality of the lead. Each activity is an example of a policy. In this sort of circumstance, an action is either permitted or required or illegal. Understanding activities as models of ethical broadness could help to regularize remedies that might frequently advance obligation and promote careful reflection on codes of conduct. "Policy" expectedly proposes that there can be legitimized exclusions because strategies are not complete guidelines. We need our approach to processing to be ethical, yet what is advisable for us to consider while developing a moral framework for the deployment of cyber resources?

Reaching out to conventional ethical researchers for help, one could identify a solid contention that exists between the leading approaches. Consequentialist hypotheses underscore the outcomes of ethical activities, whereas deontological theories accentuate rights and obligations. Undoubtedly, consequentialist speculations and deontological predictions are regularly introduced as incongruent. Rationalists occasionally delight in the contentions among good hypotheses. The nonappearance of determination among the good hypotheses leaves numerous gaps. Connected ethicists, searching for a common-sense direction, wind up entrenched in specially appointed examinations of ethical issues and the choice of appropriate policies from a different heap of standards. One can observe that ethics would benefit from bringing together theories to espouse the right conclusion.

Sharp *et al.* (2017) underscore hypotheses that call upon the different qualities of conventional ways to deal with ethics on a regular basis. Let us remember the narrative of the elephant, in which every spectator who sees just a piece of the elephant renders a depiction of the animal that differs drastically from others' portrayals. Yet, there is a general portrayal of an elephant, which an individual can understand evidently. In other words, if we could look beyond current clashing representations of ethical theories and find the elephant which incorporates them all, it might help us to further understand the subject. It could be important enough to attempt to find, if conceivable, a general portrayal of the elephant that will help us to comprehend these inconsistent depictions. In contributing to such a path, we might make a couple of strides toward an ethical approach to understanding cyber security and the related deployment of assets.

13.3.2. *Cyber security in unknown waters*

Working on an ethical approach to cyber security may be compared to outlining all necessary plans for a cruise. A mariner may outline a course to her goal by precisely spreading out the course in a straight line on a graph. Yet, occasionally there are no diagrams, and, regardless of whether there are, experienced mariners know how difficult it is to stay the course. Winds, currents, and tides are always changing. Mariners may not consistently stay on course or trim their sails correctly. Midcourse alterations are vital, legitimate, and normal. Moreover, one cannot set policies for figuring without relying to a certain extent on estimation. It is not possible for someone to precisely foresee the numerous changing elements in figuring circumstances. Unforeseen advancements will emerge if one is flexible enough to take advantage of every opportunity to move forward. Human responses to these new potential outcomes are similarly difficult to anticipate. Midcourse changes in figuring strategy are fundamental, legitimate, and ordinary. Mariners take risk direction to maintain a strategic distance from risky areas such as reefs. Certain courses should not be taken, while there are numerous different courses that are great choices, and sensible mariners may differ about which is ideal. Some may want to travel the shortest path, whereas others might want to pass by a beautiful island. Correspondingly, in registering strategy, there are approaches that must be avoided. We do not want our strategies to damage crucial human rights. In any case, given that our strategies are simple, numerous great alternatives are accessible. However, individuals may disagree about what is ideal in the real world.

13.4. The Ethical Significance of Cyber Security

Notwithstanding the different meanings associated with the term "professional," specific, general, technical, and social standards are centrally associated with an acceptable definition. Cyber security as a field of computer science is highly concerned with the application of security to computer frameworks to protect against unapproved divulgence, control, or destruction of data, as well as against denial of service or refusal of systems administration. As a result, information system security is coming to fruition.

System security is the insurance of the equipment and programming of a computer framework against vindictive projects that harm framework assets. Information security is the insurance of information on memories in computer frameworks or transmitted between networks. Cyber security professionals contribute significantly to both technical and social standards of the profession to protect valuable information and related assets as well as to facilitate the insurance of significant data and systems resources. There is a strong indication, which agrees with Brey's (2007) view, that there is a need for clarification between the protection of information and the protection of associated system-assets. In other words, system security and information security comprise cyber security.

Cyber security characterizes concerns about the insurance of three aspects of information: privacy, respectability, and accessibility. The challenge of preserving the confidentiality, integrity, and availability of information is affected by how ethical issues are thought about in the field of cyber security. As clarified before, ethics for the most part focusses on rights, damages, and interests. An answer to this inquiry can be found by investigating the connection between cyber security, rights, damages, and premiums. What ethically vital advantages would cyber security be able to yield? What might be the cost of unethical practices? What reputational damages does the infringement of ethical conduct bring to a profession or organisation?

Would cyber security be able to likewise hurt or abuse rights as opposed to ensuring that they are taken into account? The first and perhaps most evident of the damages that can result from breaks in information system security is monetary. At the point when framework security is undermined, critical equipment and programming might be harmed or debased, and administration may end up inaccessible, causing loss of time, cash, and assets. Ruptures of data security may come at a considerably higher monetary cost. Relevant information, which might be worth significantly more than the equipment on which it is stored, might be lost or degraded, and this may cause severe financial misfortunes. Stored information may likewise have individual or social value rather than economic value and can be lost when intelligence is undermined.

Any loss of framework or information security likely also causes some measure of mental or emotional strife. Breaches of security may even result in irreparable damages or demise. Such damage may occur in wellbeing frameworks, which are IT frameworks with segmented or continuous control that can have an immediately hazardous effect, such as atomic reactor control, airship and airport regulation, rocket frameworks, and medicinal treatment frameworks. The debasement of certain structures may likewise have hazardous results in a more roundabout manner. These may incorporate frameworks that are utilized for configuration, observation, fundamental decision making, or leadership. Bargains regarding the secrecy of data may cause extra damages and rights infringement.

There are obvious implications in this regard. Outsiders may bargain with the classification of data by accessing, duplicating, and spreading it. Such activities may, as a matter of first importance, abuse property rights, as Halbert (2006) emphasizes. Property rights include licensed innovation rights, which are rights to claim and use scholarly works. The information may be exclusively guaranteed by some individual who determines who can access and use the data, which can be mishandled. Also, deals of mystery may harm security rights. This can happen when information attained to fuse evidence about individuals is private. Despite the encroachment of property and assurance rights, breaks of mystery may cause additional harm because of the spread and usage of private information. For instance, dispersal of internal updates can substantially damage the reputation of online charge card trades, which ultimately undermines trust in the security of online financial trades and harms e-keeping cash as well as electronic business activity.

Arrangements for the transparency of data can negatively affect the availability of resources and hurt open door rights, particularly rights to the versatility of data and free speech. It remains advantageous to make information available to legitimate users so they can access and utilize open data. Denial of access to information and resources negatively impacts the moral rights of users in the digital age, since the possibility of interception, interruption, manipulation, and fabrication of information is increasing.

In closing down essential data associations, we might overlook the various advantages of these associations to organisations and their uses of data. Moreover, system structures have wound up being indispensable as a medium for a free conversation. Email accounts and websites are generally used to spread messages and chat with others. When access to such services is hindered, for example, through organisation-wide strikes or hijackings of goals, the right to a free conversation is infringed on. Information system prosperity attempts frequently avoid damage and secure rights, although they can also do the opposite. Broadly, attempts at prosperity might be so defensive of data and framework assets that they may prevent certain types of people from accessing data or utilizing services. Among several authors, May (2005) argues in favor of fragmented consumption in the global music industry. Attempts at prosperity may additionally be one-sided: they may wrongly keep classes of clients from utilizing a framework or may unfairly benefit certain types of clients over others. Overall, ethical contemplation should not discourage advancement, improvement, or utilization of innovation, but should encourage one to think about the potential outcomes in the event of cyber security lapses.

13.5. The Undermining of Ethical Issues in Cyber Security

As more innovations converge, individuals discuss the stresses of the digital age in terms of information security, digital wellbeing records, cyber bullying, and so on. The questionable movements of innovation and globalization emphasize essential matters that incorporate morals in cyber security. In this section, the focus will center around changes that could undermine cyber security, such as hacking, computer wrongdoing, cyber terrorism, and digital war. The accentuation on practices will include specific concentration on ethical issues.

13.5.1. *Hacking and computer wrongdoing*

In any organisation or association, ethics assumes a part and ought to be of concern with regards to cyber security. While a few sectors, for example, defence, have their own procedures to vet certifications, for an industry as various and as productive as ICT, it helps if experts can adhere to a specific code of ethics. Institutional safeguards support numerous specialist associations to hold their individuals to a gauge that guarantees the respectability of the profession. The British Computer Society (BCS), for instance, has a code of conduct all experts must keep, notwithstanding different prerequisites, for continuous professional development, training, and self-awareness in their field. Specialist groups also accentuate what makes an ethical practice in IT.

Eminently, a substantial piece of cyber security is concerned with the insurance of computer assets and information against interception, interruption, modification, and fabrication. Such activities are frequently called hacking. Hacking, as defined in this section, is the utilization of computer aptitudes to increase unapproved access to information and computer assets. Hackers are exceptionally gifted computer clients that use their abilities to expand such access and regularly frame networks or systems with different programmer groups to share learning and information. Hacking is periodically recognized more adversely as the harnessing of unapproved access for malignant purposes: to take data and programming or to degenerate information or upset framework activities. Self-distinguished hackers, in any case, distinguish between non-malignant break-ins, which they call hacking, and malevolent break-ins, or cracking. Self-recognized programmers frequently legitimize their hacking exercises by insisting that they cause no harm and instead have a positive effect. The positive impact of hacking, they contend, is that it liberates information to the advantage of all and enhances frameworks and programming by uncovering security loopholes. These contemplations are a piece of what policies detail as the hacker ethic or programmer code of ethics, which is an arrangement of specific rules that guide the movement of numerous programmers. Such standards assert that data ought to be free, entrance to systems ought to be boundless, and exercises in the Internet do not cause harm.

It has been argued (Tavani, 2003; see also Spinello, 2010 and Quinn, 2014) that various standards of the hacker ethic lack credence for sustainability. The conviction that data ought to be free runs counter to the pure thought of intellectual property or licensed innovation, for instance, and suggests that the originator of data or designer of systems would have no privileges. It would also fundamentally undermine protection and the integrity of data, as data could be altered and changed freely by any individual who might access it. People can also deny having anything to do with a derailed outcome. Moreover, the good that hacking does in finding security shortcomings may not exceed the trouble it causes.

Some authors, like Yar (2013), have contended that both hacking and cracking have a tendency to be unlawful and may be considered a type of computer wrongdoing or cyber crime (see also McQuade, 2006, and Yar 2005). However, Tavani (2003) suggests two noteworthy kinds of cyber crime that harm computer security: cyber trespassing, which is the utilization of data innovation to increase unapproved access to computer frameworks or secret key ensured sites; and cyber vandalism, which is the utilization of data innovation to release programs that upset the activities of resources or degenerate information. There is also a third sort of cyber crime that occasionally incorporates breaks of security: cyber piracy. Cyber piracy, likewise, called digital theft, is the utilization of data innovation to duplicate exclusive programming or data or to disperse such information over a network.

Digital theft is altogether more common than digital vandalism or digital trespassing because it doesn't require high aptitude, and various computer users find it morally tolerable to make copies of copyrighted software and data. Digital robbery incorporates breaks in security when it consolidates parts of copyright protections. Another sort of digital wrongdoing that combines breaches of security is deception, which includes false online identities or the adjustment of data. Computer blackmail may involve significant digital trespassing to gain passwords, automated identities, or other trade and access codes, as well as exhibitions of digital vandalism. Distinctive sorts of digital wrongdoing, for instance, child pornography or web-based harassment (cyber bullying), generally do include bursts of cyber security.

13.6. Cyber and Information Conflict

The progressive stress in cyber and national security has increased the probability of cyber terrorism, which Tavani (2003) and Quinn (2014) describe as the execution of politically impelled hacking undertakings to cause grave damages. The probability of specific attacks on information, such as debilitating systems and harming money-related or social structures, is expanding. It has been argued (Tavani, 2003; see also Whiteman *et al.*, 2006 and Quinn, 2014), that since 9/11, cyber terrorism and information conflict have become increasingly heightened.

The cyberattacks on, for example, Talk Talk, Morrisons, RBS/NatWest/Ulster Bank and Zurich Insurance Plc, depict the general results of cyber terrorism and information warfare. It is an ongoing critical concern both outside and inside affected organisations or nations. A dispute exists on the ideal degree of cyber terrorism. Where should the lines be drawn between cyber terrorism, cyber crime, and cyber vandalism? Should a youthful action that accidentally spreads a virus harming government computers be treated the same way as a cyber terrorist attack? A refinement of cyber terrorism and diverse sorts of cyber attacks may be found in a nation's politics. It's an indication that cyber terrorism contains politically impelled errands that mean to cause hurt on a global scale.

The conflicts are the direct result of human actions on cyber and information systems. Some commentators, for example, Auty (2004), have argued that not all politically enlivened cyber attacks should be called cyber terrorism. The possibility arises that some cyber analysts perceive a difference between cyber terrorism and hacktivism. The latter encompasses hacking undertakings against a website or server with the desire to aggravate regular exercises without the aim of causing bona fide harm. Denning (2001) argues that the hackers could be politically energized software engineers who participate in a kind of electronic political activism that should be perceived differently from fear-based abuse.

Mainon and Goodrum (2000) and Stallman (2010) emphasize that cyber and information battling is an enlargement of customary battling in which fighters conceptualize information and strikes on knowledge and information systems as weapons for battling. Information battling may involve the use of information media to spread reputation-damaging information, to interfere with correspondence and to hack into information systems that control primary establishment data systems, such as the WannaCry attack on NHS UK that started on 12 May 2017 and spread worldwide within hours.

The lawful outcomes of cyber security breaches indicate that morals have not been sufficiently contemplated in political circles. Both national and organisational administrations should see that there is a need for the development of institutional arrangements to advance ethical practices. It is commendable that there are several UK parliamentary activities in connection to IT and information security ethics, particularly the new movement to set up a cross-party Parliamentary Commission on Technology Ethics, as well as the provisions from the GDPR.

13.7. Ethical View of the GDPR's Cyber Security

The context of ethics and the guidelines for achieving some compelling outcomes in cyber security center on how best to create an ethical environment within the industry. The GDPR emphasizes security to provide a moral context in which institutions can operate. In compliance with GDPR, it is incumbent on system designers to be information- and security-centric. In developing a security assessment synergy for GDPR, the framework of investigation must define critical areas for performing useful security outcomes. An effective organisational self-audit encourages the use of models to identify security issues regarding risks and vulnerabilities. Gap analysis, when used over time to identify holes in systems, can help recognize dangers, problems and weaknesses that should have been logged for a verifiable trace, and suggestions for remediation.

Organisations are aspiring to comply with the GDPR, especially by considering new technologies like tokenization or encryption to ensure that existing systems would meet the expectations set out in the GDPR. The fulfillment of a gap analysis will help kickstart activity that will lead to the remediation of vulnerabilities in an acceptable moral setting. The advocacy for a security culture of defence remains a principle that helps in fulfilling maximum-security assurance irrespective of institutional complexity and the volume of operations. The GDPR expectations are fit for a working ethical climate, considering the security dimension of the complaint process.

13.7.1. *Record keeping*

Article 30 can cause worry for businesses and information assurance practitioners, yet do they know or comprehend what safety efforts have been set up? What remediation has been embraced to enhance security stature? What ongoing procedures have been set up to screen holes and dangers later? These questions must be addressed and recorded by businesses. It's reasonable to have an in-house security expert to achieve expectations in cases of blockchain technology. However, institutions should consider how technology can securely bolster operations.

13.7.2. *The "security of processing"*

The security procedure is expressed in Article 32 of the GDPR, tagged as "Security of processing." The article is short and simple; however, it contains some key information. The most applicable is "the controller and the processor shall implement appropriate technical and organisational measures to ensure a level of security appropriate to the risk" (Article 32 of the GDPR). This excerpt emphasizes working ethical culture. There is a similar reference in Article 5 to the "use of appropriate technical or organisational measures," which calls for the articulation of appropriate measures. The consequentialist and deontological approach to ethics do not in any way provide any differences to the appropriateness of a standard. In other words, creators of frameworks must comprehend the prerequisites that satisfy appropriate usage of specialized measures to guarantee security suitable for their products.

It is likewise indispensable to comprehend that the necessities mentioned in Articles 5 and 32 apply to the controllers and processors of individual information. Paragraph 1 of 5 contains four prerequisites that are controlled by propriety:

(i) The pseudonymization and encryption of individual information: If an association is handling vast volumes of personal information or sensitive classifications, this is a significant advantage. Data-in-motion has for some time been ignored, though it has been acknowledged as standard over email or for file exchanges. There now appears, all in all, to be a reasonable desire for associations to still scramble information. Execution and cost turn into an unmistakable test here, and hence incomplete depersonalization or pseudonymization becomes an integral factor. It empowers organisations to scramble highly hazardous information while minimizing costs.

(ii) The capacity to guarantee the progress of confidentiality, uprightness, accessibility, and versatility in preparing frameworks and administrations.

(iii) The ability to re-establish the openness and access to individual information conveniently in case of a physical or specialized context.

(iv) A procedure for routinely testing, surveying, and assessing the adequacy of functional and hierarchical measures for guaranteeing the security of every mode of data status within handling.

A review of the last three necessities has been kept together as they are related. What are the helpful tips one should follow when navigating an unfortunate situation? Is organisational information, along with the arrangements made to secure it, expected to change when the data is frequently in use? Is it possible to reuse data conveniently? Is there a danger of information misfortune? Catastrophe recuperation arrangements, like information replication and go down advances, are essential to organisations. Business must put in place an effective disaster recovery plan; the cost might be an issue, but the cost of noncompliance will always be enormous. These are essential inquiries to evaluate what institutions need to do and consider how working environments can be ethically contextualized for cyber security to protect the interests of stakeholders.

13.7.3. *Data ruptures*

The provision in Article 33 outlines the necessity for a data controller to instruct the supervisor regarding an individual data break. The emphasis is on what technique an organisation will use to distinguish or investigate personal data breaches. Do institutions have the essential technical and organisational mechanisms to react or proactively intervene in the case of any data ruptures? An apparent necessity for threat modelers is to identify vulnerabilities in the pre-implementation stage and prioritize hazard-recognizable proof, threat expectation, and inspection instruments. In the case of the apparent absence of required capacities, then existing staff must be trained, or assistants must be found. Extraordinary encryption and critical organisation offer layers of defense. If an individual data breach happens, yet the data have been scrambled, it isn't reportable to the supervisory authority, and a significant breach might be impending.

13.7.4. *Data protection impact assessment*

The arrangement in Article 35 defines the necessity for data protection impact assessments (DPIAs). Associations ought to have a comparable procedure set up. The former name for the process under Data Protection is the Privacy Impact Assessment. This assessment ought to be incorporated into the venture life-cycle to evaluate risk and catch any breaches. The key things to distinguish inside a DPIA are as follows:

(i) The kinds of information being prepared and if any are of touchy classifications.
(ii) The volume of information being handled, regardless of whether innovations are being utilized.
(iii) Is there any profiling or mechanized handling?

13.7.5. *Staff mindfulness program*

Article 39 outlines the necessities for a Data Protection Officer, who must guarantee that the staff are prepared on the subjects of information insurance, security, and security of information. It is the responsibility of the security unit to teach staff, provide them with an understanding of digital dangers, exemplify best practices for ensuring and anchoring information, and so on. It is not generally considered, but workers present one of the most significant risks to their associations if they are uneducated about these issues.

The security and information insurance experts must enforce the GDPR and Privacy and Electronic Communications Regulations. Of genuine concern is the developing risk of diversion methods like the influence of an email, for example, which may appear to be certifiable. There are a lot of arrangements and apparatuses that can include a layer of safety against the pernicious web. Even so, staff should additionally be prepared and given direction on the most proficient method to manage these kinds of dangers. Organisations could have the best and most recent advances; however, if staff are not savvy, then security openings and information ruptures can occur.

The GDPR provides an excellent pathway for one to deal with the comprehension of cyber security and reliable measures to satisfy security. It marks pivotal progress for institutions. The GDPR can't be executed by a specialty unit for ethical reasons, thus a joint effort from cross-specialty groups is necessary to manage issues without endangering competition in business.

13.8. Ethical Issues and Data Privacy

We now consider matters of cybersecurity, privacy, and ethics in this digital age. The administration of information as well as techniques to arrive at an ethical decision entails a myriad of possibilities. The moral view of what privacy is and its significance to the field of cyber security calls for attention. Moreover, the age of the GDPR and how it has come to us create a unique space for the subject of data privacy to be discussed in the enterprise of security. In the real world, ethics and cyber security collide frequently, and the ethics of learning cyber security cannot be overaccentuated.

13.8.1. *Privacy and its significance*

In western civilization, there exists widespread acknowledgment of the privilege to individual protection and the preservation of the right to be let alone. Privacy is hard to define, and numerous precise definitions have been presented. Frequently, the privilege of protection is distinguished by the right of people to control, access, or obstruct others from their private issues. Among a few definitions is that of Schoeman (1984, p.3), which underscores the ability that a person has to appreciate security in the sense that others have restricted access to data about them. It is a type of restricted access to the affections of their life or constrained access to their contemplations or their body. It is a definition, according to some commentators, for instance, Brey (2005), that asserts that the idea of security does not just apply to the preparing of individual data, but likewise refers to the perception of and obstruction of human practices and relations, the human body, and one's home and personal assets. In other words, Voukko (2007) and König and Schallaboeck (2012) posit that privacy is held to be significant for numerous reasons to collaborate with Brey's view.

Privacy often is esteemed as vital; it is thought to shield people from a wide range of outer dangers, for example, slander, mocking, badgering, control, shakedown, burglary, subordination, and prohibition. It presents protection as a verbalization of the central estimation of security, intended to shield individuals from a wide range of damage done by others. It has likewise been contended that protection is a vital condition for self-sufficiency. Without security, individuals cannot explore everyday life and build up their own identity since they would always be subject to the verdict of others. The privilege to security has additionally been asserted to ensure different rights, for example, the right to sexual articulation. Besides, protection has been guaranteed to have social incentive notwithstanding individual esteem. It has, for example, been asserted as fundamental for sustaining democracy because it looks after popular government.

The benefit to privacy should, however, be balanced against various rights and interests, for instance, the upkeep of open demand and national security. Security rights may similarly vacillate in different settings. There is, for example, a lesser want for privacy in the workplace or the overall public domain than there is at home. An essential standard used as a piece of security protection in Western nations is that of consent. It is customarily held that users should be actively told how organisations plan to store, use, or exchange their data and that users should be asked for their approval. People would then have the capacity to knowingly surrender their privacy to benefit their choices.

13.8.2. *Threats to privacy*

The continuing impact of Ubiquitous Computing (UC) and AI is a threat to ethical practices and confidentiality in cyber security. Both methods are pervasive. UC is an approach in data innovation that expects to move computer systems from a single workstation and install microchips into ordinary working and living conditions in an undetectable and inconspicuous way. AI is a propelled type of pervasive processing that joins remote correspondence and Intelligent

User Interfaces, which are interfaces that use sensors and intelligent algorithms for profiling and recording, in order that the interface can adjust to client standards and adapt to various circumstances.

What is indeed happening to information in the cloud? Could IoT, AI, and the like yield more challenges to security? In AI situations, individuals may have many smart, networked PCs that know about their identity and needs and perform activities or provide data given their apparent needs. It has been argued (Langheinrich, 2001; see also Palen and Dourish, 2003) that UC has unique exclusive properties that possibly undermine privacy. These properties associated with UC are invisibility, memory amplification, sensing, and ubiquity. For instance, the persistent chronicle of individuals' activities to make available logs of their past by accessing cookies or bookmarking.

With expert perception, one can add to the list to conclude that AI furthers the facilitation of similar properties. It extends the rundown of dangers associated with UC. What if the user profiling and the connectedness combine with the remote correspondence between smart items in smart cities? This question highlights the two advances and makes the protection of privacy a noteworthy test. As commentators have contended, UC and AI can make an interlaced society in which each human movement is recorded, and brilliant gadgets test individuals' activities, aims, and musings. The distinction between the private and general social circle might diminish as many smart gadgets record personal information and interface with corporate or government IT infrastructures somewhere else. Real protection shields will be expected to prevent such situations. Hopefully, GDPR compliance will be pervasive and the ethics of learning cyber security advocated.

13.9. Ethics and Research in Cybersecurity

Researching cyber security has raised moral worries for nearly as long as the subject has existed. In addition to finding solutions to ethical challenges in IT, scholars with cyber security knowledge frequently work with professional bodies to develop and implement ways of addressing ethical concerns, such as codes of ethics or practitioners' responsibilities. Research in cyber security ethics is open to a comprehensive view of perception and interpretation. The concept of making IT good for society according to the BCS, for example, raises an unobstructed view of what is "good" or "right" within the scholar-practitioner agenda. The heavy reliance on practical, ethical governance, and policy, further the support for an ethical approach to both learning and researching in the field of cyber security.

Let us concentrate mostly on what researchers should consider sufficient guidance in researching in both the ethical and moral context. The legitimate condition restrains cyber security academia to investigating the preclusion and vulnerabilities that make investigations, information gathering and the sharing of data endeavors too exorbitant to assess. Protection laws have additionally spurred robust social desire that system suppliers keep the information they have collected private. Although these desires regularly don't coordinate, they may give a reason for companies to maintain strategic distance from the cost, laws, and reputational danger that comes with allowing researchers to access network data. Improving these laws is up to privacy advocates, regulators, and law implementation institutions.

Research possesses a focal point in cyber security governance and policy. It might provide approaches to diminish and relieve the actual dangers to computers and automated systems, which end-clients have come to depend upon so intensely. Financing this research has been a real challenge for both the funders and the researchers. As arranged data frameworks wind up unavoidable, this inquiry is fundamental.

Be that as it may, a list of legal and moral vulnerabilities hangs over cyber security research. For instance, in the United Kingdom, an assortment of government and devolved parliamentary statutes either disallow exercises that would give cyber security scientists information about good frameworks and genuine assailants or feel qualms about such research exercises, causing researchers to adjust their projects or conduct them with the potential of unlawfulness.

Cyber security scientists and authorities inside the companies that engage them may likewise speculate that specific things are illicit when, indeed, they are not; but regardless, researchers, in any case, should stay away from unethical modes of doing research. Then again, if a specific course of study is lawful but ethically dubious, researchers may carry out research in that area anyway without respect to moral considerations. Moral inquiries sneak past these legitimate issues and merit researchers' consideration.

In other words, responsible research and innovation are interlaced in doing research. The subsidiary of capable study and advancement underscores the procedure that intends to guarantee that the results and methods of analysis are socially attractive, satisfactory, and maintainable. They are features essential to academic inquiries, for example, what are the benefits of the exploration, what are its dangers, what are the options, and who oversees the results of the examination? Researchers should consider those who must live with the outcomes. Scholars and practitioners must express their long-haul point of view and think on what will happen to their results outside of their labs. It is an approach that helps researchers to get better yields and limit the reactions to their results by envisioning their impact, reflecting on the reasons for the exploration, and connecting with the partners to influence the bearing of their research.

Nonetheless, researchers must frequently take the lead to change endeavors through the execution of seminars, workshops, insightful gatherings, and publications, meeting with policymakers, or educating the broader community on how research exemption influences them. The law can help to provide a sense of the interests relevant to cyber security and how privacy should intentionally guarantee security. Undoubtedly, such a legal approach will help cyber security researchers make decisions about their activities, considering broader ethical considerations. These contemplations ought to incorporate not just the clients whose exercises might be reflected in network information, but, additionally, the reputation of the researcher's institution and the interests of analysts who have provided or might want to supply information. More work is expected to build up the applicable ethical and moral structure.

13.10. Concluding Remark

Having thought about the different ethical issues in the area of cyber security, we can conclude without a doubt that moral and social aspects of cyber security are so evident and pressing that there is an urgent need for scholars and practitioners to address them. Scholars' and practitioners' advocacy for effective governance, policy in addressing the threats and vulnerabilities in security administration, as well as security experts' engagement in the field of cyber security, should be a priority. Scholars and practitioners must advocate for a comprehensive approach to security as well as accept responsibility to ensure that the frameworks they develop benefit society in an ethical manner.

Suggested Reading

Gupta, B., Agrawal, D.P. and Yamaguchi, S. (eds.). (2016). *Handbook of Research on Modern Cryptographic Solutions for Computer and Cyber Security*. IGI Global.

Jirotka, M., Grimpe, B., Stahl, B. C., Hartswood, M. and Eden, G. (2017). Responsible Research and Innovation in the Digital Age. *Communications of the ACM*, **60**(5), pp. 62–68.

Kallberg, J. and Thuraisingham, B. (2012). Towards Cyber Operations-The New Role of Academic Cyber Security Research and Education. In *Proceedings of the 2012 IEEE International Conference on Intelligence and Security Informatics (ISI), Arlington, VA, USA, June 11–14*, pp. 132–134.

Owen, R., and Goldberg, N. (2010). Responsible Innovation: A Pilot Study with the U.K. Engineering and Physical Sciences Research Council. *Risk Analysis*, **30**(11), pp. 1699–1707.

Pieters, W. and Becker, M. J. (2008). Ethics of E-Voting: An Essay on Requirements and Values in Internet Elections. In Mishra, S. S. (ed.), *E-Democracy: Concepts and Practices*. ICFAI University Press.

Shaw, I. F. (2003). Ethics in Qualitative Research and Evaluation. *Journal of Social Work*, **3**(1), pp. 9–29.

Stahl, B. C., Obach, M., Yaghmaei, E., Ikonen, V., Chatfield, K. and Brem, A. (2017). The Responsible Research and Innovation (RRI) Maturity Model: Linking Theory and Practice. *Sustainability*, **9**(6), p. 1036.

Stilgoe, J., Owen, R., and Macnaghten, P. (2013). Developing a Framework for Responsible Innovation. *Research Policy*, **42**(9), pp. 1568–1580.

References

1. Abel, G. J. (2010). Estimation of International Migration Flow Tables in Europe. *Journal of the Royal Statistical Society: Series A (Statistics in Society)*, **173**(4), pp. 797–825.
2. Arendt, H. (1958). *The Human Condition*. Chicago, IL, USA: University of Chicago Press.
3. Auty, C. (2004). Political Hacktivism: Tool of the Underdog or Scourge of Cyberspace? In *ASLIB Proceedings*, **56**(4), pp. 212–221.
4. Benveniste, É. (1969). *Le Vocabulaire des Institutions Indo-Européennes*. Collection 'Le Sens Commun'. Paris, France: Les Éditions de Minuit.
5. Brey, P. A. E. (2005). The Importance of Privacy in the Workplace. In Hansson, S. O. and Palm, E. (eds.). *Privacy in the Workplace*. Brussels, Belgium: Peter Lang.
6. Brey, P. A. E. (2007). Ethical Aspects of Information Security and Privacy. In Petkovic, M. and Jonker, W. (eds.), *Security, Privacy, and Trust in Modern Data Management*. Heidelberg: Springer.
7. Bühlmann, V. and Hovestadt, L. (2013). Introduction: Printed Physics. In: Bühlmann, V. and Hovestadt, L. (eds.), *Printed Physics: Metalithikum 1*. Vienna: Ambra.
8. Denning, D. E. (2001). Activism, Hacktivism, and Cyberterrorism: The Internet as a Tool for Influencing Foreign Policy. In Arquilla, J. and Ronfeldt, D. (eds.) *Networks and Netwars: The Future of Terror, Crime, and Militancy*. Santa Monica, CA, USA: RAND Corporation.
9. Edwards, L. and Veale, M. (2017). Slave to the Algorithm? Why a "Right to an Explanation" is Probably Not the Remedy You Are Looking For. *Duke Law and Technology Review*, **16**(1), pp. 18–84.
10. Gieryn, T. F. (1983). Boundary-Work and the Demarcation of Science from Non-Science: Strains and Interests in Professional Ideologies of Scientists. *American Sociological Review*, **48**(6), pp.781–795.
11. Halbert, D. J. (2006). Resisting Intellectual Property. New York, NY, USA: Routledge.
12. Haraway, D. J. (2008). *When Species Meet*. Minneapolis, MN, USA: University of Minnesota Press.
13. Harasim, L. (2012). *Learning Theory and Online Technologies*. New York, NY, USA: Routledge.
14. König, U. and Schallaboeck, J. (2012). *Privacy Preferences for E-Mail Messages* [Online]. Available at: http://tools.ietf.org/html/draft-koenig-privicons-02. (Accessed: September 2019).

15. Kool, L., Timmer, J. and Van Est, R. (2015). *De Datagedreven Samenleving: Achtergrondstudie.* Den Haag: Rathenau Instituut.
16. Lambert, G. (2001). *Report to the Academy: Re the New Conflict of the Faculties.* Aurora, CO, USA: The Davies Group.
17. Langheinrich, M. (2001). Privacy by Design — Principles of Privacy-Aware Ubiquitous Systems. In *Proceedings of the 2001 International Conference on Ubiquitous Computing, Atlanta, GA, USA, September 30–October 2,* pp. 273–291.
18. Lewallen, M. (2013). Cloud Computing: Lawyer's Ethical Duty to Act with Reasonable Care When Storing Client Confidences in the Cloud. *Cleveland State Law Review,* **60**(4), pp.1133–1166.
19. Mainon, D. and Goodrum, A. (2000). Terrorism or Civil Disobedience: Toward a Hacktivist Ethic. *Computers and Society,* **30**(2), pp. 14–19
20. May, C. (2005). Concentrated Industry, Fragmented Consumption: The Global Music Industry in the New Millennium. In Franklin, M. I. (ed.), *Resounding International Relations: On Music, Culture and Politics.* New York, NY, USA: Palgrave Macmillan.
21. McQuade, S. C. (2006). *Understanding and Managing Cybercrime.* Boston, MA, USA: Pearson/Allyn and Bacon.
22. Moor, J. H. (1999). Just Consequentialism and Computing. *Ethics and Information Technology,* **1**(1), pp. 61–65.
23. Palen, L. and Dourish, P. (2003). Unpacking Privacy for a Networked World. In *Proceedings of the 2003 SIGCHI Conference on Human Factors in Computing Systems, Fort Lauderdale, FL, USA, April 5–10,* pp. 129–136.
24. Quinn, M. J. (2014). *Ethics for the Information Age.* Boston, MA, USA: Pearson.
25. Schoeman, F. D. (ed.) (1984). *Philosophical Dimensions of Privacy: An Anthology.* Cambridge, UK: Cambridge University Press.
26. Schwab, K. (2017). *The Fourth Industrial Revolution.* New York, NY, USA: Crown Business.
27. Shafqat, N. and Masood, A. (2016). Comparative Analysis of Various National Cyber Security Strategies. *International Journal of Computer Science and Information Security,* **14**(1), p. 129.
28. Sharp, B., Aguirre, G. and Kickham, K. (2017). *Managing in the Public Sector: A Casebook in Ethics and Leadership.* Abingdon, UK: Taylor and Francis.
29. Spinello, R. (2010). *Cyberethics: Morality and Law in Cyberspace.* Burlington, MA, USA: Jones and Bartlett Learning.
30. Stallman, R. (2010). *The Anonymous WikiLeaks Protests are a Mass Demo Against Control* [Online]. Available at: https://www.theguardian.com/

commentisfree/2010/dec/17/anonymous-wikileaks-protest-amazon-mastercard. (Accessed: September 2019).

31. Tavani, H. T. (2003). *Ethics* and *Technology: Ethical Issues in an Age of Information and Communication Technology*. Hoboken, NJ, USA: John Wiley and Sons.
32. Tavani, H. T. (2003), Ethics and Technology: Ethical Issues in an Age of Information and Communication Technology (John Wiley & Sons, 2004). *ACM SIGCAS Computers and Society*, **33**(3), p. 1.
33. Voukko, R. (2007). Interdependence and Control at Work: Social Issues in Transforming Care Work With Mobile Technology. In *Proceedings of ETHICOMP 2007, Tokyo, Japan, March 27–29*, pp. 621–632.
34. Whiteman, D. C., Clutton, C. and Hill, D. (2006). Australian Public's Views on Privacy and Health Research. *British Medical Journal*, **332**(7552), p. 1274.
35. Yar, M. (2005). The Novelty of 'Cybercrime' An Assessment in Light of Routine Activity Theory. *European Journal of Criminology*, **2**(4), pp. 407–427.
36. Yar, M. (2013). *Cybercrime and Society*. Thousand Oaks, CA, USA: Sage.

Chapter 14

An Analysis of Data Mining Metrics to Identify and Evaluate Potential Radicalisation Utilising Social Media

Nishan Chelvachandran and Hamid Jahankhani*

Northumbria University London, UK
**Hamid.jahankhani@northumbria.ac.uk*

ABSTRACT

The prevalence, and increased use and access, of social media platforms, have cemented their function in society as an interactive communications ecosystem, generating large quantities of data about users and their interactions on and between platforms.

Social media has evolved from its initial networking premise to the digital communications platform seen today. This evolution has occured through a synergic relationship with technology and its availability and development; both of which influence the other, leading to social media becoming an integral flagstone of social communication today.

The aim of this research paper is to analyse data mined from open source social media, in this instance to ascertain if a targeted behaviour can be identified from specific keyword usage. However, the keywords are those most frequently used in two datasets, consisting of data mined from Twitter, and religious quotes from extremist publications, where both the datasets themselves and the keyword metrics gained are discussed.

The results of the analyses show that it is difficult to attribute behavioural trends through specific keyword usage. Comparatively, the metrics from the extremist publications show language relating to religious ideology, whereas the Twitter data was more closely aligned with current and trending events. It was also shown that context has an important role in identification, and that an in-depth keywords-in-context approach to analysing the keyword metrics would be an interesting project for further research.

Keywords: social media, radicalisation, psychological traits, linguistic theory, data mining, Borum's four-stage model, law enforcement Moghaddam's model, dataset

14.1. Introduction

The prevalence, and increased use and access, of social media platforms have cemented their function in society as an interactive communications ecosystem, generating large quantities of data about users and their interactions on and between platforms.

Social media has evolved from its initial networking premise to the digital communications platform seen today. This evolution has occurred through a synergic relationship with technology and its availability and development, both of which influence the other, leading to social media becoming an integral flagstone of social communication today.

The use of social media as an interactive information-sharing platform, to some, is an alternative to "mainstream media", which can be seen to be censored or biased, whereas news on social media is unfiltered and more reflective of what is happening in the world. However, paradoxically, some users also feel that the lack of rules and viral algorithms are encouraging low quality and "fake news" (Newman, 2017).

The accessibility and availability of social media has also created a direct link to many users, who utilise the platforms to obtain news and information about the world around them (The Independent, 2015). This unfiltered direct feed to individuals has enabled extremists to propagate views and radicalise individuals, an occurrence that was previously more acute and less extensive before social media (Mughal OBE, 2016).

Facebook sees on average 1.37 billion active daily users and 2.07 billion active monthly users (Facebook, 2017). Many of these users will also use other social networking platforms and interlink accounts and posts, creating online personas and affiliations across varying niches of the social media ecosystem.

These platforms also provide a cursory method to network or build a network, communications within can be moved onto other platforms seen to be more private, such as ephemeral messaging applications (Torok, 2016).

14.2. Literature Review

The quantity of data generated and stored daily by Facebook alone is approximately 600TB (Facebook, 2017). The logistics, computing power and resources required to evaluate and monitor each data byte are considerable, and in any case the endeavour would be time prohibitive. However, if data mining techniques were used to analyse the Big Data sets in a targeted manner, they could prove to be power tools against the fast-evolving threat of cyber terrorism and affiliated radicalisation. If we were able to identify the risk factors and the methodologies used by extremists utilising cyber communications platforms, the potential threat could be mitigated.

Lara-Cabrera *et al.*'s (2017) research conducts a statistical analysis of risk assessment factors and metrics to evaluate radicalisation on Twitter. Focusing on the one social media platform, they use three different data sets: keyword-based metrics, perception of discrimination and declaration of positive and negative ideas about Western Society and Jihadism. Their work concludes that using their analysis, they were able to identify Twitter users that were radicalised or at risk of radicalisation based on the terminology used and ideas expressed. They also found that more radical users tended to write longer tweets, which contradicted the expectation that introversion would be an indicative personality trait of users who were or were at risk to be radicalised.

However, though the results are promising, they rely on several sets of keywords, which are limited by linguistic definition. Twitter itself is also a more streamlined social messaging platform by design, in that its purpose is to broadcast short, character-limited sentences written by the user, or tweets, on the platform, and so does not form part of a more complex communications platform. Automated users, or bots, can also be created to generate targeted tweets which in turn could be difficult to attribute to an individual.

The data that is generated by users on a platform, chronicling projected behaviours and interactions, is a resource of which the surface has barely been scratched. Algorithmic modelling approaches to big data analytics have seen an increase and are being used for various tracking and correlative analytics on communications platforms.

To analyse metrics for language or terminology that could reflect radicalisation, extremism or the exploitation of vulnerable people on social media, these terms first need to be defined. The guidance issued by the UK government defines radicalisation as "*the process by which a person comes to support terrorism and extremist ideologies associated with terrorist groups.*" (HM Government, orr. 12/03/2015, rev. 16/07/2015). It is the UK Government's stance that it is possible to prevent vulnerable people from being drawn into terrorist-related activity through intervention. The "Prevent" strategy includes the identification and referral for appropriate interventions of those at risk of being drawn into terrorism. The intended aim of these interventions is to divert vulnerable people away from radicalisation (HM Government, orr. 12/03/2015, rev. 16/07/2015).

The "Prevent" strategy is also backed up legislatively through the Counter-Terrorism and Security Act 2015, specifically in Part 5, Chapter 1, which defines the general duties and powers of authorities to prevent people from being drawn into terrorism (HM Government, 2015).

The Terrorism Act 2000, Section 1, defines terrorism as "*an action that endangers or causes serious violence to a person/people; causes serious damage to property; or seriously interferes with or disrupts an electronic system. And that the use or threat must be designed to influence the government or to intimidate the public for the purposes of advancing a political, religious or ideological cause*". This legislation is also supplemented by the Terrorism Act 2006, Section 1, which widens the range of methods by which a terrorism offence can be committed under the 2000 act, by including the direct or indirect action or intention of the above described acts through a published statement (HM Government, 2006).

Extremism is defined by the UK Government as "vocal or active opposition to fundamental British values, including democracy, the rule of law, individual liberty and mutual respect and tolerance of different faiths and beliefs". The definition used by HM Government also includes "calls for death of members of the armed forces" (HM Government, orr. 12/03/2015, rev. 16/07/2015).

While discussing legislation, it is important to point out the nature of surveillance. The terrorism acts above give definition to what acts constitute a criminal offence under UK law, however, much of the evidence required to corroborate and increase the guilt threshold from "reason to suspect" to "beyond all reasonable doubt" would often require targeted information and intelligence about the suspected individual. Under current UK legislation, this "targeted" approach, which will interfere with a person's legal right to privacy, can only be warranted by a public body, such as the Court, or in matters relating to National Security, the UK Home Secretary. Targeted surveillance of an individual would include interception of communications and monitoring of an individual to gather intelligence on their habits and affiliations, with the purpose of collating evidence to substantiate the appropriate offence, as documented under the Warrant (HM Government, 2016).

It is for this reason that the "Prevent" strategy adopted by the UK Government relies on information on an individual and/or their activities by another party, or information gleaned from open source, publicly available information that does not breach the Data

Protection Act (now the General Data Protection Regulation) or an interception of data, which would contravene the Regulation of Investigatory Powers Act, thereby making evidence used inadmissible in court.Therefore, the researcher decided to use anonymised data in the data analysis in order to comply with appropriate legislation, as the purpose of the research is to determine whether a proof of concept can indeed be gleaned.

Jurisdiction is defined by international law as "the limits of the legal competence of a state...to make, apply, and enforce rules of conduct upon persons" (Lowe and Evans, 2006). It also concerns "the extent of each state's right to regular conduct, or the consequences of events". The difficulty underlying jurisdiction in the context of offences purportedly committed in or utilising cyberspace is attribution. The operational mechanics of the internet give users the ability to disguise their identity and location; leading to inherent difficulties in determining, under current legislative thresholds, the perpetrator and originating territory or location. While it is agreed internationally that allied states need to share information appropriately to legislate within the confines of current legislation, there is little agreement about what information can and should be shared. Academics and the legislative community have made several efforts to conduct research studies, one of which is the "Tallinn Manual", a 2-part book series which references legislation and defines jurisdiction utilising legislation used in air, in space, on land and at sea, as well as sovereignty and human rights (NATO Cooperative Cyber Defence Centre of Excellence, 2013; NATO Cooperative Cyber Defence Centre of Excellence, 2017).

The legislative conundrum concerning the jurisdiction of cyberspace means that traditional legislative definitions of crime and criminology do not fully fit with offences that culprits commit, or conspire to commit, online. Jahankhani *et al.* (2014) discuss the limitations of applying conventional legislative thinking and methodology to cyber criminality and proposes that there are two general categories of cyber crime: active and passive crimes. An active crime can be defined as that in which a criminal offence is directly committed by an individual using a computer, whereas a passive crime refers to the support and advancement of and conspiracy to an illegal activity.

Extremism is defined in a psychological context by Kruglanski *et al.* (2017) as "a *motivated deviance from general behavioural norms, and is assumed to stem from a shift from a balanced satisfaction of basic human needs afforded by moderation, to a motivation imbalance wherein a given need dominates the others*". In essence, normal behaviour is that in which the needs of an individual remain relatively balanced and in sync with each other. On the other hand, an extremist mindset is one in which one given need dominates and outweighs all others, which in turns affects other thought processes and behaviours. This makes it difficult to model with traditional methodologies, given that behavioural traits can vary greatly depending on the individual when in a state of imbalance.

14.2.1. *Psychological traits and linguistic theory*

The definitions of terrorism and extremism describe a pattern of behaviour that leads to an intention being held or an action being committed that is contrary to the legislation. However, to better identify such actions or intentions in the remit of the Prevent strategy, it is prudent to consider any psychological research and markers, to assess if they could also play a part in the identification mechanism.

Radicalisation is a multi-faceted, complex phenomenon. As such, consideration should be given to how to approach the analysis and further understanding of causal factors. De Leede *et al.* (2018) discuss the caution required when translating research findings regarding increased vulnerability to radicalisation into policies and programmes, as "*labelling certain groups as more vulnerable to radicalisation can be counter-effective as it can increase stigmatisation and feelings of estrangement*".

To make progress in developing a profiling methodology utilising the analysis of data generated on social media, psychological and social models must also be utilised to correlate data with behaviours for the purposes of profiling in a wider intelligence context.

To understand patterns of behaviour drawn from an analysis of data, an analysis of the "Big Five Personality Traits" and demographic variables should also be considered (Pang, 2017).

Both Borum's Four-Stage Model into a Terrorist's Mindset (Borum, 2011) and Moghaddam's Staircase Model (Moghaddam, 2005) propose an escalation of behaviour and trends, with each step leading to the next.

Borum's four-stage model was developed as a conceptual model to give law enforcement officials insights into the process of radicalisation, albeit to be used as a simpler starting tool (Borum, 2011).

Moghaddam's model is more descriptive in nature. It focuses on psychological over sociological factors, and outlines the route to extremism and terrorism as a staircase of stages, with fewer and fewer individuals progressing onwards as the stages increase. However, the model's first stage assumes a personalised adversity to individuals. Research into this area highlights that there are a variety of reasons as to why people engage with extremist and radical narratives. However, it is recognised in Young and Rooze's (2013) review that the model is useful in its metaphor of the staircase, as it highlights that there are a number of obstacles to overcome on the pathway to radicalisation, which prevents a greater number of individuals from becoming terrorists. It also recognises the role of morality in the individual's path to terrorism.

In a research paper authored by Lara-Cabrera *et al.* (2017), five indicators were identified and categorised into 2 groups for the purposes of their research. These two groups are personality-related indicators and attitudes- and beliefs-related indicators.

- **Personality Related Indicators:**
  - The individual is frustrated. This indicator was measured by considering swear words and the formatting of the sentence.
  - The individual is introverted. This indicator was measured by sentence strength, the shorter the sentence, the more indicative of introversion.
- **Attitudes and belief indicators**
  - Perception of discrimination.

- Expressing negative ideas about Western society.
- Expressing positive ideas about Jihadism, for example.

It is important to understand the underlying psychological and social behavioural indicators, so that a robust analysis can be completed.

14.2.2. *Social media and current events*

Social media platforms are considered an essential communication tool. Their virulence can be attributed to their ease of use and availability to complementary technology, such as smart phones.

Twitter is a social media platform with a unique model on which users post and interact with short messages known as “tweets”. These messages were originally subject to a character limit of 140 characters; however, in 2017, this was doubled to 280 characters. It is a requirement to “register” to the service to post a tweet; however, anyone can read public tweets, irrespective of registration. The platform was created in 2006, and rapidly gained popularity worldwide, with more than 100 million users posting 340 million tweets per day and handling an average of 1.6 billion search queries a day in 2012 (Twitter, 2012). By 2016, Twitter had more than 330 million monthly active users, and the company had 35+ corporate offices around the world (Twitter, 2018).

Social media has also become much more important as a news source in recent years, seeing almost a 20% rise from 2013 to 2016, with the use of print sources dropping back the same amount in the same period of time. TV as a news source has also seen an erosion from being the single most widely used source of news. Online sources (inclusive of social media) have overtaken TV in terms of reach, with at least 92% of the UK population having access to the internet (Nielsen, 2017).

The research conducted by Nielsen (2017) investigates how people find their news online, whether they go directly to a news agency or to a newspaper, to social media sources or to search engines. The results of the study state that while 47% of those surveyed say they go directly to the websites of broadcasters or newspapers, 20% find their news via various search methods, and 25% via social media methods. There is a suggestion that the digital delivery of on-demand news could lead to the formation of what is termed in the study as "filter-bubbles", in that people will only get information from a few sources that would confirm their pre-existing views. However, the study goes on to suggest that people who obtained their news from utilising search engines or social media in a search capacity were more likely to consult different and more varied sources of news than those who did not. The results of their survey however do show a proportion of users who obtain their news from social media, without necessarily "searching" or corroborating the sources, and who trust the information they receive on their news-feed or stream on their social media platform of choice.

14.2.3. *Wider relative research*

Research into the analytics of the keyword metrics of radicalisation on social media is relatively scarce; however, several wider research studies into radicalisation and the prevention of radicalisation have been conducted.

Lara-Cabrera *et al.* (2017) used risk assessment factors and metrics to evaluate radicalisation on Twitter. The study was focused on the statistical results of the data collected by analysing predetermined linguistic markers such as profanity, negative emotions and discriminatory terminology for certain behaviours, and comparing a dataset of tweets of ISIS supporters obtained from the group "Anonymous" and another dataset they compiled themselves of a random sample of Twitter users. Their research concluded that the tweets that they deemed to be more radical in nature contained more profanity and negative views about western culture and statistically were longer in length.

Torok (2016) discusses how social media has become a mainstream recruitment platform for radical extremists. The research discusses the psychological models mentioned earlier in this chapter as well as narratives from religious literature. They conclude in presenting the concept that there are three broad types of narratives that fuel violent extremism. The first occurs when a person's grievances stimulate a strong emotional response to perceived injustices. The second occurs when the person sees jihad as an avenue to actively address these grievances. The third occurs when the person commits to jihad as a goal.

It has been noted by researchers that although the rise of online criminal and extremist activities has led to social media analytics being incorporated into security practices, these analyses have not become established in academic research or intelligence practices. A study by Yang Hui (2016) discusses collection methods and analytical tools for the study of social media for intelligence and to counter violent extremism. Multiple variances of analyses are discussed in this paper, and the paper finds that the technological capabilities of social media analytics are improving. There is a need for perspectives from social science to complement social media analytics in order to provide a wider contextual basis from which to discuss the results of analyses.

De Leede *et al.* (2018) authored an interesting study into radicalisation and violent extremism focusing on women and the development of their roles in society. These ranged from passive traditional roles in a Jihadist ideological construct to more active and operations roles. The study comprehensively reviews the pathways to radicalisation, considering socio-economic issues as well as ideological narratives. The study concludes with advice about the importance of a diverse, multi-faceted approach to policy implementation, and of investing in grassroots initiatives to communicate and liaise with individuals at a local community level, whilst avoiding the marginalisation and labelling that can adversely hinder prevention. These themes are echoed in the UK Government's "Prevent" strategy.

Kruglanski *et al.* (2017) discuss the motivation factors underlying a shift towards extremism that are identified in the literature, giving examples of commonly reoccurring themes of *honour, vengeance, religion, loyalty to the leader, perks in the afterlife* and *feminism*, as detailed in assessments of specific cases in Bloom's (2005) research.

Kruglanski *et al.* (2017) acknowledge the appropriacy of these thematic indicators; however, they go further to explore an underlying theme, which they label *the quest for significance.* This is described as a fundamental desire to matter and to merit respect, which ties in with empirical psychological studies into universal human motivations such as the need for esteem, achievement, meaning and control. The paper goes on to discuss the manner in which this quest for significance could be triggered through a *deprivation of need.* This term describes how a perceived loss of significance by an individual can incite a desire to reinstate said significance by whichever mechanism. This is a technique used by recruiters looking to radicalise individuals, utilising, for example, the affront to one's social/ethnic identity through the experience of Islamophobia. The paper suggests that individuals in this situation who are in such an aggrieved position could then find themselves being directed by extremist and radical narratives. They might allow themselves to be unwittingly recruited to sate the need for significance after their perceived loss.

Mythen *et al.* (2016) discuss and critique the understanding of radicalisation and its connection with "home-grown" terrorism in the UK Government's "Prevent" strategy. The paper focuses on how specific understandings of radicalisation are constructed and operationalised in "Prevent", and how these understandings align with the world views of political parties. The authors hypothesise that a continuous focus on the role of religious ideology in the radicalisation process, as assessed in the "Prevent" strategy, blocks the recognition of other important grievances experienced by individuals involved in violent extremism.

14.3. Research Methodology

14.3.1. *Datasets*

The aim of this chapter is to analyse keyword metrics used on an open source media platform, and to assess any correlation. The analysis is used as part of a mechanism to attribute radical and exploitative behaviour to particular individuals, or to identify users that maybe show signs of exploitation or who risk being exploited by such behaviour through their social media posts. The use of keyword analytics is nothing new, and indeed is used by most social media platforms through either the identification of certain sentence structures and themes, or through the reporting mechanism on the media platform, whereby other users can flag posts and content to administrators of the platform for review and removal. However, there is little published work and research into the keyword analytics underlying the behaviour of users and the wider social landscape.

While such behaviour and psychological profiling can be attributed to an individual, individuals may utilise multiple accounts in the online space which may not relate to their actual real-world behaviour. Wider online activity and behaviour can build useful context in a larger intelligence profile, but for the purposes of this paper, the researcher will retain a narrow scope for the data analysis, in order to further explore and answer the question relating to the keyword analysis itself.

To create a control and baseline for the analysis, datasets containing social media posts from known/suspected extremist users/accounts have been analysed. Also, for the purposes of context, a dataset of known extremist published material, which would share the same ideological profile as or have a similar ideological profile to the social media posts, would be analysed as well. The researchers assert that the analysis of the keyword metrics from these two data sets could be compared with the trends identified through the wider research in the literature review. Any correlations drawn or anomalies found could then be used to direct further research, and eventually to sculpt a mechanism to help further profile thematic behaviour. Radical Islamist Extremist posts and published material were used for this data analysis; however, it is the researcher's hope that the same research methodology can be utilised. By changing the type of datasets used for the baseline and control, other targeted behaviours could be more readily assessed and analysed.

Both datasets were compiled by a US Department of Defence Research contractor, and as such, the sets used as secondary data have been deemed to be verified from a reputable source.

The first dataset is a compilation of religious and ideological texts used in ISIS English-based magazines, namely "Dabiq" and "Rumiyah" (Fraser, 2014; Wright, 2016). Both publications have been referred to as ISIS recruitment propaganda, given their ideological narrative. The former is more ideological in nature, and the latter is more urgent and deliberate in its directives (McKernan, 2016). The dataset obtained contains texts from 15 issues of "Dabiq" published between June 2014 and July 2016, and 9 issues of "Rumiyah" published between September 2016 and May 2017; a total of 2685 texts. As a baseline source for extremist terminology and keywords, the researcher believes this dataset to be extremely valuable.

The second dataset, provided by the same organisation, is a compilation of 17,000 tweets scraped from 100+ pro-ISIS user accounts on Twitter. The tweets are sourced globally and have been published since the November 2015 Paris terrorist attacks. The researcher's intention for this dataset is to provide a wider context for the keyword analysis. If the keyword analysis of the publication's dataset provides a baseline of the terminology, words and phrases regularly used in such a publication, then this can be compared with the terminology, words and phrases used in the tweets of user accounts associated with the extremist group used for this research.

By running analyses of these datasets, and by comparing the results of the datasets to each other and to the keywords and themes lifted from the research and critical literature review; the researcher should be able to corroborate the assertions made and discover potential further research avenues. The analytics of these datasets can provide profiling methodologies in a wider intelligence landscape.

14.4. Keyword Analysis

14.4.1. *Word count*

A key aspect defining the scope of analysis in this research is determining the type of analysis to be used, and which could be the best fit for the type of data to be analysed.

"Data analysis is the systematic search for meaning. It is a way to process qualitative data so that what has been learned can be communicated to others." (Hatch, 2002)

A word frequency or "word count" analysis was conducted on the datasets to define the most frequently used words in the publications and the tweets in order to glean correlative patterns through appropriately weighting emergent themes. As defined by Pennebaker *et al.* (2003), word counts are based on the belief that all people have distinctive vocabulary and word usage patterns, with these patterns becoming what are often referred to as "linguistic fingerprints". However, as highlighted by Carley (1993), there is an underlying assumption that words which are more important and have greater significance for the user would be used more often.

Miles and Huberman (1994) note that there are at least three reasons for word counting analyses, namely:

- To identify patterns more easily
- To verify a hypothesis
- To maintain analytic integrity

While this corroborates the reasoning for using this technique for the analysis of the datasets, as themes can be more readily identified in this manner, it should be also noted that there are weaknesses to word count analyses. As discussed in Leech and Onwuebuzie (2007), one drawback is that word count can decontextualize the word to a point where it is not understandable, and that in a sentence, the words before and after a key word would define the context of the phrase and the manner in which it was used, which is important when identifying and understanding themes. Another weakness is that users do not necessarily need to use a word frequently to portray important concepts.

14.4.2. *Keyword-in-context*

Another analysis technique that has been considered is that of "keywords-in-context". This technique is a data analysis method that reveals how respondents use words in context by comparing words that appear before or after "keywords" (Fielding and Lee, 1998).

This analysis method provides greater depth and context to data, which may otherwise be less rich in information, and therefore, not as appropriate for use for this research. Results from a word count or a word frequency analysis, as discussed earlier, would provide the basis of further contextual research and analysis to be conducted on the resultant data. This would allow the researcher to delve deeper into the themes and behavioural psychological traits displayed by the users from these datasets.

14.4.3. *Data analysis*

The raw data of the datasets were compiled into a Comma Separated Value Microsoft Excel spreadsheet. The researcher then imported and transposed the datasets into Nvivo. The word frequency analyses of the two datasets were conducted separately, so that they could be appropriately compared.

For each of the datasets, two types of word frequency (or word count) analyses were run. The first was an "exact match" query, in that the frequency of each specific keyword would be counted and tabulated. The second type of query was with "specialisations", which includes keywords of a similar meaning or definition into the count. The researcher conducted this second analysis with the intention of adopting some of the pros of a keyword-in-context approach. By counting other words with a similar meaning or definition and compiling them into the count, a level of context could be gleaned. It would also help dial back the potential for anomalous results.

14.5. Keyword Metric Results of the Data Analysis

The purpose for the use of the Religious Texts dataset was to act as a control and baseline for the keyword analysis. The two publications captured by researchers in this dataset are those that are named by so-called ISIS as their official publications, and are internationally recognised as being material that is authored by and for their cause. Therefore, the Religious Texts dataset was used to facilitate an accurate, pragmatic keyword analysis, and to see if the same thematic trends can be found in both theoretic and legislative terminology and these publications. This would provide a solid foundation for further research.

This dataset was obtained from a US Department of Defence Contractor. It contains 2685 religious texts scraped from multiple issues of 2 successive publications over a 3-year period. These quotes and texts are most likely representative of the arguments, themes and justification used within ISIS's ideology.

The word cloud generated from the exact keyword frequency analysis of the dataset clearly shows the terminology and recurring themes present in the publications. Religious and violent themes are evident here, which were expected from an exact analysis of keywords found in a data source based on ISIS's ideology.

Another word frequency query was run against the dataset, running exact matches with stemmed words, synonyms and specialisations. The inclusion of words with similar meanings and definitions would give a wider context to the keywords gleaned from the query, thus improving the results.

The results from the word frequency query with specialisations are similar to those from the exact match query. The "period" and "months" keywords are of interest, as this illustrates the use of and reference to key dates and timeframes; something which could be of wider interest in an intelligence context when comparing these details with posts on social media platforms.

The results of this query corroborate the assertions made previously in this paper that the word frequency query with specialisations would provide richer results with a degree of context for analysis. The word cloud also illustrates the increased diversity of the results, and together with the full set of results from which the sample was taken, would prove more useful in a subsequent and more detailed analysis of the results.

The purpose of conducting a keyword analysis on Pro-ISIS Twitter use was to provide a sample of tweets from known ISIS-supporting accounts, to assess if there were any trends or correlations that could be gleaned when the results of the keyword analysis of Pro-ISIS Twitter use were compared with the results of the keyword analysis of the dataset of texts originating from published propaganda.

The results from the exact match word frequency query illustrate the limitations that can occur with a narrow query scope. In this instance, as the data was captured from Twitter, and as the tweets themselves contain links to external sources, the keyword query has counted components of web addresses as keywords, such as "http", "www", and "com".

The keyword frequency query shows more relevant data, with mention of key locations, as well as terminology relating to religion, war and terrorism. The word count for this query is ideal to visualise the results in their entirety for the analysis. While the web address anomalies still exist within this cloud, many other keywords can be noted from the cloud. Interestingly, the themes from this dataset vary from those from the dataset of religious texts. The exact match keywords identified from this dataset can be linked to current events, and themes linked to the ideological narrative. The religious texts gleaned from the publications refer to more religious themes, rather than the nature of or location of attacks.

However, in the vein of thought of extremism and exploitation, it could be inferred that the tweets discussing current events and providing an alternative narrative to that of the mainstream media could attract individuals looking for that very alternative narrative that they have been unable to find elsewhere, and thus that the social media platform could become the gateway for further exploitation and radicalisation by directing users to other propaganda sources such as the publications which have been collated in the first dataset used in this analysis.

A word frequency query with specialisations was again also conducted on this dataset. As seen with the previous dataset, this additional query does not result in a wholly new set of analysis results, but rather provides a depth of field or context to the results.

There are some anomalies that exist in the results, due to the inclusion of the "@", a prefix for all Twitter handles, "2016", the year from which most of the tweets were scraped by the originator of the dataset, and the web address components that appear in the previous queries. The results from this query begin to show a trend within this data set, compared with the exact match query, due to the wider context and grouping of words into a singular shared theme.

The word cloud for the word frequency query with specialisations shows the larger results of the query, and shows that the most frequent keywords that appear on the tweets relate to current events or trending topics on Twitter at the time of the post. It could be that these Twitter users are utilising the mechanics of the Twitter platform to maximise the visibility of their accounts and the other tweets they have written, to gain a larger audience and attract viewership from users that may not already be subscribed to a narrative which supports their ideological objects.

14.5.1. *Analytical comparison of the keyword metrics*

The analysis itself has provided clear fundamental support for the overarching theory hypothesised; that the use of keyword metrics to identify radicalisation and exploitation on social media for use in a wider intelligence picture is indeed possible. However, more in-depth research into the keyword datasets is required. Whilst various compilations and datasets are available through some internet forums, online data repositories and indeed the "Dark Web", verifying the authenticity and trust of an unknown source is difficult. The use of untrusted and untested sources could invalidate the results and findings of the analysis. However, verified sources for such data were available, although perhaps not as readily as the research first assumed. One of the biggest factors inhibiting such analysis of keyword metrics from these platforms was the ability to source viable datasets within an appropriate timescale. The sensitive nature of the subject matter within these datasets may also deter many researchers from further study into such an area.

The analysis of these datasets show that themes can be identified through the analysis of the keyword metrics. The dataset of religious texts, as expected, showed mainly ideological themes; religious contexts and references. The dataset of tweets showed mainly keywords relating to current events or trending topics. The word frequency with specialisations showed there is a greater repository of context underlying the initial statistics gleaned from the analysis. As a next step for further research, a keyword-in-context type analysis which involves reviewing the words before and after keywords to provide greater context in the results could be a suitable stepping stone to better understand the thematic mechanics of radicalised and exploitative themes, to create a more robust and overarching mechanism and framework to apply in wider targeted thematic analysis.

14.5.2. *Legislative and jurisdiction factors interconnected with the definitions of radicalisation and extremism*

Another factor when approaching research into radicalisation, extremism and exploitation is the definition of these terms. Geographical, cultural, political and socio-economic factors can change what language or behaviour would be apportioned in these categories. One of the biggest issues facing legislatures is that of jurisdiction, and the inconsistency of legislation that exists between nation states and jurisdictions. The very nature of social media platforms and their use of the internet is that while a user can be located in one jurisdiction, whereby the language used and behaviour displayed in their social media posts could be deemed acceptable; in another jurisdiction where the same posts are viewed, they may not be. There are also linguistic considerations to be made, in that translations of phrases may not correctly articulate intent or may have lost meaning in translation. For the purposes of this research, the researcher focused on the use of English language posts and translations. This research was also carried out with reference to the Tallinn Manual of Cyber Legislation and previous knowledge held by the researcher of the similarities in the legislation and jurisdiction of the five partner countries in the Five Eyes intelligence network and affiliated agencies. As such, the use of this accepted legislative similarity provided a suitable baseline on which the analysis of the data could be based.

14.5.3. *Analysis of the social media platform and policies, and their effect on current and future data capturing*

The Facebook Data Breach occurred when analytical and political consultancy "Cambridge Analytica" made use of user profiles and data misappropriated from the Facebook platform for their own commercial purposes. This saw an overhaul of the privacy policies used by Facebook, as well as increased transparency in the security and privacy settings available to users (Cadwalladr and Graham-Harrison, 2018). Due to Facebook being a closed platform, access to which is granted via a login wall, large data scrapes for the purposes of keyword analytics would prove quite difficult, as the process would rely on the users' data and posts being posted as public. Anonymised data for academic research was previously available through Facebook and other research organisations with data sharing agreements with the platform; however, the data breach compromised the availability and use of such data.

The implementation of the GDPR has also led to the updating of data retention and privacy policies on such platforms, not only governing the data that is stored by service providers, but also making it more difficult for such information to be shared without an appropriate or proportionate cause. The nature of Twitter, which makes posts or "tweets" public as default, together with the quantity of "tweets" and the availability of the platform, mean that, for analytical purposes such as those described in this paper, large quantities of data can be obtained and utilised.

Many datasets did and do exist in online repositories, forums and exchanges on the dark web; however, their sources have to be authenticated to verify the validity of the research and the results of any analyses undertaken. The researcher found that other research organisations did hold verified datasets and were willing to share them for the purposes of academic research, as so little has been conducted on them.

14.5.4. *Review of the collated analytic data, psychological, social and legislative research*

Legislation and government guidelines provide a defined framework as to what actions constitute a criminal offence and can be defined as extremism. The dataset of extremist religious texts provides a baseline or justification for such actions, through ideological themes. What is interesting, however, is that the data collated from the Twitter dataset shows more frequent terms and keywords relating to current or trending topics on Twitter, rather than relating to the ideological themes found in the publications. Many of these tweets had links to external sites, and so, the researcher found that these tweets are using the mechanics of the Twitter platform to their advantage, maximising their outreach by linking tweets to trending topics without directly propagating ideological themes. A methodology to actively identify extremism and radicalisation on social media using keyword metrics is possible, however, further research needs to be conducted into the analysis of similar datasets. While legislation provides a definitive framework, the identification of behavioural patterns requires context to be taken into account during the analysis. A keywords-in-context approach to analysis could provide greater insight into the behaviours displayed through social media posts. However, the nature of Twitter creates a problem for such analysis. While its simplicity, accessibility and availability are reasons for the platform's popularity, the character-limited posts mean that there will tend to be links to external sites, and the use of automated accounts means that a detailed analysis could prove difficult. Another social media platform, such as Facebook for example, would more likely provide more contextual data for analysis, as users with individual accounts and groups would more likely express views when there is no limitation. However, as discussed here, there is a legislative restriction on what data can be reviewed and analysed. For the purposes of academic research, however, anonymised data samples from the platform could be used for analysis to provide a potential proof of concept.

14.6. Conclusions

Whilst the research conducted in this project achieved its defined objectives, there were some limitations that were reinforced through the analyses, although these could be addressed in further research. The concise nature of the Twitter posts at the time of capture was restrictive, with the maximum character count permissible on the platform per tweet being 140 characters. This more recently doubled to 280 characters, so many tweets on Twitter are larger, in turn providing greater contextual data.

This greater depth of context in data could provide fruitful results for future analysis. While this research identified themes and trends expressed in known extremist material and tweets rather than seeking pre-set terms, it only scratches the surface of the behavioural and profiling data that can be gleaned for use in wider intelligence and law enforcement environments.

Verifiable datasets of such a nature for use in an academic environment are difficult to obtain. Many of the accounts that posted the tweets in the dataset were deleted by Twitter for breaching their "Terms and Conditions of Use", however would reappear under a slight variation on the account name. However, the dataset used by the research accounted for these discrepancies.

Therefore, an area for further research could be the development of a dataset of datasets, whereby datasets from verified sources with data of such nature could be collated to ease and perpetuate much needed analytical research into such behavioural trends online and on social media.

More detailed keyword analytics methods could also be used on a wider range of datasets, again, to provide more context and to build a more detailed results picture from the available raw data.

References

1. Bloom, M. (2005). *Dying to Kill: The Allure of Suicide Terror.* New York, NY, USA: Columbia University Press.
2. Borum, R. (2011). Radicalisation Into Violent Extremism II: A Review of Conceptual Models and Empirical Research. *Journal of Strategic Security*, **4**(4), pp. 37–62.
3. Cadwalladr, C. and Graham-Harrison, E. (2018). *Revealed: 50 Million Facebook Profiles Harvested for Cambridge Analytica in Major Data Breach* [Online]. Available at: https://www.theguardian.com/news/2018/mar/17/cambridge-analytica-facebook-influence-us-election (Accessed: March 2018).
4. Carley, K. (1993). Coding Choices for Textual Analysis: A Comparison of Content Analysis and Map Analysis. *Sociological Methodology*, **23**, pp. 75–126.

5. De Leede, S., Haupfleisch, R., Korolkova, K. and Natter, M. (2018). *Radicalisation and Violent Extremism — Focus on Women: How Women Become Radicalised, and How to Empower Them to Prevent Radicalisation.* Brussels, Belgium: European Parliament Think Tank.
6. Facebook. (2017). *Facebook Newsroom* [Online]. Available at: https://newsroom.fb.com/company-info/ (Accessed: April 2018).
7. Facebook. (2017). *Scaling the Facebook Data Warehouse to 300 PB* [Online]. Available at: https://code.facebook.com/posts/229861827208629/scaling-the-facebook-data-warehouse-to-300-pb/ (Accessed: April 2018).
8. Fielding, N. G. and Lee, R. (1998). *Computer Analysis and Qualitiative Research.* Thousand Oaks, CA, USA: Sage.
9. Fraser, G. (2014). *To Islamic State, Dabiq Is Important — But It's Not the End of the World* [Online]. Available at: https://www.theguardian.com/commentisfree/belief/2014/oct/10/islamic-state-dabiq-important-not-end-of-the-world (Accessed: May 2018).
10. Hatch, J. (2002). *Doing Qualitative Reserach in Education Settings.* Albany, NY, USA: SUNY Press.
11. HM Government. (2006). *Section 1, Terrorism Act 2006.* London, UK: HM Government.
12. HM Government. (2015). *Counter-Terrorism and Security Act 2015.* London, UK: HM Government.
13. HM Government. (2016). *Investigatory Powers Act, 2016.* London, UK: HM Government.
14. HM Government. (2015). *Revised Prevent Duty Guidance: For England and Wales.* London, UK: HM Government.
15. Jahankhani, H., Hosseinian-Far, A. and Al-Nemrat, A. (2014). Cyber Crime Classification and Characteristics. In Akhgar, B., Staniforth, A. and Bosco, F. (eds)., *Cyber Crime and Cyber Terrorism Investigator's Handbook.* Rockland, MA, USA, Syngress.
16. Kruglanski, A. W. *et al.* (2017). To the Fringe and Back: Violent Extremism and the Psychology of Deviance. *American Psychologist,* **72**(3), pp. 217–230.
17. Lara-Cabrera, R. *et al.* (2017). Measuring the Radicalisation Risk in Social Networks. *IEEE Access,* **5**, pp. 10892–10900.
18. Lara-Cabrrera, R., Gonzalez-Pardo, A. and Camacho, D. (2017). Statistical Analysis of Risk Assessment Factors and Metrics to Evaluate Radicalisation in Twitter. *Future Generation Computer Systems,* **93**, pp. 971–978.
19. Leech, N. L. and Onwuebuzie, A. J. (2007). An Array of Qualitative Data Analysis Tools: A Call for Data Analysis Triangulation. *School Psychology Quarterly,* **22**(4), pp. 557–584.

20. Lowe, V. and Evans, M. D. (2006). *Jurisdiction in International Law.* UK: s.n.
21. McKernan, B. (2016). *ISIS's New Magazine Rumiyah Shows the Terror Group is 'Struggling to Adjust to Losses'* [Online]. Available at: https://www.independent.co.uk/news/world/middle-east/isis-propaganda-terror-group-losses-syria-iraq-a7228286.html (Accessed: May 2018).
22. Miles, M. B. and Huberman, A. M. (1994). *Qualitative Data Analysis: An Expanded Sourcebook* (2nd ed.). Thousand Oaks, CA: Sage.
23. Moghaddam, F. (2005). The Staircase to Terrorism: A Psychological Exploration. *The American Psychologist,* **2**(60), pp. 161–169.
24. Mughal, S. (2016). *Radicalisation of Young People Through Social Media* [Online]. Available at: https://www.internetmatters.org/hub/expert-opinion/radicalisation-of-young-people-through-social-media/ (Accessed: April 2018).
25. Mythen, G., Walklate, S. and Peatfield, E.-J. (2016). *Assembling and Deconstructing Radicalisation in PREVENT: A Case of Policy-Based Evidence Making?* s.l.: Sage.
26. NATO Coperative Cyber Defence Centre of Excellence. (2013). *Tallinn Manual on the International Law Applicable to Cyber Warfare.* Tallinn: NATO.
27. NATO Coperative Cyber Defence Centre of Excellence. (2017). *Tallinn Manual 2.0 on the International Law Application to Cyber Operations.* Talinn: NATO.
28. Newman, N. (2017). *Reuters Institute Digital News Report.* s.l.: University of Oxford — Reuters Institute for the Study of Journalism.
29. Nielsen, R. K. (2017). *Where Do People Get Their News?* [Online] Available at: https://medium.com/oxford-university/where-do-people-get-their-news-8e850a0dea03 (Accessed: April 2018).
30. Pang, J. S. (2017). *Understand Personality and Person-Specific Predictors of Cyber-based Insider Threat.* Singapore: Nanyang Technological University.
31. Pennebaker, J. W., Mehl, M. R. and Niederhoffer, K. (2003). Psychological Aspects of Natural Language Use: Our Words, Our Selves. *Annual Review of Psychology,* **54**, pp. 547–577.
32. The Independent. (2015). *Why Do People Join ISIS? Foreign Fighters Almost Never Recruited at Mosque, Expert Says* [Online]. Available at: http://www.independent.co.uk/news/world/middle-east/what-makes-people-join-isis-expert-says-foreign-fighters-are-almost-never-recruited-at-mosque-a6748251.html (Accessed: April 2018).
33. Torok, R. (2016). *Social Media and the Use of Discursive Markers of Online Extremism and Recruitment.* s.l.: IGI Global.

34. Twitter. (2012). *Twitter Turns Six* [Online]. Available at: https://blog.twitter.com/official/en_us/a/2012/twitter-turns-six.html (Accessed: June 2018).
35. Twitter. (2018). *About Twitter* [Online]. Available at: https://about.twitter.com/en_gb/company.html (Accessed: June 2018).
36. Wright, R. (2016). *The Hand of ISIS at Ohio State* [Online]. Available at: https://www.newyorker.com/news/news-desk/the-hand-of-isis-at-ohio-state (Accessed: May 2018).
37. Yang Hui, J. (2016). *Social Media Analytics for Intelligence and Countering Violent Extremism.* s.l.: IGI Global.
38. Young, H. F. and Rooze, M. (2013). *A Review of the Literature on Radicalisation; and What It Means for TERRA*. s.l.: TERRA.

Chapter 15

The European Union's General Data Protection Regulation (GDPR)

Sérgio Tenreiro de Magalhães

Champlain College
Burlington, VT — USA
smagalhaes@champlain.edu

Algoritmi Research Center
Guimarães, Portugal
psmagalhaes@dsi.uminho.pt

ABSTRACT

This chapter presents the General Data Protection Regulation (GDPR) approved for the European Union, which has consequences not only for all the stakeholders of the information technology industry, but also for all of those engaged in industrial or commercial activities in the European Union.

The concepts and principles of the GDPR are presented and discussed as well as the implications of this regulation in data protection and in organisational cyber security practices. The financial implications for companies are discussed and an overview of the history of recent fines and recent trends is presented.

Conclusions are drawn on the importance of compliance and a recommendation is made that organisations choose to hire the services of multidisciplinary companies specialized in GDPR compliance.

Keywords: GDPR, cyber security, personal data, DPO, IT

15.1. Introduction

The General Data Protection Regulation (GDPR) was published in the Official Journal of The European Union (EU) on the 4th of May of 2016 as "REGULATION (EU) 2016/679 OF THE EUROPEAN PARLIAMENT AND OF THE COUNCIL of 27 April 2016 on the protection of natural persons with regard to the processing of personal data and on the free movement of such data, and repealing Directive 95/46/EC (General Data Protection Regulation)" (REGULATION (EU) 2016/ 679 OF THE EUROPEAN PARLIAMENT AND OF THE COUNCIL — of 27 April 2016 — on the protection of natural persons with regard to the processing of personal data and on the free movement of such data, and repealing Directive 95/ 46/ EC (General Data Protection Regulation), 2016). This long name is itself revealing of the two major objectives of this regulation: protection and freedom of movement for the personal data of natural persons (excluding, therefore, the data of other juridical persons, like corporations). This complete name also reveals that this is not a new issue and that this regulation ends the validity of the 95/16/ EC Directive, which was more than 20 years old.

The GDPR has created an important change in the way businesses operate in Europe, no matter if they have a physical presence there or if they do not. As some of the concepts therein are hard to objectivize and/or are hard to operationalize, it has generated a lot of uncertainty, especially because the media has widely reported on the values of the fines that come with failing to implement this regulation.

While the publication of the GDPR dates from April 27, 2016, its application only became mandatory on May 25, 2018. This two-year period should have allowed for a smooth transition, but the fact is that the concerns about the application of the new regulation started much closer to the mandatory application date. A search in Google Trends shows that the public's interest on the topic was

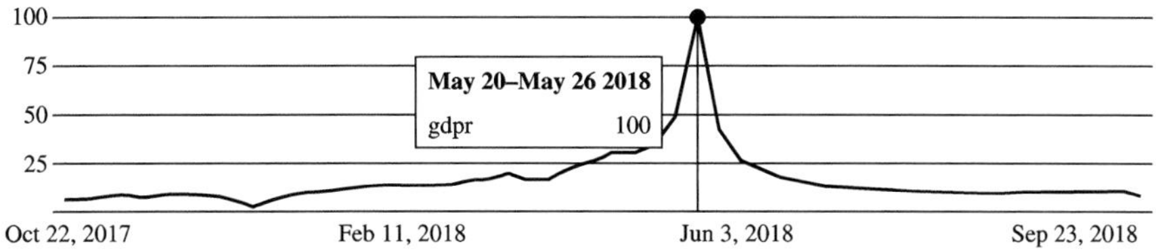

Fig. 15.1. Evolution of searches by GDPR worldwide.

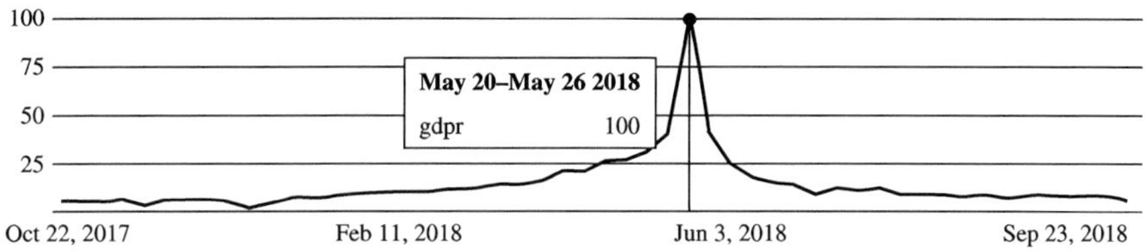

Fig. 15.2. Evolution of searches by GDPR in the USA.

focused mainly in late May 2018, both worldwide (see Fig. 15.1) and in the USA (see Fig. 15.2).

The following sections will present the legislative background, the main concepts of this new regulation with a special focus on the role of Data Protection Officer, the main implications for organisations and the current limitations of the GDPR.

15.2. Legislative Background

The GDPR is a piece of legislation that has a long history. To begin with, it replaces a directive from October 24, 1995 (Directive 95/46/EC) on the processing and movement of personal data (Directive 95/46/EC of the European Parliament and of the Council of 24 October 1995 on the protection of individuals with regard to the processing of personal data and on the free movement of such data, 1995). Therefore, the GDPR did not result from a void, even if a Directive is not a piece of legislation of the same nature as a Regulation. A Regulation is directly applicable to all European Union (EU) countries, while a Directive needs to be implemented by the countries through a national piece of legislation.

Directive 95/46/EC was actually quite advanced for its time and many of the concepts and procedures that now raise some surprise and controversy were already in it, even if the digital reality of 1995 was quite different from that of 2018.

Some of the fundamental concepts of the GDPR that Directive 95/46/EC contemplated are (Directive 95/46/EC of the European Parliament and of the Council of 24 October 1995 on the protection of individuals with regard to the processing of personal data and on the free movement of such data, 1995):

- Personal data, which is defined as "any information relating to an identified or identifiable natural person";
- Identifiable person, who is "one who can be identified, directly or indirectly";
- Consent, which is defined as "any freely given specific and informed indication of his wishes by which the data subject signifies his agreement to personal data relating to him being processed";
- Supervisory Authority, which is a national authority responsible for monitoring the application of the Directive. The existence of one or more supervisory authorities in each country of the European Community (the former name of the European Union) was mandatory.
- Right to Object. The data's subject had the right to object, in certain situations, to personal data processing. This included situations where data is handled for the purpose of direct marketing.
- Protection from automated individual decisions. Directive 95/46/EC granted protection to all persons from any relevant decisions affecting him and produced solely by automated processing.

Other legal documents that provide context to the GDPR are the Charter of Fundamental Rights of the European Union (European Parliament, European Council, and European Commission, 2012) and the Treaty on the Functioning of the European Union (European Union, 2012). Both documents grant European citizens the right to the protection of their personal data.

There are also other pieces of legislation that maintain their pertinence. Among those are:

— Directive 2000/31/EC (DIRECTIVE 2000/31/EC OF THE EUROPEAN PARLIAMENT AND OF THE COUNCIL, 2000);
— Regulation (EC) No. 45/2001 (Regulation (EC) No. 45/2001 of the European Parliament and of the Council, 2001);
— Regulation (EC) No. 223/2009 (Regulation (EC) No. 223/2009 of the European Parliament and of the Council, 2009);
— Directive 2002/58/EC (DIRECTIVE 2002/58/EC OF THE EUROPEAN PARLIAMENT AND OF THE COUNCIL, 2002);
— Directive 2011/24/EU (Directive 2011/24/EU of the European Parliament and of the Council of 9 March 2011 on the application of patients' rights in cross-border healthcare, 2011);
— Regulation (EU) No. 536/2014 (REGULATION (EU) No. 536/2014 OF THE EUROPEAN PARLIAMENT AND OF THE COUNCIL, 2014);
— The Convention for the Protection of Individuals with regard to Automatic Processing as it was amended in October 10, 2018 (Convention for the Protection of Individuals with regard to Automatic Processing of Personal Data as it will be amended by its Protocol CETS No. 223, 2018); and
— Directive 2016/680 (DIRECTIVE (EU) 2016/ 680 OF THE EUROPEAN PARLIAMENT AND OF THE COUNCIL — of 27 April 2016 — on the protection of natural persons with regard to the processing of personal data by competent authorities for the purposes of the prevention, investigation, detection or prosecution of criminal offences or the execution of criminal penalties, and on the free movement of such data, and repealing Council Framework Decision 2008/ 977/ JHA, 2016).

GDPR applies to the treatment, by any means, of personal data resulting of activities in the European Union or regarding persons living in the EU, regardless of where the treatment is made (inside or outside the EU).

15.3. Personal Data Under GDPR

GDPR defines personal data exactly as Directive 95/46/EC did, as "any information relating to an identified or identifiable natural person" and it clarifies that:

> "An identifiable natural person is one who can be identified, directly or indirectly, in particular by reference to an identifier such as a name, an identification number, location data, an online identifier or to one or more factors specific to the physical, physiological, genetic, mental, economic, cultural or social identity of that natural person" (REGULATION (EU) 2016/ 679 OF THE EUROPEAN PARLIAMENT AND OF THE COUNCIL — of 27 April 2016 — on the protection of natural persons with regard to the processing of personal data and on the free movement of such data, and repealing Directive 95/ 46/ EC (General Data Protection Regulation), 2016).

The concept of Personal Data is at the core of GDPR and is actually quite broad. While the definition does not provide any details on the extent of the underlying notion, the preamble does provide some examples of personal data, namely:

— Internet Protocol Addresses;
— Cookies;
— Radio Frequency (RFID) tags;
— Data revealing racial or ethnic origin, political opinions, religious or philosophical beliefs, or trade union membership;
— Genetic data;
— Biometric data used for authentication and/or identification;
— Data concerning health;
— Data concerning a natural person's sex life or sexual orientation

This makes it clear that any technology solutions that can indirectly lead to the identification of a person fall under GDPR, which relates to the "identifiable" component of the definition of Personal Data.

Further clarification comes from the work of the Article 29 Working Party (WP29), created by Directive 95/46/EC. WP29 issued a set of guidelines, recommendations and best practices before its work was terminated on May 25, 2018, when the European Data Protection Board (EDPB) succeeded WP29. WP29's Opinion 4/2007 focusses on the concept of Personal Data (Article 29 Data Protection Working Party, 2007, p. 4). This complex document decomposes and analyses the concept in its four parts:

— "Any information", which the WP29 believes "calls for a wide interpretation of the concept regardless of the nature or content of the information, and the technical format in which it is presented";
— "Relating to", which the WP29 feels can be approached by looking into content, purpose and result;
— "Identified or identifiable", which the WP29 considers the introduction of a context-dependent approach in the decision on what constitutes personal data, given "the means likely reasonably to be used"; and
— "Natural person", which points to an application of the GDPR mostly limited to "living individuals". It is important to notice that the chosen expression is used to refer to people already born and not yet deceased.

These clarifications are better understood through the given examples, showing that the following less obvious data is considered to be personal data under GDPR:

— Professional habits and practices;
— Customers' recording of instructions;
— Video surveillance recordings containing images of individuals;
— Any information regarding the state of a person's health, even if it can be recognized only by professionals (the example is of a child's drawing created in a neuro-psychiatric test);
— The value of a person's house;
— Car service records, which can hold personal data both from the car's owner and from the mechanic that worked on the car.
— Telephone call logs (incoming and/or outgoing);
— Vehicle GPS tracking, including those used professionally;

— Some information included in minutes of meetings, like the presence of certain individuals and the statements made.

15.4. Data Processing

Another core GDPR concept is data processing. Different people can perceive this term in different ways, so the GDPR presents a definition that is quite clear and is almost the same as Directive 95/46/EC (Directive 95/46/EC of the European Parliament and of the Council of 24 October 1995 on the protection of individuals with regard to the processing of personal data and on the free movement of such data, 1995):

> "Any operation or set of operations which is performed on personal data or on sets of personal data, whether or not by automated means, such as collection, recording, organization, structuring, storage, adaptation or alteration, retrieval, consultation, use, disclosure by transmission, dissemination or otherwise making available, alignment or combination, restriction, erasure or destruction" (Directive 95/46/EC of the European Parliament and of the Council of 24 October 1995 on the protection of individuals with regard to the processing of personal data and on the free movement of such data, 1995).

This definition only differs from the previously existing one in two words: "structuring" (added in the new definition) and "restriction" (which replaced the word "blocking"). Some components of this definition deserve special attention, due to their consequences:

— "Whether or not by automated means": The main consequence of this definition component is that the GDPR is not, as many might think, only applicable to digital data. Storing a paper that contains personal data is personal data processing, so it falls under the GDPR. This means that, for full GDPR compliance, most companies need to implement a clean desk policy, given that processing requires either a contractual/legal justification or the data subject's consent, which is given for a specific purpose. Therefore, the information is to be internally shared on a need-to-know basis and limited to the extent that is required by law, contract or consent. Being so, it shouldn't be accessible to just anyone with access to the space. For instance, cleaning crews don't need access to the data subject's data to perform their work.

— "Storage": The fact that storing personal data falls under GDPR means that organisations need to apply it not only to information that they collect after May 25, 2018, but also to all the information that was collected before that but is still being stored. Given that there has to be either a legal/contractual justification or the data subject's consent for the processing, organisations need to review all their stored data that doesn't have storage consent attached. Either there is a legal/contractual reason for continuing to store that data or else they must destroy it immediately. Asking a posteriori for consent is not a legal procedure, both because the storage is illicit until the consent is received and because contacting the data subject with the purpose of requesting the consent is a non-solicited and non-consented use of their personal data (the telephone number, e-mail address or physical address). If there is consent for storing the data, "safeguards should ensure that the data subject is aware of the fact that and the extent to which consent is given".

Processing is limited to the conditions specified in Article 6 (lawfulness of processing), which specifies that this is restricted to situations where there is consent, a legal/contractual obligation to process, the need to process in order to protect the vital interests of a person or the public interest or when the processing is done in the exercise of an official authority.

15.5. General Principles

The whole GDPR, as complex as it is, has a set of general principles that guide the entire regulation and should guide its interpretation. These can be summarized as:

— Freedom of movement of personal data inside the EU. The EU currently has in its general goals the freedom of circulation inside its borders. The Schengen Agreement created an area without internal border controls and with common visa policies and the freedom to cross between countries for leisure or for work ("The Schengen Agreement — History and the Definition," n.d.). Currently the Schengen area includes 26 countries ("Schengen Area — Visa Information for Schengen Countries," n.d.). This principle expands that concept but includes tools to facilitate that portability. Organisations must provide facilitated ways for people to collect their personal information and transfer it to another organisation.

— Limitation to purpose. The data processing has to be consistent to the purpose driving its collection. Once the definition of processing includes gathering information, this means that an organisation cannot collect information that is not justifiably needed for a legitimate purpose. Legitimacy results from informed and unambiguous consent, necessary to pursue the objectives of a contract, or to take the steps needed to enter a contract, satisfy legal obligations, perform tasks of public interest or tasks executed under official authority and protect the vital interests of the data subject, or to satisfy legitimate interests of the organisation that don't conflict with the data subject's rights and freedoms. This also enforces data minimization, which means not only that the minimum amount of data gets collected, but also that organisations must destroy information that no longer satisfies the legitimacy criteria (as storing is also a type of data processing).

— Integrity and confidentiality. Organisations are responsible for ensuring that the data is stored in such a way that guarantees, to an extent that is reasonable to expect under the current knowledge of technology, that the data does not suffer illegitimate changes (integrity) and is not disclosed without consent or legitimate necessity (confidentiality).

— Demonstrated responsibility. It is the organisation's responsibility to prove that it has collected informed consent to data processing and/or that there is a justifiable need for that processing. It is also the responsibility of the organisation to prove that it has implemented adequate processes, policies and technologies to protect the personal data under its control.

15.6. The Data Protection Officer

An important figure created by the GDPR is the Data Protection Officer (DPO). The DPO has a major role in all processes related to data in an organisation and the GDPR dedicates the entire Section 15.4 to it. There is also a Guidelines document endorsed by the European Data Protection Board (EDPB) that is extremely relevant to the interpretation of GDPR regarding DPOs, which is the Guidelines on Data Protection Officers ('DPOs'), issued in December 2016 by the Article 29 Data Protection Working Party and revised and adopted in April 2017 (Article 29 Data Protection Working Party, 2017b).

The DPO can be a person, either an employee or someone external under a contract, or an organisation contracted to take that responsibility and assume the corresponding functions. The general recommendation is that the DPO is located in the EU, although there is the possibility of the DPO being located outside the EU if the data controller and/or processor has no establishment in the European Union (Article 29 Data Protection Working Party, 2017b). Even if this is the general recommendation, a lot of thought must go into deciding the location of the DPO and/or of his team, considering not only the work he has to do on a daily basis, but also its higher-level responsibilities. It is expected that the DPO maintain a high level of proximity to the administration and that he (or it, if the role is assigned to an organisation) be involved in decisions regarding data processing. These are arguments that favor locating the DPO wherever most of the data processing activity is located and wherever decisions are made, namely the headquarters of the company. On the other hand, the DPO is the connection between the organisation and the European authorities, which favours locating the DPO in Europe. For international organisations, this is truly a challenge and there is no one-size-fits-all solution.

Obtaining the knowledge needed to act as a DPO is itself a challenge. Although most organisations would benefit from nominating a DPO, not all are obliged to do so and not all have the financial conditions necessary to hire a competent DPO. Smaller organisations that deal with smaller amounts of personal data can opt to hire an information security consultant who can help them to establish the correct procedures and assist in case a personal-data-related incident occurs. It is important that they do so, given that they still have to be compliant with the regulation. An alternative is the hiring of a common DPO by an aggregation of organisations. This can be done through consortiums, through associations (like commercial and industrial associations) or through joint contracts. However, if this is the case, organisations must be particularly careful in the choice of a DPO and about the contract conditions, given that the DPO must be able to fully satisfy the needs of all the organisations that fall under the contract. Bigger consortiums or contracts are likely to choose an organisation, instead of an individual, to act as a DPO.

Organisations are obliged to nominate a DPO in one of the following situations (REGULATION (EU) 2016/ 679 OF THE EUROPEAN PARLIAMENT AND OF THE COUNCIL — of 27 April 2016 — on the protection of natural persons with regard to the processing of personal data and on the free movement of such data, and repealing Directive 95/ 46/ EC (General Data Protection Regulation), 2016):

1. If "the processing is carried out by a public authority or body, except for courts acting in their judicial capacity". It is not clear why the legislator has decided to exempt courts from the obligation of nominating a DPO, but this is likely to be an effort to maintain the separation between legislative, executive and judicial powers. However, this does not mean that courts are exempt from following the GDPR. Relevant quotations from the regulation are:
   a. "this Regulation applies, inter alia, to the activities of courts and other judicial authorities";
   b. "The competence of the supervisory authorities should not cover the processing of personal data when courts are acting in their judicial capacity";
   c. "Supervisory authorities shall not be competent to supervise processing operations of courts acting in their judicial capacity".

2. If "the core activities of the controller or the processor consist of processing operations which, by virtue of their nature, their scope and/or their purposes, require regular and systematic monitoring of data subjects on a large scale". In this case it is necessary to clarify the meaning of "core activities", of "regular and systematic monitoring" and of "large scale" and, for that, one should consult the guidelines emanated from WP29 and endorsed by the EDPB. Unfortunately, this document does not provide clear definitions for all of these concepts, but it does exclude some situations and clearly include others. According to WP29/EDPB, core activities are the key operations executed by the organisation to pursue its objectives. For an information security professional, this definition relates closely to the concept of critical processes. So, even if a company deals with a large amount of personal data that doesn't necessarily mean that the organisation is obliged to nominate a DPO. For instance, salaries processing is not considered a core activity, therefore it does not fall into this category. Regular and systematic monitoring is any activity done, continuously or recurrently, either according to a system, a method or any organized process or as part of a plan or a strategy to track or profile data subjects, including but not limited to, over the Internet (Article 29 Data Protection Working Party, 2017b).
3. "The core activities of the controller or the processor consist of processing on a large scale of special categories of data pursuant to Article 9". Those special categories are "Processing of personal data revealing racial or ethnic origin, political opinions, religious or philosophical beliefs, or trade union membership, and the processing of genetic data, biometric data for the purpose of uniquely identifying a natural person, data concerning health or data concerning a natural person's sex life or sexual orientation". One must notice that, in general, the GDPR prohibits organisations from processing these types of data without consent from the data subject in the cases where the national law does not prohibit that consent. However, there are several exceptions, presented in paragraph 2 of article 9, mostly related to the execution of legal obligations or public interest (REGULATION (EU) 2016/ 679 OF THE EUROPEAN

PARLIAMENT AND OF THE COUNCIL — of 27 April 2016 — on the protection of natural persons with regard to the processing of personal data and on the free movement of such data, and repealing Directive 95/ 46/ EC (General Data Protection Regulation), 2016). In the cases where that processing is legitimate, the concept of large scale is critical. The guidelines for DPOs indicate that several factors must be considered to verify if a certain case can be considered large scale processing. Those factors are the number of data subjects (either in absolute numbers or as a percentage of the population), the volume of data, the range of different data, the duration of the processing activity and the geographical extent of the data activity. Examples of large scale processing include the processing of patient data in a hospital, the processing of individuals' travel data in a city transportation system, the geo-location of clients in a chain of stores and the processing of consumer data by banks and insurance companies. Examples of situations where there isn't large scale processing include patient data processed by an individual physician and the processing of criminal convictions and offenses by an individual lawyer (Article 29 Data Protection Working Party, 2017b).

The DPO "shall be designated on the basis of professional qualities and, in particular, expert knowledge of data protection law and practices and the ability to fulfil the tasks referred to in Article 39". Those tasks include informing the organisation of and advising the organisation on the obligations resulting from the GDPR, monitoring compliance, assigning responsibilities related to data protection, raising awareness, providing training to staff involved in data processing, providing advice relative to data protection impact assessment and cooperating with the supervisory authority. The DPO also needs to take into consideration the risks associated with data processing operations (REGULATION (EU) 2016/ 679 OF THE EUROPEAN PARLIAMENT AND OF THE COUNCIL — of 27 April 2016 — on the protection of natural persons with regard to the processing of personal data and on the free movement of such data, and repealing Directive 95/ 46/ EC (General Data Protection Regulation), 2016).

This means that the DPO needs to have legal and technical knowledge. Given that each country in the EU can increase the level of regulation associated with the GDPR and that some dispositions are complemented by national laws, the mandatory legal knowledge might include regulations from up to 28 countries depending on the activity of the organisation. Also, because some data processing is frequently outsourced, the DPO should have some legal knowledge regarding contracts and, if the third party is in a different country, of international law. At the same time, the DPO should possess knowledge of privacy protection techniques, which in turn demands that he possess technical knowledge in a specialized domain: information security (data security, network security, etc.). Therefore, there aren't a lot of professionals that can fulfill this task on their own. This calls for the constitution of corporations specially dedicated to this task, but that is not what is currently happening in Europe. While there isn't any data on this, the author's experience is that either companies hire one expert in either law or Information Technology (IT) or they hire the services of an existing company, usually one that already provides them with services. Again, most of those companies focus either on the technological aspects or on the legal aspects, when the GDPR calls for an integrated approach. There are only a few rare cases where legal and technological companies have come together to provide this service or when a company constitutes an interdisciplinary team that includes legal and technological experts. The recommendations of WP29/EDPB are that the DPO must also have some personal qualities like integrity and high professional ethics (Article 29 Data Protection Working Party, 2017b). While this relates to personality, it also calls for some knowledge on Social Ethics, Deontology and Theories of Justice. Therefore, ideally the DPO should have training in Philosophy. The WP29/EDPB also recommends that DPOs have knowledge of the business sector of the organisation that hires them and, if they are serving a public authority or body, that they have a sound knowledge of the administrative rules and procedures applicable to that organisation. Because raising awareness and training is one of the DPO's responsibilities, he should also have knowledge of Education and/ or Training.

In conclusion, one DPO is a super professional, with an impeccable social and professional record of "good behavior" and with a sound knowledge of several types of laws, several domains including IT, Philosophy, Education and Public Administration and the specific activity of the organisation. Again, this calls for joint teams, specialized in this activity.

One aspect of the Regulation that is very relevant for the choice of the DPO is the level of protection granted to this position. The GDPR clearly states in Paragraph 3 of Article 38 that the DPO "shall not be dismissed or penalised by the controller or the processor for performing his tasks" (REGULATION (EU) 2016/ 679 OF THE EUROPEAN PARLIAMENT AND OF THE COUNCIL — of 27 April 2016 — on the protection of natural persons with regard to the processing of personal data and on the free movement of such data, and repealing Directive 95/ 46/ EC (General Data Protection Regulation), 2016). This means that if the organisation choses to nominate a DPO from the existing staff it has to be careful to ensure that such a person has no conflict of interest and that if a situation arises where there is a need to dismiss that person no doubts will be raised regarding the reasons for the dismissal. If the DPO can correlate the dismissal with an action or a set of actions performed in the capacity of DPO, the organisation will not be able to dismiss him. This might be an incentive for organisations to hire external DPOs. Even if the protection is also applicable to them, at least there isn't any risk of misunderstandings in cases which require dismissals.

Another argument for hiring external specialized DPOs is the fact that the DPO cannot have a conflict of interest. Even if it is not clear what a conflict of interest is, the existing guidelines indicate that senior managers (such as chief executives, chief operating officers, chief financial officers, chief medical officers, heads of marketing departments, heads of Human Resources or heads of IT departments) cannot occupy this position. This restriction also applies to those in the organisation that determine the purposes or means of processing

(Article 29 Data Protection Working Party, 2017b). Therefore, it isn't easy to find someone in the organisation with the technical capacity to perform the role of DPO and someone who can do so without any conflict of interest. It is also important to notice that the issue of conflict of interest also applies to external DPOs, under a contract. The common practice of hiring a company that is already a technology supplier is frequently a violation of the GDPR. Companies that provide consultancy on the means to process data (recommendations on software adoption, database manipulation maintenance, data analytics, data collection tools, etc.) are in clear conflict of interest if they also assume the position of DPO.

15.7. Data Protection Impact Assessment

Demonstrating compliance is a pillar of the GDPR. The document is based on the notion that organisations have the responsibility to protect personal data, but it is not a naive document. The legislator understands that absolute security can only happen in a utopia and that incidents can happen regardless of what measures are in place. Therefore, organisations need to be able to prove that they have done what is reasonable, considering the underlying risk, in order to protect the data they process. The Data Protection Impact Assessment (DPIA) is the pillar tool of that demonstration.

Information security professionals know that any security plan starts with the identification of the assets to protect and a corresponding risk analysis.

The importance of the DPIA cannot be overestimated. Not only is it fundamental to the correct development of a security strategy, but it is also closely related to the fines that are associated with non-compliance. The WP29 wrote it clearly:

> "Under the GDPR, non-compliance with DPIA requirements can lead to fines imposed by the competent supervisory authority. Failure to carry out a DPIA when the processing is subject to a DPIA (Article 35(1) and (3)–(4)), carrying out a DPIA in an incorrect way (Article 35(2) and (7) to (9)), or failing to consult the compe-

tent supervisory authority where required (Article 36(3)(e)), can result in an administrative fine of up to 10M€, or in the case of an undertaking, up to 2 % of the total worldwide annual turnover of the preceding financial year, whichever is higher (Article 29 Data Protection Working Party, 2017c)

It is impossible to summarise the description of the guidelines and the procedures to follow when carrying out a DPIA and how to assess the level of the risk such that all this information fits in this section. But the guidelines (Article 29 Data Protection Working Party, 2017c) give a list of what to look for when deciding if a DPIA is needed. These items on that list deserve some consideration:

— "Evaluation or scoring of data subjects": this type of data processing can have applications in many different situations, from work performance to health insurance. Whenever the data subjects get a comparative position towards other data subjects, organisations should consider this as an indicator of high-risk processing.
— "Automated-decision making with legal or similar significant effect": automated decisions are a growing concern of legislators. The EU has a convention that covers this type of processing (Convention for the Protection of Individuals with regard to Automatic Processing of Personal Data as it will be amended by its Protocol CETS No. 223, 2018). It is important to notice that, under the GDPR, data subjects have the right to be informed that a decision was made using automated processes. They also have the right to have a human review that decision. It is also likely that in most cases humans will not change those decisions, given that companies design the automated processes to reflect the organisation's policies and humans have to follow the same criteria. This might be a concern related to machine failure or to the imprecision of the existing algorithms. In fact, machine-learning techniques have been developed quite recently and have a level of error that is unneglectable. There is no way to know how the confidence level of the algorithms

will evolve, but it makes a lot of sense to protect citizens from automatic mistakes.

— "Systematic monitoring": the whole notion of systematic monitoring has already been discussed in this chapter.
— "Sensitive data or data of a highly personal nature": the notion of sensitive data can vary according to the culture and ethics of a certain population. Health records, criminal records and data regarding sexual, political or religious orientation are usually considered sensitive data or highly personal data. But some less evident data can also be included in this category, either because of concrete temporary or regional circumstances or because they allow for indirect disclosure of highly personal or sensitive information. For instance, detailed lunch records can reveal food habits that provide clues on health problems or religious options. Other types of sensitive data are those related to personal communications, including metadata (dates, recipient, etc.) and many countries have specific laws regarding this.
— "Data processed at a large scale": the concept of large scale has already been discussed in this chapter.
— "Matching or combining datasets": this definition can be tricky. What is a dataset? This is a hard question to answer from the technological perspective. However, the spirit of the legislation seems to be that whenever there is no reasonable expectation of a common citizen to see two different sets of collected data as interrelated, then this is a red flag that elevates the risk. This type of situation, by definition, goes beyond consent, so it can only happen in special situations.
— "Data concerning vulnerable data subjects": the definition of a vulnerable data subject can change with time and space. Usually children, elderlies and people with physical or mental disabilities fall under this category. Most laws consider employees to be a group vulnerable to their employers, so organisations have to treat data related to work with extra precautions. Other situations must be considered case by case, with consideration of the sociological context of the data subjects.

— "Innovative use or applying new technological or organisational solutions": the fact that the GDPR has isolated this type of processing is a sign of the times and of the concerns that new technologies are creating. There is a fear of the unknown, so whatever is new is deemed to be particularly dangerous. Machine learning or Artificial Intelligence, combined with Big Data, are definitely a growing concern in society and so are the privacy concerns related to the Internet-of-Things. At the same time, the general population seems to accept them as part of daily life and whatever comes next is for no one to forecast, so the legislators took the safe path. WP29 includes in the description of this item biometric technologies like fingerprint and facial recognition, but it also cites the GDPR to refer to the current state of the art as the main referential for the evaluation of what is innovative (Article 29 Data Protection Working Party, 2017c). Most experts in biometrics would not consider fingerprint authentication methods an innovative technology, but a new algorithm for fingerprint biometrical authentication would definitely fall into this category. Some recent biometric technologies, like cognitive biometrics, can be of even more concern, given that they include health related data (heart beat patterns, brain activity patterns, skin conductivity, etc.) (Revett and de Magalhães, 2010).

— Processing that "prevents data subjects from exercising a right or using a service or a contract": this seems to be directed at preliminary analyses of clients, so whenever this is applied, the first item of this list ("Evaluation or scoring of data subjects") is likely to also be applied.

It seems clear that the decision on the legal obligation to do a DPIA, like the DPIA itself, should be carried out by an exempt third party with technical and legal knowledge of information technology (databases, network communications, encryption, authentication/identification, operating systems, web programming, etc.) and privacy laws and without any conflict of interest. However, even if there is no legal obligation to do a DPIA, this is still a valuable tool for any organisation and it can prove itself priceless in case of a data breach.

15.8. The Fines and the Press

The GDPR has become most famous for the value of the fines that come with the failure to comply with it. All countries must adhere to these administrative fines, which must be "effective, proportionate and dissuasive". The formal exceptions are Denmark and Estonia, which have legal systems that exclude them for the direct definition of administrative fines by an EU Regulation. However, these countries will have to apply them either through the criminal courts (Denmark) or through the supervisory authority in the framework of a misdemeanor procedure. Fines can reach 20 million Euros or, in the case of an undertaking company, 4% of the total worldwide annual turnover of the preceding year.

Following a lot of curiosity around the period when the GDPR started producing effects, the topic lost public attention (Fig. 15.1 and Fig. 15.2), but, regardless of that, the second semester of 2018 brought the first GDPR fines and, as more countries create national regulations to the GDPR and empower their national authorities, more fines are expected. Therefore, media coverage will likely increase, which will, hopefully, raise awareness and promote compliance.

The first fine applied under the GDPR after May 25, 2018 was to a hospital in Portugal in July 2018. The national authority fined the hospital due to a lack of detail in the access control systems that protect health records, which allowed for any doctor or psychologist and even some social workers to access the medical records of any patient. The hospital didn't have a policy for creation and/or deletion of account privileges, which allowed doctors who were no longer working there to continue accessing the files. The fine was of 400 thousand Euros and it is being disputed in court ("Portuguese Hospital Receives and Contests 400,000 € Fine for GDPR Infringement," 2018).

Austria has also applied a fine under the GDPR, after accusations of trying to undermine the EU regulation by passing a law that would issue warnings to first time offenders (Nielsen, 2018). The Austrian authority issued its first GDPR fine in late September and it was quite modest: 4,800 Euros (Fritz, 2018). This fine was applied to a retail establishment that had a video surveillance system that captured the sidewalk. It remains to be seen how things will progress in this country.

In November 2018, Germany applied its first fine under the GDPR and, while this wasn't of a high value it is an important case exactly because of that. The national authority fined the social media platform Knuddels.de 20 thousand Euros for a data breach of more than 300 thousand access credentials, including e-mail addresses and passwords. The fine didn't result from the breach itself but from the lack of protection of the data, given that passwords were stored in plain text. The fine was especially low due to the consideration of two facts: the financial impact of the fine on the company and the level of cooperation showed by the company in their interactions with the national authority (Pressestelle, 2018).

It is important to notice that fines regarding data protection are not new in Europe. As discussed before, there was legislation in place that required companies to protect personal data and fines were applied quite frequently. Examples of both small and large fines can be found in many countries and in a variety of business areas.

The Italian authorities have applied several fines in the past years. Examples are:

— The 10,000 Euros fine issued to a hotel in San Felice Circeo (Federico Domenichelli, 2018);
— The 32,000 Euros fine applied to the celebrity blog *5-star movement* controlled by the Rousseau Association ("M5s, dal Garante della privacy 32 mila euro di multa al blog delle Stelle," 2018);
— The 600,000 Euros fine for aggressive telemarketing applied to Fastweb ("Telemarketing aggressivo, 600 mila euro di multa per Fastweb," 2018); and
— The 960,000 Euros fine applied to the telephonic company TIM ("Violazione della privacy, multa da 960 mila euro a Tim," 2018).

Like Italy, the United Kingdom authority has issued several fines in the past years. Examples are:

— The £120,000 fine to the University of Greenwich due to a data breach that exposed almost 20,000 staff and students ("University of Greenwich fined £120,000 for breach of sensitive data," 2018); and

— The £500,000 fines (the highest fine possible prior to GDPR) issued to Equifax ("Equifax Hit With Maximum UK Privacy Fine After Mega-Breach," 2018) and to Facebook (Waterson, 2018).

Several factors should contribute to the definition of the values of fines, from the categories of the data in question to the level of collaboration with the authorities with the intent to mitigate the effects of the infringement. WP29 issued detailed but vague guidelines on this matter and the EDPB endorsed the document (Article 29 Data Protection Working Party, 2017a).

At the same time that countries are adjusting their regulations and creating/empowering their national authorities, citizens are coming together in many countries to file suits against corporations for data breaches. There are indications that consumer associations have filed lawsuits against Facebook for violations of personal data rights in Portugal, Spain, Belgium and Italy ("DECO processa Facebook e pede indemnização de até 2000 euros por utilizador," 2018).

With increasing fines, different mitigation techniques are likely to be considered and taking out insurance policies to transfer the risk is a possibility. Currently only Finland and Norway have legislation that allows insurance policies to cover GDPR fines and it is unclear if that is a possibility in eight other countries. In 20 jurisdictions GDPR fines are likely uninsurable (Leemans and Molony, 2018).

15.9. Information Technology and the GDPR

Technology is simultaneously the motor behind the need for a GDPR and a critical factor in GDPR compliance.

The proliferation of data services and data-enhanced business results from the development of IT domains like cloud technologies, social media and business analytics, the proliferation of computational devices (smartphones, Internet-of-Things, etc.) and the evolution of computer networks, not only cabled but also wireless. All these created business opportunities and enhanced the average quality of life, but also created privacy challenges that originated the need for regulatory legislation.

For companies to comply with the GDPR, they, paradoxically, will need to rely on technology, given that it is not possible to depend on humans to do all that is needed to elevate data security to acceptable levels.

One of the rights that GDPR grants to EU residents is the right to receive a copy of all the data that an organisation has on him and/or to transmit that data to another organisation, as long as that data was obtained from the data subject (actively provided or observed) and does not compromise the rights of other data subjects. This forces organisations to have integrated information systems and to develop automated forms of providing that data in a manageable format, not only due to the potentially high number of requests, but also because there is a time limit of one month, extendable in certain cases to three months, to satisfy the request (REGULATION (EU) 2016/679 OF THE EUROPEAN PARLIAMENT AND OF THE COUNCIL — of 27 April 2016 — on the protection of natural persons with regard to the processing of personal data and on the free movement of such data, and repealing Directive 95/46/ EC (General Data Protection Regulation), 2016).

Ensuring that data is not easily accessible by non-authorized parties forces organisations to both encrypt sensitive data and to implement adequate access control processes. Two of the existing (and discussed) cases of fines relate exactly to this compliance requisite. Given that there is no effective access control without effective identification and/or authentication mechanisms, organisations will need to evolve beyond the traditional password systems that suffer from the paradox that they must simultaneously be complex, so they are hard to guess, and simple, so that they are easy to remember. Biometric technologies can play a major role in this (de Magalhães, Revett, and Santos, 2008).

The right to be forgotten, when applicable, and the limitations to data storage also create a challenge. Organisations must be ready to delete any data subject's data that is no longer required to be stored, without deleting any data that actually has to be stored and without affecting the stability of their systems. Again, organisations must rely on technology to be able to do this effectively and within the legal timeframe.

Accountability is also critical under the GDPR. Organisations carry the burden to demonstrate that they have done all that is reasonably expected to protect the personal data that they process. If an incident occurs, being able to trace the data path is critical to understanding what happened and where something went wrong. Insured accountability might even demonstrate deliberate actions taken by an employee in clear disrespect for the implemented policies. For this to be possible, solutions like Private Key Infrastructures (PKI) must be implemented. PKI can ensure accountability for instance in network storage (Yumerefendi and Chase, 2007) or in e-mail communications (de Magalhães, Santos, and Nunes, 2006).

Technology is, in many ways, the protection of a digital infrastructure and, therefore, it will need to be the base for a secure organisation. Nevertheless, it is important that the independence of the DPO remains intact. Therefore, technology suppliers cannot be the organisation's DPO.

15.10. Conclusions

The revision of the main features of GDPR, of the adjacent guidelines and of the current application of this regulation show that this is a complex normative with profound implications on the way that companies do business in the EU market. However, at the same time, it is clear that many of the requirements of the GDPR were already in place before the EU passed this legislation.

In an increasingly connected world that relies on a fast growing and innovation-based technology industry, the number of incidents is likely to grow until the mindset changes and the hardware and software players realize that security by design and security as a process are part of the normal development of any solution. In the meantime, organisations will have to navigate their way between the GDPR, the particularities of each of the countries' national regulations and all the applicable regulations. The latter include not only EU regulations but also other nations' regulations, given that information services are usually offered worldwide, which means that, while dealing with the GDPR, organisations might find themselves having to deal with several different regulations. Examples of states with similar but distinct regulations are:

— The Australian Privacy Act of 1988 with all the updates made until November 2018 and its more than 300 pages (Privacy Act 1988, 2018);
— The California regulation on privacy protection (The California Consumer Privacy Act of 2018, 2018), which is likely to implicate changes in several states across the United States; and
— The Brazilian law on personal data protection, approved in August 2018 and set to be enforced in February 2020 (Lei nº 13.709, 2018).

At the same time, organisations must also adhere to business specific regulations, like the Family Educational Rights and Privacy Act (FERPA) regulations (34 CFR 99 — Family Educational Rights and Privacy, 2010) or the Health Insurance Portability and Accountability Act (HIPAA) (Health Insurance Portability and Accountability Act of 1996, 1996).

Companies definitely need to change their posture on personal data protection and understand that they must either hire a team to support them in the active protection of data or hire specialized services, as the challenges associated with this task are multidisciplinary. Companies will also need to avoid the temptation of hiring their technology suppliers as DPOs, under the penalty of not only failing to comply with the GDPR but also not being able to distinguish between what is a genuine data security concern and what is a commercially-driven concern.

References

1. Article 29 Data Protection Working Party. (2017a, March 10). *Guidelines on the Application and Setting of Administrative Fines for the Purposes of the Regulation 2016/679*. Brussels, Belgium: European Council.

2. Article 29 Data Protection Working Party. (2017b, April). *Guidelines on Data Protection Officers ('DPOs')* [Online]. Available at: http://ec.europa.eu/newsroom/document.cfm?doc_id=44100 (Accessed: September 2019).
3. Article 29 Data Protection Working Party. (2017c, April 10). *Guidelines on Data Protection Impact Assessment (DPIA) and Determining Whether Processing Is "Likely to Result in a High Risk" For the Purposes of Regulation 2016/679.* Brussels, Belgium: European Council.
4. Article 29 Data Protection Working Party. (2007, June 20). *Opinion 4/2007 on the Concept* of *Personal Data.* Brussels, Belgium: European Council.
5. Code of Federal Regulations. (2010). *34 CFR 99 — Family Educational Rights and Privacy* [Online]. Available at: https://www.gpo.gov/fdsys/granule/CFR-2010-title34-vol1/CFR-2010-title34-vol1-part99 (Accessed: September 2019).
6. Convention for the Protection of Individuals With Regard to Automatic Processing of Personal Data as It Will Be Amended By Its Protocol CETS No. 223 (2018).
7. de Magalhães, S. T., Revett, K. and Santos, H. M. D. (2008). Using Technology to Overcome the Password's Contradiction. In Gupta, M. and Sharman, R. (eds.), *Handbook of Research on Social and Organizational Liabilities in Information Security.*
8. de Magalhães, S. T., Santos, H. M. D. and Nunes, P. V. (2006). *An International Governmental Mailing System: A Requirement To Prevent Web-Enhanced Terrorism,* 8 pages.
9. *DECO Processa Facebook e Pede Indemnização de Até 2000 Euros Por Utilizador* [Online]. (2018, December 1). Available at: https://www.impala.pt/noticias/economia/deco-processa-facebook-indemnizacao/ (Accessed: September 2019).
10. *Directive (EU) 2016/680 of the European Parliament and of the Council — of 27 April 2016 — on the Protection of Natural Persons With Regard to the Processing of Personal Data by Competent Authorities for the Purposes of the Prevention, Investigation, Detection or Prosecution of Criminal Offences or the Execution of Criminal Penalties, and on the Free Movement of Such Data, and Repealing Council Framework Decision 2008/977/JHA* (2016).
11. *Directive 95/46/EC of the European Parliament and of the Council of 24 October 1995 on the Protection of Individuals With Regard to the Processing of Personal Data and on the Free Movement of Such Data, Pub. L. No. 31995L0046, OJ L 281* [Online]. (1995). Available at: http://data.europa.eu/eli/dir/1995/46/oj/eng (Accessed: September 2019).

12. *Directive 2000/31/EC of the European Parliament and of the Council* (2000).
13. *Directive 2002/58/EC of the European Parliament and of the Council.* (2002).
14. *Directive 2011/24/EU of the European Parliament and of the Council of 9 March 2011 on the Application of Patients' Rights in Cross-Border Healthcare* (2011).
15. *Equifax Hit With Maximum UK Privacy Fine After Mega-Breach* [Online]. (2018, 20 September). Available at: https://www.bankinfosecurity.com/equifax-hit-maximum-uk-privacy-fine-after-mega-breach-a-11532 (Accessed: 10 December 2018).
16. European Commission. (2001). *Regulation (EC) No 45/2001 of the European Parliament and of the Council* [Online]. Available at: https://doi.org/10.1007/978-1-137-54482-7_19 (Accessed: September 2019).
17. European Commission. (2009). *Regulation (EC) No 223/2009 of the European Parliament and of the Council* [Online]. Available at: https://doi.org/10.1007/978-1-137-54482-7_19 (Accessed: September 2019).
18. European Parliament, European Council, and European Commission. (2012). Charter of Fundamental Rights of the European Union. *Official Journal of the European Union,* **17**.
19. European Union. (2012). Consolidated Version of the Treaty on the Functioning of the European Union. *Official Journal of the European Union.*
20. European Union. (2014). *Regulation (EU) No 536/2014 of the European Parliament and of the Council.*
21. European Union. (2016). *Regulation (EU) 2016/ 679 of the European Parliament and of the Council — of 27 April 2016 — on the Protection of Natural Persons with Regard to the Processing of Personal Data and on the Free Movement of Such Data, and Repealing Directive 95/ 46/ EC (General Data Protection Regulation), Pub. L. No. 2016/679/EU, 88.*
22. Federico Domenichelli. (2018, 4 December). *Svista con la Privacy alla Reception, Stangata per un Hotel dal Garante* [Online]. Available at: https://www.latinaoggi.eu/news/cronaca/62642/svista-con-la-privacy-alla-reception-stangata-per-un-hotel-dal-garante (Accessed: September 2019).
23. Fritz, G. (2018, 10 May). *First GDPR Fine Issued by Austrian Data Protection Regulator* [Online]. Available at: https://digital.freshfields.com/post/102f39w/first-gdpr-fine-issued-by-austrian-data-protection-regulator (Accessed: 10 December 2018).
24. *Health Insurance Portability and Accountability Act of 1996, Public Law* [Online]. (1996). Available at: https://www.gpo.gov/fdsys/pkg/PLAW-

104publ191/pdf/PLAW-104publ191.pdf (Accessed: September 2019).

25. Leemans, V. and Molony, D. (2018). Are GDPR Fines Insurable? *Risk Management,* **65**(9), p. 28.
26. *Lei nº 13.709* [Online]. (2018). Available at: http://www.planalto.gov.br/ccivil_03/_Ato2015-2018/2018/Lei/L13709.htm#art65 (Accessed: September 2019).
27. *M5s, dal Garante della Privacy 32 Mila Euro di Multa al Blog delle Stelle* [Online]. (2018, 15 March). Available at: https://www.ilfattoquotidiano.it/2018/03/15/m5s-dal-garante-della-privacy-32mila-euro-di-multa-al-blog-delle-stelle/4227514/ (Accessed: 10 December 2018).
28. Nielsen, N. (2018, 5 April). *Austria Accused of Undermining New EU Data Law* [Online]. Available at: https://euobserver.com/justice/141746 (Accessed: September 2019).
29. *Portuguese Hospital Receives and Contests 400,000 € Fine for GDPR Infringement* [Online]. (2018, 26 October). Available at: https://www.natlawreview.com/article/portuguese-hospital-receives-and-contests-400000-fine-gdpr-infringement (Accessed: 10 December 2018).
30. Pressestelle. (2018, 22 November). *LfDI Baden-Württemberg Verhängt Sein Erstes Bußgeld in Deutschland Nach der DS-GVO | Der Landesbeauftragte für den Datenschutz und die Informationsfreiheit Baden-Württemberg* [Online]. Available at: https://www.baden-wuerttemberg.datenschutz.de/lfdi-baden-wuerttemberg-verhaengt-sein-erstes-bussgeld-in-deutschland-nach-der-ds-gvo/ (Accessed 10 December 2018).
31. *Privacy Act 1988* [Online]. (2018). Available at: https://www.legislation.gov.au/Details/C2018C00456/Html/Text, http://www.legislation.gov.au/Details/C2018C00456 (Accessed: September 2019).
32. Revett, K. and de Magalhães, S. T. (2010). Cognitive Biometrics: Challenges for the Future. In S. Tenreiro de Magalhães, H. Jahankhani, and A. G. Hessami (eds.), *Global Security, Safety, and Sustainability.* Berlin, Germany: Springer.
33. *Schengen Area — Visa Information for Schengen Countries* [Online]. (n.d.). Available at: https://www.schengenvisainfo.com/schengen-visa-countries-list/ (Accessed: 6 December 2018).
34. *Telemarketing Aggressivo, 600 Mila Euro di Multa per Fastweb* [Online]. (2018, 10 September). Available at: https://www.corrierecomunicazioni.it/privacy/telemarketing-aggressivo-600mila-euro-di-multa-per-fastweb/ (Accessed: September 2019).

35. *The California Consumer Privacy Act of 2018* [Online]. (2018). Available at: https://www.pbwt.com/content/uploads/2018/06/California-Consumer-Privacy-Act1.pdf (Accessed: September 2019).
36. *University of Greenwich Fined £120,000 for Breach of Sensitive Data* [Online]. (2018, 22 May). Available at: https://www.itpro.co.uk/go/31170 (Accesssed: 10 December 2018).
37. *Violazione della Privacy, Multa da 960 Mila Euro a Tim* [Online]. (2018, 29 May). Available at: https://www.corrierecomunicazioni.it/privacy/violazione-della-privacy-multa-da-960mila-euro-a-tim/ (Accessed: September 2019).
38. Waterson, J. (2018, 25 October). *UK fines Facebook £500,000 for failing to protect user data*. Available at: https://www.theguardian.com/technology/2018/oct/25/facebook-fined-uk-privacy-access-user-data-cambridge-analytica (Accessed: September 2019).
39. Yumerefendi, A. R. and Chase, J. S. (2007). Strong accountability for network storage. *ACM Transactions on Storage*, **3**(3), Article 11.

Index